McGRAW-HILL'S OUR NATION, OUR WORLD

MEETING PEOPLE

School, Self, Families, Neighborhood, and Our Country

GOING PLACES

People in Groups, Filling Needs in Communities and on Farms

COMMUNITIES

Geography and History of Cities in the United States, Canada, and Mexico

EARTH'S REGIONS

Geography and Ways of Living on Five Continents, Studying the 50 States

UNITED STATES: Our Nation and Neighbors

Chronological History and Regional Geography of the United States, Our North American Neighbors

THE WORLD

World History, Ancient Civilizations, Important Nations Today

CONSULTANTS

BARBARA BALLOU
Palo Alto, California

HELEN BAUMAN
Auburndale, Florida

BRENDA BIRCHFIELD
Knoxville, Tennessee

DR. L. JO ANNE BUGGEY
Minneapolis, Minnesota

RONALD BUSCH
Bartow, Florida

PATRICIA DRAKE
Amherst, Massachusetts

CORA DVERSDALL
Oklahoma City, Oklahoma

JUDY A. FISHER
Oklahoma City, Oklahoma

DR. N. JEROME GOLDBERG
Natick, Massachusetts

EMILY GROSSMAN
Lakeland, Florida

SANDY HANNINGTON
Yukon, Oklahoma

DR. RICHARD M. HAYNES
Tarboro, North Carolina

CAROLYN HERBST
Brooklyn, New York

DR. RONALD J. HERMANSEN
Salt Lake City, Utah

SANDY HOLT
Lakeland, Florida

JEANNE ICENHOUR
Winterhaven, Florida

SISTER M. JEANNETTE, I.H.M.
Philadelphia, Pennsylvania

ELAINE S. JONES
Woodinville, Washington

SISTER SHARON KERRIGAN
Joliet, Illinois

JEAN McGRADY
Bethany, Oklahoma

SISTER GLENN ANNE McPHEE
Los Angeles, California

ELAINE MAGNUSON
Bothell, Washington

SHERRILL MILLER
Seattle, Washington

RONNIE MOSKOWITZ
New York, New York

H. JAMES MUMMA
Novato, California

JEAN MUMMA
Novato, California

SUSAN OLDHAM
Lakeland, Florida

LEOLA OPLOH
Chicago, Illinois

FRED PEFFER
Yukon, Oklahoma

SUSIE REYNOLDS
Bethany, Oklahoma

JOANNE ROBERTSON
Redmond, Washington

BOBBIE S. SAPP
Alexandria, Virginia

SISTER ANN SCHAFER
Seattle, Washington

LYNN SKINNER
Bartow, Florida

KENNETH SUNDIN
Woodinville, Washington

SHARON WALTER
Brandywine, Maryland

Editor in Chief: Martha O'Neill
Coordinating Editor: Ann Armstrong Craig
Design Supervision: James Darby, William Dippel
Art Editors: Sydne Silverstein Matus, Alexa Ripley Barre
Photo Editor: Alan Forman
Photo Research: Ellen Horan
Production Supervision: Salvador Gonzales
Editorial Assistants: Nancy Young, Mindy Mutterperl
Outside Editing: Visual Education Corporation: Darryl Kestler
Contributing Writer: Alice Hugh Brown
Art and Design by: Boultinghouse and Boultinghouse, Inc.
Cover Design by: Alan Forman

UNITED STATES

BY Leonard Martelli, Alma Graham, George Vuicich, Cleo Cherryholmes, Gary Manson

WEBSTER DIVISION, McGRAW-HILL BOOK COMPANY

New York St. Louis San Francisco Auckland Bogotá Guatemala Hamburg Johannesburg Lisbon London Madrid Mexico Montreal New Delhi Panama Paris San Juan São Paulo Singapore Sydney Tokyo Toronto

ISBN 0-07-039815-1

1 2 3 4 5 6 7 8 9 10 KGP KGP 94 93 92 91 90 89 88 87 86 85

CONTENTS

UNIT 1 MAPPING NORTH AMERICA 12

Map: Political Map of the United States 12–13

CHAPTER 1 MAPPING THE EARTH 14

Lesson 1: **Where You Are in Time and Space** 14

Lesson 2: **The Grid on the Globe** 17

Globe: Globe with Latitude and Longitude Grid 18

Globe: Western Hemisphere 19

Globe: Eastern Hemisphere 19

Globes: Northern and Southern Hemispheres 20

Fascinating Facts: The 100th Birthday of the Prime Meridian 21

Lesson 3: **Mastering Latitude and Longitude** 22

Globes: Lines of Latitude and Longitude 22

Map: Political Map of North America 23

Lesson 4: **Geographic Dictionary: Landforms and Bodies of Water** 26

Art: Landforms of Earth 27

Lesson 5: **Weather and Climate** 31

Globe: Climate Zones 31

Chart: Climates of Earth 32

Map: Climates of North America 33

Lesson 6: **Making Maps** 34

Globe: Peeling the Globe 34

Map: Mercator Projection 35

Map: Equal-Area Projection 35

Map: Robinson Projection 35

Map: Map Drawn from Aerial Photograph 37

Fascinating Facts: The Oldest Maps in the World 38

Chapter 1 Review 39

CHAPTER 2 MAPPING OUR CONTINENT 40

Lesson 1: **Reading Maps** 40

Map: Physical Map of North America 41

Art: Finding North 42

Lesson 2: **Types of Maps** 43

Map: Political Map of the United States 43

Map: Living Resources of North America 45

Map: Population of Earth 46

Lesson 3: **Historical Maps** 48

Map: Ptolemy's Map of Earth 48

Map: European Discovery and Exploration 49

Map: Columbus's Voyages to America 50

Map: The Thirteen Colonies about 1770 51

Map: Europe before World War I 52

Lesson 4: **Using Maps** 53

Route Map: Houston to Key West 53

Mileage Chart: Houston to Key West 54

Road Map: Florida 55

Street Map: Washington, DC 56

Chapter 2 Review 57

UNIT 1 REVIEW 58

SKILL DEVELOPMENT 59

Map: The Eastern United States 59

UNIT 2 EXPLORING AND SETTLING NORTH AMERICA 60

CHAPTER 1 THE PEOPLES OF THE AMERICAS 62

Lesson 1: **The First North Americans** 62

Time Line: Early Events in North and South America 63

Map: Route of the First North Americans 64

Lesson 2: **Early Cities of North America** 66

Historical View: Tenochtitlán, the Aztec Capital 69

Lesson 3: **Other Early Cultures of North America** 71

Chapter 1 Review 75

1777

1795

CHAPTER 2 **AN AGE OF EXPLORATION** 76
Lesson 1: **Europeans Find the Americas** 76
Map: Columbus's Voyages to America 77
Map: European Discovery and Exploration 80
Lesson 2: **The Spanish and Portuguese Explore** 82
Time Line: 800s–1565 82
Map: Spanish Explorers in North America 83
Map: Spanish and Portuguese Explorers 85
People to Remember: Hernando de Soto 88
Lesson 3: **The English and French Explore** 89
Fascinating Facts: The Lost Colony 91
Time and Place: English and French Exploration of North America, Time Line and Map 93
Lesson 4: **The Search for the Northwest Passage** 95
Map: The Search for the Northwest Passage 96
Chapter 2 Review 100

CHAPTER 3 **THE ENGLISH IN NORTH AMERICA** 101
Lesson 1: **The Founding of the Southern Colonies** 101
Historical Map: Jamestown 103
Map: North American Settlements, 1630 104
Time Line: 1607–1681 105
Lesson 2: **Life on the Southern Plantations** 107
Time and Place: From the Lost Colony to the Constitution, Time Line and Map 109
Map: The British Colonies about 1770 110
Lesson 3: **The Founding of New England** 112
Chart: The American Colonies 115
People to Remember: Anne Hutchinson 117
Lesson 4: **Education and Trade in Colonial New England** 119
Lesson 5: **The Founding of the Middle Colonies** 123
Fascinating Facts: The Oldest Schools in the United States 125
People to Remember: Benjamin Franklin 128
Chapter 3 Review 129
UNIT 2 REVIEW 130
SKILL DEVELOPMENT 131
Map: European Discovery and Exploration 131

UNIT 3 **THE UNITED STATES IS BORN** 132
CHAPTER 1 **THE STRUGGLE FOR INDEPENDENCE** 134
Lesson 1: **Trouble in British America** 134
Time Line: 1765–1783 135
Lesson 2: **The American Revolution Begins** 139
Fascinating Facts: A Submarine that Fought in the American Revolution 142
People to Remember: George Washington 143
Special Feature: The Declaration of Independence 146
Lesson 3: **Winning Independence** 148
Map: The Revolutionary War 149
Lesson 4: **How the Americans Won** 155
Special Feature: The Leaders of the Revolution 158
Chapter 1 Review 162

CHAPTER 2 **GOVERNING THE NEW NATION** 163
Lesson 1: **The First Government** 163

1818

1818

Lesson 2:	**Forming a New Government**	167
Lesson 3:	**The Constitution**	170
Chart:	Our National Government	171
Lesson 4:	**Amendments to the Constitution**	173
Lesson 5:	**President Washington and the New Government**	176
Fascinating Facts:	George Washington's False Teeth	177
Fascinating Facts:	The Electoral College	178
Lesson 6:	**Jefferson to Jackson**	182
People to Remember:	Thomas Jefferson	183
Special Feature:	The Star-Spangled Banner	185
Chapter 2 Review		188
CHAPTER 3	**THE UNITED STATES EXPANDS**	189
Lesson 1:	**The Westward Movement**	189
Time and Place:	Westward Growth of the United States, Time Line and Map	191
Lesson 2:	**Frontier Life**	194
Lesson 3:	**Across the Mississippi**	197
Time Line:	1803–1830s	197
People to Remember:	Sacajawea	199
Lesson 4:	**Westward Ho!**	101
Map:	Trails West	203
Lesson 5:	**The Lone Star State**	206
Lesson 6:	**The California Gold Rush**	209
Lesson 7:	**Mexican-Americans in the West**	212
Fascinating Facts:	President for a Day	212
Chart:	Hispanic-Americans in the United States	214
Chapter 3 Review		215
UNIT 3 REVIEW		216
SKILL DEVELOPMENT		217
Time Line:	Westward Growth of the United States	217

UNIT 4	**THE UNITED STATES CHANGES**	218
CHAPTER 1	**DIVIDED STATES**	220
Lesson 1:	**Black Slavery in the United States**	220
People to Remember:	Frederick Douglass	223
People to Remember:	Sojourner Truth	224
Lesson 2:	**Slave or Free**	226
People to Remember:	Harriet Tubman	227
Bar Graph:	The North and South in 1860	228
Map:	Slave and Free States in 1861	229
Time Line:	1860–1867	231
Lesson 3:	**The American Civil War**	233
Fascinating Facts:	The Civil War Balloon Corps	234
Lesson 4:	**Reconstruction in the South**	238
Chapter 1 Review		243
CHAPTER 2	**INDUSTRY AND IMMIGRANTS**	244
Lesson 1:	**The Industrial Revolution Begins**	244
Fascinating Facts:	The Woman Who Invented the Ice Cream Freezer	250
Lesson 2:	**Industry after the Civil War**	252
Lesson 3:	**New Americans Arrive**	259
Line Graph:	Immigration: 1840–1930	259
Time and Place:	Peak Immigration Years, 1850–1920, Time Line and Map	265
Lesson 4:	**Chinese Come to the United States**	268
Lesson 5:	**Japanese and Filipinos Arrive**	276
Map:	Immigration from Asia to the West Coast	276
Chapter 2 Review		281
Bar Graph:	Immigration: 1906–1910	281

1820

1846

CHAPTER 3 **THE LAST FRONTIER** 282
Lesson 1: **The Great Plains Are Settled** 282
Lesson 2: **American Indians of the Plains** 286
Lesson 3: **Whose Land?** 290
People to Remember: Chief Joseph 293
Lesson 4: **American Indians Today** 296
Map: American Indian Communities 296
Fascinating Facts: The Oldest Corn in America 299
Chapter 3 Review 301
UNIT 4 REVIEW 302
SKILL DEVELOPMENT 303
Bar Graph: The North and South in 1860 303

UNIT 5 THE UNITED STATES IN THE MODERN WORLD 304

CHAPTER 1 **THE EARLY TWENTIETH CENTURY** 306
Lesson 1: **The United States in 1900** 306
Lesson 2: **Reformers in the United States** 308
Fascinating Facts: The First Subway in America 311
Lesson 3: **World War I** 312
Map: Europe before World War I 312
Lesson 4: **The Vote for Women** 316
People to Remember: Susan B. Anthony 319
Chapter 1 Review 320

CHAPTER 2 **THE UNITED STATES IN A CHANGING WORLD** 321
Lesson 1: **The Twenties** 321
Lesson 2: **The Great Depression and the New Deal** 324
Lesson 3: **World War II** 327
Map: Europe between the World Wars 327
Lesson 4: **The War at Home** 332
Lesson 5: **The Cold War** 335
Time and Place: The Cold War in Europe Time Line, Map of Europe after World War II 336
Lesson 6: **Equal Rights** 339
People to Remember: Martin Luther King, Jr. 341
Lesson 7: **Conflict and Compromise** 343
Lesson 8: **New Americans** 346
Lesson 9: **The Space Age** 349
Fascinating Facts: Legends about the Moon 351
Lesson 10: **Into the Future** 352
Chapter 2 Review 357
UNIT 5 REVIEW 358
SKILL DEVELOPMENT 359
Art: Interpreting Political Cartoons 359

UNIT 6 UNITED STATES GEOGRAPHY 360
Map: Physical Map of the United States 360–361

CHAPTER 1 **THE UNITED STATES TODAY** 362
Lesson 1: **What Is the United States?** 362
Map: Population of the United States 362
Map: Political Map of the United States 363
Map and Chart: United States Territories and Possessions 365
Lesson 2: **Landforms of the United States** 367
Lesson 3: **Rivers and Lakes of the United States** 372
Chart: The Longest Rivers in the United States 373
Chapter 1 Review 375

CHAPTER 2 **THE NORTHEAST** 376
Lesson 1: **The New England States** 376
Map: New England States with Key to Cities 378
Chart: New England States 379
Fascinating Facts: Making Maple Syrup 381

1851

1861

Lesson 2: **The Middle Atlantic States** 383
Map: Middle Atlantic States with Key to Cities 386
Chart: Middle Atlantic States 387
Fascinating Facts: Majestic Niagara Falls 389
Chapter 2 Review 391

CHAPTER 3 **THE SOUTH** 392
Lesson 1: **The Southeastern States** 392
Map: Southeastern States with Key to Cities 394
Chart: Southeastern States 395–396
Fascinating Facts: The Tennessee Valley Authority 397
Lesson 2: **The South Central States** 404
Map: South Central States with Key to Cities 406
Chart: South Central States 407
Fascinating Facts: New Orleans's Mardi Gras 410
Chapter 3 Review 412

CHAPTER 4 **THE MIDWEST AND WEST** 413
Lesson 1: **The Midwestern States** 413
Map: Midwestern States with Key to Cities 414
Chart: Midwestern States 415–416
Fascinating Facts: Strip Mining 418
Lesson 2: **The Mountain States** 423
Fascinating Facts: The Great Salt Lake 424
Map: Mountain States with Key to Cities 426
Chart: Mountain States 427
Lesson 3: **The Pacific States** 432
Map: Pacific States with Key to Cities 434
Chart: Pacific States 435
Fascinating Facts: Our Largest State: Alaska 436
Chapter 4 Review 441
UNIT 6 REVIEW 442
SKILL DEVELOPMENT 443
Map: United States Time Zones 443

UNIT 7 **NORTH AMERICAN NEIGHBORS** 444
CHAPTER 1 **CANADA** 446
Lesson 1: **The Geography of Canada** 446
Lesson 2: **The History of Canada** 451
Time and Place: The Growth of Canada, Map and Time Line 453
Lesson 3: **The Government of Canada** 455
Pie Chart: Languages Spoken in Canada 456
Chapter 1 Review 458

CHAPTER 2 **MEXICO AND CENTRAL AMERICA** 459
Lesson 1: **The Geography of Mexico** 459
Map: Physical Map of Mexico and Central America 459
Map: Political Map of Mexico 461
Lesson 2: **The History of Mexico** 463
Time and Place: Early Indian Peoples of Mexico, Time Line and Map 465
Lesson 3: **Central America** 468
Map: Central America and the Caribbean 472
Chapter 2 Review 473
UNIT 7 REVIEW 474
SKILL DEVELOPMENT 475
Map: Physical Map of Mexico and Central America 475

ATLAS
Physical Map of Earth 476–477
Political Map of Earth 478–479
Physical Map of North America 480
Political Map of North America 481
Physical Map of the United States 482–483
Political Map of the United States 484–485
NORTH AMERICAN NATIONS CHART 486
50 STATES CHART 487–493
PRESIDENTS AND VICE PRESIDENTS CHART 494–495
GAZETTEER 496–499
GLOSSARY 499–506
INDEX 506–511
CREDITS 511–512

MAPS AND GLOBES

Political Map of the United States 12–13
Globe with Latitude and Longitude Grid 18
Western Hemisphere Globe 19
Eastern Hemisphere Globe 19
Northern and Southern Hemisphere Globes 20
Latitude and Longitude Globes 22
Political Map of North America 23
Climate Zones Globe 31
Climate Map of North America 33
Peeling the Globe 34
Mercator Projection Map 35
Equal-Area Projection Map 35
Robinson Projection Map 35
Map Drawn from Aerial Photograph 37
Physical Map of North America 41
Political Map of the United States 43
Living Resources Map of North America 45
Population Map of Earth 46
Ptolemy's Map of Earth 48
Map of European Discovery and Exploration 49
Map of Columbus's Voyages to America 50, 77
Map of the Thirteen Colonies about 1770 51
Map of Europe before World War I 52
Route Map from Houston to Key West 53
Road Map of Florida 55
Street Map of Washington, DC 56
Map of the Eastern United States 59
Route Map of the First North Americans 64
Map of European Discovery and Exploration 80
Map of Spanish Exploration in North America 83
Map of Spanish and Portugese Explorers 85
Map of English and French Exploration of North America 93
Map of the Search for the Northwest Passage 96
Historical Map of Jamestown 103
Map of North American Settlements, 1630 104
Map of the Thirteen Colonies about 1770 109
Map of Economic Activity in the British Colonies about 1770 110
Map of European Discovery and Exploration 131
Map of the Revolutionary War 149
Map of the Westward Growth of the United States 191
Map of Trails West 203
Map of Slave and Free States in 1861 229
Map of Immigration to the United States, 1850–1920 265
Map of Immigration from Asia to the West Coast 276
Map of American Indian Communities 296
Map of Europe before World War I 312
Map of Europe between the World Wars 327
Map of Europe after World War II 336
Physical Map of the United States 360–361
Population Map of the United States 362
Political Map of the United States 363
Map of United States Territories and Possessions 365
Map of New England States with Key to Cities 378
Map of Middle Atlantic States with Key to Cities 386
Map of Southeastern States with Key to Cities 394
Map of South Central States with Key to Cities 406
Map of Midwestern States with Key to Cities 414
Map of Mountain States with Key to Cities 426
Map of Pacific States with Key to Cities 434
Map of United States Time Zones 443
Map of the Growth of Canada 453
Physical Map of Mexico and Central America 459
Political Map of Mexico 461
Map of Early Indian Peoples of Mexico 465
Map of Central America and the Caribbean 472
Physical Map of Mexico and Central America 475
Physical Map of Earth 476–477
Political Map of Earth 478–479
Physical Map of North America 480
Political Map of North America 481
Physical Map of the United States 482–483
Political Map of the United States 484–485

1912

1959

CHARTS AND GRAPHS

Climates of Earth Chart 32
Mileage Chart from Houston to Key West 54
The American Colonies Chart 115
Chart of Our National Government 171
Chart of Hispanic-Americans in the United States 214
Bar Graph of North and South in 1860 228, 303
Line Graph of Immigration: 1840–1930 259
Bar Graph of Immigration: 1906–1910 281
Chart of the United States Territories and Possessions 365
Chart of the Longest Rivers in the United States 373
Chart of the New England States 379
Chart of the Middle Atlantic States 387
Chart of the Southeastern States 395–396
Chart of the South Central States 407
Chart of the Midwestern States 415–416
Chart of the Mountain States 427
Chart of the Pacific States 435
Pie Chart of Languages Spoken in Canada 456
North American Nations Chart 486
50 States Chart 487–493
Presidents and Vice Presidents Chart 494–495

TIME AND PLACE

English and French Exploration of North America, Time Line and Map 93
From the Lost Colony to the Constitution, Time Line and Map 109
Westward Growth of the United States, Time Line and Map 191
Peak Immigration Years, 1850–1920, Time Line and Map 265
The Cold War in Europe Time Line, Map of Europe after World War II 336
The Growth of Canada, Time Line and Map 453
Early Indian Peoples of Mexico, Time Line and Map 465

TIME LINES

Early Events in North and South America 63
800s–1565 82
English and French Exploration of North America 93
1607–1681 105
From the Lost Colony to the Constitution 109
1765–1783 135
Westward Growth of the United States 191
1803–1830s 197
Westward Growth of the United States 217
1860–1867 231
Peak Immigration Years, 1850–1920 265
The Cold War in Europe 336
The Growth of Canada 453
Early Indian Peoples of Mexico 465

PEOPLE TO REMEMBER

Hernando de Soto 88
Anne Hutchinson 117
Benjamin Franklin 128
George Washington 143
Thomas Jefferson 183
Sacajawea 199
Frederick Douglass 223
Sojourner Truth 224
Harriet Tubman 227
Chief Joseph 293
Susan B. Anthony 319
Martin Luther King, Jr. 341

SPECIAL FEATURES

The Declaration of Independence 146
The Leaders of the Revolution 158
The Star-Spangled Banner 185

FASCINATING FACTS

The 100th Birthday of the Prime Meridian 21
The Oldest Maps in the World 38
The Lost Colony 91
The Oldest Schools in the United States 125
A Submarine that Fought in the American Revolution 142
George Washington's False Teeth 177
The Electoral College 178
President for a Day 212
The Civil War Balloon Corps 234
The Woman Who Invented the Ice Cream Freezer 250
The Oldest Corn in America 299
The First Subway in America 311
Legends about the Moon 351
Making Maple Syrup 381
Majestic Niagara Falls 389
The Tennessee Valley Authority 397
New Orleans's Mardi Gras 410
Strip Mining 418
The Great Salt Lake 424
Our Largest State: Alaska 436

MAPPING NORTH AMERICA

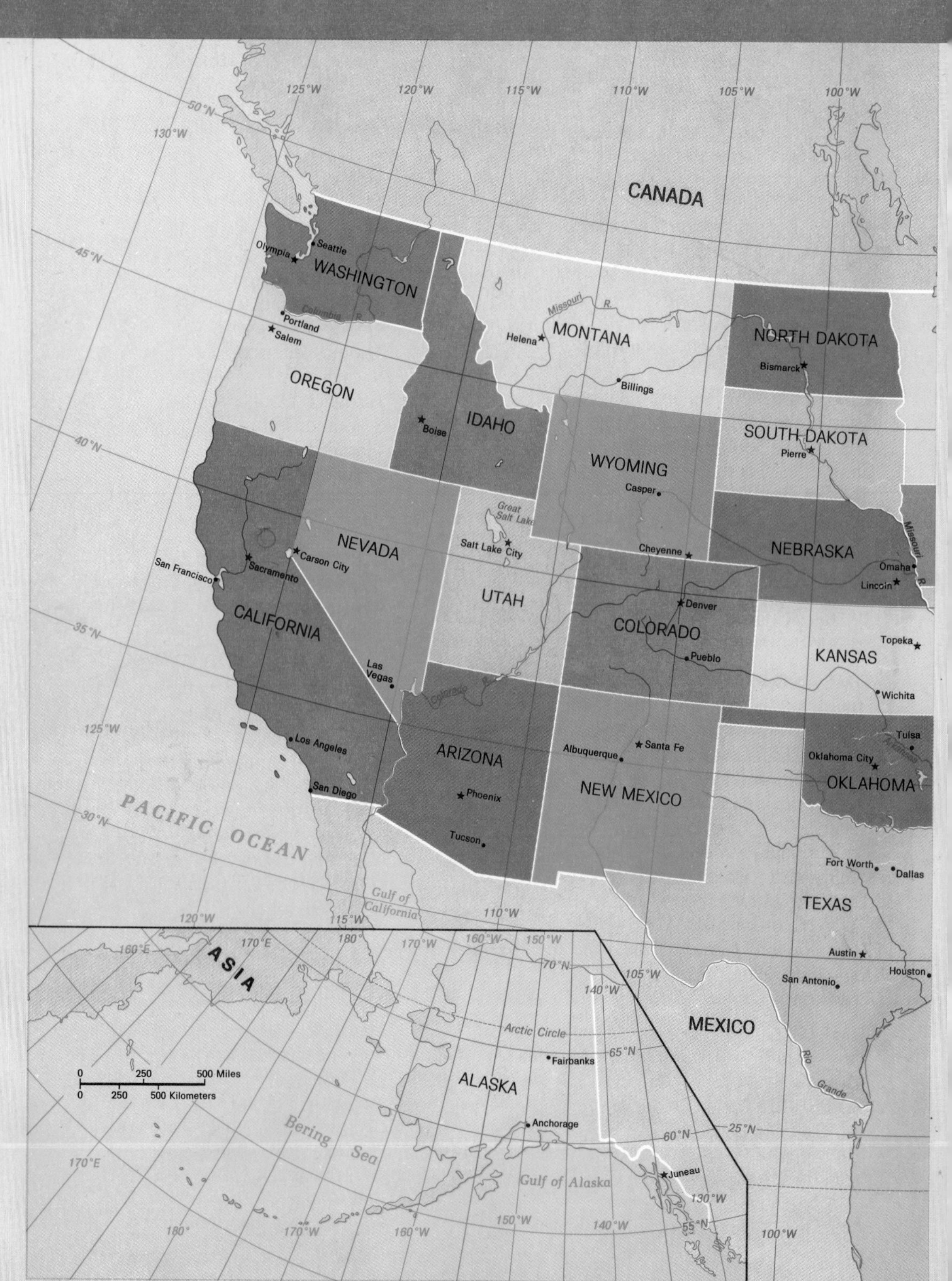

UNIT 1

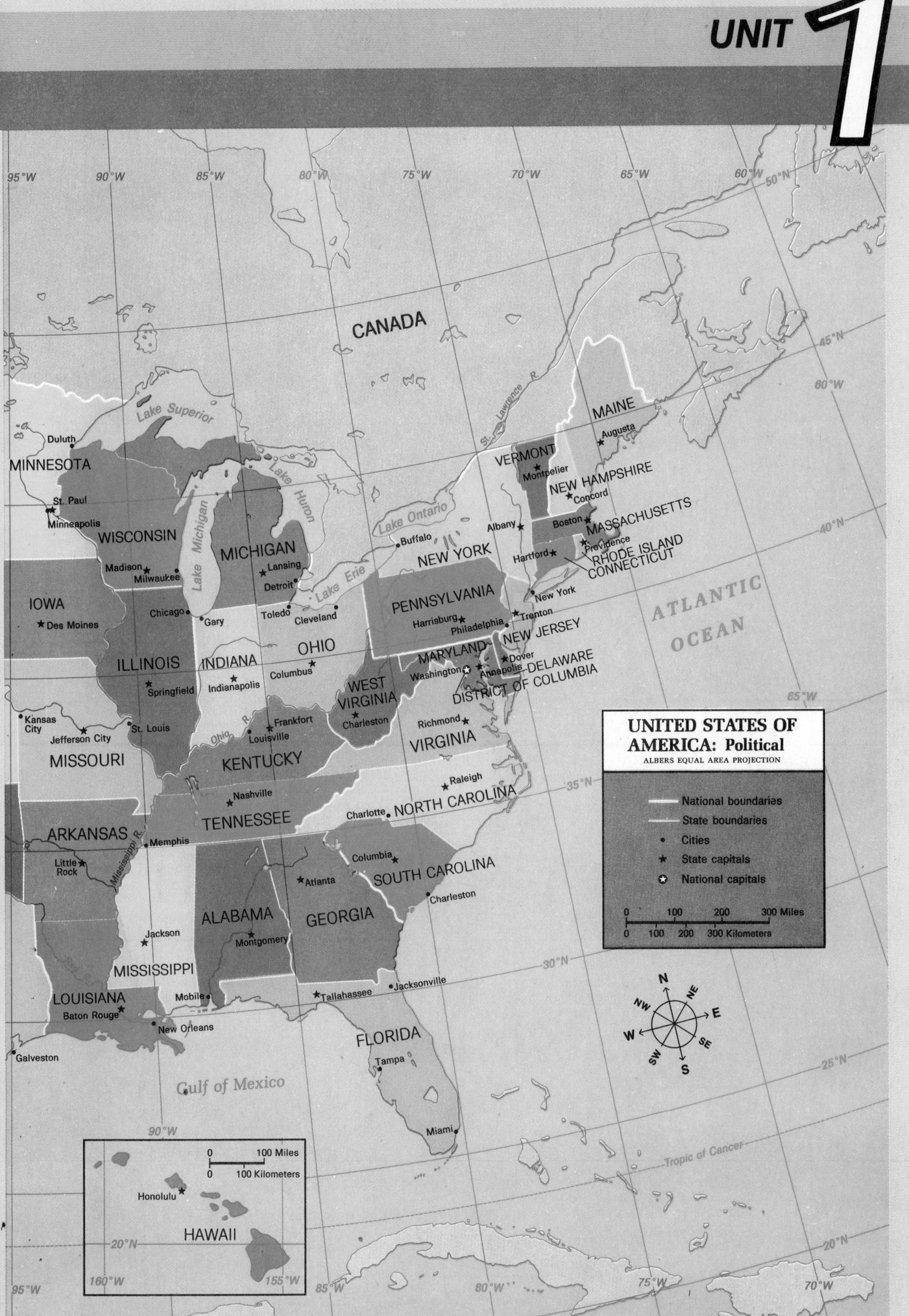
UNITED STATES OF AMERICA: Political
ALBERS EQUAL AREA PROJECTION
National boundaries
State boundaries
Cities
State capitals
National capitals
0 100 200 300 Miles
0 100 200 300 Kilometers
CANADA
ATLANTIC OCEAN
Gulf of Mexico
Lake Superior
Lake Michigan
Lake Huron
Lake Erie
Lake Ontario
St. Lawrence R.
Ohio R.
Mississippi R.
MINNESOTA
WISCONSIN
MICHIGAN
IOWA
ILLINOIS
INDIANA
OHIO
MISSOURI
KENTUCKY
TENNESSEE
ARKANSAS
LOUISIANA
MISSISSIPPI
ALABAMA
GEORGIA
FLORIDA
SOUTH CAROLINA
NORTH CAROLINA
VIRGINIA
WEST VIRGINIA
MARYLAND
DELAWARE
DISTRICT OF COLUMBIA
PENNSYLVANIA
NEW JERSEY
NEW YORK
CONNECTICUT
RHODE ISLAND
MASSACHUSETTS
VERMONT
NEW HAMPSHIRE
MAINE
HAWAII
Duluth
St. Paul
Minneapolis
Madison
Milwaukee
Lansing
Detroit
Chicago
Gary
Toledo
Cleveland
Buffalo
Des Moines
Springfield
Indianapolis
Columbus
Kansas City
Jefferson City
St. Louis
Louisville
Frankfort
Charleston
Richmond
Washington
Annapolis
Dover
Harrisburg
Philadelphia
Trenton
New York
Albany
Hartford
Providence
Boston
Concord
Montpelier
Augusta
Nashville
Raleigh
Charlotte
Memphis
Little Rock
Columbia
Atlanta
Charleston
Jackson
Montgomery
Mobile
Baton Rouge
New Orleans
Galveston
Tallahassee
Jacksonville
Tampa
Miami
Honolulu
0 100 Miles
0 100 Kilometers
Tropic of Cancer
N
NE
E
SE
S
SW
W
NW
95°W
90°W
85°W
80°W
75°W
70°W
65°W
60°W
50°N
45°N
40°N
35°N
30°N
25°N
20°N
160°W
155°W

CHAPTER 1 MAPPING THE EARTH

Lesson 1: Where You Are in Time and Space

FIND THE WORDS

continent history historian geography geographer

Today, you are sitting in a classroom. Your room is in a school. Your school is in a community. Your community is part of a state. Your state is one of 50 divisions of your nation, the United States. Most of the United States is on the continent of North America. North America is one of seven **continents,** or large masses of land, on Earth. You can use a map or globe to find your location in space.

You are also at a point in time. A clock can tell you the hour and minute. A calendar shows the day, month, and year. Can you pinpoint your position in time and space?

The United States also has a special location in time and space. It has existed for more than 200 years. This year, you will study the history and geography of the United States. **History** is the story of what happened in the past. When you study history, you learn about people and events that shaped your world.

What is happening today is a result of what people did in the past. We know about their actions because people kept written records. People who write or study records of past events are called **historians.** Historians do not report everything that happened in the past. They write about the people and events they think are most important. The founding of our nation is an important part of our history. So is the exploring of our continent, North America.

Above: Vikings from Scandinavia may have been the first Europeans to explore North America. *Below:* The signing of the Declaration of Independence in 1776 was an important event in United States history.

Most of our nation's history took place in North America. Our continent is the stage on which our history has been acted out. This year, you will learn why so many people came to North America. You will see how the land and its resources affected people's lives.

Geo- means "Earth." **Geography** is the study of physical facts about places on Earth. When you study geography, you learn about the shape of the land and water. You learn about climates and natural resources. You find out why people live in some parts of Earth and not others. Experts who study physical facts about places on Earth are known as **geographers.**

Learning geography is like going on a treasure hunt. You can find a wealth of facts by using maps and globes. You can learn special terms to help you report what you find. For the rest of this unit, you will be setting the stage for history. You will walk in the footsteps of American Indians and pioneers. Like them, you will explore the features of the land.

REVIEW

VOCABULARY MASTERY

1. In ___, we study what people did in the past.
   geography history math
2. In ___, we study physical facts about places.
   history division geography
3. North America is one of seven ___.
   countries continents nations
4. Experts who study physical facts about places on Earth are ___.
   historians pioneers geographers
5. Experts who keep records of past events are ___.
   historians geographers explorers

READING FOR MAIN IDEAS

6. Write your address on Earth. Include your street, town or city, state, nation, and continent.
7. How do people know about what happened in the past?
8. Where did most of our nation's history take place?
9. What is the meaning of *geo-* in the word *geography?*
10. Name three things people study in geography.

THINKING SKILLS

Do you think people now and people in the past thought the same things were important? Why, or why not?

WRITING SKILLS

Be a historian. Start keeping a daily record of what happens around you. Find out what was different when your grandparents were your age.

Lesson 2: The Grid on the Globe

FIND THE WORDS

globe equator hemisphere
grid latitude parallel
longitude meridian
prime meridian

A **globe** is a round model of the planet Earth. On a globe, you can see which parts of Earth are land and which are water. You can find Earth's seven continents and four oceans. On most globes, you can locate nations, states, and cities. On some, you can see rivers and mountains.

The planet Earth rotates around an axis. This imaginary line runs through the center of Earth from the North Pole to the South Pole. The North Pole is the point farthest north on Earth. The South Pole is the point farthest south.

A globe is usually mounted on a stand. It has a frame around it. This frame is attached at the points that represent the North Pole and South Pole. Notice that the globe is tilted. The North Pole is not directly on top. This is done because Earth's axis is tilted in relation to the sun.

Midway between the poles is the **equator** (ih KWAY tur). This imaginary line circles Earth around the middle. It divides the globe into two half circles, or **hemispheres** (HEM uh SFIRZ). *Hemi-* means "half." A *sphere* is a globe or ball. The part of Earth between the equator and the North Pole is the Northern Hemisphere. The part of Earth between the equator and the South Pole is the Southern Hemisphere.

Understanding Latitude and Longitude

To find places on a globe, we use directions. To go toward the North Pole is to go north. To go toward the South Pole is to go south. The direction in which the sun appears to rise is east. The direction in which the sun appears to set is west.

A globe is a model of Earth.

North, south, east, and west are the four basic directions. We need more precise directions to find places on a round surface. Suppose you were on a ship in the middle of the ocean. How would you describe your position? There are no landmarks in mid-ocean.

Now look at the pattern of lines on a globe. Some of these lines run up and down, from north to south. Some run across, from west to east. The lines cross one another to form a **grid,** or pattern of small boxes. Using this grid system, you can locate places anywhere on Earth.

First, though, you have to learn how to name and read the lines. The lines that run across the globe are called lines of **latitude** (LAT uh TOOD). Lines of latitude show how far north or south you are. The starting place for latitude is the equator. In fact, the equator itself is a line of latitude. Other lines of latitude run in the same direction as the equator. They are parallel to it. When lines are parallel (PAR uh LEL), they are an equal distance apart at every point. Latitude lines are also called **parallels.**

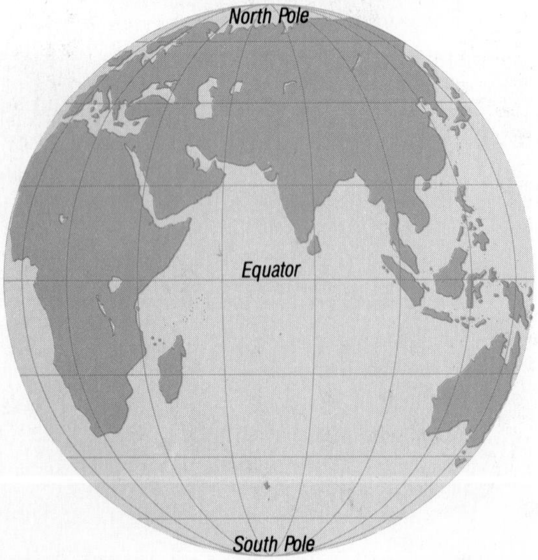

The lines that go north and south on the globe are lines of **longitude** (LON juh TOOD). Lines of longitude run from the North Pole to the South Pole. On a globe, these lines are not parallel. They meet at the poles. Lines of longitude are also called **meridians** (muh RID ee UNZ). *Meridian* means "midday." When the sun crosses a line of longitude, it is midday there.

Lines of longitude show how far east or west you are. But there is no natural starting point for longitude. In 1884, representatives of 25 nations met in Washington, DC. They agreed to start longitude at the meridian that passes through Greenwich (GREN ich), England. Greenwich is close to London. Two-thirds of the world's ships were already measuring longitude from Greenwich. Thus the Greenwich meridian became the **prime meridian,** or the starting place for longitude.

THE EASTERN HEMISPHERE

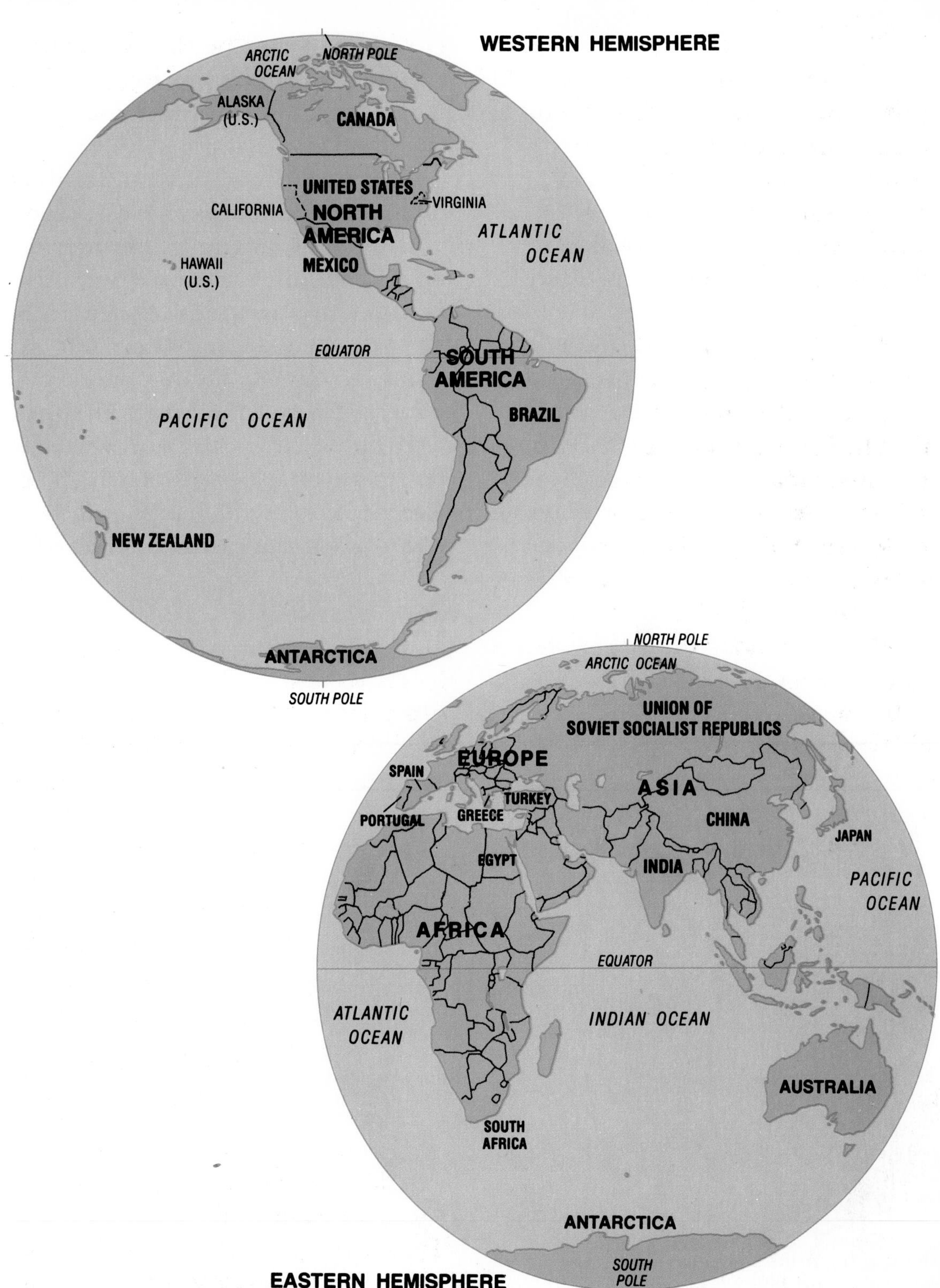
WESTERN HEMISPHERE
NORTH POLE
ARCTIC OCEAN
ALASKA (U.S.)
CANADA
UNITED STATES
VIRGINIA
CALIFORNIA
NORTH AMERICA
ATLANTIC OCEAN
HAWAII (U.S.)
MEXICO
EQUATOR
SOUTH AMERICA
PACIFIC OCEAN
BRAZIL
NEW ZEALAND
ANTARCTICA
SOUTH POLE
NORTH POLE
ARCTIC OCEAN
UNION OF SOVIET SOCIALIST REPUBLICS
EUROPE
SPAIN
ASIA
TURKEY
PORTUGAL
GREECE
CHINA
JAPAN
EGYPT
INDIA
PACIFIC OCEAN
AFRICA
EQUATOR
ATLANTIC OCEAN
INDIAN OCEAN
AUSTRALIA
SOUTH AFRICA
ANTARCTICA
SOUTH POLE
EASTERN HEMISPHERE

Remember, lATitude is distance north or south of the equATor. LONgitude is distance east or west of LONdon.

Hemispheres of Earth

The equator divides Earth into Northern and Southern Hemispheres. However, there are two ways to divide Earth into Eastern and Western Hemispheres. The first way is to follow the natural divisions of the continents. By this method, North America and South America are in the Western Hemisphere. Europe, Asia, Africa, and Australia are in the Eastern Hemisphere. Antarctica is in both the Western Hemisphere and the Eastern Hemisphere.

Since 1884, we have been able to divide the hemispheres a second way, along the prime meridian. That puts parts of western Europe and western Africa into the Western Hemisphere. It is easier to show hemispheres on globes if continents are not split.

In the next lesson, you will use the grid on the globe to find places. You will learn another way to give your address on Earth.

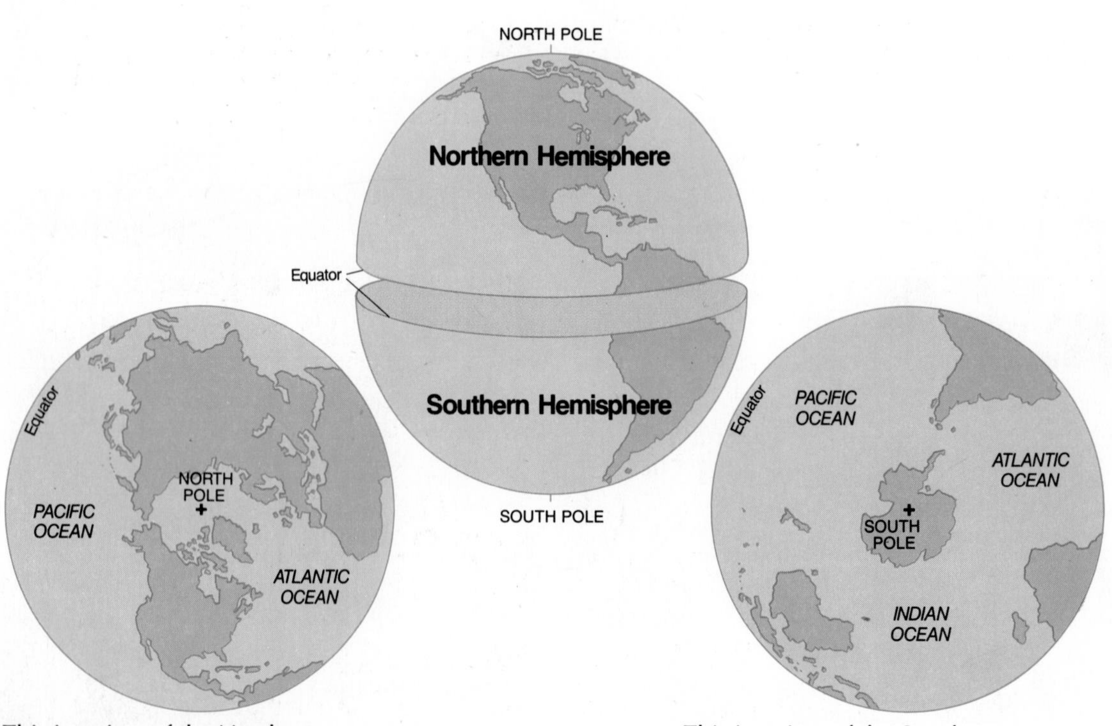

This is a view of the Northern Hemisphere from the North Pole. The equator is at the edge of the circle.

This is a view of the Southern Hemisphere from the South Pole. The equator is at the edge of the circle.

Fascinating Facts

Mapmakers have been using grids on maps since ancient times. One of the first was a Greek geographer named Ptolemy (TOL uh mee). He drew a map of Earth with latitude and longitude 1,800 years ago.

For centuries, however, there was no official starting place for longitude. Nations would start longitude in their capital city or at their chief observatory. (An observatory is a place where scientists study the stars and planets.) The French started longitude at Paris; the Danes at Copenhagen; the Swedes at Stockholm; the Italians at Naples; the Spanish at Cadiz; and the British at Greenwich.

In the late 1800s, there were more than 10 different prime meridians. To solve the problem, 25 nations sent delegates to Washington, DC. They met on October 13, 1884. They agreed that the Greenwich meridian would be the prime meridian. Thus, 1984 marked the 100th birthday of the prime meridian.

There are two ways to divide Earth into Eastern and Western Hemispheres. One is to follow the natural divisions of the continents. The other is to divide the hemispheres along the prime meridian. The photograph of Earth above was taken from outer space. The red line drawn on it is the prime meridian. You can see that the prime meridian passes through western Europe and western Africa.

REVIEW

VOCABULARY MASTERY

1. A ___ is half a globe.
   meridian parallel hemisphere
2. The ___ divides Earth into Northern and Southern Hemispheres.
   grid prime meridian equator
3. ___ starts at the equator.
   Longitude Latitude The grid
4. ___ starts at the prime meridian.
   The grid Latitude Longitude
5. Lines of latitude are also called ___.
   meridians parallels grids

READING FOR MAIN IDEAS

6. Name five things you can find on most globes.
7. Why are globes tilted?
8. What does a grid system do?
9. Tell a way to remember where latitude and longitude start.
10. What are two ways to divide Earth into Eastern and Western Hemispheres?

THINKING SKILLS

When would a map be more useful to you than a globe?

Lesson 3: Mastering Latitude and Longitude

FIND THE WORDS

degree **coordinate** **minute** **time zone**

Suppose you want to go on a trip. Find out the distance from your starting point to your goal. That is how far you must travel.

Latitude starts at the equator. It tells you how far north or south of the equator a place is.

Longitude starts at the prime meridian. Longitude tells you how far east or west of the prime meridian a place is.

Since Earth is round, it is measured like a circle. Every circle can be divided into 360 units called **degrees.** We write 360 degrees as 360°. The equator is at 0° latitude. The prime meridian is at 0° longitude. These are always the starting points.

Look at the globes below. As you remember, lines of latitude are great imaginary circles. They go around the globe parallel to the equator. They do not touch each other. They are always the same distance apart. The circles get smaller as they get closer to the North Pole and South Pole.

The lines of longitude circle the globe through the North and South Poles. All these lines meet at the poles. They are farthest apart at the equator.

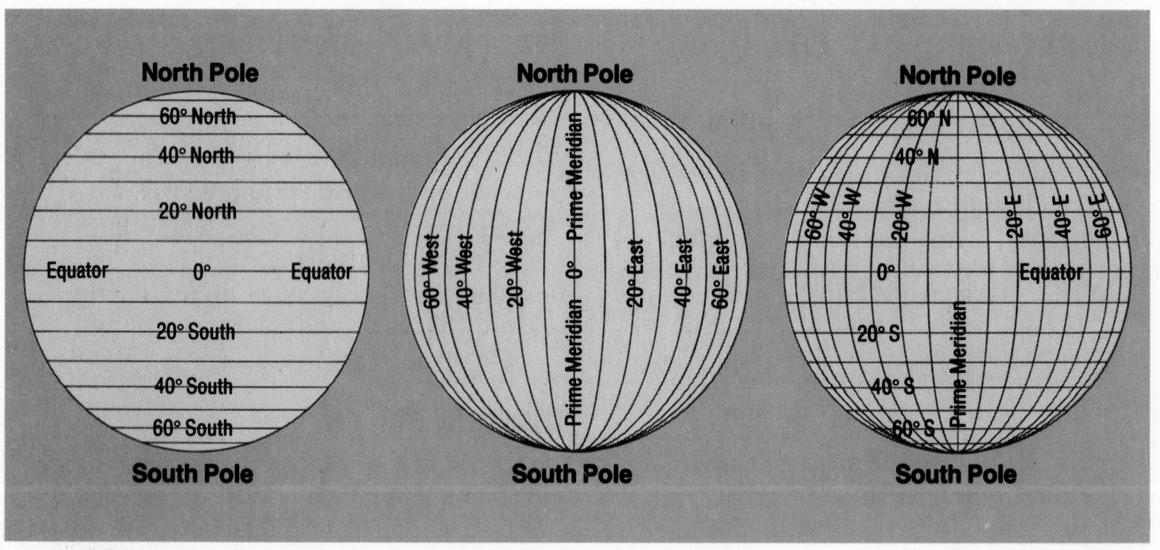

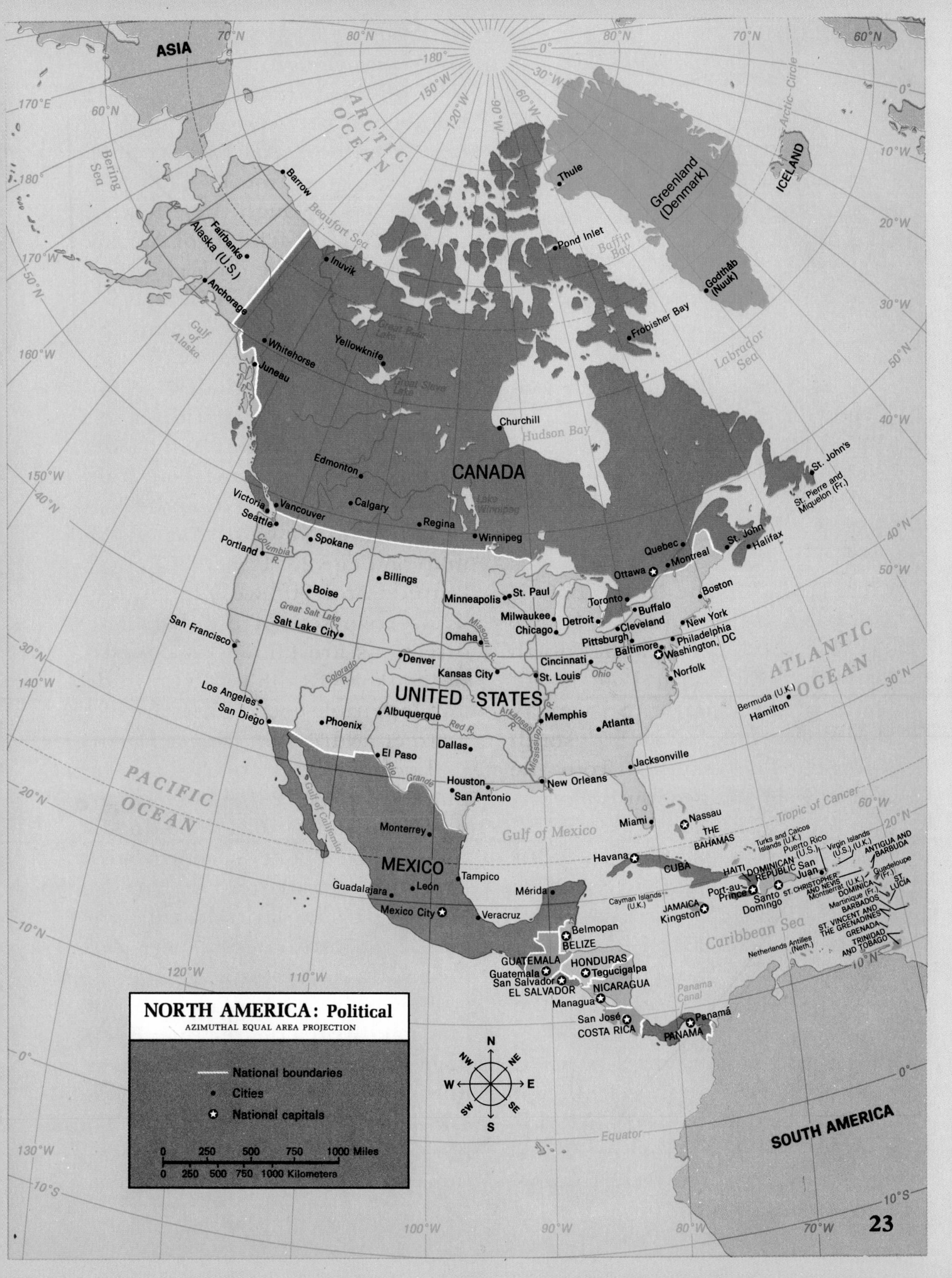

NORTH AMERICA: Political
AZIMUTHAL EQUAL AREA PROJECTION
National boundaries
Cities
National capitals
0 250 500 750 1000 Miles
0 250 500 750 1000 Kilometers
N
NE
E
SE
S
SW
W
NW
ASIA
ARCTIC OCEAN
Bering Sea
Beaufort Sea
Greenland (Denmark)
ICELAND
Thule
Baffin Bay
Godthåb (Nuuk)
Pond Inlet
Frobisher Bay
Labrador Sea
Barrow
Fairbanks
Alaska (U.S.)
Anchorage
Gulf of Alaska
Inuvik
Great Bear Lake
Yellowknife
Great Slave Lake
Whitehorse
Juneau
Churchill
Hudson Bay
CANADA
Edmonton
Calgary
Victoria
Vancouver
Seattle
Regina
Winnipeg
Lake Winnipeg
St. John's
St. Pierre and Miquelon (Fr.)
Quebec
Montreal
Ottawa
St. John
Halifax
Portland
Columbia R.
Spokane
Billings
Boise
Great Salt Lake
Salt Lake City
San Francisco
Minneapolis
St. Paul
Milwaukee
Chicago
Detroit
Toronto
Buffalo
Boston
Cleveland
New York
Pittsburgh
Philadelphia
Baltimore
Washington, DC
Omaha
Missouri R.
Denver
Colorado R.
Kansas City
St. Louis
Cincinnati
Ohio R.
Norfolk
ATLANTIC OCEAN
Bermuda (U.K.)
Hamilton
UNITED STATES
Los Angeles
San Diego
Phoenix
Albuquerque
Red R.
Arkansas R.
Memphis
Atlanta
Mississippi R.
El Paso
Dallas
Rio Grande
Houston
San Antonio
New Orleans
Jacksonville
PACIFIC OCEAN
Gulf of California
Monterrey
Gulf of Mexico
Miami
Nassau
THE BAHAMAS
Tropic of Cancer
Turks and Caicos Islands (U.K.)
Puerto Rico (U.S.)
Virgin Islands (U.S.) (U.K.)
ANTIGUA AND BARBUDA
Havana
CUBA
HAITI
DOMINICAN REPUBLIC
San Juan
Guadeloupe (Fr.)
ST. CHRISTOPHER AND NEVIS
Montserrat (U.K.)
DOMINICA
Martinique (Fr.)
ST. LUCIA
BARBADOS
ST. VINCENT AND THE GRENADINES
GRENADA
TRINIDAD AND TOBAGO
MEXICO
Tampico
Guadalajara
León
Mérida
Mexico City
Veracruz
Cayman Islands (U.K.)
Port-au-Prince
Santo Domingo
JAMAICA
Kingston
Caribbean Sea
Netherlands Antilles (Neth.)
Belmopan
BELIZE
GUATEMALA
Guatemala
HONDURAS
Tegucigalpa
San Salvador
EL SALVADOR
NICARAGUA
Managua
Panama Canal
San José
COSTA RICA
Panamá
PANAMA
Equator
SOUTH AMERICA
Arctic Circle

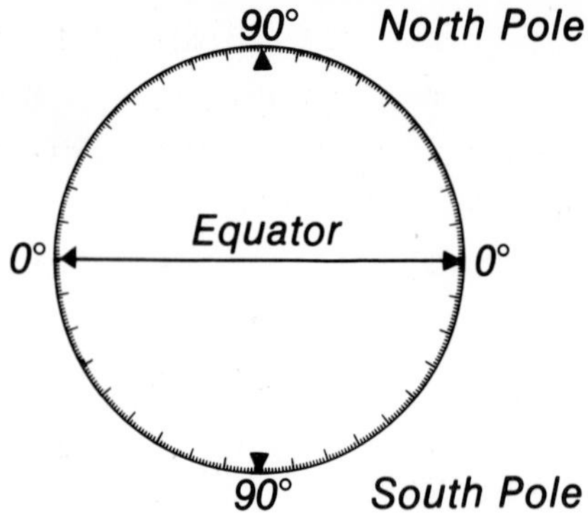

The lines of latitude and longitude form a grid system all over the globe. This grid system is used to give the location of places on Earth. Sailors use it to describe their location at sea.

You know that the equator is at 0° latitude. The North Pole is 90° north of the equator. So we say the North Pole is at 90° north latitude. The South Pole is 90° south of the equator. So we say the South Pole is at 90° south latitude. The distance from the North Pole to the South Pole is half a circle, or 180°.

New Orleans, Louisiana, is 30° north of the equator. So New Orleans is at 30° north latitude. Pôrto Alegre, Brazil, is 30° south of the equator. So Pôrto Alegre is at 30° south latitude. See the map on pages 476 and 477.

The prime meridian is at 0° longitude. Half a circle from the prime meridian is 180°. Meridians west of the prime meridian are numbered between 0° and 180° west longitude. Meridians east of the prime meridian are numbered between 0° and 180° east longitude. At the 180° line, east and west meet. The 180° line passes through the Aleutian (uh LOO shun) Islands of Alaska. Find the 180° line on a globe.

New Orleans, Louisiana, is 90° west of the prime meridian. So New Orleans is at 90° west longitude. Dacca, Bangladesh, is 90° east of the prime meridian. So Dacca is at 90° east longitude. Find New Orleans and Dacca on the map on pages 476 and 477.

Now find New Orleans on the map on page 23. It is at 30° north latitude and 90° west longitude. Those two sets of numbers and directions are known as **coordinates** (koh OR dih nits). Latitude and longitude coordinates are like a street address on planet Earth.

Look for Mexico City on the map on page 23. It is at 20° north latitude, 100° west longitude. Mexico City's coordinates can also be written as 20° N, 100° W. Using latitude and longitude coordinates, you can locate any place on Earth.

However, most places do not fall exactly on a degree line. Each degree can be further divided into 60 parts called **minutes.** We write 60 minutes as 60′. To be precise, we can state locations in degrees and minutes.

New York City is at 40° 40′ north latitude. It is at 73° 50′ west longitude.

Find out the latitude and longitude coordinates of the place where you live. Use an atlas map of your state. Find the lines of latitude and longitude that are closest to your community. Then write your new address on Earth.

Suppose your city or community is between the lines. Notice how many degrees there are between each set of lines. Divide the space into that many parts. Then guess the nearest degree.

Time Zones

Longitude is also used to figure out what time it is. Our system of time zones starts at the prime meridian. Earth has 24 **time zones.** Each zone is about 15° wide and stands for 1 hour. All places within a time zone have the same clock time.

Suppose you travel east. The time gets 1 hour later when you enter a new time zone. Suppose you travel west. The time gets 1 hour earlier when you enter a new time zone.

For example, when it is 2 P.M. in Florida, it is 1 P.M. in Louisiana. It is 12 noon in Utah and it is 11 A.M. in California. When it is 11 A.M. in California, it is 9 A.M. in Hawaii and Alaska. The times vary because Earth rotates on its axis from west to east. When day breaks in Florida, it is still night in California.

REVIEW

VOCABULARY MASTERY

1. There are 360 ___ in a circle.
   minutes   degrees   coordinates
2. There are 60 ___ in a degree.
   coordinates   minutes   seconds
3. Numbers and directions giving the latitude and longitude of a place are called ___ .
   meridians   coordinates   parallels
4. What line is at 0° latitude? What line is at 0° longitude?
5. What is a time zone?

MAP SKILLS

Look at the map on page 23.

6. What is the latitude of Houston?
7. What is the latitude of Philadelphia?
8. What is at 60° north latitude, 80° west longitude?
9. In what nation are these coordinates found: 20° N, 90° W?
10. In what state are these coordinates found: 70° N, 160° W?

THINKING SKILLS

Before 1884, there were many different prime meridians. Why was it important for nations to agree on one prime meridian for Earth?

Lesson 4: Geographic Dictionary:

Landforms and Bodies of Water

FIND THE WORDS

landform plain plateau
swamp hill mesa mountain
mountain range
mountain system valley
island peninsula ocean sea
gulf bay river source
mouth delta downstream
upstream tributary lake

If you were to travel across our country, you would see many different **landforms,** or shapes of land. In some places, the land would be flat. In others, it would be high and rugged. In still others, it would be gently rolling.

Geographers have special terms to describe Earth's landforms and bodies of water.

Plains are lands that are mostly flat. Plains are usually the most useful kind of land. Many plains have good soil for crops. Rivers flow slowly through the plains. Farming and travel are easy. Often, plains are also lowlands.

Plateaus (pla TOHZ) are flat lands that are higher than the lands around them. They are also called tablelands. The flat top of a plateau is like a plain. In fact, the Great Plains of North America are really a plateau.

Hills are lands that rise higher than the land around them. In gently rolling hills, the land is often as useful as land on the plains. But in hilly areas, the land is steeper than on the plains. A hill with steep sides and a flat top is a **mesa** (MAY suh).

A river carved the Grand Canyon out of a plateau.

LANDFORMS

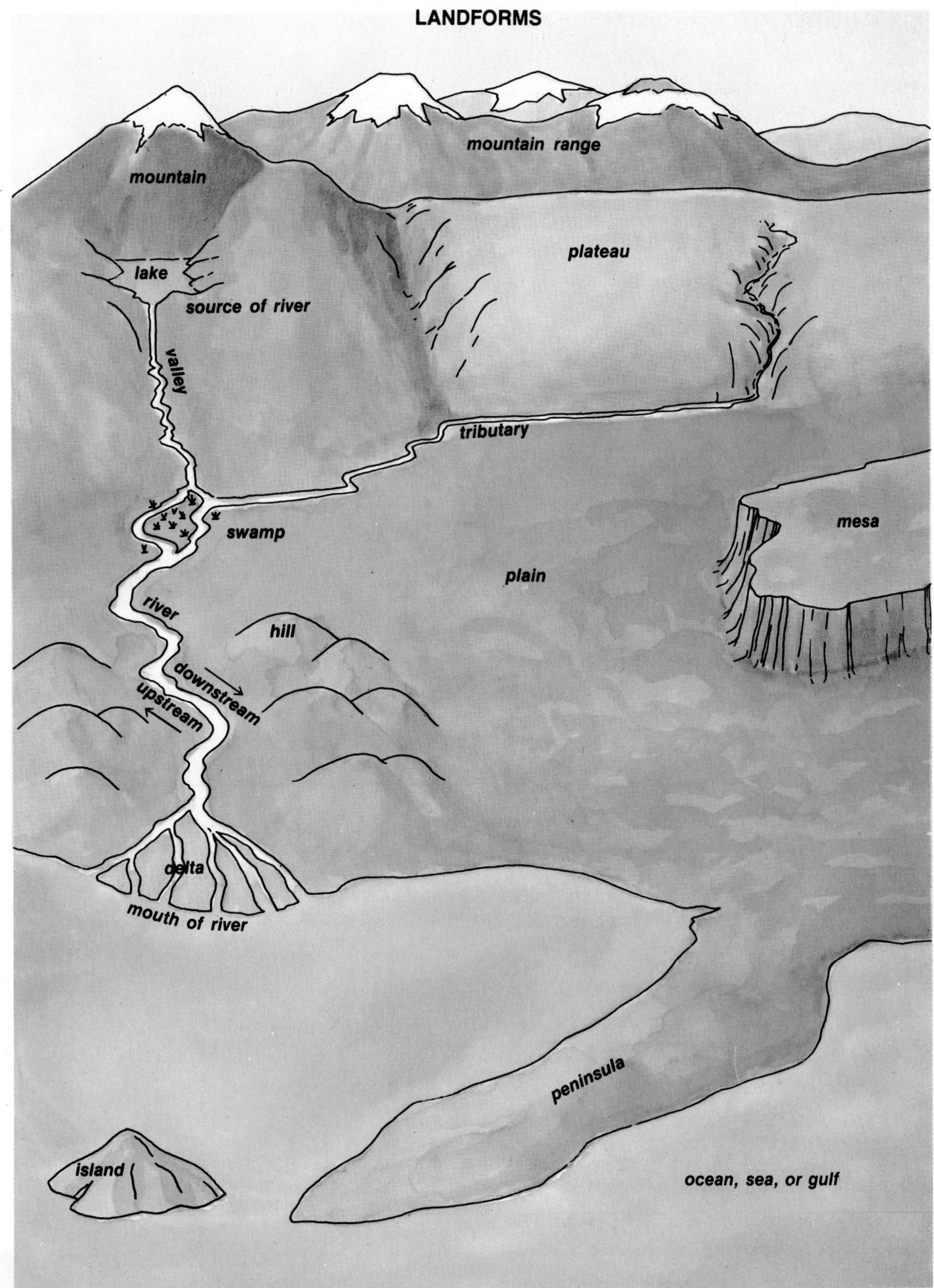
mountain range
mountain
plateau
lake
source of river
valley
tributary
swamp
mesa
plain
river
hill
downstream
upstream
delta
mouth of river
peninsula
island
ocean, sea, or gulf

Mountains are areas of very high, steep land. A mountain is much higher than the land around it. Mountain areas are seldom useful for planting crops. Usually, few people live on mountains. Mountains are often found in groups called **mountain ranges.** Huge groups of mountain ranges are called **mountain systems.** North America has two major mountain systems. The Rocky Mountains are in the west. The Appalachian (AP uh LAY chun) Mountains are in the east.

mountains

Valleys are lowlands found between a group of hills or mountains. Rivers also form valleys between higher lands. In mountain areas, people often find much useful land in valleys.

valley

Swamps are lowlands that are covered with water much of the time. Unless swamplands are drained, they are not very useful to people. But swamps are rich in plant and animal life. The Everglades is a great swamp in southern Florida.

swamp

Islands are pieces of land that are surrounded by water. The state of Hawaii is on islands in the Pacific Ocean.

Peninsulas are almost islands. They are pieces of land mostly surrounded by water. The state of Florida is on a peninsula.

island

Geographers also have terms to describe the water that covers seven-tenths of Earth's surface.

Oceans are the huge bodies of water that cover most of Earth's surface. There are four oceans: the Atlantic, Pacific, Arctic, and Indian oceans. Three oceans touch North America. Find them on the map on page 23.

Seas are much smaller than oceans. They are surrounded by land on two or more sides. A sea can be part of an ocean. Or it can be completely surrounded by land. Find the Bering Sea next to Alaska on the map on page 23.

Gulfs are much the same as seas. A gulf is a large body of water surrounded by land on two or more sides. **Bays** are also bodies of water that are mostly surrounded by land.

Rivers are bodies of water that carry water away from the land. The place where a river begins is its **source.** A river's source could be a lake or a spring. Most rivers flow into an ocean or a sea. The place where a river flows into another body of water is its **mouth.**

Sometimes, river water carries a great deal of soil. A river usually drops this soil at its mouth. This often forms a low, swampy plain shaped much like a triangle. Such an area is called a **delta.** Rivers that flow out through deltas often have many small mouths. In North America, the Mississippi River forms a delta in Louisiana.

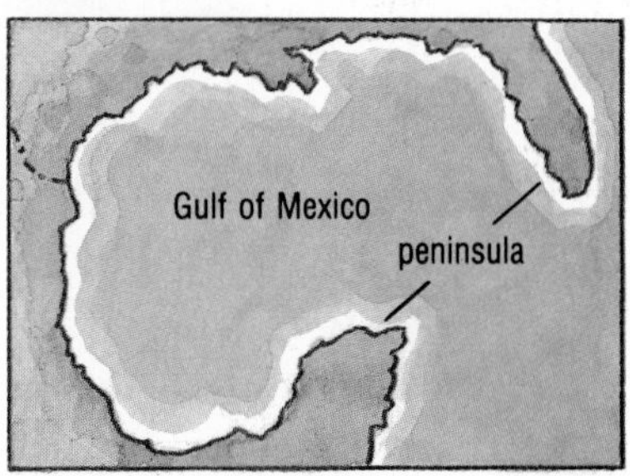

ocean

river

delta

A river flows from a higher place to a lower place. The direction in which a river flows is called **downstream.** The direction opposite to the flow of a river is called **upstream.** Rivers usually have **tributaries** (TRIB yuh TER eez). These are smaller rivers or streams that flow into a larger river.

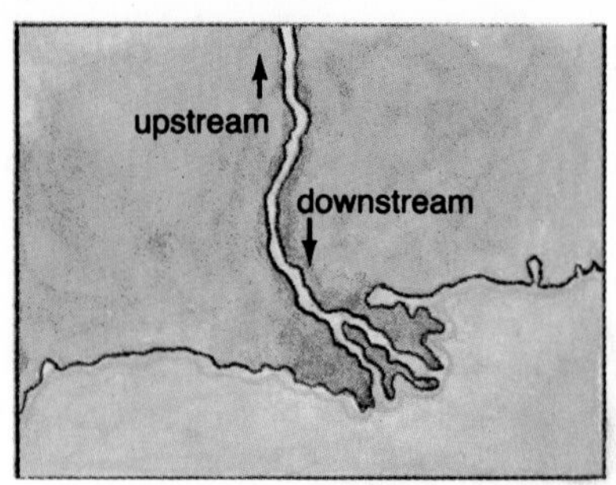

Lakes are bodies of water completely surrounded by land. Usually, the water in lakes is fresh. Fresh water has very little salt in it. There are five Great Lakes between the United States and Canada. They are the largest freshwater lakes in the world. The Great Salt Lake is in Utah. Some large salty lakes are called seas.

REVIEW

VOCABULARY MASTERY

1. A ___ can be part of an ocean.
   lake river sea
2. The top of a ___ is like a plain.
   mountain plateau peninsula
3. A group of mountain ranges is a ___.
   mountain system plateau valley
4. ___ flow into a river.
   Oceans Lakes Tributaries
5. The place where a river starts is its ___.
   mouth source tributary
6. The place where a river flows into another body of water is its ___.
   source mouth tributary

READING FOR MAIN IDEAS

7. What is usually the most useful kind of land?
8. Name two kinds of land that are less useful for people and crops.
9. How do seas differ from oceans?
10. Why is the direction in which a river flows called *downstream?*
11. What kind of water do lakes usually have?

RESEARCH AND WRITING SKILLS

Suppose you were writing a brochure to attract visitors to your state. Describe your state's landforms and bodies of water. Use an atlas, an encyclopedia, or other reference sources for information.

Lesson 5: Weather and Climate

FIND THE WORDS

temperature precipitation weather climate season

When you talk about the weather or the climate, you are talking about the air. You are speaking about how much heat and water is in the air.

The amount of heat in the air is the **temperature.** The amount of water that falls from the air is **precipitation** (pri SIP uh TAY shun). This can be in the form of rain, fog, snow, sleet, or hail.

The **weather** is the condition of the air in a place at any moment. For example, the weather may be warm and raining or cold and snowing. The **climate** is the average weather of a place over a long period of time. Usually, when you describe the climate, you are describing weather during a season of the year. A **season** is a period of the year with similar weather. Most parts of the United States have four seasons: spring, summer, fall, and winter.

The chart on page 32 shows how geographers group climates. High-latitude climates are found near the poles, between 67° and 90°. Low-latitude climates are found near the equator, between 0° and 23°. They are also called tropical climates. Mid-latitude climates are found midway between the equator and the poles. They are found at latitudes from about 23° to 67°. This climate zone has four seasons.

Now look at the map of North America on page 33. Describe the climate where you live.

Almost every climate found on Earth is found in North America. Most of these are found in the United States. There are places on Earth where the weather is always hot. There are places where the weather is always cold. In most of the United States, it is cold part of the year and hot part of the year.

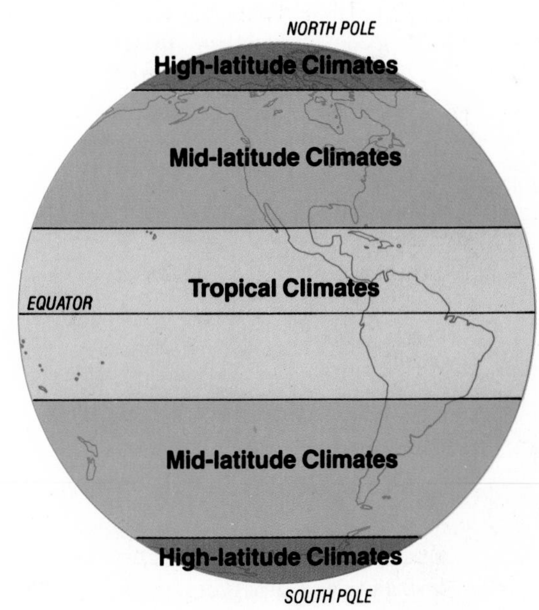

HIGH-LATITUDE CLIMATES

Climate	Winter	Summer	What is it like?
Ice cap	bitterly cold	cold	covered with permanent, thick ice
Tundra	bitterly cold, dry	cold, dry	always cold and dry; some hardy plants and animals

MID-LATITUDE CLIMATES

Climate	Winter	Summer	What is it like?
Mediterranean	mild, wet	warm, dry	a pleasant climate to live in
Humid subtropical	mild, wet	hot, wet	long summers and short winters
Marine	mild, wet	mild, wet	usually not too cold or too hot at any time of year
Continental	cold, wet	mild to hot, but wet	weather changes quickly; very hot in summer and cold in winter
Steppe (continental grasslands)	hot to cold, some rainfall	hot, some rainfall	weather changes quickly; enough rain for grasses to grow
Desert	hot to cold, but dry	hot and dry	not many plants grow except those that can store water

LOW-LATITUDE (TROPICAL) CLIMATES

Climate	Winter	Summer	What is it like?
Tropical grasslands (savanna)	hot, dry	hot, wet	always hot; covered with thick grasses and some trees
Rain forest	hot, wet	hot, wet	always hot with much rain; thickly covered with trees and smaller plants

Note: Highland areas have various local climates.

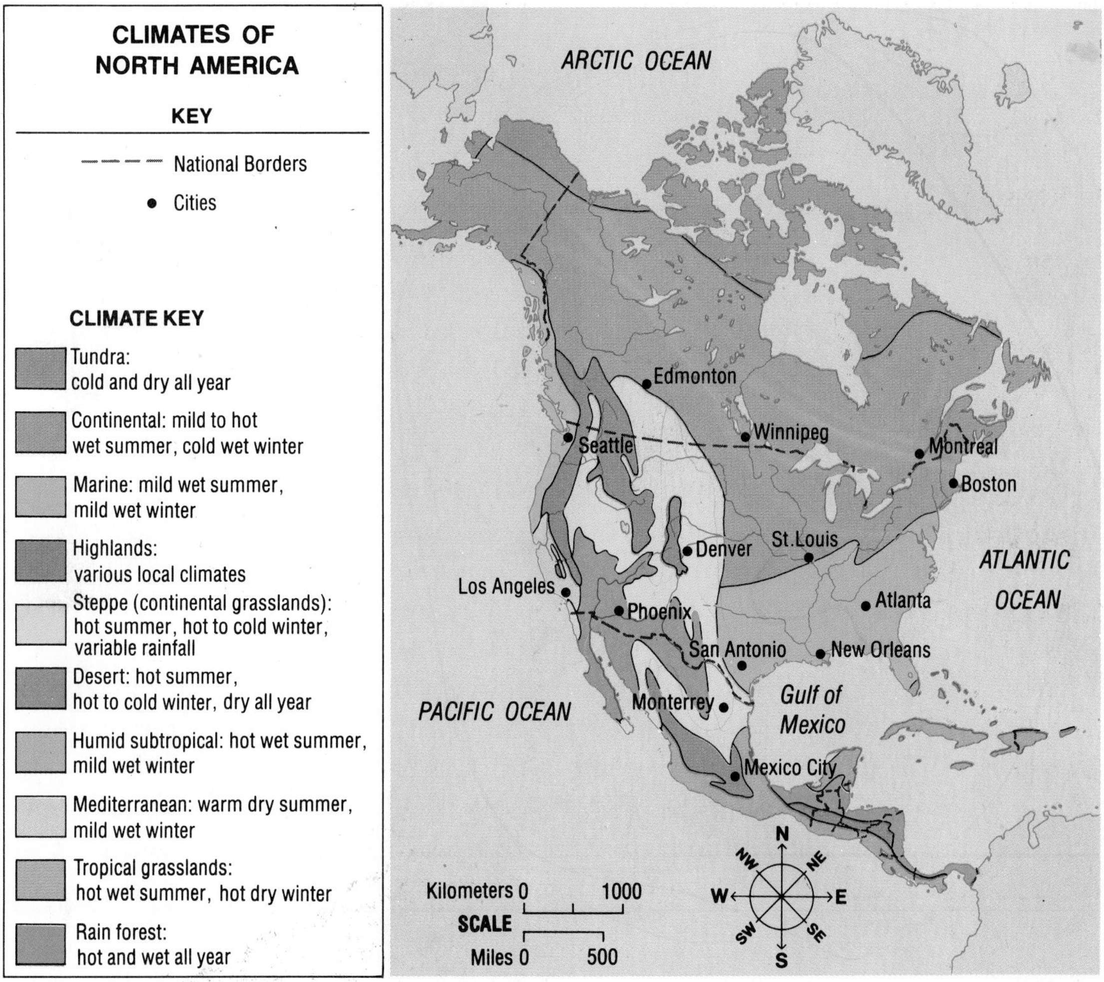

CLIMATES OF NORTH AMERICA

KEY

---- National Borders

• Cities

CLIMATE KEY

Tundra: cold and dry all year

Continental: mild to hot wet summer, cold wet winter

Marine: mild wet summer, mild wet winter

Highlands: various local climates

Steppe (continental grasslands): hot summer, hot to cold winter, variable rainfall

Desert: hot summer, hot to cold winter, dry all year

Humid subtropical: hot wet summer, mild wet winter

Mediterranean: warm dry summer, mild wet winter

Tropical grasslands: hot wet summer, hot dry winter

Rain forest: hot and wet all year

ARCTIC OCEAN
Edmonton
Winnipeg
Seattle
Montreal
Boston
Denver
St. Louis
ATLANTIC OCEAN
Los Angeles
Phoenix
Atlanta
San Antonio
New Orleans
Monterrey
Gulf of Mexico
PACIFIC OCEAN
Mexico City
Kilometers 0 1000
SCALE
Miles 0 500
N NE E SE S SW W NW

REVIEW

VOCABULARY MASTERY

1. ___ is the average condition of the air over a long period of time.
   Weather Climate Humidity
2. ___ is the condition of the air at any moment.
   Weather Climate Temperature
3. ___ is how much heat is in the air.
   Temperature Precipitation Rain
4. ___ is how much water falls from the air.
   Temperature Precipitation Heat

MAP SKILLS

Look at the map above.

5. What is the largest climate area in North America?
6. What area has no set climate?
7. What kind of climate does New Orleans have?

WRITING SKILLS

What is the weather today? Describe it in terms of both temperature and precipitation.

Lesson 6: Making Maps

FIND THE WORDS

map projection
Mercator projection
equal-area projection
interrupted projection
polar projection
aerial photograph

A globe is a fairly accurate model of Earth. On a globe, you can see the true relationship of places on our planet. Even so, globes are limited in their usefulness. They are bulky and are costly. They are good at showing the whole Earth but not at showing parts of the whole. They cannot show small areas in detail. You could not use a globe to trace your route to school.

A **map** is a flat drawing of Earth or of parts of Earth. Because maps are flat, they cannot really show the round Earth accurately. All the parts won't fit. The drawing below shows the surface of a globe being peeled off. These pieces do not make a useful map. To make a useful map, we have to change the sizes or shapes of the things we show.

There are many ways to go about doing this. We can change the sizes or shapes of pieces of land and bodies of water. We can leave off some parts of Earth so that other parts can be more accurate. The way we choose depends on what we want our map to do. The way sizes or shapes of places on Earth are changed on a map is the map's **projection** (pruh JEK shun).

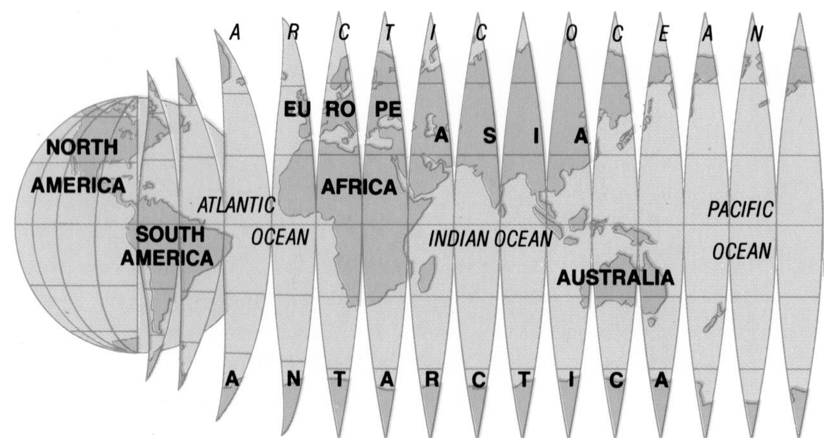

Suppose you peeled a globe like an orange. There would be many gaps. Mapmakers fill the gaps in different ways.

MERCATOR PROJECTION

On a Mercator projection, lines of longitude do not meet at the poles. They remain parallel. Near the poles, extra land and water are added.

EQUAL-AREA PROJECTION

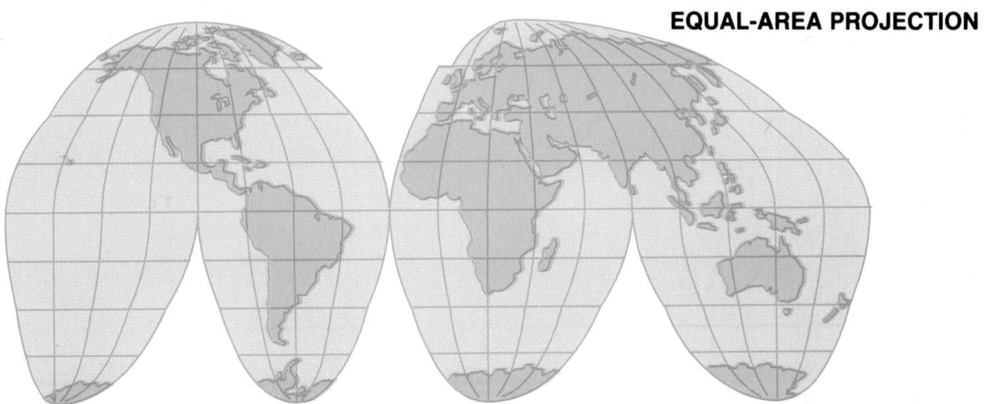

An equal-area projection changes the shape but not the size of land.

ROBINSON PROJECTION

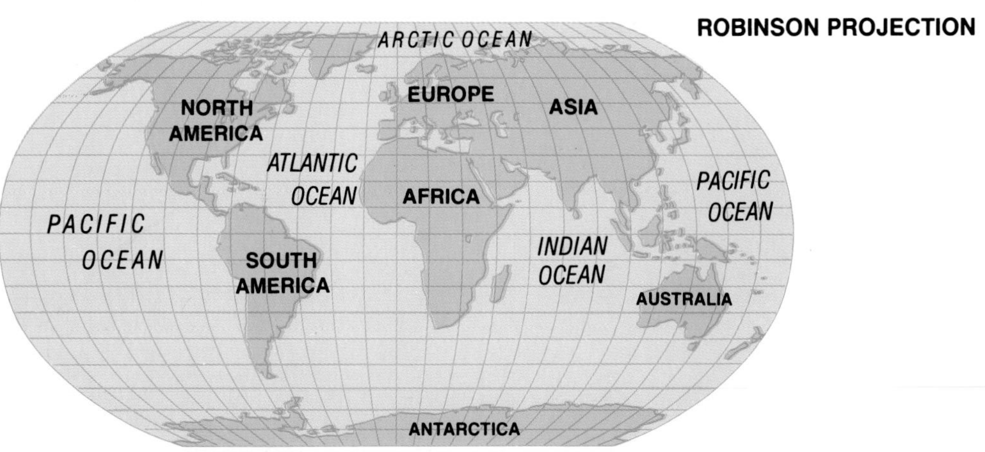

A Robinson projection shows shape and size of land quite accurately. Near the edges, however, shapes are distorted.

There are many kinds of projections. One of the most famous is the **Mercator** (mur KAY tur) **projection.** Remember, on a globe, lines of longitude come together at the poles. However, on a Mercator projection, all lines of longitude are drawn straight and parallel. This makes a Mercator map very useful to pilots of ships. It is easier for a ship to follow a straight line than a curving one.

The problem is that, on a Mercator map, the land is greatly distorted. That means it is not shown accurately. The farther land is from the equator, the greater the distortion. The map widens Earth near the poles. Extra land and water are added there. So on a Mercator projection, Greenland looks as big as South America. Actually, South America is eight times larger than Greenland. The mapmaker added land to Greenland to fill in gaps in the map.

An **equal-area projection** keeps the land areas the right size, but it changes their shapes. Toward the edges of such a map, the land looks pushed in or squashed. To make the land on this kind of map even more accurate, mapmakers use an **interrupted projection.** That means

there are gaps in the map. This changes the shape of the oceans greatly. The lines of longitude curve toward the poles.

A map of the Earth does not have to be centered on the equator. One **polar projection** on page 20 has the North Pole at the center. On this map, the Arctic areas are shown accurately. It is the land near the equator that is distorted. Airplane pilots often use this polar projection. It shows the shortest air routes between places in North America and places in Europe.

The problem of distortion becomes less important in maps of smaller areas. Today, many maps are made from **aerial** (A ree ul) **photographs.** These are pictures taken from airplanes or satellites. The maps are drawn from the photographs.

Look at the aerial photograph on page 36. It shows houses, fields, stores, a river, roads, and bridges. Then look at the map below. In drawing the map, the mapmaker used symbols. These symbols stand for real places in the community.

Notice the projection of maps you use. Equal-area projections help you see the true size of places on Earth. Suppose that

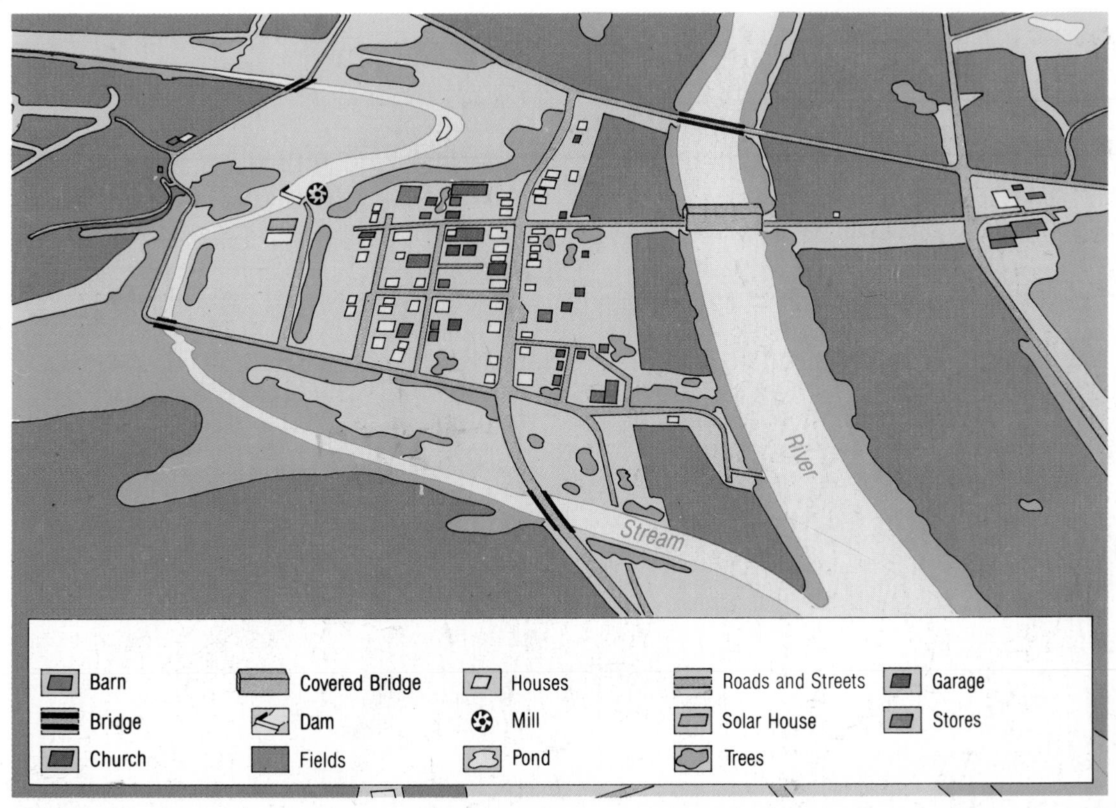

Fascinating Facts

The oldest known map is about 4,300 years old. It is a clay tablet. It was found in Babylon, an ancient city in Asia. We are not sure about what the map shows. But it seems to show someone's farm in a big valley.

The Egyptians made maps about 3,300 years ago. One of these maps shows the way to the gold mines that were to the south of the Nile River. It is the oldest treasure map in the world.

you wanted to compare the size of the plains in Europe and North America. You could not compare them accurately with a Mercator map.

Views of Earth from space help us put more things on maps. Satellites collect images of Earth by remote sensing. This shows things the eye cannot see.

Images from space can show how many plants are growing in a place. They can show when grassland turns into desert. Satellite images can reveal good fishing places in oceans. They can show oyster beds in a bay. They can even help us find minerals. With these images, we can see more of Earth than ever.

REVIEW

VOCABULARY MASTERY

1. ___ are flat drawings of Earth.
   Globes Areas Maps
2. The way sizes or shapes are changed on a map is its ___.
   globe area projection
3. In a(n) ___ projection, land near the poles is distorted.
   interrupted Mercator polar
4. In a(n) ___ projection, land near the equator is distorted.
   polar equal-area Mercator
5. A(n) ___ projection keeps all land areas the right size.
   Mercator polar equal-area

READING FOR MAIN IDEAS

6. Why can't maps show Earth accurately?
7. How do the lines of longitude run on a Mercator projection? On an equal-area projection?
8. Which kind of map projection is most useful for pilots of ships?
9. What are polar projections useful for?
10. Which kind of map projection is best for comparing the size of two land areas?

THINKING SKILLS

Imagine you are making a long trip across a wilderness. You have only a map and a compass to guide you. What kind of map should you use? Why?

CHAPTER REVIEW

VOCABULARY MASTERY

Use the words below to complete the chapter summary. Use each only once.

climate	latitude
degrees	longitude
equator	Mountains
Globes	oceans
hemispheres	Plains
Hills	prime meridian
lakes	rivers

__1__ are models of Earth. The __2__ divides Earth into two __3__. Lines of __4__ run parallel to the equator. Lines of __5__ run east and west of the __6__. Both are numbered in __7__.

The land has many shapes. __8__ are mostly flat. __9__ rise higher than the land around. __10__ are the highest land of all. Besides land, Earth has large bodies of water called __11__. On land, the __12__ and __13__ provide water. The __14__, or average weather, of an area is very important.

READING FOR MAIN IDEAS

1. What is the function of the prime meridian?
2. Why is the grid formed by lines of latitude and longitude useful?
3. Why are plains usually the most useful kind of land?
4. What is the difference between an ocean and a sea?
5. What is a map's projection?

THINKING SKILLS

6. What kind of land do you think you might like best to live on? Why?
7. Look at the climate chart on page 32. What kind of climate do you think you might like best? Why?

SKILLS APPLICATION

MAP SKILLS

Use the globe below to answer the questions. The top of the globe is north.

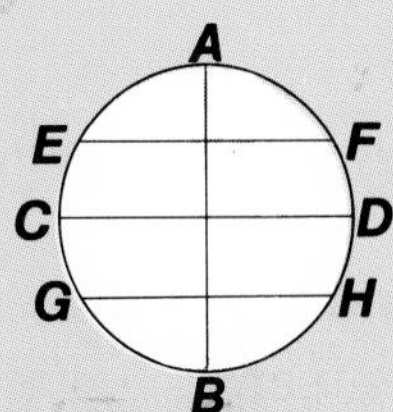

8. What is at point *A*?
9. What is line *CD*?
10. What is the part of the globe above line *CD*?
11. If line *AB* is 0°, what is it?
12. If line *AB* is 0°, which hemisphere are *F*, *D*, and *H* part of?
13. If line *AB* is 0°, which two hemispheres is *G* located in?

WRITING SKILLS

Create an imaginary state and name it. Include five landforms. Give descriptive names to the landforms. For example, the name "Cherry Valley" suggests that cherry trees grow in that valley. Name any bodies of water you include. Write a paragraph to describe these landforms in your new state.

RESEARCH SKILLS

The names of some clouds give clues as to their shapes. The following terms are parts of cloud names: *cirro*, *cumulo*, *nimbo*, and *strato*. Use an encyclopedia or dictionary to determine the complete name of each cloud. Then write a description of each cloud. Try to find a type of weather associated with each.

CHAPTER 2

MAPPING OUR CONTINENT

Lesson 1: Reading Maps

FIND THE WORDS

cartographer symbol key capital scale elevation sea level compass cardinal directions intermediate directions

People who make maps are called **cartographers** (kahr TOG ruh furz). To put information on a map, cartographers use symbols. **Symbols** are signs that stand for something else. These symbols can be lines, dots, stars, or small drawings. The map **key** lists these symbols and tells what they mean.

Cartographers are people who make maps.

Look at the map on page 23. Find the key. The white lines show national borders and dots show cities. National capitals are marked by a star. A **capital** is the city where the government of a state or nation meets.

Most maps have a **scale,** a means of measuring distances. A map scale is usually a line with kilometers and miles on it. It shows what a small distance on the map equals in real distance on Earth. Suppose that 1 inch equals 800 miles. Suppose the distance between two places on the map is 2 inches. That means the places are 1,600 miles apart.

Color can be used in many different ways on a map. Colors can help you tell land from water. They can show you where one state or nation ends and another begins. Color can also show elevation. **Elevation** is how high the land is above the surface of the oceans. The height of the ocean surface is **sea level.**

NORTH AMERICA: Physical
AZIMUTHAL EQUAL AREA PROJECTION
Elevation
Meters
Feet
Over 4,000
Over 13,120
2,000–4,000
6,560–13,120
500–2,000
1,640–6,560
200–500
656–1,640
0–200
0–656
Below sea level
Below sea level
Ice caps
Mountain peaks
National boundaries
Cities
National capitals
0 250 500 750 Miles
0 250 500 750 Kilometers
ASIA
SOUTH AMERICA
ARCTIC OCEAN
PACIFIC OCEAN
ATLANTIC OCEAN
Bering Sea
Bering Strait
Beaufort Sea
Baffin Bay
Barrow Strait
Denmark Strait
Labrador Sea
Hudson Strait
Hudson Bay
Gulf of Alaska
Gulf of Mexico
Gulf of California
Caribbean Sea
Bay of Fundy
Greenland
Iceland
Ellesmere Island
Queen Elizabeth Islands
Victoria Island
Baffin Island
Southampton Island
Aleutian Islands
ALASKA PENINSULA
Kodiak Island
Alexander Archipelago
Queen Charlotte Islands
Vancouver Island
Newfoundland
Cape Breton Island
NOVA SCOTIA
LABRADOR
BROOKS RANGE
ALASKA RANGE
Mt. McKinley
YUKON PLATEAU
COAST MOUNTAINS
ROCKY MOUNTAINS
GREAT PLAINS
CANADIAN SHIELD
Laurentian Highland
BLACK HILLS
CASCADE RANGE
COAST RANGES
SIERRA NEVADA
Mt. Rainier
Mt. Whitney
Pikes Peak
Great Basin
Great Salt Lake
Central Lowland
APPALACHIAN MOUNTAINS
Mt. Mitchell
COASTAL PLAIN
SIERRA MADRE OCCIDENTAL
SIERRA MADRE ORIENTAL
BAJA CALIFORNIA
YUCATÁN PENINSULA
CENTRAL AMERICA
ISTHMUS OF PANAMA
Panama Canal
Lake Nicaragua
Great Bear Lake
Great Slave Lake
Lake Winnipeg
Lake Superior
Lake Michigan
Lake Huron
Lake Erie
Lake Ontario
Mackenzie R.
Peace R.
Athabasca R.
North Saskatchewan R.
South Saskatchewan R.
Yukon R.
Columbia R.
Snake R.
Colorado R.
Rio Grande
Missouri R.
Platte R.
Mississippi R.
Ohio R.
Arkansas R.
Red R.
St. Lawrence R.
Cape Mendocino
Point Conception
Point Eugenia
Cape Cod
Cape Hatteras
Vancouver
Seattle
Portland
San Francisco
Reno
Los Angeles
San Diego
Denver
Winnipeg
Milwaukee
Chicago
Toronto
Montreal
Ottawa
Portland
New York
Washington, D.C.
Asheville
Dallas
Houston
Miami
Havana
Mexico City
Veracruz
Bahama Islands
WEST INDIES
Cuba
Hispaniola
Jamaica
Greater Antilles
Lesser Antilles
Leeward Islands
Windward Islands
Arctic Circle
Tropic of Cancer
Equator
N
NE
E
SE
S
SW
W
NW

Look at the scale of colors on page 41. This color key is used to show elevation. Choose a color from the scale. Find some land on the map that color. The elevation scale will tell you about how high that land is.

A map **compass** (KUM pus) is a drawing of arrows that point north, south, east, and west. It shows how directions on the map relate to real directions on Earth. North is toward the North Pole. South is toward the South Pole. East is in the direction of the sunrise. West is in the direction of the sunset. North, south, east, and west are the most important directions on Earth. They are called the **cardinal directions.** They are abbreviated: *N, S, E, W.* Between the four cardinal directions are four **intermediate directions.** These four directions are northeast, northwest, southeast, and southwest.

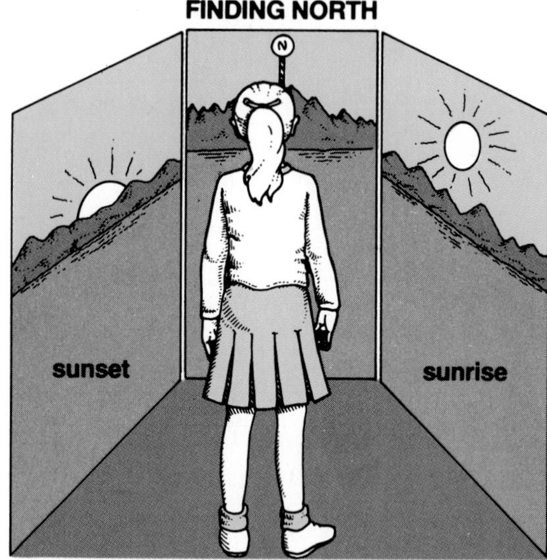

REVIEW

VOCABULARY MASTERY

1. On a map, the ___ tells distance.
   compass key scale
2. On a map, the ___ shows direction.
   key scale compass
3. The map key lists the ___.
   cartographers directions symbols
4. ___ is the height of the land.
   Elevation Direction Scale
5. ___ is the height of the surface of the ocean.
   Direction Sea level Latitude

READING FOR MAIN IDEAS

6. What word means "mapmaker"?
7. How can you find out what the symbols on a map mean?
8. What part of a map can you use to find out how wide a nation is?
9. Describe two ways in which color can be used on a map.
10. Name the cardinal directions and the intermediate directions.

THINKING SKILLS

Suppose you were lost in the woods without a compass. How could you tell which way is north?

Lesson 2: Types of Maps

FIND THE WORDS

political boundary **border**
political map
natural boundary
physical map
distribution map **resource**
product **population-density map**

Maps can give you many kinds of information. You know that a map can show directions, elevations, or the locations of nations and cities. In the last lesson, you learned two ways in which maps divide states and nations. One way is by drawing lines between them. These lines are symbols of political boundaries. A **political boundary** is a line dividing two nations or parts of nations. It is also called a **border.** Political boundaries divide the United States from Canada and Mexico. Look at the climate map on page 33. It uses dashed lines to show political boundaries.

Another way to show political boundaries is by color. Each state or nation on a map may be a different color from the ones around it. Look at the map below.

Sometimes a natural boundary also serves as a political boundary. The Rio Grande divides the United States from Mexico between about 26° and 32° north latitude and between about 98° and 106° west longitude.

Political and Physical Maps

A map that shows political boundaries is called a **political map.** Political boundaries show how people have divided up the land. Such boundaries can change over time. A **natural boundary** is a feature of Earth that divides one place from another. Rivers, lakes, oceans, and mountains are natural boundaries. Sometimes a natural boundary serves as a political boundary as well. For example, a river, the Rio Grande, divides Texas from Mexico. The Atlantic and Pacific oceans are natural boundaries and political boundaries of the United States.

A map that shows natural features of Earth is a **physical map.** A physical map shows what the surface of the Earth is like. It can show highlands and lowlands—mountains, plateaus, and plains. The elevation map on page 41 is a physical map. It uses colors to show the height of the land above sea level. The dark green lands are lowlands. You can see that there are lowlands, or coastal plains, all along the coasts of North America. The orange and brown areas are highlands. You can see that the highest lands in North America are in the West.

Distribution Maps

A **distribution map** shows the way things are spread out over an area. It can show where people live, where resources are found, or where products are made. It can show the location of forests, grasslands, and deserts. In fact, a distribution map can show the arrangement of almost anything on Earth. It can tell where something is and can often show how much is there.

Resource and Product Maps

One type of distribution map shows resources or products. A **resource** is anything on Earth

LIVING RESOURCES OF NORTH AMERICA

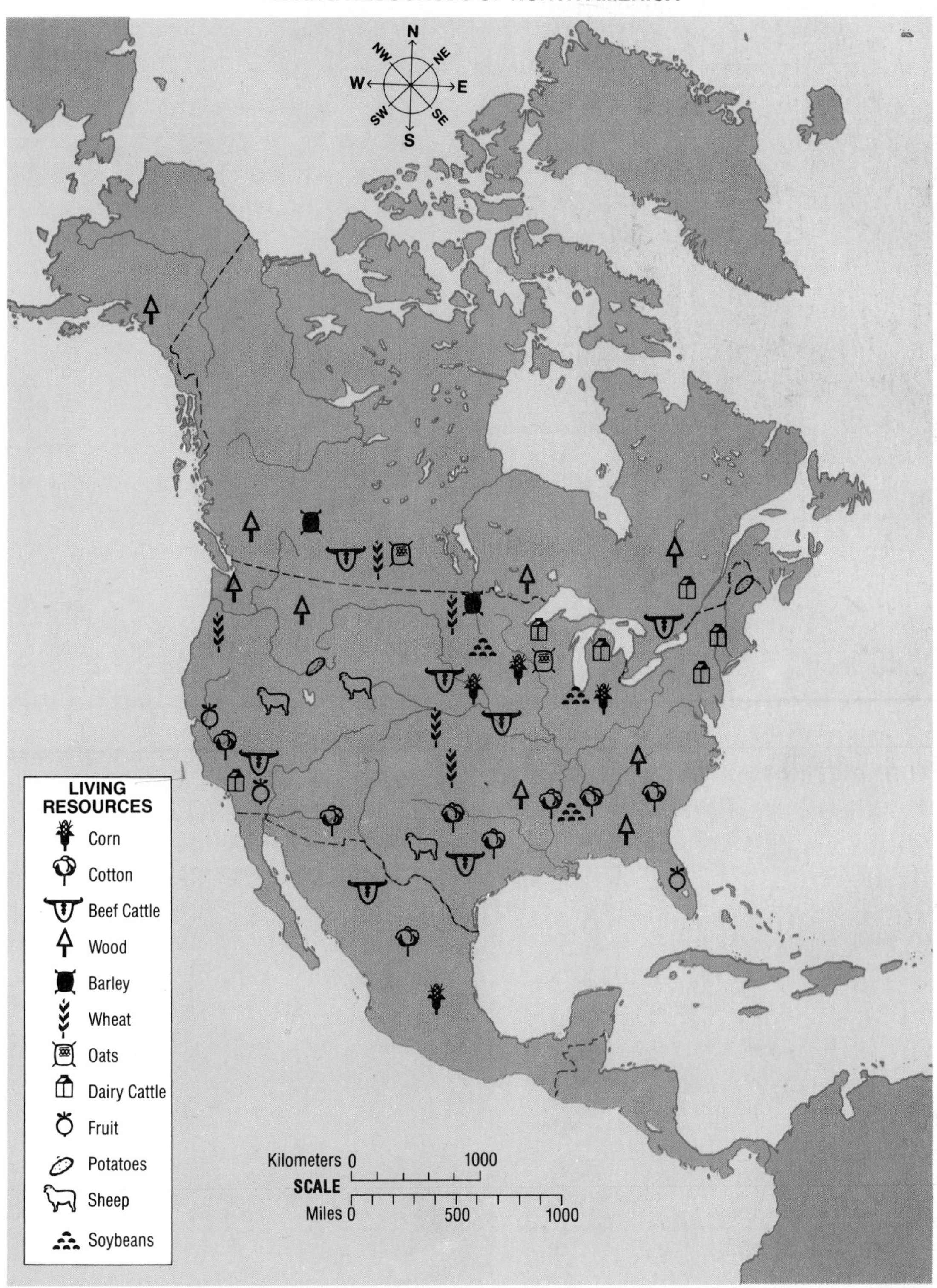

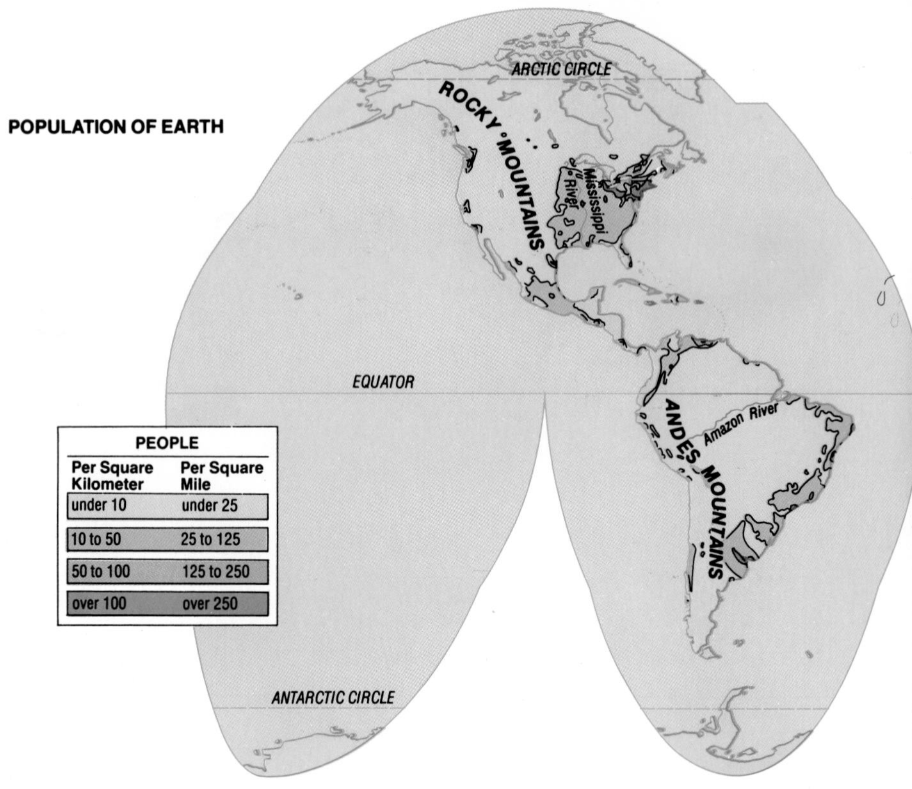

that people can use to help them live. A **product** is anything that people gather or make.

Natural resources are plants, animals, and minerals that are found on Earth. Maps can show the location of such resources. The map on page 45 shows some of the living resources of North America. Living resources include crops grown for food, wood from trees, and animal products. North America also has many nonliving resources. These include minerals such as petroleum. There are many other resources in North America besides the ones shown on resource maps in this book. Our continent's resources were an important factor in bringing so many people here to live.

Population-Density Maps

Another type of distribution map shows population density. A **population-density map** shows how people are spread out over Earth or part of Earth. It shows how many people live in each area. An area with a dense population has many people crowded closely together. An area with a sparse population has few people spread widely apart. The map above is a population-density map of Earth. From it, you can tell which parts of North America are most crowded.

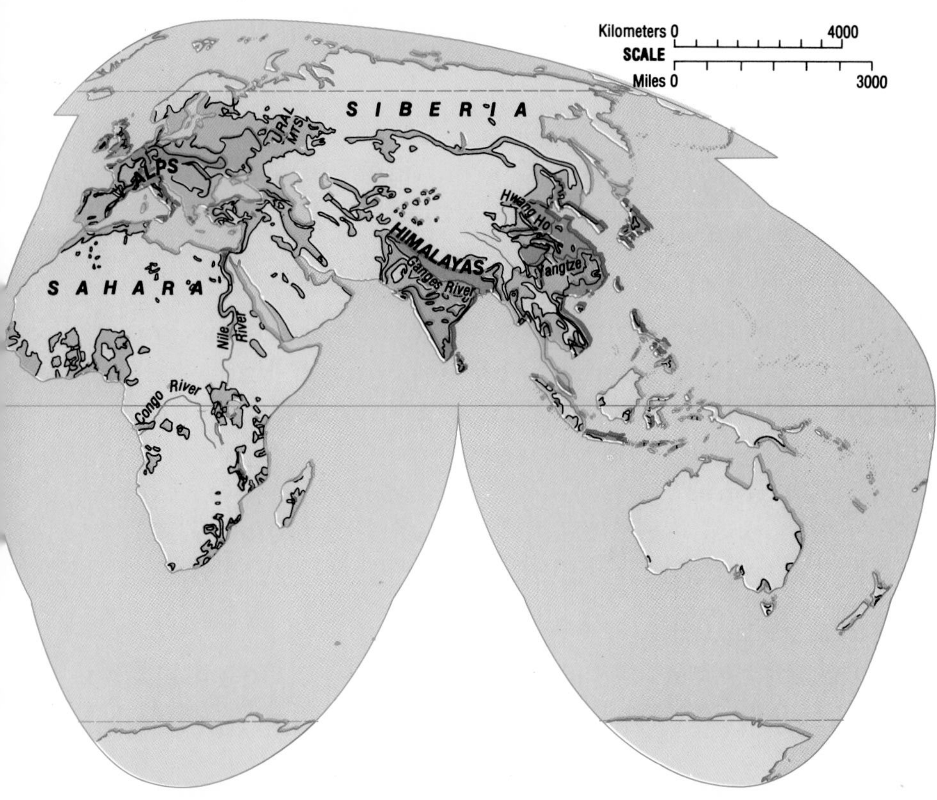

REVIEW

VOCABULARY MASTERY

1. A map that shows borders between states is a ___ map.
   physical political product
2. A ___ map shows what the surface of the Earth is like.
   population political physical
3. A ___ map shows how things are spread out over an area.
   political distribution physical
4. A ___ map shows how people are spread out over an area.
   political resource population-density
5. Plants, animals, and minerals are shown on ___ maps.
   resource physical climate

READING FOR MAIN IDEAS

6. What is another name for a border?
7. Name two ways to show divisions between states and nations on a map.
8. How does a physical map show the elevation of land?
9. What is a distribution map?
10. Name two types of distribution maps.

THINKING SKILLS

What could you learn by comparing a population-density map with a physical map? With a climate map?

Lesson 3: Historical Maps

FIND THE WORDS

historical map   route

A **historical map** shows the world as it was, or as people thought it was, in the past. In this book, you will see two different types of historical maps. Some are maps drawn in the past. Others are maps of today that show the world of the past.

Maps with Mistakes

Maps were made in the past long before scientific knowledge of Earth was available. Such maps are not accurate. However, they do show what people knew about the world in earlier times.

Despite its errors, Ptolemy's map was still being used in the 1500s.

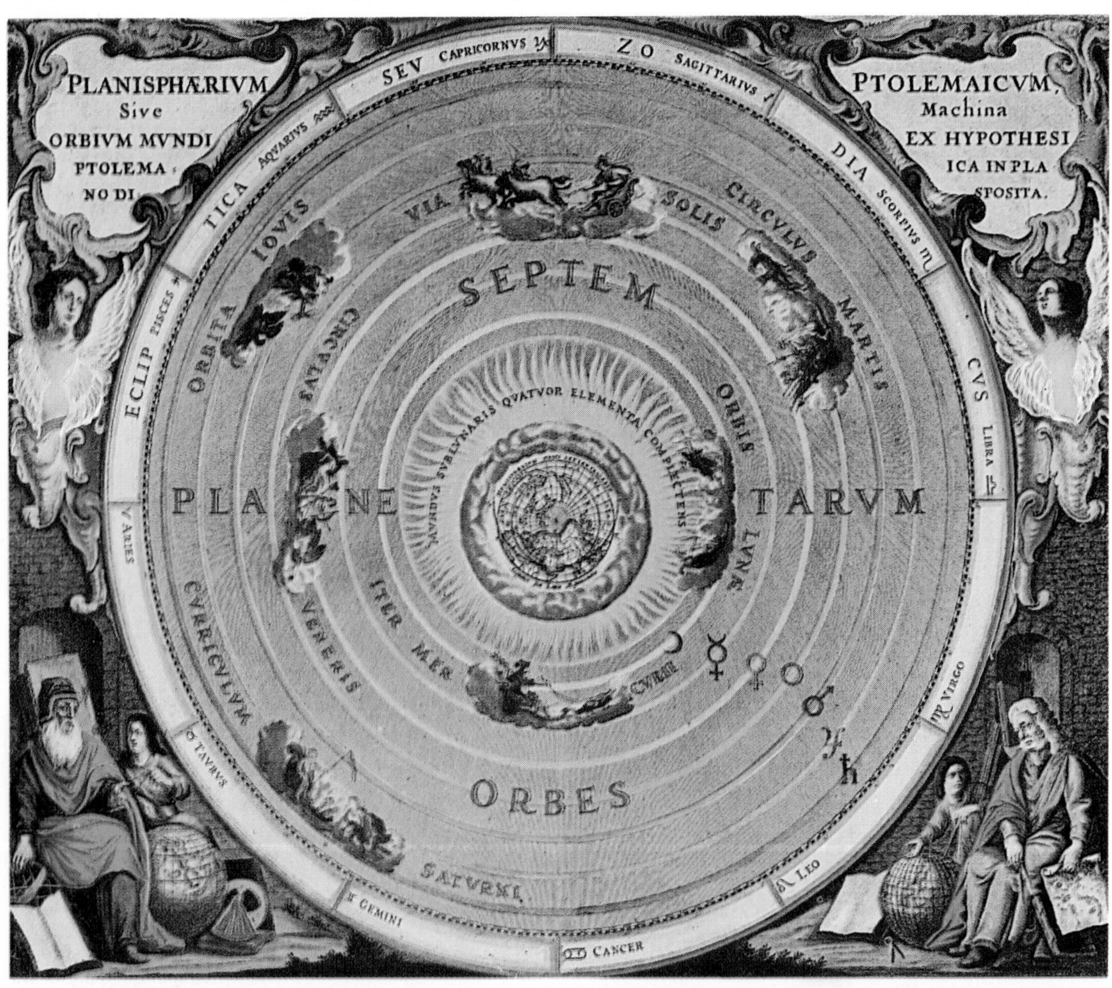

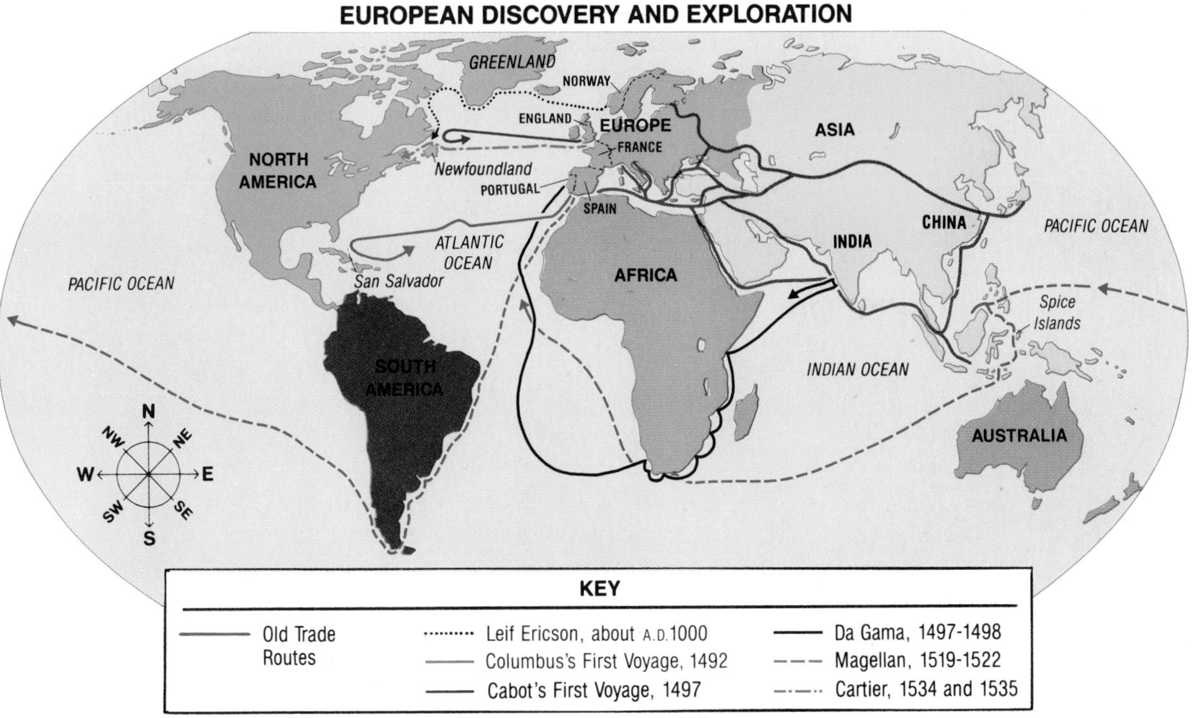

You have already read about the early Greek geographer Ptolemy (TOL uh mee). In about 150 A.D., he drew a map of the known world. Ptolemy drew his map on a grid of 360° of latitude and longitude. The trouble was, Ptolemy's known world included only three continents: Europe, Asia, and Africa. Even here, his map was full of errors. However, it was the best map people had. Ptolemy's map was used even after Columbus and Magellan proved it wrong.

In fact, a map error influenced Columbus's decision to sail west in search of Asia. In the 1400s, European mapmakers did not know about North and South America. They thought there was nothing but ocean between western Europe and eastern Asia. Like Ptolemy, they thought this ocean covered only 126° of longitude. The true distance between Europe and the Spice Islands of Indonesia is 210° of longitude!

The explorers of the 1400s and 1500s found out what the world was really like. Each new voyage across the Atlantic brought new information. The explorers drew maps or wrote reports of what they had seen. Their observations made more accurate maps possible. In 1500, Juan de la Cosa, who sailed with Columbus, drew the first map of the New World. In 1507, Martin Waldseemüller

COLUMBUS'S VOYAGES TO AMERICA

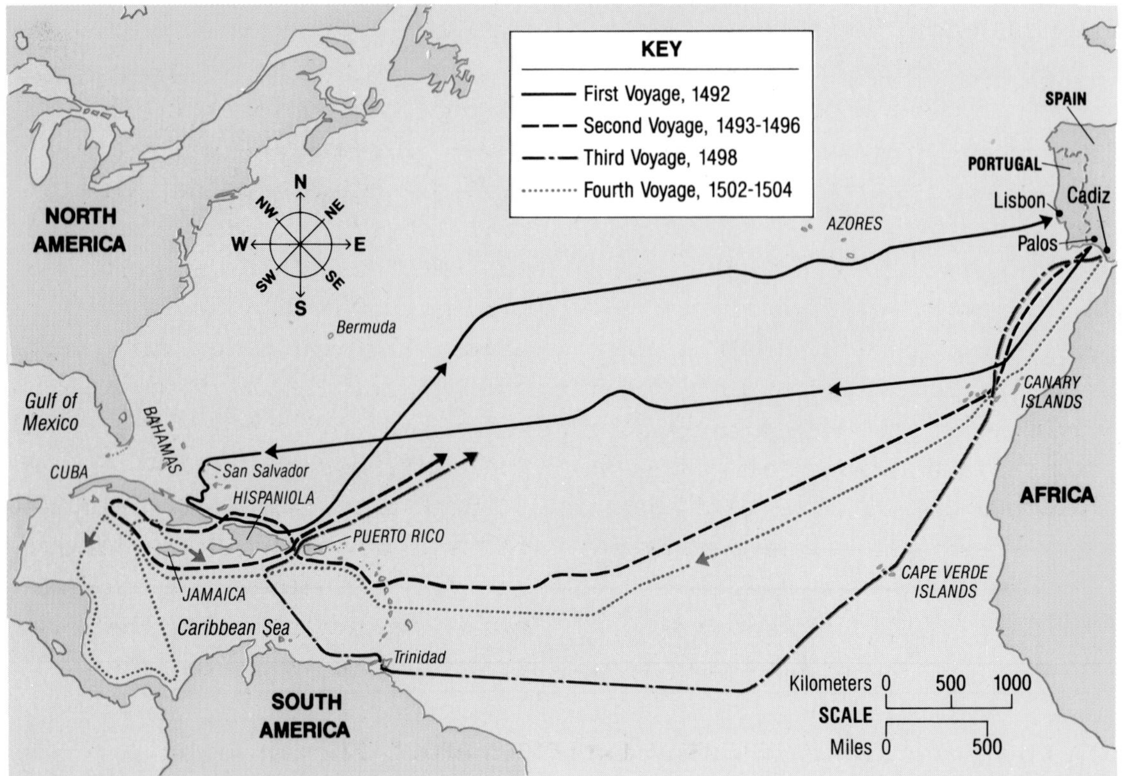

drew the first map to show America as a separate continent. His "America" was South America.

In the next 300 years, mapmaking became more accurate. More of the world became known as explorers traveled far and wide. Distances could be measured more exactly with new instruments and better methods. Cartographers began to take a scientific approach to making maps.

The World of the Past

The second type of historical map is one drawn in the present to show the past. Such a map shows the places, events, and realities of earlier times. One kind of map in this category is a route map. A **route** (ROOT) is the path someone travels from one place to another. People learned about the world through travel to unknown lands. Explorers and traders sailed over the seas. Conquerors marched across the land. Settlers followed trails to new territory.

Modern cartographers draw lines on maps to show the routes explorers followed. These lines are based on records the explorers themselves left. They show you where the explorers started. They extend across the parts of Earth that the explorers crossed. By tracing each line, you can see where an explorer went. Look at the map on page 50. You can follow the route of Columbus's ships on his voyages to the New World.

Another kind of modern historical map shows borders as they were in the past. Such a map gives an accurate picture of the world as it used to be. Today, many political boundaries are not the same as they were 50 years ago. However, maps can show how the land was divided up in the past. They can show which country claimed which land. They can show what happened as a result of wars, explorations, sales of land, or other events. For example, look at the map below. It shows the thirteen colonies about 1770. Compare this map with the map of the United States on pages 12 and 13. You can see that Georgia, North Carolina, Virginia, Pennsylvania, and New York extended their borders westward. Massachusetts lost the land that later became Maine.

Both types of historical maps—old and new—enrich our understanding of history. They help us make connections between the past and our world of today.

THE THIRTEEN COLONIES ABOUT 1770

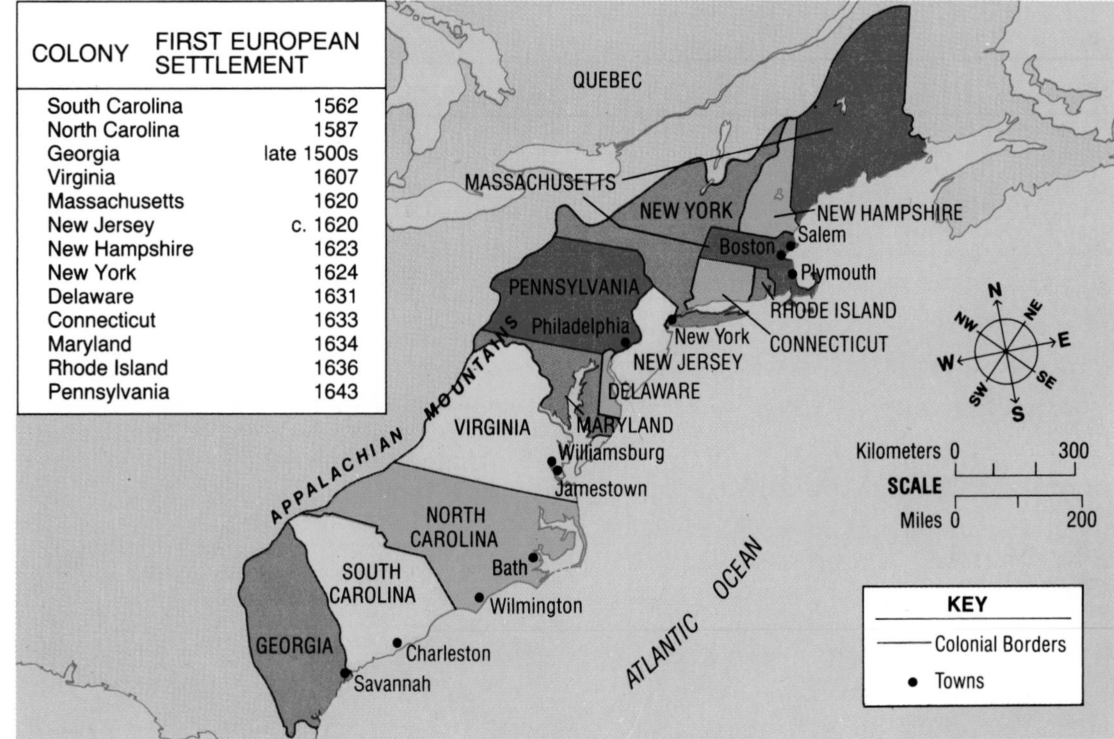

COLONY	FIRST EUROPEAN SETTLEMENT
South Carolina	1562
North Carolina	1587
Georgia	late 1500s
Virginia	1607
Massachusetts	1620
New Jersey	c. 1620
New Hampshire	1623
New York	1624
Delaware	1631
Connecticut	1633
Maryland	1634
Rhode Island	1636
Pennsylvania	1643

EUROPE BEFORE WORLD WAR I

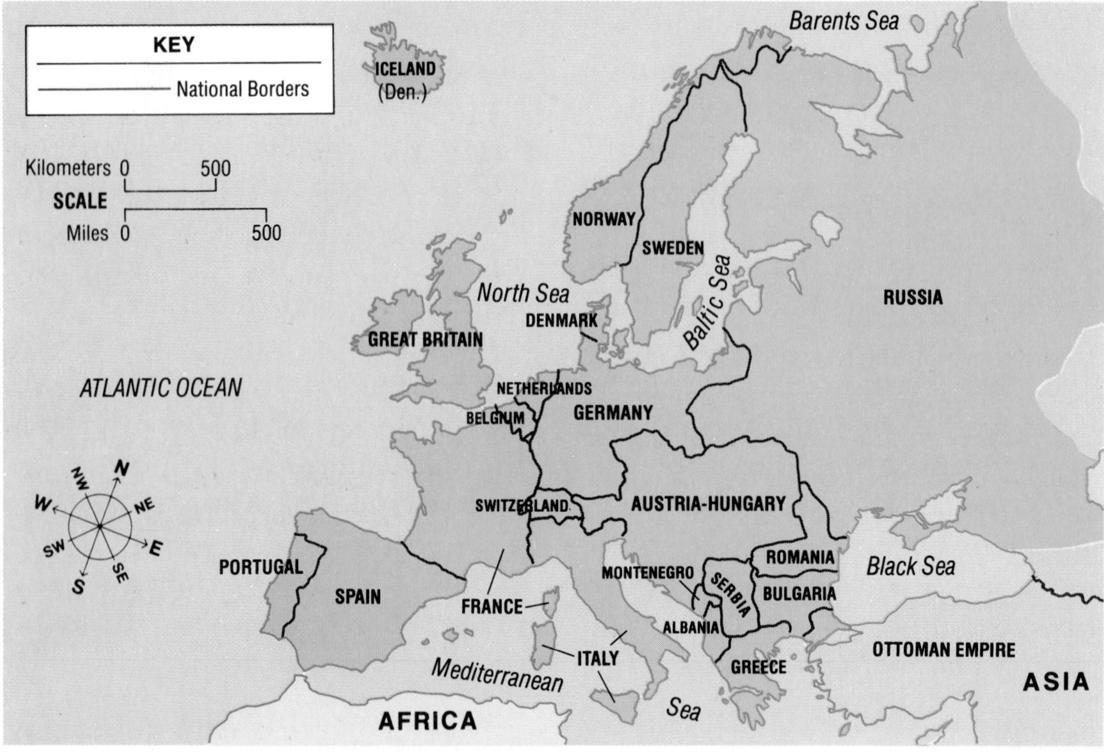

National boundaries have changed significantly since this time.

REVIEW

VOCABULARY MASTERY

1. A ____ map shows the world people saw in the past.
   physical historical resource
2. A ____ map shows the path an explorer traveled.
   resource political route

READING FOR MAIN IDEAS

3. What three continents did Ptolemy know about?
4. How do modern mapmakers know what routes explorers took?
5. Name two events that can change political boundaries.

THINKING SKILLS

6. Which continents did Ptolemy not know about?
7. What advantages do twentieth-century mapmakers have that Ptolemy lacked?
8. What could cause a nation to get smaller?
9. Suppose you discovered an island. How would you go about mapping it?
10. What unknown places might be mapped in the future?

Lesson 4: Using Maps

FIND THE WORDS

itinerary road map
mileage odometer
mileage chart plan

You have seen how maps are made. Maps have many practical uses in everyday life. Suppose you are planning a trip by car from Houston, Texas, to Key West, Florida. First, you may want to look at a map showing all the states you will pass through. Then you can plan your itinerary. An **itinerary** (eye TIN uh RER ee) is a detailed plan for a trip. It includes the route to be followed, the places to be visited, and the time to be spent.

Your trip from Houston to Key West will include visits to cities along the Gulf Coast. You will stop in New Orleans, Louisiana, Biloxi, Mississippi, and Mobile, Alabama. These are places on your itinerary. Find these cities on the map below.

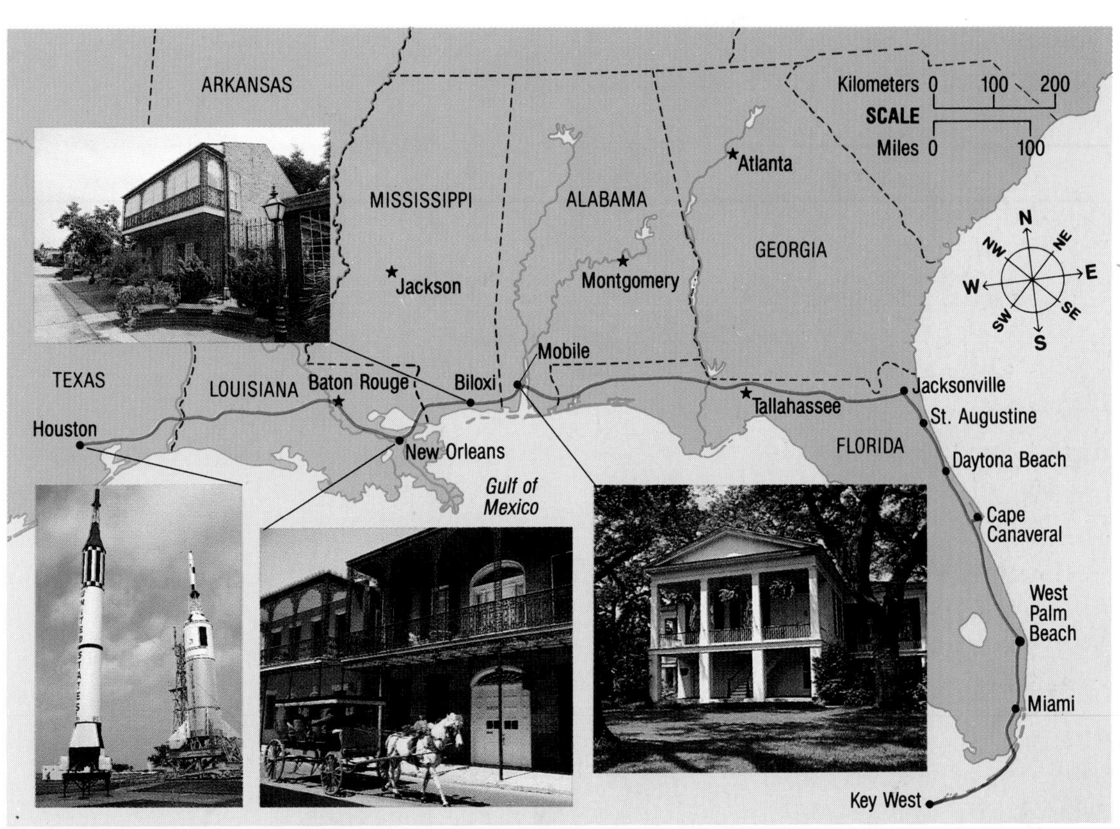

MILEAGE CHART

Approximate Mileages	Biloxi	Houston	Key West	Miami	Mobile	New Orleans	Tallahassee
Biloxi	0	356	969	808	70	87	321
Houston	356	0	1398	1237	499	365	750
Key West	969	1398	0	161	899	1053	648
Miami	808	1237	161	0	738	892	487
Mobile	70	499	899	738	0	154	251
New Orleans	87	365	1053	892	154	0	405
Tallahassee	321	750	648	487	251	405	0

To get from one city to another by car, you will need a road map. A **road map** shows highways and other important roads. It shows the location of towns and cities. Using such a map, you can find the best roads to take from one place to another. Look at the road map of Florida on page 55. What highways will you take from Tallahassee to St. Augustine?

In planning a trip by car, you also need to know the mileage between places. **Mileage** (MY lij) is distance traveled, measured in miles. The instrument on a car that records the mileage is an **odometer** (oh DOM uh tur).

When you use a distance scale on a map, you measure distance between places in a straight line. Roads often curve, following the shape of the land. A **mileage chart** shows the number of road miles from one city to another.

Look at the mileage chart at left. Put a finger on Houston at the left. Put another finger on Key West at the top. Go across and down until the fingers come together. That figure—1,398 miles—is the driving distance from Houston to Key West.

Another familiar kind of map is a plan. A **plan** is a detailed map or diagram showing how a place is laid out. A floor plan can show the layout of a new house. A seating plan for a stadium can help you match your tickets with the right seats.

A detailed map of a city, park, or neighborhood is another kind of plan. The city plan on page 56 shows central Washington, DC. Suppose you wanted to take a tour of Washington. This map could help you find your way.

A map may show the whole Earth. Or it may show a single building or city block. Maps speak in colors, shapes, symbols, and lines as well as words. The maps in this book will bring together time, place, and event. They will help you tie history and geography together.

ROAD MAP OF FLORIDA

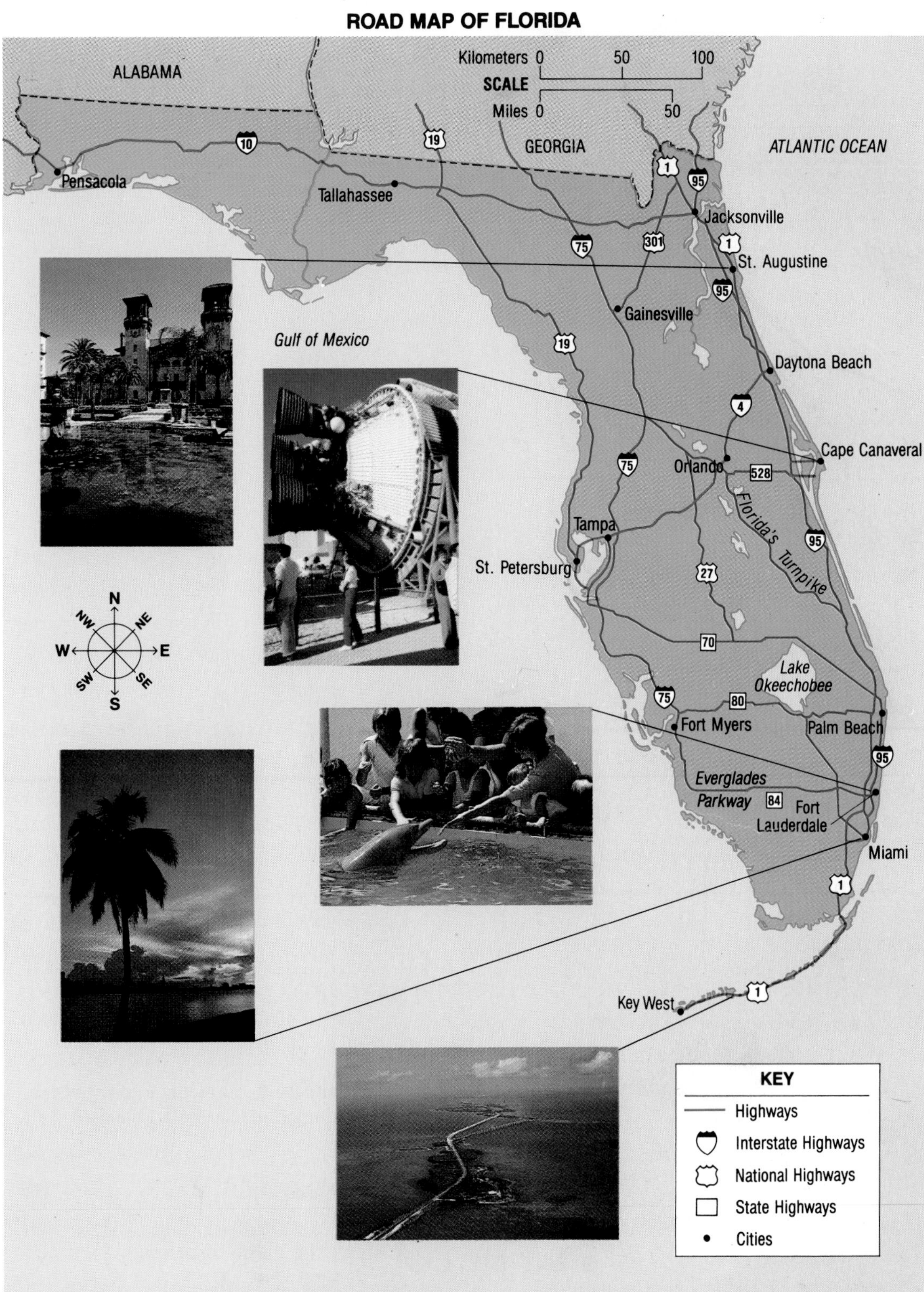

WASHINGTON, DC

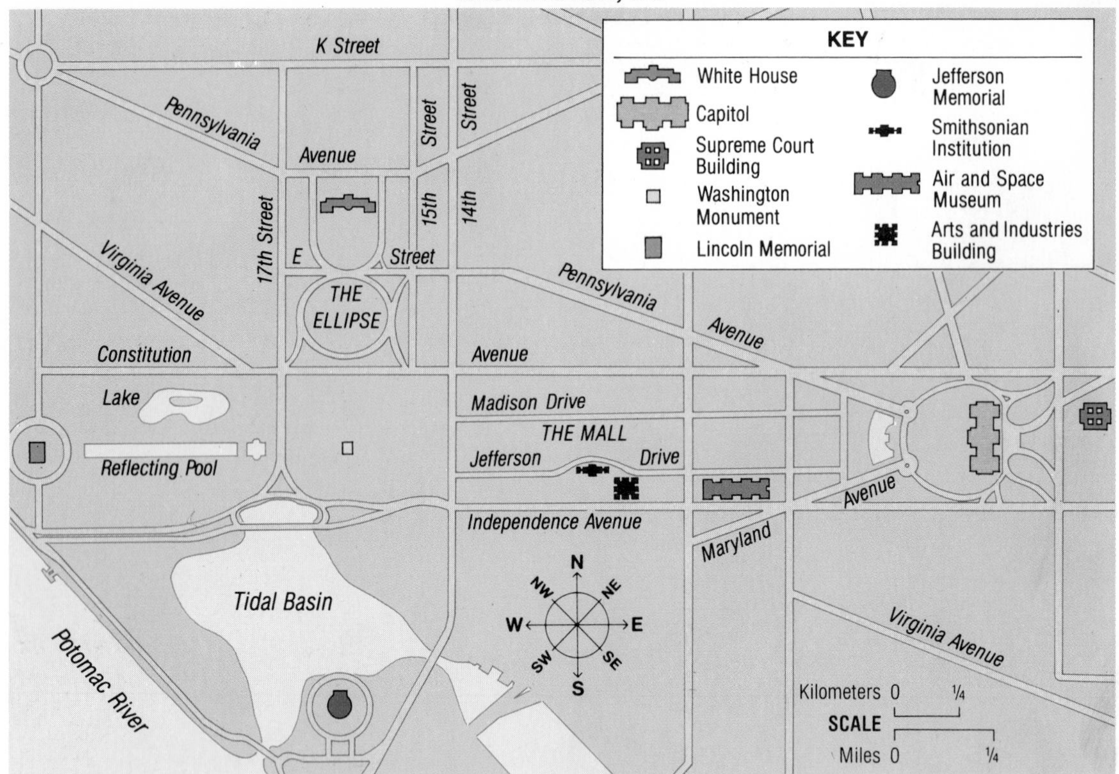

REVIEW

VOCABULARY MASTERY

1. A ____ shows the road miles between places.
   scale key mileage chart
2. A(n) ____ shows the map distance between places.
   odometer scale mileage chart
3. A(n) ____ records distance traveled in a car.
   itinerary scale odometer
4. A ____ shows highways.
   scale road map mileage chart

READING FOR MAIN IDEAS

5. Name three things that an itinerary includes.
6. What kind of map shows the layout of a place?

MAP SKILLS

7. What roads would you take from Orlando, Florida, to the Kennedy Space Center?
8. How many miles is it from New Orleans to Miami?
9. In Washington, what street would you take to get from the Capitol to the White House? From the Capitol to the Smithsonian?
10. Plan your itinerary for a trip. What maps and charts would you use?

THINKING SKILLS

When might a map scale and a mileage chart show the same distance?

CHAPTER REVIEW

VOCABULARY MASTERY

Use the words below to complete the chapter summary. Use each only once.

borders	physical map
boundaries	political map
Cartographers	scale
compass	sea level
elevation	Symbols
key	

_1_ make maps. _2_ indicate where things are located in an area. These are listed in the _3_. The _4_ shows distance on a map. Directions are shown by means of a _5_. Some maps indicate _6_, which is the height of land above _7_, or the ocean surface. There are many kinds of maps. A(n) _8_ shows the lines which divide nations or parts of nations. These lines are _9_, or _10_. A(n) _11_ shows what the surface of Earth is like.

READING FOR MAIN IDEAS

1. What is the purpose of a map compass?
2. Why is scale an important feature of a map?
3. How does a physical map show different heights? How can you tell which areas are the highest?
4. What does a population-density map show?
5. How do historical maps enrich our understanding of history?

THINKING SKILLS

6. Name some things other than those mentioned in the chapter that distribution maps can show.
7. What sorts of things could cause national borders to change?

SKILLS APPLICATION

MAP SKILLS

8. Get a map of your local area. Measure the direct distance between your home and your school. Measure the distance you actually travel to get from one to the other. Are the two distances different? Why, or why not?
9. Draw a map to show where an imaginary treasure is buried. Show and label important landmarks like roads, buildings, rivers, and so on. Include a key, scale, and compass.
10. Draw a map of North America. Show the borders of the United States, Canada, and Mexico. Label the three countries. Show and label the national capitals. Show and label important natural features. These should include oceans, other large bodies of water, and a few major rivers and mountain ranges.

RESEARCH SKILLS

11. Search through news magazines and newspapers for examples of different types of maps: physical, resource, distribution, and population-density. For each map you find, point out what is included in it. For example, for a political map tell the total area included, the type of divisions (state, city), and items included in the key.
12. Find out more about the work of a cartographer, geographer, archaeologist, or historian. At the public library, look in the card catalog under the subject, for example, *cartography.* You will also be able to get some facts from encyclopedias. Then write a job description using the information you collected.

UNIT REVIEW

VOCABULARY MASTERY

Choose one of the lists of words below. Then write a paragraph or a page using all the words from that list. You may use the words in the singular or plural. On a separate page, write the words and define them.

delta	border
island	cardinal directions
mountain	elevation
ocean	natural boundary
plain	physical map
river	political map
sea	resource
source	scale
valley	symbol

READING FOR MAIN IDEAS

1. When you study geography, what do you learn about?
2. What is a natural boundary?
3. What are the two ways of dividing Earth into Eastern and Western Hemispheres?
4. Degrees can be divided into 60 parts. What are they called?
5. What is usually the most useful kind of land?
6. Where does our system of time zones start? How many time zones does Earth have?
7. What is the difference between weather and climate?
8. Why are the shapes and sizes of things distorted on a map?
9. In what ways can a distribution map be used?
10. How did a map error influence Columbus's decision to sail west?
11. What does a map key tell us?
12. Name the cardinal directions. Name the intermediate directions.

THINKING SKILLS

13. Why are globes limited in their usefulness?
14. Suppose you wanted to tell someone the location of a place with no name. How could you do it?
15. Why do you think many cities developed near waterways?
16. Why do you think many early settlements were on plains?
17. How much do you think the presence of resources influences where people live?
18. Name the national border, mountains, ocean, river, and lake nearest to where you live.
19. Why is a Mercator map useful to pilots of ships?
20. What can you learn from a modern historical map that shows borders as they were in the past?
21. Identify exactly where you live. Give the name of your community, country, state, nation, continent, hemispheres, and planet. Include the approximate latitude and longitude for your community.

USE YOUR MAPS

Look at the climate map on page 33.

22. Name three large climate areas in the United States.
23. What is the coldest climate area shown? What is the driest?

Look at the road map on page 55.

24. What interstate highway runs north and south along Florida's east coast?
25. About how long is Interstate 4? What cities does it connect?

SKILL DEVELOPMENT

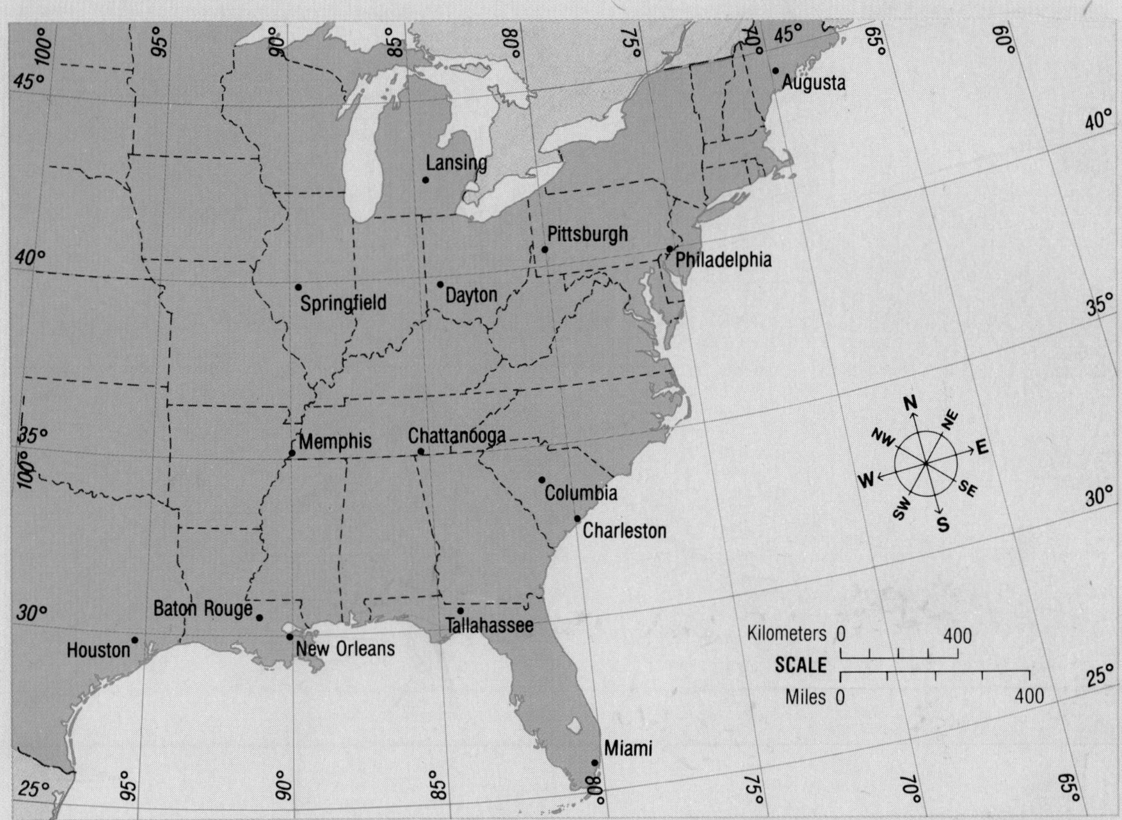

MAP SKILLS

1. Use the map above to find the cities at the following latitude and longitude coordinates:
   a. 40° N latitude, 75° W longitude
   b. 30° N latitude, 90° W longitude
   c. 45° N latitude, 70° W longitude
   d. 25° N latitude, 80° W longitude
   e. 35° N latitude, 85° W longitude
   f. 35° N latitude, 90° W longitude
2. Give the coordinates for the following cities:
   a. Houston
   b. Pittsburgh
   c. Springfield
   d. Tallahassee
   e. Dayton
   f. Baton Rouge
3. Some cities are not near intersecting lines of latitude and longitude. For example, Lansing is between 40° and 45° north latitude. Divide the space into five equal parts. Then figure out the approximate degree. It is about 43° north latitude and 85° west longitude. Use the example to locate Charleston.
4. Give the intermediate directions for each (northwest, southwest, etc.):

   a. Pittsburgh is ___ of Memphis.
   b. Charleston is ___ of Augusta.
   c. New Orleans is ___ of Columbia.
   d. Springfield is ___ of Tallahassee.

EXPLORING AND SETTLING NORTH AMERICA

UNIT 2

CHAPTER 1 THE PEOPLES OF THE AMERICAS

Lesson 1: The First North Americans

FIND THE WORDS

time line ancestors

All people have a past. This is true for groups as well as individuals. People study their past for many reasons. They want to know where they came from. They want to know how they got to be the way they are. They hope that if they get to know themselves better, they can make better plans for their future.

An American writer once said, "Those who cannot remember the past are condemned to repeat it." This means that we should try to learn from past mistakes. If we do not, we may make the same mistakes again. It is also true that we can learn from past successes.

As you have learned, history is what happened in the past. **Time lines** can help you learn history. They are charts that show important events in the order in which they happened. Time lines give you a clear idea of what happened over a certain period of time. In this book, you will read about important events in American history. See where these events fit on the time lines in your book.

Here is a time line showing some early events in North and South America.

Experts think that the first people in North America came from Asia. They came many thousands of years ago. How do you think they got here?

Look at the map on page 64. The northeastern tip of Asia is about 80 kilometers (50 miles) from the northwestern tip of North America. People may have crossed from Asia to North America by raft or boat. During the Ice Age, they may even have walked across. Then, the level of the ocean was much lower. Some of the water was frozen. This exposed a bridge of land linking the two continents. The earliest Americans probably came in small groups of families over a period of many thousands of years.

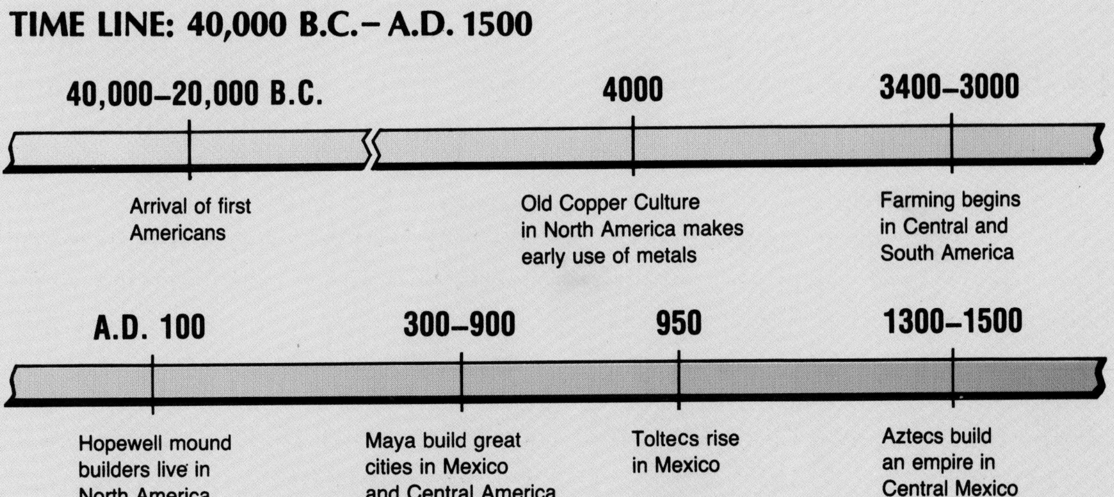

ROUTE OF THE FIRST NORTH AMERICANS

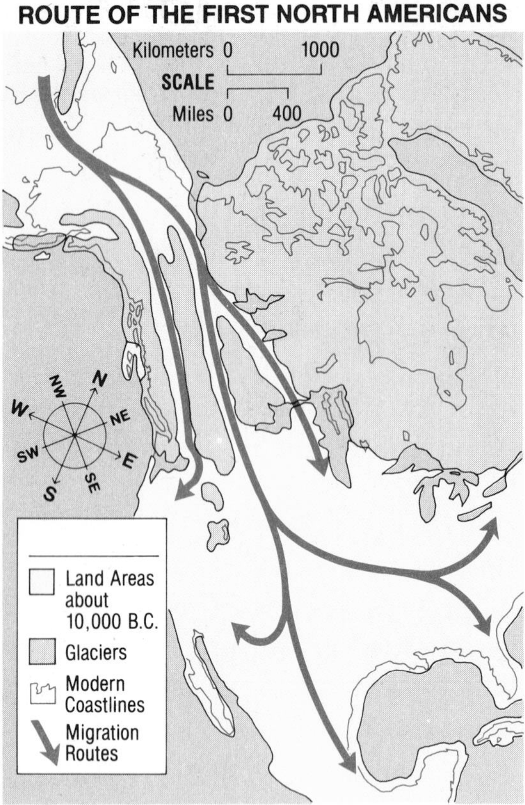

We know that the first Americans were good stonecutters and daring hunters. In Texas and New Mexico, stone and ivory spearheads have been found in the bones of animals. Some of these animals died more than 10,000 years ago. People chipped stone to make tools and weapons such as axes and spear points. They decorated some pieces with beautiful carvings. With these weapons, they hunted wild animals. Some of the animals were larger than any now living in the Americas.

Groups of people gradually moved south and east. We know this because remains of their camps have been found. They gathered around campfires for warmth and protection at night. They lived on the meat of animals they killed. They also gathered wild fruits and vegetables. They fished in the rivers and along the coasts. Some people found places they liked in North America. They decided to stay. Others moved on to Central and South America.

Wild fruits and vegetables were not always easy to find. About 5,000 years ago, people in Central and South America began to plant corn. Later, they learned to plant beans, squash, cotton, and potatoes. This was the beginning of farming in the Americas.

Can you imagine how farming might change a people's way of life? Farming people can settle in one place. They can do this because their crops give them a supply of food. Then they have more time to discover new ways of doing things. For example, they usually learn how to raise certain animals for food or skins. They may learn to make baskets of reeds or pots of clay. Settled people may begin to make cloth from cotton, from other plants, or from the hair of animals. Some discover how to melt down metals such as copper or gold. They may make tools and jewelry.

Early people in Central and South America learned how to do these things. Farming began there about 5,000 years ago. Knowledge of how to grow corn and other crops slowly spread north. Traders probably carried knowledge about farming into what is now Mexico and the United States. Sometimes traders traveled great distances to exchange goods. They also spread ideas from one culture to another.

The people who came to the Americas from Asia were the ancestors of today's American Indians. **Ancestors** are members of a person's family who lived long ago. Groups of early American Indians created their own arts and followed their own customs. Over thousands of years, many native cultures came to exist in North and South America.

American Indians now share North America with people from all over the world.

You will study some of these cultures in the lessons that follow. You will see how they developed and you will see how the coming of Europeans changed the lives of all American Indians.

REVIEW

VOCABULARY MASTERY

1. What are ancestors?
2. Define a time line.

READING FOR MAIN IDEAS

3. How might people have traveled from Asia to North America during the Ice Age?
4. How did the first Americans get food before they learned to farm?
5. How can farming change a people's way of life?

TIME LINE SKILLS

6. Look at the time line on page 63. When did farming begin in Central and South America? How many years ago was this?
7. About how many years did the Mayan culture last?
8. What are two metals early people learned to use?

THINKING SKILLS

How do we know about the life, skills, and journeys of the first Americans?

Lesson 2: Early Cities of North America

FIND THE WORDS

astronomer **mathematician** **hieroglyphics** **temple**

Did you know that cities were built in North America more than 1,600 years ago? At that time, an American Indian people called the Maya (MAH yah) began to build stone cities in Central America. Many Mayan cities have been found in Guatemala (GWAH tuh MAH luh) and on the Yucatán (YOO kuh TAN) Peninsula in Mexico. The Mayan culture was like no other. It was the most advanced culture in the Americas for about 600 years. It compared well with cultures in Europe, too.

The Maya

The Maya possessed great knowledge and important skills. They were expert **astronomers,** people who study stars. They were excellent **mathematicians,** people who study numbers. The Maya used the number zero long before it was used in Europe. They developed a calendar as accurate as the one we use today.

The Maya used **hieroglyphics** (HY ruh GLIF iks), a complicated kind of picture writing. They were also fine stone cutters. They

The Maya built pyramids with temples at the top. This is the Temple of Kukulkan at Chichén-Itzá, which is at 21° north latitude, 89° west longitude. The Egyptians used their pyramids as tombs. Mayan pyramids were religious buildings.

This is the Temple of Warriors at Chichén-Itzá in the Yucatán. It was built by the Maya and the Toltecs.

carved writing and numbers into standing slabs of stone. They also carved scenes showing their way of life. All this stonecarving was done without metal tools. Many Mayan tools were made of especially hard stone.

We know very little about how the Mayan government was organized. Most of the people lived in villages and farmed. Some helped build the great stone cities. There were also craft workers, merchants, and traders. And there were slaves. The ruling class was made up of priests and nobles.

The Maya had an organized religion with many priests. Only members of ruling-class families could become priests. A special place was created for religious ceremonies. At the center of each Mayan city was a high pyramid with a flat top. On top of the pyramid was a temple. A **temple** is a place where people worship a god or gods. Steep steps were cut in the stone leading to the top of the pyramid. Mayan priests climbed these steps. They held religious ceremonies at the top.

The Maya were peaceful farming people. They grew corn, beans, and squash. The peasants worked hard. They did not use animals to pull or carry loads. They had no plows or wheels. But they grew enough food to support the cities.

Around A.D. 900, the great age of the Maya ended. No one knows what happened. The great cities of the south were deserted. But some Mayan cities did survive in the Yucatán.

The Toltecs

Then another people rose to power in Mexico. These people were the Toltecs (TOHL teks). They gained power over the Maya in the Yucatán. The Toltecs were fierce fighters. They were very different from the peaceful Maya.

After conquering the Maya, the Toltecs settled among them. The Toltecs and the Maya influenced one another. The Toltecs added new elements to Mayan cities. The two groups built cities together. Their most beautiful cities are near the middle of the Yucatán.

Sports were popular among the Maya and the Toltecs. They played a ball game something like kickball or rugby. This game was played on a long court. Points were scored by kicking the ball through stone rings on opposite walls of the court. A ball court like this can be seen today at Chichén-Itzá (chee CHEN eet SAH) in Mexico.

The Aztecs

In the 1400s, the Toltecs were conquered by fierce Aztec warriors. The Aztecs built an empire

The Aztecs made this stone calendar. They adopted the Mayan calendar. It is as accurate as the one we use today. The carvings on this stone show the Aztec universe. These symbols tell when the Aztec world began, how it would continue, and when it would come to an end. In the center is the sun god. The symbols represent earth, air, fire, and water. The Aztec year was made up of 18 months of 20 days each. There were also extra days to complete the solar year.

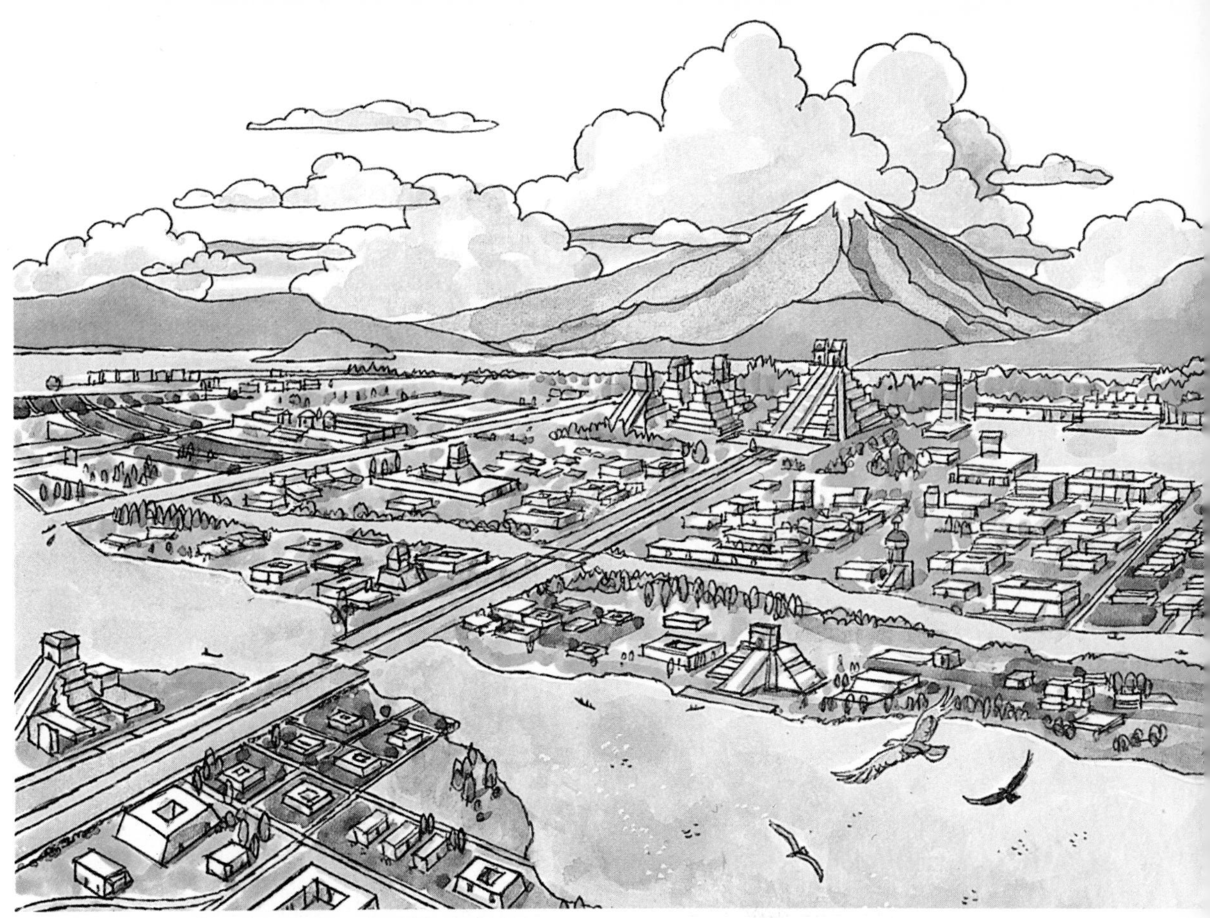

The Aztecs built Tenochtitlán on two islands in a lake. Causeways, or raised roads, were built across the water. Notice the open spaces left for canoes. Aztec pyramids have stone stairs leading to the top. You can climb them today.

that ruled several million people. They were the first people to control all of central Mexico. Their way of life was warlike and highly organized. The Aztecs made beautiful objects of gold and precious stones. They built great stone pyramids with temples on top. There, people worshiped the sun and other Aztec gods. The Aztecs also adopted the Mayan calendar. They made a great round calendar stone that still exists in Mexico City today.

The capital city of the Aztecs was Tenochtitlán (teh NOCH teet LAHN). It was founded in 1325. Tenochtitlán was a large city built on islands in a shallow lake. It was located where Mexico City is today. Tenochtitlán was built mostly of stone. Four long roads connected the island city to the land around the lake. Open spaces in the roads allowed canoes on the lake to pass through. Wooden bridges crossed the open spaces. The city also had floating gardens where vegetables, fruits, and flowers were grown.

Tenochtitlán had two central markets. All kinds of goods made in the countryside were sold there. Food products, gold and silver jewelry, lead, brass, copper, bones, shells, and feathers were sold. The Aztecs also sold colored cotton cloth, pots, pitchers, tiles, and vases of glazed and painted clay.

The Aztecs were the last great American Indian civilization to flourish in Mexico. The Aztecs built their empire between 1428 and 1519. So this great empire lasted only about 100 years. Then, in 1519, the Spanish came to Mexico. A small Spanish army easily conquered the Aztecs. The Spanish had guns and cannons. The Aztecs did not have such weapons. Also, many Aztecs died from European diseases.

Central Mexico had gone through wars and invasions before. But the Spanish conquest was different. The arrival of the Spanish was the end of rule by the native peoples in Mexico. For the next 300 years the Spanish ruled Mexico. They not only changed the government, but also the way people lived.

This old drawing shows fighting during the Spanish conquest of Mexico.

REVIEW

VOCABULARY MASTERY

1. A(n) ___ is a place where a god or gods are worshiped.
   astronomer hieroglyphic temple
2. A person who studies the stars is a(n) ___ .
   astronomer hieroglyphic mathematician

READING FOR MAIN IDEAS

3. What knowledge did the Maya have?
4. How were the Toltecs and the Aztecs alike?
5. Why did American Indian rule end in Mexico?

THINKING SKILLS

People of different cultures learn from one another. The Aztecs and the Toltecs learned much from the Maya. List some foods and some customs the United States has borrowed from other lands.

Lesson 3: Other Early Cultures of North America

FIND THE WORDS

evidence pestle adobe stockade tribe confederacy

In the area that is now the United States, there were many ancient peoples. Signs of their cultures have been found throughout the country. The things they left behind them are **evidence,** or visible proof, of how they lived.

Some of the earliest examples of metalwork anywhere in the world have been found in Wisconsin. They are copper spearheads and tools. They were made by an ancient group of people called the Old Copper Culture. We know that these people lived 5,000 to 7,000 years ago near the Great Lakes. The tools are evidence that these early people knew much about working with metal.

The ancient Cochise (KOH chees) people lived where Arizona, New Mexico, and Mexico now meet. This area is a desert. Once, however, it had a large lake. The Cochise people lived in this region for thousands of years. They began to grow corn about 4,000 years ago. They used **pestles,** or grinding stones, to grind the corn. Later, they also grew beans and squash.

The Cochise were probably the ancestors of the modern Pueblo (PWEB loh) people. About 500 years ago, Pueblo people began to dig irrigation ditches to water the land. They changed the course of streams. They made ponds to store water. That way, they could grow more crops.

The Pueblo people are best known as builders. Their homes, called pueblos, were often several stories high. They were built of **adobe** (uh DOH bee), which is sun-baked clay. Ladders were used to reach entrances on upper floors. Pueblos look somewhat like apartment buildings. Some pueblos were built on the sides of cliffs 900 years ago. Early pueblos like this can be seen in the Southwest today. Modern Pueblo people still live in that region.

About 1,900 years ago, the Hopewell mound builders lived in the Ohio and Mississippi valleys. The Hopewell people built large, high mounds of earth. We are not sure what these mounds were for. Most were used as burial places. Some were forts. Some were

The first pueblos were built on the sides of cliffs about 900 years ago. They were made of adobe, or sun-baked clay. Ladders were used to reach the upper stories of the buildings. The Pueblo people of today live in Arizona and New Mexico. Many still live in pueblos.

shaped like animals. They may have served a religious purpose.

The Hopewell Culture started as a community of farmers. Slowly, it grew into several communities that agreed to help and protect one another. The Hopewell people were great traders in art objects, sea shells, wood, copper, and food. Their communities stretched south from Wisconsin to the Gulf of Mexico. They extended west from New York to Kansas.

Another mound-building people are now known as the Temple Mound Culture. These people lived along the Mississippi River valley about 500 years ago. Their villages were surrounded by high wooden fences. The Temple Mound people built temples 33 meters (100 feet) high. These temples were shaped like pyramids with flat tops. The Temple Mound people had much in common with the earlier Maya of Mexico. They may have had contact with early Mexican cultures through trade.

One example of an early culture that survived into modern times is the Natchez Culture. The Natchez people lived near where the city of Natchez, Mississippi is today. They had a highly developed class system and religion. Their king and high priest was called Great Sun. The king's mother, if she was alive, or his sister, was the Woman Sun. She chose the king's successor from among her sons or brothers when the king died. The Natchez were

The Hopewell people built large, high mounds of earth. This is the Great Serpent Mound in Ohio. No one today is sure why the Indians built these mounds.

the strongest tribe along the lower Mississippi River when Europeans arrived. They were defeated by the French in the early 1700s. A few Natchez survivors are found today living among other tribes in the Southwest.

The Europeans arriving in the New World found many American Indians living along the Atlantic Coast. These native people belonged to Woodlands cultures.

The Woodlands peoples lived in villages. For defense, a village was often surrounded by a fence, or **stockade,** made of wooden posts. Families lived in various kinds of houses within the stockade. There was usually an open area in the center of the village.

The Woodlands peoples were organized into groups known as **tribes.** In some places, tribes formed larger groups that were called **confederacies.** There was almost constant warfare among the various groups.

The Woodlands tribes got food by gathering wild plants and by hunting and fishing. They also farmed in a way that made it impossible to stay in one place permanently. They cleared fields for farming by cutting down some trees and burning the rest. The ashes enriched the soil, but only for a few years. The richness of the soil was soon used up. As a result, the people had to move often. For this reason, and because of the constant warfare, the number of people remained small.

Here, early Indian women plant seeds while men prepare the ground. They are putting the seeds into the holes that one of the men is making with a fishbone hoe. These are Florida Indians.

The Indians of the Americas had many kinds of governments. A few tribes were ruled by one person—a king or a chief. Others had a leader whose power was controlled by a tribal council. Some tribes practiced democracy. They gave both men and women a say in tribal decision-making.

REVIEW

VOCABULARY MASTERY

1. A(n) ___ is a grinding stone.
   hieroglyphic adobe pestle
2. ___ is sun-baked clay.
   Stockade Adobe Pestle
3. A(n) ___ is a group of tribes.
   stockade adobe confederacy
4. A(n) ___ is a fence of wooden posts.
   stockade adobe pestle
5. The Woodlands peoples were organized into groups called ___.
   stockades mounds tribes

READING FOR MAIN IDEAS

6. Where did the people of the Old Copper Culture live?
7. List three crops that the Cochise people grew.
8. What kind of homes did the Pueblo people build?
9. Name two cultures that built mounds.
10. Why did the Woodlands people move from place to place?
11. Give two reasons why the number of Woodlands people remained small.

RESEARCH SKILLS

Find out what early peoples lived in your state. Has any evidence of these people been found? Use your library to find out. If you can, visit a museum.

CHAPTER REVIEW

VOCABULARY MASTERY

Use the words below to complete the chapter summary. Use each only once.

adobe	mathematicians
astronomers	stockades
confederacies	temples
hieroglyphics	tribes

Before the first Europeans arrived, American Indians had built great __1__ in Central America. These people possessed great knowledge and skill and were expert __2__ and __3__. They used a system of picture writing called __4__. Farther north, American Indians were organized into __5__ and __6__. Some lived in villages surrounded by __7__, while others lived in buildings made of __8__.

READING FOR MAIN IDEAS

1. What do time lines show?
2. Where did the first Americans probably come from? How did they get to North America?
3. How did knowledge of farming reach North America?
4. Who were the ancestors of today's American Indians?
5. What was Tenochtitlán? Describe it.
6. In what ways was Mayan culture different from other cultures of the Americas at that time?
7. Why were the Spanish able to conquer the Aztecs so easily?
8. How do we know about the metal-working skills of the Old Copper Culture?
9. The Hopewell Culture began as a farming community. What did it develop into? Where were Hopewell people found?
10. How did the Woodlands peoples clear fields for farming?

SKILLS APPLICATION

WRITING SKILLS

Writing an outline helps to organize information. You can use the information to write a paper or to give a speech. You can also use an outline to help you remember facts. The exercise below will help you prepare a study outline. It includes groups of people you studied about in this chapter.

Use a separate sheet of paper. Copy the outline as shown below. Turn to page 62. Write the chapter title at the top of your outline. This is the main title. Next you will see that the title of Lesson 1 is roman numeral *I.* on the outline. This is a *main topic* within the outline. Under each main topic, you include *subheadings,* or topics within the main topic. In this outline, the subheadings are the people described by each main topic.

In Lessons 2 and 3, you will find the information you need. Complete the outline with the names from the list below.

(title)
____

I. The First North Americans
II. People of Early Cities
  A.
  B.
  C.
III. Other Cultures of North America
  A.
  B.
  C.
  D.
  E.
  F.
  G.

Aztecs	Pueblo people
Cochise	Temple Mound Culture
Hopewell Culture	Toltecs
Maya	Woodlands people
Natchez Culture	
Old Copper Culture	

CHAPTER 2 AN AGE OF EXPLORATION

Lesson 1: Europeans Find the Americas

FIND THE WORDS

compass **trade route**

"Wednesday, October 10th, 1492. Steered west-south-west day and night, and made 59 leagues progress. Here the men lost all patience. They complained of the length of the voyage. But the Admiral encouraged them the best he could. He told them their voyage would make them rich. And he added that they had come so

far, they could not turn back. They had no choice but to go on.

"At two o'clock on Friday morning, land was discovered. They found themselves near a small island, where they saw people on the beach. The Admiral landed in a small boat with a party of his men. They found very green trees, many streams of water, and many kinds of fruit. The Admiral planted a flag on the beach and claimed the land for the King and Queen of Spain."

The "Admiral" in this story is the Italian explorer Christopher Columbus. The story comes from his diary. This voyage, in 1492, is the earliest recorded discovery of the New World by Europeans. But there is evidence that people from Europe and Asia may have come to the Americas long before.

The Vikings

Probably the first European visitors were the Norwegian (nor WEE jun) Vikings. For 300 years, these wandering, seafaring people terrorized western Europe. Sailing the rivers in their small, swift ships, they swooped down on numerous towns and churches.

COLUMBUS'S VOYAGES TO AMERICA

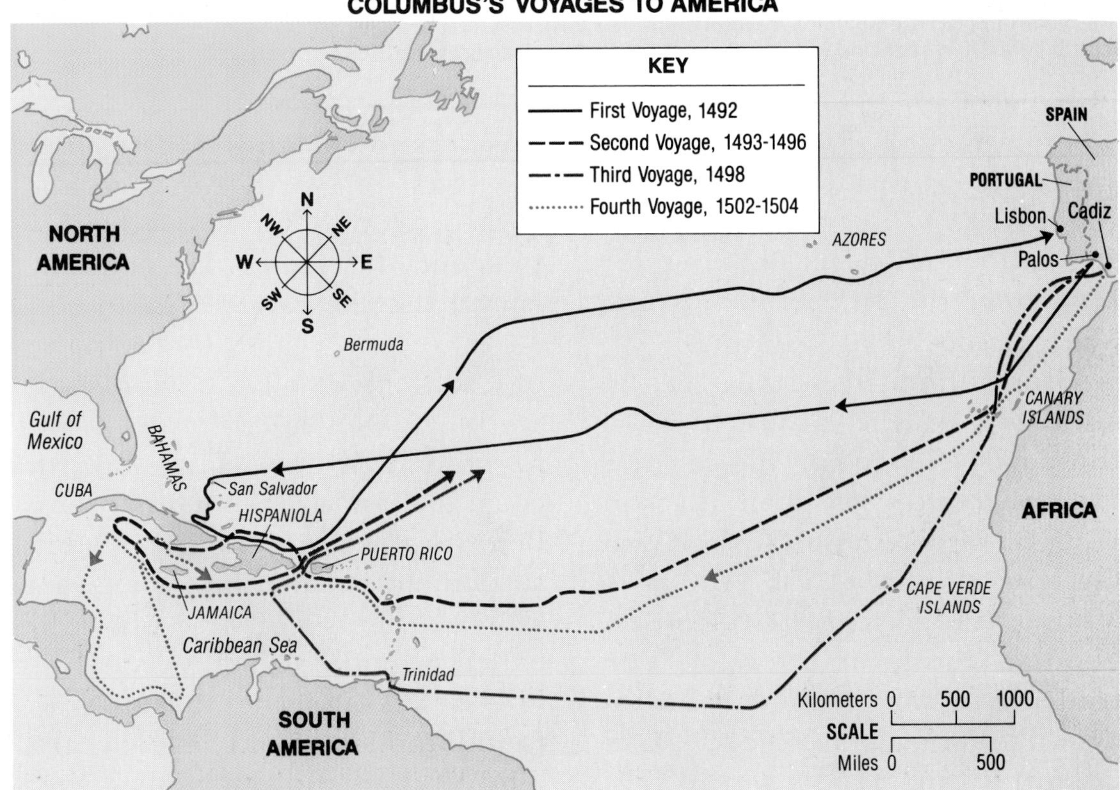

The Vikings sailed the Atlantic Ocean in ships like this. They reached Iceland in A.D. 770, Greenland in the 900s, and North America about A.D. 1000.

They attacked, took all of the valuables, and sailed off. In 770, the restless Vikings sailed west to Iceland. They were looking for land to settle. In the 900s, some Vikings moved to Greenland.

Stories handed down over the ages tell of the adventures of these early Vikings. One of their greatest heroes was Leif Ericson (LEEF ER ik sun). He lived in Greenland about A.D. 1000. A Viking trader told Leif Ericson about a land far to the west. The trader had sailed there by accident some years before. Leif bought a ship. He set out to find this unknown land. He reached the coast of North America and looked around for a good place to spend the winter. He chose an island that he called Vinland.

In recent years, the remains of a settlement have been discovered in Newfoundland. Newfoundland is an island off the coast of Canada. Some historians believe this was Leif Ericson's settlement. Other historians are still searching for the place he called Vinland.

The Viking settlement on Newfoundland lasted only a few years. The Vikings did not realize they had found a New World or pass on the news of the land they had settled. For many years, the adventures of Leif Ericson lived on only in the Viking tales.

In later years, some English sailors may have gone to the Grand Banks. This is a rich fishing area south of Newfoundland. They may have gone to catch the fish that feed there. But for the next several hundred years, Europe showed no interest in exploring the New World.

New Developments

In the 1400s, changes began to take place that increased interest in exploration. For example, scientists developed tools that helped sailors cross the oceans. One such tool is the compass. A **compass** is an instrument with a magnetic needle that always points north. These tools helped sailors know where they were and in what direction they were going. They no longer had to stay close to land to keep from getting lost. Still, sailing out of sight of land was very frightening to sailors. At that time, ships were very small.

Another important change was the growth of powerful states in Europe. France, England, Spain, and Portugal were becoming stronger. Leaders could give more attention to foreign trade.

Europeans wanted the silk and spices that were found in India and China. In the 1400s, India was called "the Indies." Trade routes to the Indies were over land. A **trade route** is a line of travel over land or water used by traders carrying goods. It took many months, and even years, to carry goods over mountains, deserts, and plains. The goods were often damaged along the way or stolen by robbers. European rulers wanted to find better trade routes to the Indies. They provided ships and money to explorers so a sea route could be found.

The Portuguese were the first Europeans to encourage exploration overseas. Prince Henry of Portugal opened a special school to train sailors and mapmakers. The Portuguese looked for a route sailing south and then to the east around Africa.

Christopher Columbus

Christopher Columbus had a different idea. He believed he could find a shorter route to Asia by sailing west instead of east. He shared the belief of many that the world was round. But he also thought the world was much smaller than it is. Many people thought Columbus was a fool. But Queen Isabella of Spain was more farsighted. She agreed to pay for Columbus's voyage.

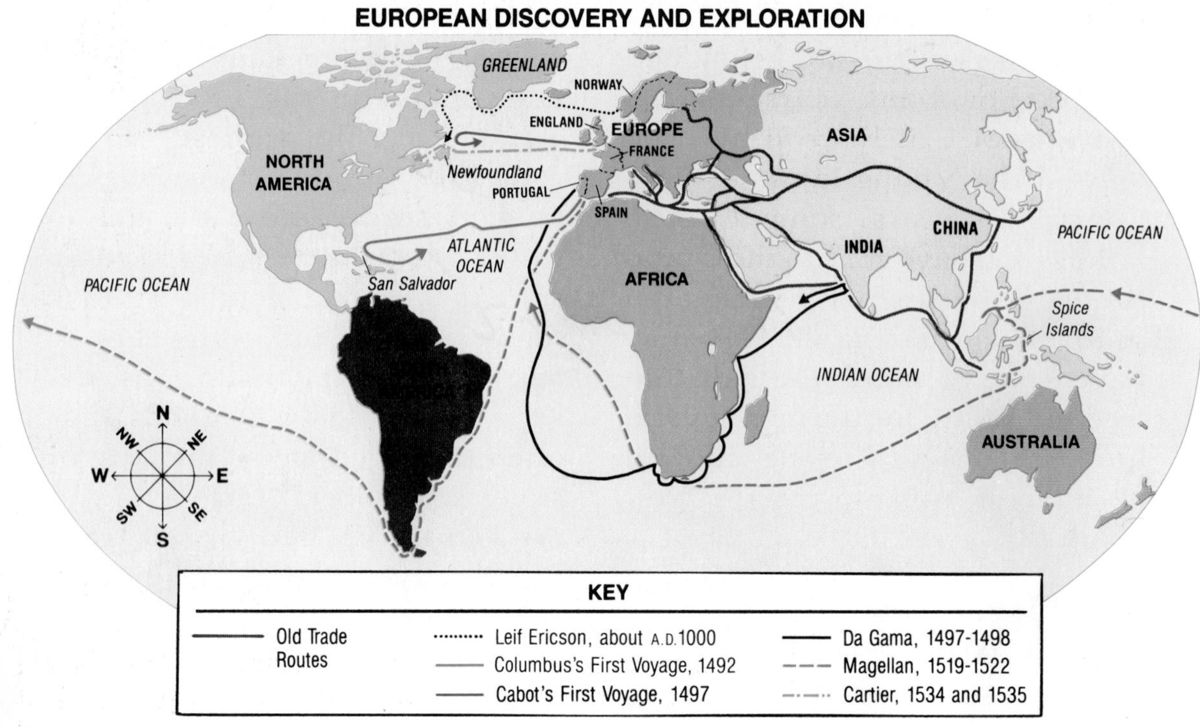

In 1492, Columbus set sail with three small ships. These were the *Niña* (NEE nyuh), the *Pinta* (PEEN tah), and the *Santa Maria* (SAHN tuh muh REE uh). Columbus and his sailors traveled 33 days across the Atlantic Ocean without seeing land. Finally, on October 12, they arrived at an island about 640 kilometers (400 miles) from the coast of Florida. It is still called San Salvador, the name Columbus gave to it. They also explored the islands of Hispaniola (HIS pun YOH luh), nearby Puerto Rico, and Cuba.

The people Columbus found on these islands were the Taino (TY noh). But Columbus called them "Indians" because he thought he was in the Indies. He returned to Spain with some of these peaceful Taino people. He also brought tobacco and a little gold. Queen Isabella and King Ferdinand were not satisfied with this cargo. They sent Columbus on three more voyages to the New World.

Columbus never found the riches he was looking for. He died in 1506, poor and unhappy. To the end, he believed that he had found the best route to the Indies. Instead, Christopher Columbus had found a whole new world.

This is a reproduction of Columbus's cabin on the *Santa Maria*.

REVIEW

VOCABULARY MASTERY

1. In the 1400s, tools such as the ___ made sailing in unknown waters easier.
   pestle compass stockade

READING FOR MAIN IDEAS

2. Who were probably the first Europeans in the New World?
3. What was Leif Ericson's settlement called?
4. Why were Europeans looking for ocean trade routes in the 1400s?
5. How did the early Portuguese plan to sail to the Indies? Which way did Columbus decide to go?

THINKING SKILLS

Columbus thought the Earth was smaller than it is. He also thought that he had sailed west to the Indies. How are these two beliefs connected?

Lesson 2: The Spanish and Portuguese Explore

FIND THE WORDS

isthmus strait mission

News of Columbus's discoveries spread quickly. Many European nations were eager to share in the imagined riches. The Portuguese king sent two explorers off on important voyages.

Vespucci and Cabral

Amerigo Vespucci (ah MAIR ih goh vess POO chee) made several trips across the Atlantic. He was looking for a passage to the Indies. The voyage he made in 1501–1502 was for Portugal. He sailed far south along the coast of South America. Trace his voyage on the map on page 85. Vespucci concluded that this land was not part of Asia. It was instead a New World.

Vespucci and other explorers wrote about their voyages to the New World. A German geographer read the stories with great interest. He drew maps based on the explorers' reports. The geographer called this new land America, after Amerigo Vespucci. When his maps were published in 1507, the name *America* became known.

A Portuguese explorer named Pedro Cabral (kuh BRAHL) sailed from Lisbon in 1500. He planned to go to India by sailing around Africa. But Cabral's ship was blown far off course. Instead of reaching India, he landed on the coast of South America. The land he found was present-day Brazil. Cabral claimed it for Portugal.

Balboa

Vasco Nuñez de Balboa (bal BOH uh) was an adventurer from

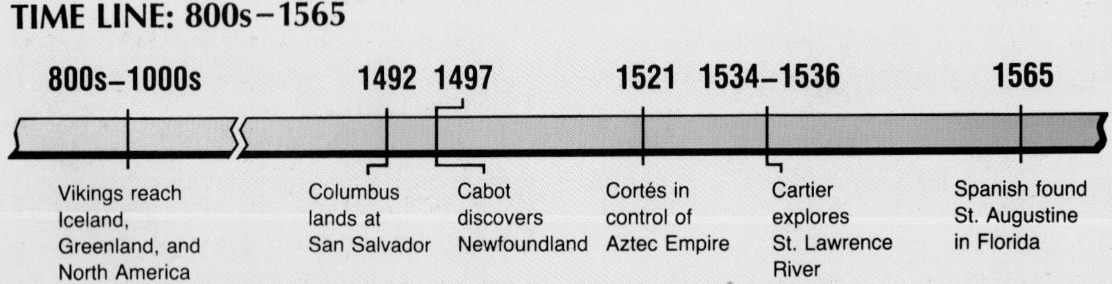

SPANISH EXPLORERS IN NORTH AMERICA

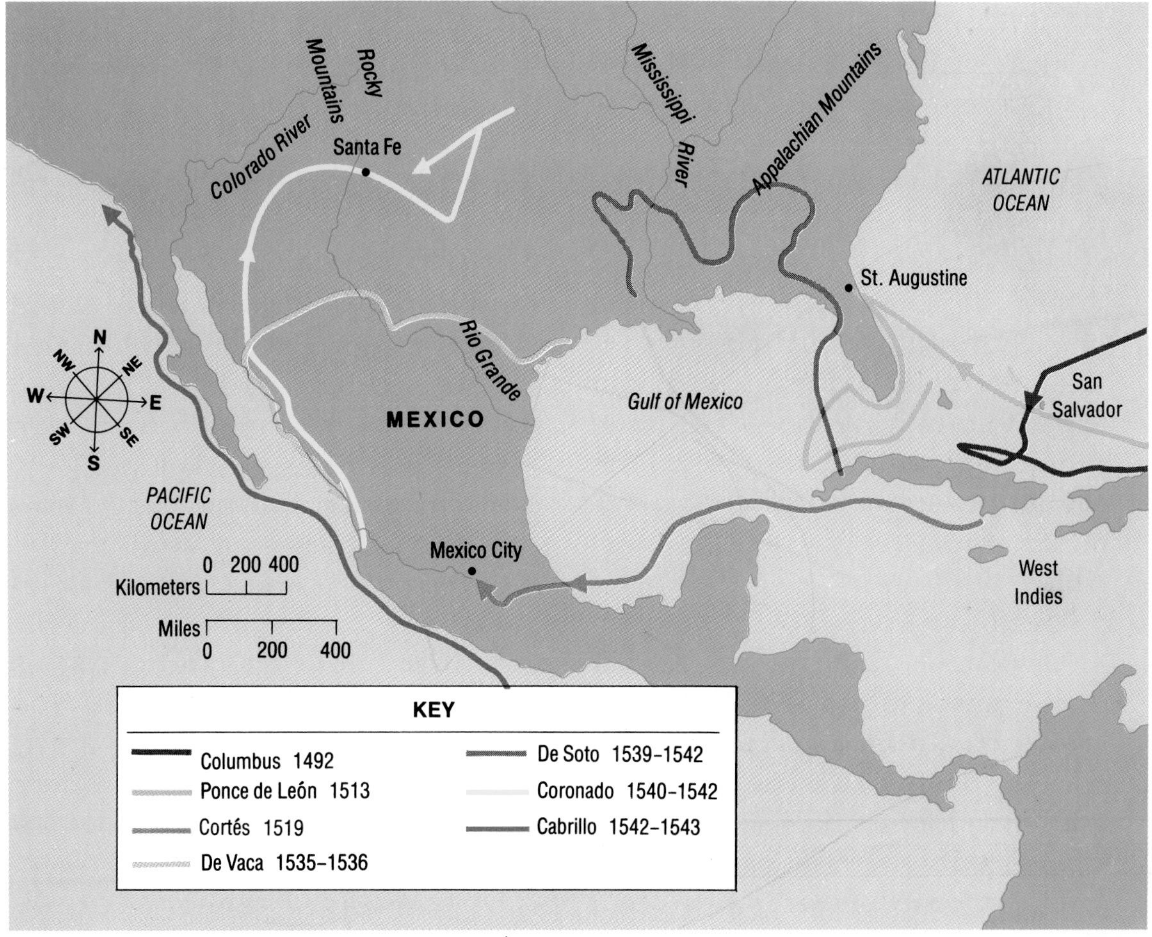

Spain. He went to what is now Panama to seek his fortune. There, he received a valuable piece of information from the local Indians. Beyond the mountains, they said, was another sea. Balboa set out with his men and with Indian guides. They had to go through swamps, through jungles, and over mountains. They crossed the **isthmus** (ISS muss) of Panama, a narrow strip of land linking North America and South America. Finally, on September 15, 1513, Balboa saw the Pacific Ocean. He was the first European to see it from the New World.

Ponce de León

Juan Ponce de León (HWAHN PON say day lay OHN) had sailed with Columbus on his second voyage to the New World. Ponce de León stayed on in the West Indies. He spent many years looking for gold. He conquered the island of Puerto Rico and became its governor. Still in search of gold, he sailed north in 1513 and discovered Florida. There, he heard stories of a marvelous "fountain of youth." It seemed that if you bathed in its water, you would never grow old. To Ponce de León, this was more wonderful than gold. He and his men searched far and wide for this fountain. They explored much of Florida, but never found the fountain of youth.

Magellan

Ferdinand Magellan (muh JEL un) was the first to succeed in doing what Columbus had hoped to do. He found a passage to the Indies. Magellan was a Portuguese explorer paid by the Spanish king. In 1519, he reached the Pacific Ocean by sailing through a strait near the tip of South America. A **strait** is a narrow channel of water connecting two larger bodies of water. The strait Magellan found is now named for him. He then crossed the Pacific to the Spice Islands in present-day Indonesia.

Magellan and his crew met with great difficulties in their travels. All but one of his five ships were destroyed during the voyage. Magellan himself was killed in a conflict in the Philippines. In 1522, the remaining ship returned to Spain. It was the first ship to sail all the way around the world. The goods it brought back to Spain were worth more than enough to pay for the whole voyage.

Cortés

The Spanish rulers heard about a rich empire in North America where Mexico is today. They sent Hernán Cortés (ehr NAHN kor TEZ) to Mexico to seek gold.

With only 500 people, Cortés conquered the great Aztec empire between 1519 and 1521. The Aztecs were fine warriors, but the Spanish had many advantages. They had guns and cannons, iron armor, swords, and horses. The Aztecs had never seen these things. The Aztecs also had enemies among the people they ruled. These people thought Cortés would free them from having to pay taxes to the Aztec emperor, Montezuma II (MON tuh ZOO muh). So they helped Cortés and the Spanish soldiers.

Probably the greatest disadvantage the Aztecs had was a story that had been handed down from generation to generation. According to this story, the ancestors of the Aztecs had once worshiped a god named Quetzalcoatl (ket SAHL KWAHT ul). He had been defeated by other gods hundreds of years before. When

SPANISH AND PORTUGUESE EXPLORERS

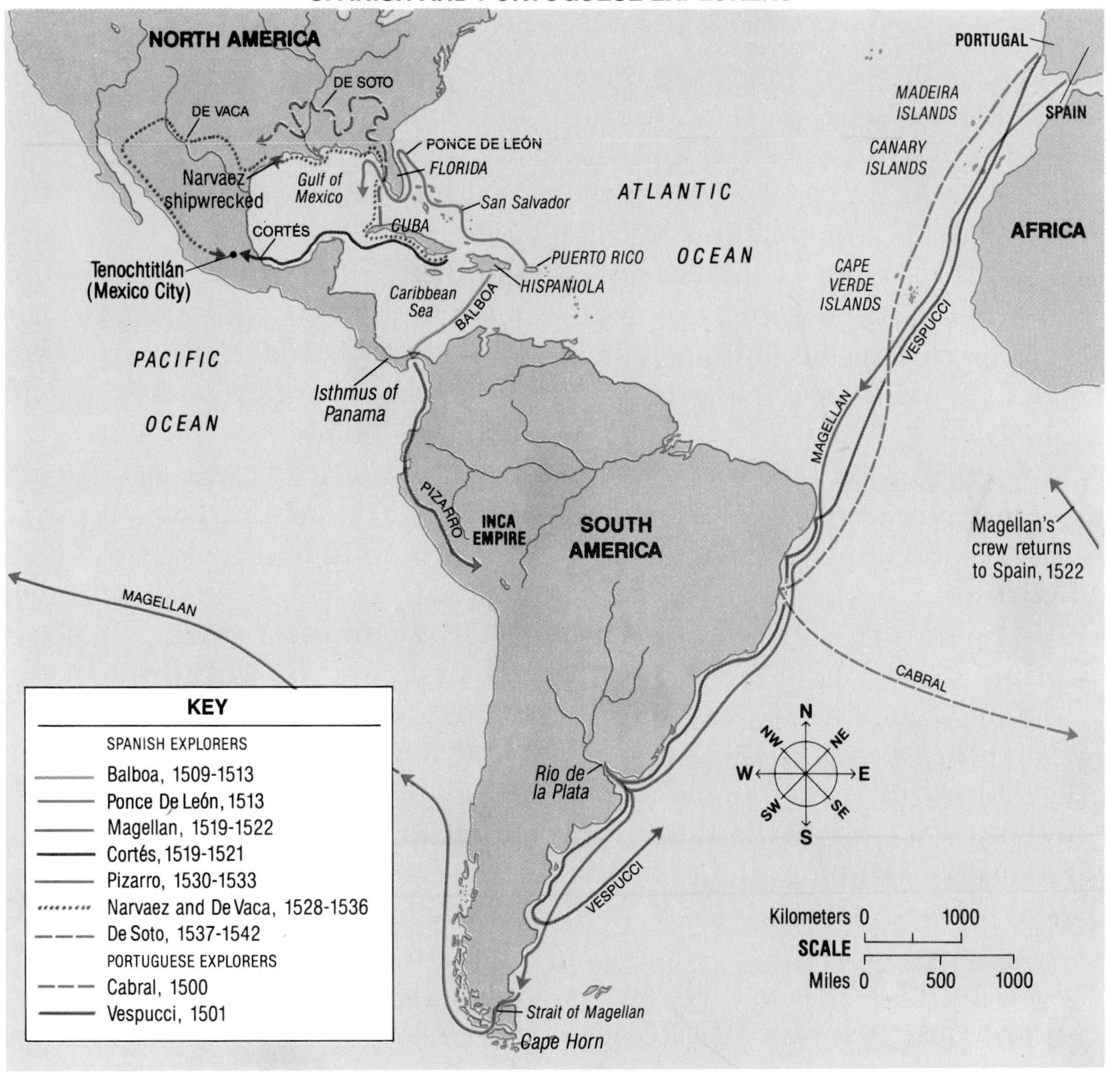

he went away he promised to return one day in great white birds that flew over the water. They would come from the direction of the rising sun.

In 1519, the Aztec emperor Montezuma heard that warriors had come to Mexico. They had come from the east in big ships with sails like white wings. Montezuma was not sure what to do. He thought the Spanish might be the ancient rulers of the Aztecs. Montezuma waited. In the end, he decided to fight. The Aztecs fought well, but it was too late. They were defeated and their empire was conquered.

Pizarro

A Spanish soldier named Francisco Pizarro (pih ZAH roh) explored the west coast of South America. There, he found an empire as great and rich as that of the Aztecs. It was the land of the Incas (ING kuz), a place now called Peru. After a long, bloody war, Pizarro and his soldiers succeeded in conquering the Incas in 1535.

By the mid-1500s, enormous amounts of gold and silver were being shipped back to Spain from Mexico and Peru. This treasure made Spain the richest nation in Europe.

Spanish explorers were eager to find other rich empires. So they traveled north from Mexico into what is now the United States. The stories of fabulous riches lured explorers far inland.

Narváez, de Vaca, Coronado

Panfilo de Narváez (PAHN fee loh duh narh VAH ays) explored what is now Florida in 1527. Afterward, he sailed his ships along the Gulf of Mexico. There, near present-day Galveston, Texas, his ships were wrecked. Four men survived the wreck and reached shore. They were Cabeza de Vaca (kuh BAY zuh day VAH kah), two other Spanish sailors, and a Black man named Estebanico (ESS tay bah NEE koh). For 6 years, they wandered across Texas. Finally, they reached Mexico City. They brought with them American Indian tales of seven "Cities of Gold."

Francisco Coronado (fran SISS koh KOR oh NAH doh) was another Spaniard who looked for a rich empire like that of the Aztecs. Between 1540 and 1542, he explored parts of Texas and Kansas. Some of the explorers traveling with Coronado discovered the Grand Canyon. But they found no cities of gold.

In 1565, the Spanish founded St. Augustine in Florida. This was the first permanent European settlement in the United States.

Roman Catholic priests from Spain were important to all the Spanish settlements. They came to the New World to teach Roman Catholic beliefs and Spanish culture to the American Indians. They built **missions,** or religious communities. There, they lived and taught the people.

The Spanish brought their laws, language, and religion to the New World. Universities were built in 1551 in Lima, Peru, and in Mexico City, Mexico. The first printing press in North America was set up in Mexico City in 1539.

Spain, by the late 1500s, had a huge empire in the Americas. Very few people lived in

The Spanish founded St. Augustine in 1565. The year before, a group of French settlers had built a fort in northern Florida. This angered the Spanish king, because Florida belonged to Spain. So he sent a group of men, under the leadership of a Spanish sea captain, to drive the French out of Florida. When the Spaniards got to Florida, they killed all the French settlers. Then they established their own settlement at St. Augustine. Florida remained under Spanish control for most of the next 250 years. Then, in 1821, Spain officially turned Florida over to the United States. St. Augustine, at 30°N, 81°W, is the oldest permanent European settlement in the United States.

some parts of the empire, such as North Mexico and Central America. But Mexico City was a thriving community. It was the center of the empire. The great homes and palaces were built by generals, bishops, and other rulers.

The ruler of the empire was the Spanish king. He was represented in the New World by the Viceroy. The Viceroy ruled in place of the king, and he had absolute power, as did the king. The colonies were considered the king's property.

People to Remember

Hernando de Soto

Hernando de Soto went to the New World in 1519 to seek his fortune. In 1530, he joined Pizarro in the conquest of Peru. De Soto did not like Pizarro's brutal treatment of the Incas. But he took his share of the Inca gold.

Later, de Soto became governor of Cuba. He had the Spanish king's permission to explore and conquer any land north of Mexico. In 1539, he and his soldiers landed on the west coast of Florida. They were looking for gold and silver.

Over the next 4 years, they traveled from the Carolinas to what is now Texas. Trace de Soto's route north and west on the map on page 85. They did not find any riches. But, in 1541, they did discover and cross a very broad river. The American Indians called the river the Mississippi, or "big river." The following spring, de Soto died near the great river he had found.

REVIEW

VOCABULARY MASTERY

1. Spanish priests built religious communities called ____.
   adobes straits missions
2. A ____ is a narrow channel of water.
   drain strait mission

READING FOR MAIN IDEAS

3. After whom was America named?
4. What did Balboa find when he crossed Panama?
5. Who was the Aztec ruler when Cortés arrived in Mexico?
6. Which Spanish expedition discovered the Mississippi River?

THINKING SKILLS

What was proved by the round-the-world voyage led by Magellan? How do you think this journey affected people's ideas about Earth?

Lesson 3: The English and French Explore

FIND THE WORDS

colony navigator circumnavigate

By the late 1500s, other European countries began to explore the New World. The French, the Dutch, and the English went farther north than the Spanish. They began to settle North America. Soon, there were Spanish, French, Dutch, and English colonies on the continent. A **colony** is a group of people who settle in a distant land. In that land, they are still ruled by their parent country.

The English and the French were eager to find gold and silver in the Americas. But they also wanted to find a shorter route to the Indies.

Cabot

A **navigator** is a person who explores by ship. To do this, the person must direct the ship's course. John Cabot, an Italian navigator, made a voyage for the English king. Cabot sailed west from Bristol, England, in 1497. He had a small ship and a crew of 18. He thought he could reach Asia by going farther to the north than Columbus. After 33 days, he landed in Newfoundland. That large island off the coast of North America is now part of Canada. Cabot, however, believed he had reached China. He saw no people on this island. He found no spices.

When he returned to England, Cabot made his report. The only wealth he had discovered was in the seas. There seemed to be an endless supply of fish. The next year, Cabot set off once more for the New World. This time he took four ships. Nobody knows what happened on the second trip. Neither Cabot nor his crew was ever heard from again.

Drake

Sir Francis Drake, an adventurer and sea captain, had a long career as a pirate. But he was a pirate who worked for the English queen, Elizabeth I. He and his men attacked Spanish ships and Spanish towns in the New World. They captured all the gold and silver they could find.

Drake was also a great explorer. The year 1577 was the beginning of Drake's most important voyage. He planned to

circumnavigate (SUR kum NAV ih GAYT), or sail around, Earth. He followed the route Magellan had taken, through a strait at the tip of South America. Then he headed north, attacking Spanish settlements along the coast. Drake collected many riches on his way.

Look at the map on page 93. It shows the routes of the French and English explorers. Find the line for Drake in the key. Now trace Drake's route around the Americas. Notice that he sailed through the Strait of Magellan instead of going around Cape Horn. Notice, too, that he stayed close to the coastline. That helped him find his way. It also meant that the sailors could go ashore to find food. Otherwise, they would have starved on the long voyage.

Continuing north in the summer of 1579, Drake came to a beautiful bay with friendly people. He called the place New Albion, meaning New England. Today, we know Drake landed on the California coast near San Francisco.

Drake sailed west. He passed the Spice Islands of Indonesia and the Cape of Good Hope at the tip of Africa. He arrived back in England in 1580. He had sailed around the world in three years. Drake was knighted by Queen Elizabeth I and became a hero.

This is Drake's Bay near San Francisco on the California coast. Sir Francis Drake and his English explorers landed there in 1579.

Fascinating Facts

Sir Walter Raleigh did not have much luck with his colonies. He sent a group of men to Roanoke Island in 1585. They soon sailed back to England. When a new shipload of colonists arrived in Roanoke, they found no one there. All but 15 of them went back to England. These 15 were never heard from again.

Raleigh sent another group to America in 1587. This group included 17 women and 9 children. Within a month after the colonists landed, Virginia Dare was born. She was the first English child born in North America.

Virginia's grandfather, John White, was the governor of the colony. He returned to England to get food and other supplies for the colony. But England was being attacked by the Spanish Armada. This was a great fleet of ships. Not until the year 1590 was White able to get back to Roanoke Island. When he returned, the colonists had disappeared. White found the word *Croatoan* carved on a post. No one has ever found out what happened to the Lost Colony.

This scene shows actors playing Sir Walter Raleigh and Queen Elizabeth I in a play.

Raleigh

The first English settlement in the New World was organized by Sir Walter Raleigh in the 1580s. Queen Elizabeth I gave him the right to start a colony there. The place chosen for the colony was Roanoke Island, now part of North Carolina. Raleigh was not able to go to America himself. England was at war with Spain. Raleigh was needed at home.

Raleigh named his colony "Virginia" in honor of Elizabeth, who was known as "the Virgin Queen." The first colonists he sent were all men. They did not succeed in keeping peace with the Indians. Food was scarce and life was very hard. After a year, the colonists returned to England. In 1587, Raleigh sent a group that included men, women, and children. It was no more successful. When a ship from England brought supplies after several years, the colonists had disappeared. No one knows what happened to them. Did they die? Did they go to live with the Indians? To this day, they are known as the "Lost Colony."

The fate of Raleigh's colony did not long discourage English settlement in the New World. Many English merchants and

This picture shows a Secotan Indian village in North Carolina as it looked in the 1500s.

nobles had heard of the great amounts of gold being shipped to Spain from America. They soon learned that the French and Dutch were also making money in the New World. The English wanted wood and tar for building ships. They wanted to grow crops that could not be grown in England.

The merchants and nobles asked the English king to grant them land to settle. The king gave them land both south and north of the Dutch claims in North America. The merchants and nobles then formed companies that outfitted ships to carry settlers to the New World. There, they meant to start English colonies. You will learn about each of these colonies in the next chapter.

The French explored areas that are now parts of Canada and the United States. They found furs and fish rather than gold.

Verrazano

Giovanni da Verrazano (VER uh ZAH noh), an Italian navigator, sailed to the New World for the French king. He, too, hoped to find a sea passage to Asia. In 1524, Verrazano landed in present-day North Carolina. Then he sailed north along the coast, discovering the bay of New York. Today, near the spot where he landed, there is a great bridge. It is named after Verrazano.

Verrazano's story did not have a happy ending. On a later voyage to Brazil, he was captured and killed by Carib people.

Cartier

Jacques Cartier (KAHR tee AY) thought the passage to Asia might be found in the north. In 1534

WHERE WE ARE IN TIME AND PLACE

ENGLISH AND FRENCH EXPLORATION OF NORTH AMERICA

1497
1524
1534–1535
1579
1587
Cabot sails from England to Newfoundland
Verrazano explores East Coast for France
Cartier discovers St. Lawrence River
Drake explores California coast
Raleigh sends colonists to Roanoke Island

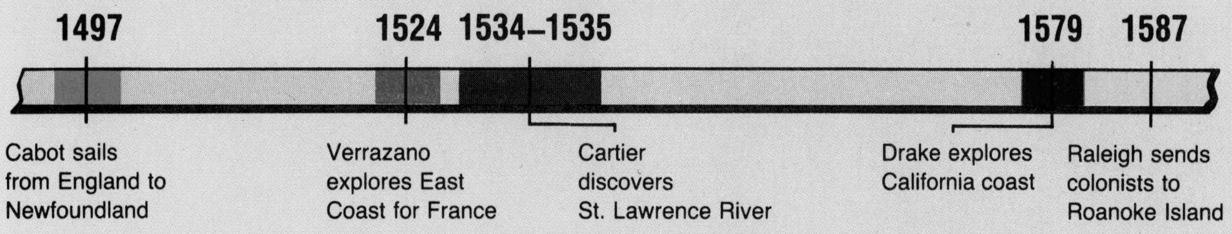

ROUTES OF THE ENGLISH AND FRENCH EXPLORERS

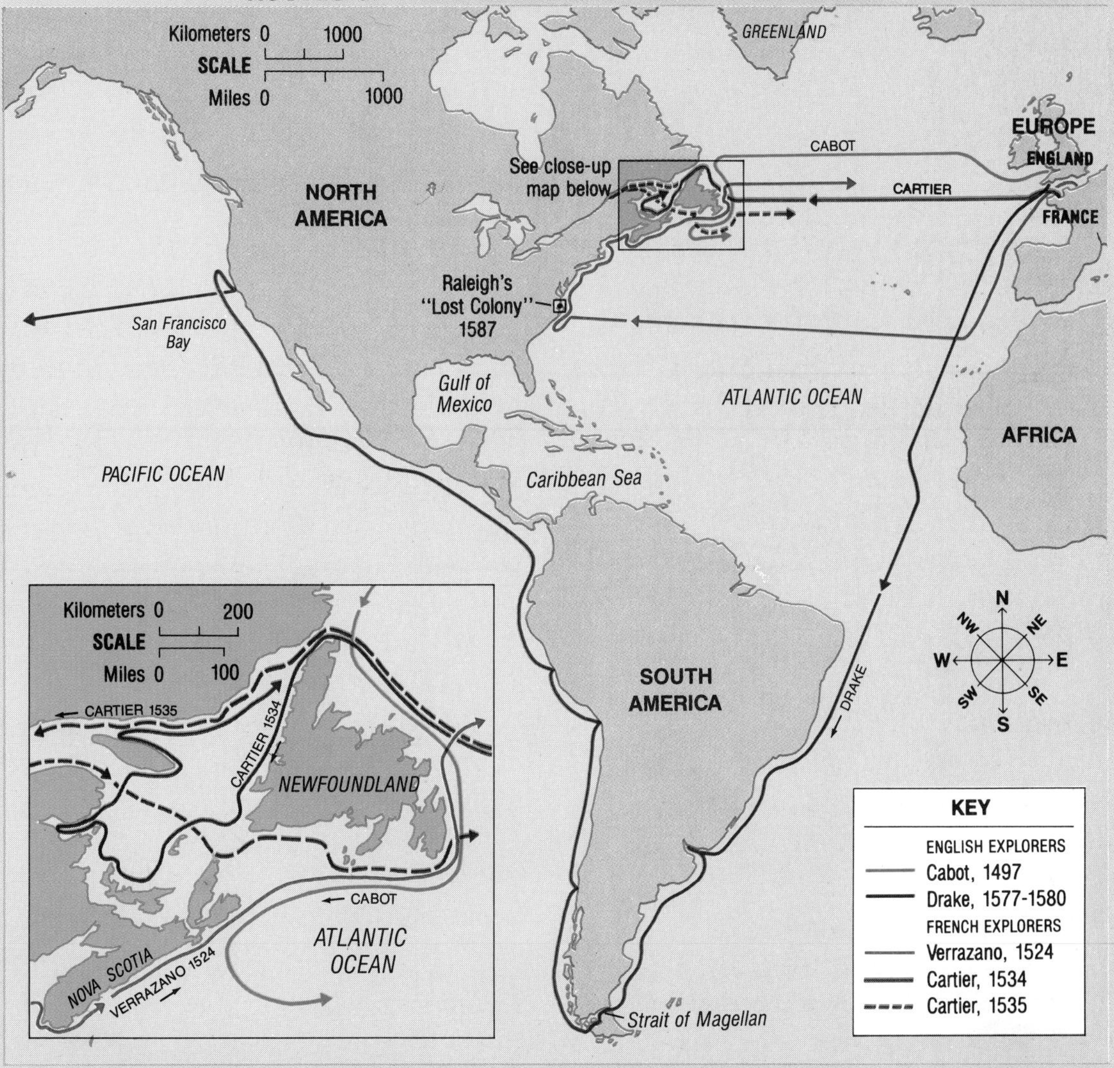

Kilometers 0 1000
SCALE
Miles 0 1000
GREENLAND
EUROPE
ENGLAND
FRANCE
CABOT
CARTIER
See close-up map below
NORTH AMERICA
Raleigh's "Lost Colony" 1587
San Francisco Bay
Gulf of Mexico
ATLANTIC OCEAN
AFRICA
PACIFIC OCEAN
Caribbean Sea
SOUTH AMERICA
DRAKE
N
NE
E
SE
S
SW
W
NW
Strait of Magellan
Kilometers 0 200
SCALE
Miles 0 100
CARTIER 1535
CARTIER 1534
NEWFOUNDLAND
CABOT
ATLANTIC OCEAN
NOVA SCOTIA
VERRAZANO 1524
KEY
ENGLISH EXPLORERS
Cabot, 1497
Drake, 1577-1580
FRENCH EXPLORERS
Verrazano, 1524
Cartier, 1534
Cartier, 1535

The Vikings were the first Europeans known to visit Newfoundland. John Cabot landed there in 1497. Jacques Cartier sailed past the island in 1534 and 1535.

and 1535, he explored the north Atlantic coast of present-day Canada. He found the mighty St. Lawrence River. The following year, he returned and sailed up the St. Lawrence. He got as far as the Indian village of Hochelaga. He called the hill there *Mont Réal* (royal mountain). Today Montreal stands there.

REVIEW

VOCABULARY MASTERY

1. A ___ is a person who explores by ship.
   colonist navigator geographer
2. A ___ is a group of people who settle in a distant land.
   colony mission tribe

READING FOR MAIN IDEAS

3. What two kinds of goods did the French obtain in North America?
4. Which explorer landed on the coast of California?
5. What were Cabot and Cartier looking for?

THINKING SKILLS

Would you like to have been along on one of the early voyages of discovery? What were some of the problems these explorers faced?

Lesson 4: The Search for the Northwest Passage

FIND THE WORDS

northwest passage **expedition**

In 1520, Magellan had found a southern route to the Indies. This was an important discovery. But it took a long time to reach Asia by sailing around South America. Many explorers believed that they could discover a better route through North America. In the 1600s, finding a northwest passage was the main goal of many explorers. This **northwest passage** would be a northern water route from the Atlantic to the Pacific. Explorers expected to find such a route through northern North America.

Jacques Cartier was the first to try. This French navigator had explored the north Atlantic coast of America in 1534–1535. He

This is a picture of Jacques Cartier's landing in Canada. Cartier sailed into the Gulf of St. Lawrence in the summer of 1534. The next year, Cartier sailed up the St. Lawrence River and claimed the land for France.

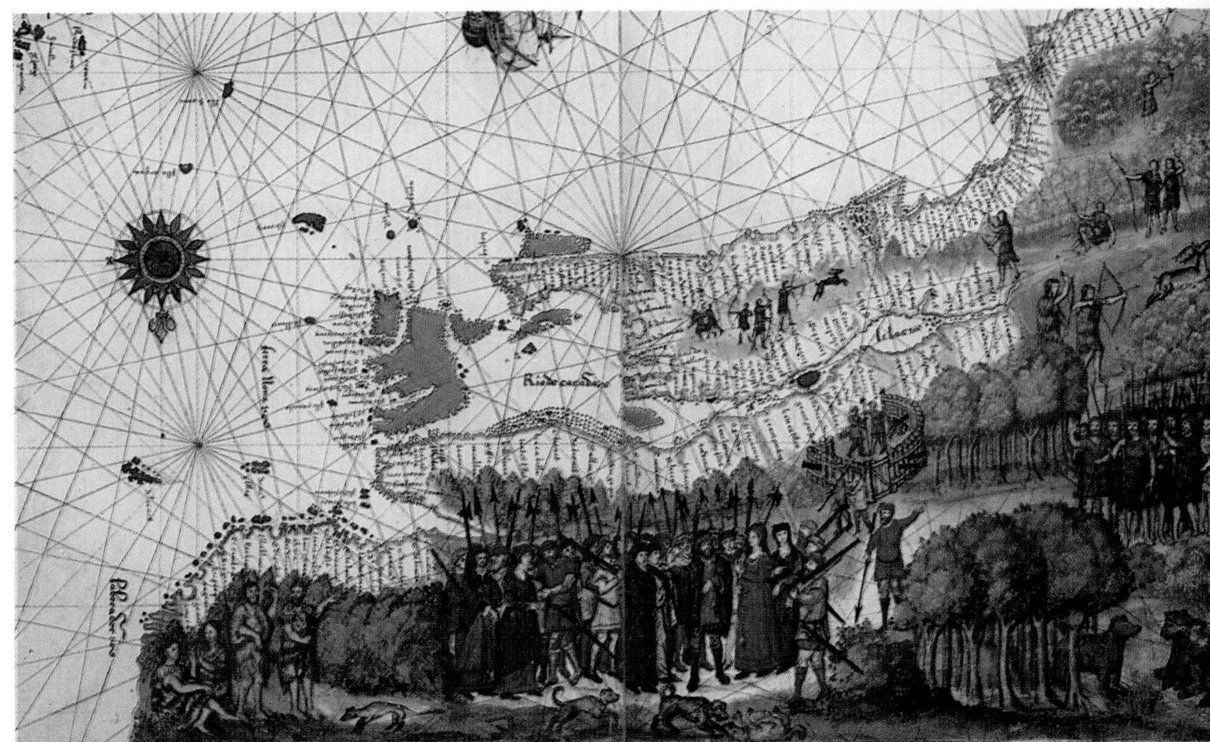

THE SEARCH FOR THE NORTHWEST PASSAGE

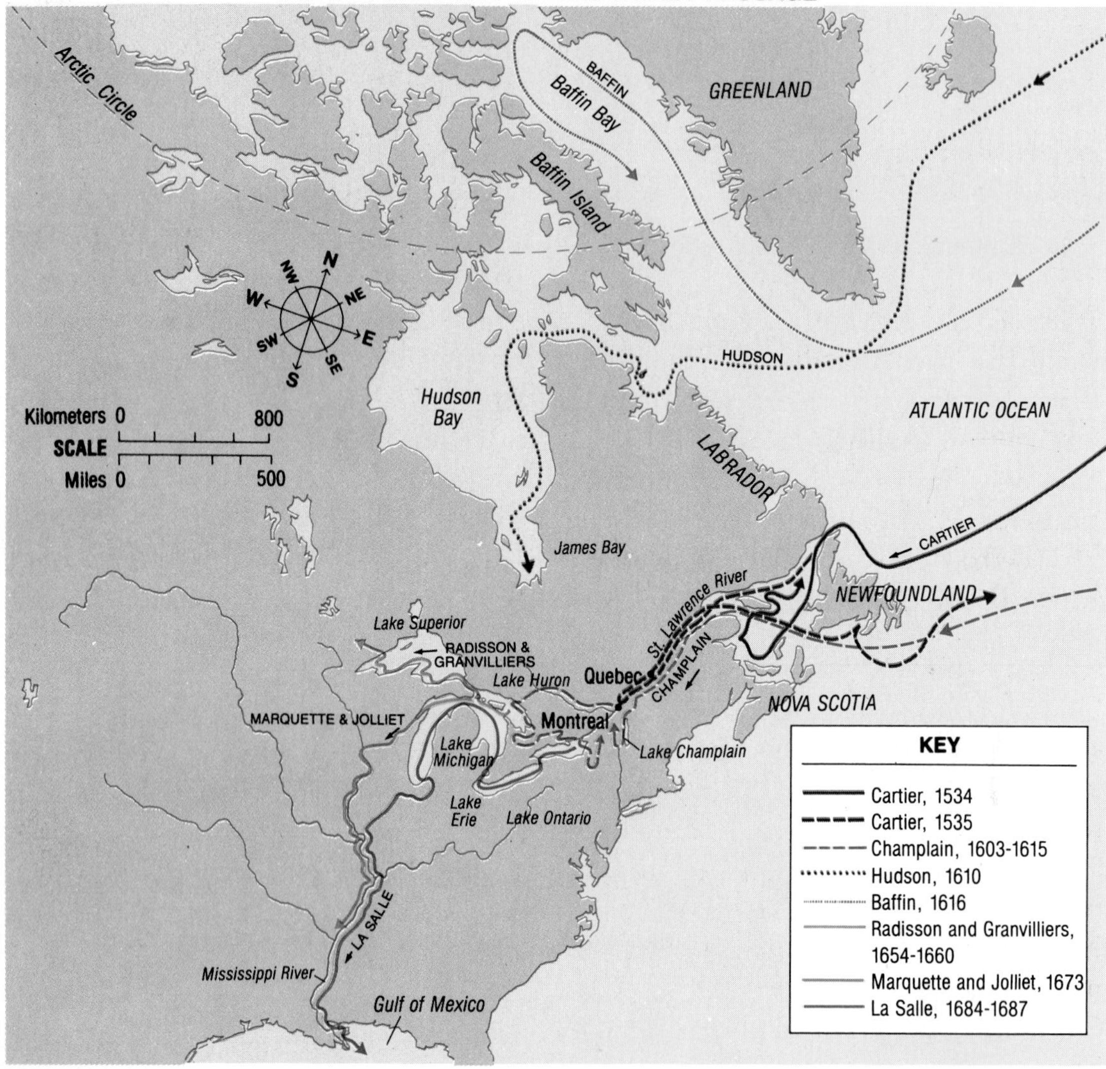

traveled up the St. Lawrence River as far as he could go. Then he ran into dangerous rapids. That was the end of Cartier's northwest passage. But Cartier did claim the land along the St. Lawrence River for France. He called it New France. Other Frenchmen were soon to follow him.

Champlain

In the 1600s, the French were ready to try their luck in the New World. They sent Samuel de Champlain (sham PLAYN) to look around for suitable places for settlement. Champlain explored the coast of what is now New England and Nova Scotia. He founded settlements on Nova Scotia and along the St. Lawrence River. The small trading post he set up on the St. Lawrence in 1608 was called Quebec (kay BEK). Today, it is a major city.

Champlain also had the idea that there must be a shortcut to Asia. He had been to Panama, crossed the isthmus, and seen the great ocean on the other side. Champlain's dream was to follow the St. Lawrence River all the way to the Pacific. He never had the chance to make this great expedition (EK spuh DISH un). An **expedition** is a journey made by a group with a definite goal. Champlain did make many smaller expeditions from Quebec. Traveling by canoe and on foot, he discovered the lake now named for him. Lake Champlain is between the present-day states of New York and Vermont. Champlain also discovered three of the Great Lakes—Lake Ontario, Lake Erie, and Lake Huron.

As the French traveled, they set up small trading posts along their way. They traded for furs with the American Indians. These native peoples trapped the animals in the great forests that covered much of the continent.

Hudson

Henry Hudson, an English captain, made four voyages to North America. He, too, was looking for a northwest passage. In 1609, Hudson made an important expedition for the Dutch. Sailing along the coast, he found the river that is now called the Hudson. He went up this river as far as present-day Albany, New York. Hudson's explorations gave the Dutch their claim to this region. They began founding settlements.

On a later voyage, Hudson went up into northern Canada. He was still looking for the northwest passage. He discovered a large body of water. Hudson thought it might be the Pacific Ocean. Now, it is called Hudson Bay. Hudson's ship was frozen there over the winter. When the ice finally melted, the crew took action. They revolted against Hudson, setting him adrift in a small boat. Hudson was never heard from again.

William Baffin, an English navigator, made two expeditions in search of the northwest passage. The first, in 1615, was to Hudson Bay. The second explored a large bay west of Greenland. We now call it Baffin Bay. Baffin returned to England discouraged. He declared that there was no northwest passage. In fact, Baffin had found the beginning of the passage but did not know it.

Marquette and Jolliet

Jacques Marquette (mar KET) was a French priest. He came to the New World to teach the American Indians about Christianity. In Michigan, he heard about a great river that flowed to the sea. He thought it might be the passage to the Pacific Ocean. In 1673, he set out to find the river with Louis Jolliet (JOH lee ET), a fur trader. Traveling by canoe, they crossed Lake Michigan. Then they continued on the Fox and Wisconsin rivers to the great river. It was the Mississippi. Marquette and Jolliet paddled down the Mississippi. Soon they realized that the river ran south, not west toward the Pacific.

La Salle and Duluth

Marquette and Jolliet turned back. But nine years later, Robert de La Salle finished the journey for them. He followed the Mississippi all the way to the Gulf of Mexico. La Salle was a French engineer. He had been sent by the king to build a line of forts across New France. La Salle claimed the Mississippi River valley for France. He named it Louisiana in honor of the French king, Louis XIV.

Another Frenchman who explored the area around the Mississippi was Daniel Duluth. He traveled around the upper part of the river in 1678–1679. Duluth claimed this region for France. Today it is the state of Minnesota.

Henry Hudson's ship was called the *Half Moon*.

La Vérendrye

The last in the line of French explorers was Pierre La Vérendrye (lah vay rahn DREE). La Vérendrye made several expeditions from Lake Superior between 1731 and 1734. He discovered the Dakotas, the western plains of Minnesota, and part of Montana. He opened up French trading routes to the west.

For more than 200 years, French, English, and Dutch explorers looked for a northwest passage. More than a few lost their lives in the search. None of them found the way to the Pacific. But they made many important discoveries. By 1750, the outlines of this continent were known.

The French explorer Robert La Salle led an expedition down the Mississippi to the Gulf of Mexico. He claimed the Mississippi River valley for France.

And what of the northwest passage? Did it really exist? Finally, in 1905, the passage was found by a Norwegian explorer. Roald Amundsen (AH mund sun) made his way by boat from the Atlantic to the Pacific. It was a difficult journey and a great accomplishment. But finding a northern route to the Indies was no longer important. What was important was to succeed where so many had failed. But it was a little easier for Amundsen. He had a map and the experience of earlier explorers to learn from.

REVIEW

VOCABULARY MASTERY

1. A journey made for a particular reason is a(n) ____.
   expedition compass colony

READING FOR MAIN IDEAS

2. What was the main goal of many explorers in the 1600s?
3. Why did the French send Champlain to the New World?
4. What was the result of La Salle's exploration of the Mississippi?
5. For what countries did explorers claim territory in North America in the 1600s?

THINKING SKILLS

Why do you think the hope of finding a northwest passage to the Pacific attracted so many explorers to the wilds of America?

CHAPTER REVIEW

VOCABULARY MASTERY

Use the words below to complete the chapter summary. Use each only once.

circumnavigated	missions
colonies	northwest passage
expeditions	trade route

Europeans traveled west with the hopes of finding a better 1 to the East Indies. Instead, they found North America. Their priests built 2 there. European nations soon set up 3 in the New World. Many 4 were organized in order to find a(n) 5 to the Pacific. Later, several explorers even 6 Earth.

READING FOR MAIN IDEAS

1. How did the growth of European states during the 1400s affect exploration?
2. How did America get its name?
3. What is the name of the narrow strip of land linking North and South America? What explorer crossed it first, and what did he see after crossing it?
4. What explorer found a passage to the Indies? What body of water is named for him, and where is it?
5. What was the first permanent European settlement in the United States? Who settled it? When?
6. Besides Spain, what three European nations explored North America?
7. Why did European nations want to settle the New World?
8. Why didn't the "Lost Colony" discourage English settlement in the New World?
9. What was the importance of a northwest passage?
10. Name the explorers who looked for a northwest passage. Who found it?

SKILLS APPLICATION

MAP SKILLS

11. Study the map on page 77. On which voyage did Columbus go farthest to the west?

Look at the map on page 93.

12. Which explorer crossed the Atlantic on the most northerly course?
13. Which explorer sailed all the way to North America's west coast?
14. Who explored Canada's Atlantic coast?

SEQUENCING SKILLS

For each group of explorers below, you need to put the events in proper **sequence,** or order. On a separate sheet of paper, write the three headings. Under each heading, write the events in the order they took place.

15. Europeans Reach New World
    - **a.** Columbus lands at San Salvador.
    - **b.** Ericson names Vinland.
16. Spanish and Portuguese Explorers
    - **a.** Magellan finds passage to India.
    - **b.** Pizarro conquers Incas.
    - **c.** Vespucci explores North American coast.
    - **d.** Coronado explores Texas and Kansas.
    - **e.** Ponce de León discovers Florida.
    - **f.** Cortés conquers Aztecs.
17. English and French Explorers.
    - **a.** Cartier finds St. Lawrence River.
    - **b.** Hudson discovers what is now Hudson Bay.
    - **c.** Cabot reaches Newfoundland.
    - **d.** LaSalle claims Mississippi River valley for France.
    - **e.** Drake sails around world.
    - **f.** Champlain sets up trading post at Quebec.

CHAPTER 3

THE ENGLISH IN NORTH AMERICA

Lesson 1: The Founding of the Southern Colonies

FIND THE WORDS

indentured servant
representative **burgess**
proprietor **debtor**

In the 1600s and 1700s, many English people settled in North America. The trip across the ocean was hard and dangerous. Life in the colonies was hard and dangerous, too. Why were so many people willing to face these dangers? For one thing, England was overcrowded. Many people were poor. In the New World, land could be had for almost nothing. People who worked hard could make a good living.

Many people came to the colonies from English prisons. Some of these prisoners had been criminals. Others had been put in prison because they could not pay back money they owed. The English authorities were glad to be rid of them. They were accepted in the colonies because the new settlements needed workers.

Many homeless children were also sent to work in North America. In England, large numbers of poor children were living on London streets. Hundreds of these children were put on ships bound for the colonies. The children had nothing to say about this. But most people did not think it was wrong. They thought the children should be glad to do useful work in the New World.

Some people left England for religious reasons. At the time, most European nations did not allow citizens freedom of worship.

Many of the people who wanted to come to the colonies could not afford to pay for the trip. One way to solve this problem was to come as an indentured servant. An **indentured** (in DEN churd) **servant** signed a contract, or indenture, with a company or a wealthy person. The servant agreed to work without pay for 7 years. In return, the employer paid for the voyage and provided food and shelter. After 7 years, the servant was free.

Virginia

In 1607, the Virginia Company founded the colony of Jamestown in Virginia. Jamestown was to be the first successful English colony in North America. But it did not begin very well.

The first colonists were a group of 120 men. They chose a spot along the James River. It was swampy and full of mosquitoes (muh SKEE tohz) that carried diseases. The water was salty and dirty. Also, winter was coming. The colonists desperately needed shelter and food. But most of the men only wanted to search for gold. They did not want to clear fields, plant crops, or build homes. There was nobody to give orders about work. A few colonists did build a small fort and some shelters.

Among these colonists was Captain John Smith. He made friends with the local Powhatan (POW uh TAN) people through Pocahontas (POH kuh HON tus), the daughter of a chief. The Powhatan people gave the colonists food that winter. Otherwise, all the colonists might have died. Even so, when spring came, only 40 of them were alive.

The following year, Captain Smith became the leader of the colony. More settlers arrived, including the colony's first women. Captain Smith made sure that everyone did his or her fair share of the work. He told the colonists, "He who will not work, will not eat." Soon, the colonists put up more buildings and planted good crops. But Captain Smith had to go back to England. While he was gone, the settlers began to quarrel again. People stopped working. And so, during the winter of 1609–1610, the colonists had little food. Over 400 colonists died in that "starving time."

Soon after, Sir Thomas Gates arrived to serve as governor of the colony. Over the next few years, he made the colonists live under

This is a drawing of Jamestown in 1607. Notice the ships on the left, called the *Discovery*, the *Susan Constant*, and the *Godspeed*. These ships brought English colonists. Jamestown was near 37° north latitude, 76° west longitude.

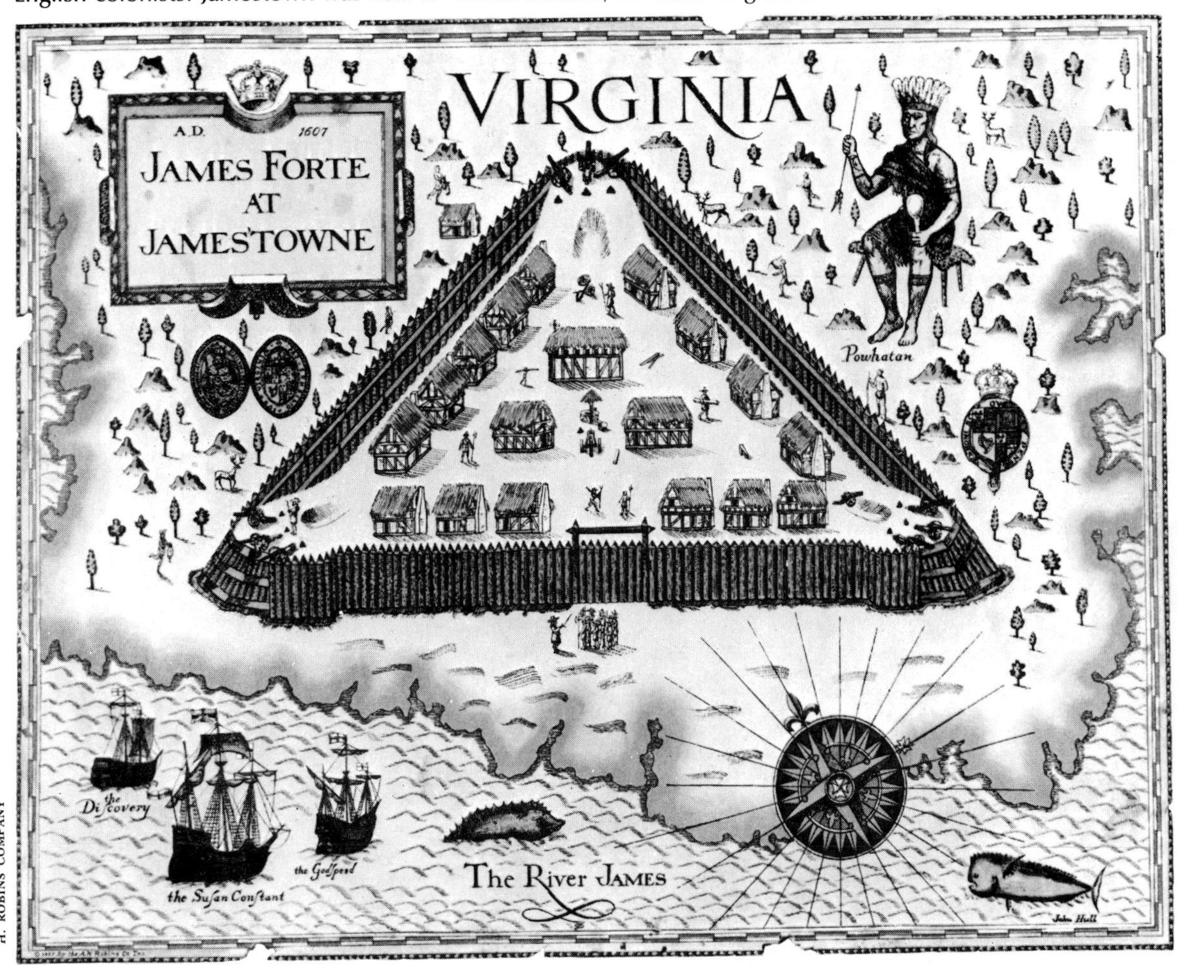

strict military rules. They were marched to the field and marched to church. People who broke the rules were punished. In this way, the colony survived, and life in Jamestown improved.

In 1616, the Virginia Company decided to divide some of its land among the colonists. Each family was given land to farm. As landowners, the colonists worked very hard.

At last, the colonists found a way to make money. A colonist named John Rolfe planted a new kind of tobacco. Virginia tobacco became popular in London. Soon, England was buying all the tobacco Jamestown could produce. It was so valuable, it was even

NORTH AMERICAN SETTLEMENTS 1630

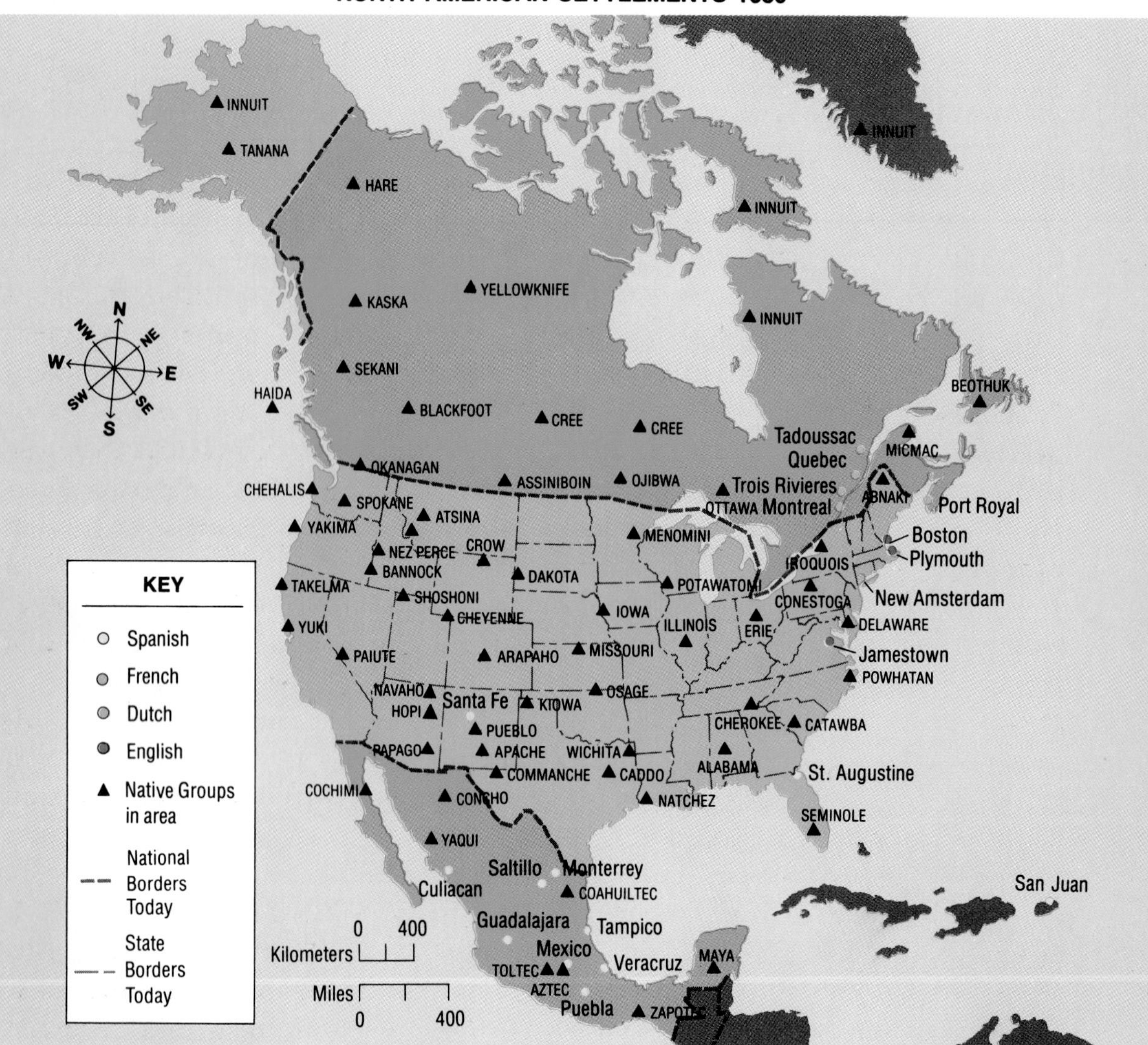

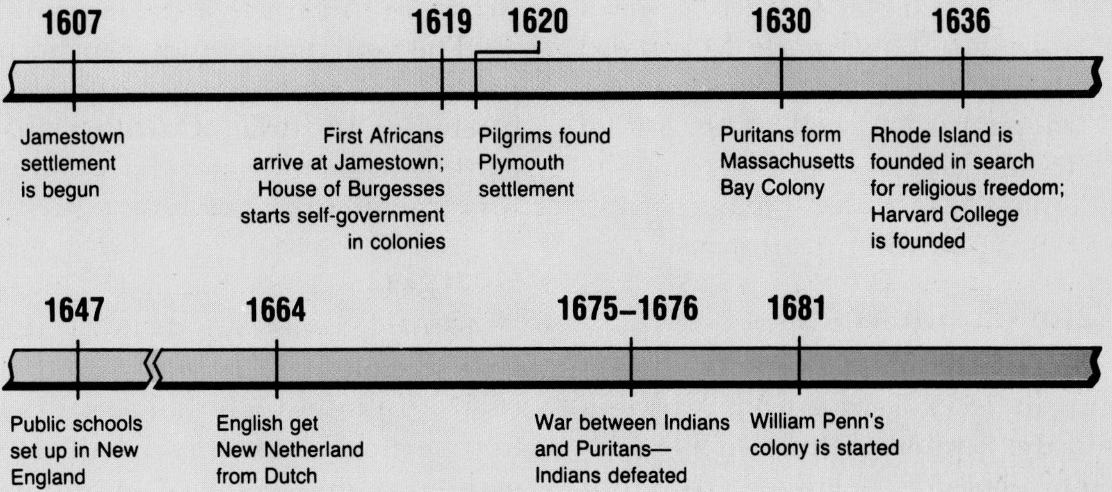

planted in the streets of the colony! This new source of wealth brought more settlers.

Among these settlers were women. Most were already married to male colonists. In 1614 John Rolfe got married, too. He married the American Indian princess Pocahontas. Then, in 1619, ships began to bring unmarried women from England to Jamestown. Most were poor women looking for a better life. As more women came, families grew and the colony became more stable.

Another thing that changed life in Jamestown was government. Before, only the governor of the colony and his council of advisers made the laws. Then, in 1619, the Virginia Company gave the White male landowners a voice in running the colony. These colonists elected representatives from among themselves. A **representative** (REP ri ZEN tuh tiv) is a person who is chosen to speak or act for a group. In the colony of Virginia, the elected representatives were called **burgesses** (BUR jis ez). The Virginia burgesses formed a group that helped make laws for the colony. This group was called the House of Burgesses. This was the start of self-government in America.

In the meantime, other colonies were founded in the South. Maryland was the first of these.

Maryland

Maryland was founded in 1634, when 200 Roman Catholic settlers landed at Chesapeake Bay. The Calvert family had received this colony from the English rulers. The Calverts were Roman Catholics. They made Maryland a safe place for Catholics and for Protestants as well. The soil of the new colony was rich, and the climate was mild. Tobacco soon became an important crop.

The Carolinas

The colony of Carolina was set up in 1665. It ran from Virginia to the border of Spanish Florida. The colony belonged to eight English lords, the Carolina Proprietors (pruh PRY uh turs). A **proprietor** is an owner.

People from Virginia settled in the northern part of the colony. These settlers raised corn and tobacco.

Charleston was founded in 1670 in southern Carolina. With its fine natural harbor, the town prospered in trade and shipping.

The northern and southern parts of Carolina had different interests. In time, Carolina became two colonies—North Carolina and South Carolina.

Georgia

Georgia was the last of the British colonies. It was founded in 1732. James Oglethorpe set the first settlement at Savannah. He wanted to give debtors an opportunity to make a new life. **Debtors** are people who owe money. At that time, they were sent to prison. Oglethorpe had high hopes for the colony. But the proprietors in England made rules that did not work well. In 1752, Oglethorpe asked the king to take over the colony.

REVIEW

VOCABULARY MASTERY

1. Define a *representative*.
2. How does a representative differ from a ruler?

READING FOR MAIN IDEAS

3. In what year was Jamestown founded?
4. What early leader said the colonists had to work if they wanted to eat?
5. What crop brought wealth to Jamestown?
6. With what group did self-government begin in Virginia?
7. What was the second permanent colony in the South?
8. Which colony was founded to give debtors a new life?

THINKING SKILLS

Why do you think most of the first Virginia colonists only wanted to search for gold?

Lesson 2: Life on the Southern Plantations

FIND THE WORDS

cash crop **indigo** **planter** **plantation** **slave**

In the Southern colonies, the main way of making a living was raising crops to sell. The South had large areas of rich soil. It had a mild climate. There were many months between the last frost of spring and the first frost of fall. These conditions made it possible to produce large crops to sell to other countries, especially to England. A crop grown to be sold is called a **cash crop.** Tobacco was the main cash crop in the South. Two others were rice and **indigo** (IN duh goh), a blue dye taken from various plants. Much later, cotton became a cash crop.

The people who owned the farms on which cash crops were

This old drawing shows what a plantation was like. High on the hill is the owner's house. Below are the slave cabins, barns, warehouses, a water mill, and a dock for ships.

raised were called **planters.** Most planters were small farmers. They had little money and only a few workers to help them. A few planters were wealthy and owned large amounts of land. They were able to raise huge crops on their large farms. These large farms were called **plantations** (plan TAY shuns). To run their plantations, wealthy planters needed many, many workers.

In the beginning, most plantation workers were indentured servants. These included both Whites and Blacks. The first Africans arrived in Jamestown in 1619. Like all indentured servants, they worked until their contracts were over. Then they became free. Some became landowners, themselves. But as time passed, planters stopped using indentured workers. It was cheaper to use the Africans who were then being brought to the colonies as slaves. A **slave** is a person who is owned by another person. To all the other people who arrived in the New World, the colonies meant freedom and opportunity. To the Blacks, they meant just the opposite.

These Black people were captured in parts of western Africa. There, they were put in chains and sold to slave traders. The slave traders brought them to America in ships. The conditions on these slave ships were horrible, and many of the Africans died. When the survivors arrived in

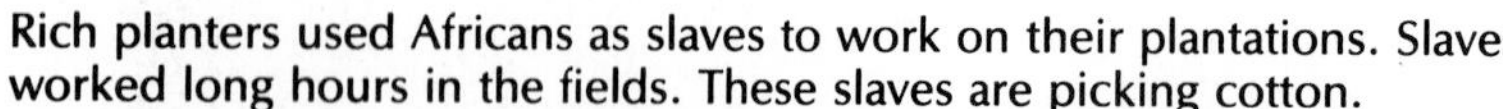
Rich planters used Africans as slaves to work on their plantations. Slaves worked long hours in the fields. These slaves are picking cotton.

WHERE WE ARE IN TIME AND PLACE

FROM THE LOST COLONY TO THE CONSTITUTION

- **1587** Raleigh founds Lost Colony in North Carolina
- **1607** Jamestown, first successful English settlement, is founded in Virginia
- **1620** Pilgrims from England land at Plymouth, Massachusetts
- **1624** Dutch settle New Netherland (later New York)
- **1630** Puritans from England found Massachusetts Bay Colony
- **1634** Catholic colony of Maryland is founded

- **1670** South Carolina is settled by English
- **1681** English king grants Pennsylvania to William Penn
- **1733** British settle colony of Georgia
- **1775–1783** American Revolution is fought
- **1789** The Constitution of the United States goes into effect

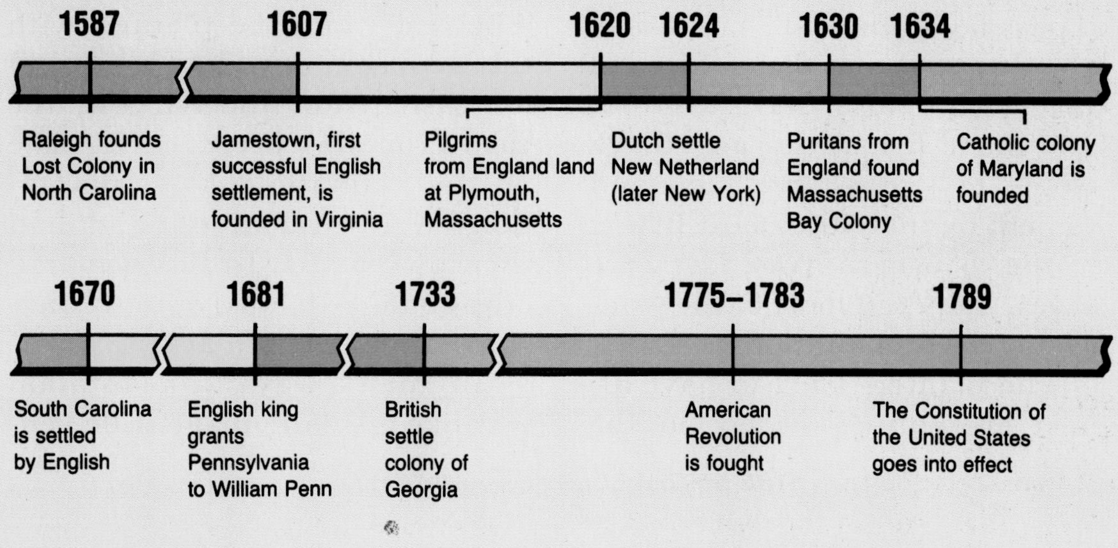

THE THIRTEEN COLONIES ABOUT 1770

COLONY	FIRST EUROPEAN SETTLEMENT
South Carolina	1562
North Carolina	1587
Georgia	late 1500s
Virginia	1607
Massachusetts	1620
New Jersey	c. 1620
New Hampshire	1623
New York	1624
Delaware	1631
Connecticut	1633
Maryland	1634
Rhode Island	1636
Pennsylvania	1643

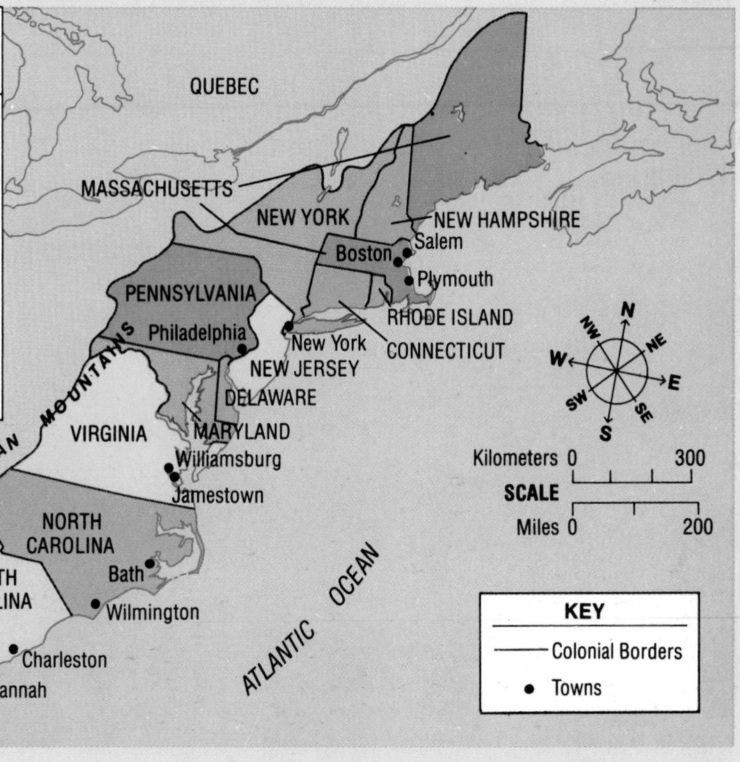

America, they were sold to buyers in slave markets. Usually, the buyer owned a slave for life.

After 1640, the colonies began to pass laws about slavery. Some laws declared that the children of slaves were also slaves. Other laws made it hard for any Black people to live as free men and women. By the 1700s, most Blacks in the Southern colonies were slaves. They did most of the work on the large plantations.

The planters tried to have almost everything needed on the plantation grown or made there. A small part of the land would be used to plant food for the planter's family and the slaves. The rest would be planted with tobacco, rice, or indigo to be sold for cash. After the harvest, the cash crop was prepared for sale on the plantation. Most plantations were near rivers and had their own docks. In this way, the crop could be loaded directly onto ships and sent to market.

In many ways, a plantation was like a small village. Life cen-

THE BRITISH COLONIES ABOUT 1770

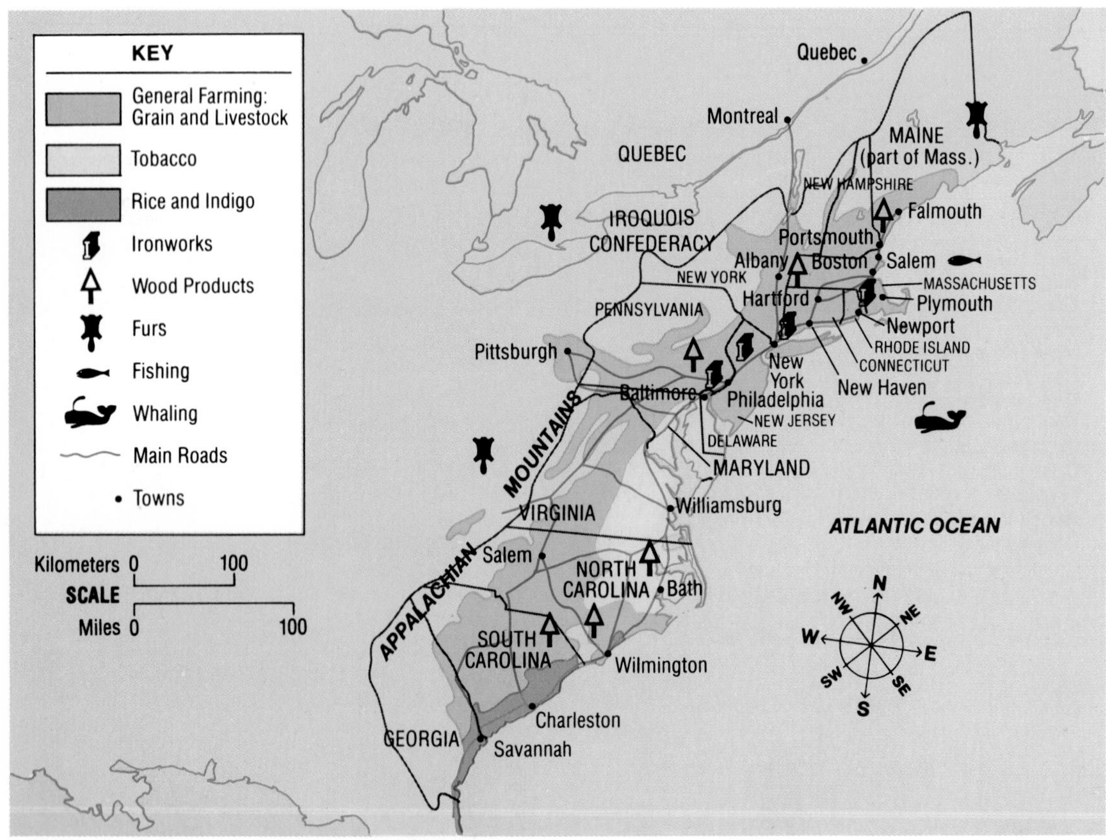

As the British colonies developed, people did many different kinds of work. Refer to this map as you study the British colonies.

tered around the planter's house. Often, this house was very large. But there were many other buildings nearby. There were stables for horses, a kitchen, laundries, and rooms for weaving and spinning. Sometimes, there was a schoolhouse for the planter's children. Sometimes, there was a mill for grinding grain. Farther away, often hidden behind trees, were slaves' cabins, storage buildings, and cattle pens.

George Mason, a Virginia planter, described how the work was handled on his father's large plantation:

"My father had among his slaves carpenters, barrel makers, blacksmiths, leather tanners, shoemakers, spinners, weavers, and knitters. His woods supplied timber for the carpenters and barrel makers, and charcoal for the blacksmiths. His cattle were killed for his own use and for sale. They supplied skins for the tanners and shoemakers. His sheep gave wool for the weavers and spinners. His carpenters built and repaired all houses, barns, and stables on the plantation."

Slaves working in the fields brought in the crops. Slaves working at trades kept the plantation running smoothly. Slaves working in the main house made life easier for their masters.

REVIEW

VOCABULARY MASTERY

Find the word that completes the sentence. Choose words from the list below.

1. A(n) ___ is a person who is owned by another person.
2. A(n) ___ is grown to be sold.
3. The ___ owned the farms on which cash crops were raised.
4. Large farms were called ___.

cash crop indigo planters
plantations slave

READING FOR MAIN IDEAS

5. Name three important crops grown in the Southern colonies.
6. What were most plantations like?
7. At first, what kind of workers were used on the plantation?
8. When did the first Africans arrive in Jamestown?
9. How did the Africans get to America?
10. Name five different jobs that people on plantations did.

THINKING SKILLS

People on plantations produced most of the things they needed. How was a plantation like a city of today? How was it different?

Lesson 3: The Founding of New England

FIND THE WORDS

Pilgrim **separatist** **Puritan** **charter**

In 1620, a tiny ship called the *Mayflower* sailed from England for the New World. Crowded together in the small ship were 102 passengers. Thirty-one were children.

Half of the *Mayflower*'s passengers were Pilgrims. The **Pilgrims** were a group of English Protestants. They believed that religious worship should be plain, simple, and strict. Their beliefs led them to separate from the Church of England. Thus, they were called **separatists** (SEP ur uh tists). In England, they had suffered because of their religious beliefs. So they had set sail for Virginia. There, they planned to start their own churches. They wanted to worship as they pleased.

After the *Mayflower* had sailed for 6 weeks, it ran into storms in the Atlantic. The ship was blown off course. Instead of arriving at Virginia, the Pilgrims landed at Massachusetts. They anchored their ship off the sandy coast of Cape Cod. For 4 weeks, most of the people stayed on the ship. Small groups set out to explore.

It was almost winter. The Pilgrim leaders knew that everyone's help was needed. Otherwise, the group would not survive. Since they were far from Virginia, they decided to stay there and set up their own government.

The Pilgrims wrote a now-famous agreement called the Mayflower Compact. They agreed that all the male Pilgrims would make the rules and laws for the settlement. They would pick their own leaders and make "just and equal laws." Women had few rights and were not allowed to sign the agreement. Still, this was one of the first times European colonists had decided to rule themselves.

The Pilgrims now sailed to an area Captain John Smith had explored some years before. Smith had named the place "Plymouth" (PLIM uth) on a map. People believe the Pilgrims landed at Plymouth Rock, a large rock on the coast. At Plymouth, the Pilgrims set up the first permanent English colony in New England.

During the first icy winter in Plymouth, half the *Mayflower*'s passengers died. Many others became sick. The food the settlers had brought with them was almost used up. Winter was no time to plant a crop. Then, in early spring, an American Indian named Samoset (SAM uh SET) visited the Pilgrims. Samoset spoke English. He had learned the language from early explorers of the area. Samoset helped the Pilgrims communicate with the Wampanoag (WAM puh NOH ahg) people who lived 64 kilometers (40 miles) away. The Wampanoag befriended the colonists.

That spring, the Wampanoag people showed the Pilgrims how to hunt wild turkey and deer. They showed the newcomers where to fish. They taught them how to plant corn and how to get sap from maple trees. The Pilgrims had a fine harvest of corn in the fall. And they were very thankful. They made a feast and invited the Wampanoag people who had helped them. This was the first Thanksgiving. Today, we celebrate this feast every year.

The next settlers to arrive in New England were another group of English Protestants called Puritans. Like the Pilgrims, they believed that the church should be plain and simple. However, the **Puritans** did not want to separate from the Church of England; they wanted to "purify" it. The Church of England was very powerful and gave the Puritans a great deal of trouble. Some Puritans were thrown into prison. As a result, some of them decided to leave England.

The Puritans received a charter from the English king to start the Massachusetts Bay Company.

The Pilgrims celebrated the first Thanksgiving with the Wampanoag people.

The early settlers of Massachusetts faced many dangers and hardships. When the Pilgrims went to church, they carried their guns. They feared attacks by American Indians.

This **charter** was a paper that gave the Company the right to run the colony. It also listed the rules by which the Company would govern. The Puritans voted to take their charter with them to the New World. The charter and the government of the Company would be in Massachusetts. Then, the king could not so easily change the charter or tell the Company what to do. In most other colonies, the charter and at least some of the government remained in England. So, from the beginning, the Puritans had more freedom to govern themselves than most early colonists had. Between 1630 and 1634, more than 10,000 Puritans came to Massachusetts. They settled eight small towns. The largest group founded the town of Boston.

Religion in New England

John Winthrop, a Puritan leader, became the first governor of the Massachusetts Bay Colony. Winthrop sailed from England in 1630. Aboard the ship, he gave a sermon about his hopes for the new colony:

"We have joined together to find a place to live under a proper form of civil and church government. In cases like this, the group is more important than any individual. Our purpose is to improve our lives in order to serve the Lord.

"We have entered into a contract with God. Now if God should hear us and bring us in peace to the place we desire, then He has accepted our contract. And He will expect us to follow it strictly. If we sink into sinful ways, the Lord will surely break out in anger against us."

The Puritans wanted to set up a kind of holy city in the New World. In this model society, everyone would live according to the teachings of the church.

The government of the Massachusetts Bay Colony was founded on these principles. The rules of the government and the church were closely tied together. Only adult males who belonged to the church could vote. Only male Puritans could be elected to serve in the government. No person could speak against the church. Yet everyone had to pay taxes to support the church.

This made life difficult for some of the people who settled in the Massachusetts Bay Colony. People of other religious beliefs were sometimes called "devil's agents." Even the Puritans had problems. They could not speak out against a Sunday sermon, for example. Merchants were sometimes brought to court because, according to the church, they were charging unjust prices. Many people who believed or simply lived differently were forced to leave the colony. The Puritans had little tolerance for people who did not think as they did.

Roger Williams, a minister, was one such person. Williams said that the government should have no power over religious matters. Some people in the Massachusetts Bay Colony agreed with him. Governor Winthrop was

THE AMERICAN COLONIES

Colony	Year Founded	First Settlement	Reason Settled
Virginia	1607	Jamestown	agriculture, trade
Massachusetts	1620	Plymouth	religious freedom, trade
New York	1626	New Amsterdam	trade
New Hampshire	1630	Portsmouth	agriculture, trade
Maryland	1633	St. Mary's	religious freedom, agriculture
Connecticut	1636	Hartford	religious freedom, agriculture
Rhode Island	1636	Providence	religious freedom
Delaware	1638	Wilmington	agriculture, trade
North Carolina	1653	Albemarle	agriculture
New Jersey	1660s	different areas	agriculture, trade
South Carolina	1670	Charleston	agriculture, trade
Pennsylvania	1682	Philadelphia	religious freedom, agriculture
Georgia	1732	Savannah	agriculture, protection from Spanish Florida

This painting shows Puritans worshiping. For the sake of their beliefs, they risked their lives in a land far from their original home.

afraid Williams's ideas might divide the colony. So he forced Williams to leave.

In 1635, Williams and his followers moved south to the area around Narragansett (NAR uh GAN sit) Bay. They bought some land from the Narragansett Indians and started the colony of Rhode Island. In Rhode Island, colonists did not have to be church members in order to vote. Colonists did not have to support any one church. Rhode Island became the first colony to have complete freedom of religious belief.

At first, most of the settlers in New England had clustered around Boston. The people of Rhode Island were not the only ones, however, to settle other areas. Later, people began to move inland. Some settlers moved west to the fertile Connecticut River valley. Another group of Puritans from London started a colony at New Haven on Long Island Sound. In 1662, the English king granted a charter that brought these two groups together to form Connecticut. Colonists also moved north from Massachusetts to found New Hampshire. By 1679, there were four growing New England colonies—Massachusetts, Rhode Island, Connecticut, and New Hampshire.

Each of these colonies had been founded for a different reason. Yet, as they grew, they had many things in common. Most of the colonists came from England or Scotland. They built towns and cities at the good harbors up and down the coast. Many people became engaged in jobs that had to do with trade and the sea.

Inland, the farmers settled in small communities. It was very dangerous to live on a small farm far from neighbors. So people lived near one another for protection. Often, the farm families had the same religion. Some of them had belonged to the same church elsewhere.

You can still see these small communities in New England today. They often have a village green and a meeting house. Long ago they also had forts.

People to Remember

Anne Hutchinson

Anne Hutchinson was also one of the founders of Rhode Island. She, too, was forced to leave Massachusetts for her religious beliefs. Hutchinson had arrived in Massachusetts with her husband and children in 1634. While she lived in Boston, she organized meetings for women. There, she discussed ministers' sermons.

Anne Hutchinson believed that each person should be free to think for herself or himself in religious matters. This was considered a dangerous idea in Massachusetts. Anne Hutchinson was put on trial in 1638. She was found guilty of questioning the authority of the ministers. So she and her family were forced to leave the colony.

Roger Williams invited her to live in Rhode Island. She and her followers settled on an island in Narragansett Bay. There, they were able to speak their minds and worship as they pleased.

The Pilgrims landed near Plymouth Rock in 1620. Today, you can visit a copy of their ship, the *Mayflower,* there. You can also visit a reconstruction of Plymouth Colony, called Plymouth Plantation. The people who work in this "living museum" dress like the Pilgrims. Plymouth, Massachusetts, is at about 42° north latitude, 70° 45′ west longitude.

REVIEW

VOCABULARY MASTERY

1. The ___ set up the first permanent English settlement in New England.
   Pilgrims   Puritans   Wampanoag
2. The English king gave the Massachusetts Bay Company a ___.
   compact   charter   government
3. People who leave one church to start a different one are called ___.
   Pilgrims   Puritans   separatists

READING FOR MAIN IDEAS

4. In what year did the Pilgrims come to America? Where did they land?
5. What important agreement did the male Pilgrims make?
6. Name three things the Wampanoag people taught the Pilgrims.
7. What was the main religious difference between the Pilgrims and the Puritans?
8. Who was the first governor of the Massachusetts Bay Colony?
9. Name two people who rebelled against Puritan rules.
10. Name the first colony to practice religious freedom.
11. List the four New England colonies in 1679.

THINKING SKILLS

12. What might have happened if the Wampanoag people had not helped the Pilgrims?
13. How were the Pilgrims like the early settlers of Jamestown? How were they different?
14. The Puritans had been treated badly in England because of their religious beliefs. When they were in power in New England, how did they treat those who disagreed with them?

Lesson 4: Education and Trade in Colonial New England

FIND THE WORDS

dame school timber lumber fishing ground export trade merchant import

The church was the center of life in New England. On Saturday afternoon, everyone began to get ready for Sunday. All work stopped. Even cooking was not allowed until sundown on Sunday. People spent much time in prayer. On Sunday, everyone went to hear long sermons in church.

On other days, the church was often used as the town hall. Villagers would meet there to pass laws, make decisions, or solve community problems.

The Puritans thought everyone should be able to read the Bible. Because of this, education was very important in New England. As early as 1647, public schools had been set up. Every community with more than 50 people had to hire a schoolteacher. In class, the children learned the Puritan religion along with their lessons. Here is part of the alphabet from the *New England Primer*. This was often the children's first schoolbook.

In *Adam's* Fall
We Sinned all.
Thy Life to mend
This *Book* attend.
The *Cat* doth play
And after slay.

A *Dog* will bite
The Thief at night.
An *Eagle's* flight
Is out of sight.
The Idle *Fool*
Is whipped at
school.

Sometimes, a woman ran a school in her home. A school like this was called a **dame school.** *Dame* means "lady." The dame was the schoolmistress. Children would come to learn the alphabet, spelling, reading, and arithmetic. As the children studied, the teacher usually went about her household chores. Often, she was also teaching older girls to weave or spin.

The Puritans believed in hard work. And they had to work hard to live in New England. The soil was thin and rocky. The time between frosts, when crops could grow, was often short. These conditions made farming difficult.

In the spring and summer, farmers worked the rocky soil to raise wheat and corn. Sometimes, there was a little extra to sell, but not often. The farmers also bred cattle and pigs. During the long winters, they trapped animals for fur and sometimes for food.

Because farming was so difficult, many New Englanders looked

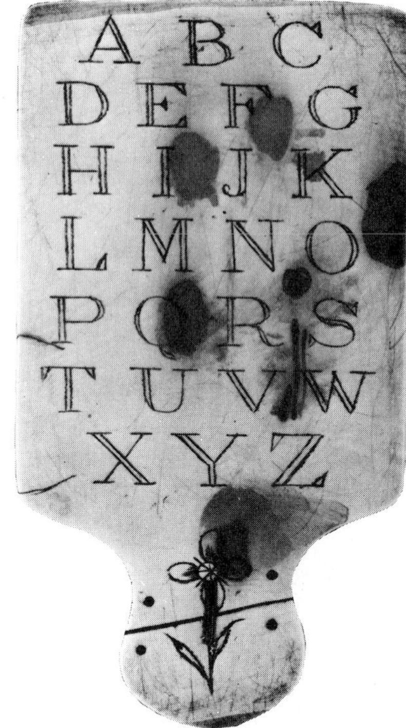

Left: Some Puritan women ran schools in their homes. *Right:* This is the kind of book a child used to learn to read.

for other ways to make a living. Many turned to the sea. Thick forests supplied plenty of wood for building ships. Wood that can be used to build things is called **timber.** Timber sawed into boards or planks is called **lumber.** At first, most ships built in New England were used for fishing. The waters of the Atlantic Coast were some of the richest fishing grounds in the world. A **fishing ground** is a part of an ocean, river, or lake where many fish are found. Many New Englanders made their living by catching fish

Boston was a busy center of trade in 1764. This watercolor shows the harbor crowded with ships. Some of these ships carried fish and grain to the West Indies. Some brought manufactured goods from England. Others brought sugar and molasses from the West Indies.

New England merchants bought fish and shipped it to the West Indies. These men are packing salted herring into barrels for shipment.

or spearing whales. The fish were then dried and salted to keep them from spoiling. Before long, New England merchants were exporting dried, salted fish. To **export** (ek SPORT) goods is to sell them to other countries. An *export* (EKS port) is a product that one country sells to another.

Sometimes, New Englanders would even sell their ships. With so much timber in the forests, they could easily build more. It was not long before shipbuilding became an important activity.

Some people built the ships out of timber. Others made ropes and sails for the ships. Still others made wooden barrels in which to pack fish, grain, and other goods. All these people were practicing different trades. A **trade** is a way of making a living by doing skilled work with the hands.

The word *trade* also stands for the business of buying and selling goods. In time, most of the ships built in New England were used by merchants for trade. A **merchant** (MUR chunt) is a person who buys goods in order to sell them for a profit. The New England merchants bought timber, cattle, and grain from farmers.

Merchants also bought fish from the fishers. Then they shipped fish and grain to the West Indies. There, they traded these foods for sugar. Then they sent the sugar to England, along with fur and timber. In England, they traded for manufactured goods. There, they filled their ships with woolen cloth, furniture, and glass. Then, they set sail for New England. Back home, the merchants sold the goods that they had imported from England. To **import** (im PORT) goods is to buy them from other countries. An *import* (IM port) is a product that one country buys from another.

Sometimes, New England merchants traded for molasses (muh LAS iz) in the West Indies. Molasses is a thick syrup that is left over after sugar is purified. New Englanders made the molasses into rum, an alcoholic drink. The rum was then used to trade for slaves in Africa. The slaves were sold in the West Indies and the Southern colonies.

By the 1700s, New England was a region with many different kinds of jobs. There was work for merchants, sailors, fishers, small farmers, and people who practiced trades and professions. New England was also a region of thriving towns and cities. By 1750, Boston's population had increased to 15,000. The New England colonies were growing fast.

REVIEW

VOCABULARY MASTERY

Match the word with the meaning.

1. export	**A.** the business of buying and selling
2. import	**B.** shipping goods overseas for sale
3. merchant	**C.** wood used for building
4. trade	**D.** a person who buys and sells goods
5. timber	**E.** buying goods from another country

READING FOR MAIN IDEAS

6. What was the center of life in New England?

7. Why was education important in New England?

8. What subjects did New England children study in school?

9. What kinds of things did the people of New England do to earn a living?

10. What kinds of things did New Englanders export? What kinds of things did they import from England?

11. What is molasses?

THINKING SKILLS

Southern planters raised only a few crops. At the same time, New Englanders were farming, fishing, and trading. Which situation is more favorable? Why?

Lesson 5: The Founding of the Middle Colonies

FIND THE WORDS

port **patroonship**
assembly **trial by jury**
Quaker **breadbasket**

New York, Pennsylvania, New Jersey, and Delaware were called the Middle Colonies. These four colonies were set in the middle, between the Southern colonies and the New England colonies. The Middle Colonies were all founded later. They had fewer people than the other colonies had.

New York and New Jersey first belonged to the Dutch. The Dutch claimed the territory when Henry Hudson explored it for them in 1609. They named their colony New Netherland. In 1624, they set up their first permanent settlement at Fort Orange (later called Albany).

Then, in 1626, the Dutch bought Manhattan Island from the Manhattan Indians for goods worth $24.00. On the southern tip of this island, they founded a fur-trading post. They called it New Amsterdam. New Amsterdam was a good port. A **port** is a place where ships take on and unload people and goods. From New Amsterdam, Dutch ships sailed in all directions, trading goods. New Amsterdam was the capital of New Netherland for 38 years.

The Dutch traded for furs with American Indian peoples in the north. Then they shipped the furs down the Hudson River to New Amsterdam. Dutch ships also sailed along the Atlantic coast. They picked up food and rum from New England. They took aboard tobacco from the Southern colonies. Then, ships filled with these goods sailed from New Amsterdam to Europe and the West Indies. From Europe, Dutch ships brought tea, cloth, and other goods.

To help bring settlers to New Netherland, the Dutch set up a system of patroonships (puh TROON SHIPS). A patroon was someone who brought 50 settlers to New Netherland. Such a person was then given a large piece of land called a **patroonship.** The patroon got a share of everything the farmers raised on the patroonship. Patroons made all the laws. And a patroon acted as the judge in almost all matters.

Dutch trading ships sailed out of New Amsterdam. They carried furs, tobacco, rum, and food to Europe and the West Indies. The ships brought tea, cloth, and other goods back from Europe. New Amsterdam was located at 40°40′ north latitude, 74° west longitude. What city is there today?

In 1664, the English captured New Netherland. The colony's Dutch governor, Peter Stuyvesant (STY vuh sunt), had ruled harshly for 17 years. He swore that he would die before giving up to the English. In fact, he gave up quietly without firing a shot. The Dutch settlers were glad to be rid of Stuyvesant. New Netherland now belonged to the Duke of York, a brother of the English king. New Netherland and New Amsterdam got a new name. What do you think it was?

At first, few English people came to New York. The people of the colony had little voice in the government. Many English people did not want to go to a colony that did not have self-government. Without more settlers, the Duke of York made little profit. Also, the people already in the colony were asking for an assembly (uh SEM blee). The kind of **assembly** they wanted was a group of representatives. At last, the duke allowed an assembly to meet. The assembly immediately passed a Charter of Liberties. It gave the colonists the same rights as all English citizens. These included the right to **trial by jury.** This right applied to a person who was being tried in a court. Such a person could only be found guilty or not guilty by others who were his or her equals.

The Duke of York gave what is now New Jersey to two friends

William Penn wanted a colony where all people could live together in peace.

Fascinating Facts

The oldest school in the United States today is the Collegiate School. It is located in New York City. It was founded in 1633 by the Dutch in New Amsterdam. Until 1775, classes were taught in Dutch. Pilgrims in Massachusetts may have taught students in classes before 1633.

Harvard College, the oldest college in the United States, was founded in 1636. It is in Cambridge, Massachusetts. Now Harvard College is part of Harvard University. It is one of America's most famous universities. Several United States Presidents attended Harvard.

named Carteret and Berkeley. The rules they made for their colony included religious freedom.

In 1681, the king of England gave William Penn a large piece of land in America. It lay between New Jersey and Maryland.

William Penn was a member of the Society of Friends. The Friends were called **Quakers** by others. They were a small group of Protestants whose beliefs caused them trouble wherever they lived. Friends believed that all people were equal and good. They lived simply. They refused to fight in wars against other human beings. William Penn wanted a colony

Farms in the Middle Colonies produced wheat, corn, and oats.

where people of all nations and religions could live in peace.

With high hopes, Penn and other Friends sailed for America. Penn's new colony was as large as England. There were many rivers and lots of rich soil. The land was covered with trees. Penn called his colony Pennsylvania, which means "Penn's woods." Pennsylvania then included the land that later became Delaware.

William Penn sent pamphlets to Europe describing his new colony. He told about its religious freedom. He described its very fine farmland. Thousands of English Friends came to Pennsylvania. Many thousands of German farmers also arrived. There were Swedish, Finnish, French, and Dutch settlers as well. Later, people came from Scotland and from Ireland.

The small colony of Delaware changed hands many times in its history. The first owners were Dutch patroons. Then, in 1635, the Dutch West Indies Company bought the land. A group of Swedes, led by Peter Minuit (MIN you it), established a settlement there. It was a fortified trading post, Fort Christina, on the site of present-day Wilmington.

In 1664, the English took over New Netherland and the Dutch possessions in Delaware. Next, Delaware was given to William Penn as part of the Pennsylvania colony. But Delaware was allowed to set up a representative assembly. By 1703, Delaware was considered a separate colony.

Farms in Pennsylvania, New York, and New Jersey soon produced large amounts of wheat, corn, and oats. These crops were shipped to New England, the South, and the West Indies. The Middle Colonies became the breadbasket of the New World. A **breadbasket** is an area that produces large amounts of grain.

Several towns of the Middle Colonies became centers of business and trade. Philadelphia and New York were the busiest and most important.

Philadelphia grew quickly under the English Friends. Like New York, it became a center of trade. Farmers sent their crops to Philadelphia. From there, merchants shipped them overseas for sale. More and more people came to Philadelphia from Europe. Soon there were ministers, bakers, bricklayers, and teachers.

Printing presses and bookstores appeared throughout the city. Some of these were owned by women. Cornelia Bradford owned and ran the *Philadelphia Mercury*. This was the third-largest newspaper in the colonies. Trade with Europe kept people in touch with European ideas.

This engraving shows a street in the center of Philadelphia in the 1700s.

People to Remember

Benjamin Franklin

The leading citizen of Philadelphia was Benjamin Franklin. Ben Franklin was born in 1706 to a poor family in Boston. When he was 17, Franklin sailed to Philadelphia. There, he became a printer. Later, he owned his own newspaper. He also published *Poor Richard's Almanac*. This little booklet gave facts about weather, farming, and business.

Ben Franklin was interested in science. In an experiment, he proved that lightning is electricity. He flew a kite on a wire during a storm. Lightning hit the kite and produced a spark on the wire.

Franklin talked to people and wrote about the problems of Philadelphia. In this way, he helped bring street lighting and paving to the city. He organized fire companies. He started the first hospital and lending library. In 1751, he helped found the Academy of Philadelphia. This became the University of Pennsylvania.

Franklin learned a great deal about all the colonies and about Europe. He would play an important role when the colonies broke away from Great Britain.

REVIEW

VOCABULARY MASTERY

1. A(n) ____ is a group of representatives.
   colony patroonship assembly
2. Members of the Society of Friends are called ____.
   Quakers patroons Dutch
3. The Charter of Liberties established the right to ____.
   trial by jury patroonship farm
4. A ____ is an area that produces a large amount of grain.
   colony charter breadbasket

READING FOR MAIN IDEAS

5. What European people first owned New York and New Jersey?
6. What did these Europeans name the present-day city of New York?
7. Who founded Pennsylvania?
8. In what way was Philadelphia like New York?

THINKING SKILLS

Imagine that you lived in colonial times. Would you have preferred living on a farm or in a city? Give reasons.

CHAPTER REVIEW

VOCABULARY MASTERY

Use the words below to complete the chapter summary. Use each only once.

assembly	Pilgrims
Burgesses	plantations
cash crops	Puritans
charter	Quakers
indentured servants	slaves
Merchants	Timber
patroonships	trade

Jamestown was the first successful English colony. There, self-government began in English America with the House of __1__. Soon, Southern planters were growing __2__ like tobacco, rice, and indigo on large farms called __3__. At first, __4__ did the work. Later, __5__ were brought in from Africa.

In New England, the __6__ came to Plymouth and the __7__ to Massachusetts Bay. The Bay Colony brought its __8__ from England. New England had a varied economy. __9__ from the forests was used to make ships for fishing. __10__ also used ships for __11__ in North America, the West Indies, Africa, and England.

New Netherland had large pieces of land called __12__. After the English took over, the Duke of York finally allowed a(n) __13__ to meet. Pennsylvania was settled by __14__.

READING FOR MAIN IDEAS

1. Why did so many English people settle in North America?
2. What were the differences between indentured servants and slaves?
3. To what religious group did many early settlers of Maryland belong?
4. Why was life difficult in the Massachusetts Bay Colony?
5. What made Pennsylvania attractive to European settlers?

SKILLS APPLICATION

MAP SKILLS

Use the map of the British colonies on page 110.

6. In 1770, how did most colonists make a living?
7. What barrier appears to be blocking westward movement?
8. Where were rice and indigo grown?
9. Which colonies had ironworks?
10. Which colonies grew tobacco?

PEOPLE TO KNOW

Match each name with a clue.

11. Anne Hutchinson
12. William Penn
13. Pocahontas
14. Captain John Smith
15. Peter Stuyvesant

A. led the Jamestown colony.
B. was a founder of Rhode Island.
C. was the governor of New Netherland.
D. founded the colony of Pennsylvania.
E. helped colonists make friends with Powhatan people.

RESEARCH AND WRITING SKILLS

Choose one of the people listed above to research. Look in encyclopedias and biographies. Write a one-page report. Be sure to include the title, author, and copyright date of a biography. Include the title and copyright date of an encyclopedia.

You will find the copyright date in the front of a book. If there is more than one date, use the latest one. Look for the symbol ©. For example, © 1985 tells you the book was published in 1985.

UNIT REVIEW

VOCABULARY MASTERY

Choose one of the lists of words below. Then write a paragraph or a page using all the words from that list. You may use the words in the singular or plural. On a separate page, write the words and define them.

ancestors	assembly
circumnavigate	burgess
colony	cash crop
compass	charter
expedition	debtor
isthmus	patroonship
northwest passage	plantation
strait	proprietor
trade route	representative
tribe	trial by jury

READING FOR MAIN IDEAS

1. Who were probably the first people to reach North America and how did they get there?
2. Name three great American Indian cultures of Mexico.
3. How did the first Americans receive the name *Indians*?
4. What changes occurred in Europe during the 1400s that increased interest in exploration?
5. What were several reasons why the Aztec empire fell?
6. Why did Roman Catholic priests come to the New World?
7. What were some of the problems of the earliest settlers of the Jamestown colony?
8. How did most people in the Southern colonies make a living?
9. Why did the Pilgrims leave England and come to the New World?
10. What was the purpose of a charter?
11. How did the Powhatan and Wampanoag Indians help the colonists?
12. Why was education important to the Puritans?
13. Why did the shipbuilding industry develop in New England?
14. What caused the Quakers so much trouble?
15. Why did the Middle Colonies come to be known as the breadbasket of the New World?

THINKING SKILLS

16. Why do farming peoples tend to have more advanced cultures than hunting peoples?
17. Why was the discovery and use of metal so important to many ancient peoples?
18. What role did religion play in the founding of the Southern Colonies, New England, and the Middle Colonies?
19. What do you think were the main differences between life in England and life in the New World?
20. How did the House of Burgesses change the government in Jamestown?

USE YOUR MAPS

21. Look at the map on page 83. What explorer reached Mexico City? What explorer crossed the Mississippi River? Who were the first to cross the Rio Grande?

Look at the map of North American settlements on page 104.

22. What American Indian group lived in what is now New York? What group lived in Florida?
23. What was the English settlement in the South in 1630? What were the two English settlements then in New England?

SKILL DEVELOPMENT

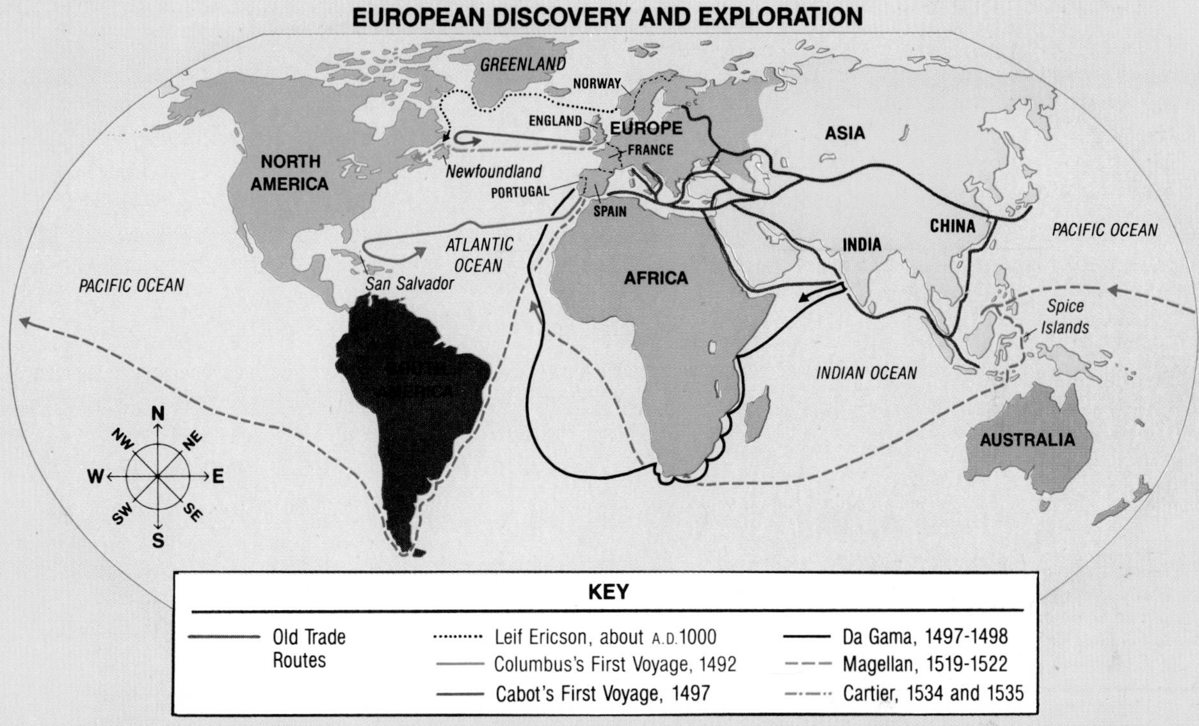

MAP SKILLS

Look at the historical map above.

1. Who was the first European explorer of North America shown on the map?
2. Who sailed around the world?
3. What continents did the old trade routes connect?
4. Who sailed to India? In what direction did he sail from the tip of Africa?
5. What explorer sailed from France to what is now Canada?
6. Who traveled farthest south? Who traveled farthest north?
7. In what direction did Cabot sail across the Atlantic Ocean?
8. Who sailed to San Salvador in 1492?

LIBRARY SKILLS

Nonfiction books have information about real people and real events. They are not fiction. Such books are located in most libraries by numbers shown on the book spines. The numbers are part of the Dewey decimal system. To learn more about explorers, look on the shelves for numbers 910 and 920. If you want detailed information about an explorer, look in the biography section.

9. Find a book about Spanish explorers. Write the book's title, author, and Dewey decimal number. Read about one explorer and write a paragraph about him. Will your paragraph be fiction or nonfiction? Explain.
10. Choose an explorer listed in the map key above. Read a biography about him.

THE UNITED STATES IS BORN

UNIT 3

CHAPTER 7 THE STRUGGLE FOR INDEPENDENCE

Lesson 1: Trouble in British America

FIND THE WORDS

revolution tax Parliament raw material manufactured goods smuggle

In the 1750s, a British traveler wrote these words about the American colonies: "There are so many differences among the Americans! There are big differences in way of life, religion, and wealth. If the Americans are left to themselves, they will be fighting each other from one end of the country to the other."

What the British traveler did not know was that the Americans had even bigger differences with Britain. Twenty-five years later, the American colonies joined together and declared that they

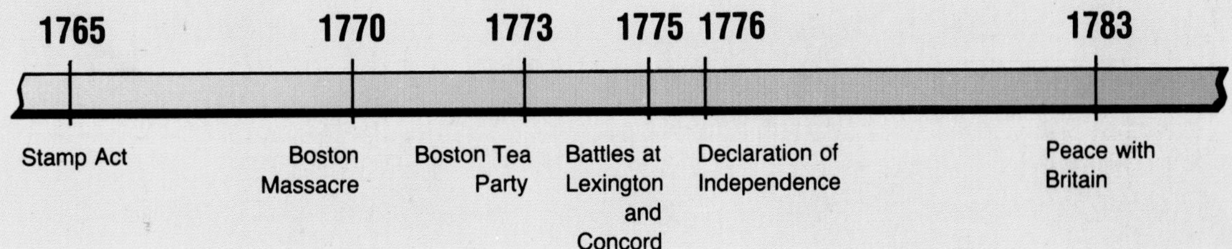

were free of British rule. Few Americans wanted war. Even so, they could not find a peaceful way to solve their problems with the British government.

The American colonists fought and won a war called the American Revolution. A **revolution** is a war in which the people of a country overthrow the government. The Americans then started a new government and a new nation called the United States of America.

Why did the colonists take such serious steps? The colonists' main complaint had to do with the **taxes** they had to pay to Britain. These were amounts of money added to the price of goods coming into or out of the colonies. The colonists had not agreed to pay these taxes. All taxes were set by the British **Parliament,** the lawmaking group. But Parliament had no American representatives in it. The Americans would not accept "taxation without representation." "We have been making our own laws for almost 100 years," said the Americans. "Now Parliament wants to make laws for us."

Britain passed laws taxing sugar, cloth, wine, and other goods. Then, in 1765, Parliament passed the Stamp Act. This law said that the colonists had to buy tax stamps. These stamps had to be pasted on all newspapers, birth certificates, wills, and other important papers. Many Americans became very angry about this tax. They refused to pay it. They warned others not to pay it. Some Americans burned the tax stamps when they arrived from Britain. Others chased the tax collectors out of town. Finally, the colonies joined together and sent a message to Britain. They asked that the stamp tax be stopped.

The British did not agree. Britain had fought a long war with France. Part of this war had been fought in the American colonies. It was called the French and Indian War. It seemed fair to the

The colonists refused to buy these tax stamps. The stamps had to be posted on all newspapers and documents.

Some colonists were so angry about taxes that they covered the tax collectors with tar and feathers to punish them.

British that the American colonies should help pay for it.

The British government did not want to use taxes only to raise money. Some taxes were also meant to encourage the colonies to trade with Britain and not with other countries. Britain, like other European countries, looked on its colonies as sources of wealth. The British wanted the colonies to produce raw materials. A **raw material** is a product that has not been improved by manufacturing. The colonies were to sell raw materials only to Britain. In turn, the colonies were to buy their manufactured goods from Britain. **Manufactured goods** are all the products that are made in factories with machines. This trade would make British manufacturers and merchants, and Britain itself, rich.

However, the colonies did not do exactly what the British government wanted. New England, in particular, did not produce many raw materials. The New Englanders often traded with other countries. Both New England and the Middle Colonies produced some manufactured goods. The South was the closest to what Britain wanted. But many Southerners were unhappy. They felt the British paid low prices for raw materials and charged high prices for manufactured goods. Many Southerners were deeply in debt to the British merchants.

In the end, the Stamp Act could not be enforced. Britain did away with it in 1766. But Parliament wanted to show that it had the right to tax the colonies. So it placed a tax on tea, glass, and other goods. It also said Americans could buy tea only from Britain. Many Americans stopped drinking tea rather than pay the tax on it. Some continued to bring it in from countries other than Britain. They had to **smuggle** it in, or sneak it past the authorities.

The British king was furious. He tried to force the colonies to obey. British soldiers were sent to the colonies to search for smuggled goods. Feelings among the colonists had been divided. There were still many who did not question Britain's right to pass these tax laws. But few Americans liked having British soldiers searching their homes and stores.

Small fights broke out between the soldiers and Americans in the cities. In March of 1770, a crowd in Boston began to poke fun at

This engraving shows the British firing on colonists during the Boston Massacre. The engraving was done by Paul Revere.

Patrick Henry of Virginia was a powerful and influential speaker in favor of a revolution.

some soldiers. Some of the colonists threw stones. The soldiers became angry and fired their guns into the crowd. Five Americans were killed. Among those killed was Crispus Attucks. He was a Black man. It was a terrible event that the colonists called the Boston Massacre. As a result of the Boston Massacre, feelings between the British and Americans became very tense. The colonists would not easily forget that Americans had been killed by the British on American soil.

REVIEW

VOCABULARY MASTERY

1. ___are made in a factory.
Taxes Manufactured goods Raw materials

2. ___have not been improved.
Imports Manufactured goods Raw materials

3. In a ___, the people overthrow the government.
Parliament revolution tax

4. Parliament added___to goods.
smuggling revolution taxes

5. To ___ goods is to sneak them past the authorities.
smuggle manufacture tax

READING FOR MAIN IDEAS

6. What is the war the colonists fought against Britain called?

7. What was the main problem between Britain and the colonies?

8. When was the Stamp Act passed by Parliament?

9. What did Parliament do after it ended the stamp tax?

10. What important event took place in March 1770?

THINKING SKILLS

The British government wanted the American colonies to help pay for their own defense. The colonists wanted to be taxed only by themselves. Which side do you think was right? Why?

Lesson 2: The American Revolution Begins

FIND THE WORDS

quarter **Continental Congress**
boycott **trench** **barricade**
grenadier

Late in 1773, something happened in Boston that had two important results. It hardened the feelings of the British against the Americans. It also united the colonists more than ever before.

In December, British ships entered Boston harbor loaded with tea. The Americans tried to send it back, but this was not allowed. The British tea was cheaper than the Dutch tea the Americans usually smuggled into the colonies. But it had a tax on it. If the Americans bought the British tea, it would mean that they agreed that Britain could tax them. Some of the people of Boston decided to protest against this tax.

On the night of December 16, 1773, they dressed up like American Indians with feathers and war paint. They climbed aboard the ships and broke open all 342 chests of tea. Then they threw the tea into the harbor. As they worked through the night, a crowd watched from the shore. There was no damage to the ships or any other trouble. One man wrote, "It was the stillest night that Boston enjoyed for many months." The British, however, were angered by "the Boston Tea Party."

The Boston Tea Party was a protest against the tax on tea.

Now the British government decided to punish Massachusetts. It closed the port of Boston to all ships. Parliament passed laws that forced the colonists to **quarter** the British troops. This meant the colonists had to let the troops stay in their homes. These things made other colonies worry. If Britain could punish Massachusetts, it could do the same to them.

In September of 1774, representatives from all the colonies met in Philadelphia to talk about the problem. This was the first meeting of the **Continental Congress.** The members decided to support the city of Boston. They agreed to **boycott,** or stop buying, British goods. A boycott—a refusal to use or buy something—is a form of peaceful protest. The Continental Congress also agreed to raise a volunteer army. The volunteers were supposed to protect the colonies if Britain used force to break the boycott.

In April of 1775, British soldiers were ordered to march out of Boston. They were to take guns and supplies the colonists had stored near the towns of Lexington and Concord. On the night of April 18, Paul Revere and William Dawes learned that British soldiers were lined up along the Charles River. They rode all night to warn the towns.

In Lexington, a group of armed Americans waited on the village green. Soon, the British soldiers were facing them, only a few yards away. A shot was fired—

The British were very angry about the Boston Tea Party. Parliament passed laws to punish the people of Massachusetts. It closed the port of Boston to all ships. It forced colonists to quarter British troops in their homes. The Americans objected greatly to this practice. This scene shows a family grieving as troops take over their house. These new laws made many colonists turn against the British.

This painting shows Americans fighting the British at Lexington, April 19, 1775. Captain John Parker led the Americans. He told his troops: "If war is to come, let it begin here." Eight Americans were killed in battle that day.

no one knows by whom. Fighting broke out. Eight Americans were killed. At Concord, farmers shot back at the British soldiers. The British soldiers had a hard time returning to Boston that night. All along the way, farmers fired on them from behind rocks and trees.

At Lexington and Concord, the American Revolution had begun.

War and Independence

The Second Continental Congress met in Philadelphia in May of 1775. Samuel and John Adams of Massachusetts, Benjamin Franklin of Philadelphia, and Thomas Jefferson of Virginia were among the representatives. The colonists had not yet decided to break away from Britain. But they realized they needed a regular army to defend themselves against the British soldiers. They also needed a leader to raise and train such an army. George Washington of Virginia had served as a colonel in the French and Indian War. The members of Congress respected his military experience. They chose him to be commander in chief of the new Continental Army.

Before Washington could take command of the army, he heard the news of the first major battle. In June 1775, British ships had arrived in Boston harbor with more troops. A battle began when

Fascinating Facts

The first submarine attack was made during the American Revolution. The submarine was named the *Turtle.* It was a tiny ship that was operated by only one person. That person not only had to guide the ship but also had to move it through the water. To move the ship, the person had to turn the propeller by hand. In 1776, the *Turtle* attacked a British warship in New York Harbor. Needless to say, the attack failed.

3,000 American volunteers came to the defense of Boston.

The Americans took up positions near a place called Bunker Hill. From there, they could watch the ships in the harbor. The night before the battle, the Americans dug **trenches,** or defensive ditches. They also set up **barricades,** defensive barriers. And they hid behind bushes and trees to stop the British from going around behind the barricades.

The next day, three British generals led 2,000 soldiers against the Americans. The British soldiers marched shoulder to shoulder. Their best fighters, called **grenadiers** (GREN uh DIRZ), were in the lead. The British thought that by attacking in such large numbers, they would make the Americans afraid. They hoped that the Americans would give up. The fighting began and went on all day. The Americans did not give up. When they ran out of bullets, they loaded their guns with scraps of metal, glass, and rocks. Many soldiers on both sides were killed or wounded.

Still, the British had better guns and more bullets. At day's end, they won the Battle of Bunker Hill. But the Americans won the glory. This battle made it clear to everyone that the Americans would not be easy to beat.

The Battle of Bunker Hill proved that Americans could stand up to the British. The Americans did not win the battle. But they fought bravely and with determination. After the battle, no one doubted that the Americans were prepared to fight for their rights.

People to Remember

George Washington

Once the fighting had started, Americans had no greater leader than George Washington of Virginia. Congress chose him to lead the army because he had more military experience than most Americans.

Everywhere, people admired Washington's courage and steadiness. These qualities were worth a great deal to a people at war. Washington's job was difficult. He had to make an army out of groups of shopkeepers and farmers. This had to be done in a short time and with very little money. As a general, Washington did make mistakes. The Americans lost more battles than they won. But Washington saw that there was more to his job than winning. He had to keep on fighting, no matter how badly the war was going. Even after the worst defeats, with his army hungry and in rags, he would not surrender. This set an example for other Americans. It gave them courage to keep on fighting.

Throughout 1775 and 1776, George Washington and his army had many problems. There were not enough supplies. Tired and hungry Americans were fighting fresh and well-equipped British troops. The Continental Army lost several battles. George Washington was desperate. He wrote to Congress: "Ten more days will put an end to the existence of our army." By the middle of December 1776, the war seemed lost.

Then, on Christmas night, 1776, Washington led a surprise attack. He and his soldiers crossed the freezing Delaware River while the enemy were celebrating the holiday. The plan worked. The Americans defeated the enemy soldiers at Trenton and at Princeton in New Jersey. At last, Americans had cause to hope.

After 6 years of struggle, the Americans won the war. Then, in 1788, the Constitution was adopted. The nation needed a leader. Again, the Americans turned to Washington. Who else was so admired? Against all odds, Washington had led the colonies to victory. He would be able to bring the colonies together as a nation. He was elected the first President of the United States.

When Washington died, Henry Lee of Virginia offered the following words about George Washington: ". . . first in war, first in peace, and first in the hearts of his countrymen."

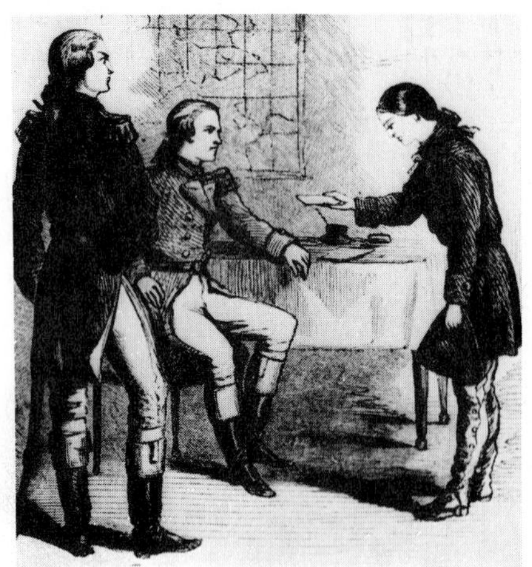

Left: Deborah Sampson joined the army disguised as a man. *Right:* Mary Ludwig Hays, called Molly Pitcher, fought at the Battle of Monmouth.

One of the Americans who fought at Bunker Hill was a Black man named Salem Poor. Poor was later praised for his bravery by several of his officers. About 5,000 Black Americans served in the American army during the Revolutionary War.

Women also fought in the Revolution. Deborah Sampson joined

Ethan Allen led a group of men from Vermont called the Green Mountain Boys. In May 1775, this group captured Fort Ticonderoga in northern New York.

the army disguised as Robert Shurtleff. She was 20 years old. She fought in several battles and was wounded in a battle near Tarrytown, New York. Her identity was discovered when she was put in a hospital in Philadelphia. Margaret Corbin fought beside her husband in a battle at Harlem Heights in New York in 1776. When her husband was killed, Margaret Corbin began firing his cannon. She fought with great bravery and was wounded three times. Mary Ludwig Hays, known as "Molly Pitcher," was a hero of the Battle of Monmouth in New Jersey. On the hot summer day of the battle, she carried the soldiers pitchers of water. Betsy Ross has gone down in history as the maker of the first American flag with stars and stripes. She created the flag, the story goes, at the request of George Washington.

This is the Liberty Bell. It was rung in Philadelphia to celebrate Independence Day, July 4, 1776. Today, it is kept in a special monument across from Independence Hall.

REVIEW

VOCABULARY MASTERY

1. Parliament forced the colonists to ___ British troops.
   quarter smuggle boycott
2. The colonists agreed to ___ British goods.
   quarter import boycott
3. The ___ were British soldiers.
   barricades continentals grenadiers
4. A ___ is a defensive ditch.
   barricade trench grenadier
5. A ___ is a defensive barrier.
   barricade trench declaration

READING FOR MAIN IDEAS

6. What were two important results of the Boston Tea Party?
7. What two things did the Continental Congress decide to do to support Boston?
8. Name the two Massachusetts towns in which the American Revolution began.
9. What two important decisions were made by the Second Continental Congress?
10. What problems did the Continental Army face during 1775 and 1776?

WRITING SKILLS

Do you think that destroying the tea in Boston was the right thing to do? Why, or why not? Give reasons.

THINKING SKILLS

The Americans lost most of the major battles of the Revolution, yet they won the war. What are the reasons for this?

The Declaration of Independence

By the middle of 1776, it seemed clear that Britain would never give the colonies the rights they wanted. Members of the Second Continental Congress decided that the colonies should declare their **independence.** That meant they would be a separate nation, free from British rule. This would be done in a document called a **declaration.** This document would give the reasons why the colonies wanted to be independent. On July 4, 1776, the final wording of the Declaration of Independence was approved by the representatives of the colonies.

The document was written by Thomas Jefferson, a young lawyer from Virginia. He had been chosen for the job because he was a good writer. Jefferson began this way:

"When in the Course of human events, it becomes necessary for one people to dissolve the political bands which have connected them with another . . ."

This first section, known as the **Preamble,** explains why the Declaration was written. It says that sometimes one group of people feels it must break away from another. The Declaration was written to tell the world that the American colonists had good reason to break away from England. Jefferson wanted to prove that this was not really a rebellion. **Rebellion** meant turning against a rightful government. But England was not the rightful ruler of the colonies. So the colonies did not owe the king their loyalty. Jefferson set out in the Declaration of Independence to explain why this was so.

The second section of the Declaration of Independence deals with the ideas that a government should be based on:

"We hold these truths to be self-evident, that all men are created equal, that they are endowed by their Creator with certain unalienable Rights, that among these are Life, Liberty and the pursuit of Happiness."

In other words, all people are equal by nature. They should all, therefore, have certain rights. These include the right to life, the right to freedom, and the right to look for happiness. The Declaration states that a government's job is to protect these rights. If a government fails in this job, the people should change or replace it.

Jefferson then declared that the king of England had failed to protect the colonists' rights. He went even further. He charged that the king had tried to establish an absolute tyranny over the colonies. That is, the king had used his power to rule in a cruel and unfair way. The king did not care about the well-being of the colonists.

In the third section of the Declaration, Jefferson listed all the wrongs the Americans had suffered. Yet, said Jefferson, in spite of their great unhappiness, the colonists had not acted hastily. They had tried again and again to change the situation. Many times, they had sent their complaints to the king. But the king had not paid any attention to them. So the representatives of the colonies decided that they must declare independence.

The final section of the document is the Declaration of Independence itself:

". . . That these United Colonies are, and of Right ought to be Free and Independent States; that they are Absolved from all Allegiance to the British Crown, and that all political connection between them and the State of Great Britain, is and ought to be totally dissolved . . . .

And for the support of this Declaration, with a firm reliance on the protection of divine Providence, we mutually pledge to each other our Lives, our Fortunes and our sacred Honor."

The Declaration of Independence was written more than 200 years ago. The goal was to explain why the American colonies were breaking away from England. The American leaders hoped that the document would win support among the colonists. Not all Americans were convinced that independence was a good thing. The leaders also hoped that some foreign nations would help the Americans.

The Declaration of Independence was successful in both of these goals. In the years since then, it has not been forgotten. It has been used many times as a model by people seeking freedom. It has always been an inspiration to the people of the United States. The stirring words of the Declaration of Independence live on.

On July 4, 1776, the members of the Second Continental Congress approved the Declaration of Independence. It was not actually signed until a month later.

Lesson 3: Winning Independence

FIND THE WORDS

strategy **Loyalist**
treaty **terms**

In 1777, the Americans had one of their biggest victories. General Burgoyne, a British officer, tried to capture the Hudson Valley of New York. His plan was to cut off New England from the rest of America. Then Britain could win the war easily. Burgoyne marched his army south from Canada. He was to be joined by British troops from New York City, led by General Howe. Burgoyne's army was large and slow. The British had trouble moving their heavy equipment along the winding, hilly roads in the wilderness. The Americans, led by Horatio Gates and others, made the going harder. They chopped down trees to block the roads. They destroyed bridges. The colonists fought like the American Indians. They attacked in small groups. They fired at the British from hiding places in the forest. The British were not used to fighting this way. They were angry and confused. When the British reached Saratoga, they were surrounded by Americans, most of whom they could not see. After

Americans fought part of the Revolution at sea.

THE REVOLUTIONARY WAR

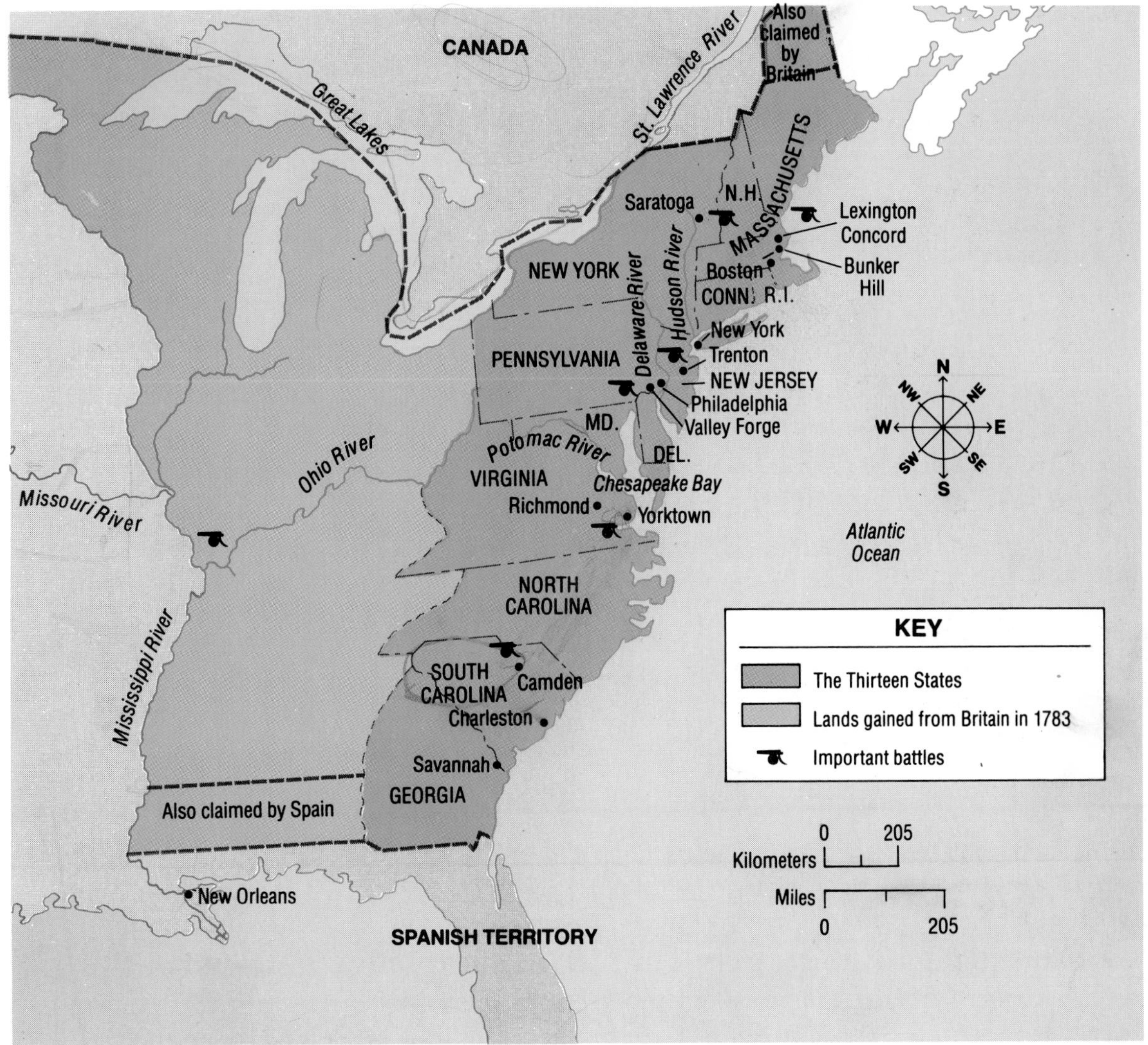

fierce fighting, Burgoyne surrendered in October 1777. Howe's army never arrived to help Burgoyne. On his own, General Howe had decided to capture Philadelphia instead.

The victory at Saratoga was a turning point for the Americans. As a result of this battle, France agreed to join the war against Britain. France had a strong army and navy.

Howe's troops spent the winter of 1777–1778 in Philadelphia. They were warm and well fed. Washington and his soldiers did not have such an easy winter. Only 32 kilometers (20 miles) away, in Valley Forge, they suffered terrible cold and hunger.

Washington and his army suffered from cold and hunger at Valley Forge. Here, Washington reviews his ragged soldiers.

The men did not have enough warm clothes. Many were barefoot. Over 3,000 died that winter from cold and disease. The women who traveled with the army tried to find food for the soldiers. They nursed the sick. They sewed and washed clothes. They buried the dead. During this "winter of despair," many soldiers lost heart and went home. But Washington did not give up. He continued to drill his soldiers. By spring, the worst had passed.

In 1778, the tide turned in favor of the Americans. The French navy captured British ships on their way to North America. This made it hard for the British to get fresh troops and supplies. Captain John Paul Jones won a series of naval victories over the British. In addition, George Rogers Clark led an army to victory against the British in the Ohio Valley.

Now the British shifted their attention to the South. Their **strategy,** or plan of action, was to cut the South off from the other states. The British captured Savannah, Georgia, in December 1778. In May 1780, they took the city of Charleston, South Carolina. The American army there, 5,000 soldiers, surrendered to the

British. It was the worst American defeat of the war. Almost the whole American army in the South was gone.

The Americans tried to regain a foothold in the South. Horatio Gates and Thomas Sumter led armies into the Carolinas. Both were stopped by the British. The outlook was not bright.

The British commander in the South was General Charles Cornwallis. He was planning to invade North Carolina. However, a small army from the Carolinas and Virginia made him think again. This army defeated Loyalist forces at King's Mountain, North Carolina. **Loyalists** were Americans who remained loyal to the British.

In this painting, a British fort surrenders to George Rogers Clark.

General Francis Marion was known as the "Swamp Fox." This was because he knew the swamps of South Carolina so well. In this picture, "Swamp Fox" Marion and his soldiers cross the Pee Dee River of South Carolina.

Cornwallis had expected more help from the Loyalists.

The victory at King's Mountain encouraged the Americans. One of their leaders, General Francis Marion, was known as the "Swamp Fox." His strategy was to hit and run. His forces would appear suddenly, attack, and then run off and hide. Because Marion knew the swamps well, he was able to lead his soldiers through them secretly. Marion's hit-and-run strategy caused much damage to the larger British forces.

Washington sent General Nathanael Greene to take command of the American forces in the South. Greene described his strategy as follows: "We fight, get beat, rise, and fight again." Under Greene's leadership, the tide of the war was turned. The Americans scored some victories and forced Cornwallis to draw back.

In the summer of 1781, Cornwallis moved his army to Yorktown, Virginia. This was a costly mistake. Yorktown was surrounded by water on three sides. The French navy defeated the

At Yorktown, American and French troops fought together to defeat the British. This painting shows General Rochambeau of France at Yorktown.

British fleet that was guarding the coast. The British could neither get supplies nor escape by sea. More than 15,000 American and French troops moved in.

Cornwallis was trapped. His soldiers were exhausted. So on October 19, 1781, Cornwallis surrendered his army to George Washington at Yorktown.

This was the final defeat for Britain. The war in America had lasted 6 years. The British were tired of it. King George III and Parliament decided to bring the soldiers home.

Two years after the surrender at Yorktown, the British and the Americans made a formal peace. They signed a **treaty,** or agreement, in Paris, France, in 1783.

The Treaty of Paris

The new nation had some skillful representatives in Paris. They were John Jay, John Adams, and Benjamin Franklin. These three men worked out the **terms,** or conditions, of the treaty. They did a very good job of protecting American interests.

John Jay insisted that the British recognize the independence of America. That had to be the first step. Otherwise, he would not even begin treaty discussions.

The British, however, hoped for a different relationship with their former colony. This relationship would not involve independence. The Americans were not interested in any other kind of relationship. They held firm.

The Americans also wanted the British out of America. They insisted that the army be withdrawn. In the end, the British gave in. They wanted to remain on good terms with the Americans. They did not want the Americans to join the French against them. The United States also had to give in on a few points. These had to do with protecting the rights of Loyalists. Americans who had supported the British would be treated the same as other Americans.

The Treaty of Paris declared that the United States was a free and independent nation. It established the borders of the new country. The United States stretched west as far as the Mississippi River. It went north to the Great Lakes and south as far as Florida. Under the terms of the treaty, Florida and New Orleans belonged to Spain.

All in all, the United States did very well. The terms the British agreed to were generous. They even allowed the Americans the right to fish off the coast of Canada. The United States had indeed won its independence.

REVIEW

VOCABULARY MASTERY

1. A ___ is a plan for achieving a goal.
treaty boycott strategy

2. A ___ is an agreement between two or more nations.
treaty revolution strategy

3. ___ were Americans who did not want to break away from Britain.
Puritans Loyalists Separatists

READING FOR MAIN IDEAS

4. Why was the American victory at Saratoga so important?

5. What was the winter of 1777–1778 like for General Howe's army? For General Washington's army?

6. What was the worst defeat of the war for the Americans?

7. What was the British strategy in the South? What was Nathanael Greene's strategy?

8. What was the final British defeat?

9. When and where was the peace treaty signed?

10. What were the borders of the United States under the treaty?

WRITING SKILLS

Do you think the Americans could have won the Revolutionary War without French help? Why, or why not? Write a paragraph and give reasons to support your answer.

Lesson 4: How the Americans Won

FIND THE WORDS

ammunition **slogan**

Few people thought the Americans could win the Revolutionary War. In 1776, the British had the world's strongest navy. They had far more money and soldiers than the Americans did. The British had factories that could produce guns, ammunition, and clothing for war. **Ammunition** includes bullets and shells fired from guns. In all ways, the British were better equipped.

The Americans seemed easy to defeat. They had no army or navy. They showed few signs that they could work well together. Many Americans were Loyalists. They wanted to keep their ties with Britain. Some fought against the colonial army. Some Loyalists

This portrait shows George Washington with the Marquis de Lafayette and Tench Tilghman. Lafayette came from France to help the colonies win their independence. He was only 20 years old when he arrived. He joined Washington's army as a major general. Lafayette became one of the heroes of the Revolution. Tench Tilghman informed the Continental Congress about Cornwallis's surrender to General George Washington at Yorktown.

escaped to Canada. Many other Americans did not care who won the war. They sold supplies to both sides.

Yet, 6 years after the fighting began, the United States had won its independence. How had this come about?

The British actually had many disadvantages. The war was not popular in Britain. Many British people agreed with the goals of the colonists. Also, Britain fought several wars in Europe not long before the American Revolution. In addition, Britain had been fighting wars in its colonies all over the world. These wars were expensive. The British people did not want to continue paying for them with high taxes.

The British navy had too few sailors and ships for all the jobs the government wanted done. The army could not get enough men to join. The British had to hire soldiers from other nations to help them fight. This, too, cost money. Britain also had to worry about enemies close at hand. France and Spain might invade Britain.

Britain had another important disadvantage. The American war was fought 4,800 kilometers (3,000 miles) away. Supplies and orders took a long time to arrive in North America. European soldiers were not used to the hot summers and cold winters of the Northern colonies. They did not like marching where there were no roads.

The Americans had some important advantages. The war was fought in their homeland. People will fight very hard to protect their own families, homes, and land. The Americans were used to the climate and land. They had learned from the American Indians how to fight effectively in the wilderness.

The Americans had a fine leader in George Washington. They also had many friends in Europe. Some of these friends came to America to fight. Americans needed the skills of these European leaders. The Marquis de Lafayette (mahr KEE duh LAH fee ET) came from France to lead part of Washington's army. Thaddeus Kosciusko (tha DEE uhs KOS ee US koh) from Poland and the German Baron von Steuben came to help train Washington's soldiers. These foreign friends admired what the Americans were doing.

The turning point in the war came in 1778. It was then that the French agreed to send soldiers and ships to help the Americans. Without French help, the Americans might not have won.

Perhaps the greatest advantage the Americans had was their desire to be free and independent of Britain. People like Thomas

Some Europeans came to help the Americans fight. The Baron von Steuben, *left,* came over from Germany. Thaddeus Kosciusko, *right,* came from Poland.

Jefferson and Thomas Paine had written of this desire in exciting words. Patrick Henry, a great speaker from Virginia, had given the Americans a **slogan,** or inspiring phrase. In the Virginia Convention, he gave a speech that became famous. It ended with these stirring words: "Give me liberty, or give me death!"

REVIEW

VOCABULARY MASTERY

1. A ___ is an inspiring phrase.
   declaration slogan treaty
2. ___ includes bullets and shells.
   Slogan Revolution Ammunition

READING FOR MAIN IDEAS

3. What was the outlook for the Americans in 1776?
4. How did the people in Britain feel about the war?
5. What may have been the Americans' greatest advantage?
6. What happened in 1778 that greatly helped the Americans?
7. Make a list of American advantages in the war.

THINKING SKILLS

Pretend you are a Loyalist during the American Revolution. What arguments will you use to persuade your friends to support Britain?

The Leaders of the Revolution

Top: In this painting, Americans raise a liberty pole. It was a symbol of liberty. *Bottom:* Samuel Adams was one of the leaders of the American Revolution.

The American Revolution did not take place only on the battlefield. Before the war and during it, Americans needed leaders. These leaders and their ideas helped shape what people thought and did about the British. The leaders helped people make up their minds about new ideas such as independence. Some wrote well or made good speeches. Others stood out because of their personal qualities, such as firmness, courage, and fairness.

Samuel Adams of Boston was one of the leaders of the Revolution. Samuel Adams wanted to unite the colonies against the British. He wrote articles and made speeches. He did what he could to make the colonists act. Adams started a **Committee of Correspondence** in Massachusetts. This group wrote letters to other groups in other colonies. These committees shared news about the British and told each other of their own plans. Adams was also the head of a group of Americans called the **Sons of Liberty.** The Sons of Liberty did many things to protest British laws and taxes. One such protest was the Boston Tea Party. They also held parades. They sang songs and danced around the Liberty Tree, a big elm near Boston. Sometimes, they would coat a British official with tar and feathers. Not everyone agreed with Samuel Adams and his followers. Some thought they went too far.

Many women worked against British rule. They formed boycott groups against merchants who supported Britain. They formed anti-tea leagues. These groups tried to get people to use drinks made from other plants in place of tea. Some women organized the **Daughters of Liberty.** The Daughters of Liberty joined the Sons of Liberty in street marches and meetings. They read newspapers out loud to people who could not read. Groups of women would spin yarn and weave cloth. They used the cloth to make uniforms and bandages for soldiers.

Mercy Warren was a writer of poems and plays who used her pen against the British. She made fun of them in her plays. She criticized the British in letters to her friend Abigail Adams. Then she had the letters printed in the newspapers for all to read. Once she wrote: "Be it known unto Britain even American daughters are politicians and patriots. They will aid the good work with their efforts."

Thomas Paine was another patriot who used his pen against the British. In January 1776, he published a small book called *Common Sense.* In it, he listed reasons why the colonies should be independent. He wrote that Britain could no longer rule the colonies. Britain was too far away. North America was too big to be ruled by a little island. Paine said other countries would trade with the colonies as long as "eating is the custom in Europe." On the last page of his book, Paine spoke of the colonies in a new way. He called them "the Free and

Top: Mercy Warren published letters criticizing the British. *Bottom:* Thomas Paine wrote a book urging independence.

Top: John Adams
Bottom: Abigail Adams

Independent States of America." Because *Common Sense* was well written, many people read it. It helped thousands of people decide that the colonies must be independent.

John Adams, a cousin of Samuel Adams, was a good speaker and writer. He worked hard and long for what he believed in. John Adams spoke out early and often against the British. As a young lawyer in Boston, he wrote newspaper stories and petitions against British laws and taxes. After the Stamp Act, he decided that independence was the only way to solve the colonies' problems. Together with Benjamin Franklin, he convinced the Continental Congress that the Declaration of Independence should be written.

On July 3, 1776, after preliminary approval of the Declaration on July 2, Adams wrote to his wife, Abigail:

"Yesterday the greatest question was decided which ever was debated in America. . . . I am well aware of the toil and blood and treasure that it will cost us to maintain this declaration, and support and defend these states. Yet through all the gloom I can see rays of ravishing light and glory."

Abigail Smith Adams was married to John Adams. She had heard that the Continental Congress might declare independence. So Abigail Adams wrote the following letter to her husband:

"I long to hear that you have declared independence. And by the way, in the new code of laws . . . I wish you would remember the ladies, and be more generous . . . to them than your ancestors. Do not put such unlimited power in the hands of husbands. Remember, all men would be tyrants if they could. If particular care and attention is not paid to the ladies, we are determined to stir up a rebellion and will not regard ourselves as bound by any laws in which we had no voice or representation."

The person who wrote the Declaration of Independence was **Thomas Jefferson.** A lawyer and planter from Virginia, Jefferson was also a fine writer. He believed that people could govern themselves and that they had a right to do so. The declaration said "all men are created equal." It said people have certain rights, given by God, which no one can take away. Among these rights, it continued, are "Life, Liberty, and the pursuit of Happiness." The Declaration went on to say that governments draw their powers from the people. When government is no longer fair and just, it said, the people have a right to change it. The Declaration of Independence appeared in many newspapers. It explained to Americans what the fighting was for. It gave them faith that independence was fair and right. They needed that faith during the years of war.

Every age has its leaders. They are people who believe in something. They are the men and women who help people make their beliefs come true.

Thomas Jefferson wrote the Declaration of Independence. *Bottom:* John Jay, John Adams, and Benjamin Franklin worked out the terms of the treaty in which Britain formally recognized American independence.

CHAPTER REVIEW

VOCABULARY MASTERY

Use the words below to complete the chapter summary. Use each only once.

boycott	quarter
Continental Congress	revolution
Loyalists	taxes
Parliament	treaty

The colonists living in British America began a(n) __1__ in the 1770s. The quarrel started because the British __2__ wanted to make the colonists pay __3__. The British also wanted to __4__ troops in the colonists' homes. The colonists met together in the __5__ and organized a(n) __6__ of British goods.

After years of fighting, a(n) __7__ ended the war. The Americans had won even though they lacked many supplies. In addition, many American __8__ had supported Britain.

READING FOR MAIN IDEAS

1. Why did the colonists destroy British tea?
2. Why was the Declaration of Independence written?
3. In the Revolutionary War, how did the battle at Saratoga mark a turning point for the Americans?
4. What were the conditions of the Treaty of Paris?
5. Name several of the disadvantages the British had in the Revolutionary War.

THINKING SKILLS

6. Suppose you were a third party trying to make peace between Britain and the colonies *before* 1776. What would you suggest to help solve the problem?

SKILLS APPLICATION

MAP SKILLS

Look at the map on page 149.

7. What was the western border of the new nation?
8. What divided the United States from Canada along much of the border?
9. In what states were the battles of Camden and Yorktown fought?
10. In what state were the battles of Lexington and Concord fought?

CAUSE-AND-EFFECT SKILLS

A *cause* makes something happen. An *effect* is what happens as a result. Look at the example below. Then use your textbook as directed.

Cause: Parliament put a tax on many British goods sent to the colonies.
Effect: Some colonists staged the Boston Tea Party as a protest.

11. **Cause:** Paul Revere and John Dawes warned colonists that British troops were coming to Lexington and Concord.
    Effect: ______ See page 140.
12. **Cause:** Americans showed their strength by defeating the British at Saratoga.
    Effect: ______ See page 149.
13. **Cause:** The British signed the Treaty of Paris in 1783.
    Effect: ______ See page 154.

RESEARCH AND WRITING SKILLS

Select one of the people discussed in this chapter. Prepare a one-page report on him or her. To do so, use encyclopedias, almanacs, or biographies. List your sources. Include the title, author, and copyright date of a biography. Include the title and copyright date of an encyclopedia.

CHAPTER 2 GOVERNING THE NEW NATION

Lesson 1: The First Government

FIND THE WORDS

government
Articles of Confederation

During the Revolutionary War, the 13 American colonies were all working for the same goal. They had to win the war. When the fighting was over, the differences between the colonies became important again. The colonies were now states in one nation. Some states earned money from farming. Others were centers for shipbuilding and trade. Some states had slaves, while others did not. Some states claimed large areas of land to the west. Others had no western lands. In the years

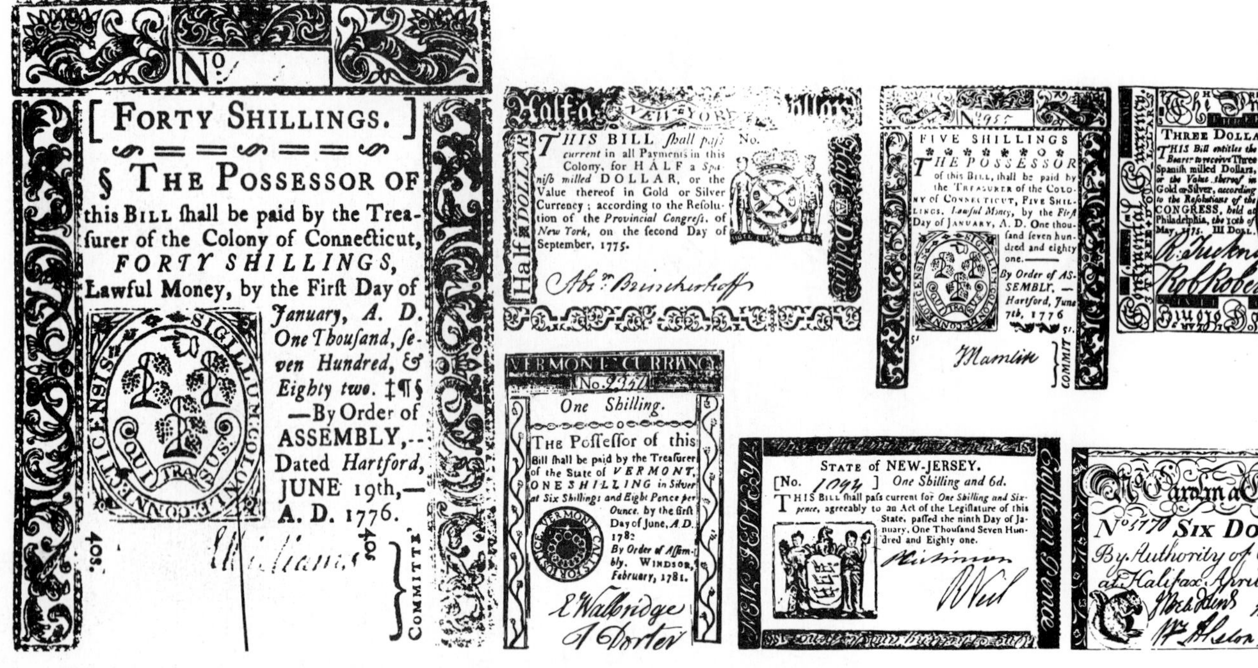

Under the Articles of Confederation, each state could issue its own money.

after the war, each state wanted to take care of its own interests. Each one already had its own government. So some states began passing laws that harmed other states. One state, for example, might tax all products coming from other states near it.

Articles of Confederation

But there was a government over all the states. A **government** is the system by which laws are made and enforced. The first government of the United States was set up in 1781. At that time, all the states agreed on the **Articles of Confederation.** According to this agreement, the national government was to be made up of a congress with one house. This new Congress was much like the earlier Continental Congress. Each state had one vote in Congress.

The Articles of Confederation gave Congress certain powers. Congress could set up post offices, charge postage, and coin or print money. Congress could trade with American Indian groups to the west. It also had the power to raise an army and make peace treaties.

Under the Articles of Confederation, the states agreed to work together. However, each state also had its own individual government. These state governments remained stronger than the government of the nation as a whole.

Farmers attacked the tax collectors during Shays's Rebellion.

In addition, there were some important powers that Congress did *not* have under the Articles of Confederation.

To begin with, Congress could not make trade agreements that would go against any state laws. More important, Congress did not have the power to tax the states. It could only *ask* the states to pay their share of expenses. The state governments collected the money. Then they turned it over to Congress, if they chose to. Many states did not choose to pay. Congress found it difficult to pay the war debts and meet all the other national expenses.

There was an even bigger problem with the Articles of Confederation. Congress could not change any part of the Articles unless every state agreed. Since the states had different interests, they could not all agree on any changes. So Congress remained weak. Some foreign governments thought they would need a separate treaty with each state.

Many Americans came to feel that such a weak government could not hold the United States together. The states might all go their own ways. Then they would not be able to defend themselves against foreign nations.

Some Americans were afraid that there would be another revolution. After the war, times were very hard. Trade had not completely started up again. There was very little money to rebuild businesses and factories. Farmers could not sell their crops. People in all states were having trouble paying their taxes. The worst problem was in Massachusetts. The farmers in that state were very poor. The Massachusetts government often took a farmer's land as payment for taxes owed. The farmers tried to stop this by legal means but could not.

Then, in January of 1787, Daniel Shays took stronger action. He led a group of farmers in an attack on a government building where weapons were stored. But troops fired on the farmers. Daniel Shays and the farmers did not have weapons with which to defend themselves. They gave up the attack and fled. The windows of John Adams's house were broken during this uprising. But he understood the feelings of the farmers. Adams wrote to Thomas Jefferson that Shays's Rebellion was the act of a desperate people.

Many people were worried. They were afraid such things might happen again if they did not have a strong and fair government. Everything the colonies had fought for might be lost.

REVIEW

READING FOR MAIN IDEAS

1. What did the new states want when the war was over?
2. What agreement set up the first government of the United States?
3. Why did the first American government have trouble paying its bills?
4. Why was it hard to change the first national government?
5. What event made people worry about the future of the United States?

THINKING SKILLS

The first national government of the United States did not work well. What do you think was its greatest weakness? Give your reasons.

Lesson 2: Forming a New Government

FIND THE WORDS

Constitution federal
compromise ratify
antifederalist right federalist

In May 1787, 55 representatives chosen by their states met in Philadelphia. They came to discuss the problems of the Articles of Confederation. They soon decided that they would have to rewrite the Articles. For 4 months, they talked and argued about what the government of the United States should be like. When they were through, they had written the **Constitution** of the United

George Washington was the president of the Constitutional Convention.

States. This was a new plan of government for the new nation. George Washington was the president of the Constitutional Convention. James Madison probably influenced the outcome most.

The representatives at the Constitutional Convention faced one major problem. They had to give the new government enough power to do the necessary jobs. But they did not want to give it too much power. If the government had too much power, it might take away the people's freedom. The Convention did not want the new government to behave as the British government had behaved before the American Revolution.

The representatives tried to solve this problem in several ways. One way was to carefully divide the powers of government. Some were given to the **federal,** or national, government. Others were given to the state governments. The federal government was given the powers to print money and make treaties. The federal government could also collect taxes directly from the people for certain things. State governments were allowed to pass laws about education, traffic, cities, and other things inside their borders. They could also collect taxes to pay for services they provided.

The representatives also had to make many compromises. There is **compromise** when people on both sides of an argument agree to give in a little. Then each side gets part of what it wants. For example, the large states wanted the number of votes in Congress to be based on population. The more people a state had, they felt, the more votes it should have. The small states did not agree. They wanted all states to have the same number of votes. Otherwise, they feared, the large states would have too much power over the small ones. The representatives decided that there would be two parts to Congress. One part of Congress would be based on population. In the other part of Congress, each state would have two votes.

There were other compromises. One solved a problem for the states that had slaves. These states wanted slaves to count as part of their population. In this way, they could have more votes in Congress. Yet they did not want slaves to count if there was a tax based on population. The compromise was to count only three out of every five slaves.

The Constitution was finally finished. Now it was up to the states to **ratify,** or approve, it. If nine states ratified the Constitution, it would become law. Everywhere, people were talking

JOIN, or DIE.

Benjamin Franklin published this cartoon. The sections of the snake are the states.

about it. The people who were against the new Constitution were called **antifederalists.** They were afraid of a strong national government. They did not think enough powers were left to the states. Many people wanted the Constitution to spell out the rights of the people. A **right** is a just claim to have or do something. Laws can protect a person's rights from other people and from the power of government.

The **federalists** supported the new Constitution. They believed that a strong national government was necessary. Then, they said, other nations would respect and trust the United States. They felt this would be good for trade and business. Also, they argued, the United States would be better able to defend itself. Federalists agreed that if the Constitution were ratified, they would back changes to protect the people's rights.

The federalists won. By June of 1788, nine states had accepted the Constitution. The Constitution would become the law of the land. Between 1788 and 1790, the other four states joined the Union.

REVIEW

VOCABULARY MASTERY

1. When people on opposing sides each give in a little, they reach a ____.
   Constitution compromise ratification

2. Nine states had to ____ the Constitution to make it law.
   oppose compromise ratify

3. The ____ government is the government of the nation.
   Constitution federal state

4. The ____ opposed the Constitution.
   antifederalists federalists ratifiers

5. The ____ favored the Constitution.
   antifederalists federalists compromisers

WRITING SKILLS

Imagine you were a leader in the government of a large, rich state when the Constitution was proposed. How would you have felt about the Constitution? Why? Give your reasons.

Lesson 3: The Constitution

FIND THE WORDS

legislative executive judicial
check Congress
House of Representatives
elect Senate bill
President veto
Supreme Court justice
appoint unconstitutional

The writers of the Constitution divided the powers of government between the federal government and the states. They also divided the powers of the federal government itself. The Constitution set up a government with three separate branches, or parts.

One branch makes the laws. This is the **legislative** branch.

The second branch carries out the laws. This is the **executive** branch of government.

The third branch settles questions about what the laws mean. This is the **judicial** branch.

Each branch has some—but not all—of the power needed to run the country. Each branch has some power to **check,** or limit, the other two. This keeps any one branch of the government from becoming too strong.

The legislative branch is called **Congress.** Congress is made up of two houses, or parts. The **House of Representatives** is the part that is closest to the people. The number of representatives a state has depends on its population. States with more people have more representatives than those with fewer people. Representatives are **elected,** or chosen by vote, every 2 years by the people of their area. The other part of Congress is the **Senate.** There are two senators from each state. They are elected every 6 years by all the people of their state.

Representatives and senators discuss proposals for new laws. These are called **bills.** For a bill to become a law, both parts of Congress must agree on it.

Through the laws it makes, Congress controls trade between states and with other nations. It has the right to print money. It decides how much money people must pay in taxes to the federal government. Congress also has the right to declare war. These are very important government powers.

The executive branch is headed by the **President.** The President is the leader of the whole nation. The President is elected by the people every 4 years. When the Constitution of the United States was written, no other nation

OUR NATIONAL GOVERNMENT

LEGISLATIVE THE CONGRESS	EXECUTIVE THE PRESIDENT	JUDICIAL THE SUPREME COURT AND LOWER COURTS
1. Suggests and passes the laws	1. Makes the laws of Congress work	1. Settles questions about the laws
2. Approves judges and heads of department chosen by the President	2. Suggests new laws and may veto laws	2. May rule that the President or other official has acted illegally
3. May accuse executive or judicial officials of wrongdoing	3. Chooses judges and heads of government departments	3. Settles questions about treaties
4. Approves treaties	4. Makes treaties with other nations	
5. Has the right to declare war	5. Is Commander in Chief of the Armed Forces	

elected its leaders. Those in power in other nations did not think the people were wise enough to choose good leaders.

The President must sign bills before they can become law. The President directs the people who carry out the laws of the nation. Some of these people collect taxes. Some of them settle problems with other nations and make treaties with them. Others have duties such as giving licenses to radio and television stations. The President is also the commander in chief of the armed forces.

The President may suggest new bills to Congress. But Congress must approve them before they can become law. The President also has the power to **veto,** or stop, a bill passed by Congress. Presidents can veto bills they think are not good for the nation. Congress can try to pass such a bill again. After a veto, a bill can become law only if two-thirds of both houses of Congress approve.

The judicial branch includes courts in all parts of the nation. The highest court in the land is called the **Supreme Court.** The

Today, you can see the original documents that shaped American government.

Supreme Court has nine members, called **justices.** They are not elected. The President **appoints,** or selects, them. The Senate must approve the President's choices. Justices of the Supreme Court may serve for life.

The Supreme Court can decide that a law passed by Congress or by a state is **unconstitutional.** Such a law does not fit in with the ideas and purposes of the Constitution. No one has to obey a law that the Supreme Court has called unconstitutional. The Supreme Court can also decide if an action of the President is unconstitutional.

The Constitution set up a government that would endure.

REVIEW

VOCABULARY MASTERY

1. The President has the power to ___ bills.
   check veto appoint
2. Members of the Supreme Court are called ___.
   representatives senators justices
3. Congress is the ___ branch of the federal government.
   legislative executive judicial
4. The President heads the ___ branch.
   legislative executive judicial
5. The Supreme Court is the highest part of the ___ branch.
   legislative executive judicial

READING FOR MAIN IDEAS

6. Name the two houses of Congress.
7. What must happen before a bill can become law?
8. How can a bill be passed after the President vetoes it?
9. How are the members of the Supreme Court chosen?
10. What does it mean to say that a law is unconstitutional?

THINKING SKILLS

Each branch of the federal government has some power to check the other two. Do you think this is a good idea? Why, or why not?

Lesson 4: Amendments to the Constitution

FIND THE WORDS

amendment **Bill of Rights**
bail **fine** **suit**
naturalize **repeal**

Built into the Constitution is a way of changing it. Such a change is called an **amendment.** Amendments are hard to make. Three-fourths of the states must ratify an amendment before it can become part of the Constitution.

In trying to get people to accept the Constitution, the federalists promised to make changes in it. These changes would describe the rights of the people. In 1791, 3 years after the Constitution was ratified, the first 10 amendments were added. These amendments make up the United States **Bill of Rights.** Since 1791, the Bill of Rights has been very important in the history of the United States. It safeguards individual rights and freedoms from the power of government.

Bill of Rights

Here are some of the main points of the Bill of Rights. You can see in them what early Americans meant by the word *freedom.*

Amendment 1: Congress will make no law that (a) sets up a religion, helps one religion over another, or takes away a person's right to believe in and practice a religion; (b) takes away the freedom of newspapers to print the news or takes away a person's right to say what he or she thinks; (c) tries to stop people from getting together in a peaceful crowd and complaining about the government.

Amendment 2: The people's right to keep weapons cannot be taken away.

Amendment 3: In peacetime, no soldiers can be quartered in someone's house without the agreement of the owner. In wartime, laws must be passed if this is to be allowed.

Amendment 4: The government cannot search people's homes and property without a good reason. The courts must give permission for a search.

Amendment 5: People cannot be made to say anything against themselves in court. People cannot have their lives, freedom, or property taken away except according to the laws.

The Bill of Rights gave people the right to a trial by jury. It gave people the right to know the charges being made against them. It gave people the right to a lawyer to defend them against the charges.

Amendment 6: People accused in court of committing a crime have the right to a public trial. They have the right to have a fair jury hear and decide the case. They have the right to know why they are being tried. They have the right to have a lawyer defend them.

Amendment 7: People have the right to a jury in court cases that involve disagreements about amounts of money over $20.

Amendment 8: **Bail,** money pledged to get out of jail while awaiting trial, should not be too great. **Fines,** money paid as punishment for crimes, should not be too large. Punishments cannot be cruel or strange.

Amendments 9 and 10: If a right is not mentioned in the Constitution, that does not mean the people do not have it. Any rights not given to the federal government in the Constitution belong to the states or to the people.

Additional Amendments

Sixteen other amendments have been added to the Constitution since the Bill of Rights. These amendments have made it possible for the Constitution to meet the needs of a changing nation.

Amendment 11: A **suit,** or legal action, against a state must be judged in a court in that state.

Amendment 12: Electors will vote for the President and Vice President separately.

Amendment 13: Slavery is abolished, or done away with.

Amendment 14: All people born in the United States or naturalized here are citizens of the United States. They are also citizens of the states where they live. **Naturalize** means to give the rights of a citizen to someone who came to the United States from a foreign country.

All citizens must be treated equally under the law.

Amendment 15: No citizen can be denied the right to vote because of race or color.

Amendment 16: Congress has the power to collect a tax on income.

Amendment 17: Senators are to be elected directly by the people.

Amendment 18: Making or selling alcoholic beverages is illegal.

Amendment 19: No citizen can be denied the right to vote because she is a woman.

Amendment 20: Presidents will take office on January 20; members of Congress will take office on January 3.

Amendment 21: Amendment 18 is **repealed,** or is no longer in effect.

Amendment 22: No person can be elected President more than two times.

Amendment 23: The people living in the District of Columbia have the right to vote for the President and Vice President.

Amendment 24: Citizens do not have to pay a tax to vote in national elections.

Amendment 25: If a President dies, the Vice President becomes President and appoints a new Vice President. If the President is seriously ill and cannot do the work, the Vice President then becomes Acting President.

Amendment 26: Citizens can vote at age 18.

REVIEW

VOCABULARY MASTERY

1. A change in the Constitution is a(n) ____.
bill amendment fine

2. A ____ is money paid as punishment for a crime.
right bail fine

3. People pay ____ to get out of jail while awaiting trial.
fines bail suits

4. If a law is ____, it is done away with.
amended ratified repealed

READING FOR MAIN IDEAS

5. What are the first 10 amendments called?

6. Which amendment gives people the right to speak freely?

7. Which amendments give people the right to trials by jury?

8. Which amendment prohibits bail and fines that are too large?

9. Which amendment did away with slavery?

10. Which amendment gave women the right to vote?

THINKING SKILLS

Are there any rights that you think are important that are not in the Bill of Rights? If so, what are they?

Lesson 5: President Washington and the New Government

FIND THE WORDS

secretary Cabinet candidate currency credit neutrality political party

Once the Constitution was approved, the new government had to be set up. Members of Congress were elected from the states. Electors were chosen to vote for the President. It was no surprise that every one of them voted for George Washington of Virginia. He had led the nation in war. Now he was to lead it in peace. John Adams of Massachusetts was elected Vice President.

On April 30, 1789, President Washington took the oath of office in New York City. It was an exciting day. Cannons roared and church bells rang. A crowd shouted, "Long live George Washington!" The people were eager to see the President who had "the look and figure of a hero." The new President must have thought about the welcome as he settled down to work. He

George Washington was elected the nation's first President. An arch of laurel branches was made to welcome him to New York.

Fascinating Facts

Probably the most famous false teeth in the world belonged to George Washington. Most people thought they were made of wood. But wooden teeth would have rotted much faster than real teeth.

In fact, George Washington's false teeth were made of gold and ivory. His dentist made them in 1795.

On June 19, 1981, Washington's famous teeth were reported missing in Washington, DC. They were stolen from the Smithsonian Institution. If you happen to find a pair of false teeth, here is how you will know if they belonged to Washington. Inside the teeth are the words: "This was the Great Washington's teeth."

had to oversee the building of a government from a set of plans—the Constitution. The task was difficult. There was no example to follow. As one member of Congress said, "We are in a wilderness without a single footstep to guide us."

But George Washington had a clear idea of what he wanted to do. He wanted to win the respect of the people for the Presidency. He wanted to get people to trust the federal government. He wanted the nation to rebuild its business and trade. He wanted the United States to stay at peace with other nations.

The Cabinet

Congress soon set up departments to help the President. The first were the Department of State, the Department of the Treasury, and the Department of War. The heads of these departments were called **secretaries.** Together with the Attorney General and the Postmaster General, they met often with Washington. They talked about the problems of government and gave the President their advice. This group became known as the **Cabinet.** Since then, every President has had a Cabinet. The Cabinet members help the President carry out the nation's laws.

The members of the first Cabinet did not always agree with one another. Alexander Hamilton, the Secretary of the Treasury, thought the nation should be ruled by rich people and government officials. He wanted a strong federal government that could help and protect trade and business. Thomas Jefferson, the Secretary of State, thought the United States should be a nation of independent farmers. He wanted the federal government to stay small. He thought Hamilton would make America like Great Britain, with its ruling upper class. The ideas of both leaders were important to the development of the nation.

Fascinating Facts

How should the President of the United States be chosen? That was one of the questions facing the writers of the Constitution. Some thought that Congress or the state legislatures should select the President. Others favored a direct vote by the people. In the end, a compromise was reached. An Electoral College, made up of electors chosen by the states, would elect the President.

Each state was to have as many electors as it had members of Congress. For example, a state with two senators and six representatives got eight electors.

The Electoral College system is far from perfect. Now the person with the most popular votes in each state gets all of the state's electoral votes. It is a winner-take-all system. Three times in our nation's history, the person who received the most votes of the people did not become President. Another candidate received the most electoral votes and so was elected. A **candidate** is someone who runs for an office.

Although many complain about it, people cannot seem to agree on a system to replace the Electoral College.

Hamilton's Plans

Alexander Hamilton studied the nation's problems. He saw that the United States was deep in debt. The people, the states, and the nation owed money. But the **currency,** paper money issued by the government, was almost without value. Hamilton knew the United States must pay what it owed. If it did not, its currency would not be accepted. Business and trade would be hurt.

Alexander Hamilton believed he had to make people trust the credit of the government. **Credit** is the belief that someone who owes money will repay it. Hamilton wanted the national government to pay its own debts and the debts of the states as well. The Southern states were not happy with this because their debts were small. The New England states supported the plan because they had large debts from the war to pay.

Hamilton got what he wanted by compromise. The South, led by Jefferson, accepted Hamilton's plan. In return, the North, led by Hamilton, agreed to let the national capital be located in the South. The District of Columbia, between Maryland and Virginia, was the site chosen.

Next, Hamilton asked Congress to set up a national bank. The government would keep its money in this bank. The bank would control how much money other banks could lend. Some people were against the bank. They felt the government did not have the right to set up a bank. Hamilton argued that the Constitution said that Congress could do what was necessary to carry out its powers. Congress accepted Hamilton's idea. It voted for the

The First Bank of the United States was set up in Philadelphia in 1791. At first, there was a great deal of opposition to the bank.

Alexander Hamilton was the first Secretary of the Treasury. He asked Congress to set up a national bank.

First Bank of the United States. As trade became greater, people had more money in their pockets. More people trusted Hamilton's plans.

Foreign Affairs

The early days of the country were a dangerous time. The United States was a baby giant in the family of nations. There was often a difference between what the country wanted to do and what it could do. Soon after Washington took office, Great Britain and France went to war. France had helped the United States defeat Britain in the Revolutionary War. Should the United States now help France?

Thomas Jefferson, the Secretary of State, wanted to help France. But President Washington and Alexander Hamilton agreed that the nation could not afford another war. In 1793, Washington issued a Proclamation of Neutrality. **Neutrality** is not taking sides in a war. Washington wanted the United States to stay out of problems between other nations. He repeated this idea in his famous Farewell Address in 1796.

Neutrality did not solve the problems the United States had with European nations. Both the French and the British attacked American ships. The differences between Jefferson and Hamilton became greater. Jefferson did not want to allow British ships to trade with the United States. Hamilton and Washington knew

George Washington was elected President again in 1792. This painting shows his second inauguration ceremony, at Independence Hall in Philadelphia. An inauguration is the ceremony at which an official takes the oath of office.

that to stop British ships would destroy American trade.

Finally, Washington sent John Jay, the Chief Justice of the Supreme Court, to Britain to solve the problems. The United States and Britain signed the Jay Treaty. But in the treaty, Britain did not promise to leave American ships alone. As a result, many people, including Jefferson, were against the treaty. Jefferson resigned as Secretary of State because of it. The British did promise in the treaty to remove their troops from forts in the Northwest Territory. British troops had stayed there after the Revolutionary War had ended. The treaty also prevented, for a while, a war that could have destroyed the young nation.

Political Parties

The differences between Alexander Hamilton and Thomas Jefferson in the 1790s were not just arguments between two people. The first national political parties in the United States grew out of their conflict. A **political party** is a group of people who have similar ideas about how the government should be run. They join together and support candidates for public office. The followers of Hamilton became known as the Federalist Party. They were not necessarily the same people as the federalists who had backed the Constitution in the 1780s.

Those who supported Thomas Jefferson were called the Republican Party. This group was later called the Democratic-Republican Party and, still later, the Democratic Party. The Democratic Party of today is descended from it. The present-day Republican Party has nothing to do with the Republicans of the 1790s. It is an entirely different group that was founded much later. From early days, though, the United States has had two major political parties. This has made it easier to elect governments.

In 1796, George Washington said he would not run again for the Presidency. The Federalists then chose Vice President John Adams to be their candidate for President. Thomas Jefferson was the presidential candidate of the Republicans. Adams won and became the second President.

While John Adams was President, the United States had more problems with France. Alexander Hamilton wanted Adams to lead the nation into war with France. When Adams refused, Hamilton worked against his reelection. In this way, the Federalist Party was divided. As a result, the Republican candidate, Thomas Jefferson, was elected President in 1800. Hamilton's followers, the Federalists, were never again strong enough to elect a President.

REVIEW

VOCABULARY MASTERY

1. The heads of government departments were called____.
War Hawks political parties secretaries

2. A____is a group of people that run candidates for public office.
cabinet political party currency

3. ____is paper money issued by the government.
Neutrality Credit Currency

4. ____is the belief that someone who owes money will repay it.
Neutrality Credit Doctrine

5. The heads of government departments form the____.
Cabinet Secretariat Doctrine

READING FOR MAIN IDEAS

6. What were George Washington's main goals as President?

7. How did Thomas Jefferson and Alexander Hamilton differ in their ideas about government?

8. What major problem did Hamilton have to deal with as Secretary of the Treasury?

9. What was the Jay Treaty?

10. How did the first two political parties begin?

RESEARCH SKILLS

Today, the President's Cabinet is much larger than it was under Washington. Find out how many and which government leaders are now Cabinet members. Use an encyclopedia or other source suggested by your teacher.

Lesson 6: Jefferson to Jackson

FIND THE WORDS

inaugurate **survey**
War Hawk **casualty**
Monroe Doctrine

Jefferson became the third President of the United States in 1801. He did not win the election easily, however. He and Aaron Burr each received 73 electoral votes. The House of Representatives then had to decide between the two. It took 36 ballots before Jefferson was chosen as President. Jefferson, like Washington, served two terms.

This was the first time a Democratic-Republican had been elected President. The Federalists expected a disaster. They feared that Jefferson would overturn all the laws they had passed. Instead, Jefferson tried to make peace. He declared, "We are all Republicans, we are all Federalists." Jefferson's election was called "the revolution of 1800." However, it was a peaceful revolution.

President Adams did not stay in Washington to see Jefferson become President. He was afraid that Jefferson's election would mean the end of the nation.

Thomas Jefferson became President of the United States in 1801. This is the way the Washington, DC, area looked at the time.

People to Remember

Thomas Jefferson

Thomas Jefferson was a person of many talents and interests. He was a scientist, inventor, architect, diplomat, writer, musician, and farmer. He was also the third President of the United States.

Jefferson was born into a wealthy Virginia family. In 1776, he represented his colony at the Second Continental Congress in Philadelphia. Jefferson excelled as a writer. He was chosen to write the Declaration of Independence.

When Jefferson went back to Virginia, he helped set up a government for the new state. He also served as governor. As a private citizen, he studied the plants, animals, climate, and geography of the region. He designed his own home.

In 1785, Jefferson went to France as the United States' diplomatic representative. When he returned home, President Washington asked him to serve as Secretary of State. Jefferson was elected Vice President in 1796. He became President in 1801.

The last years of his life were spent back at Monticello. He had a huge library there that became the foundation of the Library of Congress. In addition, Jefferson founded the University of Virginia.

On July 4, 1826, exactly 50 years after the Declaration of Independence was signed, Thomas Jefferson died. His good friend, John Adams, died on the same day.

Jefferson was the first President to be **inaugurated,** or sworn into office, in the new capital of Washington. The city was designed by Pierre-Charles L'Enfant, a French-born architect. L'Enfant modeled the new city after Paris, including marble buildings and many parks and fountains. But he believed that Washington should reflect the open spirit of America. There were to be broad avenues and lots of open space.

One of the people hired to **survey** the new city, or measure its land, was Benjamin Banneker. He was the first Black to receive a Presidential appointment. Banneker was also a mathematician and scientist, and the author of an almanac.

In 1801, the city of Washington was mostly swamps and fields. Cows and pigs wandered about at will. There was no inaugural parade that year on Pennsylvania Avenue. The street was then only a muddy path.

The War of 1812

While Jefferson was President, the United States continued to have problems with Britain and France. Britain and France were at war. Each country had announced that any ship trading with the other side would be captured. American ships were caught in the middle.

There were members of Congress who wanted the United States to go to war with Britain. They were called the **War Hawks.** War finally broke out in 1812, while James Madison was President. Madison gave three reasons for going to war. The British were interfering with American shipping. They were boarding the American ships and taking away sailors. They were encouraging American Indians to attack American settlements.

The War Hawks believed that the Americans could drive the British out of Canada. Then Canada could become American territory.

Not everyone wanted war, however. States that depended on trade—the New England States, New York, and New Jersey—were against it. The War Hawks came mostly from the South and the West. They felt the British were blocking their expansion. They thought defeating the British would be easy. But the War Hawks were wrong about American strength. The American army was unprepared, and the navy was very small. In spite of this, the American navy did very well. One ship, the *Constitution,* sank at least two British ships. It was known as "Old Ironsides" because its sides were covered with metal.

However, the power of the British forces was too great. At sea, their navy destroyed many American ships. On land, the British had even more success. In August 1814, they marched on the city of Washington, setting fire to many buildings. Dolley Madison, the President's wife, stayed in the White House until the last minute. Just before the British arrived, she carried away a famous portrait of George Washington.

The burning of the city of Washington was the low point of the war for the Americans. Events soon took a turn for the better. The British tried to capture Baltimore and to invade the United States from Canada. But both

The Star-Spangled Banner

On September 12, 1814, the British attacked Fort McHenry in Baltimore. Over the fort flew a large American flag. The battle went on all day and all night.

Francis Scott Key, a young American lawyer, watched the battle from a ship offshore. During the night, he could see the flag by the light of "bombs bursting in air." But sometimes the smoke got too thick, and he could not see. Had the fort surrendered? Had the British won? In the morning, "by the dawn's early light," Key saw the flag. He knew that the Americans had not given up.

Key realized how much the flag meant to him. Afterward, he wrote a poem, "The Star-Spangled Banner." That poem, set to music, has become our national anthem.

"Oh, say! can you see, by the dawn's early light,
What so proudly we hailed at the twilight's last gleaming,
Whose broad stripes and bright stars, through the perilous fight,
O'er the ramparts we watched were so gallantly streaming?
And the rockets' red glare, the bombs bursting in air,
Gave proof through the night that our flag was still there.
Oh, say, does that star-spangled banner yet wave
O'er the land of the free and the home of the brave?"

This painting shows the *Constitution* during the War of 1812.

attempts failed. It became clear that neither the British nor the Americans were winning the war.

A treaty of peace was signed on Christmas Eve of 1814. Unfortunately, news of the peace did not travel fast enough. On January 8, 1815, the British army attacked New Orleans. In less than half an hour, more than 2,000 British soldiers had been killed or wounded. The Americans suffered very few **casualties,** or dead and injured. The man who led the Americans to victory was General Andrew Jackson. He became known as the "hero of New Orleans." The fame and popularity he gained helped him win the Presidency years later.

The War of 1812 ended in a draw. Neither side won. But the United States came out of the war a stronger nation. The war brought the nation together. It gave the American people new pride. They soon forgot the individual defeats. What mattered was that America had stood up to the world's greatest naval power. The United States could now take its place among the nations of the world. The War of 1812 is called the "Second War of American Independence."

The War of 1812 had another result—this one quite unexpected. Relations between the United States and Britain improved. Each side now realized that war was not a quick and easy way to settle their differences. They were more willing to discuss their problems.

James Monroe was President during the Era of Good Feelings. During these years from 1817 to 1825, the two big political parties of today came together. The Federalist Party had disappeared from national politics.

The United States had shown that it was the most powerful nation in the Western Hemisphere. In 1823, President Monroe stated the **Monroe Doctrine.** He said the United States would not allow European nations to set up any more colonies in the Americas.

In 1828, Andrew Jackson of Tennessee was elected President. He was the first President to come from a state west of the Appalachian Mountains. Jackson was also the first President to come from the "ordinary people." He was called "the people's choice." On his inauguration day, 10,000 people went to Washington to celebrate. After his inauguration, Jackson threw open the White House to everyone. So many people came that the President himself had to flee.

The election of Jackson was a symbol of the growing power of the western part of the nation. Many Americans were moving west. Businesses were growing throughout the country. The United States had won its independence. It had set up a strong government under the Constitution. A time of great growth and change had begun.

REVIEW

VOCABULARY MASTERY

1. The President of the United States is ___ in January.
   ratified elected inaugurated
2. A ___ is someone injured or killed in an accident or war.
   Loyalist casualty grenadier
3. To ___ is to measure the land.
   survey quarter boycott

READING FOR MAIN IDEAS

4. Thomas Jefferson and Aaron Burr each received 73 electoral votes in 1800. How was the new President chosen?
5. How did the Federalists feel about the election of Jefferson?
6. What three reasons did President Madison give for going to war against Britain in 1812?
7. What did the War Hawks want?
8. Which states were against the War of 1812? Why?
9. Which side won the War of 1812?
10. What was the Monroe Doctrine?

THINKING SKILLS

Why is the War of 1812 often referred to as the "Second War of American Independence"?

CHAPTER REVIEW

VOCABULARY MASTERY

Use the words below to complete the chapter summary. Use each only once.

amendments	federal
antifederalists	federalists
Articles of Confederation	judicial
Bill of Rights	legislative
bills	President
checked	ratified
Constitution	unconstitutional
executive	veto

At first, the new nation was governed under the __1__. Later, a new __2__ for the __3__ government was written. It was supported by the __4__ and opposed by the __5__. All the states __6__ it. The new government had __7__, __8__, and __9__ branches. These branches __10__ each other. For example, the Congress could pass __11__, but the __12__, head of the executive branch, could __13__ them. In addition, the Supreme Court could find laws __14__. Soon, 10 __15__ known as the __16__ were added to the Constitution to protect freedom.

READING FOR MAIN IDEAS

1. What was the main problem the members of the Constitutional Convention faced?
2. Name the three branches of the federal government and describe how each one works.
3. What is the difference between the House of Representatives and the Senate?
4. Why did Alexander Hamilton want the national government to pay its own debts and the debts of the states?
5. Why did the states disagree about going to war in 1812?

SKILLS APPLICATION

DICTIONARY SKILLS

Words often have more than one meaning. You need to know how a word is used each time you see it. Read the dictionary entries below. Then answer the questions that follow.

bill (BIL), *n.* 1. a piece of paper money. 2. a paper showing the amount of money owed. 3. a written plan for a new law. 4. a written public notice.
check (CHEK), *v.* 1. to stop. 2. to limit. 3. to make a mark on paper.
credit (CREH dit), *n.* 1. the belief that someone who owes money will repay it. 2. the money in a bank account. 3. a plan for buying now, paying later. 4. honor, praise.

6. How many meanings does *bill* have? Which definition fits its use in this chapter?
7. Write a sentence using *bill* to show that meaning.
8. What is the difference between the first and second definitions for *check*? Which definition matches its use in this chapter?
9. According to the chapter, who does the checking? What do they check?
10. What meaning of *credit* is used first in this chapter?
11. When the government keeps its money in a national bank, which definition of *credit* fits?
12. Look up the word *Cabinet* in your Glossary. Write the definition. Then look up *cabinet* in a dictionary. Write a definition that shows another meaning for *cabinet*.
13. Write a sentence using *Cabinet* to show the meaning used in your textbook.

CHAPTER 3 THE UNITED STATES EXPANDS

Lesson 1: The Westward Movement

FIND THE WORDS

frontier pass blaze
pioneer territory
land speculator

In North America, "the West" has meant different things at different times in history.

To the early European explorers in North America, the West was the Atlantic Coast. As settlements grew, the West became the area where settlements ended and the woods began.

For about 100 years, only a few Europeans crossed the Appalachian Mountains. These mountains formed a barrier to settlement. They were like a wall blocking the way west. At the time of the American Revolution, the Appalachians were the gate to the western frontier. A **frontier** is an unsettled area at or beyond the edge of a settled area.

Daniel Boone was a hunter, explorer, and soldier. He was the first White person to lead a group of settlers through the Appalachian Mountains.

In the South, there is a narrow **pass,** or low place, in the Appalachians. It is near the spot where the states of Virginia, Kentucky, and Tennessee meet. The Cherokees and Shawnees had used the pass for hundreds of years and had opened up trails around it. White people called the pass the Cumberland Gap.

In 1775, Daniel Boone and a group of woodcutters cleared a road through the Cumberland Gap. They joined and widened the Indian trails. They **blazed** the trail by cutting marks in trees. Boone's trail was called the "Wilderness Road." It was 480 kilometers (300 miles) long. Many hunters, trappers, and farmers began to move west along this footpath.

The early settlers who moved west came to be known as pioneers. **Pioneers** are the first people to settle a new region. The pioneers on the Wilderness Road traveled in groups of at least 100 people. There was safety in numbers. The pioneers took along only what they could carry. Their food was dried corn, corn meal, dried apples, and dried string beans. On a good day, they would walk 8 miles. About every 3 days,

Many people traveled west in covered wagons. They faced a long, hard journey over poor roads and across rivers. They often traveled in groups. There was safety in numbers. These pioneers took along only what they could carry. Most of them were farmers.

WHERE WE ARE IN TIME AND PLACE

WESTWARD GROWTH OF THE UNITED STATES

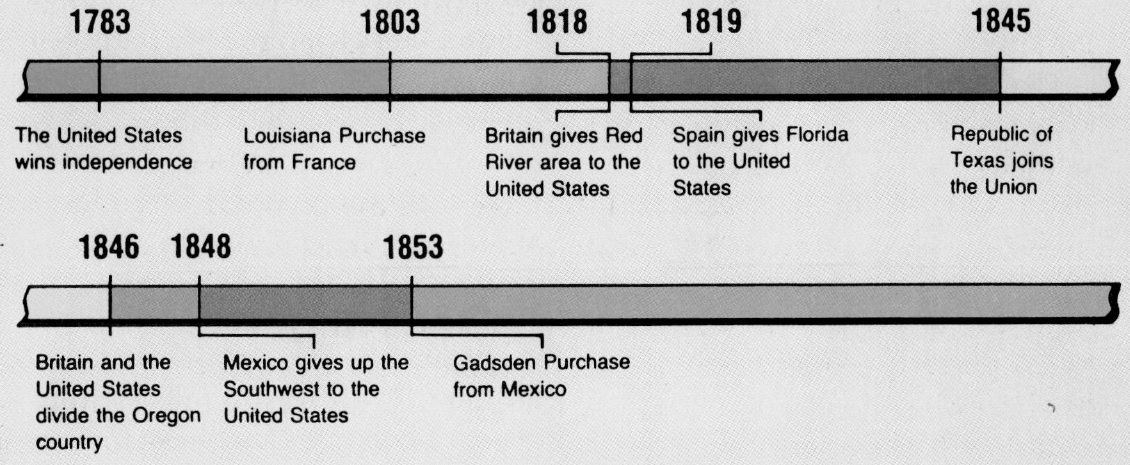

WESTWARD GROWTH OF THE UNITED STATES

BRITISH POSSESSIONS
Oregon Territory Ceded by Britain 1846
Ceded by Britain 1818
Portland
Oregon Trail
California Trail
Louisiana Bought from France 1803
Chicago
The Old Northwest
New York
Washington, D.C.
San Francisco
Old Spanish Trail
Independence
St. Louis
Ceded by Mexico 1848
Santa Fe Trail
The United States 1783
ATLANTIC OCEAN
Santa Fe
Mississippi River
San Diego
Gila River Trail
El Paso
Texas Joins the Union 1845
Atlanta
Bought from Mexico 1853
PACIFIC OCEAN
San Antonio
New Orleans
Florida Ceded by Spain 1819
Gulf of Mexico
MEXICO

KEY
Trails to the West in 1845
Forts
Cities

N NE E SE S SW W NW

SCALE
Kilometers 0 200 400 600
Miles 0 200 400 600

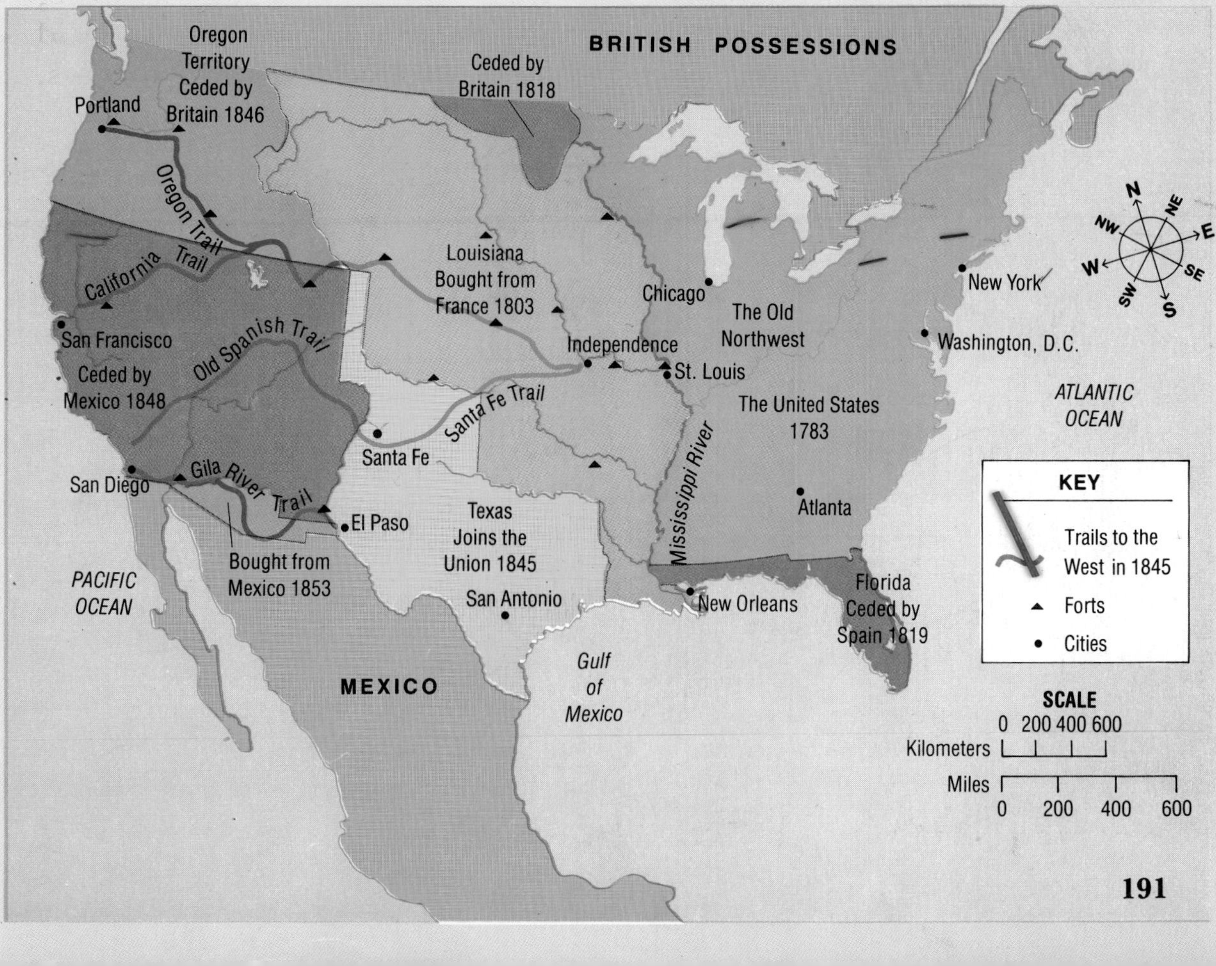

When the pioneers reached their destination, they had to clear the land and build places to live. Men, women, and children helped turn the wilderness into a home.

they stopped for a day. Then, men hunted and women cooked.

The pioneers used plants that grew along the trail for food or medicine. Someone who had been cut could die if the cut became infected. People then did not know about using stitches to close a wound. So a pioneer would rub a poison ivy leaf inside the cut. This made the skin swell up, closing the cut inside.

Most of the pioneers were farmers. They had to harvest their crops in the fall. They had to arrive in time for spring planting. This meant that they traveled in winter.

By the end of the Revolution, the United States stretched from the Atlantic Ocean to the Mississippi River. Many settlements had been established west of the Appalachians. By 1790, there were 74,000 people in Kentucky and 36,000 people in Tennessee. The United States did not then include Florida, which belonged to Spain.

In the 1780s, the government decided to make it easier for people to settle the Old Northwest. This frontier region extended west from the Appalachians to the Mississippi River. It stretched north from the Ohio River to the Great Lakes. Find the Old Northwest on the map on page 191. Look south of the Great Lakes.

The government divided the land and offered it for sale at very low prices. It passed laws about the rights of settlers. The Northwest Territory was then set up. A **territory** was an area with a government but with less independence than a state. When a part of this territory had 60,000 people, it could become a state.

Some of the first Americans to move to the Old Northwest were **land speculators.** They came to buy land cheaply so they could sell it later for a profit. But most of the early settlers came to stay. Most were poor farmers. They wanted land on which to build a home and start a farm. These pioneers faced a long, hard trip over poor roads and across rivers. They faced dangers from the Miami, Sauk, and Fox. These American Indian peoples fought to keep the settlers away from their hunting lands. The pioneers knew life would be hard but believed that times would improve.

By 1820, the United States had about 10 million people. About 2½ million lived between the Appalachians and the Mississippi. New states west of the Appalachians had joined the Union. Kentucky became a state in 1792 and Tennessee in 1796. Mississippi, Alabama, Ohio, Indiana, and Illinois were states by 1819.

REVIEW

VOCABULARY MASTERY

1. An unsettled area beyond the edge of a settled area is a ____.
   frontier pioneer territory
2. The early settlers in the West are called ____.
   frontiers land speculators pioneers
3. A ____ has a government but is less independent than a state.
   nation territory frontier

READING FOR MAIN IDEAS

4. What was an important barrier to early settlement of the West?
5. What route did Daniel Boone help start?
6. What kind of food did the pioneers eat along the trail?
7. Why did land speculators move to the West?
8. What was the first state west of the Appalachians?

RESEARCH SKILLS

Find books in your library about pioneer life in the West. Choose a book to read and make a report.

THINKING SKILLS

A frontier can be an unexplored region, such as outer space. Or it can be an undeveloped area of knowledge. What frontier would you like to explore? Why?

Lesson 2: Frontier Life

FIND THE WORDS

livestock **porridge**

The work on the frontier was shared by all. Men, women, and even children cleared the forest and turned it into farmland. They planted food, raised livestock, and hunted wild animals. **Livestock** are farm animals.

The frontier cabin was a sort of factory. There, raw materials were made into things that could be used. Wood from the forest was made into tools. Cotton, flax, or wool was spun into thread. The thread was then woven into cloth. The cloth was made into blankets and into shirts and other clothes. Hogs and cattle were butchered at home. The meat was salted and saved to be eaten later. Corn and other grains were made into breads, puddings, or porridges. A **porridge** is a souplike food made from grain or peas. Cream was churned into butter. Animal fat was made into soap and candles.

There was plenty of room in the wilderness for new settlers. With the help of neighbors, they could put up a log cabin in a day.

A woman who lived in the Old Northwest in the early 1800s told what it was like:

"We did most of our work in the summer kitchen. That was where we had the big brick oven. We used to fire it twice a week and do a sight o' baking all at once. We'd make a hot fire in the oven. Then, when the bricks were heated through, we'd scrape out all the coals with a big iron scraper. We would dump the coals into the fireplace. Then we'd shove in the roast and fowls, the pies, and bread. At other times, we'd use the open fireplace.

"It was so easy, since we had no screens, to let the flies spoil everything. My mother just wouldn't have it so. We weren't allowed to bring apples into the house in summer. Apples attracted flies. If any of us dropped a speck of butter or cream on the floor, my mother would run for a cloth to wipe it up. At mealtime, someone stood and fanned to keep the flies away while the other people ate.

"In warm weather, we washed outdoors. We used our well water. We'd draw a barrel of water and put one shovel of ashes into it. It would just suds up like soft water, so white and clean. Our starch was of two kinds. It was made from a dough worked round and round until it was smooth. Or it was made from grated potato cooked to the right consistency.

"My mother used to spin. She made beautiful fine thread. I used to love to watch her work at the spinning wheel. I can close my eyes and see Ma standing over there spinning a thread as far as from here to the bed.

"When I was eight years old, she wove me a plaid dress of which I was very proud. I remember the pattern. There were eight threads of brown, then one of red, one of blue, one of red, then brown again. It made the prettiest flannel. That dress lasted me for years."

Like the earlier settlers in the 1600s and 1700s, the western pioneers had to depend on their neighbors. Life on the frontier could be lonely. For the pioneers,

The frontier home was a sort of factory. There, raw materials were made into useful things. This woman is dipping candles, which were made from animal fat.

working together often provided a welcome chance for a social gathering. Visiting was important to people who often lived 5 or 6 kilometers (3 or 4 miles) apart. A man from Ohio told how the pioneers worked and played together when he was a boy.

"Houses and barns were raised by the collection of many neighbors together on one day. Men rolled up the logs in a clearing. They grubbed out the underbrush. Then they cut the logs for a house or barn. When such a gathering of men took place, the women also shared a job. There was quilting, sewing, or spinning of thread for some poor

Life on the frontier could be lonely. Corn husking was an occasion for a social event.

neighbor. This would bring together a mixed party. Usually, after supper there would be a dance or at least plays. These filled a good part of the night. The evening wound up with the young fellows seeing the girls home in the short hours or, if they went home early, sitting with them by the fire."

In later years, life became easier for the pioneers. The government built post roads and canals. Small trading posts became towns and then cities. Farmers could sell their crops to buy the goods they had made before or had done without. The children of the pioneers saw and enjoyed these better times.

REVIEW

READING FOR MAIN IDEAS

1. Who did the work on the frontier?
2. How was the frontier cabin like a factory?
3. How did the pioneers make clothing? List three steps.
4. How did the pioneers save meat?
5. What were soap and candles made from?

THINKING SKILLS

The lesson describes some things that pioneer neighbors did together. What other things can you think of?

Lesson 3: Across the Mississippi

FIND THE WORDS

envoy **interpreter**

Thomas Jefferson became President of the United States in 1801. He served two terms in office. Probably his greatest contribution as President was the Louisiana Purchase.

When Jefferson became President, France owned much of the land west of the Mississippi River. It also owned the port city of New Orleans. New Orleans was very important to American farmers living west of the Appalachians. They wanted to send their goods down the Mississippi and ship them from New Orleans. This was easier than sending them east over the mountain roads.

In 1803, Jefferson sent two envoys to France to try to buy New Orleans. An **envoy** (AHN voy) is someone who represents one government in dealing with another. To the Americans' surprise, the French ruler, Napoleon, offered to sell the whole Louisiana Territory. This was all the French land west of the Mississippi. The envoys could not ask Jefferson what to do. It would take weeks or months to get an answer from the United States. If they delayed, Napoleon might change his mind. On their own, the American envoys offered Napoleon $15 million for the Louisiana Territory. Napoleon accepted.

Napoleon needed money to pay for his wars in Europe. He also knew he did not have the power to keep this land. Few French people lived outside New Orleans.

When the news of the deal reached the United States, the reaction was mixed. Some people were strongly opposed. Jefferson decided to ask Congress for the money to buy the territory. He

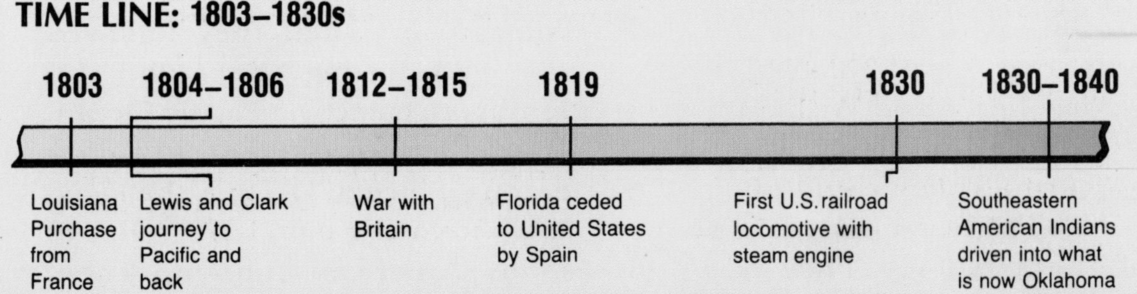

Lewis and Clark met many American Indians during their explorations. Most of them were friendly. They provided food, supplies, and information for the explorers. Lewis and Clark were interested in learning about the different Indian peoples who lived in the West. They studied the customs and languages of the Indians.

asked Congress to think of the future of the nation. The new territory would double the size of the United States. Congress finally agreed, and Louisiana became part of the United States. Look at the map on page 191. The Louisiana Territory stretched from the Mississippi to the Rocky Mountains. It reached from the Gulf of Mexico all the way up to the Canadian border.

No one knew the exact borders of the new territory. No one knew what the land was like. The following year, President Jefferson sent two army officers, Meriwether Lewis and William Clark, to explore Louisiana. They were to learn all they could about the land, climate, animals, and plants of the territory. They were to study the language and ways of the American Indians of the area. They were to map the rivers. They were to go beyond the new territory, all the way to the Pacific Ocean.

Lewis and Clark set out from St. Louis, Missouri, in May of 1804. They took about 40 people along on their expedition. The first winter was spent at Fort Mandan in present-day North Dakota.

During the summer of 1805, the explorers crossed the Rocky Mountains. Then they followed the swift-flowing Snake and Columbia rivers to the Pacific Ocean. It was a very difficult and dangerous journey. Along the way, the explorers had the help of many American Indians. Then,

People to Remember

Sacajawea

During the first winter of their expedition, Lewis and Clark met a young Shoshone (shuh SHOH nee) woman. Her name was Sacajawea (SAK uh juh WEE uh). She had been captured by a rival tribe many years before. Now she was far from her people. Sacajawea was married to a French-Canadian fur trapper named Toussaint Charbonneau. (too SAN SHAR boh NOH).

The explorers invited Sacajawea and her husband to join them on their westward expedition. Charbonneau knew the languages of the river Indians. Sacajawea knew the Shoshone tongue. They could act as interpreters. An **interpreter** is a person who explains what is being said in another language.

Sacajawea soon earned the respect of the explorers. She helped them in many ways. In time of danger, she acted calmly and quickly.

When Lewis and Clark reached the Rocky Mountains, they looked for the Shoshone people. They found out that Sacajawea's brother was now the chief of the Shoshone. The Indians agreed to help. They provided horses and showed the way across the mountains.

Without Sacajawea's help, Lewis and Clark's famous expedition might not have succeeded.

on December 3, 1805, they reached the Pacific. William Clark carved his name and the date on a tree to mark the occasion.

The Lewis and Clark expedition ended in St. Louis 9 months later. It had covered 12,800 kilometers (8,000 miles) of unknown territory. During the whole trip, Lewis and Clark made notes of what they saw and learned. They collected samples of plants, rocks, and soil. They brought back much valuable information about the vast territory the nation had purchased. Lewis and Clark also led the way for the millions of settlers who would follow.

The Louisiana Territory was the biggest, but not the only,

border change. In 1818, the border between Canada and the United States was set westward to the Rocky Mountains. The United States and Britain also agreed to share the Oregon country. In 1819, the United States bought Florida from Spain.

More and more Americans moved into the new lands. Thus, they came into contact with the American Indian peoples who had lived there for thousands of years. There were fierce battles as the American Indians tried to keep the settlers away. These battles were usually followed by treaties. In these treaties, the American Indian peoples would agree to give up some of their lands. In return, the United States government promised to protect their rights to their remaining lands.

Cotton was becoming an important crop in the South. Thousands of settlers crossed the Appalachians looking for good cotton lands. Several American Indian groups lived in the Southeast, the area between the Appalachians and the Mississippi. Most of these American Indians were farmers. Some, like the Cherokees (CHERH uh keez), had become used to European ways. They owned cotton lands and cattle. The Cherokees had developed their own system of writing for their language. They also had schools and a newspaper. These things did not make any difference to the American settlers who wanted the Cherokees' lands. In 1830, Congress passed a law ordering all American Indians to move west of the Mississippi. Congress promised them that the lands of the Great Plains would be theirs forever.

So the American Indian peoples of the eastern United States were moved from their homes. Many were sent to dry, treeless places very different from the woodlands they knew. President Andrew Jackson sent the army to force out those who would not leave. The Cherokees were forced to make the long march west in the middle of winter. One-fourth of them died of hunger, cold, and sickness along the way. This march is known today as the "Trail of Tears."

It may be hard to understand how Americans treated the Indians as they did. After all, Americans said they stood for equality

The Cherokees had their own system for writing their language. This sign is in English and Cherokee.

Congress ordered all American Indians to move west of the Mississippi. Their march west is known today as the "Trail of Tears."

and justice for all. But ideals are goals to strive for. Each generation of Americans has moved closer to these ideals. In this book, you will see how this has happened. You will also see that Americans still have a long way to go. Each generation has its own set of goals to achieve.

REVIEW

READING FOR MAIN IDEAS

1. Why did Jefferson want to buy New Orleans for the United States?
2. What did Jefferson do when he heard that his envoys had offered to buy the whole Louisiana Territory?
3. What were Louis and Clark sent to do in the Louisiana Territory? What woman guided them?
4. How did Florida become part of the United States?
5. Why were American Indians in the southeastern United States ordered to move west of the Mississippi?

THINKING SKILLS

6. Do you think Jefferson's envoys were right to buy Louisiana without the President's approval? What would you have done if you were Jefferson?
7. Suppose the Louisiana Territory had not been bought. How would our history have been different?

STUDY SKILLS

The Cherokees were one of five southeastern Indian groups known as the Five Civilized Nations. Find out the names of the other four. Where do most of their descendants live today?

Lesson 4: Westward Ho!

FIND THE WORDS

missionary **wagon train** **emigrant**

When the Far West was a frontier, its deserts, mountains, and rivers were explored by hardy fur trappers. Trappers often lived and worked along with American Indians. Many trappers caught beavers by the streams and rivers of the Oregon country. They sold the fur from beavers and other animals to trading companies. These companies then sent the furs to the East and to Europe. Jim Beckwourth, a Black man, was a famous mountaineer and trapper. He also became a chief of the Crow tribe.

Jim Beckwourth was a mountaineer and trapper. He also became a chief of the Crow tribe.

Oregon Trail

In the 1820s and 1840s, many other people began using the trappers' trails. Most pioneers heading west followed routes that had been worked out by other travelers. The Oregon Trail was the route to the northwest. It was a difficult trail, 3,220 kilometers (2,000 miles) long. Along the way, pioneers left furniture, books, and whatever they felt they could do without. The trail was hard enough without the extra load.

The Oregon Trail started near the town of Independence on the Missouri River. It followed the Platte River across the plains and then crossed the Rockies. The last part went along the Snake and Columbia rivers. Find and trace the Oregon Trail on the map on page 203.

Farmers, traders, and missionaries followed this trail to Oregon. **Missionaries** are people who travel to a new area to spread religion. In the 1830s, a group of missionaries settled in the Willamette Valley of Oregon. Among

TRAILS WEST

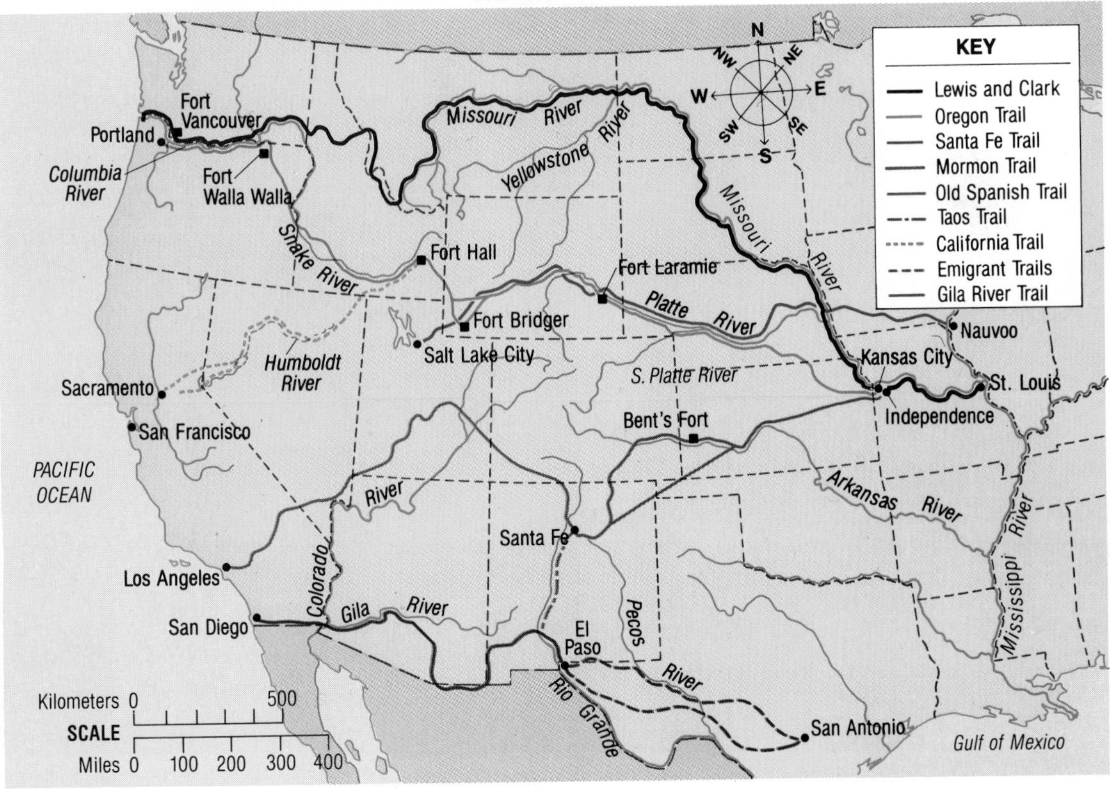

them were Narcissa Prentice Whitman and Elizabeth Hart Spaulding, the first women to cross the Rocky Mountains.

The new settlers sent back word of Oregon's rich soil, forests, and rivers. Between 1843 and 1845, more than 4,000 people made their way west along the Oregon Trail. By 1845, there were 5,000 Americans living in the Oregon country.

The pioneers traveled west in covered wagons pulled by oxen or mules. The wagons formed groups, or **wagon trains,** to travel across the country. Each wagon train had about 60 wagons. A wagon train was led by a captain called a wagonmaster.

Wagon trains usually left from Independence, Missouri. The trip west took about 6 months. There were many dangers. Sometimes, there were attacks by the American Indians of the Great Plains. But the everyday dangers were worse. The summer sun blazed down. The ovenlike heat dried out the wooden parts of the wagons. The spokes in the wheels would often break or fall out. Animals and people sometimes drowned crossing streams. Bad drinking water and spoiled food weakened the pioneers. Then, as

By the 1820s and 1840s, pioneers were using trappers' trails to go west. The Oregon Trail was one of these routes.

a result, deadly diseases could sweep through wagon trains.

By the middle 1840s, Americans in the Oregon country asked to join the United States. In 1846, Britain agreed to give up its claims to much of the area. Oregon became part of the United States because so many American pioneers had moved there.

California Trail

Some of the pioneers turned off the trail at the Snake River. They headed southwest on the California Trail. The California Trail followed the Humboldt River. It crossed the Nevada desert and the Sierra Nevada. Many pioneers settled in the Sacramento Valley. At the time, California was owned by Mexico. People who went there were called emigrants. An **emigrant** is a person who leaves one country or region to settle in another.

Most Americans knew little about California. In 1842–1844, the American government sent out groups under Captain John C. Frémont. They were to explore the West. Kit Carson and other scouts led the way. Frémont published reports on his trips. These reports made many Americans want to move to California.

Mormon Trail

The Mormons were one of the largest groups to travel west. The Church of Jesus Christ of Latter-day Saints had been founded in 1830 by Joseph Smith. He and his followers, called Mormons, tried to settle in several different places. Each time they were chased away. People did not understand the Mormons' beliefs. In Nauvoo, Illinois, trouble broke out between the Mormons and their neighbors. Joseph Smith was jailed and then killed by a mob.

The Mormons found a new leader in Brigham Young. He wanted to take them out into the wilderness away from other people. Then the Mormons could follow their own religious beliefs. In the winter of 1846–1847, the Mormons were forced to leave Nauvoo. After a stop in Iowa, they headed west along a route parallel to the Oregon Trail. Their route became known as the Mormon Trail.

In 1847, the Mormons settled at the Great Salt Lake, in what is now Utah. They called their new home in the desert, Deseret. Through hard work, the Mormons turned this desert area into a rich and productive land.

REVIEW

VOCABULARY MASTERY

1. A(n) ___ is someone who leaves one nation to settle in another.
   missionary emigrant envoy
2. A(n) ___ is a person who travels to a new area to spread religion.
   missionary emigrant envoy

READING FOR MAIN IDEAS

3. What did trappers like Jim Beckwourth do in the West?
4. Which trail did pioneers take to the northwest? To the southwest?
5. How did the pioneers going to the West travel?
6. How did the United States acquire the Oregon country?
7. Why were settlers going to California called emigrants?
8. Why did Brigham Young lead the Mormons off into the wilderness?

WRITING SKILLS

Pretend you are a pioneer on the Oregon Trail. Write a diary entry describing one day of your journey.

STUDY SKILLS

Was your state part of the Louisiana Purchase or of the Oregon country? If not, how did it become part of the United States? Use an encyclopedia to find out.

Lesson 5: The Lone Star State

FIND THE WORDS

land grant **empresario**

Southeast of the Great Salt Lake, Americans were settling other Mexican lands. Much of this area is now called the American Southwest. Look at the map on page 203. Draw an imaginary line from San Antonio, Texas, through Santa Fe, New Mexico, to San Francisco, California. South of this line, Spanish-speaking missionaries, soldiers, ranchers, and farmers had settled.

Stephen F. Austin brought many settlers to Texas.

In 1821, the people of Mexico won their independence from Spain. They welcomed American trade and settlement in their northern lands. The Mexican government gave an American,

In 1821, after winning independence from Spain, Mexico welcomed American settlement in its northern lands. In this painting, a group of pioneers stops to set up camp along the way.

The Texans won their independence from Mexico in the Battle of San Jacinto. In this painting, Sam Houston accepts the surrender of Santa Anna.

Stephen F. Austin, a large **land grant,** or free land. It was to be used for settling 300 families in Mexico. Austin and other **empresarios,** or land agents, brought many Americans to Texas. The Santa Fe Trail became an important trade route. Long trains of pack mules carried goods between Independence, Missouri, and Santa Fe. By 1830, 20,000 Americans lived in Texas.

Some of the Americans became ranchers. They copied the houses and ways of the Mexican ranchers. They rounded up the wild cattle and horses that roamed the prairies. Others became owners of large cotton plantations.

By 1834, the Americans outnumbered the Mexicans in Texas. They felt they could no longer live under Mexican laws. On March 2, 1836, the Texans declared their independence. But the Mexicans were not ready to give up their northern region. Santa Anna, the Mexican leader, marched into Texas with a large army. He surrounded the Alamo, a former mission in San Antonio. Inside the Alamo were 187 Americans. They would not surrender. The Mexicans stormed the walls of the mission and killed all the Americans. Among those who died were Davy Crockett, a famous frontiersman from Tennessee, and Jim Bowie, who invented the Bowie knife. The battle cry of the Texans became famous. It was: "Remember the Alamo!"

A small army of Texans, led by Sam Houston, took up the fight. Their chance came a month later at San Jacinto (SAN hah SIN toh). With cries of "Remember the Alamo," the Texans surprised and defeated part of Santa Anna's army. Santa Anna was captured. Houston forced him to sign a treaty giving Texas its independence.

For 9 years, Texas was an independent nation, the Republic of Texas. It was called the Lone Star Republic because there was only one star on its flag. Texas had its own constitution and president. Then, in 1845, Texas joined the United States as the 28th state in the Union.

The border between Texas and Mexico had not been settled, however. In 1846, Mexican and American soldiers shot at each other in the area under dispute. At that time, many Americans were interested in gaining California and other lands in the Southwest. In 1846, the United States declared war on Mexico.

The war with Mexico lasted 2 years. After many battles, American soldiers captured Mexico City. In 1848, Mexico and the United States signed the Treaty of Guadalupe Hidalgo. The Rio Grande became the border between Texas and Mexico. All of what is now California, Nevada, and Utah became part of the United States. Most of Arizona and parts of New Mexico, Colorado, and Wyoming were also added. Today, 48 of the 50 states border each other. This main part of the United States was almost complete in 1848. The last piece of it was added in 1853 with the Gadsden Purchase from Mexico. The United States wanted this area of southern Arizona and New Mexico to build a railroad.

REVIEW

READING FOR MAIN IDEAS

1. What did Stephen Austin do to attract settlers to Texas?
2. When and why did Texans declare their independence from Mexico?
3. What does the battle cry "Remember the Alamo!" mean?
4. How did Sam Houston help Texas gain its independence?
5. How did the United States gain the area south of Oregon and west of Texas?

THINKING SKILLS

How did the defeat at the Alamo help the Texans win the war?

Lesson 6: The California Gold Rush

FIND THE WORDS

prospector **forty-niner**

"It was a clear, cold morning in January. I shall never forget that morning. As I was taking my usual walk, my eye was caught by a glimpse of something shining in the bottom of a ditch. There was about a foot of running water there. I reached my hand down and picked it up. It made my heart thump, for I felt certain it was gold. The piece was about half the size and the shape of a pea. Then I saw another piece in the water. . . ."

The exact date was January 24, 1848. The place was a ditch near the Sacramento River in California. James Marshall, a Scottish carpenter, had made a very exciting discovery.

News of the gold spread quickly to all parts of the United States and the world. A new wave of pioneers rushed to the Far West. They became **prospectors,** people hunting for gold.

Newspapers in the East were filled with stories about the rich gold deposits in California. Guidebooks told people what to take. They listed these supplies: a shotgun, horseshoes, pots, a

A new wave of pioneers rushed to California to look for gold. These gold seekers were called *prospectors*. Many thousands of hopeful people traveled to California in search of instant riches. Few of them found what they sought, and many returned home disappointed. Some, however, stayed in California to become farmers or laborers or to start businesses.

San Francisco became an important center of trade almost overnight. Thousands of people came to the town during the gold rush. These people needed food, shelter, and supplies. Later, they needed homes, banks, churches, and schools.

water barrel, a lantern, bars of lye soap, a rubber knapsack, a harmonica, a pick, and a pan.

Farmers left their fields. Ships lay deserted in San Francisco Bay as sailors ran into the hills to hunt for gold. Other people came overland. They traveled from the East, first by railroad and then by steamboat. They crossed the Great Plains in wagons and on mules. Others, including some foreigners, came by sea.

In 1849, more than 80,000 hopeful newcomers arrived in California. They were called the **forty-niners.** They crowded into mining camps with names like Red Dog, Poker Flat, and Grub Gulch.

Life for the forty-niners was very different from the stories they had heard. A Philadelphia schoolteacher described it:

"We made $3.00 each today. This life has affected my health. Our diet consists of hard tack (a hard biscuit made of flour and water), flour we eat half cooked, and salt pork. Sometimes, we have some salmon which we buy from the Indians. Vegetables are not to be found. Our feet are wet all day while a hot sun shines down upon our heads. The very air parches the skin like the hot air of an oven.

"After our day of labor, we lie down in our clothes. We rob our feet of their boots to make a pillow out of them. Near morning, there is always a change in the temperature, and several blankets become necessary. The feet and hands of a newcomer become blistered and lame. Besides all these causes of sickness, the worries of so many men who leave their families to come to this land of gold, all work to the same result.

"We are quickly beginning to realize that our chances of making a fortune are about the same as those of drawing a prize in a lottery."

By the middle of the 1850s, many forty-niners had left. Most left poor. Some traded a bag of gold dust for a ticket home by ship. Some stayed to work as laborers for big mining companies. These businesses had heavy equipment for mining gold. Some stayed to farm the rich valleys of the area. Others stayed to work in the towns that had sprung up all over California.

California was a land of natural beauty and resources. It bordered the Pacific Ocean. There were miles of fertile land for farming. There were huge forests. These resources provided many people with the means to make a living.

San Francisco had become an important center of trade almost overnight. Thousands of people had come to the town during the gold rush. These people needed food, shelter, and supplies. More and more ships arrived with goods. The newcomers needed lawyers to arrange the sale of property. They needed banks. Soon, homes, churches, and schools were being built.

The gold rush was over. But it had opened up yet another part of the American West.

REVIEW

READING FOR MAIN IDEAS

1. In what year was gold discovered in California?
2. How did the prospectors come to California? What were they called?
3. What was life like in the gold fields?
4. Where did all the gold seekers go after the gold rush?
5. How was mining done after the gold rush?
6. What town did the gold rush make important?

THINKING SKILLS

Who do you think really became rich from the gold rush?

Lesson 7: Mexican-Americans in the West

FIND THE WORDS

mestizo **citizen**
Hispanic **Communism**

There were about 80,000 Mexican-Americans living in California and the Southwest in the 1850s. These Spanish-speaking people were the pioneers of what had been the frontier of northern Mexico. They founded and settled many of the western cities that have Spanish names today. Most of these people were **mestizos** (mess TEE zohz). These are people with Indian, Spanish, and sometimes Black ancestors.

The 1848 treaty with Mexico promised the Mexican-Americans "all the rights of citizens of the United States." A **citizen** is a person who is a member of a particular nation.

The Mexican-Americans were soon outnumbered in their own land. Before the gold rush, most of the people in California were Spanish-speaking. By 1850, there were 380,000 people in California. Now only about 15 out of every 100 were Spanish-speaking. The same thing happened in Texas and Arizona. As more and more English-speaking people came, the Mexican-Americans became a small part of the population. This meant the Mexican-Americans had less power. It was harder for them to protect their rights and their property. Spanish-speaking Americans were not

Fascinating Facts

Who was our 12th President? Any list will show you that Zachary Taylor was. But Davis Rice Atchison could also claim to have been our 12th President. Here is how.

James K. Polk was our 11th President. His term ended at midnight on Saturday, March 3, 1849. But, for religious reasons, Zachary Taylor did not want to be sworn in on a Sunday. So the country could have been without a President or Vice President for one day, Sunday, March 4, 1849.

But the law at the time filled the office. The law said that when the offices of President and Vice President are empty, the president pro tempore (for the time being) of the Senate becomes President. Atchison was president pro tempore of the Senate at that time. So Davis Rice Atchison was President of the United States for a single day.

San Antonio was an important city when Texas became a state in 1845.

treated as well as the English-speaking people in many ways.

Throughout these years, the Mexican-Americans continued to press for their rights. A few were elected to positions in government. Many joined organizations to discuss problems they shared as Mexican-Americans. Spanish-language newspapers encouraged people to vote. They told them to have pride in their language and to learn English, as well.

After 1910, there were political problems in Mexico and few jobs. Many jobs were open in the United States at that time. Many more Mexicans now moved into the part of the United States near Mexico. This group reminded the older Mexican-Americans of their ties with Mexico.

Today, there are about 15 million people of Spanish background in the United States. That is about 6 out of every 100 people in the nation. People of Spanish background, language, and culture are called **Hispanics.**

Hispanic-Americans share the Spanish language. They also share other parts of Spanish culture. But they are not all the same, just as other Americans are not all alike. Most of the Hispanic-Americans have come from countries settled by Spain more than 400 years ago.

State	Number of Hispanic people in 1980
CALIFORNIA	4,500,000
TEXAS	3,000,000
NEW YORK	1,700,000
FLORIDA	900,000
ILLINOIS	600,000
NEW JERSEY	500,000
NEW MEXICO	500,000
ARIZONA	400,000
COLORADO	300,000
MICHIGAN	200,000

Mexican-Americans make up the largest Hispanic group in the United States today. Puerto Rican–Americans are the second-largest Hispanic group. Puerto Rico (PWEHR toh REE koh) is on islands southeast of Florida. It was taken by the United States from Spain during the Spanish-American War of 1898. Puerto Rico is not a state, but all Puerto Ricans are citizens of the United States. Many Puerto Ricans have migrated to mainland North America. Many now live in New York City.

Many Cubans came to the United States in the 1960s and afterward. They left Cuba after the Cuban government became Communist in 1959. **Communism** is a system under which the government owns and runs all businesses. Many Cubans have settled in Florida. Most of them have become American citizens.

This chart shows where many Hispanic-Americans live. Many live far from Mexico.

REVIEW

VOCABULARY MASTERY

1. Most Mexican-Americans in the 1850s were ____.
   Spaniards mestizos Texans
2. A ____ is a person who is a member of a particular nation.
   citizen mestizo foreigner
3. People of Spanish background are called ____.
   citizens foreigners Hispanics

READING FOR MAIN IDEAS

4. How did Mexican-Americans become outnumbered in the West?
5. What is the largest Hispanic group in the United States?
6. What state has many Cubans?

RESEARCH SKILLS

Does your state have many Hispanic-Americans? If so, find out to what group or groups they belong.

CHAPTER REVIEW

VOCABULARY MASTERY

Use the words below to complete the chapter summary. Use each only once.

blazed	missionaries
emigrants	pass
frontier	pioneers
land grant	Territory
Land speculators	wagon train

In the 1770s, the Appalachian Mountains formed the western __1__. A group of woodcutters __2__ a trail through a __3__ in the Appalachians called the Cumberland Gap. The first settlers who moved west are known as __4__. Later, the United States government set up an area known as the Northwest __5__. __6__ bought land in this area so they could sell it later for profit.

In the 1820s and 1840s, many pioneers traveled west by __7__. These included farmers, traders, and __8__. People who settled in California when it was still part of Mexico were called __9__. The Mexican government gave Stephen F. Austin a __10__ in Texas.

READING FOR MAIN IDEAS

1. What was the extent of the Louisiana Purchase?
2. What was the purpose of the Lewis and Clark expedition?
3. Name three of the trails used by pioneers heading west.
4. What did the United States get in the Treaty of Guadalupe Hidalgo?
5. How did San Francisco become an important center of trade?

THINKING SKILLS

6. What did "the West" mean in 1607? In 1783? In 1803? In 1848?

SKILLS APPLICATION

MAP SKILLS

Look at the map on page 192.

7. In what town did the trails to the West begin?
8. Which trail extends west from the Santa Fe Trail?
9. What clues tell you the trails were made going west and not east?
10. When did the last part of the West become part of the United States?

WRITING AND DRAWING SKILLS

11. Pretend you are living during the westward movement. Prepare an advertisement urging people to move to the new western lands. Remember, an advertisement must be brief and to the point. Include artwork if you choose.
12. German immigrants introduced Conestoga (KON uh STOH guh) wagons to this country. Many of these wagons were used during the westward movement. Find a picture of one in an encyclopedia or other source. Make a drawing of it to share with the class.

SEQUENCE SKILLS

Put the events below in the proper sequence, or order. Rewrite them on a sheet of paper and add the year for each event.

a. Gold is discovered in California.
b. Lewis and Clark begin to search for the Pacific Ocean.
c. Daniel Boone clears "Wilderness Road."
d. Britain gives up its claim to much of the Oregon country.
e. Captain Fremont and Kit Carson lead explorers into California.

UNIT REVIEW

VOCABULARY MASTERY

Choose one of the lists of words below. Then write a paragraph or a page using all the words from that list. You may use the words in the singular or plural. On a separate page, write the words and define them.

appoint	emigrant
bill	empresario
Congress	frontier
Constitution	interpreter
government	land grant
House of Representatives	missionary
President	pioneer
Senate	territory
Supreme Court	wagon train

READING FOR MAIN IDEAS

1. What two events that occurred in Boston helped lead to the American Revolution?
2. What was the first major battle of the American Revolution?
3. How did the members of the Constitutional Convention finally come to agreement?
4. How can the Constitution be changed?
5. Why does each branch of the federal government have some power to limit the other two?
6. Why has the meaning of "the West" changed since the discovery of America?
7. Why were land speculators interested in the West?
8. How did many Americans travel to Oregon?
9. Why was California settled as quickly as it was?
10. Name the natural borders of the Old Northwest.

USE YOUR MAPS

11. Look at the map of the Revolutionary War on page 149. In what state is Bunker Hill? Saratoga?
12. List the original 13 states.
13. Look at the map on page 191. Name five important western trails.
14. Has the shape of Florida changed since 1819?
15. Has the shape of Texas changed since 1845?

THINKING SKILLS

16. What do you think the colonists hoped to gain by boycotting British goods?
17. What part of British America remained loyal to Britain after 1776?
18. George Washington believed that it was more important to keep on fighting than to win particular battles. Do you think he was right or wrong? Why, or why not?
19. Under the Articles of Confederation, each state had one vote in Congress. Discuss what that meant.
20. Do any parts of the Bill of Rights seem less important today?
21. Why is it important that justices of the Supreme Court can serve as long as they live?
22. What did Jefferson mean when he said "We are all Republicans, we are all Federalists"?
23. How did the War of 1812 change the nation?
24. Why do you think people moved to the frontier even though life was so hard there?
25. Why do you think the Mormons chose to settle in the wilderness near the Great Salt Lake?

SKILL DEVELOPMENT

WESTWARD GROWTH OF THE UNITED STATES

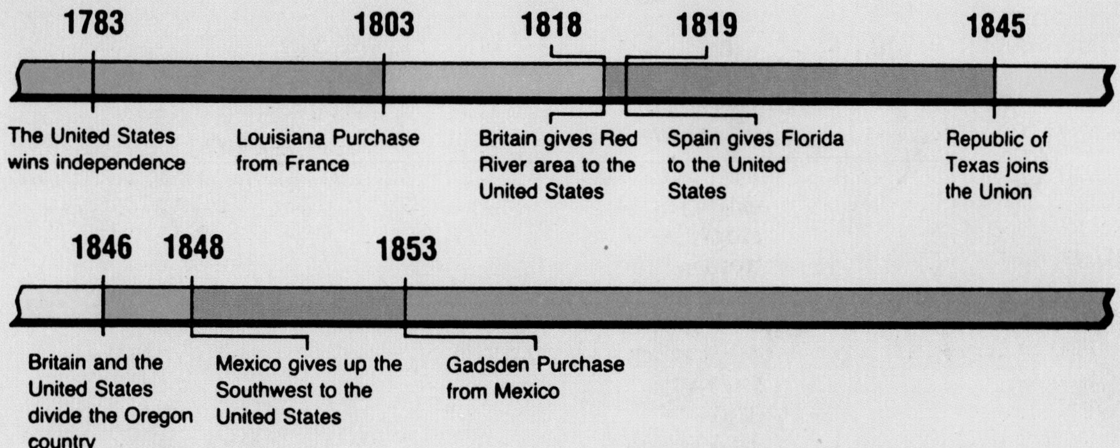

TIME LINE SKILLS

What is a *time line*? Look it up in the Glossary. Write the definition on a sheet of paper. Then, answer these questions about the time line above.

1. What does this time line show?
2. When did Texas join the Union?
3. Did Texas join before or after Mexico gave up the Southwest?
4. How many years after the Louisiana Purchase did Spain give up Florida?
5. How many years does this time line include?

MAP AND CHART SKILLS

6. Draw a map that shows the westward expansion of the United States. Label each area with its name and the date it was added. Include the United States (1783), Louisiana Purchase (1803), British Cession (1818), Florida (1819), Texas (1845), Oregon Territory (1846), Mexican Cession (1848), and Gadsden Purchase (1853).
7. Make a chart with the title "Westward Expansion of the United States." Set it up like this:

Section	Date	How Added

In the first column, list each of the eight parts added to the United States (see question 6). Add the dates under the second column. Then complete the third column.

8. 1789 — 1797 — 1801 — 1809 — 1817

This time line lists some important dates concerning leaders in the United States. What happened in each of these years? Give this time line a title.

RESEARCH AND WRITING SKILLS

Choose one of the areas listed in question 6. Search in an encyclopedia or other source book. Find out how and why the area was acquired. Include other information of interest to you. Prepare a brief report. List your sources.

THE UNITED STATES CHANGES

UNIT 4

CHAPTER 7 DIVIDED STATES

Lesson 1: Black Slavery in the United States

FIND THE WORD

abolitionist

In the years after 1619, the first Blacks were brought to the Southern colonies as indentured servants. They had to work for about 7 years to earn their freedom. But as time passed, more and more Blacks were brought to the colonies as slaves.

Slaves could not earn their freedom by their work. They could be set free only by their master, the person who owned them. Slaves usually had to work their whole lives without any pay. Only a very few slaves were allowed to buy their freedom. They earned

Slaves often had to use their free time to do their own chores. Families had little chance to rest or to be together. Times of relaxation were rare.

the money from work their masters let them do for other people.

Most of the Blacks sold in the colonies were captured in Africa. After their capture, they were packed into the holds of ships. A hold is the part of a ship below decks where goods are stored. There, the Africans were crowded very close together. On the voyage, many became sick and died. Others jumped overboard. They

Blacks were sold at auction to the buyer who offered the highest price. Members of Black families were often separated at auctions. They were sold as slaves to different masters. Husbands and wives were parted. Children were sold away from their parents. Blacks had to have great courage, character, and strength of spirit to endure this and survive.

If slaves tried to escape, they were hunted down. If caught, they could be punished harshly or even killed. Some people made a living hunting down runaway slaves. They collected the reward money offered by the slave owners. This old picture shows runaway slaves going down a road in a large group. If slaves had really tried to escape this way, they would have been easily caught. They traveled at night. They hid or disguised themselves. They had to plan very carefully and to stay alert.

drowned in the sea rather than be slaves. However, most of them were chained down and could not escape.

In most parts of the United States in the early 1800s, Blacks had no rights at all. They did not have the right to vote. It was against the law for them to go to school with Whites. In some states, it was even against the law for them to learn to read and write. Slaves did not have the right to come and go as they pleased. To leave their master's land, they had to have a pass. This was a paper from their master giving written permission. Slaves were often separated from their families when they were sold. They had to work very long hours. If they did not do as they were told, they could be whipped. If they tried to escape, they were hunted down. If caught, they were punished harshly or even killed.

Until about 1800, there were slaves in almost every state in the United States. But slaves were not a big part of the Northern way of life. Northern factories hired workers. They did not use slaves. However, many Northern factories paid low wages. Often young children worked long hours. By 1850, all Northern states had made slavery illegal.

On the Southern plantations, however, most of the field workers were slaves. One out of every four families owned slaves. But out of the 5 million Southern Whites, only about 10,000 families owned most of the slaves. These people often had large plantations. They were very rich.

People to Remember

Frederick Douglass

Frederick Douglass became one of the most powerful abolitionist speakers of his time. Douglass had been born a slave. His master's wife taught him to read and write when he was a child. The lessons stopped when the master found out. Teaching a slave to read and write was against the law. After that, Douglass knew that he had to escape. "I will run away," he wrote. "I will not stand it. I would rather be killed running than die as a slave."

Frederick Douglass did manage to escape. He borrowed the clothes and papers of a free Black sailor. He got safely to the North in 1838.

At first, he lived quietly. Runaway slaves could be punished harshly and sent back to their old masters. Soon, however, Douglass joined the American Anti-Slavery Society. He spoke at their meetings. Douglass was an excellent speaker. In 1847, he set up his own newspaper, *The North Star.* During the Civil War, he urged Blacks to join the Union Army. Many did. After the Civil War, Douglass never stopped fighting. He continued to try to win equal rights for his people. He also fought for the rights of all people in the United States. In 1895, on the day he died, he spoke for women's right to vote.

The few Black people in the United States who were free, educated, and successful were very important. Some of them were among the first to attack slavery. In 1827, the first Black newspaper was set up. It was started by the Reverend Samuel E. Cornish and John Russwurm. They called the paper *Freedom's Journal.* David Walker was a free Black who lived in Boston. He wrote a small book known as *Walker's Appeal.* In it, he urged slaves to run away. Walker said to White Americans: "We must and shall be free, I say, in spite of you."

Several free Blacks became wealthy during the 1700s and 1800s. Paul Cuffe of Massachusetts owned a fleet of ships and much land in New England. James Forten of Philadelphia was a sail manufacturer with 50 employees. A free Black owned one of the largest ranches in Texas.

Black inventors were also important. Norbert Rillieux invented a new way of making sugar in the 1840s. Lewis Temple invented a new harpoon, or spear, for whaling.

In the 1840s, several Blacks returned to the United States from Europe with degrees in medicine. They set up medical practices and became well known. James McCune Smith was one such doctor.

People to Remember

Sojourner Truth

Sojourner Truth was a very important speaker against slavery. She also fought for women's rights. She often compared the situation of slaves to the situation of women. She saw many similarities, and she called attention to them.

Like Frederick Douglass, Sojourner Truth had been born a slave. Unlike him, she lived in New York, and in 1827, that state passed a law freeing slaves. Her name in slavery had been Isabella Baumfree. She changed it to Sojourner Truth. A *sojourner* is someone who stays in a place only for a short time. Sojourner Truth was going to travel around the nation spreading "the truth."

At one women's rights meeting, men in the audience were shouting. They were making fun of the women who were speaking. At first, Sojourner Truth sat quietly. One male speaker after another got up and spoke against women's rights. It was becoming more and more difficult to continue the meeting. Then, Sojourner Truth stood up. She attacked the male speakers with powerful words. Here is part of what she said:

"That man over there says that women need to be helped into carriages, and lifted over ditches, and to have the best place everywhere. Nobody ever helps me into carriages, or over mud puddles, or gives me any best place!"

She raised herself to her full height of 6 feet. She spoke in a voice like rolling thunder:

"And ain't I a woman? Look at me, look at my arm! I have ploughed, and planted, and gathered into barns, and no man could head me! And ain't I a woman? I could work as much and eat as much as a man—when I could get it—and bear the lash as well! And ain't I a woman? I have borne 13 children, and seen most of them sold off to slavery. When I cried with my mother's grief, none but Jesus heard me. And ain't I a woman?"

During the Civil War, Sojourner Truth worked hard for the Union side. She raised money for gifts to make life easier for the soldiers. Sometimes she went to the camps to deliver the gifts and to encourage the soldiers.

Other Black women did important work during and after the war. Frances Ellen Watkins Harper was an abolitionist and poet. She wrote one of the earliest novels by a Black American woman. The sculptor Edmonia Lewis was the child of a Chippewa mother and a free Black father. She studied art in Rome after the war. Madam Sissieretta Jones was a coloratura soprano. She sang in Europe and South America.

Here is a description of slavery on a Virginia plantation in 1778. It was written by a British soldier.

"The slaves are called up at daybreak. They barely have time to swallow a mouthful of hominy or hoe cake. They immediately go out to the fields, where they do hard labor without stopping until noon. Then they get barely an hour to eat hominy and salt pork. If their master is very kind, he may give them a little milk or rusty bacon twice a week. Or he may give his slaves an acre of ground, where they can grow their own food on Saturday afternoons. After their noon dinner, the slaves return to work in the fields until dark.

"At dark, their work is still not over. They must then strip tobacco or husk corn until late evening. They eat their last meager meal and then lie down to rest. They sleep on benches or on the ground in crowded shacks.

"These poor creatures must submit to all manner of insult and injury without resisting. If they dare to defend themselves, the law directs the Negro's arm to be cut off."

The only power the Blacks had came from their strength as individuals. To endure slavery, they had to be strong in mind and spirit. Some of them fought back actively and suffered for it.

But even in the early 1800s, there were many **abolitionists** (AB uh LISH un ists). These were people who wanted to abolish, or do away with, slavery. Some were Southerners. William Lloyd Garrison and the Grimké sisters were Northerners. Garrison wrote against slavery in his Boston newspaper, *The Liberator,* in the 1830s. In 1838, Angelina Grimké spoke to the legislature of Massachusetts about equal rights for Blacks and women. The struggle for freedom had begun.

REVIEW

READING FOR MAIN IDEAS

1. What was the position of the first Blacks brought over to the American colonies?
2. In what way could slaves obtain their freedom?
3. Why were most slaves unable to read and write?
4. According to a description of slavery written in 1778, what was life like for slaves?
5. Who were the abolitionists?

RESEARCH SKILLS

Crops are not grown in the winter. Find out what slaves did in the winter.

Lesson 2: Slave or Free

FIND THE WORDS

tariff fiber cotton gin secession

During the first half of the 1800s, the North and the South grew in different ways. In the North, cities became centers of wealth and manufacturing. There were many workers with different skills. In the South, there was little manufacturing. Most of the people were farmers. The wealth of the South came largely from plantation crops. These crops included tobacco, cotton, rice, and sugar cane. Slaves did much of the work on the plantations.

Meanwhile, the West was growing fast. Western farmers grew grain and corn and raised cattle and hogs. New businesses came to Western cities, such as Chicago and Cincinnati. These cities became centers where Western products were sold and shipped to the East. Many of the Western territories became new states.

As these changes took place, one question became more and more important. Who would control the federal government in Washington? Would Congress make laws mainly for the benefit of the North, with its banks, factories, and cities? Or would it make laws in favor of the South, with its plantations, slaves, and smaller population? New states were joining the Union. It became very important to know whether these new states would vote with the North or with the South in Congress.

The routes that escaped slaves used to travel north were called the Underground Railroad. In this picture, a group of runaway slaves arrive at one of the "stations." These were safe hiding places along the routes to freedom.

People to Remember

Harriet Tubman

Harriet Tubman was born a slave on a farm in Maryland. All her life, she had one great wish. She wanted to be free.

One day, Harriet Tubman ran away. Like many runaway slaves, she escaped on the Underground Railroad. This was a system of secret routes to the North with hiding places along the way. The slaves stayed at safe "stations" during the day. At night, they traveled with a "conductor" to the next "station."

After a dangerous journey, Harriet Tubman reached Pennsylvania. This was a free state. But she knew she had to go back. She had to help other slaves escape. So Harriet Tubman joined the Underground Railroad as a conductor.

Harriet Tubman returned to the South many times. She may have led as many as 300 slaves to freedom. Slave owners offered a $40,000 reward for her capture. But Harriet Tubman was never caught. She was a person of courage and determination. She said: "I was the conductor of the Underground Railroad for 8 years. I never ran my train off the track, and I never lost a passenger."

Look at the bar graph on page 228. It shows some of the big differences between the North and the South in 1860.

The map on page 229 shows which states were "free" and which were "slave." Free states did not allow slavery. Slave states did.

The map also shows the territories. The territories could be either slave or free. It depended on what the people living there wanted. New territories that joined the Union as free states voted with the North. Those that joined as slave states voted with the South. The section that had the most votes in Congress would control the federal government. So the North and the South were divided over keeping a balance of free states and slave states.

There was another big problem dividing the North and the South. It was the **tariff,** or tax, placed on goods brought into the

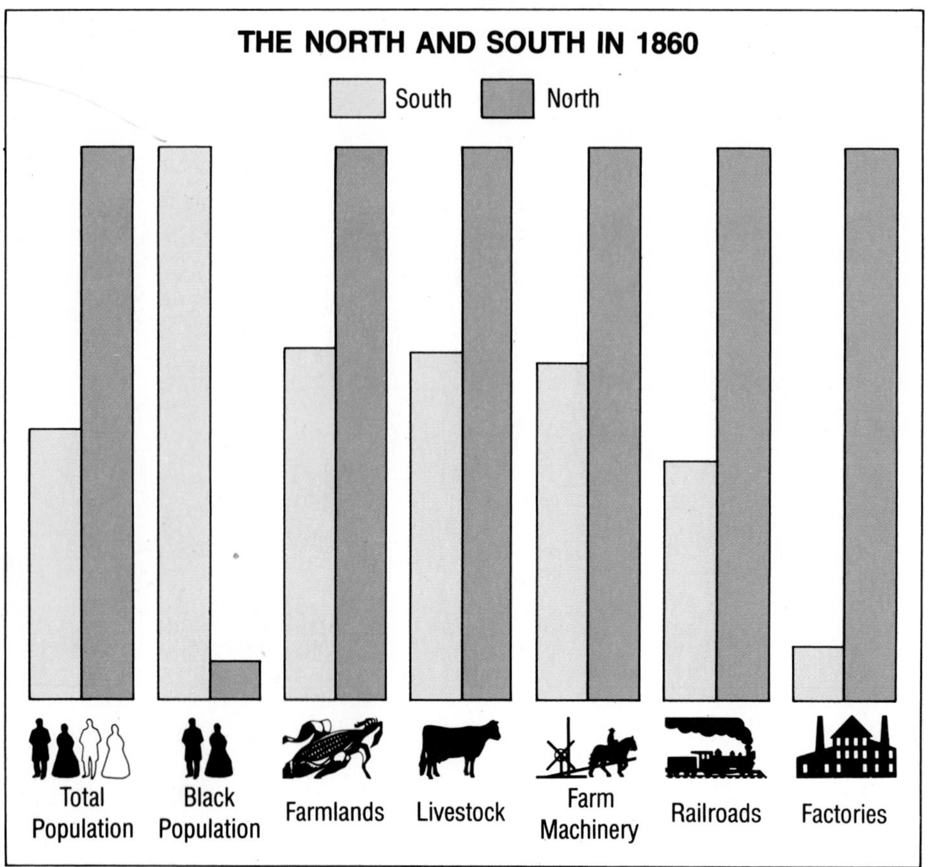

United States from Europe. Goods made in European factories were usually cheaper than those made in Northern factories. Northern factory owners did not want to have to compete with these cheaper European goods. The North wanted Congress to set a high tariff.

The South did not want a high tariff. Southerners did not manufacture many goods. Thus, they had to buy manufactured goods from outside the South. A high tariff just made these manufactured goods more expensive. It did not help the South. Also, the Europeans did not only sell manufactured goods. They also bought Southern cotton, tobacco, and other crops. They paid higher prices for these things than the Northerners did. This trade with Europe was the main source of wealth in the South. A high American tariff tended to hurt such trade. Thus, it tended to hurt the South. The tariff was another major cause of conflict between the North and the South.

SLAVE AND FREE STATES IN 1861

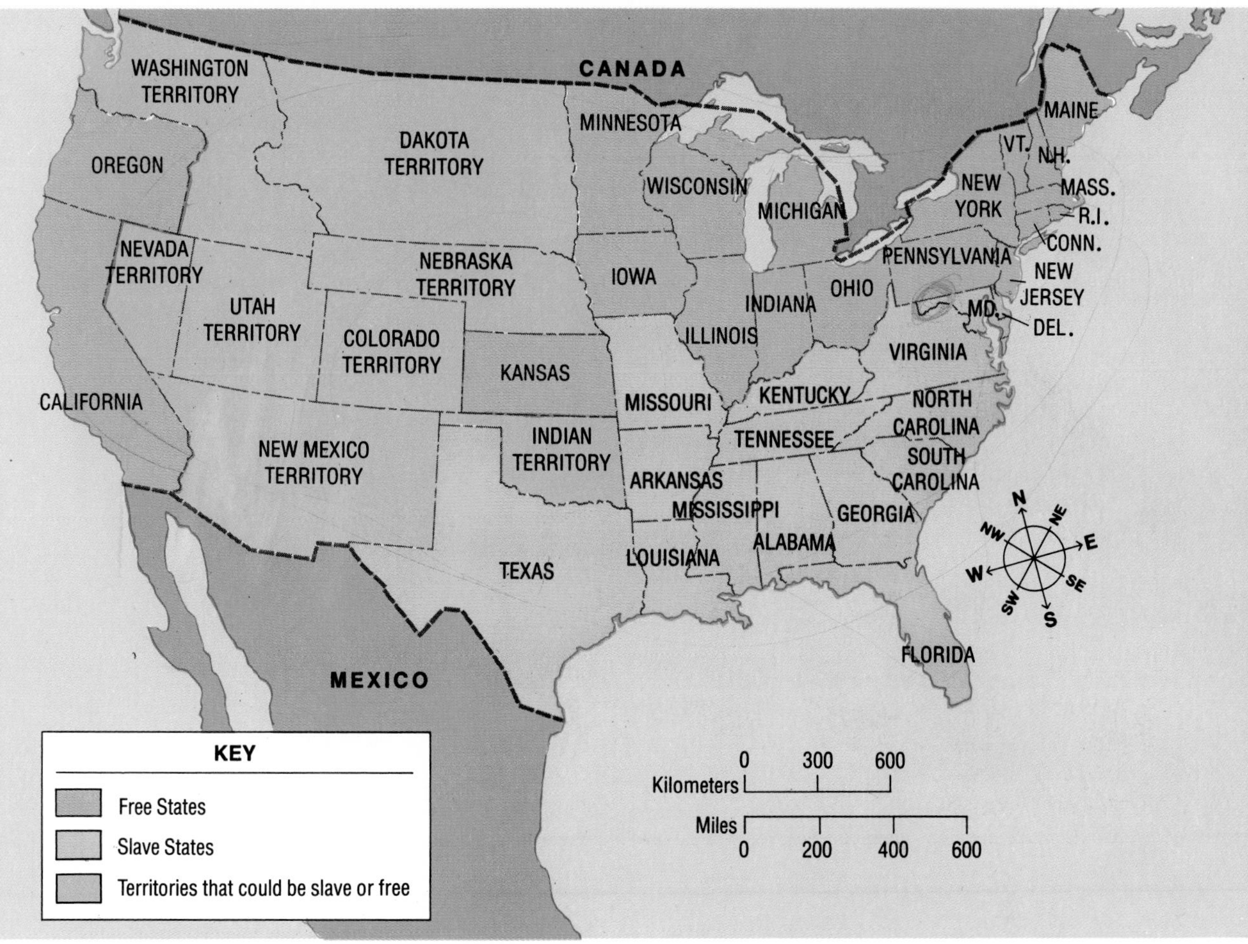

Slavery, however, was the main thing dividing the North and the South. In the late 1700s, some cotton was grown in the South. But the seeds had to be picked from the cotton **fiber,** or threads, by hand. This could not be done quickly enough for planters to make a real profit. At that time, slavery was becoming less important to the Southern economy. Then, in 1793, Eli Whitney invented the **cotton gin.** This new machine cleaned the seeds from the cotton fibers 10 times faster than a human worker could. Cotton then became a great source of wealth. The number of slaves in the South increased. There were fewer than 1 million slaves in 1800. But there were more than 3 million by 1850. Slaves were needed to raise the cotton. Their work was also important in growing tobacco and rice.

But in the North and elsewhere,

Cotton grows around the seeds of the cotton plant to protect them. When cotton is picked, two-thirds of its weight is in seeds. The seeds must be removed before the cotton can be used. It takes a long time to remove them by hand. This is because the fibers are twisted around the seeds. A cotton gin cleans the seeds from the cotton much more quickly. A great many slaves were used in the South to pick the cotton. Now mechanical pickers are used. Here slaves are using a cotton gin.

in the world, feelings about slavery had changed. Slavery was now looked upon as wrong. It was seen as an injustice to those who were slaves. Britain freed the slaves in its colonies in 1833. In the United States, the movement to abolish slavery became very strong in the North. But the stronger the abolitionist movement grew, the more strongly Southerners defended slavery.

Many important citizens and lawmakers in the North spoke out against slavery. William Lloyd Garrison founded a newspaper, *The Liberator,* in Boston. In it, he wrote articles attacking Congress for being so slow to take action against slavery. In 1852, Harriet

The stronger the abolitionist movement became, the more White Southerners defended slavery. In this picture, an 1860 abolitionist meeting is broken up.

TIME LINE: 1860–1877

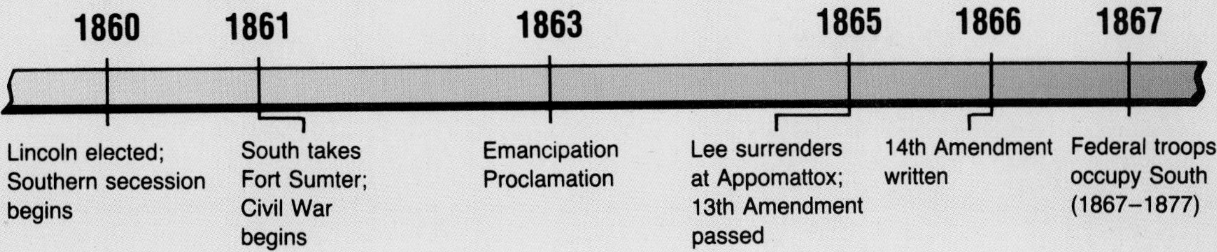

Beecher Stowe wrote a book about slavery in the South. It was called *Uncle Tom's Cabin.* It made many Northerners aware of the terrible things that slaves suffered.

With the Presidential election of 1860, the conflict between the North and the South grew worse. Abraham Lincoln, a member of Congress from Illinois, was nominated for President by the Republican Party. The Republicans were against slavery. The Democrats of the South were for it. Because the Democrats were divided, it was almost certain that the Republicans would win.

Many Southerners began to talk about **secession** (si SESH un). This meant they wanted to secede, or withdraw, from the United States. These Southerners said that the United States was created when the states agreed to form a new nation. And just as they could join the Union, they could leave it.

On December 20, 1860, after Lincoln was elected President, South Carolina seceded. Within 4 months, six other states seceded. They were Georgia, Florida, Alabama, Mississippi, Texas, and Louisiana. Later, Virginia, Arkansas, North Carolina, and Tennessee joined them. These states formed a new nation called the Confederate States of America. They elected Jefferson Davis president of the Confederacy.

Lincoln took office in March 1861. In his first speech, he said he would not break the laws that protected slavery. But he also said

Abraham Lincoln was elected President of the United States in 1860.

Jefferson Davis was President of the Confederate States of America.

The Confederates captured Fort Sumter and raised their flag.

that he did not think the Confederate States could leave the Union. He said that the Confederacy had no legal right to destroy the government. The President, he said, had a duty to "preserve, protect, and defend" the government.

Lincoln said that he would keep control of all federal property in the South, especially forts. The Confederacy wanted Union soldiers to leave the forts. In Charleston, South Carolina, there was a federal fort called Fort Sumter. The Confederacy ordered the soldiers there to leave. The commander of the fort refused. The Confederates then fired cannons at the fort on April 12, 1861. The Civil War had begun. Southerners call this the War between the States.

REVIEW

VOCABULARY MASTERY

1. The ___ cleaned the seeds from cotton faster than workers could.
   fiber   cotton gin   tariff
2. A ___ is a tax on goods brought in from other nations.
   fiber   secession   tariff

READING FOR MAIN IDEAS

3. List three issues that divided the North and the South.
4. Why did some Southerners believe that their states had the right to leave the Union?
5. What nation did 11 Southern states form? Who was the president of this new nation?

THINKING SKILLS

Do you think the Civil War had to happen? If so, why? If not, how could it have been avoided?

Lesson 3: The American Civil War

FIND THE WORDS

blockade volunteer draft
Emancipation Proclamation
civilian

The Civil War lasted from 1861 to 1865. It was the bloodiest war people in the United States had fought up to that time. On one side, the South, or the Confederacy, fought for Southern independence. These Southerners wanted to protect states' rights and the Southern way of life. On the other side, the North, or the Union, fought to preserve the federal union.

The North had many advantages. Three-fourths of the nation's wealth was produced in the North. Northern factories made everything the Union Army needed. There were 22 million people in the North. There were fewer than 9 million in the South. The North had most of the nation's ships, banks, factories, and railroads.

The South did have important

At first, states had little trouble getting soldiers for the armies. Later, as the war dragged on, states began paying money to volunteers.

Fascinating Facts

Today, balloons are used mostly as toys. But during the Civil War, balloons were serious business. The Union army had a balloon corps. Observers were sent up in baskets hung from big hot-air balloons. They signaled people below with important information. They could see where the Confederate Army was. They could tell the Union Army where to direct its cannon fire.

advantages. Most battles would be fought on Southern territory. Confederate soldiers would fight bravely to defend their homes. Union soldiers would have to fight in unfriendly and unfamiliar territory. Many of the nation's high-ranking army officers were from the South. That meant that the Confederate Army would have better generals. The South also had cotton. Many European nations needed that cotton to make cloth. Those nations might help the South in order to get cotton.

General Robert E. Lee

President Lincoln knew how important European trade was to the South. So the first war action he took was to order the Union Navy to blockade Southern ports. To **blockade** a port is to keep ships from entering or leaving it. Throughout the war, the South had a hard time getting supplies through the Union blockade.

On July 21, 1861, the first major battle took place between the Union Army and the Confederate Army. The Union Army had hoped to capture Richmond, Virginia, the capital of the Confederacy. They thought they could win the war quickly. But the Confederate Army met them at Bull Run, a small creek between Washington and Richmond. The Union Army was defeated in this first battle of Bull Run. The North began to realize that it would be a long war.

For 2 years, things went badly for the Union Army in the East. The Union soldiers were led by General George McClellan. He knew how to organize and train

The Emancipation Proclamation freed slaves living in areas still under Confederate rule. Here, freed slaves leave the plantations as troops pass by.

troops. But he was slow to attack. The Confederate armies were led by General Robert E. Lee and General Thomas "Stonewall" Jackson. These great generals won many battles. In the West, the Union Army did somewhat better under General Ulysses S. Grant.

In the North and in the South, many soldiers were **volunteers.** That meant that they joined the army of their own free will. The South also had a **draft.** That is a law that requires people to join the armed forces. The North did not start to draft soldiers until 1863. But the Northern draft law was different. Anyone who did not want to fight could avoid the draft by paying $300 to the government. This was unfair to poor people. They could not afford to pay so much money. At that time, many workers did not make that much in a whole year. Many riots broke out in New York and other cities in the North over the draft issue.

The abolitionists hoped that the war would free the slaves. They thought that free Blacks should be armed to fight with the North against the South. Blacks had fought bravely in the Revolution and in the War of 1812. But some White people did not know this. They thought that Blacks would not fight. Finally, President Lincoln allowed the Blacks to be armed. They proved once again to be brave soldiers. There were 186,000 Blacks who fought in the Union Army.

Lincoln believed that if he freed the slaves, many more Black soldiers would fight for the Union. Also, Lincoln did not want Europe to support the South. Many

At Gettysburg, there was a long, hard battle. Both sides lost thousands of soldiers. From that point on, the tide turned against the South. Gettysburg, Pennsylvania, is at 39°50′ north latitude, 77°15′ west longitude.

Europeans opposed slavery. Thus, if he freed the slaves, Europe would sympathize with the North. So, on January 1, 1863, Lincoln issued the **Emancipation Proclamation.** This document freed only those slaves living in the parts of the South still under Confederate rule. The Thirteenth Amendment, passed in 1865, freed all the slaves.

By July 1863, Union forces, under General Grant, controlled the Mississippi River. Texas, Arkansas, and most of Louisiana were now separated from the rest of the Confederacy. In the East, the Union Army met the Confederate Army at Gettysburg, Pennsylvania, on July 1, 1863. General Meade commanded the Union troops. The Confederates were under General Lee. There was a long, hard battle. Each side lost about 25,000 soldiers. But the Union Army had won. The tide now turned against the South.

In November 1863, Lincoln made a famous speech at the Gettysburg battlefield. It is called the Gettysburg Address. In it, Lincoln said that the soldiers buried there had given their lives so that "government of the people, by the people, for the people shall not perish from the earth."

The war continued for almost 2 more years after Gettysburg. In 1864, Lincoln made General Grant head of all the Union armies. The South was steadily losing ground. Finally, the two armies met at Petersburg, Virginia. They fought from trenches for months. Then, on April 2, 1865, General Lee retreated. On April 9, 1865, Lee surrendered to Grant at Appomattox (AP uh MAT uks), Virginia. The war was over.

The American Civil War was the first "modern" war. In the past, most wars had been fought by small, specially trained armies. **Civilians,** those people not in the armed forces, did not have much to do with those wars. In the past, generals tried to defeat each other's armies in the field. But in the Civil War, the civilian population suffered more than ever before. For the first time, huge armies with heavy cannons and equipment moved over vast areas and through cities. Over 600,000 people died, and 400,000 were wounded.

General Ulysses S. Grant was President of the United States from 1869 to 1877.

REVIEW

VOCABULARY MASTERY

1. The opposite of a draft army is a ___ army.
volunteer civilian blockade

2. To ___ a port is to keep ships from entering or leaving it.
volunteer emancipate blockade

3. ___ are people not in the armed forces.
Volunteers Civilians Draftees

READING FOR MAIN IDEAS

4. What were some of the North's advantages in the Civil War? What advantages did the South have?

5. Why is the American Civil War often considered the first "modern" war?

STUDY SKILLS

Pick one of the generals named in this chapter. Look him up in the encyclopedia. What was his most famous battle? What was he known for?

Lesson 4: Reconstruction in the South

FIND THE WORDS

reconstruction
Freedmen's Bureau **Black Codes**
carpetbagger **scalawag**
segregation

At the end of the Civil War, the North was well-off. But the South was largely ruined. Factories in the North had grown rich making and selling supplies to the Union Army and Navy.

In the South, factories and farms lay in ruins. Many cities and towns had been destroyed. More than 250,000 Southern men and boys had died in the war. Many others had been wounded. Food was scarce, and Confederate money was worth nothing.

Slaves were now free. They had to find ways to support themselves, but there were few jobs in the South. This meant that Blacks and poor Whites now

This picture shows a square in the center of Charleston, South Carolina.

After the war, much of the South was in ruins.

tried to get the same jobs. For this reason, many poor Whites resented the Blacks. Also, few Blacks had money to buy their own land. Many had to stay on plantations and other farms. Often, they were working for people who had been slave masters. Most Blacks, who had nothing under slavery, remained very poor as free people.

President Lincoln felt sympathy for the South. He saw that the South had suffered very much. He planned to provide money, food, and supplies for the **reconstruction,** or rebuilding, of the South. But 5 days after the surrender at Appomattox, Lincoln was killed. He was shot by a Southern White who blamed him for destroying the South. Andrew Johnson became President. Johnson wanted to carry out Lincoln's Reconstruction plan. However, Congress had its own plans.

In 1865, the federal government set up the **Freedmen's Bureau.** This agency was to help former slaves learn a new way of life. The bureau gave out goods and clothing. It set up schools in which Black men, women, and children could learn to read and write.

Meanwhile, several Southern states passed laws called **Black Codes.** These laws kept Blacks from voting, serving on juries, and carrying guns. In some states, Blacks were allowed to work only as house servants or farmhands.

Congress did not like what was happening in the South. In 1867, federal troops were sent to run parts of the South. State elections were held in which Black men voted for the first time. Men who had been Confederate leaders during the war were not allowed to vote. No women—White or Black—were allowed to vote.

New state governments were elected. They were made up of Black men and of White Southern men who had not taken part in the war. Some Northerners who had come south after the war also took part in the new state governments. The White Southerners who could not vote resented these officeholders. They called the Northerners **carpetbaggers.** A carpetbag was an old-fashioned type of suitcase made of carpet cloth. The former Confederates had a name for the White Southern officeholders, too. They were called **scalawags** (SKAL uh wagz).

Blacks had never held positions in government. Between 1876 and 1880, 14 Blacks were elected to Congress. The first two United States Senators were from Mississippi. Hiram Revels, a free Black, was a minister. During the Civil War, he had helped organize Black regiments in the Union Army. Blanche Bruce, a slave who escaped during the war, had started a school for Blacks in Missouri. Both men had held government offices in Mississippi.

Not all Blacks who held office were so well qualified. Many had little experience to guide them. Often, the carpetbaggers and scalawags took advantage of them.

During the Reconstruction period, Congress sent to the states three important new amendments to the Constitution. These were the Thirteenth, Fourteenth, and Fifteenth Amendments. All were approved by the states.

The Thirteenth Amendment abolished slavery. The Fourteenth Amendment made the Blacks citizens. It also said that all citizens must be treated equally under the law. The Fifteenth Amendment said that no citizens could be stopped from voting because of their race or color.

In 1877, the last federal troops left the South. The South had suffered under Reconstruction. Many of the White Southerners resented the way they had been treated. Despite the new amendments, Black Southerners were gradually put down again. Laws were passed that provided for the **segregation,** or separation, of Southern society into two parts on the basis of race. For example, Whites and Blacks were to go to separate schools. But the schools for Blacks were not as good as the schools for Whites. Special rules were set up that prevented Blacks from voting.

In 1865, the federal government set up the Freedmen's Bureau. This agency was to help former slaves learn a new way of life. The bureau gave out goods and clothing. It set up schools for Black people. Here, women learn how to make a living by sewing.

Under the laws of segregation, Whites and Blacks went to separate schools. Segregation in Southern schools continued until the 1950s and 1960s.

Booker T. Washington thought that the best way for Blacks to establish themselves was to learn skilled work. To help them do this, he set up the Tuskegee Institute for the education of Blacks.

In the North and the South, educated Blacks tried to stop segregation. They did this in many different ways.

Booker T. Washington believed that Blacks should try to gain skills and become good workers. He thought that when Blacks had money, businesses, and skills, equal rights would follow. Booker T. Washington was able to win support for his ideas from wealthy people. He set up the Tuskegee Institute in Alabama. At first, the institute trained people for practical jobs, such as bricklaying, shoemaking, and dairy farming. Later, George Washington Carver, a great Black scientist, worked and taught there. He developed hundreds of new products from peanuts, sweet potatoes, soybeans, and cotton.

Another Black leader, W.E.B. DuBois, had different ideas. He said that Blacks must learn to do more than lay bricks, make shoes, raise cows, and grow crops. He believed that Blacks had to stand up against laws that made segregation possible. These laws said that Blacks could not enjoy the same rights as other citizens. So these laws had to be changed.

REVIEW

VOCABULARY MASTERY

1. ___ were Northerners who came south after the Civil War.
   Carpetbaggers Scalawags Freedmen
2. ___ were Southern Whites who took part in the Reconstruction governments.
   Carpetbaggers Scalawags Freedmen
3. ___ separated Southern society into two parts.
   Reconstruction Segregation Freedmen

READING FOR MAIN IDEAS

4. Why did many poor Whites resent the newly freed slaves?
5. What federal agency helped the former slaves?

THINKING SKILLS

After the Civil War, some people wanted to divide the plantations among the former slaves. Do you think this was a good idea? Would it have been fair? Why, or why not?

CHAPTER REVIEW

VOCABULARY MASTERY

Use the words below to complete the chapter summary. Use each only once.

abolitionists	Freedmen's Bureau
civilians	secession
cotton gin	segregation
draft	tariff
fibers	volunteers

Slavery began in the United States in 1619. When the __1__ was invented in 1793, the number of slaves greatly increased. This machine separated the cotton __2__ from the seeds. More slaves were needed to raise the cotton and work the machines.

Northern __3__ opposed Southern slavery. The North and the South also disagreed on the __4__ on imported goods. Southern __5__ took place after President Lincoln was elected.

When the American Civil War began, many soldiers joined as __6__. There were also __7__ laws that required people to join the armed forces. Many soldiers and __8__ suffered from the war.

After the American Civil War, the __9__ was set up to help former slaves. But after Reconstruction, the Southern states passed new __10__ laws.

READING FOR MAIN IDEAS

1. List three things the law did not allow slaves to do.
2. List three ways that the North and the South were different in the early 1800s.
3. Why did Southern states secede from the Union?
4. Why did President Lincoln order the Union Navy to blockade the Southern ports?
5. What rights did Blacks gain in the South during Reconstruction?

SKILLS APPLICATION

TIME LINE SKILLS

Look at the time line on page 231.

6. The Civil War ended when General Lee surrendered his troops. What year was that?
7. How many years did the Civil War last?
8. How long did federal troops remain in the South?
9. The Emancipation Proclamation freed slaves only in Confederate parts of the South. How many years later were all slaves freed?
10. Lincoln was assassinated in 1865. How long after his election was that?

RESEARCH AND WRITING SKILLS

The following people all used the written word to fight against slavery. Match the people with their publications. Select one person to find out more about.

11. William Lloyd Garrison	A. *Uncle Tom's Cabin*
12. Reverend Samuel E. Cornish and John Russworm	B. *The North Star*
	C. *Freedom's Journal*
13. Harriet Beecher Stowe	D. *The Liberator*
14. Frederick Douglass	

15. Use research notes to prepare a report on Angelina Grimké, Eli Whitney, Harriet Tubman, Robert E. Lee, or Sojourner Truth. Use encyclopedias, almanacs, or biographies. Take notes on facts such as date of birth, place of birth, education, major accomplishment, a special interest or hobby, and date and place of death. Your notes on each fact should be *10 words or less.* List your sources.

CHAPTER 2 INDUSTRY AND IMMIGRANTS

Lesson 1: The Industrial Revolution Begins

FIND THE WORDS

revolution reaper thresher
mass production division of labor
interchangeable parts
assembly line locomotive
process ingenuity

A **revolution** is not always a war to change a government. It can be any great change in the way people think, work, or live. The earliest human beings hunted, fished, and gathered wild plants for their food. Then people learned to plant crops and raise animals. For thousands of years, most people herded flocks or raised food on farms.

Until the mid-1700s, most work was done with muscle. People and animals pulled, pushed, and carried heavy loads. Only a few other sources of power were used. Running water made waterwheels go around. Rushing wind made the blades of windmills turn. This water and wind power also ran machines that could grind grain into flour. Windmills also furnished power to pump water and saw wood.

Farm Machines

Then, in a single century, new machines changed the way most work was done. At first, power to move the machines was still furnished by a horse. Cyrus McCormick showed farmers his new invention in 1831. It was a horse-drawn reaper. A **reaper** is a machine that cuts down a crop and drops it in piles. A worker could cut 50 times more wheat with a reaper than by hand. Almost 50 years earlier, a Scottish inventor had invented a threshing machine. The **thresher** separated the seeds, or grains, of wheat from the rest of the plant. Using reapers and threshers, farmers could harvest much more wheat. So, much more wheat was planted and grown. Reapers and threshers were soon followed by corn planters, huskers, and other farm machines.

The Steam Engine

The Industrial Revolution was made possible by the power of steam. In Scotland, James Watt had invented a practical steam engine in 1769. Fuel was burned in a furnace. It heated water in a boiler. The heat turned the water to steam. Then the steam was condensed. Great pressure built up. Machine parts were moved by the force of the steam.

In the early 1800s, steam engines were improved. Soon they could furnish power for farm equipment, such as threshers. They could also drive factory machines. They could be used to raise coal out of mines. Steam engines could even provide power to move ships and railroad trains.

Home and Factory

For thousands of years, people made goods by hand. They worked in their homes or in small shops. Sometimes one person worked alone, using a few simple tools. Sometimes an assistant or other family members helped.

Suppose you had lived in those days. Suppose you wanted to make a wool shirt. First, you would cut

Before the Industrial Revolution, people canned food by hand. How do you think this job is done today?

The steam engine changed the way work was done in textile mills. Machines driven by steam power could work much faster than people could. The use of machines made mass production possible.

the wool off the sheep. Then, you would wash and dry it. Next, you would dye the wool. You would spin it into thread. After that, you would weave the thread into cloth. Finally, you would use thread and cloth to sew a shirt. You would make the whole product, from beginning to end.

In the 1700s and 1800s, inventors found new ways to make things with machines. Now, one machine could do as much work as many different people. Using machines, people could work much faster. They could make many more goods. The age of mass production had arrived. **Mass production** is making a great many goods by using machines.

Machines changed more than the amount of work done and the speed. Machines also changed the workplace and the way work was done. Before, business owners sometimes used workers who did the work in their own homes. Family members worked together there. Now, business owners were building factories to house their new machines. So workers started to work outside the home. They began to work with strangers in the factories. Some New England women went to work in cloth factories called textile (TEX tyl) mills.

In factories, work was divided up. Different workers did different jobs. This way of working is called the **division of labor.** Suppose a factory made wool shirts. One set of people would cut the wool and bring it to the factory. There, other people would wash and dry the wool. Still other people would dye it. Then spinners would use machines to spin it into thread. Finally, weavers would use other machines to weave it into cloth. Steam engines supplied the power to run the spinning and weaving machines.

With each worker doing a different job, more goods could be made in less time. Cash registers were among the products made this way.

The Assembly Line

In 1798, Eli Whitney built a factory to make guns. Whitney had already invented the cotton gin. Now he had another important idea. He wanted the parts from one gun to fit any other gun

Eli Whitney's gun factory changed the way goods were made. It was Whitney's idea to use interchangeable parts.

made in his factory. Before, each worker had made all the parts of a single gun. The parts for one gun would not fit any other gun. Now, each worker would make many copies of one part. The copies would be the same size and shape. That meant one part could change places with any other like it. So the copies were called **interchangeable** (IN tur CHAYN juh bul) **parts.** Workers making one part needed less skill than workers making a whole gun.

Eli Whitney's idea spread. Today, because of Whitney, we have assembly lines. An **assembly line** in a factory is a line of workers and machines. Every worker or machine does a different thing to the product. No one person makes a whole product. Instead, each product is made by many people and machines, one step at a time. Interchangeable parts are used in products made on an assembly line.

Cities and Railroads

The growth of factories also led to the growth of towns and cities. Factory owners needed a supply of workers. They built their factories in places where workers could be found. Then, more workers moved to places where there were factory jobs. Going to work in a factory usually meant leaving a farm.

More people were traveling away from home to work. More products were coming out of factories. So better transportation was needed to move people and materials around. Before, sailors had needed wind to push a ship across the water. Other travelers had needed horses to pull a wagon over the land. The first railroads had horse-drawn cars. They were used to carry minerals from mines. Then, in 1830, the first steam railroad in the United States started to run. The railroad tracks were only 21 kilometers (13 miles) long. But something revolutionary had happened. A steam locomotive called *Tom Thumb* was moving under its own power! The word *locomotive* means "able to move from place to place." The **locomotive** of a train contains the engine. It is strong enough to pull or push the other railroad cars.

Soon, workers were putting down thousands of miles of railroad tracks. Other workers were digging canals to connect large eastern rivers and lakes. By the 1840s, steamboats moved across the inland waterways. Steamboats and railroads carried raw materials from around the country to factories in the North.

There, workers processed the raw materials. To **process** something is to make it ready for sale

Steam power drove the engines of early railroads. Trains carried raw materials to factories and took finished goods away. This train got stuck in the snow.

or for use. Cotton was spun into thread and woven into cloth. Raw sugar was refined, or made pure. Meat was cut up, cleaned, and packed. Then, the railroads and steamboats carried processed goods from the North to other parts of the United States. Steam transportation gave factories a much bigger market for their goods.

The Telegraph

As you can see, there were great changes in the ways people made and moved goods. There was also a great change in the way people sent messages. In 1844, Samuel Morse perfected the telegraph. The telegraph could send messages across many miles. These messages traveled over wires

This drawing shows the progress made in travel and communication. How many signs of progress can you see?

LIBERTY AND UNION NOW AND FOREVER

GLORY TO GOD IN THE HIGHEST ON EARTH PEACE GOOD WILL TOWARD MEN.

as electric signals. A newspaper reporter described the impact of this new invention. He was in Washington, DC, getting a report of the Democratic National Convention in Baltimore. He wrote:

"Never before was anyone aware of what was happening in a distant city 40, 100, or 500 miles away. For example, it is now exactly 11 o'clock. The telegraph announces as follows: '11 o'clock—Senator Walker is *now* answering Mr. Butler on the adoption of the two-thirds rule.' It takes quite a mental effort to realize that this is a fact that *now* *is* and not one that *has been.* The telegraph is a most wonderful achievement."

By 1860, 80,000 kilometers (50,000 miles) of telegraph wires joined the different parts of the nation.

There were many other inventions in the first half of the 1800s. New ways of making steel were being used. Ways to mold rubber into firm shapes were found. New inventions ranged from the tricycle to the safety pin. A new kind of printing press came into use. It could print thousands of newspapers and books in an hour.

Fascinating Facts

Americans love ice cream. The United States manufactures enough frozen dessert each year to feed every American 23 quarts apiece! In the summer of 1790, George Washington spent $200 on ice cream. And in 1812, Dolley Madison served homemade ice cream at the White House.

Making ice cream was a long, hard job. Someone had to beat the cream, sugar, and flavorings by hand in a wooden pot. At the same time, the pot had to be jiggled up and down in a pan of ice and salt. Ice was hard to get in the days before refrigerators. And it took hours of work to make ice cream.

Nancy Johnson of New Jersey changed all that. In 1846, she invented the hand-cranked ice cream freezer. This freezer was a bucket with a paddle inside and a crank for a handle. The cream mixture went in a container in the middle.

Ice and salt were packed around the edges. Then one person could turn the crank that moved the paddle that beat the cream and shook the ice and salt around it.

Today, we can buy ice cream from pushcarts, grocery stores, and ice cream parlors. Over 500 different flavors have been invented. We can eat ice cream in cones, cups, sodas, sundaes, and banana splits. And we owe it all to the ingenious Nancy Johnson!

The United States had a wealth of natural resources. The people had plenty of native cleverness, or **ingenuity** (IN juh NOO uh tee). The years before the Civil War brought new inventions and steam power. With new equipment, fewer farmers were needed to raise large crops. Some workers began to leave the farm for the factory. Around the factories, cities began to spread. People, goods, and messages were being moved faster than ever before. The pace of life had quickened. At home and on the job, people's way of life was changing. The Industrial Revolution had begun.

REVIEW

VOCABULARY MASTERY

1. A ___ cuts down a crop and drops it in piles.
   thresher reaper locomotive
2. A ___ separates the grains of wheat from the rest of the plant.
   thresher telegraph reaper
3. ___ are exact copies of one another.
   Threshers Reapers Interchangeable parts
4. To ___ something is to prepare it for sale or use.
   telegraph process interchange
5. Each worker on a(n) ___ does a different job.
   thresher reaper assembly line
6. The ___ means that work is divided up among different people.
   revolution mass production division of labor
7. Making many goods at once by using machines is ___.
   division of labor mass production revolution
8. The engine of a train is in the ___.
   thresher reaper locomotive
9. Successful inventors have a lot of ___.
   ingenuity process interchangeable parts
10. A ___ can be a great change in the way people live.
    process division of labor revolution

READING FOR MAIN IDEAS

11. Who first had the idea of interchangeable parts?
12. Who invented the reaper? Who perfected the telegraph?
13. What new systems of transportation used the steam engine?
14. How was most work done before modern machines were invented?
15. Describe how work is done on an assembly line.

THINKING SKILLS

16. Why did people begin to move from farms to cities? How did farm machines and factories help bring this move about?
17. Which invention mentioned in this lesson do you think was most important? Why?
18. How do you think computers are going to change the way people work?
19. Write a paragraph about what life would be like without modern communications technology.

Lesson 2: Industry after the Civil War

FIND THE WORDS

industry **manufacture**
industrial **construction**
entrepreneur **refine**
patent **skyscraper**

The word **industry** has three meanings. People can be praised for their industry. That means long, steady effort to get work done. People can work in a certain industry. The garment industry makes a certain kind of product. The tourist industry supplies services and promotes trade. A nation can also have a lot of industry. That means it has many large businesses that manufacture goods for sale. *Manufacture* comes from Latin words meaning "made by hand." But to **manufacture** products is to make raw materials into finished goods by using machines.

A country that manufactures and sells many goods is called an **industrial** (in DUS tree ul) nation. The United States became an industrial nation in the years

Steel supports raised elevated railroads over city streets. Tunnels were dug underground for subway trains.

after the Civil War. Factories were being built everywhere. More and more of the nation's work was being done with machines. Using machines, people could produce many more goods and services. With machines, they could travel longer distances. They could send messages faster than ever before.

Energy was no longer supplied only by wind and water. Now, engines ran on steam. Before, people used surface sources for building materials. Mostly, they used wood. Now, they began to take fuels and building materials out of the ground. Minerals from the earth were the raw materials of a new industrial age.

Many construction workers were needed to build the Flatiron Building in New York. Work on the 20-story skyscraper was finished in 1902.

An Age of Steel

People used steam engines to drain water and lift coal out of mines. Coal is mostly carbon. Carbon is a better fuel than wood. It gives off much more heat when it is burned. Coal and iron are also used in making steel. The carbon makes the iron very hard and strong. The eastern United States had a lot of iron ore and coal. So steelmaking became an important industry. Soon, steel bridges replaced wooden bridges. These strong steel bridges could carry railroad tracks over wide rivers and valleys. Steel supports made it possible to build tracks high over city streets. Steel was also used to build factories, machines, and railroad cars.

When work moved from homes to factories, workers moved to cities from farms. The growth of Chicago shows how fast this movement took place. In 1860, Chicago had only 106,000 people. It had 20 times that many people 50 years later, in 1910. That meant over 2 million people were living in one place. They needed homes, schools, and stores. There was work in **construction** (kun STRUK shun), or building. There was work in manufacturing and trade. There was work providing services. Many new businesses were started. There was a lot of money to be made.

Manufacturing and construction were at the heart of the new age. The most important new material was steel. Andrew Carnegie came to Pennsylvania from Scotland when he was a child. His first job was winding thread in a cotton factory. He made $1.20 a week. Later, he worked for the Pennsylvania Railroad. Since people often had to travel overnight, he introduced sleeping cars. Then, he started his own iron and steel business. He realized how important steel was going to be. By 1900, he owned a steel company, coal and iron mines, steamboats, and railroads. His factories were making one-fourth of the steel in the United States. His company was worth 500 million dollars. He was the richest steel manufacturer in the world.

American Entrepreneurs

A person like Carnegie is called an entrepreneur (AHN truh pruh NUR). An **entrepreneur** is someone who sees an opportunity and sets up a new business. Entrepreneurs have to be good managers. They have to be willing to take risks. The late 1800s were good years for entrepreneurs in the United States. With so much growth and change, it was a good time for businesses to start.

Railroads were one new business in which large fortunes could be made. Three rich and powerful railroad owners were Cornelius Vanderbilt, Collis P. Huntington, and Jay Gould.

Other new industries grew up around petroleum, or oil. In 1859, E. L. Drake drilled the first American oil well. Then the crude oil from the well had to be refined. To **refine** petroleum is to purify it. This is done by heating it to separate its substances. An industry was started to do this work.

At first, petroleum was used to make kerosene (KER uh SEEN). The kerosene was used as an oil for lamps. Then, in 1873, George Brayton of Boston built an engine that ran on kerosene. Later, petroleum was used to make gasoline. Not until 1889 did a German, Gottlieb Daimler (GOT leeb DYM lur), build the kind of gasoline engine we use now.

The Rockefeller fortune was made in petroleum. John D. Rockefeller began working when he was still a child. He earned $3.50 a week as a clerk in a grocery store. Then he started a business selling fruits and vegetables. With partners, he went into the oil-refining business when he was 24. His company was called Standard Oil. By 1911, this company produced, refined, and distributed most of the nation's petroleum. John D. Rockefeller lived to the ripe old age of 98. At

Petroleum, or crude oil, gushed out of this oil well. Petroleum has to be refined before it is useful as fuel.

John D. Rockefeller started the Standard Oil Company. His company produced, refined, and sold most of the nation's petroleum.

the time he died, he was the richest person in the United States.

With so much money being made, people needed banks. The Morgan family of Massachusetts made a fortune by investing money and making loans. J. P. Morgan built the family business into an empire of wealth. He controlled banks, steel, and railroads. His banks provided money to run factories and develop mines.

American Inventors

Inventors were also very important to the new age. In 1876, Alexander Graham Bell took out a patent on a new invention—the telephone. A **patent** is an official paper from the government. It gives the inventor all rights to the invention for a certain number of years. Using the telephone, people could speak to one another over long distances.

American inventors were full of new ideas. They figured out practical ways to do things. In 1879, Thomas Alva Edison invented a long-lasting light bulb. Then he developed a new system to supply buildings with electric power and light. "Nothing that's good works by itself," he said. Edison also invented the record player and the first practical movie camera and projector. He took out over 1,300 patents on inventions during his life!

Elisha G. Otis invented the first safety elevator in 1853. The invention of elevators had important results. People no longer had to walk up and down stairs. That meant they could live and work in taller buildings. It was now possible to build very tall buildings by using a framework of steel. Such a building seemed to scrape against the sky. So it was called a **skyscraper.** The world's first skyscrapers were built in the United States. The first modern

Thomas Alva Edison was one of the world's greatest inventors. He invented the electric light bulb, the movie camera, and the record player. Edison also developed a new system of supplying buildings with electric power. This would make the light bulbs work. "Nothing that's good works by itself," said Edison. During his life, he took out over 1,300 patents on inventions.

skyscraper went up in Chicago in 1883. Its steel framework supported both the floor and the walls. Then, beginning in 1887, electric elevators were used.

The Nation Grows

Now, cities could grow upward as well as spread out. That meant that people could live closer together than ever before. City people were not like independent farmers, living far apart. They were crowded together. Most had to depend on other people's businesses for jobs. People also had to rely on one another more. As cities grew larger, more services were introduced. Larger schools were needed. Hospitals were built. Some small shops expanded and became department stores. There were fire and police departments. There were also telegraph and telephone companies. There were power stations that produced or

Telephone wires strung from posts carried people's words over long distances. As telephone companies grew, the lines of communication stretched farther.

generated, electricity. The 1880s brought the nation's first electric streetcar.

Manufacturing businesses also grew larger. Workers could make many more goods with machines. Large companies could buy more raw materials for less money. Also, it cost less per item to make many goods at one time. That meant large companies could sell their products at a lower price. Since the products were cheaper, more people could buy them. Then more trains and ships were needed to move products around.

Railroads brought distant parts of the country closer together. In 1860, the United States had 56,000 kilometers (35,000 miles) of railroad track. By 1900, almost six times as much track had been laid. This was more than in all of Europe. Now the United States had cities, factories, and railroads. It had communications and banking. It had steam engines and electric power. It had petroleum, coal, and steel. By 1900, the United States had become the largest industrial nation in the world!

REVIEW

VOCABULARY MASTERY

Fill in the blanks. Use the words in the list below.

1. A(n) ___ protects an inventor's rights to an invention.
2. A(n) ___ nation manufactures many goods.
3. One meaning of the word ___ is "hard work."
4. To ___ petroleum is to purify it.
5. A person who sets up a new business is a(n) ___.

entrepreneur industrial
industry patent refine

READING FOR MAIN IDEAS

6. How did cities in the United States change after the Civil War?
7. What material was important for building bridges, railroads, and skyscrapers? Why?
8. What new fuels were used?
9. Who invented the telephone? The light bulb? The record player?
10. Why were the late 1800s good years for entrepreneurs?

THINKING SKILLS

11. In the late 1800s, many factory and construction workers were needed in cities. Is this still true today?
12. Suppose you were an entrepreneur living in the late 1800s. In which industry would you try to make your fortune? Why?

WRITING SKILLS

Find out three new things about one of the inventors or entrepreneurs in this lesson. Use an encyclopedia. Then write a one-page report.

Lesson 3: New Americans Arrive

FIND THE WORDS

immigrant **wave** **famine** **tenement**

The United States was growing and developing very fast. In 1845, Texas joined the Union. By 1848, the nation had added on the whole West Coast. This meant there was much more land to farm. There were cities to build. There were railroad tracks to put down. There was work to be done in factories and mines.

The United States was still a young nation. The population in the mid-1800s was not large. But now the nation stretched from the Atlantic Coast to the Pacific Coast. American companies advertised in Europe for people to come to the United States. Many new Americans were needed to develop this vast land.

The United States has been called "a nation of immigrants." An **immigrant** is a person who comes to settle in a new country. Except for American Indians, all Americans came to the United States from other parts of the world. In 1587, Sir Walter Raleigh sent settlers from England to North Carolina. They started a colony on Roanoke (ROH uh NOHK) Island. Their leader returned to England for supplies. When he came back 4 years later, the colonists had disappeared!

Now, immigrants have been coming to the United States for

IMMIGRATION 1840 to 1930

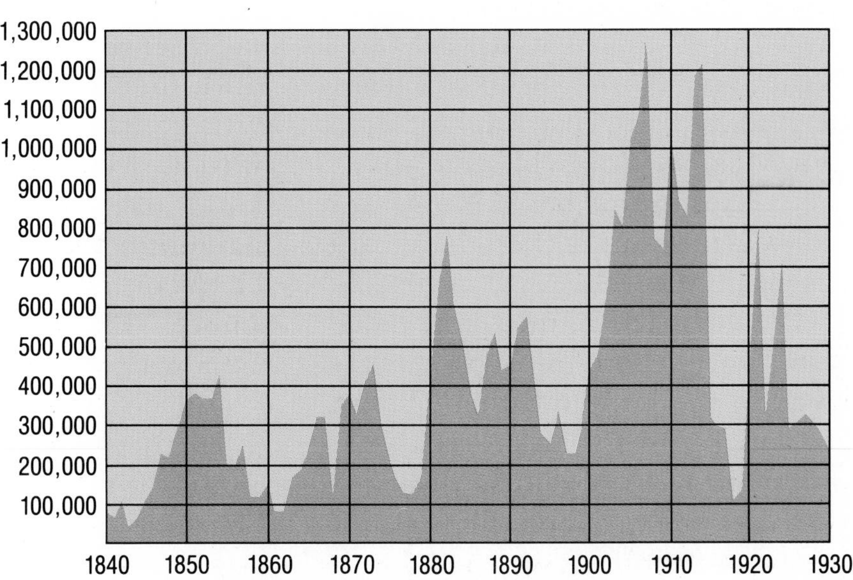

This picture shows a group of European immigrants getting off a ship in New York City. They brought their belongings with them to the United States. They came to America to start a new life.

400 years. Like the lost colonists of Roanoke, they faced dangers and hardships. They often risked their lives. They had to be very brave and determined. This is still true of immigrants coming to the United States today. Many of these new immigrants are from Southeast Asia, Central America, and Mexico. You will read about them later in this book. Now, you will learn about some of the earlier immigrants.

Between 1815 and 1915, more than 30 million immigrants arrived in the United States. These settlers came for many reasons. Some left home because they did not have enough food. Others left because of fighting in their land. Some wanted the freedom to say what they thought and to worship as they pleased.

Most immigrants came because they saw the United States as a land of opportunity. Some had heard stories about cheap land, high pay, and streets paved with gold. Here, they could work hard to make a better life. They could use their skills and their ingenuity. They could earn money. They could send their children to school. Then, they could work their way up in the world. They would be Americans.

In the 1600s and 1700s, most immigrants had been English. There were also many Dutch, French, Germans, Scotch-Irish,

Spanish, and Swedes. Then, in the 1800s, many more immigrants arrived. They came in two great waves. A **wave** of immigrants is a large group of people arriving around the same time. People from Europe seemed to move like an ocean wave toward America's shores.

The First Wave

The first great wave of immigrants arrived between 1815 and 1860. Five million people came then. Most came from Northern Europe. The greatest numbers came from Ireland and Germany.

The first Irish who came were poor. Families would save up to send their younger members to the United States. There, the young people would find jobs. Then they could send money home. With the money, the whole family could move to the new land. Then, in 1846, crops failed in Ireland, Holland, and Germany. In Ireland, the potato crops were ruined. Potatoes were the chief source of food. This terrible time was known as the potato famine. A **famine** is a serious shortage of food that lasts for a long time. During the potato famine in Ireland, many people starved. Half a million died of hunger and disease. Within 10 years, $1\frac{1}{2}$ million Irish people left for America.

This picture was taken around 1900. It shows immigrants waiting in New York to enter the United States.

The Irish immigrants landed in port cities on the East Coast. Most were farmers. But they could not afford to move to the country or buy farms. So they remained in cities like Boston, New York, and Philadelphia. There, they got the hardest jobs at the lowest pay. Irish men dug canals, built roads and railroads, and worked in coal mines. Irish women worked as servants or in textile mills.

Most Irish immigrants were Roman Catholics. They had moved to a country where most people were Protestants. The Protestants did not like or trust the Catholics. Many businesses would not even hire the Irish. Business owners put up signs that said: "No Irish need apply." In spite of these hardships, the Irish

COMING TO AMERICA.

RETURNING FOR A VISIT.

Over $1\frac{1}{2}$ million Irish people came to America. This old cartoon shows an Irish immigrant about to leave Dublin for New York. After a few years in America, he is rich enough for a trip back.

managed to succeed. Later, many made money in business. Others rose to high positions in education, politics, and law.

Millions of immigrants came from Germany to the United States. Most German immigrants were better off than the Irish. After the famine, many came for political reasons. Some of these had started a revolution to change their government. They left home because their revolution had failed. Most of the Germans had money enough to move to the Middle West and buy farms. Many others started businesses in cities such as Milwaukee, Chicago, and Detroit. The Germans were expert farmers and successful entrepreneurs. They brought many gifts to the United States. They even gave us the American hamburger!

Next came the Swedes, Norwegians, and Danes. They settled on the farmland and prairies of the Middle West. These people were hardy pioneers. Some lived in rough sod huts made of clumps of earth. To them, a log cabin seemed like a luxury. Many farmed. Some worked in the forests, cutting wood. The Danes helped to develop the dairy industry. Some Norwegians went all the way to the West Coast. Other Norwegians stayed in the East to work on the docks. They were excellent sailors.

Many immigrants came to America from Germany. The German family in this painting lived on a farm in the Middle West.

Many families from Norway, Sweden, and Denmark settled in the Middle West. They were hardy pioneers. Some of them lived in rough sod huts made of clumps of earth. Many were farmers, but some worked in the forests. This photograph shows some pioneers in front of their sod hut in Nebraska. Nebraska extends from 40° to 43° north latitude and from 95° to 104° west longitude.

The Second Wave

The second great wave of immigrants came between 1890 and 1920. During those years, most immigrants came from Southern and Eastern Europe. Italians and Greeks began to arrive. So did Austrians, Poles, Hungarians, and Russians. All were coming in search of a better life. After 1900, as many as 15,000 immigrants would arrive in a single day!

Poor people in southern Italy had a very hard life. Some workers in Sicily made only 8 cents a day. People had to live in straw houses. Some even lived in caves and tombs. Different problems faced the Jews. They came from many parts of Europe. There, they were often treated badly because of their religious beliefs.

The new immigrants arrived in the United States with high hopes. Yet most faced many problems in the new land. Most had worked on farms. Now they were crowded together in cities. They moved into poor areas that earlier immigrants had left. There, they lived in overcrowded apartment buildings called **tenements.** Families often had to share one small, dark room. The living conditions were so bad that sickness spread. Many of the children died.

The second wave of immigrants had a very hard time. At first, most could not speak English. To other Americans, their clothes looked different. Their languages sounded strange. Some earlier immigrants resented them. They did not want new immigrants in their neighborhoods.

The new immigrants were far from home. They were tired after traveling so far. Often, they did not know where to go or where to stay. They did not know how to find jobs. Swindlers cheated many immigrants. They promised to find them jobs and places to live. Then, after taking the immigrants' savings, they would disappear.

The immigrants of the second wave learned painful lessons. The streets of America were not paved with gold. But they, too, succeeded by determination and hard work. The Poles realized their dream of owning land and homes. Many Jewish immigrants became great merchants, business leaders, and scientists. The Italians built subways and skyscrapers. They worked in factories and mines. They practiced crafts and opened shops and stores. Italians won success in business, banking, government, and the arts.

Many immigrants believed in education. They sent their children to school. They knew their children could get better jobs if they could read and write.

WHERE WE ARE IN TIME AND PLACE

PEAK IMMIGRATION YEARS: 1850–1920

1850–1855	1881	1882	1888–1889	1910–1914	1920
1½ million immigrants from Ireland and Germany	125,000 immigrants from Canada	40,000 immigrants from China; Chinese Exclusion Act passes	4,500 immigrants from Pacific islands	2½ million immigrants from southern and eastern Europe	52,000 immigrants from Mexico

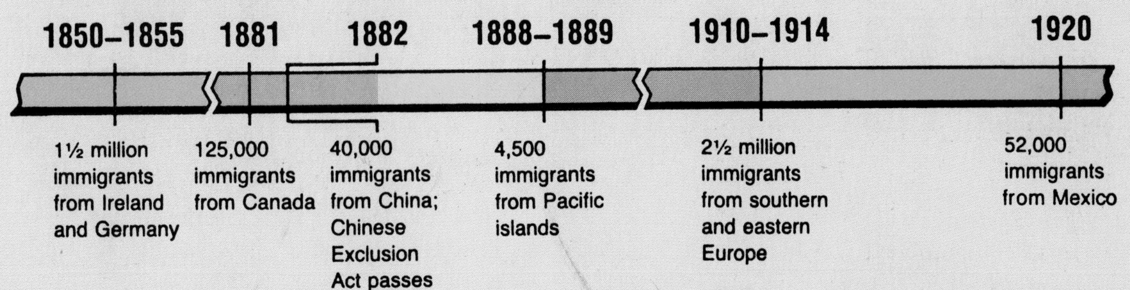

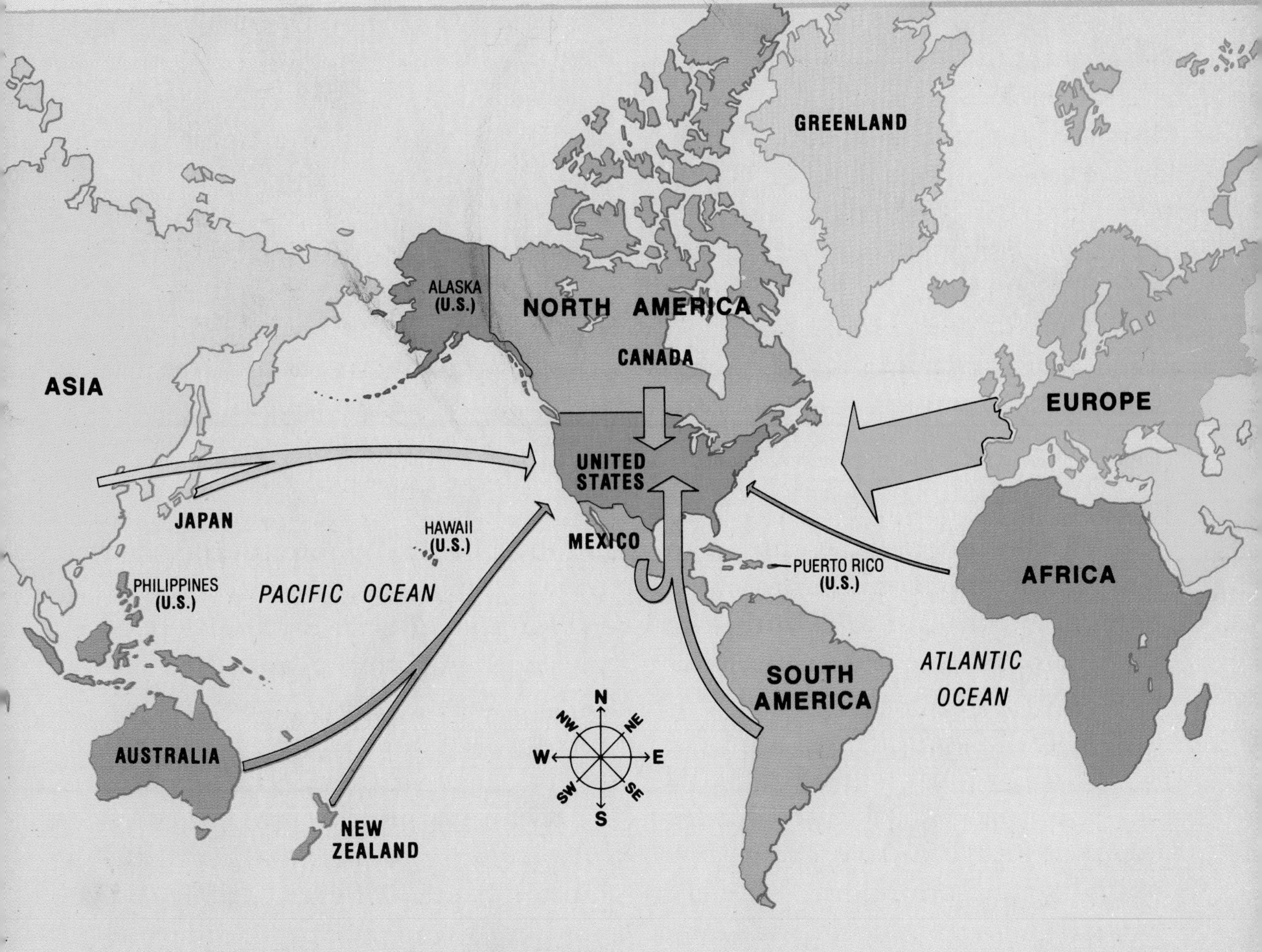

Factory work provided jobs for many immigrants. Many women and some children worked in textile mills. The pay was low and the hours long.

This picture of a Chinese immigrant family is unusual. For many years, there were few Chinese women and children in the United States.

Not all immigrants came from Europe. Immigrants from Asia helped to open up and build the West. In the next lessons, you will learn about the Asian immigrants.

With the hard work and skills of the immigrants, United States farming and industry grew. For many years, immigrants were needed to help do the nation's work. Even when they were needed most, they were not always welcomed. Later, when there were fewer jobs, resentment against the immigrants grew. Some people said the immigrants had no skills. Others said immigrants worked for low wages and took away other workers' jobs.

Some people thought that the immigrants were making the United States different. They did not like or want people of different races, religions, and languages. In 1882, a law was passed to keep

Chinese workers from entering the United States. Later laws greatly limited immigration from all of Asia and from Southern and Eastern Europe as well. These laws favored the first wave of immigrants who were from England and Northern Europe.

The Statue of Liberty was dedicated in New York harbor in 1886. The statue is a symbol of America's welcome to immigrants. It was dedicated 4 years after Chinese immigration was banned. The Statue of Liberty was a gift to the United States from the people of France. American schoolchildren collected pennies to raise the money to build the base. For this great statue, a Jewish poet, Emma Lazarus, wrote a poem. It ended:

"Give me your tired, your poor,
Your huddled masses yearning
  to breathe free,
The wretched refuse of your
  teeming shore;
Send these, the homeless,
  tempest-tost to me,
I lift my lamp beside the golden
  door!"

REVIEW

VOCABULARY MASTERY

Fill in the blanks. Use the words in the list below. You may use a word more than once.

Many Irish ___ left Ireland during the potato ___. Many later ___ lived in ___, or crowded apartment buildings.

famine tenements immigrants

READING FOR MAIN IDEAS

1. How many immigrants came to the United States between 1815 and 1915?
2. From what part of the world did most of the first wave of immigrants come?
3. Where did most of the Irish immigrants settle?
4. From what parts of the world did most of the second wave of immigrants come?
5. Give three reasons why immigrants came to the United States.
6. What were some problems that immigrants faced? Name at least three.
7. Why were laws limiting immigration passed after 1882?

CHART SKILLS

8. In what 10-year period between 1850 and 1920 did immigration rise the highest?
9. In what 10-year period did immigration fall the most?

MAP SKILLS

10. Many immigrants came to the United States between 1850 and 1920. From what continents did they come?

THINKING SKILLS

Try to find out when your ancestors first came to the United States. From what country or countries did they come?

Lesson 4: Chinese Come to the United States

FIND THE WORDS

sojourner benevolent enterprise transcontinental stereotype

Not all immigrants to the United States came from Europe. Immigrants also came from Asia. Most of them crossed the Pacific Ocean to the West Coast. The earliest Asian immigrants to arrive were the Chinese. Some people believe Chinese explorers may have discovered America before Columbus did.

In the Ch'ing Dynasty (1644–1911), a law forbade the Chinese to leave their land. Then, around the mid-1800s, European nations began to interfere in China's affairs. They wanted to control China's trade. The British attacked China's coast. They took over the port of Hong Kong. The Chinese government lost much of its power. Civil wars broke out. People's homes were burned. Many of the Chinese people were left hungry and poor.

Settlers and Sojourners

One of the first Chinese to leave for America during these years was Chum Ming. He was a young merchant. He landed in California in 1847. Then, in 1848,

This old picture shows Canton harbor in China. At the time, the flags of many western nations flew over the town. These nations all wanted control of China's rich trade. Their struggle for control led to war in China. Some Chinese left for America. Canton is now called Guangzhou. It is at 23°07′ north latitude, 113°15′ east longitude.

the California gold rush began. Chum Ming was one of the first to find gold. He sent the news back to China. Between 1848 and 1850, about 800 Chinese came. By 1860, 35,000 Chinese immigrants had arrived in America.

In the 1800s, whole families from Europe came to the United States. But in those days, not many women went to the "Wild West." Most of the early Chinese immigrants were men and boys. They came to the United States to work for pay. They wanted to send money home and to save money, too. Then they could go back to their families someday. Some early Chinese immigrants planned to return to China as soon as they could. They were called sojourners (soh JURN urs). A **sojourner** is someone who plans to live in a place only for a short time. Many Chinese came as settlers. They hoped to stay.

Immigrants with Enterprise

Chinese family members had a strong sense of duty and loyalty to each other. This made it very hard for sons and husbands to leave. But family and group loyalty helped the immigrants when they arrived in the United States. The Chinese already in the United States started self-help societies. They met new immigrants at the boat. They helped newcomers find homes and jobs. The self-help societies represented different districts in China. These societies formed the Chinese Benevolent (buh NEV uh lunt) Association. The word **benevolent** means "showing kindness and good will."

The Chinese immigrants were hard, steady workers. They were known for their industry and enterprise (EN tur PRYZ). Someone with **enterprise** uses new ideas and extra effort to reach a goal. Even so, many people were prejudiced against them. Special laws and rules were passed to drive them out of many businesses. So Chinese immigrants started greatly needed service industries. They opened laundries, stores, and restaurants. The restaurants served the best-prepared food in the old West.

Views of life in the Chinese community of Virginia City, Nevada, in 1877. They include a shoemaker, a laundry, a restaurant, and a barber.

The Miners

At first, most Chinese immigrants worked for mining companies. In 1860, there were 83,000 miners in California. Of these miners, 24,000 were Chinese. The Chinese miners were good at teamwork. Some groups owned their own small mines. Many Chinese worked mining claims that other miners had given up. They used dams and pumps to drain water out of riverbeds.

The work of all the miners brought great wealth to California. In turn, California gold helped pay for the nation's growth. Later, Chinese immigrants mined gold, silver, and coal in other Western states.

The Railroad Builders

Chinese immigrants also built much of the railroad linking the East and the West. This was the first railroad to cross the continent of North America. Thus, it was called a **transcontinental** (TRANS KON tuh NEN tul) railroad. Building it was a hard and dangerous job. One set of tracks was to start in Omaha, Nebraska, and go west. The other set of tracks was to start in Sacramento, California, and go east. Somewhere between these two towns, the tracks had to meet.

Chinese workers started in Sacramento in 1865. Irish workers started in Omaha. The Chinese laid tracks from California across

Chinese immigrants built the western part of the transcontinental railroad. They worked from dawn to dusk 6 days a week. They laid tracks over mountains and deserts. They performed many heroic feats.

the mountains to Utah. They worked from dawn to dark, 6 days a week. They brought their own food, tents, and supplies.

The Chinese railroad builders carried out amazing feats. Sometimes, they cut roadways in solid rock at dizzying heights. Sometimes, they dug tunnels beneath great banks of snow. Some miners froze to death. Finally, in Utah, in 1869, the Irish and Chinese railroad builders met. Immigrants to North America had connected the East Coast and West Coast!

Farm and Factory

Some of the Chinese in America decided to farm. In China, they had learned to drain swamps and irrigate dry land. In the valleys of California, they turned much poor land into good farmland. Some started small farms near California cities. Each morning, they sold flowers, fruits, and vegetables from door to door. The descendants of some of these growers raise million-dollar crops today.

Some Chinese immigrants developed new and better kinds of plants. Ah Bing developed the Bing cherry. Luey Gim Gong bred a new kind of orange. It ripened slowly and stayed juicy and sweet. Florida fruit growers began to raise and sell this kind of orange.

The Chinese also worked in factories. Some worked in woolen mills. Others made shoes or clothes. Some started their own shoe or garment factories.

American businesses needed many new workers to do all the work in the West. Some American business managers went all the way to China to hire the Chinese. But sometimes businesses used Chinese workers for other reasons. In 1875, Chinese workers were brought east to Massachusetts to work in a shoe factory. They were being used to replace employees who were on strike.

Religion was very important to Chinese immigrants. Here are two Chinese houses of worship in San Francisco. One is a traditional Chinese temple, called a joss house. The other is a Chinese Methodist church.

This created very bad feelings among the workers the Chinese replaced.

Problems with Stereotypes

Some people distrusted the Chinese simply because they were different. The Chinese looked different from most other Americans. Their language sounded strange to Europeans. They wore different clothes and ate different foods. They also lived apart in special sections of American cities. Other Americans would call a Chinese community "Chinatown." The Chinese seemed very foreign and hard to understand.

Also, many people had strange ideas about the Chinese. Some sailors said that the Chinese cared nothing for human life.

This idea was a stereotype. A **stereotype** (STEH ree oh TYP) is a false idea about a group. It is a belief that everyone in that group is much the same.

The bad things people believed about the Chinese were not true. Many Chinese worked for low pay because they had no choice. They were thousands of miles from home. They had to work to live. Their pay was low because people took advantage of them. They lived in their own communities for companionship. Also, they faced discrimination elsewhere. They were safer among friends.

Chinese-Americans in the United States keep their ancient culture alive. Here, in New York City's Chinatown, young people celebrate the Chinese New Year. The Chinese year begins in January or February. The exact time depends on the date of the new moon. Each year in the Chinese calendar is named after an animal. For example, 1986 is the year of the tiger and 1987, the year of the rabbit.

In 1873, a depression hit the United States. A depression is a time when prices fall and companies go out of business. Many people lose their jobs. In 1873, some people in the West blamed the Chinese for the depression. They believed the Chinese were taking their jobs. Actually, this was not true. The Chinese had done much work that other workers were not willing to do. Even so, some Chinese were killed and their homes were burned.

Then, in 1882, Congress passed the Chinese Exclusion Act. The word *exclusion* (eks KLOO zhun) means "keeping out." This law said that no more Chinese workers could come to the United States. It also said that the Chinese in the United States could not become citizens. In many states, laws were passed saying that Chinese could marry only Chinese. But the Exclusion Act kept Chinese women out. Also, the men were often threatened and harassed. Many left. From 1890 to 1920, almost half the Chinese who lived in the United States left the country.

Success

Some Chinese stayed in the United States. Many managed to succeed. One of them, Yung Wing, was born in China in 1828. He came to the United States in 1847. In 1854, he graduated from Yale University. He was the first Chinese to graduate from an American college. He also became a citizen. Later, he represented the Chinese government. For 11 years, he brought other Chinese students to study in the United States.

By the time Yung Wing died in 1912, other Chinese were following his lead. Some entered professions, such as dentistry and law. Others started successful businesses. Joe Shoong built a small shop into a large chain of stores. Thomas Foon Chew turned a family business into a nationwide company.

The Chinese Exclusion Act was finally ended, or repealed, in 1943.

REVIEW

VOCABULARY MASTERY

Match each word with its opposite.

1. benevolent	**A.** fact
2. enterprise	**B.** settler
3. sojourner	**C.** local
4. stereotype	**D.** unkind
5. transcontinental	**E.** laziness

PEOPLE TO KNOW

Match the name with the clue.

6. Ah Bing	**A.** bred a sweet, juicy orange.
7. Chum Ming	**B.** started a large chain of stores.
8. Luey Gim Gong	**C.** educated Chinese students in the United States.
9. Joe Shoong	**D.** found gold in California in 1848.
10. Yung Wing	**E.** developed a new kind of cherry.

READING FOR MAIN IDEAS

11. In the 1800s, why did Chinese immigrants come to the United States? Give three reasons.

12. What is the difference between a sojourner and a settler?

13. What did the Chinese self-help societies do?

14. What kinds of businesses did Chinese immigrants start?

15. Why did so many Chinese leave the United States after 1882?

THINKING SKILLS

16. Why were most of the early Chinese immigrants men?

17. Why do you think business managers wanted Chinese workers in the "Wild West"?

18. Chinese workers were often paid less than other workers. What kinds of problems did this cause?

19. What is the difference between a fact and a stereotype?

20. What do you think was the most important work the early Chinese immigrants did? Why?

RESEARCH AND WRITING SKILLS

Some big cities have a Chinese community called Chinatown. What can you find out about Chinatown in New York, Boston, Los Angeles, or San Francisco? Write a report.

Lesson 5: Japanese and Filipinos Arrive

FIND THE WORDS

discrimination alien

In 1898, the United States took possession of two island groups in the Pacific Ocean. These were the islands of Hawaii and the Philippines. These islands were in the same ocean as Japan. Each island group was to give the United States new citizens.

The Japanese

It was around the middle of the 1800s that foreigners began to buy land in Hawaii. Planters came from Europe and the United States. They started plantations to grow sugar cane. Workers came to these plantations first from China and later from Japan. By 1896, there were over 20,000 Japanese people in Hawaii. They were the largest group there.

FROM ASIA TO THE WEST COAST

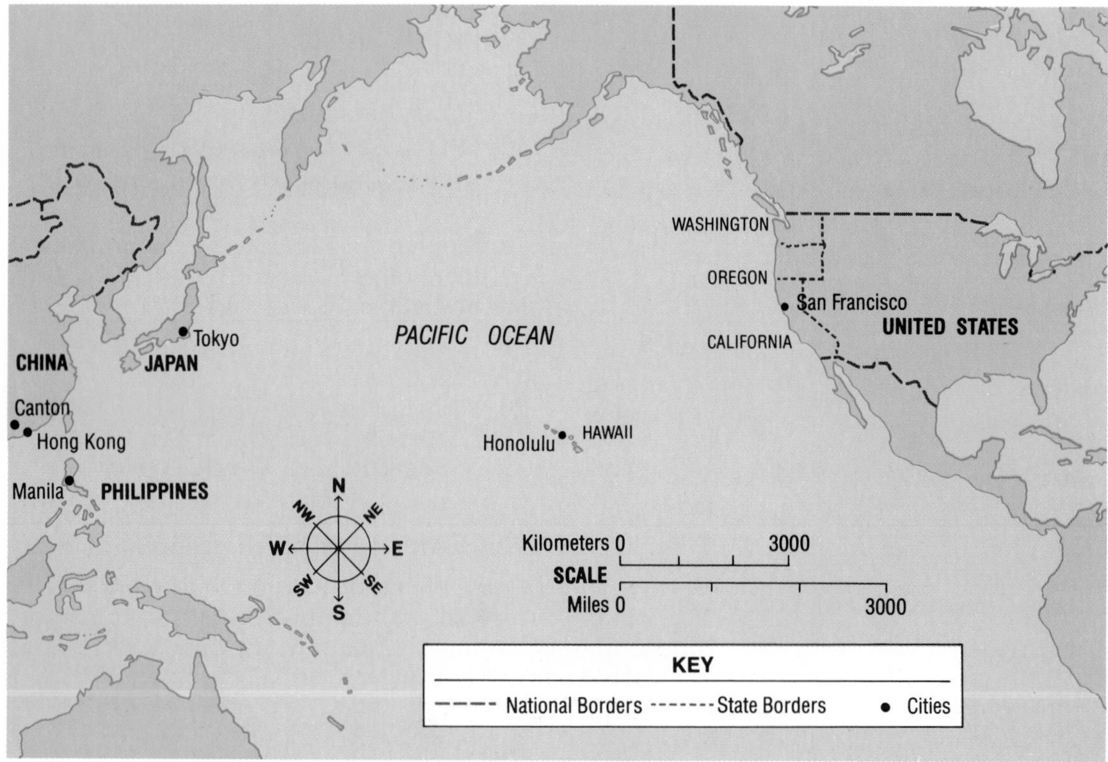

Right: The port of Honolulu, Hawaii, had only a few small houses in 1821. By the 1850s, foreign planters were buying up Hawaiian land.

Below: There were many more buildings in Honolulu in 1875. Soon, thousands of people came to Hawaii from China and Japan. They worked on large plantations growing sugar cane.

By the late 1880s, Japanese immigrants had started to come to the United States. Most came after the Chinese Exclusion Act was passed. In those years, many Chinese immigrants went back to China. The Japanese immigrants took their place. They did many jobs that the Chinese had once done. Some Japanese workers canned fish or fruit. Others worked on farms or in mines. From 1901 to 1910, nearly 130,000 Japanese arrived. The year in which the most Japanese immigrants came was 1907. In 1907, 27,000 men and 3,000 women came from Japan to the United States.

But feelings against the Japanese were strong. In 1906, there were 93 Japanese children in school in San Francisco. City leaders decided to put these students in a separate school for Asians. The Japanese government protested this insult. President Theodore Roosevelt then stepped in. He got the schools in San Francisco to take the Japanese students back. But he also worked out an agreement with the Japanese government. This was called the Gentleman's Agreement of 1907–1908. This agreement stopped Japanese immigration to the United States.

However, this agreement did not stop discrimination against the Japanese. To *discriminate* (dis KRIM uh NAYT) is to treat some

This Japanese family keeps its traditions but also tries out new ways. In California, Asian men wore boots instead of sandals to protect their feet when they worked in the mines.

The Japanese knew how to use and preserve the resources of their land. Immigrants brought these skills to California, where they grew rice, vegetables, and fruit.

people less well than others. Thus, **discrimination** means treatment that is unequal or unfair.

In 1913, California passed the Alien Land Law. This law said that aliens could not own California farmland. An **alien** (AY lee un) is simply someone who came from another country. A foreigner who becomes a citizen ceases to be an alien. But Japanese people were not allowed to become American citizens then. So the Alien Land Law stopped them from buying farmland.

Even so, many Japanese immigrants managed to get land. Sometimes they rented land. Sometimes they bought swampland. They drained this swampland and grew good crops on it. The Japanese planted crops that needed human labor. They did not plant the kinds of crops that were harvested with machines. Soon, Japanese farmers were growing strawberries, celery, peppers, cabbages, and artichokes. The Japanese farmers were the first to successfully grow rice on the West Coast.

One very successful Japanese farmer was George Ushijima (OO shi JEE muh). He was a hard worker who saved his money. In 1898, he bought land at the mouth of the San Joaquin (san WAH keen) River. He and other Japanese drained this land and turned it into good farmland. As time passed, George Ushijima bought more and more land. He planted potatoes in his fields. By 1920, he owned or rented 13,000 acres of

Most Japanese immigrants to the United States were men. Many were skilled in crafts. This picture shows a Japanese carpenter at work.

farmland. When he died in 1926, he was rich. People called him "the potato king."

In 1924, the United States Congress passed a new immigration law. As a result, no more Chinese or Japanese immigrants could enter the country. At this time, most Japanese in the United States were men.

In the 1920s, Filipinos farmed in Hawaii and on the United States mainland. Today, farmers in the Philippines use modern farm machines.

The Filipinos

In 1898, the United States went to war with Spain. Because of this war, Spain gave up the Philippine Islands to the United States. These islands are in the Pacific Ocean, south of Japan. The people of these islands are called Filipinos (FIL uh PEE nohz).

When the United States took over the Philippine Islands, some Filipinos resisted. They were led by Emilio Aguinaldo (a MEE lee oh AHG ee NAHL doh). For 3 years, these Filipinos fought a war against the United States. The United States won the war. But before the fighting ended, a million Filipinos died.

The Gentleman's Agreement of 1907–1908 kept Japanese workers out of the United States. At that time, sugar planters in Hawaii began hiring Filipinos. By the early 1920s, there were over 25,000 Filipinos in Hawaii.

In the 1920s, there was also a lot of work to be done on California farms. The 1924 immigration law kept out most Asians. But the Philippines were then owned by the United States. By 1930, over 100,000 Filipinos had immigrated to Hawaii and the United States mainland.

The Filipinos on the West Coast were treated much as the Chinese and Japanese had been. Their work was needed. But in bad times, they were blamed for taking other workers' jobs away. Laws in some states limited what Filipinos were allowed to do. Laws like that do not exist today.

Today, the Philippines is an independent nation. Now, many Filipinos are immigrating to the United States once more.

United States Citizenship

Immigrants can become United States citizens if they meet certain requirements. They must be at least 18 years old. They must have been lawfully admitted to the country as permanent residents. They must have lived in the United States for 5 years. This time can sometimes be shortened to 30 months.

New citizens must be able to speak, read, and write simple English. They must sign their names in English. All people applying for citizenship must pass a test on United States history and government. Classes are held to help people study.

New citizens must be people of good character. They must believe in the principles set forth in the Constitution. They must pledge allegiance to their new country and must obey its laws. Immigrants who meet all of the requirements can be naturalized. That means they are granted full citizenship in the United States.

Good citizenship does not mean the same thing in all countries. In a society that is not free, it may mean following orders without asking questions. In the United States, it means taking part in our representative democracy.

REVIEW

VOCABULARY MASTERY

1. What does *discrimination* mean? Give an example.
2. When does a foreigner living in the United States cease to be an *alien*?

READING FOR MAIN IDEAS

3. Where are Japan, Hawaii, and the Philippines?
4. Name three jobs the Japanese did in the 1880s on the West Coast.
5. What was the Gentleman's Agreement of 1907–1908?
6. What was the Alien Land Law?
7. How did Japanese farmers get land? What crops did they grow?
8. List at least five requirements that naturalized U.S. citizens must meet.

THINKING SKILLS

Suppose you went to live in a country where people did not speak English. What kind of work could you do?

CHAPTER REVIEW

VOCABULARY MASTERY

Use the words below to complete the chapter summary. Use each only once.

assembly lines
immigrants
interchangeable parts
mass production
Revolution
stereotypes

Even before the American Civil War, the Industrial __1__ had begun. Eli Whitney's idea of using __2__ at his factory made __3__ possible. Other inventions followed that could do the work of many people. The age of __4__ had arrived.

Many __5__ came to the United States. They were often treated unfairly because of unjust __6__.

READING FOR MAIN IDEAS

1. What are interchangeable parts? How did they contribute to the Industrial Revolution?
2. Why was steel considered the most important new material of the Industrial Revolution?
3. Why did many immigrants risk their lives to come to America?
4. Describe the life of a new immigrant in the United States.
5. List some ways that the Chinese immigrants contributed to the growth of California.

THINKING SKILLS

6. Why was the railroad important to a large nation like the United States?
7. What changes did the telegraph and telephone bring?
8. Why does an industrial nation need banks?
9. What are two ways of becoming a citizen of the United States?

SKILLS APPLICATION

GRAPH SKILLS

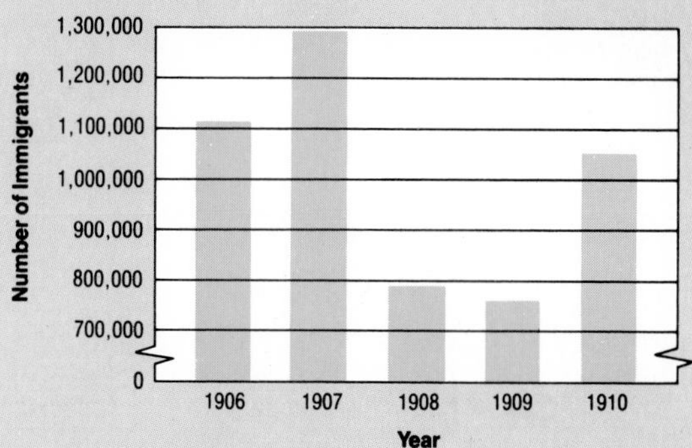

The bar graph above shows the number of immigrants entering the United States from 1906 through 1910.

10. In which year did the most immigrants come to the United States?
11. About how many immigrants arrived in 1906?
12. In how many years did more than a million immigrants arrive?

Look at the line graph on page 259.

13. In how many 10-year periods did immigration rise above 700,000?
14. During what 10-year period did immigration first rise above 500,000?
15. During what 20-year period did the most immigrants arrive?
16. Compare the line graph with the bar graph above. Which one gives more detailed information about specific years? Which one gives information over a longer period of time?

TIME LINE SKILLS

Make a time line listing inventors and their inventions between 1831 and 1875. Include these inventions: light bulb, reaper, safety elevator, telegraph, and telephone.

CHAPTER 3 THE LAST FRONTIER

Lesson 1: The Great Plains Are Settled

FIND THE WORDS

sod locust longhorn

From 1865 to 1900, the land west of the Mississippi was settled. Before the Civil War, few people wanted to live on the Great Plains. The area between the Mississippi River and the Rocky Mountains was called the "Great American Desert." Settlers just wanted to get across it on their way to California and Oregon. But after the Civil War, people began moving onto the Great Plains to stay.

In 1862, the Homestead Act helped open up the Great Plains. This law gave free land to settlers. All they had to do was live on the land and work it for 5 years. Many farmers quickly claimed their land. With it, they claimed

There were not enough trees on the Great Plains to provide wood for houses, so settlers built houses made of sod. To use the materials at hand to fill your needs is to be resourceful. Notice the animal grazing on the hillside.

a very hard life. There were few trees on the Great Plains to provide wood. Thus, they built houses made of prairie sod. **Sod** is soil held tightly together by the roots of grass. The settlers lived through bitter winters and blazing-hot summers. They had to struggle to plant their fields. The prairie sod was very tough. Sometimes, farmers would have to chop the sod with an ax before they could plow the soil underneath. And then grass fires, locusts, or hail could wipe out a year's work in a few days. **Locusts** are swarming insects that often eat crops.

Farming on the Great Plains was best done by big machines. These machines could easily turn over the tough sod. However, many farmers could not afford such machines. Without them, they could barely raise enough crops to stay out of debt. Little by little, the small farms were combined into larger ones. Some "sodbusters," as ranchers called the farmers, gladly sold out. They moved to the cities to find better-paying work. But farming was established on the Great Plains. Before long, much of the area was planted in wheat and corn.

In the Southwest, cattle ranching became important in the 1870s. Tough, half-wild cattle called **longhorns** were a main source of beef for markets in the East. These cattle could be turned loose

At the end of a cattle drive, cowhands herded the longhorns into boxcars. The cattle were then shipped east. The days of the cattle drives did not last long, though. By the 1880s, this way of life had almost disappeared.

One of the best-known Black cowhands in the West was Nat Love.

to feed on the millions of acres of unclaimed grassland. Ranchers did not have to pay for feed. They did not even have to build shelters for the cattle. Every spring, the cowhands would round up the animals. Then they would start the long drive north to the railroad towns in Kansas. The cowhands took their time. If the drive moved slowly enough, the cattle often gained weight on the way to market. Then they could be sold for more money in Kansas. Finally, the cattle were herded onto trains and shipped east to stockyards in Chicago, Kansas City, or Omaha. After spending most of their pay, the cowhands headed for home. They were soon ready to do it again the next year.

The days of the cattle drives did not last long. By the 1880s, this way of life had almost disappeared. The invention of barbed wire was the most important reason. With barbed wire, farmers could build fences to keep cattle out of their fields. Before long, even old cattle trails were blocked by fences. The open range was mostly closed. Cattle raising changed. Ranchers, too, used barbed wire—to fence their cattle in. Penned in small areas, the cattle could be fattened with grain from farms. Ranching was more expensive than in early days. It became a big business. This helped to make life in the West more settled.

Towns and cities grew up. They attracted more and more people. In 1850, there were only half a million people living west of the Mississippi. In 1890, there were almost 9 million.

The people who settled the Great Plains were different from each other in some important ways. But they also had some things in common. Although many were immigrants, they came to share a common language—American English. They shared many beliefs about what was good and right. They shared beliefs about the land. They agreed that the land should belong to someone. They believed that it should be used for something.

There were people living in the West who did not share many of these beliefs. These were the native peoples of the Great Plains. The Plains peoples were among the last of the American Indians to lose their freedom and their old ways.

The last parts of the United States were also added as the Great Plains were being settled. In 1867, the United States government bought Alaska from Russia. Hawaii was added to the nation in 1898. It would be many years before Alaska and Hawaii became states. But the present-day borders of the United States were finally complete.

REVIEW

WATCH YOUR WORDS

1. ___ is soil held tightly together by the roots of grass.
Fiber   Longhorn   Sod

2. The tough, half-wild cattle of the Southwest were called___.
scalawags   longhorns   locusts

READING FOR MAIN IDEAS

3. When were the Great Plains of North America settled?

4. What law helped open the Great Plains to settlers?

5. Why did the Great Plains farmers often build sod houses?

6. When did the United States get Alaska and Hawaii?

7. How did the invention of barbed wire change life in the Southwest?

WRITING SKILLS

Pretend you are a cowhand on a cattle drive. Write a diary that covers 5 days on the trail. Tell things that happen. Say what life on the trail is like.

Lesson 2: American Indians of the Plains

FIND THE WORDS

buffalo bison carcass

Between the Mississippi River and the Rocky Mountains lived many different groups of American Indians. The Comanches (kuh MAN cheez) lived in northern Texas. The Kiowas (KY oh wayz) and Southern Cheyenne (shy AN) lived in Kansas and eastern Colorado. The Pawnee (paw NEE), Crow, Northern Cheyenne, and several Sioux (SOO) groups lived in Nebraska, the Dakotas, Wyoming, and Montana. These were only some of the many American Indian peoples living on the Great Plains.

Originally, the Plains peoples were farmers and hunters. They lived in villages and grew corn, squash, and beans. In the summer, the Indian men left their villages to go hunting. They returned in the fall to harvest their crops.

The main animal hunted by the Plains Indians was the **buffalo,** a large animal related to ordinary cattle. Its proper name is **bison** (BY sun). In earlier times, the American Indians hunted buffaloes on foot. They did not yet have horses. Spanish explorers first brought horses to North America. Some horses escaped and became wild. As the years passed, herds of wild horses grew and wandered over the grasslands. By the early 1700s, the Plains peoples had learned to capture and ride them. From then on, hunting was easier. The vast buffalo herds had to move in order to eat. They also moved south or north during certain parts of the year. With horses, the Plains peoples could follow them. They could stay close to the animals that provided almost everything they needed.

Zona Thunderhawk is a Sioux teacher at the Standing Rock Reservation in North Dakota. Here she describes how the Sioux used buffaloes:

"Our braves hunted the buffalo because it had plenty of meat. They never killed for sport. The men shot the buffalo and brought it to camp. Then it was mostly up to the women to do what they had to do. The older women taught the younger ones to prepare everything for the year.

Plains Indians holding a council meeting. The men sat in a circle to show that all were equal. The Plains Indians spoke many different languages. They used sign language to talk with people from other tribes.

"First, we skinned the buffalo. We staked out the hide and dried it on the ground. We then removed all the meat off the bones. Some we ate fresh. But most of it we dried to eat in the winter. We even used the muscles—the muscles of the leg that people throw away today. We cut them into long strips and dried them. And even the windpipe, we cut and dried that, too. Because we never knew when we might be without food in the wintertime. We always prepared for the long winter months.

"When the hides were dry, we sewed them together to make into tents. We boiled the muscles and hoofs and spread the slimy stuff on the tents. This hardened and kept the rain out of the teepee. Our clothing was made from hides as well. For thread we used sinew (SIN yoo), the stringy part of the buffalo's muscles. Sinew was also used for rope and bowstrings.

"We used the tail of the animal. We put it in the pot until all the meat was cooked off the bones. The little bones we used as playthings. There are holes in them. We laced them and gave them to the children to play with. The horns of the beast were carved into spoons, chisels, and other tools. Other bones were cut into pieces and boiled. We made a kind of bone grease out of this. This lard was then stored in a pouch made from the buffalo's stomach.

"We scraped all the fur from the hide. The longest hair from

The Plains Indians used all parts of the buffaloes they hunted. They lived in tepees, or cone-shaped tents, made of dried buffalo hides. (*Tepee* comes from the Dakota word *tipi*, meaning "dwelling.") They wore clothes made of buffalo hides. They slept on mattresses stuffed with buffalo fur. They ate with spoons made of buffalo horn. They were highly resourceful in using the buffalo and wasting nothing. Look at this picture. How many uses of the buffalo can you see?

the front of the buffalo was saved for mattresses. Tanned buffalo skins were sewed and stuffed with the fur. It made a soft mattress.

"We used everything. I mean everything. When we ate, if there was grease on our hands or on our lips, we wiped it off and put it on our hair. It oiled our hair. It made our hair grow thick and long.

"But the buffalo was hard to catch. Our chief would go up on the high hills to fast and pray for food for his people. Our chief was guided by mighty spirits. He always put the widows and fatherless children first. They ate first. Braves and their families got their share later."

The railroads dealt the first blow to the culture of the Plains people. Railroad workers needed food. Hunters like Buffalo Bill Cody were hired to shoot buffaloes to feed the workers. After the railroads were built, settlers came to the Great Plains in great numbers. They wanted protection from the American Indian peoples. The Army quickly saw that killing buffaloes was one way to control the Plains peoples. So settlers were encouraged to shoot buffaloes. Passengers shot the animals from train windows just for sport. Millions of buffaloes were killed for their hides or their tongues. The tongues were shipped back to restaurants in the East. The

The Army saw that it could control the Plains peoples by killing buffaloes. So the Army encouraged settlers to shoot the animals. There were special trains just for buffalo "hunters." The Indians had hunted one buffalo at a time, with bows and arrows. Sometimes they concealed themselves in wolfskins to get close to the herd. Such hunters ran a risk of being killed. By contrast, hunters on trains, armed with guns, ran no risk at all. The buffaloes had no chance.

carcasses (KAHR kuh sez), or dead bodies, were left rotting on the Great Plains.

In the early 1800s, there were about 60 million buffaloes. Sometimes, a single herd would stretch from horizon to horizon. About 100 years later, only a few were left, in a national park. The American Indians of the Great Plains found themselves without the animals that supported their culture. Soon, they would also be without their land.

REVIEW

VOCABULARY MASTERY

1. The Plains peoples depended on the ____.
railroad beaver buffalo

2. *Buffalo* is another word for____.
carcass bison sinew

READING FOR MAIN IDEAS

3. How did the Plains peoples get their horses?

4. What did the Plains peoples use buffalo hides for?

5. How much of the buffalo did the Plains peoples use?

6. What groups killed many buffaloes?

THINKING SKILLS

Why were the American Indian cultures destroyed when the buffalo was destroyed?

Lesson 3: Whose Land?

FIND THE WORD

reservation

Not all the Plains peoples were friendly with one another. For example, the Sioux were given that name by one of their neighbors. *Sioux* comes from a word meaning "snake in the grass" or "enemy." The Sioux call themselves *Dakotas*. *Dakota* means "ally" or "friend."

The Plains peoples often fought over the right to hunt in, plant on, or travel across a certain territory. Each tribe tried to protect some areas of land for its members. But all the members of a tribe had equal rights to the land. The idea of *owning* the land was completely strange to these people. For many people in Europe and the United States, land was something to own. It was owned just as one owns a tool or a house. Land belonged to the person who bought it or claimed it. The owners could do whatever they wanted with it. No one could come onto their property without their permission.

This difference in values caused many misunderstandings. Often, settlers would offer to buy some land from American Indians. They

Not all the Plains peoples were friendly with one another. The title of this painting is *When Sioux and Blackfeet Meet*. These Indians were excellent riders. They went into battle carrying shields of buffalo hide. As weapons, they used bows and arrows, tomahawks, and lances. Showing bravery in battle was more important than killing the enemy.

The Plains peoples made treaties with the United States government. Settlers broke these treaties again and again. This painting shows the Pawnee at a treaty council. They finally were forced to move from Nebraska to Oklahoma.

would give gifts, usually blankets, guns, coffee, or whiskey. The American Indians thought they were allowing the settlers to use the land. The settlers thought they were buying it. Too late, the American Indians discovered that they could no longer move freely on the land. They began to realize what land ownership meant.

Some American Indians would "sell" land used by other tribes. They thought that no individual person could sell land or even give it away. They thought that no other American Indian had to honor such a sale. Settlers did not understand this. They became angry when other American Indians continued to use the land. They went to courts and to the Army to get support.

Until the 1880s, many fierce battles were fought between the U.S. Army and the Plains peoples. These battles were followed by treaties with the United States government. In these treaties, the Plains people agreed to stop fighting. They also agreed to give up some of their lands. In return, the government promised to protect the rights of the American Indians to their remaining lands.

These treaties were broken again and again by settlers. The settlers were backed up by the United States government and the Army. The American Indians fought hard. But without food or freedom to hunt, the Plains peoples could not resist for long.

American Indians in different regions had been fighting with settlers for 300 years. With the settling of the Great Plains, the struggle was almost over.

American Indian Reservations

As the United States grew, American Indians steadily lost their lands. Settlers pushed west, starting farms and founding towns. The United States government felt it had to protect the settlers. It also tried to see that they got the lands they wanted. To do these things, the government had to deal with the American Indians. Until 1871, Congress treated American Indian tribes as independent nations. After 1871, Congress said the American Indians were no longer independent. But they were not made American citizens either. It was not until 1924 that they finally became citizens and were given the right to vote.

In 1824, the government established the Bureau of Indian Affairs (BIA). The BIA was set up to manage the **reservations.**

American Indians pass cultural traditions and crafts on to their children. Here, a Navaho boy learns how to make turquoise and silver jewelry.

People to Remember

Chief Joseph

The Nez Percé (NEZ PURS) people lived in the northwest part of the United States. In the late 1800s, many White settlers moved into this area. They wanted the Indian lands. In 1876, the United States government told the Nez Percé they had to leave Oregon. They were to move to a reservation in Idaho. Chief Joseph, the leader of the Nez Percé, agreed to go. He knew his people would suffer terribly if they resisted the government.

Just before the move, however, some Nez Percé horses were stolen. In revenge, angry warriors killed some White settlers. Chief Joseph knew that this meant war with the United States. He left immediately with a handful of warriors and several hundred women, children, and old men. He thought his people would be safe in Canada. They traveled more than a thousand miles over very rough territory. The United States Army followed them every step of the way. Finally, only a few miles from the Canadian border, the Army caught up with the Nez Percé.

Chief Joseph surrendered. "I am tired of fighting," he said. "Our chiefs are killed. The old men are all dead. It is cold and we have no blankets. The little children are freezing to death. . . . Hear me, my chiefs! I am tired. My heart is sick and sad. From where the sun now stands, I will fight no more forever."

These were areas of land set aside for American Indians. The BIA sent agents to the reservations. They were supposed to see that the American Indians had enough food, warm clothing, and other necessities. The American Indians needed such help because reservation land was often poor and hard to farm. The American Indians could no longer hunt for food, and now they could not grow good crops. They had to rely on White traders for food and other goods. Often these traders cheated the American

In school, Navaho children learn about their culture. They also study history, geography, English, and arithmetic. The Navaho are the largest Indian tribe in the United States. Their reservation extends from Arizona into Utah and New Mexico. Their ancestors farmed, like the neighboring Pueblo people. In fact, their name, *Navahu,* means "great planted fields." Today, the Navaho own and operate coal mines, a lumber mill, and an electronics company.

Indians. Some agents from the BIA cheated them, too.

The government set up schools on the reservations. In the schools, American Indian children were often not allowed to use their own language. They were taught to read and write only in English. They studied the same subjects that other children in the United States did. The schools wanted to make the American Indians more like other people in the United States. They wanted them to live as most Americans did. Then, it was thought, American Indians would fit in. They would not be a "problem" anymore. In fact, this idea lay behind most of the government programs and laws. Here is an example:

In 1887, the government passed a law to divide up land that was owned by whole tribes. Smaller pieces of this land would be owned by individual American Indians, instead. The government hoped this would make American Indians want to become farmers. Then they would be more like other Americans. But many American Indians did not want to be farmers. They wanted to hunt and gather their food, as they had done in the past. Besides, owning land individually and plowing up the earth went against their beliefs. Confused and bitter, many American Indians sold their little plots of land. When the money was gone, they had nothing. In a period of about 30 years, American Indians lost or sold about 90 million acres. This

The reservation land is better for raising sheep than other animals. Children do most of the herding. This herder is in Monument Valley in southeastern Utah. Some of the sandstone formations there are 300 meters (1,000 feet) high. Monument Valley is near 37° north latitude, 110° west longitude. Many Navaho are sheep ranchers or farmers. But more and more of them are becoming engineers, technicians, and teachers. They value a good education.

was about two-thirds of the land that they had owned.

In 1934, the government again allowed whole tribes to own reservation lands. In some cases, it gave groups of American Indians loans to buy back reservation land that had been sold. The government tried to improve education and medical care. It also allowed American Indians to practice more of their old ways.

REVIEW

READING FOR MAIN IDEAS

1. Different ideas about landownership caused a great deal of conflict in the Great Plains. How were the ideas of the American Indians different from those of the White settlers?
2. What group fought the American Indians?
3. Who usually broke the agreements about the American Indians' lands?
4. Who was Chief Joseph? Why did he agree to leave the lands of his ancestors?
5. How did Congress treat the American Indian tribes until 1871?
6. When did American Indians become citizens of the United States?
7. What is a reservation?
8. What government agency was set up to manage reservations? What was it supposed to do?
9. What was the goal behind the government's school and land policy toward the American Indians?

THINKING SKILLS

Do you think the government was right or wrong in trying to make American Indians like other Americans? Give reasons for your answer.

Lesson 4: American Indians Today

FIND THE WORDS

quinine **malaria**

Today, there are about 275 reservations in the United States. Many American Indians still live on reservations. There, much of their way of life is like that of other people in the United States. But the old cultures are still alive. They are being passed on to the young with pride. Children are learning their people's tribal songs and dances. They study ancient arts and crafts. And they, in turn, will pass this culture on to their children.

Still, life for most American Indians on reservations is not as good as it should be. Many people are poor and cannot get good

AMERICAN INDIANS TODAY

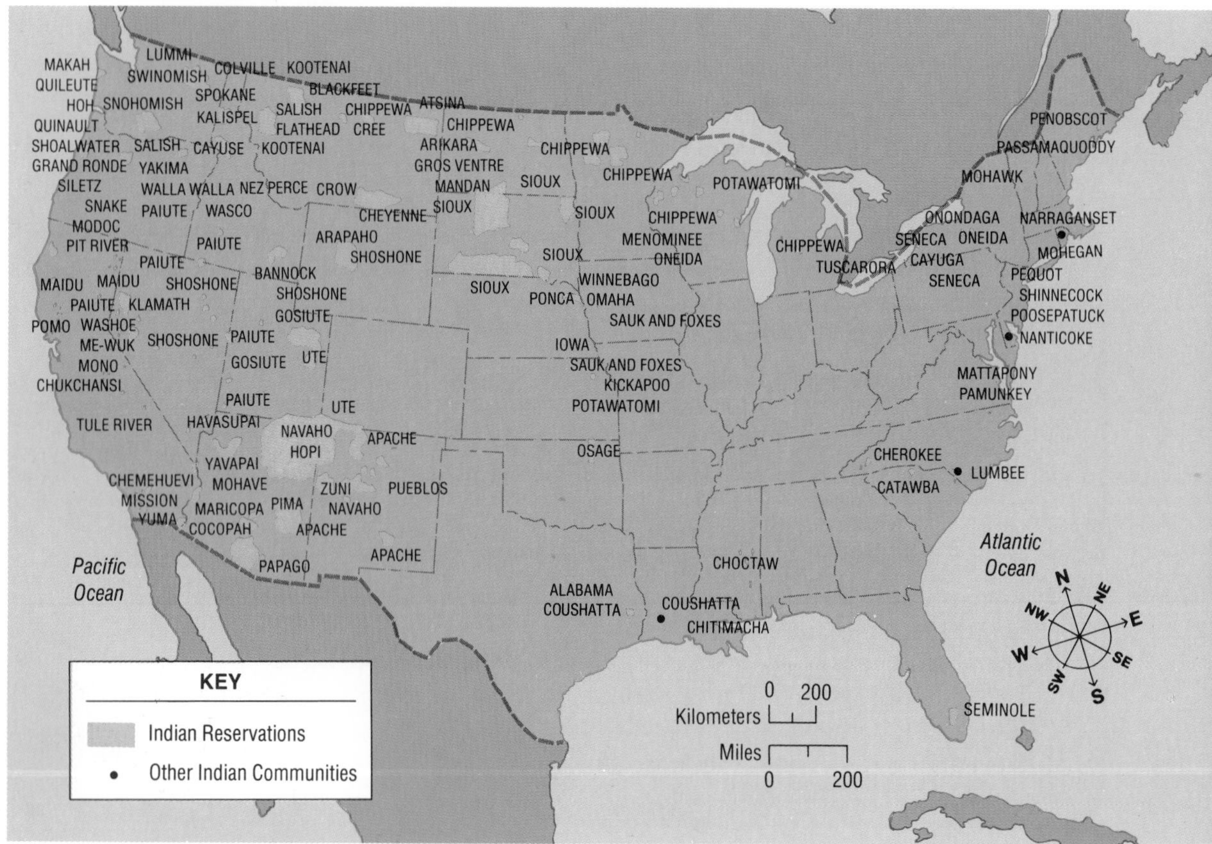

jobs. They do not have good medical care. And many, even though they do go to school, do not have good educations.

One of the most important things you can learn about American Indians is this: Any statement that begins "All American Indians are" is probably false. It is almost impossible to make true general statements about American Indians. There are too many cultural groups. There are too many differences among the groups. For example, there are nearly 100 different American Indian languages and religions.

Today, there are about 1.4 million American Indians in the United States. Separate communities can be found in almost every part of the country.

American Indians have made many contributions to North America and to the world.

The settlers in Jamestown and Plymouth might have starved to death without the help of American Indians.

The native peoples of North America introduced settlers to corn, beans, squash, melons, pumpkins, and other fruits and vegetables. From the native peoples of Central and South America came sweet potatoes, white potatoes, peanuts, tomatoes, chocolate, and many more farm products.

Try to imagine what your life would be like without even some of these things. Corn, potatoes, and beans are very important foods. Today, millions of people throughout the world depend on these basic foods.

American Indians influenced the early settlers in other ways, too. While the American states were still colonies, the Iroquois

The Hohokam Indians are believed to be the ancestors of the Pima Indians of today. The Hohokam people lived in Arizona for at least 1,500 years. Their art, pottery, tools, and homes have been found dating from 300 B.C. to A.D. 1200. The Hohokam also made irrigation canals. They farmed the desert centuries before the Europeans came. This painted bowl dates from about A.D. 900.

American Indians invented the canoe, an ideal boat for lake and river travel.

tribes had an advanced form of government. It was called the Iroquois Confederacy, or the Six Nations. There were representatives from all the tribes. They took part in decisions that affected more than one tribe. In 1754, Benjamin Franklin wrote to colonists who were thinking of forming a union. "It would be strange," he said, "if Six Indian Nations can have a union like this and we can't. They have made it work. We need such a union. . . ."

American Indians have also made contributions to medicine. For hundreds of years, they have used plant roots and herbs as medicines. Many of these medicines came to be used by European settlers. Willow bark is a good example. It was used for hundreds of years by several tribes. What we know as aspirin is made from an ingredient the American Indians got from willow bark. At least 59 drugs have come from wild plants that American Indians used as medicines. One of these drugs is **quinine** (KWY nyn). Made from the bark of a tree, it is used to treat **malaria** (muh LAIR ee uh). That is a disease spread by mosquitoes.

The rubber ball came from South American Indians. North American Indians invented lacrosse, a popular sport.

We now use many other things the American Indians invented. We also often use the native names for them. For example, we use the canoe, kayak (KY yak), hammock, and toboggan. We also use parkas, pipes, and cigars—all from the American Indians.

The English language is full of American Indian words. Many animals are called by their native names. Chipmunks, skunks, moose, opossums, and raccoons are just a few such animals. Many tree names, such as hickory, catalpa, and pecan, are also American Indian. Foods such as succotash, barbeque, squash and potatoes were named by American Indians. Words as different as *bayou, hurricane,* and *totem* have their roots in American Indian languages.

States, towns, lakes, and rivers all over the United States have American Indian names. There are many of these names and they are very familiar. As a result, we tend to forget where they came from. Ohio, Chicago, Kansas, Miami, Mississippi, Omaha, Peoria, Seattle, Tallahassee, Tucson, and Wichita are American Indian names.

We can find American Indian contributions in almost every part of American life. American society continues to benefit from the many tools and ways of doing things invented by the Indians. Even more important are some of the values taught by the American Indians. One of these is the American Indians' deep love and respect for the land and the whole world of nature.

Fascinating Facts

You might think that popcorn is a modern invention. But American Indians were popping corn long before Columbus came to America. In fact, American Indians were the first to grow and develop popcorn and all the other types of corn.

Thousands of years ago, the Indians discovered corn plants growing wild. The ears of wild corn were very small—no bigger than strawberries. To increase their size, the Indians planted only the kernels from the larger plants. They also crossed one type of corn with another to improve it further.

Indians saved the lives of many early settlers by showing them how to grow corn. Today, corn is the most valuable crop grown in the United States.

American Indian children like to learn about their people's past.

REVIEW

READING FOR MAIN IDEAS

1. What three American Indian foods do millions of people in the world now depend on?
2. Name the American Indian group that had a very advanced form of government.
3. What important medicine for malaria was first used by American Indians?
4. Name a sport invented by American Indians.
5. Where did the names Canada and Mexico come from?

MAP SKILLS

6. Is there an American Indian reservation in Texas?
7. What American Indian group lives in southern Florida?
8. In which states do the Navaho people live?

RESEARCH SKILLS

9. Get a map of your state. Make a list of towns, rivers, mountains, and other features that have American Indian names.
10. Did the area you live in once belong to an American Indian people? Who were they? If you don't know, look up your state in the encyclopedia.

CHAPTER REVIEW

VOCABULARY MASTERY

Use the words below to complete the chapter summary. Use each only once.

bison	malaria
buffalo	quinine
carcasses	reservations
locusts	sod

The first settlers of the Great Plains built houses made of __1__. The farmers faced many problems. Sometimes __2__ would destroy their crops.

The American Indians of the region depended on the __3__ to live. Its proper name is __4__. Sometimes the settlers would kill these animals and leave the __5__ to rot. As the United States grew, the American Indians steadily lost their lands. They were forced to live on __6__. The American Indians made many contributions to modern medicine. They used __7__ to treat __8__.

READING FOR MAIN IDEAS

1. What were some of the problems that the settlers of the Great Plains faced?
2. Why was the buffalo so important to the survival of the American Indians of the Great Plains? By 1900, only a few buffalo were left. How did this happen?
3. Explain how the Plains peoples lost their land to the American settlers.
4. Why is it almost impossible to make a true general statement about American Indians?
5. Describe the government schools on the reservations. What was the purpose of these schools?
6. List some of the contributions that the American Indians made to modern medicine.

SKILLS APPLICATION

MAP SKILLS

Look at the map on page 296.

7. In what part of the nation are most reservations located?
8. What part of the United States appears to have the fewest American Indians today?
9. What one group has reservations from Michigan through Montana?
10. What American Indian communities are in Louisiana?
11. Where do the Catawba live?

WRITING SKILLS

An outline shows how the parts fit into the whole topic. Copy the outline below on a sheet of paper. Use words from the list to complete it.

beans	Kansas	pecan
canoe	kayak	pumpkin
catalpa	melon	raccoon
Chicago	Miami	Seattle
chipmunk	moose	squash
corn	Omaha	toboggan
hickory	parka	

I. American Indian Contributions
   A. Foods
      1.
      2.
      3.
      4.
      5.
   B. Animal Names
      1.
      2.
      3.
   C. Inventions
      1.
      2.
      3.
      4.
   D. Place Names
      1.
      2.
      3.
      4.
      5.
   E. Tree Names
      1.
      2.
      3.

UNIT REVIEW

VOCABULARY REVIEW

Choose one of the lists of words below. Then write a paragraph or page using all the words from that list. You may use the words in the singular or plural. On a separate page, write the words and define them.

Black Codes	construction
carpetbagger	entrepreneur
Emancipation Proclamation	ingenuity
Freedmen's Bureau	manufacture
reconstruction	patent
scalawag	reaper
segregation	thresher

READING FOR MAIN IDEAS

1. Name three people who escaped slavery and later spoke out publicly against slavery.
2. What was the Underground Railroad?
3. What event marked the beginning of the American Civil War?
4. How long did the American Civil War last?
5. What are the Thirteenth, Fourteenth, and Fifteenth Amendments?
6. List some of the inventions of the early 1800s. Tell how each contributed to the Industrial Revolution.
7. Who invented the elevator? Why was this invention so important?
8. Why has the United States been called "a nation of immigrants"?
9. What is the Statue of Liberty a symbol of?
10. What was life like in a tenement?
11. What was the Chinese Exclusion Act? When was it passed? When was it repealed?
12. Why did many Filipinos immigrate to Hawaii in the early 1900s?
13. What was the Homestead Act? How did this law help the settlement of the Great Plains?
14. What happened to the Plains people as the American settlers moved west?
15. In what year were American Indians given the right to vote?
16. Describe the land that was given to the American Indians after they were forced to leave their own territory.

THINKING SKILLS

17. Do you think the fast growth in industry after the Civil War was related to the Northern victory? Give reasons for your answers.
18. In what ways was the Civil War a turning point in American history?
19. The assembly line made mass production possible. How do you think the assembly line affects the workers? Give reasons for your answer.
20. How did the locomotive change life in the United States?
21. Many immigrants lived difficult lives after they came to the United States. Was it worth leaving their old countries? Explain your answer.
22. How can stereotypes limit a person's opportunities?
23. The United States government has established requirements and procedures that immigrants must follow to become naturalized citizens. Which ones do you think are most important? Why?
24. The American Indians suffered greatly as the American settlers moved west. Could this suffering have been avoided? Explain your answer.

SKILL DEVELOPMENT

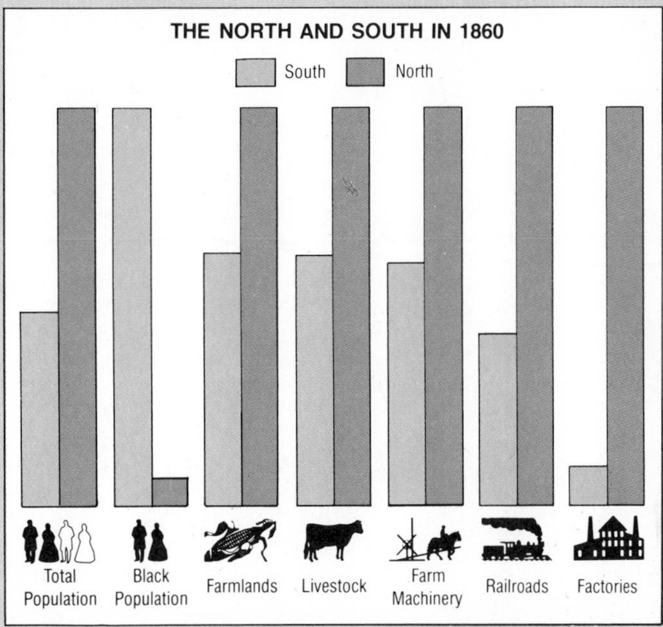

GRAPHING SKILLS

A *bar graph* helps you compare things quickly. There were big differences between the North and South at the time of the Civil War. The bar graph above lists resources for the North and South. Use the graph and information from this unit to answer the questions.

1. Did the North or South have the most resources?
2. What was the South's largest resource? How was this resource mostly used in 1860?
3. What was the South's smallest resource? What problems did that cause during the war?
4. Who had the largest number of railroads? How did that help during the war?
5. Look at the South's two largest resources. How were these two resources a major cause of conflict between the North and South?

PROBLEM-SOLVING SKILLS

Complete the chart below on a piece of paper. Briefly explain which solution the North and South wanted for each problem. Refer to Lesson 2 for help.

A Nation of Opposites

Problems	Solutions	
	North	South
New Territories (slave/free)		
Tariffs (high/low)		
Slavery (keep/end)		
Union (remain/secede)		

MAP SKILLS

Draw a map of the United States during the Civil War. Label the following and show them in different colors: the Confederacy, the Union, the slave states remaining in the Union.

THE UNITED STATES IN THE MODERN WORLD

UNIT 5

CHAPTER 1 THE EARLY TWENTIETH CENTURY

Lesson 1: The United States in 1900

FIND THE WORDS

migration subway congestion reformer

In 1900, the United States was a rapidly growing nation. Industry and business were expanding. The cities were getting bigger. Huge numbers of immigrants were coming into the cities from abroad. Many people were also leaving the farms. In particular, many Black people left farms in the South. They were seeking a better life in cities in the North.

This movement of people from one place to another is **migration** (my GRAY shun). City governments had to spend large sums of money to provide services for all these new people. At that time, people needed to live near where they worked. There were few ways to travel long distances to work. Besides, few people could afford a long trip every day. So people had to live in the center of the city. Builders had to construct higher buildings to house everyone. High buildings were also put up for business offices. Construction became a very important industry.

As the cities grew larger and more crowded, new means of transportation came to be used. The horse-and-buggy days were ending. Now, in the early 1900s, factories were making cars. City streets soon became crowded with traffic. The streets had to be paved as more people rode on buses and trolley cars. Bridges and tunnels were built to carry the streets across rivers. Tracks for trains were also built in tunnels underneath some cities. These underground railroads were called **subways.** As crowds of people, cars, and buses filled the streets, a new problem arose. This crowding of vehicles and people on city streets is called **congestion.**

In the early 1900s, there were few laws in the United States telling people how to run businesses. Because of this, there were many abuses. Children often worked long hours in factories. They had to work to help support their families. Sometimes, big companies drove smaller companies out of business by cutting prices. Sometimes, large companies sold spoiled food to stores that sold it to the poor. What is more, many people were not treated justly. Women were not allowed to vote. Blacks, American Indians, and other minority groups were not treated as full citizens. Some people in the United States protested against these conditions. These protesters were called reformers. A **reformer** is someone who tries to change things for the better.

REVIEW

VOCABULARY MASTERY

1. The crowding of streets with vehicles and people is called____.
   migration construction congestion
2. ____ is the movement of people from one place to another.
   Migration Reform Congestion
3. People who try to change things for the better are____.
   migrants reformers minorities

READING FOR MAIN IDEAS

4. Many new people came to the cities around 1900. Where did they come from?
5. What did migration force city governments to do?

THINKING SKILLS

Today, do most people still live in the centers of large cities? If not, where do they live?

Lesson 2: Reformers in the United States

FIND THE WORDS

muckrakers **Progressives**

There are many advantages to living in an industrial nation. An industrial nation produces more goods. The goods can be sold at a lower price. In an industrial society, many people can buy things that once only the rich could afford to buy.

But the growth of industry in the United States brought some problems, as well. There were people who wrote about the problems and about other things they thought were wrong. They wanted to bring wrongdoing to public attention. They were called **muckrakers** (MUK RAY kurz).

One of the muckrakers was Ida Tarbell. She was concerned that some businesses and industries were becoming too big. She feared that big business would be able to control society and take advantage of people. Ida Tarbell wrote a book about this problem. The book told about the Standard Oil Company. Standard Oil had become so big that it forced many other oil companies out of business. The company was then able to make people pay whatever price it asked for its oil. Ida Tarbell's book also explained how the oil company used other businesses to make itself even larger. Standard Oil was run by John D. Rockefeller.

Ida Tarbell was a muckraker. She wanted to bring wrongdoing to the attention of the public. She wrote a book about the Standard Oil Company. In it, she explained how this big company controlled the oil industry. She told how it took advantage of the people.

Another muckraker was Lincoln Steffens. He wrote a series of magazine articles that became known as "The Shame of the Cities." In the series, Steffens wrote about how politicians helped big business take unfair advantage of smaller businesses. He also described how politicians were cheating the people in order to help industries grow and prosper.

Other muckrakers wrote about different kinds of unfair conditions. While the rich built palaces, other citizens had barely enough to eat. Factory workers

This cartoon shows huge companies called trusts dominating the United States Senate. At the time, senators were elected by state legislatures. And state legislators could be influenced by rich companies in their state.

were at their jobs 12 hours a day, 6 or 7 days a week. They seldom earned more than 15 cents an hour. Some children began working when they were 8 or 10 years old. Here is a description of the unfortunate conditions at one factory that used child labor:

"I shall never forget my first visit to a glass factory at night. It was a big wooden structure, so loosely built that it had no protection from draft. It was surrounded by a high fence with rows of barbed wire stretched across the tops. The foreman of the factory explained to me the reason for the fence. 'It keeps the young imps inside once we got 'em for the night shift,' he said. The young imps were, of course, the boys employed. There were about 40, at least 10 of whom were less than 12 years of age."

Poor people on farms lived no better. In the South, Blacks and Whites had to rent land in order to farm. Often, most of their crops went to the landlord as payment for use of the land. These farmers did not have enough money left to pay for good food and housing.

Muckrakers were responsible for making the nation aware of many bad conditions. Thanks to them, people in the United States learned that meat and medicines were often unhealthful.

In the early 1900s, a group of people started a movement to correct some of these injustices. These people were known as **Progressives.** The Progressives did not want to destroy American business. They understood that big business is important because it produces much wealth. But the Progressives wanted to make sure that everyone was treated fairly by the law. They wanted ordinary people to have a voice in government. They also wanted to make sure that everyone had a chance to earn a good living.

As President, Theodore Roosevelt helped the Progressives bring about important reforms.

The Progressives were able to bring about important reforms. In part, this was because a President of the United States, Theodore Roosevelt, came to support many of their views. Roosevelt understood some of the problems of the poor. He tried to fight injustice. He wanted to make the government work for everyone.

Roosevelt's program became known as the Square Deal. Under his leadership, the government acted to stop many harmful business practices. It tried to improve some of the poor living conditions of that time.

In 1906, Roosevelt and the Progressives in Congress were able to get the Meat Inspection Act passed. Under this law, the government could inspect all meat transported between states. It could stop any bad meat from being shipped. In the same year, the Pure Food and Drug Act was passed. It kept businesses from manufacturing, transporting, or selling medicines and foods that might be harmful to people. Roosevelt was also concerned about saving natural resources. He ordered that 60 million hectares (150 million acres) of government forest land be set aside.

Fascinating Facts

The first subway in America was built in New York City in 1866. The tunnel was 312 feet long and 9 feet wide. The subway had one train that moved on metal tracks. A big fan at one end of the tunnel pushed the train to the other end of the tunnel. Then the fan was run backwards. It then pulled the train back.

Alfred Beach was the builder. He did not have permission from the city to build a subway. So he built it in secret in just 58 nights. City officials were very displeased. So the project was eventually closed and forgotten about.

In 1912, a crew was digging a tunnel for another subway under New York. Suddenly they went through the tunnel of Beach's subway. There sat the train, still waiting for passengers after half a century.

It could not be sold to private businesses or individuals. These lands were to be used as national parks and forest preserves.

Another leader of the Progressives was Florence Kelley. Florence Kelley was a leader of the National Consumers League. She brought public attention to the hardships and unhealthful conditions of child labor. She worked to help women receive pay equal to that of men. Kelley also worked against businesses that had dangerous or unsanitary working conditions.

Today, many people are still fighting for some of the things Florence Kelley wanted. These people especially want women to receive equal pay for equal work. They want equality for all Americans, regardless of their race, origin, religion, or sex.

REVIEW

READING FOR MAIN IDEAS

1. What leading muckraker wrote about the Standard Oil Company?
2. What muckraker wrote a series of articles about the influence of big business on politicians?
3. What group of people tried to correct the injustices?
4. What President favored reforms?
5. What was the Square Deal?
6. What group did Florence Kelley lead?

THINKING SKILLS

Have all the things the Progressives fought for been won? If not, which problems that they were concerned with still remain?

Lesson 3: World War I

FIND THE WORDS

alliance assassinate Central Powers Allied Powers neutral U-boat armistice

Americans did not pay much attention to Europe during the early 1900s. Many Americans were surprised when war broke out in Europe on July 28, 1914.

At this time, five nations dominated Europe. They were Great Britain, France, Germany, Austria-Hungary, and Russia. Two other nations, the Ottoman Empire and Italy, were also important. But they were less powerful. All these nations were rivals in many ways. They competed not just in Europe but all over the world. Britain and France had huge empires, with land on almost every continent. Russia had huge amounts of land in Europe and Asia, but no colonies. Germany and Italy had only a few colonies. Yet all these nations thought they needed colonies. They were very afraid of any

EUROPE BEFORE WORLD WAR I

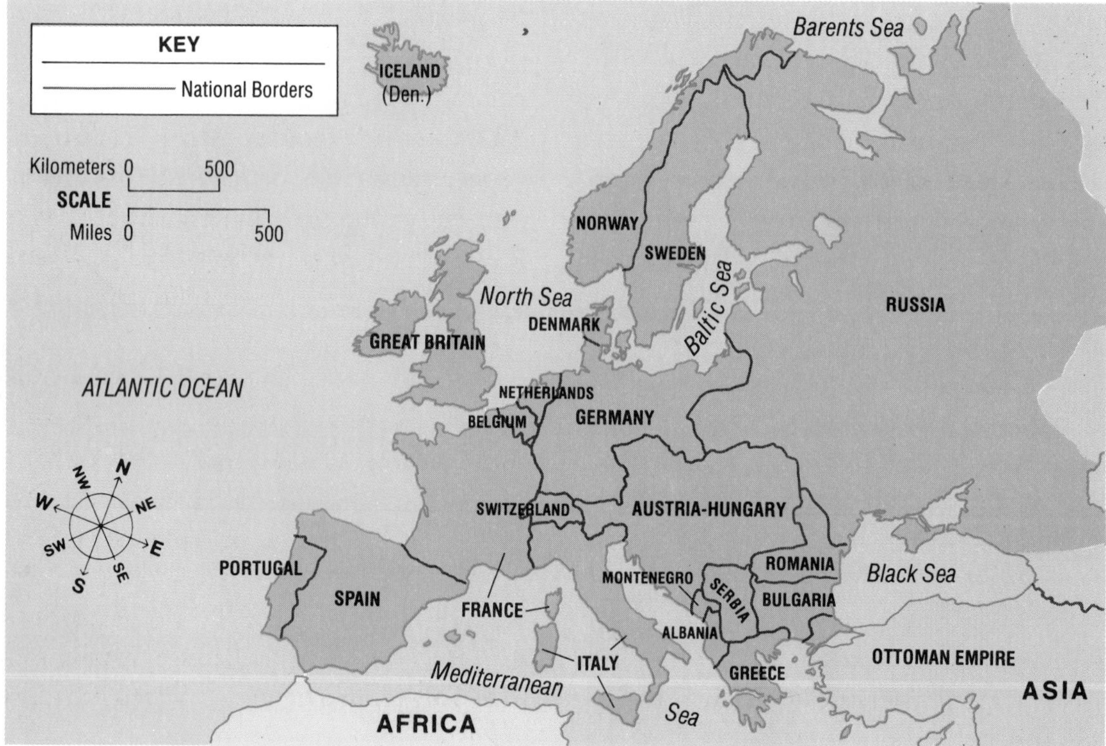

other nation's gaining power where they were already powerful.

The powerful nations of Europe feared each other. Each nation was afraid that two or more powerful nations might gang up on it in war. As a result, these nations formed alliances. An **alliance** (uh LY uns) is an agreement that nations make with each other. The partners in such an agreement are called *allies* (AL EYEZ). In effect, nations that are allies will fight for each other. They say, "For protection, we will stick together. An attack on one of us is like an attack on all of us." There were two great alliances in Europe. On one side were Britain, France, and Russia. On the other were Germany, Austria-Hungary, and Italy.

Then, in June 1914, the son of the emperor of Austria-Hungary was **assassinated** (uh SAS uh NAY tid), or killed. The killer was a Serbian. The Austro-Hungarian government blamed the small nation of Serbia for the murder. On July 28, 1914, it declared war on Serbia and sent an army into that nation. Germany supported Austria-Hungary. Within a week, Russia, France, and Great Britain had entered the war against Germany and Austria-Hungary. The Ottoman Empire and Bulgaria later joined Germany and Austria-Hungary. They were known as the

The United States entered the war in 1917. The government sold bonds to help pay for the war. This poster was aimed at immigrants.

Central Powers. Italy changed sides and supported Russia, France, and Britain. These nations were known as the **Allied Powers.** They were also joined by Japan.

At first, the United States was **neutral.** That meant it did not take sides in the war. President Woodrow Wilson had been elected in 1912. He urged Americans to be "neutral in fact as well as in name." However, this was not easy. The United States had long had close ties with Britain and France.

The fighting in Western Europe soon became trench warfare. Long lines of trenches and barbed wire faced each other all across France. From these trenches, large numbers of soldiers attacked each other. They were trying to gain small pieces of land. Poison gas, airplanes, and tanks were used in war for the first time. Hundreds of thousands of soldiers died.

The submarine, another new weapon, helped bring the United States into the war. German submarines, called **U-boats,** began to sink all ships sailing to Britain or France. In May 1915, the ocean liner *Lusitania* was sunk by a U-boat. More than a thousand people died, including many Americans. The United States government protested. As a result, the German government ordered the U-boats to stop attacking passenger liners.

In February 1917, almost 2 years later, the German government announced that the U-boats would again attack all ships around Britain. As a result, the United States broke off relations with Germany. In March, the United States government learned that the Germans were trying to get Mexico into an alliance. The Germans promised to help the Mexicans get back the land they lost to the United States in 1848. All Mexico had to do was enter the war on Germany's side if the United States declared war on Germany. Americans were shocked and angry.

Finally, in April, President Wilson asked Congress to declare war on Germany. This was done on April 6, 1917.

The United States entered the war at a time when the Allied Powers needed help. U-boats were sinking many Allied ships. Allied armies made unsuccessful attacks on the German trenches. The czar (ZAHR), or emperor, of Russia was overthrown. The new government in Russia took Russia out of the war. This freed German troops to fight in France.

But the United States soon brought new strength to the Allied armies. About 1.4 million American soldiers fought in Europe. In 1918, the Americans helped stop the German armies when they attacked in the spring. In the summer, the Allies launched many successful attacks in which Americans fought bravely. Finally, the Central Powers could fight no more. Early in November, Austria-Hungary surrendered and the German government fell. The war ended when an **armistice** (AHR muh STIS), or agreement to stop fighting, was signed on November 11, 1918.

During the war, President Wilson had wanted "14 Points" as a

President Wilson wanted to use "14 Points" as a basis for peace. He also wanted to set up a League of Nations.

basis for peace. He called for open treaties instead of secret treaties. He also called for freedom of the seas and a limit on the weapons nations could have. He wanted European culture groups to have their own nations. And he wanted to set up a League of Nations. Wilson's points were fair to all nations. But the nations that won the war did not want to be fair. They wanted to punish the nations that lost. As a result, the Treaty of Versailles (vur SY) that ended the war was very harsh. Germany was forced to admit guilt for the war. It had to pay money to the Allied Powers. The United States Senate disapproved of the conditions and rejected the treaty. As a result, the United States made a separate peace with the Central Powers.

REVIEW

VOCABULARY MASTERY

1. The United States fought on the side of the____.
   neutrals Central Powers
   Allied Powers
2. To ____ someone is to kill for political reasons.
   reform assassinate muckrake
3. An ____ is an agreement to stop fighting.
   armistice assassination alliance
4. A(n) ____ is an agreement nations make to protect each other.
   armistice migration alliance
5. The ____ helped bring the United States into World War I.
   armistice assassination U-boat

READING FOR MAIN IDEAS

6. What were the two groups of nations that fought in World War I called?
7. Who was President of the United States during World War I?
8. Name three new weapons used in World War I.
9. What did Wilson want as the basis for peace?
10. What treaty ended the war?

THINKING SKILLS

Did the United States have good reasons for entering World War I? Why, or why not?

Lesson 4: The Vote for Women

FIND THE WORDS

suffrage **suffragist**

Before World War I, many efforts to correct bad conditions and injustices in the United States had succeeded. Laws had been passed to limit the power of big business. New laws protected children from being used as cheap labor. Women had worked hard for these laws. There were other reforms made in law and in government as well.

The Declaration of Independence had stated that all men were created equal. But half the nation's citizens were women. They were still not treated equally. Until 1920, most women did not have the right to vote.

During the 1800s and early 1900s, the role of women was the subject of much heated discussion. People had been taught to believe that a woman's place was in the home. Girls were often told that they were too weak in mind and body to go to college.

Until 1920, most women did not have the right to vote. These women are demonstrating to get the vote.

But many women proved that these beliefs were wrong. A determined few did go to college. Some women went on to become doctors, lawyers, scientists, and business managers. Women continued to do many things that some people believed only men could do. Maria Mitchell discovered Mitchell's Comet in 1847. She was later professor of astronomy at Vassar College. In 1849, Dr. Elizabeth Blackwell graduated from medical school at the head of her class. She was the first woman in the United States to earn a medical degree. In 1879, Mary Baker Eddy founded the Church of Christ, Scientist. She also started her own newspaper, the *Christian Science Monitor*. In 1926, Gertrude Ederle (A dur lee) swam the English Channel. She broke all the earlier records set by men. And, in 1932, Amelia Earhart became the first woman to fly a plane across the Atlantic alone. She was also the first person to fly alone from Honolulu to California.

There was a shortage of workers during World War I. For the first time, many women had the chance to work outside the home. During wartime, women were hired for jobs that were usually done by men. They worked in factories making tools, weapons, and explosives. They refined petroleum and metals. They made airplane and automobile parts. They ran farms. They worked on the railroads. They did everything that was necessary to support the war effort at home.

More women than ever before were taking those jobs that were open to them. Many became secretaries and clerks. Some held jobs as bank tellers, nurses, and teachers. But after the war, women lost the better-paying factory jobs. High level jobs in all areas were also reserved for men. Women were not even considered for such jobs. Many people believed men should earn money and women should raise families.

Women sometimes disagreed with each other about whether or not women should hold jobs. But most women did agree that they should have the right to vote. For a long time, women had been fighting for suffrage. **Suffrage** means the right to vote. People who fight for the right to vote are called **suffragists.**

Millions of women who worked in the United States wanted better jobs. They wanted higher wages and better working conditions. These women believed that the vote would give them the power to bring about these changes. They also realized that, with the right to vote, they could help correct some other injustices.

For example, during the 1800s, married women were not allowed to own property in most states. Even those who worked did not really own their earnings. Under the law, everything a woman had belonged to her husband. One of the causes of the American Revolution was the colonists' complaint about taxation without representation. Yet, 125 years later, working women had to pay taxes without being represented in any law-making bodies.

Some women, such as Alice Paul, told people about their cause by leading marches and demonstrations. Often the women who took part in these events were laughed at and insulted. Some were beaten and jailed. But they did not stop fighting for their rights. Other women worked through the political system. Carrie Chapman Catt organized women to work in local political districts. She had 2 million women working in a national campaign. All this effort finally paid off. Also, many people realized that women had helped win the war. So in 1920, the Constitution was changed. The Nineteenth Amendment gave women across the nation the full right to vote in elections.

Winning the right to vote brought women closer to the American ideal of equality for all. But it did not solve all their problems. Many still believed that women and men were not equal. Women could vote. But few women were elected to office. Many opportunities were still denied to women.

Pictured are Carrie Chapman Catt, Julia Ward Howe, and Alice Paul. They were early suffragist leaders.

People to Remember

Susan B. Anthony

Susan B. Anthony was the great leader in the movement for women's suffrage. For 60 years, she worked tirelessly for women's rights.

The suffrage movement had started in 1848 in Seneca Falls, New York. There, Elizabeth Cady Stanton and Lucretia Mott held the first Women's Rights Convention. At Seneca Falls, women declared that men and women are created equal.

The partnership of Susan B. Anthony and Elizabeth Cady Stanton was the movement's vital center for half a century. Together, they founded the National American Woman Suffrage Association.

Susan B. Anthony gained fame nationally by voting in the 1872 presidential election. Anthony believed she had the right to vote as a citizen and a person. She was arrested for breaking the law.

Over the years, Anthony carried her message all around the country. By the early 1900s, the women's suffrage movement had grown larger. Women began to win limited voting rights in some states.

Susan B. Anthony died in 1906. Fourteen years later, in 1920, the Nineteenth Amendment was passed. It was named the "Anthony Amendment" in her honor. It says that "the right of citizens of the United States to vote shall not be denied or abridged by the United States or by any State on account of sex." Thanks to the efforts of Susan B. Anthony, American women won the right to vote.

REVIEW

READING FOR MAIN IDEAS

1. Who was the first American woman to earn a medical degree?
2. What jobs did women hold during World War I? List five kinds.
3. When and where did the women's suffrage movement begin in the United States?
4. Who was Susan B. Anthony?
5. What amendment to the Constitution gave women the right to vote?

THINKING SKILLS

How old do you have to be to vote today? How long have people this age had the right to vote?

CHAPTER REVIEW

VOCABULARY MASTERY

Use the words below to complete the chapter summary. Use each only once.

alliances	migration
Allied Powers	muckrakers
armistice	Progressives
assassinated	reformers
Central Powers	suffragists

In 1900, cities were growing in part because of _1_ from the farms. All these new people created problems for the cities. The _2_ tried to change things for the better. The _3_ wrote about the problems created by big business. The _4_ founded a political movement to help solve the problems.

World War I began when an Austro-Hungarian leader was _5_. The European nations were divided into two _6_. Germany, Austria-Hungary, and the Ottoman Empire were the _7_. Their opponents were called the _8_. In 1918, a(n) _9_ was signed. It ended World War I.

In 1920, women's right to vote was approved in the United States. This was because of the efforts of the _10_.

READING FOR MAIN IDEAS

1. Describe the new means of transportation the cities came to use around 1900.
2. Name two leading muckrakers and tell what they did.
3. What is a U-boat? Why were they important in World War I?
4. Why did President Woodrow Wilson ask Congress to declare war on Germany?
5. Name two early suffragist leaders. Tell how they fought for women's right to vote.

SKILLS APPLICATION

SUMMARIZING SKILLS

A **summary** helps you remember specific facts. It gives you that information in brief form. Read the paragraph below. When you finish, write a summary of it. Be sure it includes the main ideas of the paragraph.

Alice Paul was born in New Jersey in 1885. Unlike many women of her time, she went to college. She earned a Ph.D. in social work. Later, she earned three law degrees. Like other women of her time, she could not vote. Dr. Paul wanted to change that. First, she worked in England to help women there gain the right to vote. Then, she came back to the United States. Paul organized hunger strikes and protest marches. Sometimes she and her marchers were jailed. Not everyone agreed with her methods of protesting. Others thought it silly that women should protest at all. Dr. Paul's efforts and those of many others were finally successful. In 1920, Congress approved the Nineteenth Amendment to the Constitution. This gave the women of the United States the right to vote.

RESEARCH AND SUMMARIZING SKILLS

Find out more about one of these leaders: Susan B. Anthony, Elizabeth Cady Stanton, Lucretia Mott, Julia Ward Howe, Carrie Chapman Catt, Abigail Scott Duniway. Use an encyclopedia and other library books. Then write a one-paragraph summary of your findings.

TIME LINE SKILLS

Make a time line of World War I showing four events leading up to the United States's declaring war on Germany.

CHAPTER 2 THE UNITED STATES IN A CHANGING WORLD

Lesson 1: The Twenties

FIND THE WORDS

suburb advertising Prohibition

The 10 years between 1919 and 1929 were thought of as good years for the United States. Many people were making money. Business was booming. It seemed that the day would soon come when every American citizen could live in comfort.

New products were being manufactured. Radios offered exciting home entertainment. Refrigerators were introduced that used electric motors instead of blocks of ice to cool food. People bought electric vacuum cleaners and washing machines. Many of these new products made housework much easier.

Henry Ford started manufacturing cars on an assembly line. The assembly line made it possible to build more cars at a faster rate. Each worker put on one part as cars moved down the line. Ford lowered prices until many more people in the United States could afford to buy a car. More cars meant more jobs for workers. More cars meant that more and better roads were needed. Dirt roads were paved with concrete and asphalt. Motels were built to give travelers a place to sleep along the roads. Families could now easily travel long distances to visit each other. People no longer had to live near their work. Many people moved from the city to the suburbs. A **suburb** is a community near a city where people who work in the city live.

In the 1920s, advertising became an important new business. **Advertising** is telling people about products or services. Businesses advertised on signs, in newspapers and magazines, and on radio. Through advertising, businesses tried to get people to buy their products. Advertising suggested that the more people bought, the happier they were bound to be.

It did seem as though people were happy in the 1920s. These years have been called the Roaring Twenties or the Jazz Age. In 1919, the Eighteenth Amendment to the Constitution had been approved. This amendment made it illegal to make or sell alcoholic beverages. This was known as **Prohibition** (PROH uh BISH un). But some people drank alcoholic beverages anyway. They broke the law. Gangsters got rich supplying them with alcohol. There were also some dishonest people in the federal government when Warren G. Harding was President. When their wrongdoing was found out, some important government leaders went to jail.

Many of the changes of the

Left: Amelia Earhart flew across the Atlantic as a passenger in 1928. In 1935, she became the first pilot to fly solo from Honolulu to California. *Below:* George Herman ("Babe") Ruth hit 60 home runs in 1927, setting a season record. Babe Ruth was the most famous sports hero of his time.

1920s were reflected in entertainment. Going to the picture show became very popular. In turn, the movies helped spread new ways of acting and dressing. During the 1920s, Harlem in New York City became a center for Black artists, musicians, and writers. Harlem jazz clubs became popular and famous throughout the nation. Duke Ellington and Count Basie were two of the greatest jazz musicians.

Things were changing very fast in the 1920s. Some Americans wanted things to stay the same. They reacted to change by attacking new people and ideas. Many had bad feelings about foreigners. So the government placed limits on the number of immigrants in 1921 and 1924.

The good times of the 1920s did not reach most of the people in the United States. In some industries, such as coal mining, workers often did not have jobs. Farmers' earnings did not rise. Most factory workers continued to be underpaid. Many women worked long hours for low wages in laundries and textile mills. Very few people in the United States were truly well-off.

The twenties were also a time of heroes who often seemed larger than life. Gertrude Ederle swam the English Channel. Amelia Earhart was a brave aviator and one of the pioneers of flight. Baseball player Babe Ruth was the most famous sports figure of the age. The greatest hero was Charles A. Lindbergh. In 1927, this young aviator became the first pilot to fly across the Atlantic alone.

REVIEW

VOCABULARY MASTERY

1. The law against drinking alcohol was known as ___.
   suffrage amendment Prohibition
2. ___ is telling people about products and services.
   Advertising Entertainment Prohibition

READING FOR MAIN IDEAS

3. List four new products that were manufactured during the 1920s.
4. Who started manufacturing cars on an assembly line?
5. What area of New York became a center for Blacks in the arts?

THINKING SKILLS

What was life like for most working people in the 1920s?

RESEARCH AND WRITING SKILLS

Find out more about one of these people: Count Basie, Amelia Earhart, Gertrude Ederle, Duke Ellington, Charles A. Lindbergh, Babe Ruth. Use an encyclopedia and other library books. Then write a one-page report.

Lesson 2: The Great Depression and the New Deal

FIND THE WORDS

Great Depression **stock** **drought** **bonus** **erosion** **session**

In 1929, the booming good times of the twenties quickly came to an end. The period that followed was known as the **Great Depression.** A depression is a time when many businesses fail. Many workers do not have jobs. The Great Depression lasted for 10 years. It was one of America's most difficult periods.

There were many reasons for the Great Depression. During the 1920s, many people bought stocks. **Stocks** are shares in a company. The prices of stocks kept going up. Many people thought this would continue forever. They put all their money into stocks. Then, in October 1929, the prices of stocks began to fall. Many people who had bought stocks on credit could not pay for them. They sold stocks at lower and lower prices. Whole fortunes were wiped out.

Business owners became frightened. Factories began to

During the Great Depression, bread lines kept many people from starving. A drought and dust storms destroyed land, machinery, and homes.

produce fewer goods. Stores ordered fewer goods. Workers had to be laid off. As people lost their jobs, they bought fewer goods. This made prices drop and caused more factories to close. People had to take their savings out of the banks in order to live. Many banks then had to close. They soon had no money left.

These were terrible times for the nation. To make matters worse, in the early 1930s there was a terrible drought (DROWT) in the Great Plains. A **drought** is a period of little or no rainfall. During a long drought, land and crops are ruined. In the 1930s, dust storms destroyed land, machinery, and homes. These storms also killed farm animals. Thousands of people had to leave their farms and go to the cities to look for work. But there was no work.

At first, the federal government did little to help people. President Herbert Hoover and others believed that people should solve their own problems. At the time, many veterans were asking for the government to pay them a **bonus.** This was an extra payment that would be a reward for fighting in World War I. Many poor veterans came to Washington and formed a "Bonus Army." Some camped out near the Capitol. After a time, President Hoover ordered the Army to remove the veterans. Troops forced the unarmed men to leave and burned their camp. To many, this was a sign of the government's lack of concern for the people's suffering.

In 1932, Franklin D. Roosevelt was elected President of the United States. He promised a "New Deal" to cure the nation's problems. Roosevelt brought many advisers to Washington to find ways to help. These advisers were often called the "Brain Trust." Congress soon passed laws to help banks, industry, farmers, workers, and the unemployed. The Tennessee Valley Authority (TVA) was set up. This government company built dams to control floods and provide electricity. The TVA improved a vast area.

In 1935, Roosevelt began the second part of the New Deal.

Franklin D. Roosevelt promised a "New Deal" to solve the nation's problems.

More help was given to the unemployed and to farmers. The right of workers to join labor unions was protected. Housing was built for the poor. The Social Security Act set up a system of pensions for retired people. Money was taken out of working people's salaries. It was used to make monthly payments to older people when they stopped work. Another program protected natural resources, especially soil. At the time, there was very bad erosion in the United States. Soil **erosion** is the washing away or blowing away of the soil.

President Roosevelt did not succeed at everything he tried. The Supreme Court declared some of his programs unconstitutional. In 1937, Roosevelt tried to add extra judges to the Supreme Court. These judges supported his programs. But his plan was defeated. A special **session,** or meeting, of Congress that same year refused to pass the laws he wanted. In 1938, the President campaigned against opponents in his own party. Most were reelected.

The New Deal did succeed in helping millions of people who were suffering because of the Great Depression. Because of the New Deal, the role of the federal government in the economy and society grew. However, the Great Depression did not fully end until World War II began.

REVIEW

VOCABULARY MASTERY

1. ___ is the washing away or blowing away of soil.
Drought   Erosion   Depression

2. A___is a share in a company.
stock   bonus   session

3. A ___ is an extra payment given as a reward.
stock   bonus   session

4. A(n) ___ is a period of little or no rainfall.
drought   erosion   depression

5. A meeting of Congress is called a(n) ___.
depression   erosion   session

READING FOR MAIN IDEAS

6. What were the bad times after the 1920s called?

7. When did the prices of stocks begin to fall?

8. What happened on the Great Plains in the 1930s?

9. What was President Franklin Roosevelt's program called?

10. When did the American economy fully recover from the bad times?

THINKING SKILLS

Suppose you were President when a depression started. Make a list of things you could do to help.

Lesson 3: World War II

FIND THE WORDS

dictator Axis
concentration camp
isolationism
Allies atomic bomb

The Great Depression that hit the United States in the 1930s was worldwide. Nations everywhere felt its effects. The Depression years caused great changes, especially in Germany.

After World War I, a democratic government had been set up in Germany for the first time. But the Treaty of Versailles that ended the war had taken land and resources from Germany. It had made the Germans pay more money than they could afford to the winning nations.

During the 1920s and 1930s, the German government could not solve the people's problems. The Great Depression was especially bad there. The German people became angry and resentful. They felt they were being treated unfairly.

EUROPE BETWEEN THE WORLD WARS

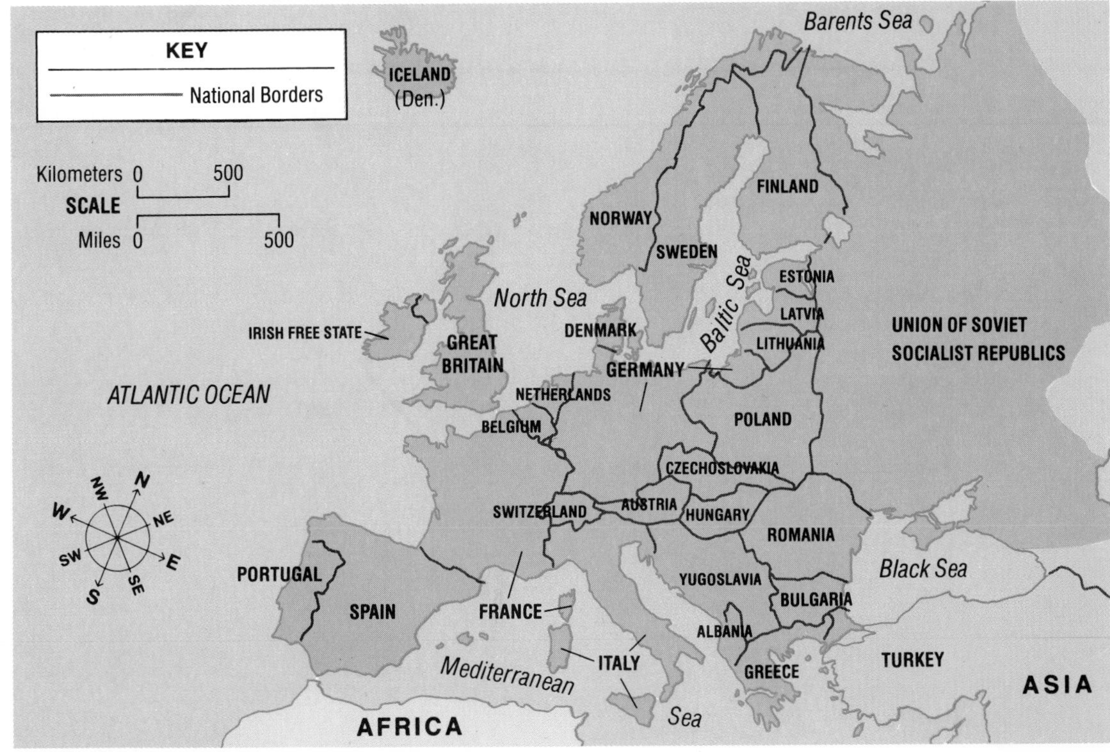

Adolf Hitler became a powerful leader in Germany. He told the Germans that they were better than any other people in the world. He said Germany's problems were caused by the Treaty of Versailles and by Jewish people. Hitler said that the solution was to get more land and to get rid of the Jews. Some Germans were so unhappy and in such a bad situation that they believed what Hitler said.

Hitler was the head of the Nazi (NAHT see) Party. Hitler and the Nazis were able to take over the German government. Hitler became a dictator. A **dictator** is a ruler who has complete power over a government. In Germany, Hitler and the Nazis controlled everything. The Germans lost the rights they had gained under their democratic government. Hitler began building an army. He began preparing for war.

In Italy, another dictator, Benito Mussolini, had seized power. Mussolini was the leader of the Fascist (FASH ist) Party. Conditions in Italy were also bad. The Italian people thought that the Treaty of Versailles did not give them enough land. So Italy took over lands in Africa.

Hitler and Mussolini joined forces. They began to attack other European nations. They began to take over other nations' land. Their partnership was called the **Axis.** Japan later joined the Axis.

On September 1, 1939, the German army marched into Poland. World War II had begun. Britain and France declared war on Germany. But Germany was better prepared for war than the other nations were. Between 1939 and 1941, Germany conquered most of Europe. The German army took over Poland, Norway, Czechoslovakia, the Netherlands,

Adolf Hitler became a powerful leader in Germany. He used huge rallies to stir up the patriotism of the German people.

Benito Mussolini seized power in Italy. He joined forces with Hitler to attack other European nations.

Denmark, Belgium, and France. Great Britain stood alone against the Nazis. Soon the Germans started bombing British cities.

Throughout Europe, Hitler had special prisons built for the Jews and others he was trying to destroy. These prisons were called **concentration camps.** Millions of people died in them. By the time the war ended, the Nazis had murdered 6 million Jews. Hitler also had several million other people who opposed him killed.

At first, the United States wanted to stay out of the war. Many people felt that the nation should worry only about itself. They thought it should not get involved with the problems of other nations. Such a policy was called **isolationism** (EYE suh LAY shuh NIZ um). But by that time, isolationism was no longer practical. American businesses were trading with other nations. Thus, the United States was affected by events in those nations.

During the 1930s, the Japanese were trying to build an empire in Asia. Japan, too, was becoming an industrial nation. The Japanese needed raw materials and markets for their goods. They wanted to control lands in southeast Asia. These lands had rich resources such as petroleum, rubber, and tin. They also grew many foods Japan needed. Japan went to war against China in 1931. By the late 1930s, Japan controlled all the coastal provinces of China.

Thousands of Japanese-Americans joined the United States armed forces in World War II. These soldiers are being honored for bravery.

But the United States did not want Japan to control China and southeast Asia. The United States wanted those areas to remain open to American trade. The Japanese would not have allowed that. Relations between Japan and the United States became worse.

On December 7, 1941, the Japanese made a surprise attack against the United States Navy base at Pearl Harbor in Hawaii. Thousands of Americans were killed or wounded. Many American ships were destroyed. The next day, the United States declared war on Japan.

The United States then joined forces with Britain and the Soviet

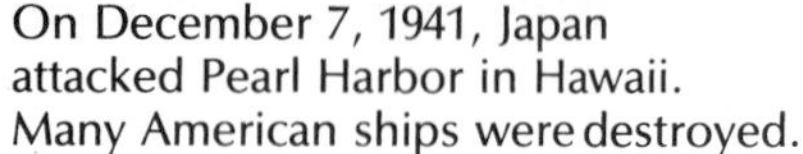

On December 7, 1941, Japan attacked Pearl Harbor in Hawaii. Many American ships were destroyed.

The bravery of Soviet soldiers impressed many Americans. Here, United States soldiers and Soviet soldiers meet after the defeat of Germany.

Union to fight Germany and Italy. This group was called the **Allies.** Once again, war reached around the world. Now it was truly a world war.

The United States and the Soviet Union had not been friendly for some time. The problems went back to the time of World War I. The Soviet Union had become Communist after a revolution in 1917. Many Americans did not like the Communists.

During the war, the bravery of Soviet soldiers changed many Americans' ideas about the Soviet Union. When the Germans attacked the Soviet Union in June 1941, the Soviets were nearly defeated. They retreated as far east as Moscow before they finally stopped the Germans. Millions of Soviet citizens died. But the Germans could not get the Soviet Union to give up. This made Americans think less about Communism and more about courage. Many Americans hoped that, after the war, the United States could remain friendly with the Soviet Union.

On May 8, 1945, the war ended in Europe. Germany finally surrendered. The Allies had already defeated Italy. Now they were preparing to invade Japan. The new President of the United States was Harry Truman. Truman wanted the war to end quickly. That way, he thought, fewer American troops would die. By this time, the United States had built the most powerful weapon the world had ever seen. This weapon was the **atomic bomb.** It used the power of the splitting atom. Truman decided to use this weapon against Japan.

On August 6, 1945, the United States dropped the atomic bomb on the Japanese city of Hiroshima (HIR uh SHEE muh). Over 100,000 people were killed immediately. Three days later, a second bomb destroyed Nagasaki (NAH guh SAH kee). Japan surrendered, and World War II was over.

Soon after the war began, the Allies started to plan for peace when the war would be over. In 1941, President Roosevelt and British Prime Minister Winston Churchill signed the Atlantic Charter. They wanted to protect weak nations from stronger ones. They wanted to prevent the use of force and to ensure peace. In 1943, the United States, Britain, China, and the Soviet Union called for an international organization for peace. Planning for the new organization was done over the next 2 years. Finally, in 1945, the Charter of the United Nations was signed at San Francisco. The United Nations has worked since then for peace and cooperation among all nations. The headquarters of the United Nations is in New York City.

REVIEW

VOCABULARY MASTERY

1. Hitler had the Jews put into____.
isolation   the Axis
concentration camps

2. ____ is the policy of staying out of other nations' affairs.
Isolationism   Nazism   Fascism

3. A ____ is a person who controls everything in a nation.
dictator   Nazi   Fascist

4. In World War II, the United States fought on the side of the____.
Allies   Axis   dictators

5. Germany, Italy, and Japan formed the____.
Allies   Axis   isolationists

READING FOR MAIN IDEAS

6. What kind of government did Germany have right after World War I?

7. What group did Adolf Hitler lead?

8. What nation stood alone for a time against the Axis?

9. What happened at Pearl Harbor on December 7, 1941?

10. What was the relationship between the United States and the Soviet Union during World War II?

GET THE DATE STRAIGHT

Match the event with the date.

11. World War II began.	**A.** May 8, 1945
12. Pearl Harbor was attacked.	**B.** September 1, 1939
13. The war ended in Europe.	**C.** August 6, 1945
14. Hiroshima was bombed.	**D.** December 7, 1941

THINKING SKILLS

How might history have been different if the Axis had won World War II?

Lesson 4: The War at Home

FIND THE WORDS

ration **integration**
relocation camp **Nisei**

During World War II, almost everyone in the United States contributed to winning the war. They helped in different ways.

While millions of men were fighting overseas, women stepped into important jobs in industry at home. This had also happened during World War I. Again, women proved that they could do the work as well as men. Some women became welders. Others drove trucks, worked in construction, and did thousands of other jobs. Women also joined the armed forces in great numbers. There were thousands of women in the Army and the Army Air Corps. After the war ended, the soldiers came back to their jobs. Again, many women lost their wartime jobs. But American industry was changing. Women still worked in some jobs that were filled only by men before. During the war, women had been needed as workers. After the war, many women wanted to keep on working outside the home.

Many American women supported the war effort by working in factories on the home front.

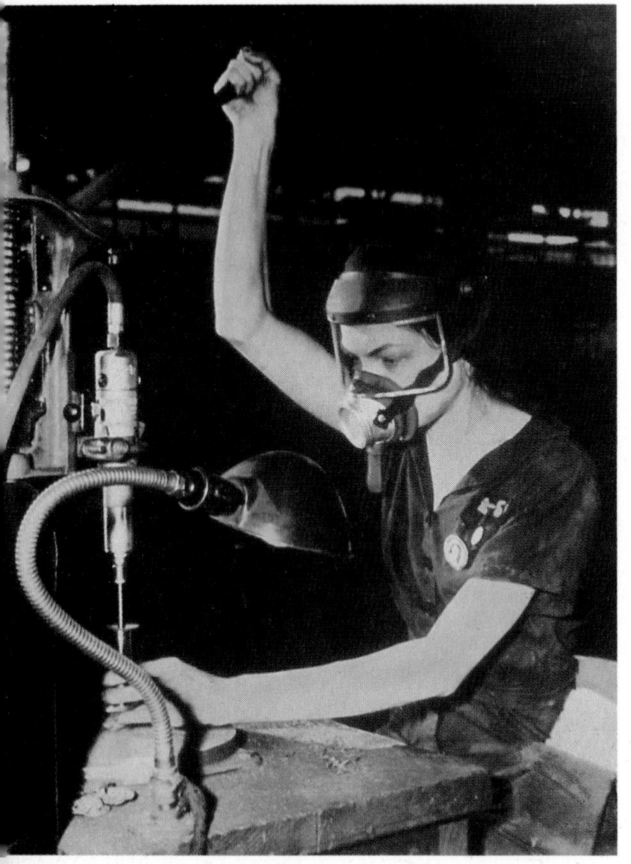

During World War II, factories stopped producing ordinary goods so that they could manufacture war materials. Automobile manufacturers began building airplane engines, tanks, and army trucks. Textile manufacturers were developing new materials, such as nylon. Americans were learning to do without many things they had been used to having. The government told people that they must use less of goods such as meat, butter, and gasoline. Such goods were **rationed** (RASH und). That meant that the amount a person could buy was limited. The government gave out ration coupons. These had to be used along with money to buy things. Each person had only so many coupons. When they were used up, people had to do without the rationed goods.

The United States gave the other Allies many weapons and supplies to use in fighting Germany and Japan. In 1944, the United States built over 60,000 planes and 45,000 tanks. Many Americans went overseas to fight in the war. Over a million of them were killed or wounded in Europe and the Pacific.

During World War II, many of the soldiers who fought and died for their country were Black. Yet Black people still did not have all the rights and freedoms that other Americans had. Even in the Army, Black soldiers had to live in separate barracks and fight in separate units. After the war, President Harry Truman ordered the **integration** of the armed forces. That meant that there would no longer be segregation, or separation by race, in the armed forces.

BLACKS IN WORLD WAR II

About 1 million Blacks served their nation in the armed forces in World War II. For the first time, Blacks were allowed to join the Marines and to train as officers and Air Force pilots. The blood bank, developed by a Black doctor, Charles Drew, saved many lives. After the war, the armed forces were integrated.

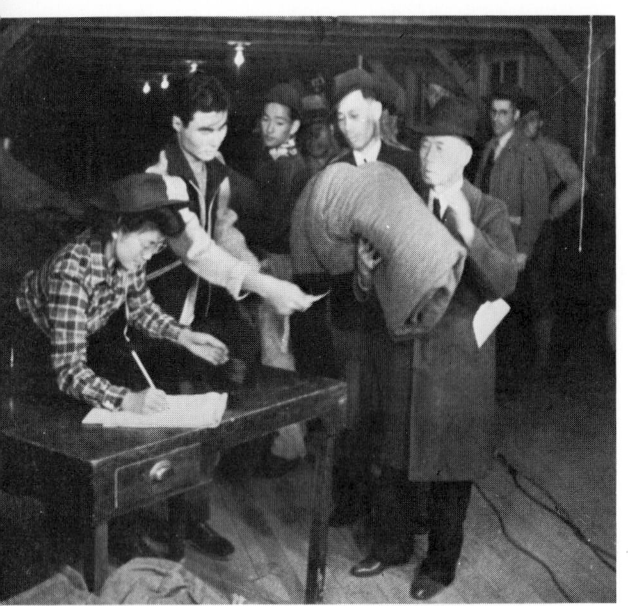

The United States government sent thousands of Japanese-Americans to relocation camps located far from the West Coast.

Because of the war with Japan, some people in the United States began to distrust Japanese-Americans. Some people suspected the Japanese-Americans of spying for the Japanese government. In 1942, the government removed thousands of Japanese-Americans from their homes on the West Coast. They were placed in special prison camps called **relocation camps.** These relocation camps were located far from the West Coast. Men, women, and children were imprisoned in these camps. Treatment of Japanese-Americans was harsh and unfair. Yet in spite of it, they continued to be loyal and good American citizens. The people born in the United States of Japanese parents were called **Nisei** (NEE SAY). About 8,000 Nisei joined the armed forces and fought bravely for their country.

American scientists were also working for the war effort. They developed the atomic bomb in 1945. This powerful weapon began a new age in the history of the world.

REVIEW

VOCABULARY MASTERY

1. The Nisei were put into____.
   concentration camps
   relocation camps   isolation
2. To____goods is to limit the amount people can buy.
   ration   relocate   integrate
3. President Truman ordered the____ of the armed forces.
   segregation   relocation
   integration

READING FOR MAIN IDEAS

4. Who did many jobs at home while the soldiers were fighting overseas?
5. Name two groups that were not treated equally during the war.

THINKING SKILLS

How can war help citizens who are discriminated against to improve their situation?

Lesson 5: The Cold War

FIND THE WORDS

cold war economy socialism capitalism free enterprise

By the end of World War II, the Soviet Union and the United States had become rivals. They did not agree about what should happen in certain countries. The Soviet Union wanted Communist governments in Poland and other Eastern European nations. The United States wanted democratic governments there. But the Soviet Union had its army in Eastern Europe. The American army was in Western Europe. So the Soviets helped Communists take over the governments in Eastern European countries. Soon, Poland, Hungary, Bulgaria, Romania, and Albania had Communist governments. Later, Yugoslavia and Czechoslovakia fell under Communist rule.

Meanwhile, in Asia, a civil war was going on. The Soviet Union and the United States took sides in this war. This war was fought in China between Chinese Communists and Chinese Nationalists. The Soviet Union supported the Communists. They were led by Mao Tse-tung (MOW tzay DUNG). The United States supported the Nationalists. Chiang Kai-shek (JYANG KY SHEK) was leader of that side. Chiang's government was weak. It did not have the support of most Chinese. Partly for this reason, the United States began withdrawing its support of the Nationalists in 1948. In 1949, the Communists won. The Nationalists withdrew to Taiwan (TY WAHN). This is a large island off the coast of China. There, the Nationalists set up a separate Chinese government. For many years, the United States did not recognize the Communist government of China. It dealt only with Taiwan.

By 1949, the Soviet Union had

Dwight D. Eisenhower commanded Allied forces in Europe in World War II. A national hero, "Ike" was elected President in 1952.

WHERE WE ARE IN TIME AND PLACE

THE COLD WAR IN EUROPE

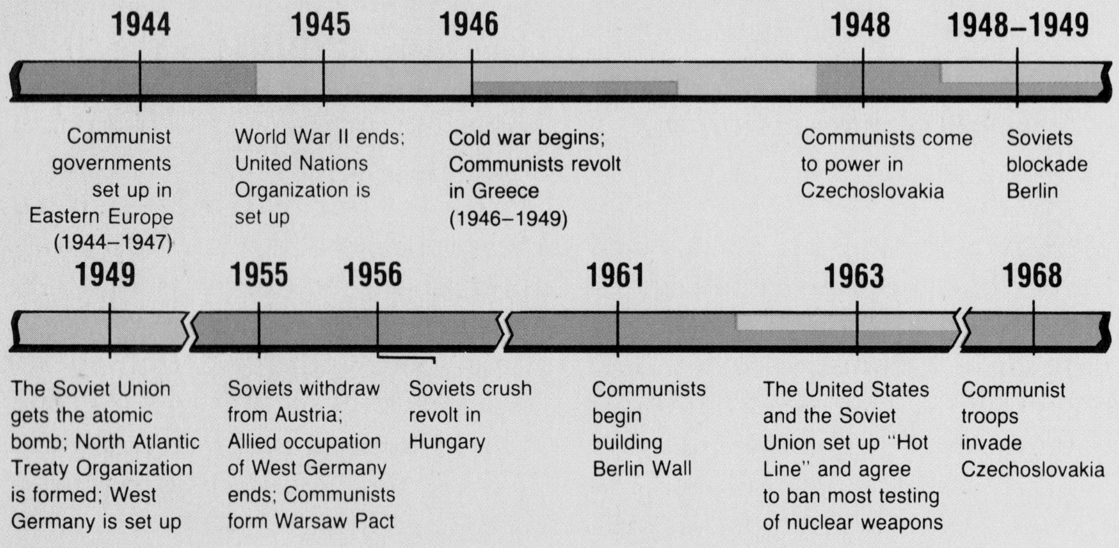

KEY
National Borders
Members of NATO
Members of the Warsaw Pact

Kilometers 0 500
SCALE
Miles 0 500

N NE E SE S SW W NW

ATLANTIC OCEAN
Barents Sea
ICELAND
UNITED KINGDOM OF GREAT BRITAIN AND NORTHERN IRELAND
IRELAND
North Sea
NORWAY
SWEDEN
FINLAND
Baltic Sea
DENMARK
UNION OF SOVIET SOCIALIST REPUBLICS
NETHERLANDS
BELGIUM
EAST GERMANY
WEST GERMANY
POLAND
CZECHOSLOVAKIA
SWITZERLAND
AUSTRIA
HUNGARY
ROMANIA
PORTUGAL
SPAIN
FRANCE
YUGOSLAVIA
Black Sea
BULGARIA
ALBANIA
ITALY
TURKEY
GREECE
Mediterranean Sea
AFRICA
ASIA

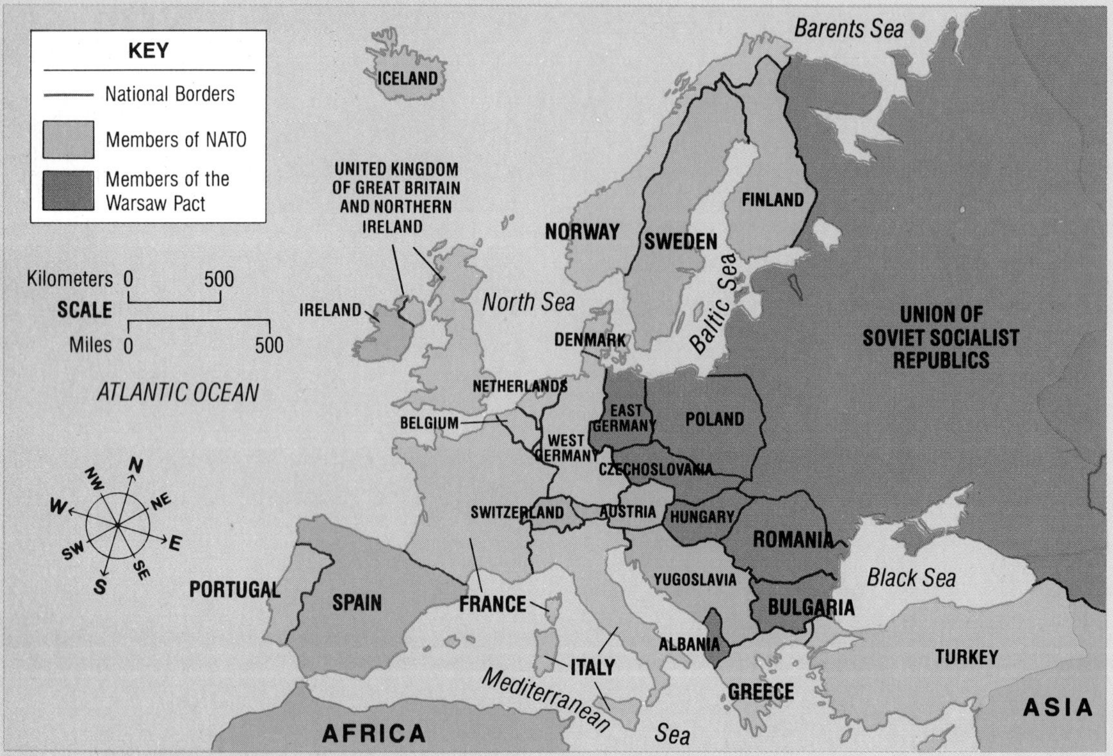

developed an atomic bomb. The United States was no longer the only nation in the world with this weapon. Both nations realized that if they fought each other now, they could destroy much of the world. They began to wage a new kind of war—a war without fighting. It was called the **cold war.**

The United States and the Communist nations disagreed about what kind of economy was best. An **economy** is the way in which people produce and distribute goods and services.

The Communists believed in an economy controlled by the government. This kind of economy is called **socialism.** In a socialist economy, the government decides what products are produced and who gets them.

Most Americans believed in an economy run by private individuals and businesses. This kind of economy is called **capitalism** or **free enterprise.** In a capitalist economy, business leaders decide what to produce. People decide what they want to buy.

The Communists wanted to destroy capitalism. They said it was unfair to workers. Most Americans disagreed. They believed that socialism gave too much power to the government. Communist governments denied their people many rights and freedoms.

Many Europeans and Americans were worried about an attack by the Soviet Union. In 1949, 10 European nations joined the United States and Canada to form a military alliance. It was called the North Atlantic Treaty Organization (NATO). An attack on any member nation would be treated as an attack on all. In 1955, the Soviet Union and Communist nations of Europe also formed an alliance. This was the Warsaw Pact.

American troops fought in the Korean War, 1950–1953. About 33,000 Americans died in this war. Korea is between 33° and 43° north latitude and between 124° and 131° east longitude.

In the 1950s, the United States became involved in conflicts in different parts of the world. One of these conflicts was the Korean War. After World War II, Korea was split into two parts. The part north of 38° north latitude became North Korea. It had most of the factories. The part south of 38° north latitude became South Korea. It had most of the good farmland. Then, in 1950, the Korean War began. Communist North Korea attacked South Korea. United Nations troops, mostly from the United States, were sent to help South Korea. China and the Soviet Union supported the Communists in North Korea. Finally, in 1953, there was an armistice. It drew a border between the two Koreas close to the boundary of 1950.

There was also a civil war in Cuba. There, the Communists were led by Fidel Castro. Castro gained control of Cuba in 1959.

John F. Kennedy was elected President in 1960. In 1961, he started the Alliance for Progress to combat poverty in Latin America. It was poverty that made many people support Communism. In 1961, the United States supported an invasion of Cuba by anti-Communists at the Bay of Pigs. This attack failed, and Castro became stronger. In 1962, the Soviet Union began to build missile bases in Cuba. The United States protested and began a blockade of Cuba. The Soviet Union backed down and withdrew the missiles. The world had come very close to nuclear war.

The missile crisis had another result. The United States and the Soviet Union opened up a "Hot Line" in 1963. If another crisis arose, leaders of the two nations could discuss it and keep a war from happening by accident. Also in 1963, the two nations agreed to ban most testing of nuclear weapons. Many other nations also joined in this agreement.

REVIEW

VOCABULARY MASTERY

1. Capitalism is also called____.
free enterprise socialism
economics

2. Socialism is a kind of____.
free enterprise nationalism
economy

3. The ____ is the struggle between the Soviet Union and the United States that began after World War II.
free enterprise economy
cold war

READING FOR MAIN IDEAS

4. What parts of Europe and Asia did the Communists take over shortly after World War II?

5. What is the difference between capitalism and socialism?

6. Over what nation did the Soviet Union and the United States almost fight a war in 1962?

THINKING SKILLS

Why was it hard for Korea to be split into two parts?

Lesson 6: Equal Rights

FIND THE WORDS

civil rights

American citizens often pledge allegiance to their country. When they do this, they speak of a nation that believes in "liberty and justice for all." These are the values that the United States stands for. These values have been called the American Dream.

Some citizens do not feel that they share fully in the American Dream. These people suffer from discrimination. This means that they are not given the same opportunities as other people.

Blacks in the United States have always been victims of discrimination. For years, some of the states had laws that said Blacks had to attend separate schools from Whites. When Blacks rode on public buses, they had to sit in the back. As you learned before, this separation of people by race is called segregation.

In the North, there were few laws establishing segregation, but it existed all the same. In many parts of the nation, Blacks were kept from voting in elections. Blacks were also discriminated against in employment. It was hard for them to get good jobs.

During the 1950s and 1960s, Black leaders fought against the segregation laws in the South. Their struggle was known as the civil rights movement. **Civil rights** are rights that belong to people because they are citizens. In 1954, Black leaders succeeded in getting the Supreme Court of the United States to declare segregation in public schools illegal.

In 1955, a Black woman, Rosa Parks, refused to give up her seat on a bus in Montgomery, Alabama. She was arrested. Some

Rosa Parks and Dr. Martin Luther King, Jr., fought to win civil rights for Blacks in America during the 1950s and 1960s.

Henry Cisneros's family came from Mexico. He is now the mayor of San Antonio, Texas.

March Fong Eu, a Chinese-American, was elected Secretary of State in California.

people became determined to do something. They started a movement to end segregation in public transportation. Blacks in Montgomery began a boycott of the city buses. They did this to protest having to sit in the back. A boycott is a refusal to use goods or services until a change is made. The bus boycott was led by Dr. Martin Luther King, Jr., a Black minister. A year after the boycott started, the bus company gave in. Buses were losing money. So Blacks could sit anywhere they chose.

In 1964 and 1965, Congress passed civil rights laws. These laws made discrimination illegal in jobs, education, voting, and public facilities. Over the next years, Blacks made more progress. Some were elected to high public office. Jesse Jackson, a Black minister, ran for President in 1984.

There are other groups in the United States who faced discrimination. They, too, have struggled to win equality. American Indians asked the government to pay for land it had taken away from them years before. Mexican-Americans worked in the Southwest to make schools provide special help to children who spoke only Spanish.

Women have also worked to overcome injustices. Even when women did the same jobs as men, they were usually paid less. Often, women were not given promotions. Unmarried women could not get loans from banks even if they had high-paying jobs.

Many women and men worked to oppose discrimination. They won major improvements for

People to Remember

Martin Luther King, Jr.

When Rosa Parks was arrested in Montgomery, a Black minister led the boycott of public buses. His name was Martin Luther King, Jr. He was pastor of the Baptist Church of Montgomery.

The boycott of the buses was so successful that the company gave in. Blacks won the right to ride anywhere they liked on the buses. Black drivers were also hired. The name of Martin Luther King became known across the nation.

Martin Luther King was a peaceful man. He taught his followers that the best way to win equality was through peaceful protest, or nonviolent demonstration. This meant that people were not to fight each other. They were not to destroy property. Instead they were to demonstrate in groups. They were to boycott businesses that did not treat them fairly. They were to sit in at restaurants that would not serve them and use restrooms that had been designated "For Whites Only." More than once, Dr. King and his followers were sent to jail for their activities. In some places, their peaceful protests were met with violence.

In 1957, Dr. King founded the Southern Christian Leadership Conference. This organization arranged protests and spread Dr. King's ideas of nonviolence.

In August 1963, American civil rights leaders organized a gigantic march on Washington. More than 250,000 people joined the march. They sat and stood peacefully in the great mall. They listened to many speeches. But the speech most remembered is that of Dr. Martin Luther King, Jr. It is called his "I have a dream" speech.

"I have a dream that one day this nation will rise up and live out the true meaning of its creed: 'We hold these truths to be self-evident; that all men are created equal.'

"I have a dream that one day on the red hills of Georgia the sons of former slaves and the sons of former slaveowners will be able to sit down together at the table of brotherhood.

"I have a dream that my four little children will one day live in a nation where they will not be judged by the color of their skin but by the content of their character."

In 1964 Dr. King received the Nobel Prize for Peace for his efforts.

In 1981, Sandra Day O'Connor became the first woman to serve on the Supreme Court.

Daniel Inouye, a Japanese-American, is a United States senator from Hawaii.

women in education, jobs, credit, and other fields. In the 1980s, women achieved important firsts in national leadership. Sandra Day O'Connor was appointed to the Supreme Court. Geraldine Ferraro was the Democratic Party candidate for Vice President in 1984.

People were also concerned with protecting the family. They wanted to strengthen the rights of women who worked at home.

The United States has made many improvements in social conditions. Such changes come because Americans believe in justice for all.

REVIEW

READING FOR MAIN IDEAS

1. What is discrimination?
2. What are civil rights?
3. In what year did the Supreme Court declare segregation in the public schools illegal?
4. How did Blacks in Montgomery, Alabama, get the bus company to end segregation?
5. Who was Martin Luther King, Jr.?
6. Who was the first woman appointed to the Supreme Court?

RESEARCH AND WRITING SKILLS

Find out more about the American Indians. How did they lose their lands? What promises did the government make and break? Find facts in an encyclopedia. Then write a report.

Lesson 7: Conflict and Compromise

FIND THE WORDS

escalate **embargo**

The Soviet Union and the United States became more friendly after the Cuban missile crisis of 1962. However, the American struggle against Communism continued. In 1961, President Kennedy began to increase the American role in Vietnam. Communists in North and South Vietnam were fighting the anti-Communist government of South Vietnam. The Soviet Union and China supported the Communists. The United States backed South Vietnam.

In 1964, American warships became involved in fighting with the North Vietnamese in the Gulf of Tonkin. Congress passed a resolution backing the actions of President Lyndon Johnson. In 1965, President Johnson began to **escalate,** or greatly increase, American involvement in the war. American planes started to bomb North Vietnam. At one time, over 500,000 American troops were in Vietnam. Over 50,000 Americans were killed there.

Many Americans began to oppose the role of the United States in the war. To many, the leaders of South Vietnam seemed little better than the Communists. Huge antiwar demonstrations were held.

A turning point came early in 1968. It was the time of the Asian New Year, called Tet. The Communists started a whole series of attacks. This was known as the Tet offensive. The Communists showed great power and will to fight. Even more Americans began to oppose the war. President Johnson stopped the American bombing of North Vietnam. Peace talks between the United States and North Vietnam began.

After President Richard Nixon took office in 1969, he began to withdraw troops from Vietnam very slowly. Huge antiwar demonstrations continued in the United States.

In 1970, President Nixon sent American troops across the South Vietnamese border into Cambodia. The Communists had been hiding troops and supplies there. Many Americans protested against this widening of the war. Four students were killed in an antiwar demonstration at Kent State University in Ohio. This increased protests even more. In 1971, it became clear that the war had also spread to Laos, a small neighboring country.

In the Vietnam War, civilians suffered the most. Heavy bombing and fighting forced many people to leave their homes.

In 1972, the North Vietnamese began a major attack. President Nixon ordered the bombing of North Vietnam to start again. The ports of North Vietnam were also mined and blockaded. But the withdrawal of American troops continued. Peace talks seemed to be succeeding. Finally, in January 1973, a peace agreement was signed. American prisoners of war were released. All American troops were withdrawn from Vietnam.

Despite the peace agreement, fighting continued between the Communists and the South Vietnamese for 2 years. In 1975, the South Vietnamese government fell. Vietnam was soon united into one Communist nation. Cambodia and Laos came under Communist rule.

In spite of the Vietnam War, the United States became more friendly with the Soviet Union. A 1967 treaty allowed each nation to set up offices in the other. One treaty banned the use of arms in outer space (1967). Another banned the use of nuclear arms on the seabed (1972). A 1969 treaty sought to stop the spread of nuclear weapons. In 1972 and 1973, President Nixon exchanged visits with the Soviet leader. A number of agreements were signed, including one to limit nuclear weapons. President Nixon also visited China in 1972. This visit improved relations between the United States and China. In 1979, under President Jimmy Carter, the United States set up diplomatic relations with China.

Since World War II, the United States has also been involved in the conflict between the Arabs and the Israelis (iz RAY leez). This conflict has taken place in the Middle East. In 1948, the United States supported the founding of the Jewish state of Israel in Palestine. After the Six-Day War in 1967, the United States supplied weapons to Israel. The United States also supported Israel in the Yom Kippur War of 1973. As a result, Arab nations put an **embargo,** or ban, on oil sales to the United States. Beginning in 1973, the American government helped bring about agreements between Israel and Egypt and Syria. With President

Carter's help, Israel and Egypt signed a peace treaty in 1979. However, this did not solve the problem of the Arabs of Palestine. In 1948, they had lost their country. Many also lost their homes.

A revolution in Iran created many problems for President Carter. Many Iranians were angry because the United States had supported their former ruler, the shah. In 1979, a group of Iranians seized the American embassy in Tehran. They held the Americans there as hostages. It was more than a year before their release.

In the mid-1970s, the influence of the Soviet Union in Africa and elsewhere began to increase. Communist Cuba also sent troops to Africa. President Ronald Reagan took office in 1981. He began to stress the danger of Communist actions. Like President Carter, Reagan condemned the Soviet Union for sending troops into Afghanistan.

In El Salvador, rebels have been fighting a civil war against the government.

In Central America, government instability caused much concern. President Reagan criticized the Soviet Union and other Communist countries for sending arms into El Salvador and Nicaragua. In the Caribbean, American troops landed on Grenada in October 1983. The island's government had been overthrown. An organization of Caribbean states asked the United States to help restore democracy.

REVIEW

READING FOR MAIN IDEAS

1. Which side did the American government support in the Vietnam War?
2. Which President sent many American troops to fight in Vietnam?
3. The Vietnam War spread to two neighboring nations. What were these nations?
4. Which American President helped bring about a peace treaty between Egypt and Israel?
5. What is an embargo?

THINKING SKILLS

What was the reaction of the American people to World War II? How did the reaction to the Vietnam War differ?

Lesson 8: New Americans

FIND THE WORDS

quota **national-origins system** **refugee** **sponsor**

In 1921, the United States Congress passed an immigration law. This law limited the number of people who could come to the United States to live. It was the first time such a limit had been set on immigration.

In 1924, Congress passed another immigration law. This set up a system of immigration that was to last until the 1960s. Starting in 1929, only 150,000 immigrants could enter the country each year. The law also said how many people could come from each foreign nation. Each nation had a different quota. A **quota** is a certain share of the whole amount. Each nation's quota was based on its share of the United States population in 1920. This was known as the **national-origins system** of immigration.

Over the years, many immigrants had come to the United States from Europe. Particularly in the earlier years, most had come from Northern and Western Europe. So the proportion of the United States population from those areas was high. Thus, the nations of Northern and Western Europe had high quotas. In more recent years, more immigrants had started to come from Southern and Eastern Europe. However, the proportion of the total United States population from those areas was still fairly low. Thus, the nations of Southern and Eastern Europe had lower quotas. Asians and Africans were not allowed to immigrate at all.

The national-origins system affected the sources of immigration and helped reduce it overall. Immigration was also discouraged by the Great Depression of the 1930s. During that time, there were few jobs to be had in the United States. So not many immigrants wanted to come. Then World War II was fought. The war made it difficult for people to move about freely. After the war, new immigration laws were passed. Some American soldiers serving overseas had married foreigners. In 1946, they were allowed to bring their families to the United States.

In 1948, 1950, and 1953, Congress passed more special immigration laws. These laws helped refugees (REF yoo JEEZ) come to the United States. **Refugees** are people who leave their country to

More than 300,000 people fled from Vietnam in boats. These boat people waited to be rescued.

In 1980, a boatlift brought thousands of Cubans to Florida.

escape danger or death. Most of the refugees were from Germany, Hungary, the Soviet Union, Poland, and Yugoslavia. Many of them were Jews. They wanted to live in freedom and to worship as they pleased. A 1952 law set up quotas for nations in Asia and other areas.

New Immigration Laws

In 1965, Congress changed the basic immigration law. A new system of quotas was set up. Each year, 170,000 immigrants could come from the Eastern Hemisphere. Each year, 120,000 could come from the Western Hemisphere. Thanks to this law, many Asians could come to the United States again. Many Asians came from India, Korea, and the Philippines. Later, many came from Vietnam, mostly South Vietnam.

In 1978, Congress changed the immigration laws once more. The separate quotas for the two hemispheres were dropped. There was still a limit of 290,000 immigrants a year. But now people could come from any part of the world.

Cuban and Vietnamese Refugees

Several times, Congress has let large numbers of refugees enter the United States. In 1959, a Communist government took over in Cuba. Thousands of Cubans left their country. Many came to the United States as refugees. In 1980, the Cuban government said that others who wanted to leave could do so. Hundreds of boats left Florida to pick up refugees from Cuba. This "boatlift" brought more than 100,000 Cubans to the United States.

In 1973, the United States withdrew its troops from Vietnam. Soon, a Communist government gained power there. Then, thousands of Vietnamese left their homeland. Many feared for their lives because they had helped the Americans.

There were also many Chinese people living in Vietnam. Later, the Vietnamese government forced many of them to leave. More than 300,000 people fled from Vietnam on boats. Many times, these "boat people," as they were called, had nowhere to go. They often suffered great hardships. Between 1975 and 1979, the United States took in over 200,000 refugees from Vietnam. In recent years, refugees have also fled from wars in Cambodia and Laos.

Since 1980, the number of refugees trying to enter the United States has increased. The Refugee Act of 1980 opened the door to people who fear persecution in other countries. People have come from South and Central America, and from the Caribbean.

A New Start

Almost all immigrants have problems when they come to a new land. Many must learn a new language. All have to find new jobs and homes. Immigrants also have to find new friends.

The United States government helps refugees learn English. It also helps find sponsors for them. A **sponsor** is someone who agrees to be responsible for one or more refugees. Sponsors help refugees find homes and jobs. They help them make a new start. Thanks to American sponsors, many refugees are making new lives.

REVIEW

VOCABULARY MASTERY

1. Under the national-origins system, each nation had a____.
   refugee sponsor quota
2. ___ are people who leave their countries to escape danger or death.
   Refugees Sponsors Quotas

READING FOR MAIN IDEAS

3. When was the national-origins law passed? What did it say?
4. What events limited immigration in the 1930s and 1940s?
5. From what nations have many refugees come to the United States in recent years? Name two.
6. What did the Refugee Act of 1980 do?

THINKING SKILLS

How have immigrants helped to make the United States a stronger nation?

Lesson 9: The Space Age

FIND THE WORD

satellite

"That's one small step for a man, one giant leap for mankind." With these words, American astronaut Neil Armstrong became the first person to walk on the moon. Neil Armstrong and Edwin Aldrin reached the moon on July 20, 1969, on the *Apollo 11* mission. This exciting moon landing was the high point of America's space program.

The space age began on October 4, 1957. On that day, the Soviet Union put the first satellite, *Sputnik I,* into orbit around the Earth. An artificial **satellite** is an object sent into space to orbit Earth or another heavenly body. Other Soviet successes in space followed. The Soviets put the first satellite into orbit around the moon in 1959. In 1961, they sent the first person into space. He was Yuri Gagarin.

The Soviet space program was a challenge to the United States. The first American satellite was *Explorer I.* It went into orbit on January 31, 1958. In May 1961, President John F. Kennedy said that the United States would put a person on the moon "before this decade is out." During that same month, Alan Shepard became the first American to travel in space. In 1962, John Glenn became the first American to orbit the Earth.

American astronaut Neil Armstrong was the first person to walk on the moon.

After the *Apollo 11* mission in 1969, American astronauts made five more landings on the moon. The United States then sent astronauts on long trips in Earth orbit aboard Skylab, a space station. The space shuttle, a combined spacecraft and airplane, will be the main American space effort of the 1980s. In April 1981, the first successful flight of the space shuttle *Columbia* took place. Two

Left: Sally K. Ride was the first American woman in space. *Middle:* In April 1981, the space shuttle *Columbia* blasted off on its first round-trip flight. *Right:* Astronaut Guion Bluford was the first Black American in space.

new space shuttles were launched in 1983 and 1984, the *Challenger* and *Discovery*. Their crews included America's first Black and first female astronauts. On one important mission, the astronauts succeeded in rescuing two broken satellites from space and bringing them back to Earth.

Meanwhile, the Soviets continued their space program. The Soviets stressed long flights in orbit. They did not send people to the moon. In 1975, an American Apollo spacecraft docked with a Soviet Soyuz craft. This joint mission showed that the two nations could work together in space.

The space age has included much more than the exciting trips people have made into space. American and Soviet spacecraft have studied the moon, the planets, and the sun. The Soviet Union concentrated on the planet Venus. The United States sent many Mariner spacecraft to Mars. The American Viking spacecraft landed on Mars in July 1976. The American Pioneer and Voyager spacecraft sent back beautiful pictures of Jupiter and Saturn.

Some of the most important spacecraft have stayed close to the Earth. Every day we see pictures of the Earth sent back by weather satellites. These have been of great help in predicting the weather. Telephone calls and live television pictures come from overseas through communications satellites. Scientific satellites study the Earth and the skies. Military satellites spy on other nations.

Some people have questioned the huge amounts of money spent on space. They suggest that we should pay attention to problems here on Earth, instead. Yet the space program has brought many new inventions. They have made our lives better. Besides this, space is the last frontier. It is a challenge to people everywhere. President Kennedy said it very well in 1962:

"We choose to go to the moon in this decade and do the other things, not because they are easy, but because they are hard; because that goal will serve to organize and measure the best of our energies and skills. . . . Many years ago the great British explorer George Mallory, who was to die on Mount Everest, was asked why did he want to climb it, and he said, 'Because it is there.' Well, space is there, and . . . the moon and the planets are there, and new hopes for knowledge and peace are there."

Fascinating Facts

What is a lunatic? *Luna* is a Latin word meaning moon. So a lunatic is a person who is "Moonstruck." For many centuries some people believed that sleeping in moonlight could make a person crazy. Even today, people believe that a full moon makes people nervous and more likely to do strange things.

Astronauts found the moon to be a dead world without air or water. But for thousands of years, people believed that some form of life existed on the moon.

Many early peoples believed that the moon was a powerful god or goddess. Even today, people in some parts of the world worship the moon.

REVIEW

READING FOR MAIN IDEAS

1. In what year did people first land on the moon? Who were they?
2. What nation put the first satellite into orbit around the Earth?
3. Which American President set the goal of reaching the moon?
4. What is the main American space effort of the 1980s?
5. Name two kinds of satellites that affect our lives every day.

THINKING SKILLS

List some arguments for and against space travel.

Lesson 10: Into the Future

FIND THE WORDS

**energy nuclear energy
solar energy environment
conservation recycle
pollution acid rain
inflation productivity
deficit republic**

In November of 1984, Ronald Reagan was reelected President of the United States. He pledged to continue the program he had begun in his first term. In the first four years, he tackled the problems of the American economy. He cut taxes and some areas of government spending, hoping to increase private savings and investment. However, he increased spending on national defense. He wanted America to be strong and prepared.

In the 1984 election, President Reagan won the electoral votes of 49 states. It was the largest margin of victory in the history of the United States. He had asked people whether they were better off than when he took office. Many believed that they were. The nation's economy was in good shape. Unemployment was down. Prices were no longer rising. Many Americans once again felt proud of their nation.

In November 1984, Ronald Reagan was reelected President of the United States. In this picture, President Reagan takes the oath of office from the Chief Justice of the Supreme Court.

Violence in America

Only three years earlier, on March 30, 1981, Americans were shocked to hear that President Reagan had been shot. A gunman had fired six shots at him as he left a hotel in Washington, DC. Fortunately, the President recovered from his wound.

But many Americans asked themselves: "What is happening to us? How can we protect our leaders?" People remembered their shock on November 22, 1963. Then, President John Kennedy was shot and killed in Dallas, Texas. The nation and the world mourned for days. The leaders of nations from all over the world flew to Washington. They wanted to show their feelings for the dead President and for the American people.

But there were many shocks awaiting the American people during the 1960s. Dr. Martin Luther King, Jr., the leader of the civil rights movement, was shot and killed on April 4, 1968. This happened in Memphis, Tennessee. Two months later, Robert Kennedy was shot and killed in Los Angeles, California. Robert Kennedy was the brother of President John Kennedy. He was running for President, himself, when he was assassinated.

Americans were reminded again and again about violence in the United States. But people did not seem to know what to do about it. Some said that all guns should be banned. Others said that taking guns away from people would mean that only criminals would have guns. But most people felt that something had to be done to stop violent crime.

Energy for the Future

A nation with as much industry and transportation as the United States faces an important challenge. It needs energy to keep everything running. **Energy** means power. Electricity is a form of energy. It makes light bulbs, refrigerators, record players, televisions, and air conditioners work. Gasoline is burned to provide energy. It powers our cars, trucks, and airplanes. Coal, a mineral, is another source of energy. It is burned for heat.

The United States is a land rich in natural resources. Water, petroleum, and coal are resources. They have been used to produce the energy the nation has needed. But as the population of the United States grows larger, the nation needs more and more energy. The petroleum in the United States cannot provide as much energy as the nation needs. So the United States has begun to buy more than half the petroleum it uses from other nations.

Many Americans think we should make more use of solar energy. This house is heated by the sun. The roof panels collect solar energy.

Many Americans are concerned about the nation's future energy needs. Some think that **nuclear** (NOO klee ur) **energy,** energy made in atomic reactors, is the answer. Others want to make more use of **solar** (SOH lur) **energy,** energy from the sun. Most agree on the need to use energy more wisely.

Resources and the Environment

The natural resources of the United States give its people more than just energy. People breathe the air. They drink the water and use it in many other ways. They grow food in the soil. They cut wood and hunt animals in the forests. Americans do not just use the waters and the land in practical ways. They enjoy the rivers, lakes, forests, and mountains of the nation, too. All these things—the air, the water, the land, and the plants and animals—are natural resources. These natural surroundings make up the **environment.**

In the past, Americans have acted as though there were no end to the forests and other resources. Americans now know that if they use up too many resources, soon there will not be any left. That is why the **conservation,** or careful use, of natural resources is so important. One way to conserve resources is to **recycle** them, or use them again. Tin and paper, for example, can be saved and recycled.

There are other dangers to the environment. An important problem is **pollution,** the putting of wastes into the air and water. When automobiles and factories burn gasoline and coal, certain waste products get into the air. These wastes can harm living things. When people breathe polluted air, they can get sick. The use of unleaded gasoline in cars can help. So can cleaning devices on the furnaces of factories.

Some factories throw their waste products into nearby bodies of water. These wastes often pollute the water. They harm and sometimes kill fish and plants. People who drink such water or eat its fish can also be affected.

Acid rain is another form of pollution. **Acid rain** forms when rain mixes with gases in the air. These gases are produced when factories burn coal. When acid rain falls on forests and lakes, it harms the trees and the fish.

In recent years, a lot of effort has gone into cleaning up our lakes and rivers. It takes a long time, but progress is being made. Protecting our natural environment is an important challenge for the future.

Economic Problems

In recent years, the United States and other nations have suffered from inflation. **Inflation** is a drop in the value of money. It means that the same goods cost more. You have learned that the United States buys much of its petroleum from other nations. In past years, increases in the price of this imported petroleum added to inflation.

Inflation has also been created by a decline in productivity in the United States. **Productivity** refers to how many goods a worker can make. In large part, this depends on how good factories and machines are. In recent years, workers' wages have been going up. But workers have not been producing any more goods. Thus, to pay the higher wages, companies have increased the prices of their goods. Rising prices cause inflation.

A major economic problem today is the national deficit. A **deficit** occurs when people spend more money than they have. Governments often borrow money to pay for their programs and meet expenses. But borrowed money must be paid back. Interest must also be paid on the loans. In the last few years, the deficit of the United States has skyrocketed. In 1984, it reached $200 billion.

The problems of the economy are all connected. Solving them will be a challenge for the future.

The American People

The United States is a republic. A **republic** is a representative democracy, a government in which people elect their leaders. Most Americans believe in majority rule.

Many people believe that America's natural beauty should be protected from too much development.

People with disabilities can live active lives. *Left:* These women are using sign language to communicate. *Right:* How are these children communicating?

This means that the majority—the largest group—decides who will run the government.

However, most Americans do not believe that the majority should have complete power. They believe that all citizens have rights. Rights protect minorities—the smaller groups—from the power of the majority.

The United States includes people of different races, religions, and culture groups. It includes older people and people with disabilities. The rights of all these many people have to be safeguarded. This is a challenge for the future, too.

Along with rights, Americans have the responsibility to protect their freedoms. They have the duty to be good citizens.

REVIEW

VOCABULARY MASTERY

1. ___ is a decrease in the value of money.
   Investment Scarcity Inflation
2. ___ refers to how many goods a worker can make.
   Investment Productivity Energy
3. ___ means power.
   Inflation Productivity Energy

READING FOR MAIN IDEAS

4. Name four sources of energy.
5. What is acid rain?
6. What causes a national deficit?
7. What is a republic?

WRITING SKILLS

Write a paper on a problem discussed in this lesson. Suggest a solution.

CHAPTER REVIEW

VOCABULARY MASTERY

Use the words below to complete the chapter summary. Use each only once.

advertising	energy
atomic bomb	Great Depression
civil rights	isolationism
conservation	pollution
drought	satellites

During the prosperous 1920s, __1__ told people about the many new products. The __2__, however, brought hard times in the 1930s. Also, there was __3__ on the Great Plains, which ruined farmland.

In spite of the policy of __4__, the United States entered World War II. It fought on the side of the Allies. A new weapon, the __5__, helped end the war.

Since World War II, the United States has made great progress. In 1964 and 1965, Congress passed laws to protect __6__. The United States and the Soviet Union have put many __7__ into space. New forms of __8__ are being developed. One of the problems we still face is __9__. Americans know that __10__ will help to protect the environment.

READING FOR MAIN IDEAS

1. Why did suburbs grow in the 1920s?
2. The Great Depression lasted for 10 years. List at least 5 things that happened in the United States during that period.
3. Why did the United States wait to enter World War II? Why did the United States finally enter the war?
4. What is a cold war?
5. List some of the events of the civil rights movement.
6. Why did the United States send troops to fight in Vietnam?

SKILLS APPLICATION

RESEARCH AND WRITING SKILLS

7. The following were each the first to be involved in an airplane or spacecraft experience: Neil Armstrong, Amelia Earhart, Yuri Gagarin, Charles A. Lindbergh, Sally Ride, Alan Shepard, Guion Buford, Jr. Choose one of them to do a research report on. In your report, include the person's occupation, what he or she was the first to do, when the event happened, and results of the event.
8. Write a descriptive paragraph telling about something you would like to be the first person to do. Explain how you would go about accomplishing your goal.

CHART SKILLS

Make two charts labeled "World War I" and "World War II." On the first, make two columns headed "Allied Powers" and "Central Powers." On the second, put columns for "Allies" and and "Axis." List each nation under the correct column: Austria-Hungary, Serbia, Russia, Germany, France, Great Britain, Ottoman Empire, Bulgaria, United States, Italy, Japan, Soviet Union. Put a star by the nations that fought in both wars.

DICTIONARY SKILLS

Use a dictionary to find the meanings of these words or parts of words: *geo-*, *thermo-*, *solar*, *nuclear*, *fossil*. Write a definition for each energy-related word such as *geothermal* and *fossil fuel*. Look for them as subheadings under *energy* in an encyclopedia. Then write a sentence or two describing each type of energy.

UNIT REVIEW

VOCABULARY MASTERY

Choose one of the lists of words below. Then write a paragraph or page using all the words from that list. You may use the words in the singular or plural. On a separate page, write the words and define them.

civil rights	conservation
muckrakers	environment
Progressives	nuclear energy
reformer	pollution
suffrage	recycle
suffragist	solar energy

READING FOR MAIN IDEAS

1. List some of the problems of the early 1900s.
2. Who were the Progressives? What did they do?
3. In what ways did President Theodore Roosevelt go about fighting injustice?
4. Did the United States sign the Treaty of Versailles? Why, or why not?
5. Name three suffragist leaders.
6. What does the Nineteenth Amendment say?
7. Did the good times of the 1920s reach everyone? Give reasons for your answer.
8. What was life like in the United States during the Great Depression?
9. Explain what the Tennessee Valley Authority was.
10. What was the New Deal?
11. Why was Germany so successful at the beginning of World War II?
12. What happened on August 6 and August 9, 1945?
13. What is the American Dream? Is this dream a reality for all Americans?
14. Who was the Black woman who, in 1955, was arrested for refusing to give up her seat on a bus in Montgomery, Alabama? What were the results of this action?
15. Why did the Arab nations put an embargo on oil sales to the United States?
16. How have immigration laws changed since 1920?
17. List some of the accomplishments of the United States' space program.

THINKING SKILLS

18. Why were the muckrakers, the Progressives, and the reformers so important in United States history?
19. Was World War I called by that name when it was being fought?
20. Women took over men's jobs during both world wars. Do you think this helped the suffrage movement? Explain your answer.
21. How were relocation camps like concentration camps? How were the two different?
22. Why do you think so many people protested the involvement of the United States in the Vietnam War?
23. Many Americans believe we should continue to explore outer space. Others feel we should spend the money to solve problems at home. What do you think? Why?
24. The United States has many problems to solve. What do you think is the most important problem? What would you do to solve it?
25. Suppose you were writing a history of the twentieth century. What do you think were the five most important things that happened between 1900 and the present? Tell why.

SKILL DEVELOPMENT

FACT AND OPINION SKILLS

A *fact* states the truth. An *opinion* states what someone believes to be true. A cartoon shows the way someone interprets facts. It states an opinion. A *political cartoon* states an opinion about someone or something that concerns politics.

Cartoon A tells a story about voters.

1. What is its message?
2. Which statements in the cartoon are facts?
3. Which statement is an opinion?
4. Do you agree or disagree with the opinion? State your reason.
5. Which of the following is a fact? Which is an opinion?
   a. My vote doesn't count. It doesn't make any difference.
   b. Elections have been won or lost by a single vote.

Reprinted by permission of Newspaper Enterprise Association.

Cartoon A

Cartoon B was one of the first political cartoons in the United States. Benjamin Franklin drew it in 1754 during the French and Indian War. People then believed a cut-up snake could live if it was put back together.

6. What does the snake represent?
7. What is the message of Cartoon B?
8. In the cartoon, N.E. represents four New England colonies. Identify these four and the other seven shown.
9. What part of Franklin's cartoon is fact? What part is opinion?
10. Draw your own political cartoon. Look for examples in newspapers. Use a symbol as Franklin did. Be brief and to the point.

Cartoon B

UNITED STATES GEOGRAPHY

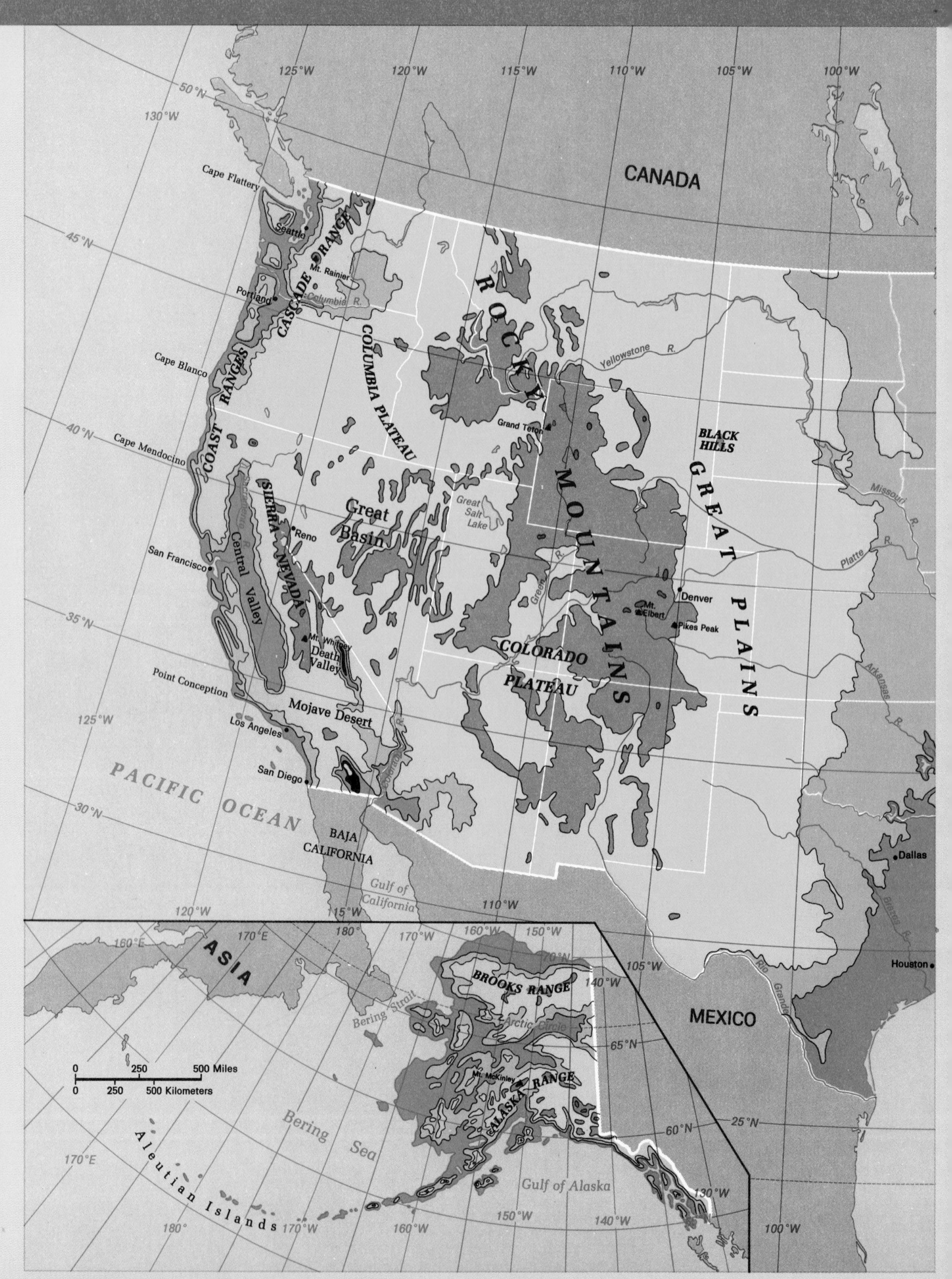

UNIT 6

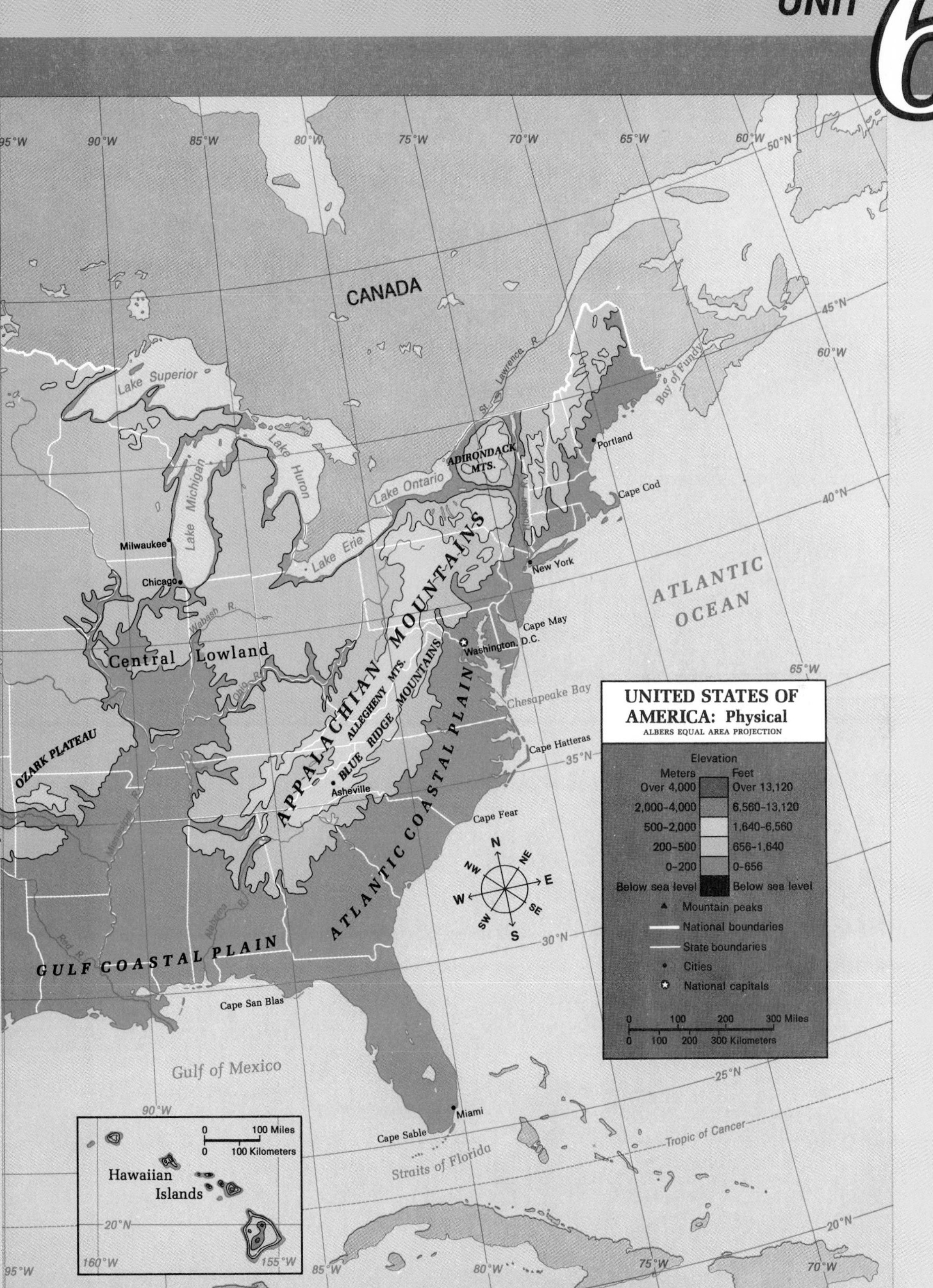

CANADA
Lake Superior
Lake Michigan
Lake Huron
Lake Ontario
Lake Erie
St. Lawrence R.
Bay of Fundy
ADIRONDACK MTS.
Portland
Cape Cod
Milwaukee
Chicago
New York
ATLANTIC OCEAN
Wabash R.
Central Lowland
APPALACHIAN MOUNTAINS
ALLEGHENY MTS.
BLUE RIDGE MOUNTAINS
Cape May
Washington, D.C.
Chesapeake Bay
Ohio R.
OZARK PLATEAU
ATLANTIC COASTAL PLAIN
Asheville
Cape Hatteras
Cape Fear
Mississippi R.
Alabama R.
Red R.
GULF COASTAL PLAIN
Cape San Blas
Gulf of Mexico
Miami
Cape Sable
Straits of Florida
Tropic of Cancer
Hawaiian Islands
0 100 Miles
0 100 Kilometers
UNITED STATES OF AMERICA: Physical
ALBERS EQUAL AREA PROJECTION
Elevation
Meters Feet
Over 4,000 Over 13,120
2,000-4,000 6,560-13,120
500-2,000 1,640-6,560
200-500 656-1,640
0-200 0-656
Below sea level Below sea level
Mountain peaks
National boundaries
State boundaries
Cities
National capitals
0 100 200 300 Miles
0 100 200 300 Kilometers
N NE E SE S SW W NW
95°W 90°W 85°W 80°W 75°W 70°W 65°W 60°W
50°N 45°N 40°N 35°N 30°N 25°N 20°N
160°W 155°W

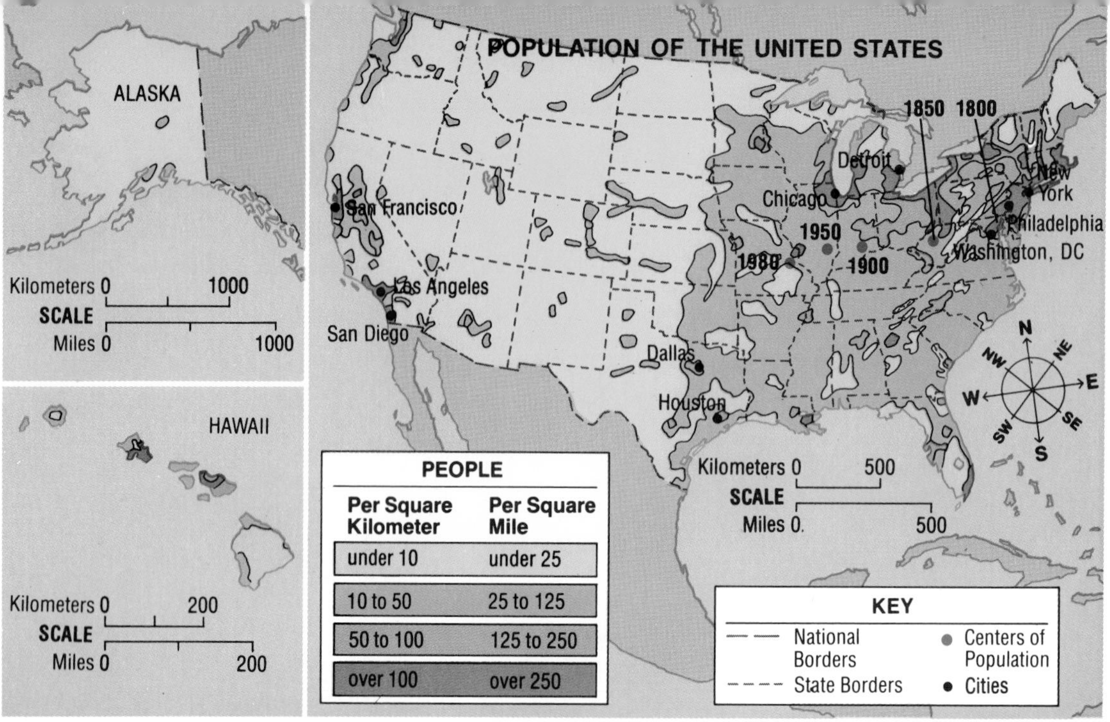

POPULATION OF THE UNITED STATES

ALASKA

Kilometers 0 1000
SCALE
Miles 0 1000

HAWAII

Kilometers 0 200
SCALE
Miles 0 200

San Francisco
Los Angeles
San Diego
Dallas
Houston
Chicago
Detroit
New York
Philadelphia
Washington, DC
1850 1800
1950
1980
1900

Kilometers 0 500
SCALE
Miles 0 500

N NE E SE S SW W NW

PEOPLE

Per Square Kilometer	Per Square Mile
under 10	under 25
10 to 50	25 to 125
50 to 100	125 to 250
over 100	over 250

KEY

National Borders	Centers of Population
State Borders	Cities

CHAPTER 

THE UNITED STATES TODAY

Lesson 1: What Is the United States?

FIND THE WORDS

subregion **federal district** **commonwealth** **territory** **possession** **urban area** **rural area** **census**

Suppose someone asked you to describe the geography of the United States. That would not be easy because the United States is a big country. In land area, it is the third-largest nation in the world. It is so large that it includes many different kinds of landforms and many different climates.

It is easier to understand what the United States is like if we divide it up. In this book, we have divided the country into three major regions. They are the Northeast, the South, and the Midwest and West.

UNITED STATES

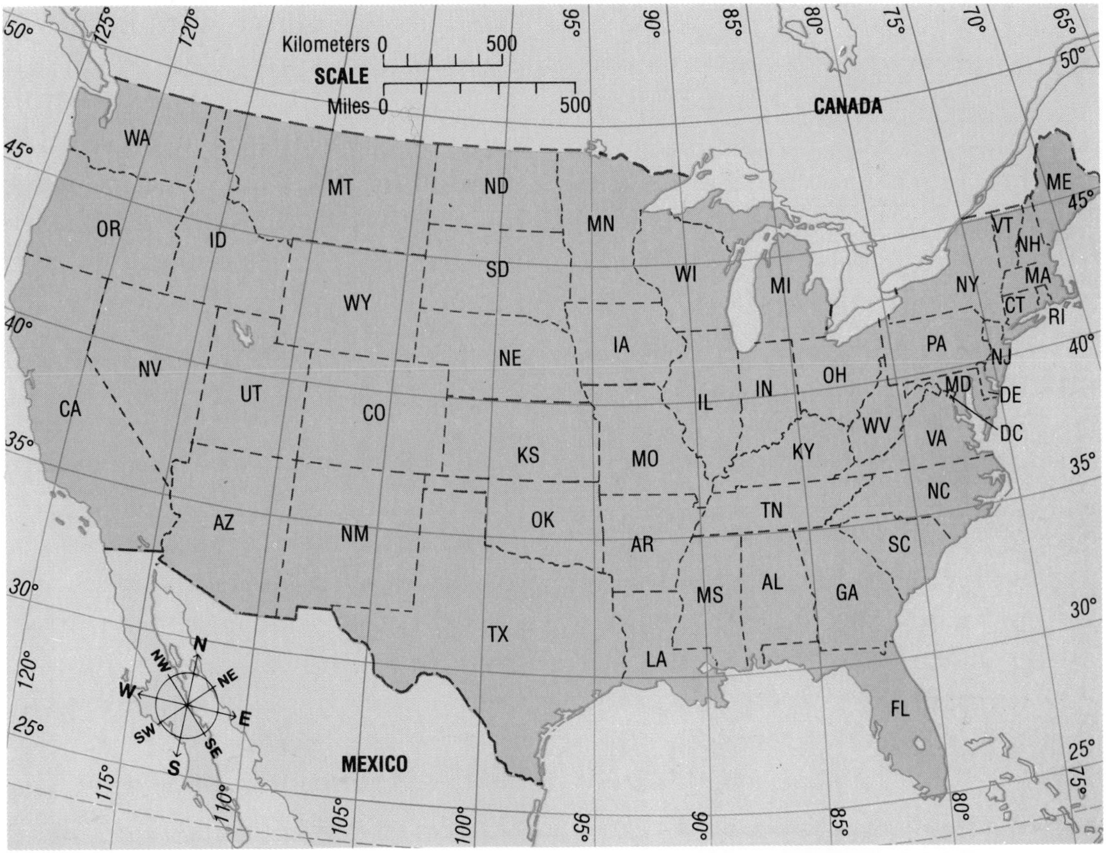

KEY

States:

- AL Alabama
- AK Alaska
- AZ Arizona
- AR Arkansas
- CA California
- CO Colorado
- CT Connecticut
- DC District of Columbia
- DE Delaware
- FL Florida
- GA Georgia
- HI Hawaii
- ID Idaho
- IL Illinois
- IN Indiana
- IA Iowa
- KS Kansas
- KY Kentucky
- LA Louisiana
- ME Maine
- MD Maryland
- MA Massachusetts
- MI Michigan
- MN Minnesota
- MS Mississippi
- MO Missouri
- MT Montana
- NE Nebraska
- NV Nevada
- NH New Hampshire
- NJ New Jersey
- NM New Mexico
- NY New York
- NC North Carolina
- ND North Dakota
- OH Ohio
- OK Oklahoma
- OR Oregon
- PA Pennsylvania
- RI Rhode Island
- SC South Carolina
- SD South Dakota
- TN Tennessee
- TX Texas
- UT Utah
- VT Vermont
- VA Virginia
- WA Washington
- WV West Virginia
- WI Wisconsin
- WY Wyoming

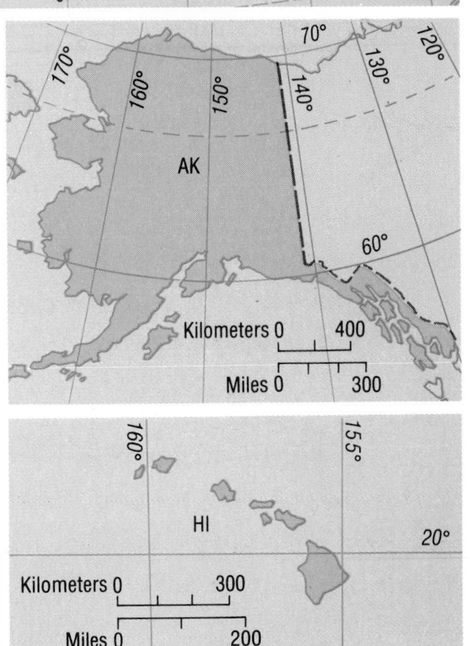

These three regions are still quite large for study. So we have further divided each one into two or three subregions. A **subregion** is a part of a region.

The Northeast includes the New England and the Middle Atlantic States. The South is made up of the Southeastern and South Central States. There are three subregions of the Midwest and West. They are the Midwestern, Mountain, and Pacific States.

Divisions of the United States

Dividing the United States into regions and subregions makes study easier. But this is not the way the country is really divided.

The 50 states are the major political divisions of the United States. Each state has its own government that makes laws. Yet each state also participates in the federal government. States do this by sending representatives to Congress. The people who live in each state must obey the laws of the federal government.

One American city, Washington, DC, is not in any state. It lies within a federal district called the District of Columbia. This **federal district** is a special area set aside for the nation's capital by the Constitution. The city of Washington and the federal district are exactly the same size. Having the capital in a federal district keeps it neutral. It belongs to the whole nation, not to a particular state.

There are several other divisions of our country. A **commonwealth** is an area that governs itself but is not a state. Puerto Rico (PWEHR toh REE koh) is now the only United States commonwealth. The people who live there are American citizens.

The two other political divisions of the United States are territories and possessions. **Territories** and **possessions** belong to the United States but are not part of the nation. Some have their own governments. Guam in the Pacific Ocean is one example. The Virgin Islands in the Caribbean are another. The people who live in Guam and the Virgin Islands elect their own legislatures. They are also American citizens.

Several other territories and possessions are governed by various departments of the United States government. The people who live there are not American citizens. Wake Island and the Midway Islands in the Pacific Ocean are examples of this kind of territory.

Where Do People Live?

About 75 out of every 100 Americans live in urban areas. **Urban areas** are towns and cities with more than 2,500 people.

UNITED STATES TERRITORIES AND POSSESSIONS

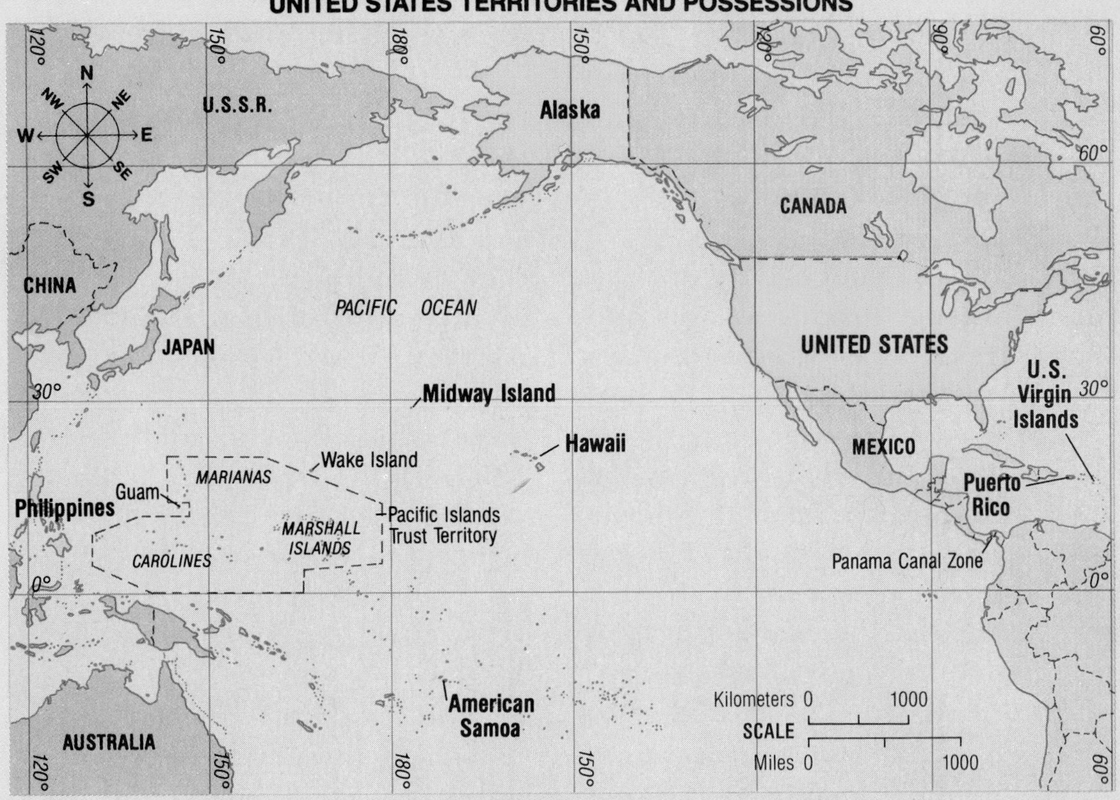

Name	Acquired	Present Status
Alaska	1867	State (1959)
Midway Island	1867	Possession
Hawaii	1898	State (1959)
Guam	1898	Territory
Philippines	1898	Independent (1946)
Puerto Rico	1898	Commonwealth (1952)
Wake Island	1899	Possession
American Samoa	1899	Territory
Canal Zone	1903	U.S./Panama control
Virgin Islands	1916	Territory
Marshall, Caroline & Mariana Island groups	1947	Pacific Islands Trust Territory (U.N.)

About 25 out of every 100 Americans live in rural areas. **Rural areas** include farmlands and country towns and villages with fewer than 2,500 people.

As the numbers above show, Americans are not evenly distributed among urban, rural, and farm areas. They are not evenly spread across the nation either. A population-density map shows how people are distributed in an area. The map on page 362 shows where the people of the United States lived at the time of the last census. Every 10 years, the government takes a **census,** or count, of the population.

Look at the map and the map key. The most heavily populated regions are colored red. Areas with few people are colored yellow. Much of this land is in the western part of the United States.

Find one of the red circles on the map. Look at the date beside the circle. At that time, that area was the center of population for the United States. That means that as many people lived north of the circle as lived south of it. As many lived east of the circle as lived west of it. Centers of population are shown for 1800, 1850, 1900, 1950, and 1980. As you can see, the center of population for the nation has been moving west. In 1850, it was in West Virginia; in 1980, it was in Missouri.

The centers of population shown on the map are for the 48 states between Canada and Mexico. They do not include the states of Alaska and Hawaii or the islands of Puerto Rico.

REVIEW

VOCABULARY MASTERY

1. An area such as New England or the Mountain States is called a ____.
   commonwealth territory subregion
2. The majority of Americans live in ____.
   urban areas rural areas federal districts
3. A ____ map shows where people live.
   population-density territory rural-area

READING FOR MAIN IDEAS

4. What parts of the United States are *not* states?
5. Why is the capital of the United States located in a federal district, not in one of the states?

THINKING SKILLS

Why has the center of population of the United States been moving west? Where do you think the center of population of the United States will be in 20 years? Give reasons for your answer.

Lesson 2: Landforms of the United States

FIND THE WORDS

geographic region **fertile**
dairy cattle **prairie**
petroleum **transportation**
beef cattle **mining** **logging**
arid **irrigation**

We can also divide the United States into geographic regions. **Geographic regions** are large areas where the landforms, or shapes of land, are similar. There are six geographic regions in the United States: Atlantic and Gulf coastal plains, Appalachian Mountains, Central Lowland and Great Plains, Rocky Mountains, Great Basin, and Pacific Coast Ranges and lowlands.

Look at the map on page 480. You can see that geographic regions do not stop at political borders. For example, the Great Plains stretch from Canada through the United States. The Rocky Mountains also extend from Alaska through Canada and into the southern part of the United States. In this lesson, we will study only the geographic regions of the United States.

Seen from the air, this American farmland looks like a giant patchwork quilt.

The Atlantic and Gulf Coastal Plains

A narrow plain runs along the East Coast of the United States from New England to Florida. It is known as the Atlantic Coastal Plain. In the south, the plain becomes much broader. It continues west of Florida as the Gulf Coastal Plain. The Gulf Coastal Plain extends along the coast of the Gulf of Mexico.

The coastal plains are low and rather flat. Much of the land of the plains is **fertile** land. That means the soil is good for growing crops. In the north, farmers grow vegetables and raise **dairy cattle.** These are cattle that produce milk. In the south, the major crops are fruit, vegetables, cotton, and rice.

In some places along the coasts, there are very large swamps. The swamps are thick with plants.

Some of the oldest and largest cities in the United States are on the coastal plains.

The Appalachian Mountains

West of the Atlantic Coastal Plain are the Appalachian Mountains. Beginning in Canada, these mountains extend south to Georgia and Alabama. They extend for 2,570 kilometers (1,600 miles).

The Appalachians are millions of years old. They are older than the Rockies, the other major mountain system in the United States. Through the years, the Appalachians have been worn down by wind and weather. Most of the tops are rounded, and the sides are not steep.

Fishing boats at dawn on the Gulf Coast. Shrimps, oysters, and other seafood from these waters are shipped all over the United States.

The Great Smoky Mountains, on the North Carolina-Tennessee border, are part of the Appalachians. They are named for the smoky haze that often covers them.

The Central Lowland and Great Plains

This region lies in the center of the United States. It stretches from the Appalachians to the Rocky Mountains and from Canada to the Gulf Coastal Plain. The Central Lowland and Great Plains region is one of the largest areas of flat land in the world. Of course, the region is not completely flat. From the Appalachians, the Central Lowland slopes downward to the Missouri River. Then the ground rises again across the Great Plains to the Rocky Mountains. In fact, the Great Plains are really a plateau, a mile high in some places.

There are also some rolling hills in this region. Only the Black Hills in South Dakota and northeastern Wyoming are very high, though.

Originally, much of the northern and western part of this plains area was prairie (PRER ee). A **prairie** is a large area of flat or rolling grassland. It has fertile soil and few trees. It makes excellent farmland.

The plains east of the Missouri River are called the Central Lowland. The Central Lowland has some of the most fertile land in the world. On these plains, farmers grow corn, soybeans, and wheat. These important crops feed people in our nation and around the world.

Farmers also raise dairy cattle in the Central Lowland. Products such as cream, butter, and cheese are made from milk that the cattle produce.

The Central Lowland is rich in petroleum. **Petroleum** is a thick, dark liquid found under the earth. It is used for fuel and for making plastics and other products.

Many large cities are located in the Central Lowland. Cities are often built on level land because transportation is better there. **Transportation** is the movement of people or goods. It is easier to build roads, railroads, and airports on level land than in hilly areas.

Extending west of the Missouri River are the Great Plains. This area receives less rain than the Central Lowland. Much of the land is covered with grass. Large herds of cattle are raised on these plains. They are **beef cattle,** raised for their meat. People also use their hides, or skins, to make leather.

In addition, farmers grow large amounts of wheat on the Great Plains.

The Rocky Mountains

The Rocky Mountains are the largest, highest mountains in the United States. They have jagged peaks, steep sides, and deep valleys. They are much younger than the Appalachian Mountains. The Rocky Mountain system runs from Alaska to northern New Mexico. Alaska's Mount McKinley, the highest peak in North America, is in the Rockies. It rises 6,194 meters (20,320 feet) above sea level.

Some of the people who live in the Rocky Mountains earn their living by mining and logging. **Mining** is taking minerals out of the ground. **Logging** is cutting down trees for wood. The Rocky Mountains also attract visitors who come there for vacations.

The Great Basin

West of the Rockies is a large area of high, mostly level land. It is called the Great Basin. This land receives little rain. Much of it is desert. It is **arid,** or dry. The land is, therefore, not good for farming. Only irrigation allows farmers to grow food. **Irrigation** is supplying land with water that comes from somewhere else.

The Pacific Coast Ranges and Lowlands

Along the Pacific Coast of the United States there are moun-

Oranges are one of the important crops that grow in California's valleys. In the fertile plains and valleys along the Pacific Coast, farmers also grow lettuce, grapes for making wine and raisins, and many other kinds of fruits and vegetables. The mild, sunny climate provides a long growing season, especially in southern California.

tains, valleys, and coastal plains. Some of the mountains are close to the ocean. They are called the Pacific Coast Ranges. Other mountains, farther inland, separate the Coast Ranges from the Great Basin. These mountains are the Sierra Nevada.

The plains along the Pacific Coast are narrow. Look at the map on page 480, especially in the area of California. Between the Coast Ranges and the Sierra Nevada are large, fertile valleys. Here, farmers grow many different fruits and vegetables.

REVIEW

VOCABULARY MASTERY

1. The Rocky Mountains are one of the ___ regions of the United States.
   political plains geographic
2. ___ is the movement of goods and people.
   Irrigation Transportation Logging
3. ___ are raised for meat.
   Dairy cattle Beef cattle Soybeans
4. Much of the Great Plains was originally ___.
   prairie desert forest
5. ___ is an important occupation in mountain areas.
   Logging Transportation Agriculture

READING FOR MAIN IDEAS

6. How do geographic boundaries and political borders differ?
7. Where are some of the oldest cities in the United States found?
8. Where are the Appalachian Mountains located?
9. What part of the United States is one of the largest areas of flat land in the world?
10. Where are the Rocky Mountains located?

THINKING SKILLS

Many people live in the eastern half of the United States and on the West Coast. Fewer people live in between. What reasons can you think of for this?

Lesson 3: Rivers and Lakes of the United States

FIND THE WORDS

drain **river system**
drainage basin **glacier**

Rivers are very important to people. River valleys often have much fertile land that is suitable for farming. Rivers also provide a way to go from place to place. Before many roads were built, rivers were one very important means of transportation. For these reasons, many towns and cities have been built beside rivers.

Rivers of the United States

You have probably heard of the Mississippi, the Missouri, and the Ohio rivers. You may know about the Colorado and the Rio Grande (REE oh GRAND). Find these rivers on the map on pages 360 and 361. These rivers drain

An aerial view of the Mississippi River at New Orleans. By the time it reaches this point in Louisiana, the river is very wide and moving slowly.

LONGEST RIVERS IN THE UNITED STATES

Rivers	Length in km	Length in miles
Mississippi	3,779	2,348
Missouri	3,969	2,466
St. Lawrence	2,935	1,824
Rio Grande	2,913	1,810
Yukon	2,781	1,728
Arkansas	2,240	1,392
Colorado	2,240	1,392
Columbia	1,875	1,165
Snake	1,661	1,032
Red	1,629	1,012

Added together, the lower Mississippi and the Missouri rivers form the longest river in North America and the third-longest river system in the world.

a large part of the country. When a river **drains** a land area, it carries away all the water that runs off that land.

Notice that many rivers of the United States flow into one another. The Yellowstone River flows into the Missouri River and the Missouri flows into the Mississippi. They are part of the Mississippi River system. A **river system** is a group of rivers that flow into another river.

The land area drained by a river system is called a **drainage basin.** Drainage basins receive their water from rain and snow.

The landforms in each area determine which way the rivers flow. Mountains divide the land. Rivers on different sides of mountains flow in different directions.

The longest river in the United States is the Mississippi. It begins in northern Minnesota in Lake Itasca. It wanders south and is joined by tributaries, or smaller rivers, along the way. The Mississippi's most important tributaries are the Missouri and the Ohio rivers.

The Central Lowland and Great Plains are drained by the Mississippi and its tributaries. The

Mississippi River system drains an area of 3,255,615 square kilometers (1,157,000 square miles). The river then empties into the Gulf of Mexico. There is a delta where the river meets the gulf. A delta is an area of rich soil at the mouth of a river. It is usually shaped like a triangle.

Lakes of the United States

The Great Lakes are the most important group of lakes in the United States. There are five of them: Lake Erie, Lake Huron, Lake Michigan, Lake Ontario, and Lake Superior. The lakes touch on the states of New York, Pennsylvania, Ohio, Michigan, Indiana, Illinois, Wisconsin, and Minnesota. The United States–Canada border runs through four of the lakes. Only Lake Michigan is within the United States.

The Great Lakes are very deep. They were carved out by great glaciers more than 10,000 years ago. A **glacier** is a thick mass of ice that moves slowly. At one time, much of North America was covered by glaciers. Today, many ships travel the Great Lakes carrying people and goods.

We have many other lakes in our nation. Most lakes develop naturally. They are areas in which rainwater or water from rivers collects. A few lakes in the southern and western parts of the country have been created by people. A lake can form behind a dam built to hold river water back.

Most lakes have fresh water. The Great Salt Lake of Utah, however, is saltier than the ocean. The rivers that run into it carry tiny amounts of salt. No rivers run out of the Great Salt Lake. When the air dries up the lake water, the salt stays behind.

REVIEW

VOCABULARY MASTERY

1. Rivers that flow into one another make up a ____.
   river system drainage basin tributary
2. Rivers carry rainwater from a(n) ____.
   ocean drainage basin glacier
3. A thick mass of slow-moving ice is called a ____.
   drainage basin glacier tributary

READING FOR MAIN IDEAS

4. Why are many towns and cities built beside rivers?
5. What determines which way a river flows?
6. Where are the Great Lakes located?

MAP SKILLS

Look at the map of Midwestern states on page 414. Locate five United States cities on the shores of the Great Lakes.

CHAPTER REVIEW

VOCABULARY MASTERY

Use the words below to complete the chapter summary. Use each only once.

arid	mining
dairy cattle	petroleum
fertile	prairies
irrigation	river system
logging	subregions

The United States can be divided into regions and smaller ___1___. Much ___2___ land is located in the Coastal Plains and the Great Plains. The Great Plains were once ___3___. In the Great Basin west of the Rocky Mountains, most of the land is ___4___. Farming in the Great Basin is possible only with ___5___.

Farmers in the Coastal Plains grow vegetables and raise ___6___. The Coastal Lowland region is rich in ___7___. Two important activities in the Rocky Mountains are ___8___ and ___9___.

Many rivers in the United States flow into one another. They are part of a ___10___.

READING FOR MAIN IDEAS

1. What is a federal district?
2. Describe one of the major geographic regions of the United States.
3. Why are the tops of the Appalachian Mountains rounded off?
4. Why are rivers so important?
5. Why are the Great Lakes so deep?

THINKING SKILLS

6. Identify your geographic region. Pretend that you are about to move to another region. What changes could you expect in your lifestyle? Consider urban versus rural living, climate, outdoor activities, and so on.

SKILLS APPLICATION

MAP SKILLS

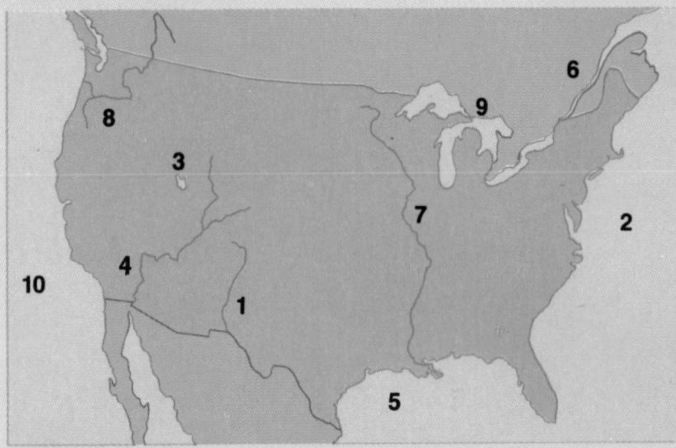

7. The numbers on this map stand for important bodies of water in North America. Match these numbers to the bodies of water listed below.

Pacific Ocean	Rio Grande
Mississippi River	St. Lawrence River
Gulf of Mexico	Great Salt Lake
Atlantic Ocean	Colorado River
Columbia River	Great Lakes

Look at the population density map on page 362.

8. What parts of the United States are heavily populated?
9. What parts have few people? Why do you think this is so?
10. Find New York City, Los Angeles, Chicago, and Philadelphia. They are the nation's largest cities. Are these cities surrounded by areas of high population density? Explain your answer.
11. Find three other areas of high population density in the United States. Name the city that is the center of each of these areas.
12. In what state was the center of population in 1980?

CHAPTER 2 THE NORTHEAST

Lesson 1: The New England States

FIND THE WORDS

commerce hydroelectric power commercial wood pulp mine quarry textile bog poultry urbanized commuting

The original English settlers gave the New England area its name because it reminded them of England. There are six states in this subregion: Maine, New Hampshire, Vermont, Massachusetts, Connecticut, and Rhode Island.

Features of the Land

Most of New England is covered by mountain ranges and a rolling plateau. The mountains, running north to south, are called the Appalachian Highlands.

East of the mountains lies the

rocky New England Plateau. It stretches from the mountains to the ocean, where it forms a high, rugged coastline. In eastern Massachusetts, however, the coastal area is low and flat and the beaches are sandy. This area is part of the Atlantic Coastal Plain.

The Appalachian Highlands are made up of two mountain ranges, separated by a river valley. The ranges are the White Mountains and the Green Mountains. Mount Washington in the White Mountains is the highest peak in the Northeast.

New England's longest river is the Connecticut River. It flows from northern New Hampshire, forming the border between Vermont and New Hampshire. It passes through Massachusetts and Connecticut. It then empties into Long Island Sound, off the Atlantic. Most New England rivers flow into the Atlantic.

Speaking about New England weather, the writer Mark Twain once said: "The weather is always doing something there. . . . In the spring I have counted one hundred and thirty-six different kinds of weather inside of twenty-four hours." He was joking, but he meant to stress how fast New England weather can change.

New England weather can be very harsh. The area has a continental climate. Winters are cold and wet. Summers are mild to hot, and wet, and fall comes early.

Weather along the coast is affected by ocean currents. The very cold Labrador Current comes down from the north. The warm Gulf Stream flows up from the south. Where the cold current meets the warmer one, fog is formed. That is why the coast of New England is often blanketed in thick fog.

Economic Activity

From its early history, New England has been a center of commerce and industry. **Commerce** (KOM urs) is the buying and selling of goods. Types of industry have changed over the years. Yet fishing, the manufacture of clothing, and paper and wood products are still important. New England's rivers have provided much of the power for its industries. Energy from the rivers' running water is used to produce electricity. This is called **hydroelectric power.**

One of New England's most valuable resources is the Atlantic Ocean. It has long been used for shipping, fishing, and vacationing. Commercial fishing started early there. A **commercial** (kuh MUR shul) activity is one done for profit. Fishers catch many kinds of fish and shellfish in the fishing grounds of the Atlantic.

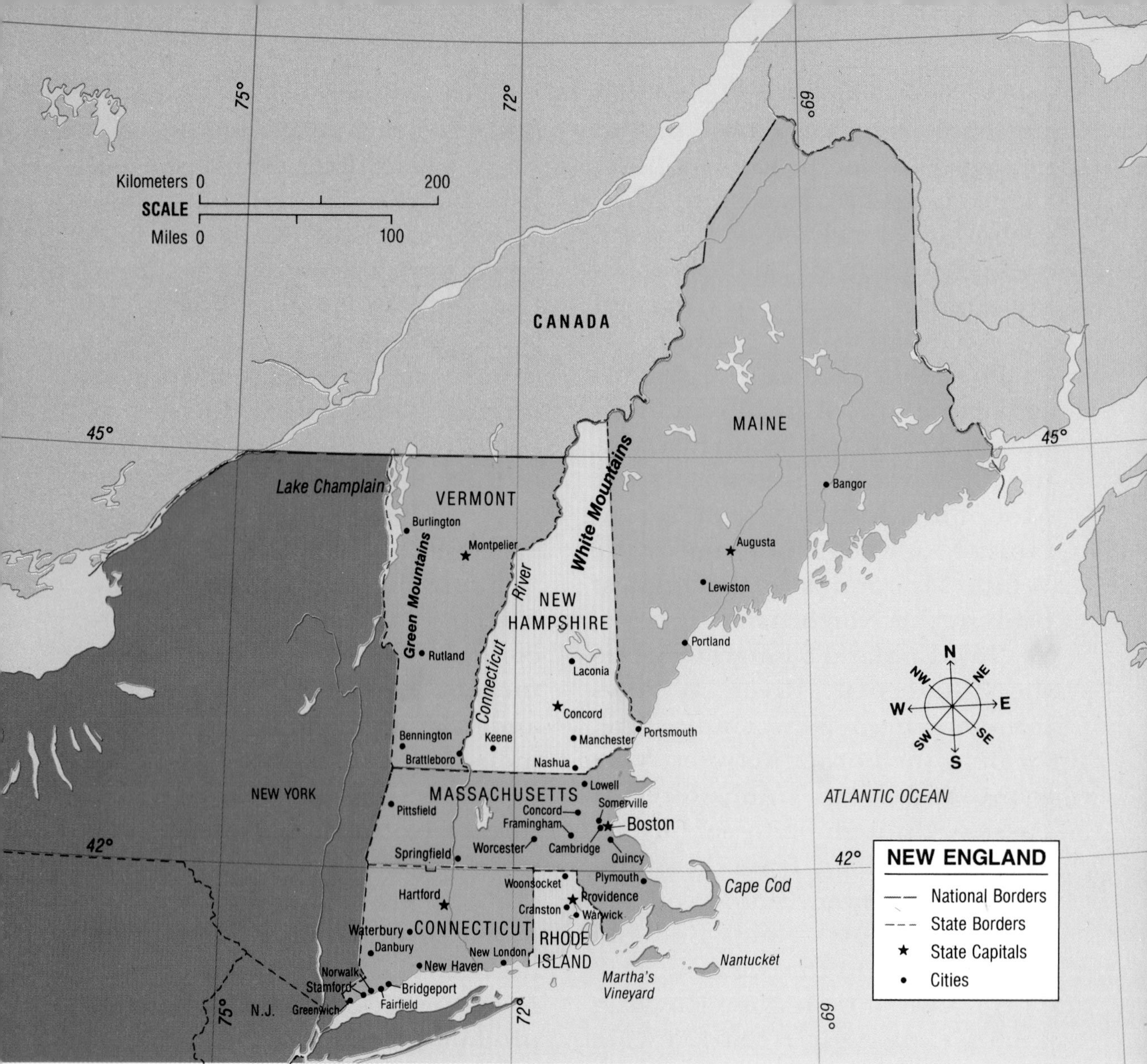

Key to Cities Shown on the Map

Population under 100,000
★Augusta (ME) .... 44°N, 70°W
Bangor (ME) .... 45°N, 69°W
Bennington (VT) .... 43°N, 73°W
Brattleboro (VT) .... 43°N, 73°W
Burlington (VT) .... 44°N, 73°W
Cambridge (MA) .... 42°N, 71°W
Concord (MA) .... 42°N, 71°W
★Concord (NH) .... 43°N, 72°W
Cranston (RI) .... 42°N, 71°W
Danbury (CT) .... 41°N, 73°W
Fairfield (CT) .... 41°N, 73°W
Greenwich (CT) .... 41°N, 73°W
Keene (NH) .... 43°N, 72°W
Laconia (NH) .... 44°N, 72°W
Lewiston (ME) .... 44°N, 70°W
Lowell (MA) .... 43°N, 71°W
Manchester (NH) .... 43°N, 72°W
★Montpelier (VT) .... 44°N, 73°W
Nashua (NH) .... 43°N, 71°W
New Bedford (MA) .... 42°N, 70°W
New London (CT) .... 41°N, 72°W
Norwalk (CT) .... 41°N, 73°W
Pittsfield (MA) .... 42°N, 73°W
Plymouth (MA) .... 42°N, 70°W
Portland (ME) .... 44°N, 70°W
Portsmouth (NH) .... 43°N, 71°W
Quincy (MA) .... 42°N, 71°W
Rutland (VT) .... 44°N, 73°W
Somerville (MA) .... 42°N, 71°W
Warwick (RI) .... 42°N, 71°W
Woonsocket (RI) .... 42°N, 72°W

Population 100,000–499,000
Bridgeport (CT) .... 41°N, 73°W
★Hartford (CT) .... 42°N, 73°W
New Haven (CT) .... 41°N, 73°W
★Providence (RI) .... 42°N, 71°W
Springfield (MA) .... 42°N, 73°W
Stamford (CT) .... 41°N, 74°W
Waterbury (CT) .... 42°N, 73°W
Worcester (MA) .... 42°N, 72°W

Population 500,000–999,000
★Boston (MA) .... 42°N, 71°W

Population 1,000,000 or over
None

THE NEW ENGLAND STATES

State	Population/ Admitted to the Union	Area Sq. mi.—Sq. km.	Capital	State Bird	State Flower	State Flag
Connecticut (CT) Constitution State	3,166,500 **1788**	5,009 12,973	Hartford	 Robin	 Mountain Laurel	
 **Maine (ME)** Pine Tree State	1,158,300 **1820**	33,215 86,027	Augusta	 Chickadee	 White Pine Cone and Tassel	
Massachusetts (MA) Bay State	5,786,400 **1788**	8,257 21,386	Boston	 Chickadee	 Arbutus	
 **New Hampshire (NH)** Granite State	982,400 **1788**	9,304 24,097	Concord	 Purple Finch	 Purple Lilac	
 **Rhode Island (RI)** Ocean State	959,300 **1790**	1,214 3,144	Providence	 Rhode Island Red	 Violet	
Vermont (VT) Green Mountain State	529,100 **1791**	9,609 24,887	Montpelier	 Hermit Thrush	 Red Clover	

After the fish are caught, they must be prepared for market. Food processing employs many people.

The forests of Maine, Vermont, and New Hampshire are another important resource. Some trees are cut down and ground into **wood pulp,** which is used to make paper. Other trees are turned into building material. Logging provides many jobs, especially in Maine and New Hampshire.

New England is known for its stony soil. This makes farming difficult. Some stones, however, are valuable. Granite, marble, and slate are found in Vermont. Workers dig these stones from mines and quarries. **Mines** are holes or tunnels dug under the ground. **Quarries** are open pits from which stone is taken. Granite, marble, and slate are used as building materials.

The **textile** industry, which makes woven or knitted cloth, has a long history in New England. The area was once a manufacturing center for cotton and woolen textiles. Now many of our cotton textiles are produced in the South. New England is still a leader in the woolen industry, though. It also produces leather goods.

Other industries of the subregion include metalworking, electronics, printing, and publishing. Finally, there is tourism. The tourist industry contributes much to New England's economy. Many people come to the area for sports and recreation.

Farming is not a major economic activity in New England. Much of the soil is rocky and hilly. Yet some products do very well. Two-thirds of all the cranberries sold in the United States come from bogs near Cape Cod in Massachusetts. A **bog** is like a swamp or marsh. It is flooded to help the plants grow.

Potatoes are the main crop of Maine. Vermont is famous for its maple syrup. Did you know that tobacco is grown in New England? It comes from the Connecticut River valley.

Throughout New England, you will find dairy and poultry farms. **Poultry** (POHL tree) farmers raise chickens. The land can support these types of agriculture. The large cities on the coast provide a market for the products.

The People of New England

Over 12 million people live in the New England States. Three out of every four live in urban areas. Massachusetts, Connecticut, and Rhode Island—the three southern states—are heavily urbanized. An area is **urbanized** when its communities are close together. Large numbers of people live in urbanized areas. Many

Fascinating Facts

You probably like maple syrup on your pancakes or waffles. Perhaps you know it is made from the sap of maple trees. But do you know how the syrup is produced?

The process begins in early spring. Orchard owners drive spouts into the trunks of sugar maple trees. Freezing nights followed by warmer days cause sap to flow from these spouts.

The sap is collected, then put into long vats called evaporators. These machines boil the sap until it has the right thickness, color, and flavor.

Maple sugar is made by the same process. But the sap must be boiled longer to make maple sugar.

The average tree yields 38 to 76 liters (10 to 20 gallons) of sap. You need about twice that much sap to make 1 gallon of syrup. Many maple trees are required for the syrup on your pancakes.

of them work in a city and live in one of its suburbs, or surrounding communities. Every day, they travel between the suburbs and the city. This traveling back and forth from one community to another is called **commuting** (kuh MYOOT ing).

Most of the large cities in New England are along the coast. Inland and to the north, this is a subregion of small towns. One-fourth of the population lives in and around these small towns.

The typical New England town is built around a village green. This is a grassy area central to the town's activity. Around the green, you may find a church, a town hall, houses, a few stores, and restaurants.

The largest and most important city in New England is Boston. Boston is the capital of Massachusetts. It is a port city and an important center of commerce. Many places in Boston are linked with the early history of our nation. Samuel Adams and his friends planned the Boston Tea Party in Faneuil Hall. Paul Revere set off on his famous ride after two lanterns appeared in the Old North Church to show

The city of Cambridge, Massachusetts, at 42° N, 71° W, is the site of Harvard University.

that the British were coming.

Other major New England cities include New Haven and Hartford, Connecticut, and Providence, Rhode Island.

Places to See

The scenery of New England attracts many visitors. There are beautiful national parks: White Mountain National Forest in New Hampshire, Acadia National Park in Maine, and the Cape Cod National Seashore. In autumn, many tourists come to see the leaves. The cold nights and sunny days produce woodlands bursting with brilliant reds, oranges, and yellows.

There are also many historic sites. You can visit Plymouth Rock, where the Pilgrims landed. You can relive colonial history at Plymouth Plantation or at Salem in Massachusetts. You can visit battlefields on which the fight for American independence began. You can explore an old-time New England seaport in Mystic, Connecticut.

REVIEW

VOCABULARY MASTERY

1. The ___ industry is important in New England.
   citrus cotton textile
2. Granite and marble are taken from ___.
   mines quarries textiles

READING FOR MAIN IDEAS

3. What are summers and winters like in New England?
4. Why have rivers been important in New England?
5. Why is farming difficult in New England?

RESEARCH AND WRITING SKILLS

Since colonial times, many New Englanders have gone to sea. Some were traders; others fished or hunted whales. Do research and write a report on one of these New England occupations.

Lesson 2: The Middle Atlantic States

FIND THE WORDS

piedmont fall line rapids
falls growing season
truck farming mixed farming
mineral bituminous coke
anthracite natural gas
finance communications
megalopolis

The Middle Atlantic States include six states and a federal district. They are New York, New Jersey, Pennsylvania, Delaware, Maryland, West Virginia, and the District of Columbia.

This subregion is not large. Yet it is a busy area with many major industries and large cities. Like New England, it holds an important place in the early history of our nation.

Features of the Land

The landforms of the Middle Atlantic States can be divided into three groups: the Appalachian Mountain system, the Piedmont Plateau, and the Atlantic Coastal Plain.

The Appalachian Mountain system runs from New York

Baltimore residents are proud of their "Harbor Place," a major renovation of the city's inner harbor area. Baltimore is at 39° north, 77° west.

through the northern part of New Jersey. It sweeps across Pennsylvania into West Virginia. The system has several ranges: the Adirondacks, Catskills, and Alleghenies. Find the Adirondack and Allegheny mountains on the map on pages 360 and 361.

East of the Appalachian Mountain system is the Piedmont (PEED mont) Plateau. This rolling land slopes gently down from the mountains. **Piedmont** means "lying at the foot of the mountains." Some of the soil here is very fertile. The plateau is separated from the coastal plain by the **fall line.** This is a place where the level of the land drops, and the rivers form rapids and falls. **Rapids** are rocky places where a river drops down gradually. **Falls,** or waterfalls, are places where a river drops steeply and suddenly from one level to another.

Many of the area's rivers provide hydroelectric power. The waterfalls and rapids have been used to produce energy. Cities have grown up along the fall line. Philadelphia, Baltimore, and Washington all lie along the fall line at the edge of the Piedmont Plateau.

The coastal plain covers most of New Jersey, all of Delaware, and the eastern part of Maryland. Millions of people live in large cities on this low, flat plain.

Water has played a major role in the history of the Middle Atlantic States. Four of them—Maryland, Delaware, New Jersey, and New York—are on the Atlantic Ocean. Two large bays, Delaware Bay and Chesapeake Bay, cut deeply into the Atlantic coastline. The ocean and bays have been a commercial and recreational resource for the Middle Atlantic region.

Two of the Great Lakes border this subregion. They are Lake Erie and Lake Ontario. Between them flows the Niagara River, best known for the spectacular Niagara Falls.

Great rivers flow across the Middle Atlantic States. The Ohio River drains the Appalachian Mountains to the west. The Hudson cuts down through New York State. Beginning in the Adirondack Mountains and ending in New York Bay, the Hudson River is over 500 kilometers (300 miles) long. The Hudson River is connected to the Great Lakes by canals. This water route was very important in the growth of the Midwestern part of the nation.

The Delaware and Susquehanna (SUSS kwuh HAN uh) rivers flow mainly through Pennsylvania. There is a lot of shipping on the Delaware. The Susquehanna and the Potomac rivers empty into Chesapeake Bay. The nation's capital, Washington, DC, lies on the east bank of the Potomac River.

The Middle Atlantic States can be divided into two climate zones. The southeastern, coastal part of the subregion has a humid subtropical climate. In winter, it is mild and wet; in summer, hot and wet. The rest of the subregion has a continental climate. The summers are mild to hot, and wet. Winters are cold and wet, but not as harsh as in New England. The Middle Atlantic States have a longer growing season than New England. The **growing season** is the time between the frosts of spring and the frosts of autumn, when crops can best be grown.

Steelmaking is a major industry in Pennsylvania, where 25 percent of the nation's steel is made.

Economic Activity

Agriculture, or farming, is one source of income in the Middle Atlantic States. Along the coastal plain, much of the soil is too sandy to grow many crops. Inland, large areas of the Piedmont Plateau have fertile soil.

The subregion has many dairy and poultry farms, especially in New York and Pennsylvania. Truck farming is another important type of agriculture. **Truck farming** means growing different kinds of vegetables for sale. The large urban areas of the subregion provide markets for these foods. Truck farming is an important activity in New Jersey.

Mixed farming is also practiced in this subregion. **Mixed farming** means raising a combination of animals, grain, and hay. The grain and hay are fed to the animals. The animals are then sold on the market for cash.

Several types of fruit are grown in the Middle Atlantic States. Southeastern New York is known for its apple orchards. Grapes are a major crop around the Finger Lakes region of New York. Blueberries, cranberries, and peaches are grown in New Jersey.

The Middle Atlantic States are highly industrialized. Leading industries include petroleum refining, chemicals, textiles, clothing,

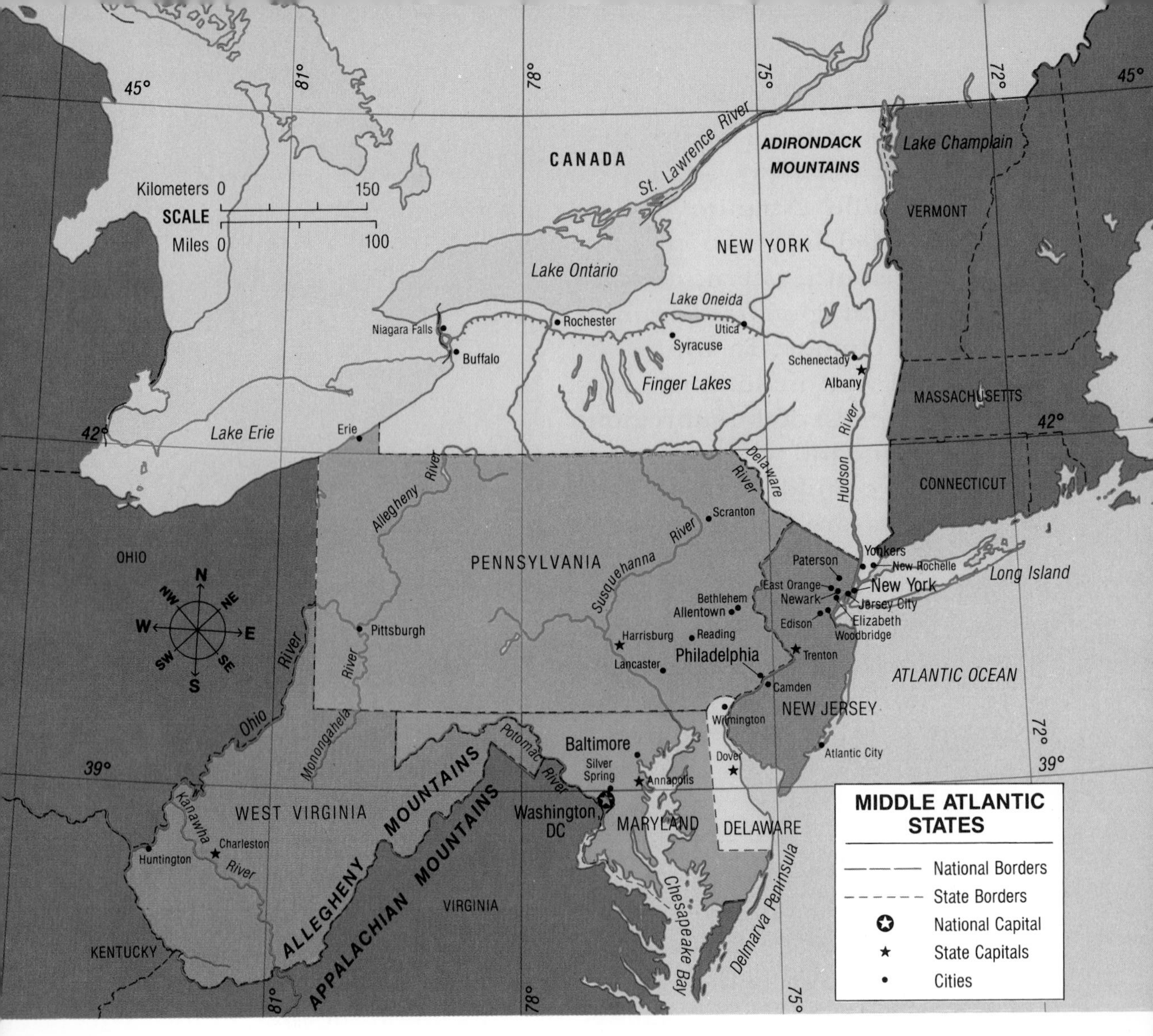

Key to Cities Shown on the Map

Population under 100,000
★Annapolis (MD) .... 39°N, 76°W
Atlantic City (NJ) .... 39°N, 75°W
Bethlehem (PA) .... 41°N, 75°W
Camden (NJ) .... 40°N, 75°W
★Charleston (WV) .... 38°N, 82°W
★Dover (DE) .... 39°N, 76°W
East Orange (NJ) .... 41°N, 74°W
Edison (NJ) .... 41°N, 74°W
★Harrisburg (PA) .... 40°N, 77°W
Huntington (WV) .... 38°N, 82°W
Lancaster (PA) .... 40°N, 76°W
New Rochelle (NY)......... 41°N, 74°W
Niagara Falls (NY) .... 43°N, 79°W
Reading (PA) .... 40°N, 76°W
Schenectady (NY) .... 43°N, 74°W
Scranton (PA) .... 42°N, 76°W
Silver Spring (MD) .... 39°N, 77°W
★Trenton (NJ) .... 40°N, 75°W
Utica (NY) .... 43°N, 75°W
Wilmington (DE) .... 40°N, 76°W
Woodbridge (NJ) .... 41°N, 74°W

Population 100,000–499,000
★Albany (NY) .... 43°N, 74°W
Allentown (PA) .... 41°N, 76°W
Buffalo (NY) .... 43°N, 79°W
Elizabeth (NJ) .... 41°N, 74°W
Erie (PA) .... 42°N, 80°W
Jersey City (NJ) .... 41°N, 74°W
Newark (NJ) .... 41°N, 74°W
Paterson (NJ) .... 41°N, 74°W
Pittsburgh (PA) .... 40°N, 80°W
Rochester (NY) .... 43°N, 78°W
Syracuse (NY) .... 43°N, 76°W
Yonkers (NY) .... 41°N, 74°W

Population 500,000–999,000
Baltimore (MD) .... 39°N, 77°W
✪Washington (DC) .... 39°N, 77°W

Population 1,000,000 or over
New York (NY) .... 41°N, 74°W
Philadelphia (PA) .... 40°N, 75°W

THE MIDDLE ATLANTIC STATES

	Population/ Admitted to the Union	Area Sq. mi.—Sq. km.	Capital	State Bird	State Flower	State Flag
Delaware (DE) First State	613,200 **1787**	2,057 5,328	Dover	Blue Hen Chicken	Peach Blossom	DECEMBER 7, 1787
Maryland (MD) Old Line State	4,324,400 **1788**	10,577 27,394	Annapolis	Baltimore Oriole	Black-eyed Susan	
New Jersey (NJ) Garden State	7,552,700 **1787**	7,836 20,295	Trenton	Eastern Goldfinch	Purple Violet	
New York (NY) Empire State	17,555,500 **1788**	49,576 128,402	Albany	Bluebird	Rose	
Pennsylvania (PA) Keystone State	11,887,200 **1787**	45,333 117,412	Harrisburg	Ruffed Grouse	Mountain Laurel	
West Virginia (WV) Mountain State	1,983,000 **1863**	24,282 62,890	Charleston	Cardinal	Rhododendron	

and food processing. Machinery, ships, automobiles, and aircraft are built here.

Coal is the most important mineral resource of the subregion. A **mineral** is a substance found in the ground that is not a plant or an animal. The Appalachian Mountains in Pennsylvania and West Virginia have the richest coal fields in the nation.

There are two kinds of coal. **Bituminous** (bi TOO muh nus) coal is soft coal. It is used to make coke. **Coke** is used as a fuel in the furnaces that produce steel.

The second type of coal is **anthracite** (AN thruh SYT). Anthracite is hard coal. When it burns, it does not pollute the air very much. This coal was once widely used for heating homes. As other fuels became popular, coal was used less. In recent years, the United States has faced fuel shortages. So coal from this subregion has become more important again.

Natural gas is one of the fuels that replaced anthracite. **Natural gas** is a mixture of gases found in the ground. There are reserves of natural gas in the Appalachian Mountains of Pennsylvania and West Virginia.

Petroleum, another fuel, is also found in the subregion. The first oil well was drilled in Titusville, Pennsylvania, in 1859. A small amount of petroleum still comes from this area. But it is no longer a major producer of petroleum.

In Pennsylvania, steel is a major industry. The city of Pittsburgh has long been the nation's iron and steel center. Coal is mined nearby. Iron ore is shipped across the Great Lakes from Minnesota and Michigan. Both coal and iron ore are needed to make steel. Today, however, much of the nation's steel comes from foreign countries. Some of Pittsburgh's steel mills have closed down.

Commercial fishing is an important economic activity in New York, New Jersey, and Maryland. The Chesapeake and Delaware bays are known for their shellfish.

New York City is a world center of finance and communications. **Finance** is the science of money management. It includes banking. It also includes buying and selling stocks and bonds. **Communications** include radio, television, newspapers, and magazines. Advertising and book publishing are also centered in New York.

Tourism thrives in the Middle Atlantic States. There are many scenic parks, mountain areas, and sandy beaches. Much of the nation's early history took place in this subregion. The nation's capital is also located there.

Fascinating Facts

Niagara Falls is not the highest waterfall in the world. But that does not bother the more than 4 million people who visit it every year. They have come to see the beauty and power of the Niagara River as it drops straight down 51 meters (167 feet).

Niagara Falls is on the border between the United States and Canada. Each nation owns the falls on its side. Both nations use some of the river's waterflow for hydroelectric power. Fortunately for tourists, the United States and Canada have agreed to leave enough water to keep the falls flowing.

People of the Middle Atlantic States

Many large cities lie along the coast of the Middle Atlantic States. The population density of the area is very high. More than 40 million people live there. The area is called a megalopolis (meg uh LOP uh lis). A **megalopolis** is an area that has several large cities close together.

New York is the most important city in the area. Its bustling port handles much of the nation's foreign trade. It is a major center of commerce and transportation. Wall Street is the main street of the financial district. Wall Street traders buy and sell shares in the nation's businesses. New York is not all business, though. It offers outstanding museums, theater, art, music, and dance. New York's many fine colleges and universities contribute much to the life of the city. So does the United Nations. The headquarters of this international organization are in New York. World leaders visit the city every year. People from many nations and cultures have made New York their home. They have helped make it an exciting and varied city.

Philadelphia is another great city of the Middle Atlantic. It has one of the world's busiest ports. Philadelphia played a leading role in the early history of the United States. The Continental Congress met there. The Declaration of Independence was signed there. From 1790 to 1800, Philadelphia was the nation's capital.

Three rivers come together at Pittsburgh in southwestern Pennsylvania. These rivers—the Allegheny, Monongahela (muh NON guh HEE luh), and Ohio—helped make Pittsburgh a great industrial center. Pollution from its industry once made Pittsburgh the "Smoky City." But today, the air and water are cleaner.

Baltimore, Maryland, is another major port. In the last few years, the harbor area has been rebuilt. The new stores and restaurants attract many visitors.

Washington, DC, has two main industries: government and tourism. Government work employs most of the people in the area. Tourists come to see how the government works. The White House and the Capitol, where Congress meets, attract visitors from all over the world.

Places to See

The great cities of the subregion each offer something different. New York has towering skyscrapers and the Statue of Liberty. Philadelphia has the Liberty Bell, which rang to announce American independence. It has Independence Hall, where the nation's founders met and planned America's future.

The city of Washington, DC, of course, has the White House and the Washington Monument. However, no trip to the city would be complete without a stop at the Smithsonian Institution. Really a group of museums and art galleries, the Smithsonian has been called the "nation's attic." It has a little of everything—from dinosaurs to spacecraft. Its collections include more than 30 million items.

REVIEW

VOCABULARY MASTERY

1. In ___ farming, different kinds of vegetables are grown for sale.
   poultry dairy truck
2. New York City is an important center of ___.
   truck farming communications minerals

READING FOR MAIN IDEAS

3. Name the three groups of landforms found in the Middle Atlantic States.
4. What part of the Middle Atlantic region is called a megalopolis? Why?
5. Give three reasons why people come to New York City.

RESEARCH AND WRITING SKILLS

Choose a city in the Middle Atlantic States. Do research on this city. Write a description of it. Then give three reasons why you would like to live there.

CHAPTER REVIEW

VOCABULARY MASTERY

Use the words below to complete the chapter summary. Use each only once.

commerce	mines
commercial	mixed farming
communications	poultry
commuting	quarries
finance	textile
megalopolis	truck farming
mineral	urbanized

The New England States are heavily __1__. They have long been a center of __2__. Many people live in the suburbs and go to work by __3__. There are many __4__ farms in New England. The __5__ industry in New England produces woolen goods. Workers dig granite, marble, and slate from __6__ and __7__. Another important activity in New England is __8__ fishing.

The area of the Middle Atlantic States is often called a(n) __9__ because so many people live there. New York City is a center of __10__ and __11__. Agriculture is an important source of income for many areas in the Middle Atlantic States. Both __12__ and __13__ are practiced in this subregion. There are also large __14__ deposits, which supply many kinds of fuel.

READING FOR MAIN IDEAS

1. What influences the weather along the coast of New England?
2. Why is the ocean along the Atlantic coast a valuable resource?
3. What are the major economic activities of New England?
4. Describe the two climate zones of the Middle Atlantic States.
5. What is the most important city in the Middle Atlantic States? Why?

SKILLS APPLICATION

CHART SKILLS

Look at the state charts on pages 379 and 387.

6. Which New England state has the most people? Is it also the largest state in that region?
7. Which is the only New England state that did not enter the Union during the 1700s? In what year did it enter?
8. Name the largest Middle Atlantic state. Does it also have the largest population?
9. Compare the two state charts. Do the New England or the Middle Atlantic states tend to have more land area?

CAUSE-AND-EFFECT SKILLS

Complete the exercise on cause and effect below.

10. **Cause:** See Lesson 1.
    Effect: Coastal New England is often blanketed in thick fog.
11. **Cause:** New England's soil is very stony.
    Effect: See Lesson 1.
12. **Cause:** The Hudson River and the Great Lakes are connected by canals.
    Effect: See Lesson 2.
13. **Cause:** Many areas of the Piedmont Plateau have fertile soil.
    Effect: See Lesson 2.
14. **Cause:** The Middle Atlantic States have many large cities close together.
    Effect: See Lesson 2.
15. **Cause:** The United Nations headquarters is in New York.
    Effect: See Lesson 2.

CHAPTER 3 THE SOUTH

Lesson 1: The Southeastern States

FIND THE WORDS

silt tidewater barrier islands fertilizer hurricanes bauxite hardwood softwood citrus fruit sunbelt service industries

The Southeast is made up of nine states: Virginia, North Carolina, South Carolina, Georgia, Florida, Kentucky, Tennessee, Alabama, and Mississippi. These states are east of the Mississippi River. About 45 million people live in the subregion. Much of the area is rural. Yet many major cities are found here as well. Find cities with a population over 100,000 on the map on page 394.

Features of the Land

The Southeast is an area of mountains, rolling hills, and

plains. The landforms you learned about in the Middle Atlantic States continue into this subregion. The Appalachian Mountains sweep through the area from Virginia to Georgia. Mount Mitchell, the highest peak in the Appalachians, is in North Carolina. It rises 2,037 meters (6,684 feet) above sea level.

The Appalachians include several smaller ranges. Farthest east are the Blue Ridge Mountains. Between North Carolina and Tennessee lie the Great Smoky Mountains. On the west are the Cumberland Mountains, which are really a plateau. Rivers that cut deeply through the area have made the plateau look ruggedly mountainous.

Between the mountains and the coastal plain lies the Piedmont Plateau. It includes parts of Virginia, the Carolinas, Georgia, and Alabama. The area is mostly flat or rolling, with some hills. Many rivers run through this plateau. As in the Middle Atlantic States, the fall line is the eastern border of the Piedmont Plateau. Here there are waterfalls and rapids. Many large cities have grown up along this line.

The Atlantic and Gulf coastal plains lie along the eastern and southern border of this subregion. In some places, the coastal plain is very wide. The entire state of Florida is on the coastal plain.

In the western part of the region, the coastal plain changes. This area is called the Mississippi Alluvial Plain. The land here was lifted up from the Gulf of Mexico in the not too distant past. Compared with other areas, the soil is quite young. This lowland is covered with silt from the Mississippi River. **Silt** is rich soil carried by a river. In western Mississippi, these conditions have created a highly fertile farming area.

The Southeast is bordered on the east and south by large bodies of water. These are the Atlantic Ocean and the Gulf of Mexico.

Inland, along the coastal plain, are many swamps. Swamps are lands mostly covered by water. Many types of plants and animals live and grow in swamps. The Everglades National Park in southern Florida and the Okefenokee (O kuh fuh NOH kee) Swamp in Georgia are two of the nation's largest swamps.

Swamps are covered by water all of the time. **Tidewater** areas are covered by water only part of the time. When the tide is high, the land is flooded. When the tide is low, the water drains from the land. The coast of Virginia around Norfolk is a tidewater area.

Off the coast of North Carolina are the Outer Banks. These are barrier islands. **Barrier islands** are thin, sandy islands. They are

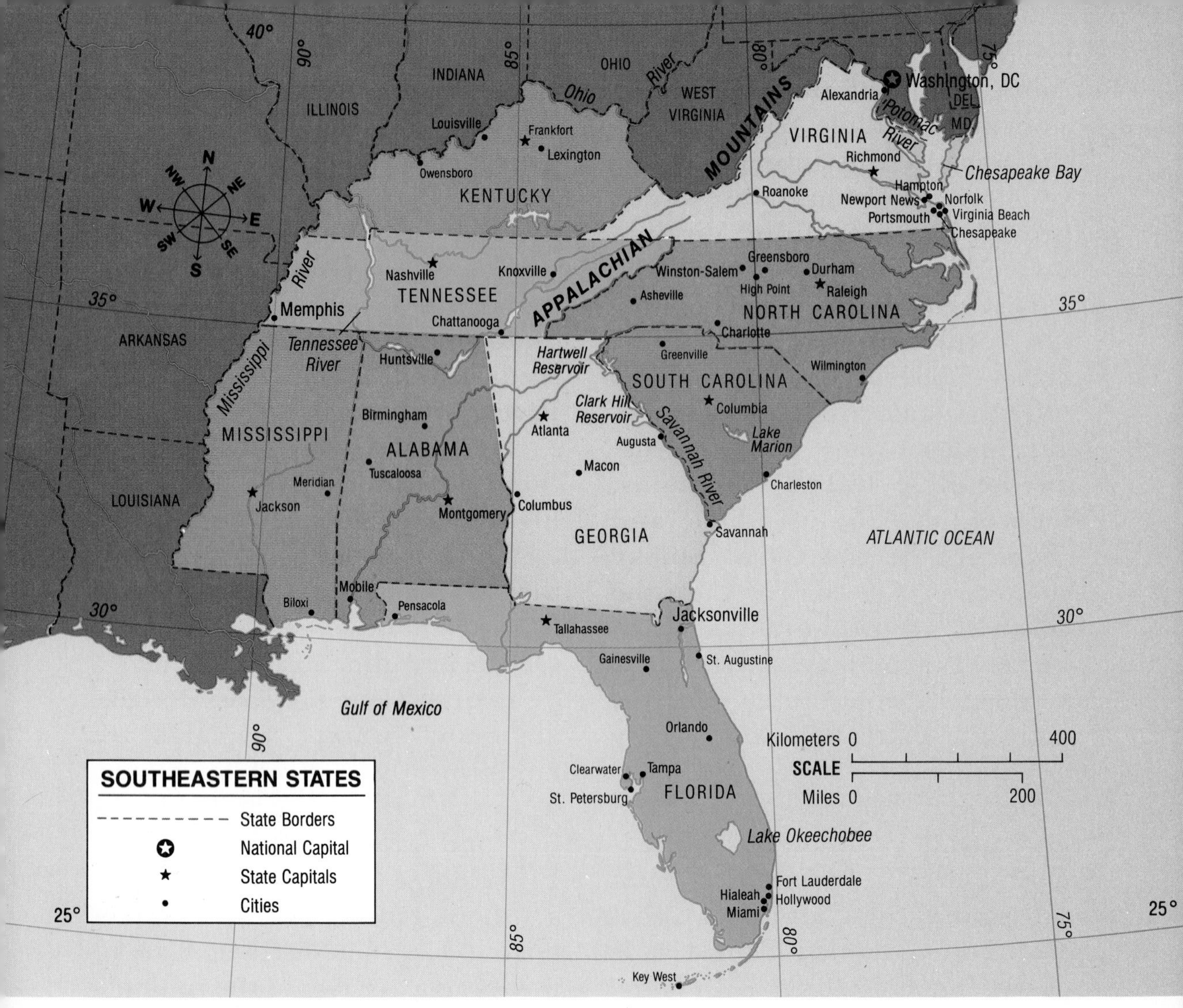

Key to Cities Shown on the Map

Population under 100,000

- Asheville (NC) .... 36°N, 83°W
- Augusta (GA) .... 33°N, 82°W
- Biloxi (MS) .... 30°N, 89°W
- Charleston (SC) .... 33°N, 80°W
- Clearwater (FL) .... 28°N, 83°W
- ★Frankfort (KY) .... 38°N, 85°W
- Gainesville (FL) .... 30°N, 82°W
- Greenville (SC) .... 35°N, 82°W
- High Point (NC) .... 36°N, 80°W
- Key West (FL) .... 25°N, 82°W
- Meridian (MS) .... 32°N, 89°W
- Owensboro (KY) .... 38°N, 87°W
- Pensacola (FL) .... 30°N, 87°W
- St. Augustine (FL) .... 30°N, 81°W
- ★Tallahassee (FL) .... 30°N, 84°W
- Tuscaloosa (AL) .... 33°N, 88°W
- Wilmington (NC) .... 34°N, 78°W

Population 100,000–499,000

- Alexandria (VA) .... 39°N, 77°W
- ★Atlanta (GA) .... 34°N, 84°W
- Birmingham (AL) .... 34°N, 87°W
- Charlotte (NC) .... 35°N, 81°W
- Chattanooga (TN) .... 35°N, 85°W
- Chesapeake (VA) .... 37°N, 76°W
- ★Columbia (SC) .... 34°N, 81°W
- Columbus (GA) .... 32°N, 85°W
- Durham (NC) .... 36°N, 79°W
- Fort Lauderdale (FL) .... 26°N, 80°W
- Greensboro (NC) .... 36°N, 80°W
- Hampton (VA) .... 37°N, 76°W
- Hialeah (FL) .... 26°N, 80°W
- Hollywood (FL) .... 26°N, 80°W
- Huntsville (AL) .... 35°N, 87°W
- ★Jackson (MS) .... 32°N, 90°W
- Knoxville (TN) .... 36°N, 84°W
- Lexington (KY) .... 38°N, 85°W
- Louisville (KY) .... 38°N, 86°W
- Macon (GA) .... 33°N, 84°W
- Miami (FL) .... 26°N, 80°W
- Mobile (AL) .... 31°N, 88°W
- ★Montgomery (AL) .... 32°N, 86°W
- ★Nashville (TN) .... 36°N, 87°W
- Newport News (VA) ..... 37°N, 76°W
- Norfolk (VA) .... 37°N, 76°W
- Orlando (FL) .... 29°N, 81°W
- Portsmouth (VA) .... 37°N, 76°W
- ★Raleigh (NC) .... 36°N, 79°W
- ★Richmond (VA) .... 38°N, 78°W
- Roanoke (VA) .... 37°N, 80°W
- St. Petersburg (FL) ...... 28°N, 83°W
- Savannah (GA) .... 33°N, 82°W
- Tampa (FL) .... 28°N, 83°W
- Virginia Beach (VA) ..... 37°N, 76°W
- Winston-Salem (NC) .... 36°N, 80°W

Population 500,000–999,000

- Jacksonville (FL) .... 30°N, 82°W
- Memphis (TN) .... 35°N, 90°W

Population 1,000,000 or over

- None

THE SOUTHEASTERN STATES

	Population/ Admitted to the Union	Area Sq. mi.—Sq. km.	Capital	State Bird	State Flower	State Flag
 **Alabama (AL)** Yellowhammer State	4,011,100 **1819**	51,609 133,667	Montgomery	 Yellowhammer	 Camellia	
 **Florida (FL)** Sunshine State	10,824,700 **1845**	58,560 151,670	Tallahassee	 Mockingbird	 Orange Blossom	
 **Georgia (GA)** Empire State of the South	5,790,800 **1788**	58,876 152,489	Atlanta	 Brown Thrasher	 Cherokee Rose	
 **Kentucky (KY)** Bluegrass State	3,742,200 **1792**	40,395 104,623	Frankfort	 Kentucky Cardinal	 Goldenrod	
Mississippi (MS) Magnolia State	2,629,800 **1817**	47,716 123,584	Jackson	 Mockingbird	 Magnolia	
 **North Carolina (NC)** Tar Heel State	6,168,200 **1789**	52,586 136,198	Raleigh	 Cardinal	 Flowering Dogwood	

THE SOUTHEASTERN STATES	Population/ Admitted to the Union	Area Sq. mi.—Sq. km.	Capital	State Bird	State Flower	State Flag
South Carolina (SC) Palmetto State	3,278,800 **1788**	31,055 80,432	Columbia	Carolina Wren	Carolina Jessamine	
Tennessee (TN) Volunteer State	4,762,400 **1796**	42,244 109,412	Nashville	Mockingbird	Iris	
Virginia (VA) Old Dominion	5,614,600 **1788**	40,815 105,711	Richmond	Cardinal	Dogwood	

called barrier islands because they separate the shoreline from the ocean.

The Mississippi, the longest river in the United States, borders on the Southeastern States. It forms a water highway through the center of the nation. Goods from the Midwest travel along the Mississippi to the Gulf of Mexico. The Mississippi is also important because of the richness of the soil around it. Many crops can be grown on the Alluvial Plain. Other major rivers of the subregion include the Ohio, the Cumberland, and the Tennessee.

Most of the Southeast has a humid subtropical climate. Summers are hot and wet. Winters are mild, but also wet. Temperatures in the Appalachian Mountains are generally cooler than along the coast. The tip of Florida has a tropical grasslands climate, with hot, wet summers and hot, dry winters.

The Southeast has plenty of rain. There is usually more than 100 centimeters (39 inches) every year. It is rainiest on the coast. The rain and the warm temperatures produce a long growing season. Even the northern parts of the subregion have 200 days free of frost. In Florida, some crops are harvested three or four times a year.

Yet the area's climate has some drawbacks. Soil usually rests in the winter. During this time, nourishing substances can build up. These substances will be used later by growing plants. A short winter or no winter at all means the soil gets little rest. The heavy rains also wash away substances needed by plants. As a result, fertilizer must be put on the soil to make it productive. **Fertilizer** adds minerals to the soil. It makes the soil more fertile.

Sometimes hurricanes occur in this subregion. **Hurricanes** are severe tropical storms, with very high winds and often heavy rains. The Mississippi Lowland is a path for many of these storms. Hurricanes form in the Caribbean Sea in late summer and early fall. The storms move onto the continent along the Gulf of Mexico and do a lot of damage.

The Southeast has many valuable resources. Its soil and its mild climate are very good for agriculture. Its rivers and coastal waters are used for transportation, fishing, hydroelectric power, and recreation. There are also some important minerals. Virginia, Kentucky, Tennessee, and Alabama all have coal in the Appalachian Highlands. Much of the nation's bituminous coal comes from this area. Iron is found in Alabama, along with limestone. These minerals are used in making steel. Bauxite is also found in Georgia and Alabama. **Bauxite** is a mineral used to make the light and useful metal aluminum. The production of aluminum is a key industry in Alabama, Tennessee, and Kentucky.

Another mineral found in the Southeast is phosphate rock. Phosphate is used to make fertilizer. Both Florida and Tennessee have phosphate.

Forests are a major living resource of the subregion. The long

Fascinating Facts

At one time, the Tennessee River overflowed regularly. This caused serious floods that led to property damage and loss of lives. But the Tennessee Valley Authority, or TVA, changed all that.

The TVA was set up by the federal government in 1933. Its job was to control flooding, to make the river easier for ships to use, and to provide hydroelectric power. The TVA has accomplished all three tasks. No damage from floods has occurred since the TVA dams were built. The river has been deepened and improved in many ways. River traffic has increased. And the TVA supplies inexpensive electric power to Tennessee and to parts of Virginia, North Carolina, Georgia, Alabama, Mississippi, and Kentucky. The TVA tamed the river and put it to work.

growing season and plentiful rain make forests grow quickly. Trees can be cut within 25 years of planting. This is half as long as in New England. In the northern part of the subregion, the forests have hardwood trees, such as oaks and maples. A **hardwood** is a tree that loses its leaves in the fall. In the southern part of the subregion, softwood trees, such as pines, are common. A **softwood** is a tree with cones and needles. Both lumber and wood pulp are produced from the forests of the Southeast.

Economic Activity

Farming contributes much to the economy of the Southeast. In the 1800s, cotton was the major crop, and there were many large plantations. Cotton is still grown in Mississippi, Alabama, Georgia, South Carolina, and Tennessee. But the Southeast of today has many other crops.

Tobacco is grown mostly in the north and east of the subregion. North Carolina and Kentucky produce over half of the nation's tobacco crop. Virginia, South Carolina, Georgia, and Tennessee also grow tobacco.

Florida raises more citrus fruits than any other state. **Citrus fruits** are fruits such as oranges, grapefruit, lemons, and limes. Farmers in Florida also grow sugar cane. Sugar cane is a tall, thick-stemmed plant from which sugar can be made.

Many other fruits and vegetables come from the Southeast. Farmers grow corn to sell and to use as feed for animals. Soybeans are another important crop. In some places, soybeans have replaced cotton. Farmers in the Southeast also grow grains such as rice and wheat. Peanuts and pecans are raised throughout this subregion. Georgia is the nation's leading peanut producer.

Some farmers raise animals to sell. Both hogs and poultry are raised in the Southeast.

Of course, farming is not the only way the people of the Southeast are employed. Industry is important in this subregion. Manufacturing employs about a third of the people who work. This is higher than the national average. Many factories have moved here since World War II. The warm climate means lower costs for heating. Wages and taxes have also been lower than in other areas. Today, however, the Southeast faces new competition from foreign industry.

Both the cotton and woolen textile industries thrive here. Synthetic fibers such as nylon and Dacron are also manufactured. Louisville, Kentucky, and Richmond, Virginia, are two centers

An orange grove in central Florida. The Florida climate is good for growing citrus fruits, but frosts sometimes occur and severely damage the crops.

of the chemical industry. Steelmaking is important in Alabama.

Forests, as you remember, are a key resource of the Southeast. Some trees are ground into wood pulp. Turning this wood pulp into paper is an important industry. Trees are also cut for lumber. Some of this wood is made into furniture. North Carolina is a leader in the furniture industry.

The tobacco grown throughout the subregion is processed locally. Both Virginia and North Carolina produce many tobacco products.

Fishing is big business along the Atlantic and Gulf coasts. The catch includes oysters, crabs, shrimp, red snapper, and many other fish. Food processing also employs many people. Consider the citrus industry, for example. Grapefruit grown in Florida must be prepared for market. Some fruits are picked and shipped whole. Others are made into juice. Still others are canned or frozen.

Tourism is a major industry in the Southeast, especially in Florida. Florida's warm weather and miles of beaches make it popular with visitors all year round. Throughout the subregion are many areas of patriotic and historical interest.

The mild climate draws not only visitors but people who come to stay. Many retired people move to the Southeast, especially to Florida. Florida is part of the **sunbelt,** the warm, sunny area that stretches across the southern part of the United States. The sunbelt extends from Florida to California. Because of migration to the sunbelt, service industries there are growing fast. **Service industries** help people but do not make products. They carry out activities such as serving meals, providing transportation, and giving medical care.

People of the Southeast

The Southeast is a growing area. Much new business and industry has developed in this area. People have moved here because of the job opportunities. Retired people also account for some of the growth. Many people have moved to large cities. Yet one-third of the population still lives in rural areas. Blacks make up one-fifth of the population of the Southeastern States.

The Southeast has many exciting cities. One of the largest in the subregion is Atlanta, Georgia. This state capital continues to grow very rapidly. Industries such as clothing, metal goods, chemicals, furniture, and airplanes are based here. Atlanta is a center of commerce and transportation as well. Many air, rail, and highway routes come together in Atlanta. The city also offers a variety of cultural, historical, and recreational activities.

In the neighboring state of Alabama is the city of Birmingham. An iron and steel manufacturing center, Birmingham is Alabama's largest city. It also serves as the area's commercial and financial center. Textiles,

Atlanta, Georgia, at 34° north latitude, 84° west longitude, is a stylish and fast-growing center of commerce, industry, and transportation.

chemicals, furniture, and lumber are just a few of Birmingham's products. Birmingham also has many historical sites and cultural attractions. In spring, displays of roses and dogwood blossoms draw visitors to the city.

One of the liveliest cities in the Southeast is Miami, Florida. There are over 1½ million people in Miami. Many have come from Cuba to live in the United States. Another important part of the population is made up of retired people.

Miami is one of the great tourist cities of the world. People are attracted by Miami's warm temperatures and sandy beaches. Tourism is the city's major industry, but it is not the only industry. Service industries and the manufacture of clothing are important as well. Also, Miami is a major transportation center.

Louisville, Kentucky, an inland city, has a special claim to fame. It is the home of the Kentucky Derby. Every May since 1875, horses have raced at Churchill Downs. Louisville, the state's largest city, sits on a bend of the Ohio River.

Memphis, Tennessee, is located on the banks of the Mississippi River. It is not surprising that it is a center of commerce and industry. Cotton, lumber, and many other products are sold

A street in "Little Havana," Miami's Cuban section. Miami is at 26° N latitude, 80° W longitude.

here. Memphis is also known in the musical world. W. C. Handy, the "Father of the Blues," lived in Memphis.

Charleston, South Carolina, is one of the oldest cities in the United States. It lies between two rivers that flow into the Atlantic Ocean. Its location makes it an important Atlantic seaport. The government has a submarine base and a navy yard there. For the tourist, Charleston offers a variety of historic attractions. It is famous for its handsome 18th century streets and houses.

Places to See

Many people visit the Southeast because of the beaches along

Above: The Space Museum at Huntsville, Alabama, 35° north latitude, 87° west longitude. *Below:* A glimpse of a bygone age in Charleston, South Carolina, 33° north latitude, 80° west longitude.

the Atlantic and Gulf coasts. Virginia Beach in Virginia, Myrtle Beach in South Carolina, Miami Beach and West Palm Beach in Florida, and Gulfport in Mississippi are among the fine resorts. Cape Hatteras National Seashore in North Carolina has over 100 kilometers (70 miles) of coastline.

The plant and animal life of the swamplands brings visitors to the Everglades National Park in Florida. Alligators, egrets, ospreys, green turtles, and manatees are just a few of the exotic birds and animals to see. The Everglades is the nation's third-largest national park. Inland, other state parks offer hiking, camping, and a variety of wildlife to see. The Great Smoky Mountains National Park is one such place.

Anyone interested in American history will want to visit Williamsburg, Virginia. Here you can see just how people lived and worked in colonial times.

Those interested in the technology of today and tomorrow should visit the Kennedy Space Center. It is located at Cape Canaveral, Florida. Some of the most important early space flights were launched here. Huntsville, Alabama, calls itself "The Space Capital of the Universe." It is the home of the Alabama Space and Rocket Center. Here, scientists have performed key experiments in space travel.

The Kentucky Derby is held every year at Louisville, Kentucky, 38° N latitude, 86° W longitude.

And for those who just want to have fun, there is Walt Disney World in Florida. There, the Magic Kingdom offers camping, hiking, swimming, and a large amusement park. The Epcot Center, which opened in 1982, gives a glimpse of what the world of tomorrow may be like.

REVIEW

VOCABULARY MASTERY

1. ___ helps make the land along a river more fertile.
   Bauxite Tidewater Silt
2. Transportation is considered a(n) ___ industry.
   urban service sunbelt

READING FOR MAIN IDEAS

3. What kind of climate does most of the Southeast have?
4. Why is fertilizer needed to help crops grow in the Southeast?
5. What are two reasons that many factories have been built in the South since World War II?

RESEARCH SKILLS

Choose a state in the Southeast. Find out the following facts about the state: How many people live in the state? What is the capital? What are other important cities? What are the state's main crops and industries? What landforms, bodies of water, or natural resources make the state interesting?

Lesson 2: The South Central States

FIND THE WORDS

gorge steppe tornado sulfur magnesium sorghum dry farming petrochemical

There are only four states in the South Central subregion: Arkansas, Louisiana, Oklahoma, and Texas. Yet about 1 out of every 10 people in the United States lives here. Almost all of this area is west of the Mississippi River.

Features of the Land

There are four major landform areas in the South Central States. The largest is the Gulf Coastal Plain. All of Louisiana and about half of Arkansas and Texas are on this plain. The plain consists mostly of rolling grasslands. There are also swamps in the Mississippi delta.

The Ozark Plateau stretches north from central Arkansas. Rivers there have formed **gorges,** or deep valleys. This makes the plateau look mountainous.

The third landform area is the Central Lowland, a huge plain. This covers parts of Oklahoma and northeastern Texas.

Most of western Texas is on the Great Plains, the fourth landform area. The Texas Panhandle is a strip of Texas between Oklahoma and New Mexico. It is one of the flattest areas in the United States.

The South Central States are bordered by several great bodies of water. To the south is the Gulf of Mexico. To the east is the Mississippi River.

Other important rivers run through the subregion. The Rio Grande forms the border between Texas and Mexico. *Rio Grande* means "big river" in Spanish. This river rises in Colorado and empties into the Gulf of Mexico. The Arkansas River also begins in Colorado. It flows through Oklahoma and Arkansas before joining the Mississippi River. The Red River runs through all four states in the subregion. Its name comes from the red-colored soil it carries with it as it flows.

Most of the South Central States have a humid subtropical climate. Summers are hot and quite humid. Winters are mild and wet. There are frosts, but not severe ones. The growing season is long. Along the coast, the rainfall can be as much as 150 centimeters (60 inches) a year.

Western Texas and Oklahoma have a steppe climate. A **steppe** is a continental grassland, or grassy plain. Summers are hot and dry. Winters are variable. They may be warm or very cold and windy. Rainfall and snowfall vary here, too.

The southwest part of Texas has a desert climate, dry all year long. Summers are very hot. Winter temperatures vary. Farmers here must irrigate the land in order to grow crops.

These four states are part of an area known as "Tornado Valley." A **tornado** is a small but very severe windstorm. From a distance, it looks like a dark funnel standing on its narrow end. Tornadoes occur most often in spring and summer. These storms have been known to shatter large trees and lift automobiles high in the air.

The South Central States have many resources. The most important of these is petroleum. Large deposits of petroleum are found in Louisiana, Texas, and Oklahoma. The early oil wells were drilled on land. Many still are. Eastern Texas has over 25,000 wells. Lately, these fields have been producing more and more natural gas. Natural gas is often found near petroleum deposits.

Petroleum deposits also exist under the Gulf of Mexico. Today, large offshore platforms are set on the water's surface. They hold the drills that reach down through the water and earth to the petroleum. These fields are small, but there are many of them. They produce a lot of petroleum.

Oil rigs drill for petroleum along the Gulf coasts of Texas, Oklahoma, and Louisiana.

The South Central States have many minerals, too. Louisiana has four of the largest salt mines in the world. With Texas, it leads the country in salt production. Three-fourths of the nation's sulfur comes from the Gulf Coast of Texas. **Sulfur** is a yellow mineral used widely in the chemical industry. Louisiana also has much sulfur.

Freeport, Texas, produces large amounts of **magnesium.** This light, strong metal is taken out of seawater. It is used in making airplanes and spacecraft.

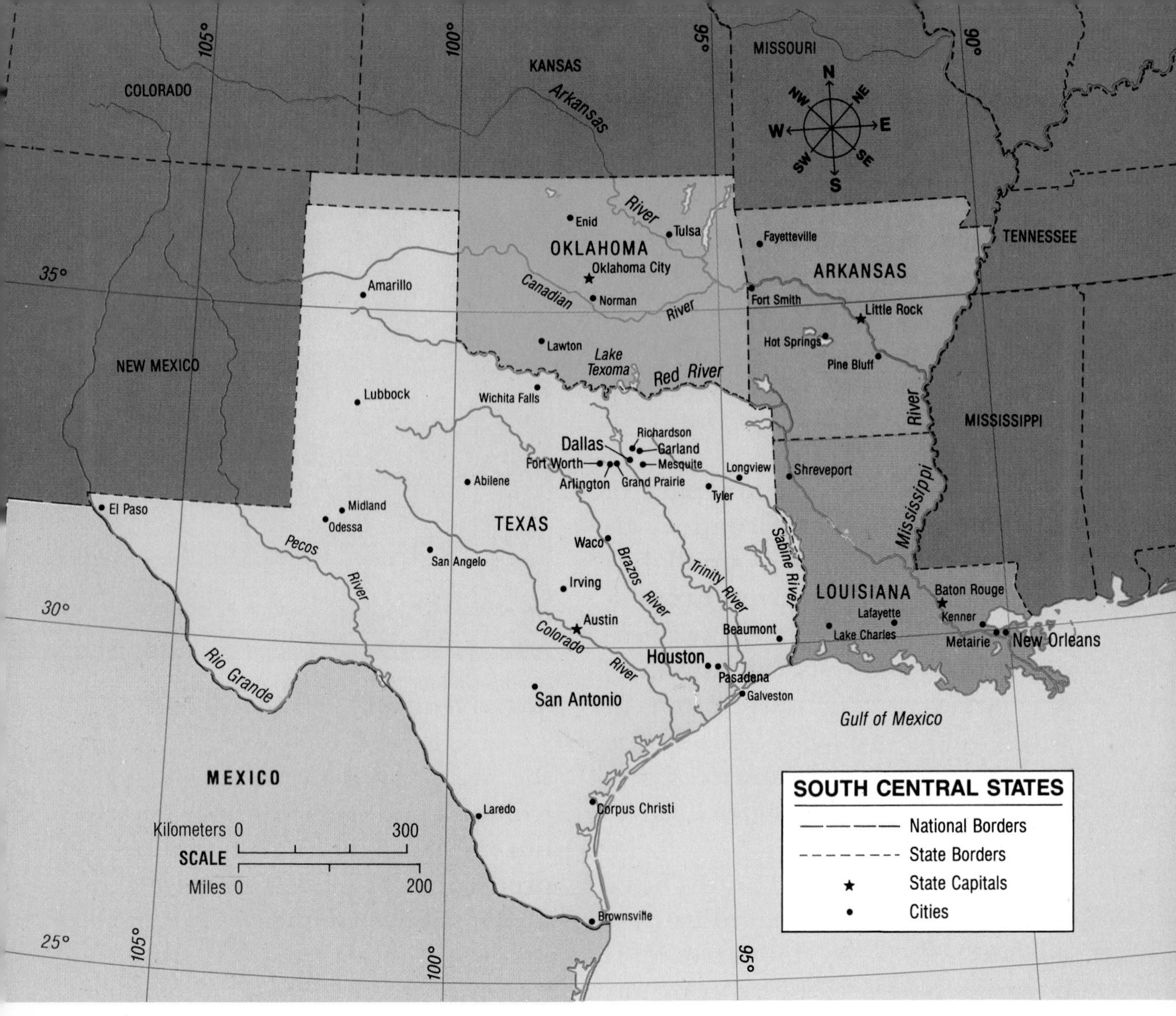

Key to Cities Shown on the Map

City	Latitude	Longitude
Population under 100,000		
Abilene (TX)	32°N,	100°W
Brownsville (TX)	26°N,	98°W
Enid (OK)	36°N,	98°W
Fayetteville (AR)	36°N,	94°W
Fort Smith (AR)	35°N,	94°W
Galveston (TX)	29°N,	95°W
Grand Prairie (TX)	33°N,	97°W
Hot Springs (AR)	34°N,	93°W
Kenner (LA)	30°N,	90°W
Lafayette (LA)	30°N,	92°W
Lake Charles (LA)	30°N,	93°W
Laredo (TX)	28°N,	99°W
Lawton (OK)	35°N,	98°W
Longview (TX)	32°N,	95°W
Mesquite (TX)	33°N,	97°W
Midland (TX)	32°N,	102°W
Norman (OK)	35°N,	97°W
Odessa (TX)	32°N,	120°W
Pine Bluff (AR)	34°N,	92°W
Plano (TX)	33°N,	97°W
Richardson (TX)	33°N,	97°W
San Angelo (TX)	31°N,	100°W
Tyler (TX)	32°N,	95°W
Wichita Falls (TX)	34°N,	98°W
Population 100,000–499,000		
Amarillo (TX)	35°N,	102°W
Arlington (TX)	33°N,	97°W
★Austin (TX)	30°N,	98°W
★Baton Rouge (LA)	30°N,	91°W
Beaumont (TX)	30°N,	94°W
Corpus Christi (TX)	28°N,	97°W
El Paso (TX)	32°N,	106°W
Fort Worth (TX)	33°N,	97°W
Garland (TX)	33°N,	97°W
Irving (TX)	33°N,	97°W
★Little Rock (AR)	35°N,	92°W
Lubbock (TX)	34°N,	102°W
★Oklahoma City (OK)	35°N,	98°W
Pasadena (TX)	30°N,	95°W
Shreveport (LA)	33°N,	94°W
Tulsa (OK)	36°N,	96°W
Waco (TX)	32°N,	97°W
Population 500,000–999,000		
Dallas (TX)	33°N,	97°W
New Orleans (LA)	30°N,	90°W
San Antonio (TX)	29°N,	99°W
Population 1,000,000 or over		
Houston (TX)	30°N,	95°W

THE SOUTH CENTRAL STATES

	Population/ Admitted to the Union	Area Sq. mi.—Sq. km.	Capital	State Bird	State Flower	State Flag
Arkansas (AR) Land of Opportunity	2,315,700 **1836**	53,104 137,539	Little Rock	 Mockingbird	 Apple Blossom	
 **Louisiana (LA)** Pelican State	4,503,600 **1812**	48,523 125,675	Baton Rouge	 Brown Pelican	 Magnolia	
 **Oklahoma (OK)** Sooner State	3,250,300 **1907**	69,919 181,090	Oklahoma City	 Scissor-tailed Flycatcher	 Mistletoe	
 **Texas (TX)** Lone Star State	15,566,000 **1845**	267,336 692,397	Austin	 Mockingbird	 Bluebonnet	

Bauxite is another mineral found in this subregion. The nation's most important bauxite mines are near Little Rock, Arkansas. As you know, bauxite is used to produce aluminum.

Water plays a key role in the life of the South Central States. Major ports have grown up along the Gulf of Mexico. Many varieties of fish and shellfish live in Gulf waters. The Mississippi River has been an important commercial waterway since the nation began.

Almost half of Louisiana and Arkansas is covered by forests. Forests are a major resource in the subregion. Fur-bearing animals are another resource. Muskrat, mink, raccoon, and other furs come from Louisiana.

Economic Activity

The South Central States make up one of the leading agricultural areas in the United States. The favorable climate allows farmers here to grow many different types of crops. Raising animals is big business, too.

Cotton was once the major crop in the South. Many southern states are growing less cotton today. For Texas, however, it is still the leading crop. Texas produces more cotton than any other state in the nation. Cotton is grown along the coastal plain. The dry climate there helps cut down on the insect pests that attack the crop elsewhere.

Farmers grow several types of grains in this subregion. Arkansas, Louisiana, and Texas are three of the leading rice-growing states. Winter wheat is grown in Oklahoma and central Texas. This type of wheat is planted in the fall. Its strong roots are not damaged by cold temperatures. In spring, the wheat begins to grow. By early summer, it is ready to be harvested.

As in the Southeast, soybeans have replaced cotton on many farms. Farms in Arkansas, in Louisiana, and on the coastal plain of Texas grow soybeans. Another crop raised in this area is sorghum. **Sorghum** is a grassy plant used as food for animals and to make syrup. Sugar cane is also grown in this subregion. Louisiana is a leading producer.

Citrus fruit is grown in Louisiana, southern Texas, and Arkansas. In Texas, there are many citrus farms along the Rio Grande. Vegetables grow well in this area, too. If necessary, farmers can use water from the river to irrigate the land.

In places with little rain, dry farming is used to grow crops. In **dry farming,** the land is plowed in rows that go around hills instead of up and down. This way, the soil holds more of the moisture. Only plants that need little water are raised, and only half of the land is planted each year.

Much of the land now used for dry farming was used for cattle ranching before. Texas still leads the United States in beef cattle production. Sheep are also raised. Both Oklahoma and Louisiana have sheep and cattle ranches.

The South Central States have many industries. Most important is the petrochemical industry. **Petrochemicals** are chemicals made from petroleum or natural gas. Products as varied as medicine, paint, fertilizer, and plastics are made from petrochemicals.

The production of aluminum is a major industry in Arkansas as well. Both Oklahoma and Texas are known for the manufacture of aircraft and spacecraft. Other industries in the subregion include meat processing and electronics.

Louisiana leads the Southern states in the production of high-quality timber. Both Louisiana and Arkansas are heavily forested. Furniture, paper products, and building materials are made from this wood.

Have you ever ordered "gulf shrimp" in a restaurant? The Gulf Coast, especially Louisiana, is famous for its shrimp, oysters, and other seafood. Fish and shellfish from this area are shipped all over the United States.

Tourism is important to the South Central States. Some of

Texas is known worldwide for its huge cattle ranches and its cowboy traditions.

the visitors to these states come for the Gulf Coast beaches. Others enjoy the scenic beauty of the national parks. In the woodlands that cover much of Louisiana and Arkansas, there is camping and hunting. Historic cities such as San Antonio and New Orleans also attract many tourists.

The People of the South Central States

About 26 million people live in these four states. Texas has a large Hispanic population. Louisiana has the largest group of French-speaking people in the country. About 3 out of 10 people in Louisiana are Black. American Indians make up 5 percent of Oklahoma's population.

The subregion has some very big cities. About three-fourths of the population live in urban areas. Yet, in western Texas and Oklahoma, there are large areas that have few people.

Houston, Texas, is the fifth-largest city in the United States. It is one of the fastest-growing cities as well. Though not on the coast, Houston is the third-busiest port in the nation. A deep ship channel, 80 kilometers (50 miles) long, connects Houston to the Gulf of Mexico. Oil refining, the petrochemical industry, and metal industries are important here. Outside the city is the Lyndon B. Johnson Space Center, where astronauts are trained. "Mission control" is located at this space center.

Fascinating Facts

The Mardi Gras in New Orleans may be the biggest party in the world. *Mardi Gras* means "Fat Tuesday." It is the day that comes before Ash Wednesday, the opening of the solemn season of Lent.

In New Orleans, "Fat Tuesday" is just the peak of several weeks of merrymaking. Organizations called *krewes* hold parties and parades leading up to this day. Masked, costumed people ride large, colorful floats through the streets. Music and singing go on night and day. This is an opportunity to hear some of the exciting jazz bands for which New Orleans is so famous. New Orleans is the city where jazz began.

At midnight on Tuesday night, all the merriment ends and the season of Lent begins.

Dallas is the second-largest city in Texas. It has always been a center of trade and manufacturing. Cotton trading, the aircraft industry, electronics, and banking are all important in Dallas.

San Antonio, Texas, has its own special flavor. Originally settled by Spanish people, the city has retained its Hispanic heritage. Many San Antonians speak both Spanish and English. Today, San Antonio is a center for food processing, transportation, and many different types of manufacturing.

New Orleans, Louisiana, is one of the most fascinating cities in the South. The nation's second-busiest port, it lies on the Mississippi River. About half a million people live in New Orleans. Natural resources such as oil, natural gas, salt, sulfur, and forests are found around New Orleans.

Places to See

Big Bend National Park in Texas is located along the Rio Grande. The rushing river waters have formed deep canyons here. The Hot Springs National Park is in Arkansas. The park is named for its 47 warm mineral springs.

History lovers will want to visit the Alamo in San Antonio. This church, which was once used as a fort, holds a special place in Texas history. More than 180 brave Texans died defending it in 1836, in the Texas war of independence from Mexico.

New Orleans, Louisiana, offers music, good food, and fun. Jazz was born and still thrives in this city. Its fine old houses, famous restaurants, and jazz clubs draw many visitors. The French Quarter of New Orleans is very attractive. There, much of the original city still survives.

REVIEW

VOCABULARY MASTERY

1. People in the South Central States are sometimes threatened by ___ .
   gorges steppes tornadoes
2. Which of these is *not* a mineral?
   sulfur sorghum magnesium

READING FOR MAIN IDEAS

3. What is the most important resource in the South Central States?
4. Why is the Gulf of Mexico important to the South Central States?
5. What was once the major crop in the South? What other crops are also grown in the region today?

THINKING SKILLS

What are some things that make New Orleans different from many other cities in the United States? Why is there a strong French influence in this city?

CHAPTER REVIEW

VOCABULARY MASTERY

Use the words below to complete the chapter summary. Use each only once.

bauxite	softwood
citrus fruit	sulfur
Hardwood	sunbelt
Hurricanes	tornado
magnesium	

The __1__ is a warm and sunny area that stretches across the southern part of the United States. The region can experience violent weather conditions. __2__ often occur in the Southeast. In the South Central States, a __3__ can severely damage homes and property.

Much __4__ is grown in Florida. Forests are a major resource of the Southeast. __5__ trees, such as oak and maple, grow in the north, while __6__ trees, such as pines, grow in the south. The South Central States have large deposits of __7__, __8__, and __9__.

READING FOR MAIN IDEAS

1. What are the advantages and disadvantages of the climate in the Southeastern States?
2. How has farming in the Southeast changed since the 1800s?
3. Why are many people moving to the sunbelt?
4. How were the gorges of the Ozark Plateau formed?
5. Describe dry farming.

THINKING SKILLS

6. Of all the major cities in the Southeast or South Central States, which would you like most to live in? Briefly describe the city and tell why you would like to live there.

SKILLS APPLICATION

MAP SKILLS

Look at the political map on page 406.

7. These states are west of what major river?
8. What other rivers flow along or through the South Central States?
9. About how many miles is it from Austin to Little Rock? How many kilometers?
10. Is Baton Rouge northeast or southeast of San Antonio?

WRITING SKILLS

Below is an outline summarizing some of what you learned in Lesson 1 of this chapter. Complete this outline. Then continue the outline for the South Central States. Include the same headings and subheadings.

Southern States

I. Southeastern States
- A. Major Landforms
  - 1.
  - 2.
  - 3.
  - 4.
- B. Climate
  - 1.
  - 2.
- C. Resources
  - 1. nonliving
    - a.
    - b.
    - c.
    - d.
    - e.
    - f.
    - g.
  - 2. living
    - a.
    - b.
    - c.

CHAPTER 4 THE MIDWEST AND WEST

Lesson 1: The Midwestern States

FIND THE WORDS

lock front blizzard
renewable resource
strip mining

The 12 large Midwestern States lie in the center of the nation. They are Ohio, Michigan, Indiana, Wisconsin, Illinois, Minnesota, Iowa, Missouri, North Dakota, South Dakota, Kansas, and Nebraska. Six of these states border the Great Lakes. The other six are west of the Mississippi River.

Pioneers from the East began to settle this subregion in the late 1700s. They traveled west in covered wagons, looking for land and a new life. Later, the Midwest became the home of many people who came directly from Europe to settle there.

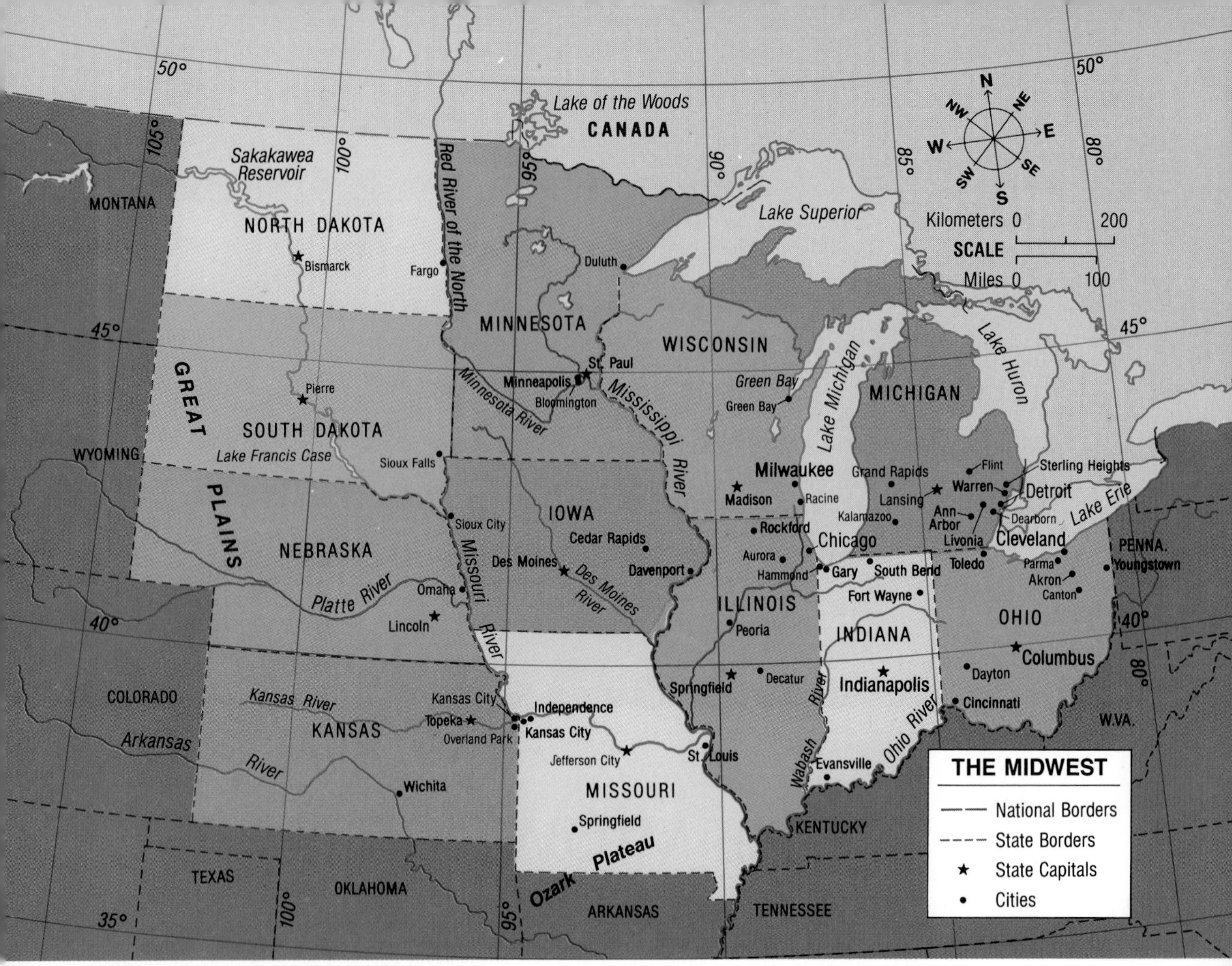

Key to Cities Shown on the Map

Population under 100,000

Aurora (IL) .... 42°N, 88°W
★Bismarck (ND) .... 47°N, 101°W
Bloomington (MN) ...... 45°N, 93°W
Canton (OH) .... 41°N, 81°W
Dearborn (MI) .... 42°N, 83°W
Decatur (IL) .... 40°N, 89°W
Duluth (MN) .... 47°N, 92°W
Fargo (ND) .... 47°N, 97°W
Green Bay (WI) .... 45°N, 88°W
Hammond (IN) .... 42°N, 88°W
★Jefferson City (MO) ... 39°N, 92°W
Kalamazoo (MI) .... 42°N, 86°W
Overland Park (KS) ... 39°N, 95°W
Parma (OH) .... 41°N, 82°W
★Pierre (SD) .... 44°N, 100°W
Racine (WI) .... 43°N, 88°W
Sioux City (IA) .... 43°N, 96°W
Sioux Falls (SD) .... 44°N, 97°W

Population 100,000–499,000

Akron (OH) .... 41°N, 82°W
Ann Arbor (MI) .... 42°N, 84°W
Cedar Rapids (IA) ...... 42°N, 92°W
Cincinnati (OH) .... 39°N, 85°W
Davenport (IA) .... 42°N, 91°W
Dayton (OH) .... 40°N, 84°W
★Des Moines (IA) .... 42°N, 94°W
Evansville (IN) .... 38°N, 88°W
Flint (MI) .... 43°N, 84°W
Fort Wayne (IN) .... 41°N, 85°W
Gary (IN) .... 42°N, 87°W
Grand Rapids (MI) ..... 43°N, 86°W
Independence (MO) ... 39°N, 94°W
Kansas City (KS) .... 39°N, 95°W
Kansas City (MO) ...... 39°N, 95°W
★Lansing (MI) .... 43°N, 85°W
★Lincoln (NE) .... 41°N, 97°W
Livonia (MI) .... 42°N, 83°W
★Madison (WI) .... 43°N, 89°W
Minneapolis (MN) .... 45°N, 93°W
Omaha (NE) .... 41°N, 96°W
Peoria (IL) .... 41°N, 90°W
Rockford (IL) .... 42°N, 89°W
St. Louis (MO) .... 39°N, 90°W
★St. Paul (MN) .... 45°N, 93°W
South Bend (IN) .... 42°N, 86°W
★Springfield (IL) .... 40°N, 90°W
Springfield (MO) .... 37°N, 93°W
Sterling Heights (MI) .. 43°N, 83°W
Toledo (OH) .... 42°N, 84°W
★Topeka (KS) .... 39°N, 96°W
Warren (MI) .... 43°N, 83°W
Wichita (KS) .... 38°N, 97°W
Youngstown (OH) ...... 41°N, 81°W

Population 500,000–999,000

Cleveland (OH) .... 42°N, 82°W
★Columbus (OH) .... 40°N, 83°W
★Indianapolis (IN) .... 40°N, 86°W
Milwaukee (WI) .... 43°N, 88°W

Population 1,000,000 or over

Chicago (IL) .... 42°N, 88°W
Detroit (MI) .... 42°N, 83°W

THE MIDWESTERN STATES

State	Population/ Admitted to the Union	Area Sq. mi.—Sq. km.	Capital	State Bird	State Flower	State Flag
Illinois (IL) Land of Lincoln	11,527,900 **1818**	56,400 146,076	Springfield	 Cardinal	 Native Violet	
 **Indiana (IN)** Hoosier State	5,506,800 **1816**	36,291 93,994	Indianapolis	 Cardinal	 Peony	
Iowa (IA) Hawkeye State	2,921,500 **1846**	56,290 145,791	Des Moines	 Eastern Goldfinch	 Wild Rose	
Kansas (KS) Sunflower State	2,413,400 **1861**	82,264 213,064	Topeka	 Western Meadowlark	 Sunflower	
 **Michigan (MI)** Wolverine State	9,197,400 **1837**	58,216 150,779	Lansing	 Robin	 Apple Blossom	
 **Minnesota (MN)** Gopher State	4,231,000 **1858**	84,068 217,736	St. Paul	 Common Loon	 Pink and White Lady's Slipper	

THE MIDWESTERN STATES	Population/ Admitted to the Union	Area Sq. mi.—Sq. km.	Capital	State Bird	State Flower	State Flag
Missouri (MO) Show Me State	5,037,200 **1821**	69,686 180,487	Jefferson City	Bluebird	Hawthorn	
Nebraska (NE) Cornhusker State	1,610,600 **1867**	77,227 200,018	Lincoln	Western Meadowlark	Goldenrod	
North Dakota (ND) Flickertail State	674,200 **1889**	70,665 183,022	Bismarck	Western Meadowlark	Wild Prairie Rose	
Ohio (OH) Buckeye State	10,824,300 **1803**	41,222 106,765	Columbus	Cardinal	Scarlet Carnation	
South Dakota (SD) Sunshine State	707,300 **1889**	77,047 199,552	Pierre	Ring-necked Pheasant	American Pasqueflower	
Wisconsin (WI) Badger State	4,833,800 **1848**	56,154 145,439	Madison	Robin	Wood Violet	WISCONSIN 1848

Features of the Land

The Midwestern States cover more than 1,982,714 square kilometers (765,530 square miles). This makes the area almost six times as large as the Middle Atlantic States. Yet the population is not much larger than that of the Middle Atlantic States.

The major landform of the subregion is the Central Lowland. This expanse of rolling plains stretches from central Ohio to central Kansas. It covers all or part of the 12 Midwestern States.

The western section of the subregion is part of the Great Plains. This includes part of Kansas, Nebraska, and the Dakotas. Much of the land here is dry grassland.

Hills are few and far between in the Midwest. In southern Missouri, there is the hilly Ozark Plateau. In South Dakota are the Black Hills, which are in fact mountains. One of these mountains, Harney Peak, is the highest point east of the Rocky Mountains. Mount Rushmore, carved with the heads of four Presidents, is also in the Black Hills.

The Great Lakes are the largest group of freshwater lakes in the world. Canals and rivers link the Great Lakes. Some lakes are higher than others. Canals raise or lower ships traveling from one lake to another. They do this by means of locks. A **lock** is an enclosed section of a canal that works like an elevator. The water level in the lock can be raised or lowered. The ship in the lock also goes up or down to the new level.

The Great Lakes are connected to the Atlantic Ocean by the St. Lawrence Seaway. The seaway was built in 1959 so that large ships could reach the Great Lakes. Now ships from all over the world can sail inland as far as Duluth, Minnesota.

Many thousands of smaller lakes are found in Minnesota, Wisconsin, and Michigan. Wisconsin has more lakes for its size than any other place in the world.

Most of the Midwest is drained by the great Mississippi River system. The Mississippi River begins in northern Minnesota and flows south to the Gulf of Mexico. On its way south, the Mississippi River is joined by other rivers. The two largest are the Missouri and Ohio rivers.

Most of the Midwest has a continental climate. Winters are cold and snowy, and summers are hot and humid.

In the Midwestern States, the weather often changes suddenly. This is because of cold fronts from the north. A **front** is a large mass of air that moves into an area. Cool, dry air comes from Canada. Warm, moist air comes from the

Gulf of Mexico. When the cold front from Canada meets the warm front from the Gulf, weather changes occur. Sometimes, the change brings violent weather. In spring and summer, there may be thunderstorms and even tornadoes. **Blizzards,** or heavy snowstorms with very high winds, can also strike this subregion.

The rich, dark soil of the Midwest is one of the subregion's resources. It is very good for farming. In the northern part of the Midwest, the soil is not as good for farming, but trees do very well. These forests are a valuable renewable resource. A **renewable resource** is something that can be replaced after it is used. People can replace forests by planting more trees.

There are important mineral resources in the Midwest as well. Minnesota and Michigan have the nation's biggest deposits of iron ore. Michigan also boasts the world's largest limestone quarry. Coal is found in Illinois and Ohio. Missouri has large amounts of lead ore. North Dakota has important petroleum reserves. There is even gold in the Black Hills of South Dakota.

Economic Activity

The farmers of the Midwest grow enormous amounts of corn and wheat. That is why this area is called the breadbasket of the nation. Food grown here is sold all over the world.

Corn is the leading crop of the subregion. The area where it is grown is called the corn belt. This area has rich soil and long, moist summers. It stretches west from Ohio to Nebraska and north into Michigan and southern Wisconsin. The corn belt is a good place

Fascinating Facts

Strip mining is mining that is done aboveground. It involves stripping off the top layer of dirt and rock to get at a mineral deposit. It is used when the mineral lies near Earth's surface. We get much of our coal and up to 90 percent of our iron and copper this way.

Strip mining requires heavy equipment, such as power shovels, bulldozers, and trucks. Also, there may be drilling and blasting. Sometimes explosives are needed to break up the rock. Strip mining works best on flat land, where the deposits tend to be flat, too. This makes it easier to strip-mine a large area.

Strip mining is less expensive than underground mining, but many people do not like it. It leaves the land ugly, and it erodes the soil. For this reason, many states have passed laws about strip mining. These laws require companies to clean up and replant the land after the mining is finished.

The Midwest is called America's breadbasket because of its corn and wheat crops.

to raise livestock or to fatten up animals raised elsewhere. Farms in the corn belt also grow hay, barley, oats, and soybeans.

The wheat belt is in the drier western part of the Midwest. Wheat does not need as much moisture as corn. Kansas and Nebraska grow winter wheat. It is planted in the fall but stops growing during the winter. In the spring, it starts growing again and is harvested in midsummer.

Spring wheat is grown in the Dakotas, where the winters are more severe. The wheat is planted in the spring and harvested in the fall. Kansas and North Dakota lead all other states in the production of wheat.

The dairy belt is centered in Wisconsin, "America's dairyland." But it also includes Michigan and Minnesota. This area has cooler, drier summers than the corn belt. Corn does not grow as well. Instead of feeding their animals corn, farmers let them graze. The cattle are raised for their milk rather than for their meat. Some of the milk is sold in the cities, but much of it is made into butter, cheese, and other dairy products. Wisconsin produces more cheese than any other state.

The Midwestern States also have many industries and large cities. Some of the industries are connected to agriculture. Meat packing is one of these industries.

In the meat-packing plants, workers kill livestock raised in the corn belt. Then they prepare the meat for the market.

The Midwest prepares and packages the food it grows. Companies can and freeze vegetables. They also grind wheat to make flour, bread, and breakfast cereals. Minneapolis and Kansas City both grind wheat into flour and ship it off to grocery stores and supermarkets around the nation.

Another important industry is the manufacturing of farm machinery. Today, machines are doing more and more of the work on the farms. Advanced machinery makes American farming the most efficient in the world.

The Midwest is well known for its steel production. The iron ore, coal, and limestone needed to make steel are all found near the Great Lakes. Most of the steel is produced at the southern end of Lake Michigan and along the shore of Lake Erie. The largest steelworks is in Gary, Indiana.

Detroit, Michigan, is the car capital of America. Automobile assembly plants and parts factories are also found in other areas of the Midwest.

A car factory in Detroit, Michigan, at 42° north latitude, 83° west longitude.

Petroleum is refined in Kansas, Illinois, and North Dakota. Mining and processing of copper take place in northern Michigan. Akron, Ohio, is the center of the nation's rubber industry.

There are many service industries in the Midwest, too. These include retail stores, banking, transportation, and entertainment. Chicago is a national leader in wholesale and retail sales. Many mail-order houses have their headquarters there.

Trade and commerce in the Midwest has been helped by a very good transportation system. The canals, rivers, and Great Lakes link up much of the area. Good highways allow trucks to move farm and factory goods quickly and cheaply. About a third of the nation's highways are in the Midwest.

The People of the Midwest

About 59 million people live in the Midwestern States. That is a little over one-fourth of the nation's population.

During the 1800s, many people came to the Midwest from northern Europe. The largest groups were German, Swedish, and Norwegian. Later, Poles, Italians, and Greeks came, too. Today Blacks, Hispanics, and other minorities also live in the Midwest.

The Tulip Festival in Muskegon, Michigan, is a tradition passed on by early Dutch settlers. Muskegon is at 43° N latitude, 86° W longitude.

Some of the most important U.S. cities are in the Midwestern States. Most are either near the Great Lakes or on a large river.

Chicago, on Lake Michigan, is the largest city in the Midwest. It is the third-largest city in the nation. About 3 million people live there. Chicago is the transportation hub of the nation. More trains go into and out of Chicago than any other city in the country. Chicago's O'Hare Airport handles more passengers than any other airport in the United States. Along Lake Michigan is a spectacular line of skyscrapers. The city now boasts the world's tallest building, the Sears Tower.

The Midwest's second-largest city is Detroit. It lies between Lakes Huron and Erie. The old downtown area of Detroit has been completely rebuilt. This new city center draws many people.

Milwaukee is also on Lake Michigan. Many German people settled there in the mid-1800s. The important port city of Cleveland is on Lake Erie. Cleveland has one of the nation's leading symphony orchestras.

Some other major cities grew up on rivers. The twin cities of Minnesota—Minneapolis and St. Paul—as well as St. Louis, Missouri, lie on the Mississippi River. Cincinnati, Ohio, is on the Ohio River. Omaha, Nebraska; Kansas City, Kansas; and Kansas City, Missouri, are all on the Missouri River.

Places to Go

Mount Rushmore in South Dakota is one of the most interesting places to visit. It honors four of our Presidents. Carved in rock are the faces of Washington, Jefferson, Lincoln, and Theodore Roosevelt.

In Indianapolis, Indiana, the Indianapolis 500 is considered the World Series of car racing. Racing-car drivers come from around the world to compete in this famous event.

Outside of Cincinnati, Ohio, is the Great Serpent Mound. This is a huge earth sculpture, shaped like a snake. It was built by the Adena-Hopewell people about 1,000 years ago. Many people have studied it, but no one knows exactly what the purpose of the mound was.

REVIEW

VOCABULARY MASTERY

1. In a ____, a ship can be raised or lowered from one level of a canal to another.
tidewater lake lock

2. ____ are snowstorms with high winds.
Tornadoes Blizzards Hurricanes

READING FOR MAIN IDEAS

3. Why is the Midwest important even to Americans who do not live there?

4. What industries are important in the Midwestern States?

5. List four groups of European peoples who have settled in the Midwest.

THINKING SKILLS

Some people are moving out of Midwestern cities to other regions. In some parts of the Midwest, there are not as many jobs as there used to be. What do you think can be done to keep jobs and people in the Midwest? Give as many practical suggestions as you can.

Lesson 2: The Mountain States

FIND THE WORDS

altitude timberline Continental Divide canyon salt pan uranium geyser

The Mountain States stretch from Canada to Mexico. They include the states of Montana, Wyoming, Colorado, New Mexico, Idaho, Utah, Arizona, and Nevada. The spectacular Rocky Mountains give this area some of America's most beautiful scenery. The great national parks draw many tourists every year.

Features of the Land

The eight Mountain States are so large that New England could fit into any one of them. Together they make up about a quarter of the land area of the United States.

The main landforms of the subregion are mountains and plateaus. The Rocky Mountains are the largest mountain system in North America. These high, rugged mountains stretch from Alaska south to New Mexico. Like the Appalachians, the Rockies are made up of different mountain ranges. These include the Bitterroot, Wind River, Wasatch, and Sangre de Cristo ranges.

The Rockies are relatively young mountains. They were formed much later than the Appalachians. Nature has not had time to wear down their peaks.

The highest peaks in the Rockies are in Colorado. This state has 54 peaks over 4,200 meters (14,000 feet) high. Mount Elbert, the highest, has an elevation of 4,400 meters (14,431 feet).

Trees will not grow above a certain **altitude,** or height, in the mountains. The point at which they stop growing is called the **timberline.** At higher altitudes, the soil beneath the surface stays frozen all year. Only low-growing plants and shrubs can root in the shallow surface soil.

A high ridge in the Rocky Mountains forms the backbone of the North American continent. This ridge is called the **Continental Divide.** Rivers east of the Continental Divide flow toward the Atlantic Ocean. Rivers west of it flow toward the Pacific Ocean.

The Colorado River is west of the Continental Divide. It rises in the Rocky Mountains of Colorado and flows southwest into the Gulf of California. The Gila and Snake rivers also flow west toward the Pacific. The North

Platte, Yellowstone, and South Platte rivers rise east of the Continental Divide. These rivers flow east to the Missouri River. The Missouri and Arkansas rivers flow east into the Mississippi. The Rio Grande and Pecos River flow southeast into the Gulf of Mexico.

The rest of the subregion consists of plateaus. On the north is the Columbia Plateau; on the south, the Colorado Plateau. West of the Rockies lies the Great Basin, a desert that covers most of Nevada and Utah.

The high surfaces of these plateaus are deeply cut by streams and rivers. As a result, there are many canyons. A **canyon** is a deep, narrow valley with steep sides. The Grand Canyon is on the Colorado Plateau. The Grand Canyon was carved over millions of years by the Colorado River. Its walls show us what Earth's crust is made up of. Different types of rocks form layers in the canyon. The layer at the bottom contains some of the oldest rock in the world.

The climate of the Mountain States is dry. Precipitation is less than 50 centimeters (20 inches) a year. Drought, or lack of rain over a long period of time, is a continuing problem. There are three climate zones: steppe, desert, and highlands. In general, summers are hot and dry. Winters are cold except in the desert areas of Arizona and New Mexico. In the mountains of Colorado and Wyoming, summers tend to be cool. The Rockies' peaks are covered with snow year-round.

The Mountain States are rich in mineral resources. Many of the early settlers went there to find gold and silver. Today gold is still mined in the Rockies, and there are silver mines in Idaho, Utah, and Montana.

Fascinating Facts

Most lakes have fresh water. The Great Salt Lake of Utah, however, is saltier than the ocean. The rivers that run into the lake carry tiny amounts of salt. No rivers run out to carry off this salt. So the lake water evaporates, but the salt stays behind. The salt has built up over the years. Only brine shrimp and some small plants can live in it. Tourists enjoy swimming in the Great Salt Lake because the salt in the water makes them float very easily, like corks.

There are other small, salty lakes in the Great Basin. Some salt lakes have dried up altogether. What remains are **salt pans,** areas of land covered with salt. The soil there is too salty to grow crops.

In recent years, the Great Salt Lake has been expanding. Unusually heavy rains and snows have caused severe flooding. The level of the lake is higher now than ever before.

The world-famous Grand Canyon is located near 36° N, between 112° and 114° W.

Copper is the area's most important mineral today. Most of it is low-grade. That means that much ore has to be dug up and crushed to get small amounts of copper. Copper is mined in Montana, Utah, Nevada, New Mexico, and Arizona. Lead and zinc are mined in Idaho and Montana.

The most important uranium deposits in the United States are in the Colorado Plateau. **Uranium** (yoo RAY nee um) is a heavy metal used to produce atomic energy. Wyoming leads the nation in the production of uranium.

Just about every kind of mineral used in modern industry is found somewhere in the Mountain States. Nevada is a major source of tungsten. Molybdenum (muh LIB duh num), a metal used in the manufacture of steel, comes from Colorado. New Mexico has natural gas and petroleum. Wyoming and Colorado have petroleum and coal. Coal is also found in Utah and Montana.

Water and sunlight are also sources of energy. Dams provide water power as well as water for irrigation. Both water power and sunlight are used to generate electricity. The Hoover Dam is the most famous dam in the United States. Located on the Colorado

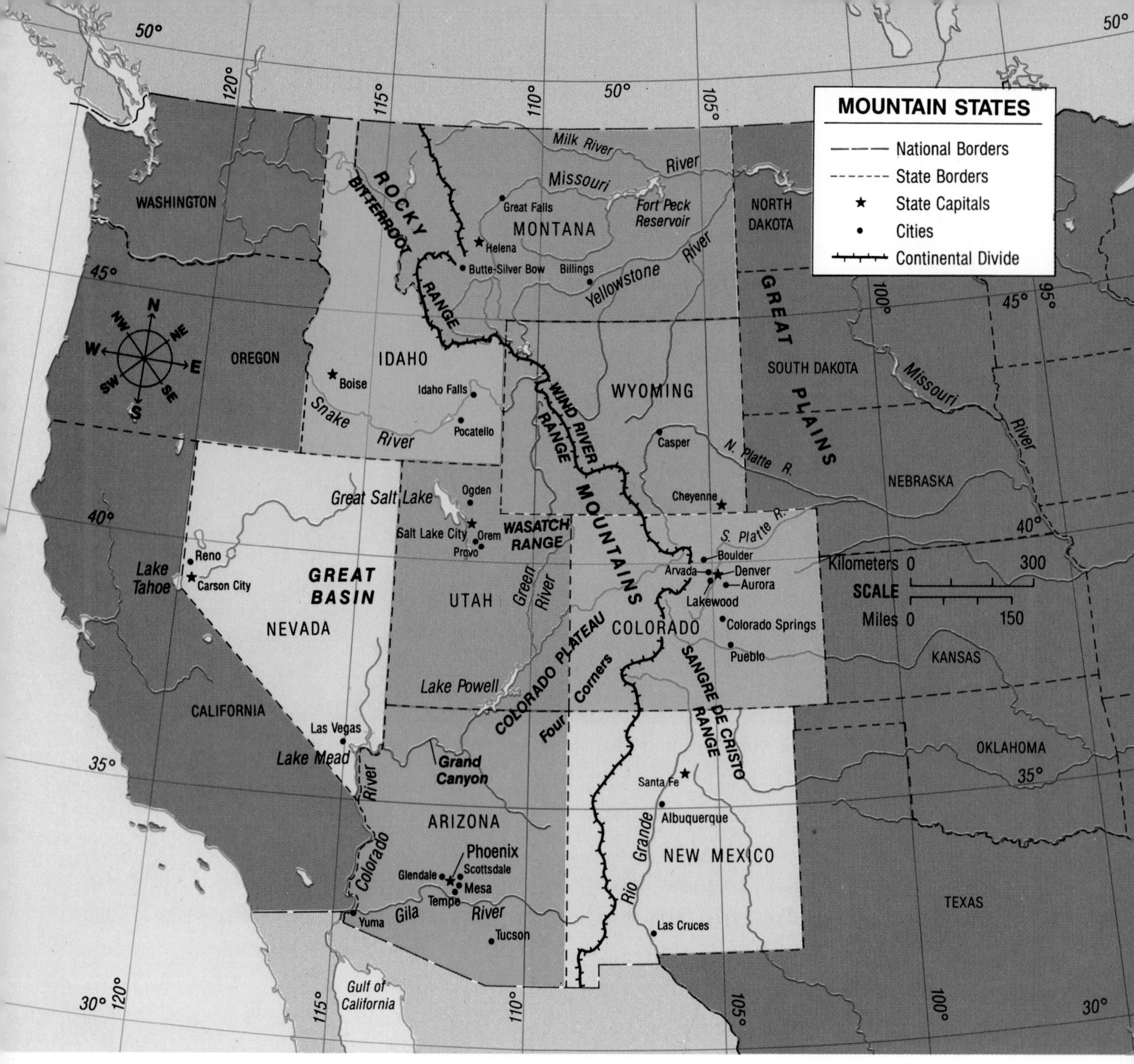

Key to Cities Shown on the Map

Population under 100,000

Arvada (CO) .... 40°N, 105°W
Billings (MT) .... 46°N, 108°W
Boulder (CO) .... 40°N, 105°W
Butte-Silver Bow (MT) 46°N, 113°W
★Carson City (NV) .... 39°N, 120°W
Casper (WY) .... 43°N, 106°W
★Cheyenne (WY) .... 41°N, 105°W
Glendale (AZ) .... 34°N, 112°W
Great Falls (MT) .... 48°N, 111°W
★Helena (MT) .... 47°N, 112°W
Idaho Falls (ID) .... 44°N, 112°W
Las Cruces (NM) .... 32°N, 107°W
Ogden (UT) .... 41°N, 112°W
Orem (UT) .... 40°N, 112°W
Pocatello (ID) .... 43°N, 113°W
Provo (UT) .... 40°N, 112°W
★Santa Fe (NM) .... 35°N, 106°W
Scottsdale (AZ) .... 34°N, 112°W
Yuma (AZ) .... 33°N, 115°W

Population 100,000–499,000

Albuquerque (NM) ..... 35°N, 107°W
Aurora (CO) .... 40°N, 105°W
★Boise (ID) .... 44°N, 116°W
Colorado Springs (CO) 39°N, 105°W
★Denver (CO) .... 40°N, 105°W
Lakewood (CO) .... 40°N, 105°W
Las Vegas (NV) .... 36°N, 115°W
Mesa (AZ) .... 33°N, 112°W
Pueblo (CO) .... 38°N, 105°W
Reno (NV) .... 40°N, 120°W
★Salt Lake City (UT) .... 41°N, 112°W
Tempe (AZ) .... 33°N, 112°W
Tucson (AZ) .... 32°N, 111°W

Population 500,000–999,000

★Phoenix (AZ) .... 34°N, 112°W

Population 1,000,000 or over

None

THE MOUNTAIN STATES

State	Population/ Admitted to the Union	Area Sq. mi.—Sq. km.	Capital	State Bird	State Flower	State Flag
Arizona (AZ) Grand Canyon State	2,965,000 **1912**	113,909 295,024	Phoenix	Cactus Wren	Saguaro (Giant Cactus)	
Colorado (CO) Centennial State	3,128,100 **1876**	104,247 270,000	Denver	Lark Bunting	Rocky Mountain Columbine	
Idaho (ID) Gem State	1,002,100 **1890**	83,557 216,413	Boise	Mountain Bluebird	Syringa (Mock Orange)	
Montana (MT) Treasure State	814,800 **1889**	147,138 381,087	Helena	Western Meadowlark	Bitterroot	
Nevada (NV) Silver State	957,400 **1864**	110,540 286,299	Carson City	Mountain Bluebird	Sagebrush	
New Mexico (NM) Land of Enchantment	1,413,700 **1912**	121,666 315,115	Santa Fe	Roadrunner	Yucca Flower	
Utah (UT) Beehive State	1,637,600 **1896**	84,916 219,932	Salt Lake City	Sea Gull	Sego Lily	
Wyoming (WY) Equality State	536,000 **1890**	97,914 253,597	Cheyenne	Meadowlark	Indian Paintbrush	

River, it generates much of the subregion's electricity. Lake Mead in Nevada was created when the Hoover Dam was built.

Economic Activity

The mining and processing of minerals is the major industry of the Mountain States. Gold, silver, copper, lead, zinc, and uranium have already been mentioned. Other minerals, such as potash, phosphate rock, sodium carbonate, and potassium salts, are also mined there.

However, there are fewer mining jobs today than there used to be. Machines have taken over more and more of the work. Other important industries in the subregion include food processing, electronics, and the manufacture of machinery. Colorado and Arizona are the two leading manufacturing states of the area.

The beautiful, rugged scenery of the Mountain States draws skiers, climbers, and hikers.

The Mountain States have also provided a home for the high-technology industries. They make everything from computers to airplanes, spacecraft, and missiles. The very first testing of the atomic bomb was done in New Mexico.

Tourism also brings money into the area. Millions of visitors come every year to enjoy hiking, camping, fishing, and hunting and to visit the national and state parks.

Since the days of the pioneers, transportation has been difficult. The mountains are high and the land is rugged. Unlike the Midwestern States, the Mountain States have no network of canals and rivers for shipping goods. But travel is improving. Railroads and new highways have been cut through the mountains. Air travel makes the smaller cities and towns less remote.

Ranching is the most important agricultural activity in the Mountain States. Both sheep and cattle are raised. The best grazing lands are in the valleys and mountain slopes of the Rockies and the grasslands of the Great Plains east of the Rockies. Many of the mountain areas can only be grazed in the summer. In winter, sheep and cattle have to be brought down to lower altitudes.

With so little rain, much of the land cannot be farmed. Only a small part of it is used for crops. Farmers grow wheat in parts of the north that are not too dry. Montana grows more wheat than any other state outside the Midwest. Barley, hay, oats, sorghum, and peas are also grown. Many ranchers grow hay to feed their livestock during the winter.

Irrigation makes it possible to raise crops in some other areas. The irrigated land is used for potatoes, beets, alfalfa, hay, and various fruits and vegetables. Idaho produces more potatoes than any other state in the nation. Cotton is grown on irrigated land in Arizona and New Mexico. It is the largest cash crop in these two states.

People of the Mountain States

The Mountain States have fewer people than any other subregion. About 12 million people live in this area. That is about 5 percent of the nation's population. The rugged land and low rainfall have discouraged settlement in the past. Crops can be raised only in a few areas. Transportation has been difficult. But

An American Indian woman who is a carpenter. Indians today are in many professions.

things are changing. Today, the Mountain States are the fastest-growing subregion in the nation. People are moving to the area for jobs and for the warmer, drier climate.

Many older people move to the sunbelt after they retire. Southern Arizona and New Mexico are in the sunbelt.

More American Indians live in the Mountain States than in any other subregion. Most of them live on reservations set up by the government. Many Spanish-speaking people also live in the Mountain States, mostly in New Mexico and Arizona.

"This Is the Place" Monument in Salt Lake City, Utah, commemorates the decision by Mormon leader Brigham Young to build the Mormon capital there. Salt Lake City is at 41° north latitude, 112° west longitude.

Denver is Colorado's largest city. It lies at the heart of a busy, fast-growing area that stretches from Colorado Springs to Cheyenne, Wyoming. Known as the Mile-High City, Denver is 1,609 meters (5,280 feet) above sea level. It started out as a mining town. Today, Denver is an important center of transportation, manufacturing industries, and government offices.

Salt Lake City in Utah was settled by the Mormons in 1847. Most of the state's population still live in and around the city. Seven out of ten people in Utah are Mormons.

Some of America's fastest-growing cities are in the sunbelt. Phoenix, Arizona, is a center of the aircraft and electronics industries. Tucson, also in Arizona, is another rapidly growing industrial center. Albuquerque, New Mexico, is the trading center of a large cattle- and sheep-raising area. Los Alamos, the nuclear research station, is nearby.

Places to See

Yellowstone National Park, in the northwest corner of Wyoming, is the oldest and largest of the nation's national parks. People come from all over the world to see Yellowstone's geysers, hot springs, and waterfalls. **Geysers** are hot springs that shoot water and steam into the air. The most famous geyser is called Old Faithful. It got its name because it blew off steam "faithfully" every 65 minutes or so. Old Faithful stayed on schedule for more than 100 years.

The Grand Canyon National Park in Arizona is one of the nation's top tourist attractions. Glacier National Park in northern Montana is known for its rugged mountains and large glaciers. In Carlsbad Caverns National Park in New Mexico, you can visit the world's largest underground caves. In Utah, you can see the Great Salt Lake. Many small rivers empty into it. It is the largest saltwater lake in North America.

Old Faithful, a famous geyser at Yellowstone National Park, erupts every 65 minutes or so.

REVIEW

VOCABULARY MASTERY

1. The ___ is the ridge that forms the backbone of North America.
   timberline   Continental Divide   Grand Canyon
2. Old Faithful is the most famous ___ in the Mountain States.
   geyser   canyon   waterfall

READING FOR MAIN IDEAS

3. What are the two main landforms of the Mountain States?
4. What kinds of resources are found throughout the Mountain States? List some of these resources.
5. Why has traveling usually been difficult in the Mountain States? How do people travel between towns and cities in this subregion?

RESEARCH AND WRITING SKILLS

Choose one of the national parks in the Mountain States. Write a brief report about it. Include information about the size of the park and its wildlife, landforms, and other attractions.

Lesson 3: The Pacific States

FIND THE WORDS

earthquake fault volcano
lava erupt tundra
permafrost aerospace industry

Five states of the United States have coasts on the Pacific Ocean. These Pacific States are California, Oregon, Washington, Alaska, and Hawaii.

Four of these states—Alaska, Washington, Oregon, and California—are on the West Coast of North America. California has the largest population of any state. Alaska has the smallest population but the most land. It is more than twice the size of Texas.

The state of Hawaii is the only state that is not part of the North American continent. It is on islands in the Pacific Ocean, west of Mexico.

Features of the Land

Mountains are a feature shared by all five Pacific States. Mountains extend down the Pacific Coast of North America from Alaska to California. The Rocky Mountain system begins in Alaska. It includes the Brooks Range, which stretches across northern Alaska, and the Alaska Range, in the southern part of the state. The Alaska Range has some of the highest mountains in North America. The highest of all, Mount McKinley, has an elevation of 6,194 meters (20,320 feet). Lowlands and valleys lie between these two mountain ranges. The Yukon River, the longest in the Pacific States, flows across this area.

Two chains of mountains run through the Pacific States south of Alaska. The ranges near the ocean are low mountains called the Coast Ranges. The Coast Ranges begin in northern Washington with the Olympic Mountains. In southern Oregon and northern California, they are called the Klamath Mountains.

San Francisco Bay interrupts the range. Then the mountains continue on down the coast of California. In some places, their rocky cliffs drop straight down to the ocean.

In southern California there is a narrow plain next to the ocean. Los Angeles, San Diego, and many other cities have grown up there. Much of the population of California lives on this plain.

Higher mountains lie inland, to the east. In Washington and Oregon, these inland mountains are called the Cascade Range. In

California, they are known as the Sierra Nevada, which means "snowy range" in Spanish. Mount Whitney in the Sierra Nevada has an elevation of 4,418 meters (14,494 feet). It is the highest mountain in the 49 states south of Alaska.

Between the coastal and inland ranges are fertile valleys. The Puget Sound–Willamette River valley runs through Washington and Oregon. California has the great Central Valley.

California also has deserts. Most of them are in the southeastern part of the state. The Mojave (moh HAH vee) Desert, the largest desert in California, has almost no rainfall.

Also in this area is Death Valley. Death Valley is the lowest place in North America. It is 86 meters (282 feet) below sea level. On July 10, 1913, Death Valley had the highest temperature ever recorded in the United States—57° Celsius (134° Fahrenheit).

Death Valley got its name in 1849. Some Americans on their way to the California Gold Rush tried to take a shortcut across the desert valley. They did not make it. The party ran out of food and water and died under the scorching sun.

Earthquakes occur often in California. An **earthquake** is a quick movement of Earth's surface that causes the ground to shake and tremble. In 1906, a great earthquake destroyed much of the city of San Francisco.

Most earthquakes occur along faults. A **fault** is a crack in Earth's surface. The land along a fault tends to move suddenly. That sudden movement is what causes earthquakes.

The biggest and longest of California's faults runs north to southeast for 1,200 kilometers (750 miles). That is almost the whole length of the state. This fault is called the San Andreas Fault. Most of the state's faults are in southern California. That is why there are more earthquakes there.

The state of Hawaii consists of eight large and many small islands out in the Pacific Ocean. These islands were created by volcanoes. A **volcano** is an opening in Earth through which hot, melted rock and gases can shoot up. The melted rock is called **lava.** Each time a volcano **erupts,** or shoots out lava and gases, the lava flow hardens. This builds up a mountain around the volcano. The Hawaiian islands are volcanoes that pushed up out of the sea over the centuries.

Hawaii extends the farthest south of any state. Its southernmost point is only 19° north of the equator. Alaska extends farther north than any other state.

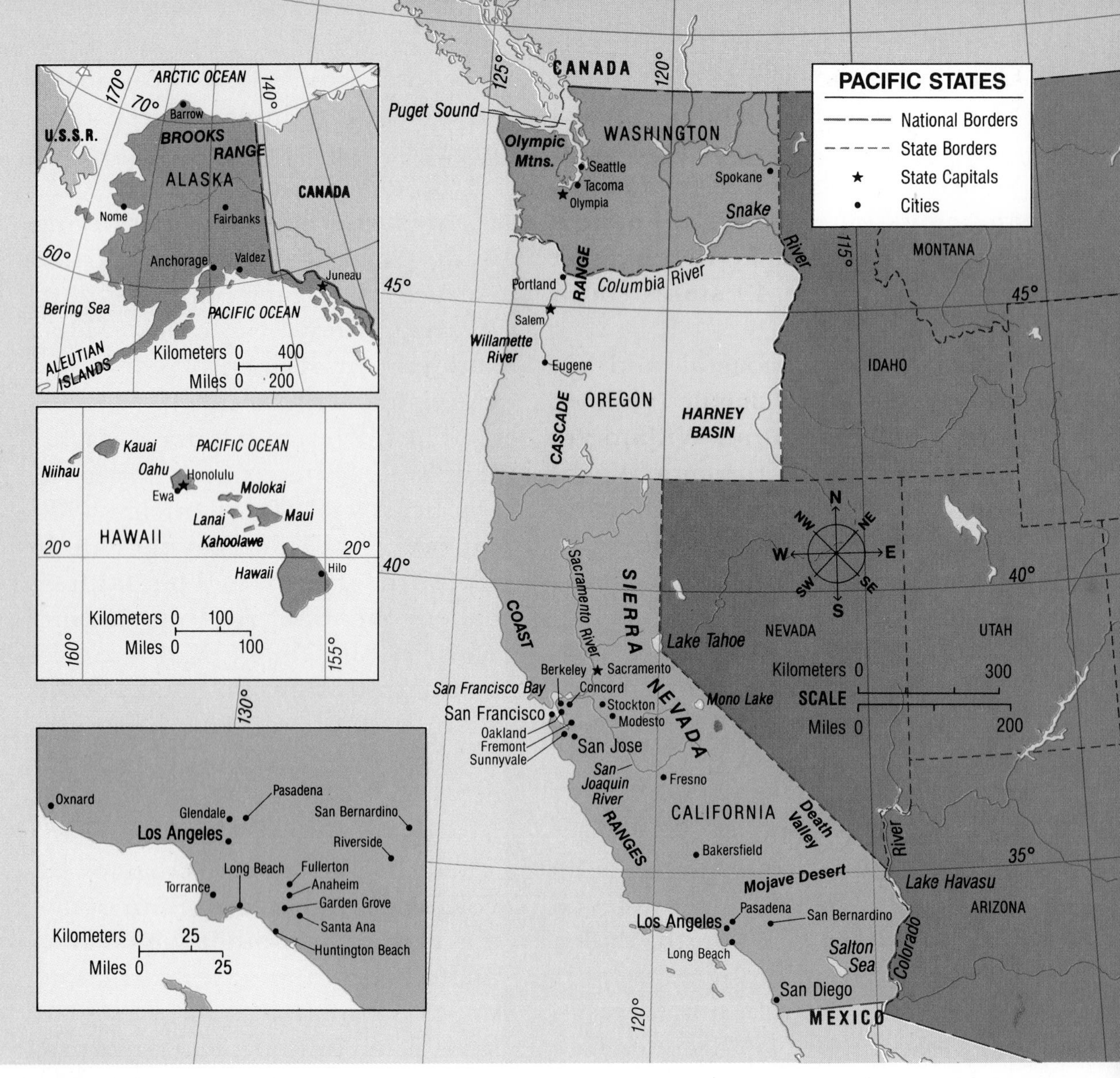

Key to Cities Shown on the Map

Population under 100,000
- Barrow (AK) .... 71°N, 156°W
- Fairbanks (AK) .... 65°N, 148°W
- Hilo (HI) .... 20°N, 155°W
- ★Juneau (AK) .... 58°N, 135°W
- Nome (AK) .... 65°N, 165°W
- ★Olympia (WA) .... 47°N, 123°W
- ★Salem (OR) .... 45°N, 123°W
- Valdez (AK) .... 61°N, 146°W

Population 100,000–499,000
- Anaheim (CA) .... 34°N, 118°W
- Anchorage (AK) .... 61°N, 150°W
- Bakersfield (CA) .... 35°N, 119°W
- Berkeley (CA) .... 38°N, 122°W
- Concord (CA) .... 38°N, 122°W
- Eugene (OR) .... 44°N, 123°W
- Ewa (HI) .... 21°N, 158°W
- Fremont (CA) .... 38°N, 122°W
- Fresno (CA) .... 37°N, 120°W
- Fullerton (CA) .... 34°N, 118°W
- Garden Grove (CA) ... 34°N, 118°W
- Glendale (CA) .... 34°N, 118°W
- ★Honolulu (HI) .... 21°N, 158°W
- Huntington Beach (CA) .34°N, 118°W
- Long Beach (CA) .... 34°N, 118°W
- Modesto (CA) .... 38°N, 121°W
- Oakland (CA) .... 38°N, 122°W
- Oxnard (CA) .... 34°N, 119°W
- Pasadena (CA) .... 34°N, 118°W
- Portland (OR) .... 46°N, 124°W
- Riverside (CA) .... 34°N, 117°W
- ★Sacramento (CA) .... 39°N, 122°W
- San Bernardino (CA) . 34°N, 117°W
- Santa Ana (CA) .... 34°N, 118°W
- Seattle (WA) .... 48°N, 122°W
- Spokane (WA) .... 48°N, 117°W
- Stockton (CA) .... 38°N, 121°W
- Sunnyvale (CA) .... 37°N, 122°W
- Tacoma (WA) .... 47°N, 122°W
- Torrance (CA) .... 34°N, 118°W

Population 500,000–999,000
- San Diego (CA) .... 33°N, 117°W
- San Francisco (CA) ... 38°N, 122°W
- San Jose (CA) .... 37°N, 122°W

Population 1,000,000 or over
- Los Angeles (CA) ...... 34°N, 118°W

THE PACIFIC STATES

State	Population/ Admitted to the Union	Area Sq. mi.—Sq. km.		Capital	State Bird	State Flower	State Flag
Alaska (AK) Last Frontier	462,700 **1959**	586,400	1,518,776	Juneau	Willow Ptarmigan	Forget-me-not	
California (CA) Golden State	25,298,100 **1850**	158,693	411,014	Sacramento	California Valley Quail	Golden Poppy	
Hawaii (HI) Aloha State	1,021,100 **1959**	6,450	16,706	Honolulu	Nene or Hawaiian Goose	Hibiscus	
Oregon (OR) Beaver State	2,715,800 **1859**	96,981	251,181	Salem	Western Meadowlark	Oregon Grape	
Washington (WA) Evergreen State	4,291,300 **1889**	68,192	176,617	Olympia	Willow Goldfinch	Coast Rhododendron	

Point Barrow, Alaska, is only 19° south of the North Pole.

Because Alaska is so far north, much of its land is tundra. **Tundra** is treeless land with permanently frozen subsoil. Only the surface layer of soil thaws in the short months of summer. Thus, only plants with shallow roots, such as mosses and lichen, can grow there. The ground underneath that stays frozen all year long is called **permafrost.**

As you can see, the climate of the Pacific States varies greatly from place to place. The area north of San Francisco has a cool, wet, marine climate. It rains there a good deal of the time, even in the summer months. Some places in Oregon and Washington have over 252 centimeters (100 inches) of rain a year.

In southern California, the weather is warmer and drier. Here, the Mediterranean climate brings summers with little moisture and mild, wet winters. The mountain ranges tend to block the moisture from the ocean. Much of this moisture falls on the mountains as rain or snow. Thus, many parts of the Central Valley have to be irrigated. East of the high Sierra Nevada, there is very little rain. Southeastern California is almost all desert.

More than a third of Alaska is north of the Arctic Circle. There, it is bitterly cold. During winter, it is dark most of the time. In summer, it is light all day and all night. That is when northern Alaska becomes the land of the midnight sun.

Hawaii is in the tropical climate zone. Fruits can grow year-round. The islands get plenty of rain, too. On the slopes of Mount Waialeale (wy AH lee AH lee), on the island of Kauai (KOW eye), it can rain 350 days a year.

Fascinating Facts

Alaska is a land of extremes. It is the largest state in the nation but has the smallest population. It is also the fastest-growing state.

Alaska boasts the northernmost point in the United States: Point Barrow. It also has the highest peak in North America: Mount McKinley. In Alaska, you can find both bubbling hot springs and slow-moving glaciers. There are vast stretches of ice fields but also active volcanoes. You can see dramatic fjords or a rain forest. Fjords (FYORDZ) are deep, narrow inlets carved by glaciers many thousands of years ago.

The northern part of Alaska lies above the Arctic Circle. In winter, it is always night. The people living there do not see the sun from late November until well into January. In summer, however, this becomes the land of the midnight sun. Then, the sun never sets.

For all five states, the Pacific Ocean is an immensely valuable resource. Goods are traded with Asia and even with Europe and Africa through the Panama Canal. Fishing is important all along the Pacific Coast. Tourists are attracted by the sandy beaches of Hawaii and the beautiful coastline of California.

Alaska is rich in minerals. In the late 1890s, people went there to find gold. Today, Alaska's most important resource is petroleum. The petroleum is found in northern Alaska, where coastal waters are frozen most of the year. To get the oil to market, a giant pipeline was built. The Alaska pipeline carries the oil 1,290 kilometers (800 miles) to the ice-free port of Valdez. Alaska can ship 2 million barrels of oil a day. California also has deposits of petroleum and natural gas. Some of the oil is found offshore.

Great forests are found in Washington, Oregon, and California. The rain and rich soil make the trees grow straight and tall. Over half the nation's lumber comes from the Pacific States. Giant redwoods grow in northern California and Oregon. Some of these trees are 1,500 years old.

The Alaska pipeline carries petroleum 800 miles, from oil fields on the Arctic coast at 70° N to the ice-free port of Valdez, Alaska, at 61° N.

Economic Activity

The industries of the states along the Pacific are varied and constantly changing. By itself, California produces more goods than any other state. The greater Los Angeles area is one of the nation's most rapidly growing industrial centers.

Washington and Oregon also have much industry. From the lumber of the great forests come many wood products. These include furniture, plywood, paper, and wood shingles.

There are also many fisheries and canning factories. Tuna are caught along the Pacific Coast. So are salmon, though they are also trapped as they travel up rivers to lay their eggs.

Washington and southern California are the centers of the aerospace industry. The **aerospace industry** includes airplanes, missiles, and spacecraft.

South of San Francisco in California is an area known as "Silicon Valley." Its name comes from the silicon chips that are used in computers. Silicon Valley is headquarters for California's important computer industry.

Hollywood is still the film capital of the world. The moving-picture industry got its start there in the early 1900s. Today, many television shows are also produced in Hollywood.

Lumbering is a major industry in the Pacific States of Washington and Oregon.

Many jobs in Alaska depend on the state's rich supplies of petroleum, minerals, timber, and fish. In the economy of Hawaii, tourism ranks first.

California is the leading agricultural state in the nation. It grows just about everything. Good soils and a warm, dry climate help make the Central Valley and California lowlands productive. Irrigation is used in many parts of California.

California leads the nation in the production of peaches, pears, grapes, strawberries, lemons, tomatoes, lettuce, carrots, and other fruits and vegetables. It produces one-fifth of the nation's oranges. It even grows cotton. California also has many ranches and farms that raise beef and poultry.

Agriculture is important in Washington and Oregon as well. Wheat is a major crop. Washington and Oregon also produce dairy products, vegetables, and fruit, such as apples, peaches, pears, and cherries. Washington grows more apples than any other state. Cattle are also raised there.

Hawaii has a climate that allows crops to grow all year long. On the islands there are 810,000 hectares (2 million acres) of farmland. Farmers grow sugar cane, coffee, pineapples, and other fruit. Cattle are raised on the largest island, also called Hawaii.

People of the Pacific States

California has more people than any other state. Already, more than 25 million people live there, and thousands more are arriving each year. The new Californians come from Asia, Mexico, and other parts of the United States. More than 4 million Hispanics live in California. Spanish has become the state's second language. Most Californians live in the cities and suburbs. In fact, 9 out of 10 Californians live in urban areas.

Alaska has only 500,000 people. This is the smallest population of any state in the nation. Alaska is growing fast, though. American Indians and the Innuit and Aleuts (Eskimos) make up more than 20 percent of Alaska's population. The Aleuts (AL ee OOTZ) live in the Aleutian (uh LOO shun) Islands west of the mainland.

Hawaii is growing fast, too. Now more than 1 million people live there. Hawaii is a mix of many people and races. Polynesians were the earliest Hawaiians. Later, people came from Japan, China, the Philippines, and the United States. Hawaii is the only state where Whites are not in the majority.

Three of the nation's largest cities are in California. In 1984, Los Angeles became the second-largest city in the nation. It is a great port and industrial center. It is also a city of culture and sports. In the summer of 1984, the Summer Olympics were held in Los Angeles.

The islands of Hawaii were formed by volcanoes. They are near 20° N and between 155° and 165° W.

San Diego is another booming city. Engineering and shipbuilding industries and a naval base are important there. San Diego also has a world-famous zoo.

San Francisco is one of the nation's most beautiful cities. It is built on steep hills. Large bridges connect it to the land north and east of San Francisco Bay.

Portland is Oregon's largest city and its chief industrial and commercial center. Located on

Children celebrate the Chinese New Year in San Francisco's famous Chinatown. About 82,000 people of Chinese descent live in San Francisco. Many Chinese people came to California during the Gold Rush of 1849. Others came during the 1860s to help build railroads.

the Columbia River, it is one of the Pacific States' major ports.

Seattle, Washington, is on Puget Sound. It is a great port as well as an industrial city. Its major industries are aerospace and lumber.

Places to See

California's Yosemite (yoh SEM uh tee) National Park has breathtaking scenery and the highest waterfall in North America. It attracts many hikers and campers. Sequoia National Park, also in California, has some of the oldest trees in the world.

San Francisco is a favorite place to visit because there is so much to see and do. Its top attractions include the Golden Gate Bridge, the cable cars, and Chinatown.

REVIEW

VOCABULARY MASTERY

1. Earthquakes in California occur along a ___ line.
   tundra fault volcano
2. The mountains that build up around volcanoes are made of ___.
   lava permafrost tundra

READING FOR MAIN IDEAS

3. What feature does the land of the Pacific States have in common with the Mountain States?
4. Why is the Pacific Ocean important to all the Pacific States?
5. Give three reasons that people move to California.

THINKING SKILLS

The climate in the Pacific States varies greatly from state to state, and even within some of the states. How does climate affect the way people live in different parts of this subregion? What Pacific State has the kind of climate you like best? What state's climate do you like least? Give your reasons.

CHAPTER REVIEW

VOCABULARY MASTERY

Use the words below to complete the chapter summary. Use each only once.

altitude	geysers
canyons	lava
earthquakes	permafrost
erupted	timberline
faults	volcanoes

Many __1__ occur in California, especially where there are __2__, or cracks in Earth's surface. The islands of Hawaii were formed by __3__. These __4__ when gases and melted rock called __5__ pushed up out of the sea over many centuries.

In the Mountain States, rivers have cut deeply into plateaus and created __6__. There are also hot springs, or __7__, that shoot water and steam high into the air.

The __8__ is the point where trees stop growing. Above this __9__, only low-growing plants and shrubs can grow. In northern Alaska, the ground beneath the surface of Earth remains frozen all year long and is called __10__.

READING FOR MAIN IDEAS

1. Why does weather often change suddenly in the Midwestern States?
2. What is the leading crop of the Midwestern States? Why is this subregion good for growing this crop?
3. What is the "backbone" of the North American continent? How does it affect river flow?
4. What is the major industry of the Mountain States? What is the most important agricultural activity?
5. Why do earthquakes occur more often in Southern California than in Northern California?

SKILLS APPLICATION

MAP SKILLS

Look at the political map on page 414.

6. Which states border the Great Lakes?
7. Which Midwestern States does the Missouri River flow along or through?
8. For which states does the Mississippi River form the border?
9. What state is in two parts?
10. Which city is closest to 40° north latitude and 90° west longitude?

CHART SKILLS

Look at the chart on page 435.

11. The Pacific States include our newest states. Name them and give the year they joined the Union.
12. The largest Pacific State is also the largest of all states. Which is it, and how large is it?
13. Look at the other state charts in this unit. Rank Hawaii and the smaller states from smallest to largest. List the area for each.
14. Copy the chart below on a separate sheet of paper. Then fill in the blanks. Use an encyclopedia. Look under "Mountains."

Mountain	State	Height	
		feet	meters
MT. McKINLEY			
PIKES PEAK			
MT. WHITNEY			
MT. RAINIER			
MT. LOA			
BORAH PEAK			
HUMPHREYS PEAK			
MT. HOOD			

UNIT REVIEW

VOCABULARY MASTERY

Choose one of the lists of words below. Then write a paragraph or a page using all the words from that list. You may use the words in the singular or plural. On a separate page, write the words and define them.

canyon	bauxite
drain	logging
drainage basin	mine
gorge	mineral
prairie	petroleum
rapids	quarry
silt	renewable resource
steppe	strip mining
tidewater	uranium
tundra	wood pulp

READING FOR MAIN IDEAS

1. What are the six geographic regions in the United States?
2. Explain what the Mississippi River system is.
3. How are most lakes formed?
4. What are some of the ranges that make up the Appalachian Mountain system?
5. What is the climate of most of the Southeast? Name and describe the severe storms that can be found in this climate.
6. What are some resources of the Southeast?
7. What makes western Mississippi such a fertile farming area?
8. Why is the Midwest known as the breadbasket of the nation?
9. Name several important rivers in the South Central subregion.
10. In what states is cotton grown?
11. Why is Chicago the transportation hub of the nation?
12. Where is the Continental Divide?
13. Which resources of the Mountain States are important to industry?
14. What is the San Andreas Fault?
15. When does northern Alaska become the land of the midnight sun?

THINKING SKILLS

16. The Hudson River is linked to the Great Lakes by a system of canals. Give several reasons why this waterway was important to the development of the Midwest.
17. Why is Wisconsin called "America's dairyland"?
18. Why do the Mountain States have fewer people than any other subregion? Why is this changing?
19. Why is winter wheat grown in Oklahoma and central Texas?
20. Give reasons for the great variety of industry in the Pacific States.

USE YOUR MAPS

Look at the maps on pages 378, 386, 394, 406, 414, 426, and 434.

21. What New England states are on the Atlantic coast?
22. What bodies of water form borders for New York State?
23. What river divides South Carolina from Georgia?
24. List three cities on the Gulf of Mexico.
25. What rivers form borders for South Central states?
26. What bodies of water form state borders in the Midwest?
27. Name three ranges in the Rocky Mountain system.
28. Name two rivers in California.

SKILL DEVELOPMENT

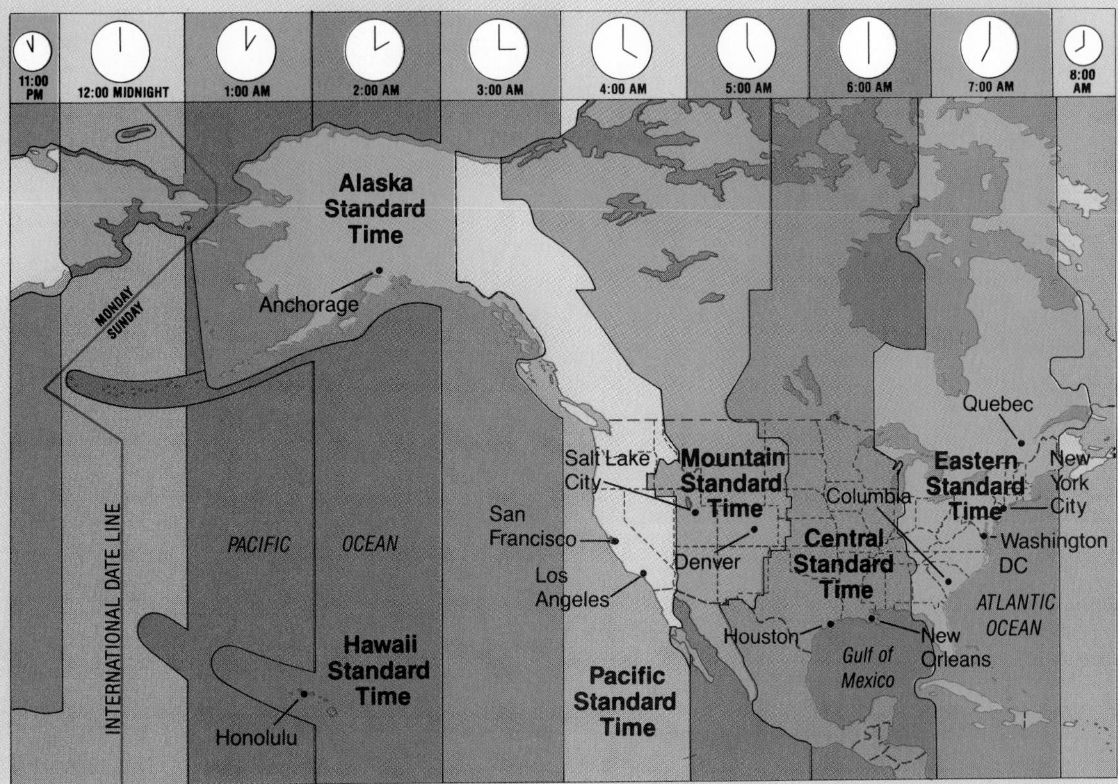

MAP SKILLS

There are 24 time zones in the world. This is because Earth makes one complete rotation every 24 hours, or day. The map above includes time zones for North America.

1. How many time zones are in North America?
2. Start in Los Angeles. How many time zones do you cross going to Washington, DC? (Do not count Los Angeles.)
3. When it is noon in Houston, is it earlier or later in Denver?
4. When it is 3 P.M. in New Orleans, what time is it in
   a. San Francisco? c. Quebec?
   b. Anchorage?
5. When it is 11 A.M. in Salt Lake City, what time is it in
   a. Honolulu? b. New York?
6. Suppose you are eating lunch at noon in Columbia, South Carolina. Your pen pal is eating an 8 A.M. breakfast now. What state is your pen pal in?
7. Suppose you are in San Francisco. It is 2 P.M. there. A friend will call you at 6 P.M. Eastern time. How long must you wait?

RESEARCH AND WRITING SKILLS

The map above shows the *International Date Line*. Look in an encyclopedia for an explanation of it. Then write a question about it using the map.

NORTH AMERICAN NEIGHBORS

UNIT 7

CHAPTER 1 CANADA

Lesson 1: The Geography of Canada

FIND THE WORDS

province maritime
Canadian Shield geologist
taiga

Canada is the largest nation in North America. It is the second-largest nation in the world. Only the Soviet Union is bigger. Canada covers 9,992,330 square kilometers (3,831,033 square miles) of the North American continent.

In the south and northwest, Canada is bordered by the United States. The two nations are separated by political boundaries. The border between southern Canada and the northern United States stretches the entire width of the continent.

Three of Earth's four oceans form natural boundaries for Canada. The Atlantic Ocean is to the east. The Pacific Ocean is to the southwest. Canada's northern boundary is the Arctic Ocean. It is frozen much of the time.

Altogether, Canada has more than 241,500 kilometers (150,000 miles) of coastline. This is the longest coastline of any nation in the world.

Canada's Regions

Canada has five geographic regions. They are the Atlantic Coast region, the St. Lawrence Lowlands, the Laurentian (lor REN chun) Plateau, the Great Plains, and the Western Mountain region.

Just as the United States is divided into states, Canada is divided into provinces and territories. Like a state, a **province** is part of a nation. It has its own land, people, and government. A territory is part of a nation, too, but it has less power than a state or province.

Canada has 10 provinces. The Atlantic Coast region includes the 4 provinces on Canada's east coast. These provinces are New Brunswick, Nova Scotia, Prince Edward Island, and Newfoundland. The first three of these are sometimes called the Maritime Provinces. The word **maritime** means "on or near the ocean." The province of Newfoundland is actually closer to Ireland than it is to British Columbia on Canada's Pacific Coast.

The land in the Atlantic Coast region is mostly gently rolling meadows with many rivers and lakes. There is also a low range of hills. This region has a continental climate.

The St. Lawrence Lowlands region is named for the St. Lawrence River. This is Canada's smallest region. However, it has the most people and the largest cities of any region. The southern parts of the provinces of Ontario and Quebec are in the St. Lawrence Lowlands.

More than half of Canada is on the Laurentian Plateau. This region is also known as the **Canadian Shield.** That is because it is U-shaped like a shield. Most of Quebec and Ontario are in this region. The Canadian Shield stretches across Canada from Newfoundland south to the Great Lakes and northwest to the Beaufort (BOH furt) Sea. This vast region is covered by large forests except in the far north. That is a tundra region, where the climate is too cold for trees to grow.

The Great Plains region contains the three prairie provinces of Manitoba, Saskatchewan, and Alberta. The plains here are part of the same Great Plains that stretch across part of the United States. The northern part is covered by forests. The southern part is a flat, grassy prairie.

The Western Mountain region includes both the Rocky Mountains and the Coast Mountains that extend along the western coast of North America. The province of British Columbia is in this region. Warm winds that blow off the Pacific Ocean give the coastal region a milder climate than the rest of Canada.

Natural Resources

Canada's land and water are its two most important natural resources.

Canada has thousands of lakes and rivers. In fact, it has more lakes than any other nation in the world. Canada's lakes and rivers hold more fresh water than those of any other nation. Many fish live in this water. This water also provides power for both Canada and the United States. Hydroelectric plants generate electricity that is used on both sides of the border.

Canada's most important waterway is the St. Lawrence River. It is part of the St. Lawrence Seaway, which connects the

The St. Lawrence Seaway has a series of canals and locks. Using these artificial waterways, ships can be raised or lowered to the next body of water.

Great Lakes with the Atlantic Ocean. Early explorers from Europe used the river and lakes to go into Canada. Today, the river and lakes are used to transport goods. Oceangoing ships can sail into the Great Lakes through the St. Lawrence Seaway. These ships carry many goods to and from Canada. This trade is important to Canada's economy.

Fishing is important to Canadians who live on the Atlantic and Pacific coasts. The Grand Banks is one of the richest fishing grounds in the world. It is a shallow part of the Atlantic Ocean located off the southeastern coast of Newfoundland.

Canada's land is vast. Geologists have found that much of this land contains valuable minerals. A **geologist** is a scientist who studies Earth's physical structure. Important minerals found in Canada include iron ore, coal, nickel, silver, copper, zinc, uranium, petroleum, and natural gas.

As an industrial nation, Canada makes good use of these minerals. The minerals are processed and then used to make steel, automobiles, trucks, heavy machinery, and other goods.

Canada is able to grow more food than its people use. The soil in the Great Plains region is very fertile. There, farmers grow wheat, corn, and oats. Eastern Canada has many dairy farms. The mild climate of British Columbia is good for growing crops, especially fruits and vegetables.

Canada's vast forests are one of its richest resources. The timber shown here will be made into many different wood and paper products.

Ranching is also a big industry in Canada. Sheep and cattle are raised on ranches in the prairie provinces.

Forests in Canada provide vast quantities of timber. The **taiga** is the forested area south of the tundra. Many wood products come from this timber. Half of the world's newspapers are printed on paper from Canadian forests.

The Canadian People

For such a big country, Canada has few people. About 25 million people live there. Most of them live in cities near the United States border. Toronto and Montreal are Canada's two largest

An Innuit mother and her baby in northern Canada. Many of Canada's 25,000 Innuit live in towns and have adopted a modern way of life.

cities. Both are located in southeastern Canada. Vancouver, in British Columbia in the west, is Canada's third-largest city.

Few people live in northern Canada. Most of the people who do are Eskimos. They are properly called *Innuit* (IN yoo it), their word for "people." There are also about 370,000 North American Indians in Canada. Many of them live on reservations. Others live and work in the cities. About 2 percent of Canadians are American Indian or Innuit.

Most Canadians have European backgrounds. About 45 percent have British ancestors. About 29 percent are of French descent. English and French are the two official languages of Canada. All official notices are printed in both languages.

In recent years, people have come to Canada from Asia, Africa, and Latin America. Many different peoples now live in Canada. Like the United States, Canada is a nation of immigrants.

REVIEW

VOCABULARY MASTERY

1. A ___ in Canada is similar to a state in the United States.
   region   territory   province
2. The ___ Provinces are by the sea.
   Prairie   Maritime   Great Lakes

READING FOR MAIN IDEAS

3. List the five geographic regions of Canada. Write one distinguishing feature of each.
4. What is Canada's most important waterway?
5. Name five of Canada's resources.
6. Where do most Canadians live?

THINKING SKILLS

Although Canada is the second-largest nation in the world, it has fewer people than many smaller nations. Why do you think this is? Do you expect this to change in the future? Why?

Lesson 2: The History of Canada

FIND THE WORDS

voyageur	**portage**	**intendant**
seigneur	**habitant**	**dominion**

Canada's earliest settlers came from Asia thousands of years ago. The descendants of these people still live in Canada. They are the Canadian Indians.

The Innuit are descendants of later settlers from Asia. They began moving to Canada about 2,000 years ago.

Experts say that the Vikings were the first Europeans to sail to North America. They landed in Newfoundland before A.D. 1000. They did not stay long.

Europeans who later rediscovered Canada were looking for a sea route to Asia. In 1497, John Cabot sailed west from England and landed in Newfoundland. His voyage marked the beginning of English interest in America.

In 1535, Jacques Cartier sailed up the St. Lawrence River. He tried to start a French settlement but failed. However, more French explorers and settlers followed him. In 1608, Samuel de Champlain founded Quebec and started the colony of New France on the St. Lawrence River. He made friends with the Indians and bought furs from them. Soon, many Europeans were eager to buy Canadian furs.

The Fur Trade

Fur trading was New France's most important business. Indians did the actual trapping. French **voyageurs** (vwah yah ZHURZ) were hired by the fur companies

In this painting, a French *voyageur* is shown bargaining with members of an Indian tribe. Voyageurs were daring French traders who traveled deep into the wilderness to buy furs from the Indians. They traveled by river, filling their canoes with furs before returning to the French trading posts along the St. Lawrence. There, they sold the furs to traders from Europe.

In this engraving, the British are shown attacking the French on the cliff above Quebec. You can see the French firing down on them from above. The French were defeated after a fierce battle in which many men were killed.

to carry furs by boat to towns on the St. Lawrence River. Then the furs were shipped to France.

Indians taught the voyageurs how to make canoes out of birch bark and how to live off the land. To get from one body of water to another, voyageurs carried their canoes over land. This is called **portage** (POR tij).

By law, the French king owned all the land in New France. He appointed a governor for the colony. The governor was called an **intendant** (anh tahn DAHN). However, seigneurs controlled the land. A **seigneur** (san YUR) was a French nobleman who lived on the land. **Habitants** (ah bee TAHN) were settlers who worked for the seigneur. In exchange for land, they gave the seigneur part of their crops and livestock.

The Fight for Canada

The English did not want to be left out of Canada. Some English fur traders went to Hudson Bay. In 1670, they started their own fur company, called the Hudson's Bay Company. It became a powerful force in Canada.

In 1754, England, now called Britain, went to war with France. They were fighting to see which nation would rule Canada. This war lasted until 1759. Most North American Indian groups sided with the French. That is why the war was known as the French and Indian War. However, the most powerful Indian group, the Iroquois, were allies of the British.

The strongest French fort was at the top of a steep hill in Quebec. The British knew that if they

WHERE WE ARE IN TIME AND PLACE

THE GROWTH OF CANADA

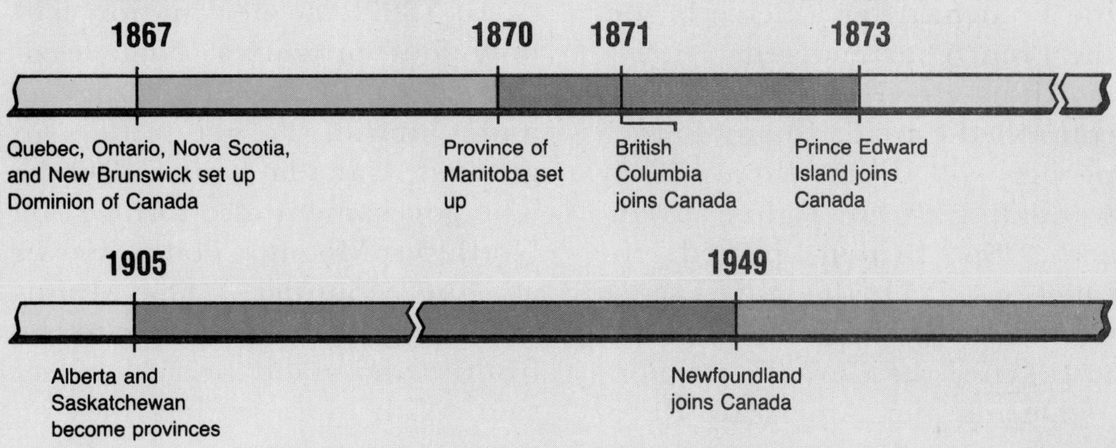

POLITICAL MAP OF CANADA

KEY
National Borders
Provincial Borders
National Capital
Provincial Capitals
Cities

could capture Quebec, they would win the fight for Canada. They climbed the cliff and surprised the French. After a fierce battle, the French surrendered.

Although Great Britain now controlled Canada, many French people still lived there. They wanted their full rights as citizens. So Britain passed the Quebec Act. This law gave French Canadians the right to vote and to practice the Catholic religion.

During the American Revolution, many Americans who were loyal to Britain moved to Canada.

Independent Canada

Canada became independent in 1867. It got its own constitution. However, this constitution was written by the British Parliament. Canada kept close and friendly relations with Britain. It was called a **dominion,** a self-governing nation in the British Commonwealth of Nations.

In 1867, the new nation had only four provinces: Nova Scotia, New Brunswick, Quebec, and Ontario. To get settlers to go west, Canada built railroads. The government also formed the Northwest Mounted Police, known as "the Mounties." The Mounties brought law and order to the frontier and made the settlers feel safe. With more settlers moving west, the provinces of Manitoba, British Columbia, Saskatchewan, and Alberta were formed.

Today, Canada has close relations with both the United States and Great Britain. Canada and the United States are good neighbors. The border that divides these two nations is the longest friendly border in the world.

REVIEW

VOCABULARY MASTERY

1. ___ transported furs by boat to towns on the St. Lawrence River.
   Voyageurs Seigneurs Habitants

2. In New France, ___ controlled the land and ___ farmed it.
   voyageurs habitants seigneurs

READING FOR MAIN IDEAS

3. What trade attracted the French and English to Canada in the 1600s?
4. What groups fought in the French and Indian War? How long did this war last? Who won the war?
5. When did Canada become independent?
6. How did the government encourage Canadians to settle in the west?

THINKING SKILLS

Why do you think Canada remained loyal to Britain while the 13 American colonies rebelled against British rule? Why do you think Canada could gain independence peacefully?

Lesson 3: The Government of Canada

FIND THE WORDS

prime minister **premier**
bilingual **referendum**

Canada today is divided into 10 provinces and 2 territories. The map on page 453 shows the provinces and territories of Canada and their capitals.

Most American states were territories or parts of territories before they became states. Canada's two territories are in the far north. They are the Northwest Territories and the Yukon Territory. Few people live there because it is so cold.

Canada's Democracy

Canada's national capital is Ottawa in the province of Ontario. This is where Canada's national, or federal, government is located. A federal government is one that unites all the provinces or states in a nation.

Like the United States, Canada has three different levels of government. They are the federal government, the provincial governments, and the local governments. Towns and cities are run by local governments.

Also like the United States, Canada is a representative democracy. The Canadian people vote for officials who run the government at all levels.

The Canadians have a federal legislature. It meets in Ottawa and makes the laws for all of Canada. This legislature is called the Parliament (PAHR luh munt). It is somewhat like the United States Congress. The Canadian Parliament has two houses. Members of the House of Commons are elected, but members of the Senate are appointed.

The bustling city of Calgary, Alberta, at 51° north latitude, 114° west longitude. The discovery of petroleum has made Calgary a boom town.

Quebec, at 47° north latitude, 71° west longitude, is the center of French-speaking Canada.

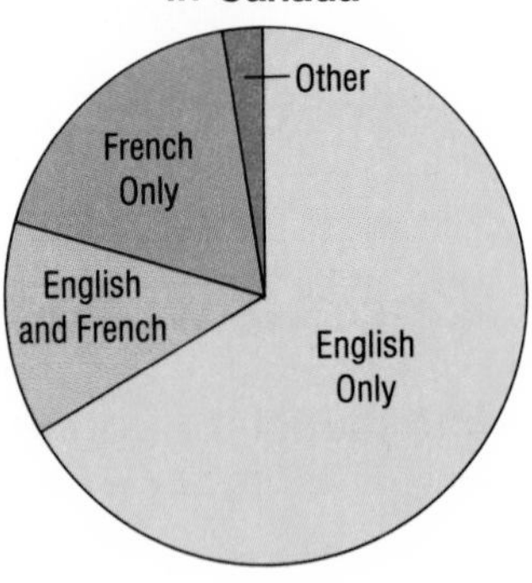

Canada has two major political parties, the Conservative Party and the Liberal Party. Each has its own ideas about what the government should do. There are also several smaller parties.

Each party has its own leader. The leader of the party that wins the majority of seats in Parliament becomes the prime minister. The **prime minister** is the national leader of Canada. In many ways, the Canadian prime minister is like the American President. However, in Canada, the people do not elect the prime minister directly.

Each province has its own legislature, which makes laws for the province. Each province also has its own leader, called a premier. The **premier** (prih MIR) of a province is like a state governor.

The Quebec Problem

One of Canada's biggest problems concerns the province of Quebec. This is where most of Canada's French-speaking people live. For a long time, many of these people have felt they were not being treated equally with the English Canadians.

In the late 1960s, some Quebec politicians started a new political party. It was called the Parti Québécois (pahr TEE KAY bay KWAH), or PQ for short. The PQ wanted Quebec to stop being a Canadian province. It wanted Quebec to become an independent nation. Canada's prime minister at the time believed Canada should be a bilingual nation. **Bilingual** (by LING gwul) means "using two languages." He thought this would help make all

Canadians equal. Instead, the plan angered many English-speaking Canadians in the west. They did not want to have to learn the French language.

In 1976, the PQ won the elections in Quebec. The PQ's leader was now Quebec's premier. He made French the official language of Quebec. This made English-speaking people in Quebec unhappy. Some large companies left Montreal in Quebec for Toronto in Ontario.

In 1980, Quebec held a referendum on the issue of independence. A **referendum** is a vote to decide an important question. By a large majority, the people of Quebec voted to remain part of Canada.

Facing the Future

There are also some disputes between people in the east and west of Canada. The west has many minerals and few people. The east has many people and old industries that need help. In the west, the economy is generally strong. In some places in the east, many people cannot find work. Some easterners feel that money earned from petroleum and from other businesses in the west should be used to help the east. People in the west say that they should be allowed to keep the money they have earned. The federal government is trying to find solutions to these problems. Meanwhile, Canada continues to grow and prosper as a nation.

REVIEW

VOCABULARY MASTERY

1. The leader of the majority party in Parliament becomes Canada's ____.
   premier president
   prime minister
2. The leader of a province is a ____.
   governor premier prime minister
3. In a ____, the people vote to decide an important question.
   compromise referendum
   province

READING FOR MAIN IDEAS

4. What is the "Quebec problem"? What are some effects it has had?
5. How do Canada's east and west differ?

MAP AND TIME LINE SKILLS

6. Look at the map and time line on page 453. How many provinces and territories does Canada have?
7. Which became a province first, British Columbia or Newfoundland?
8. What province or territory extends farthest north? Farthest south?

THINKING SKILLS

Compare and contrast the government structure of Canada with that of the United States.

CHAPTER REVIEW

VOCABULARY MASTERY

Use the words below to complete the chapter summary. Use each only once.

dominion	premier
Geologists	prime minister
habitants	province
intendant	seigneurs

In 1608, Samuel de Champlain started the colony of New France. The king of France appointed a(n) __1__ to govern the colony. However, the __2__ controlled the land. The settlers were called __3__. Later, the British took control. Canada became an independent nation in 1867. As a(n) __4__, Canada was part of the British Commonwealth of Nations.

Today, the __5__ is the national leader of Canada. Each __6__ has its own __7__. Canada's land and water are important resources. __8__ have found many minerals in western Canada.

READING FOR MAIN IDEAS

1. What is a province?
2. What does *maritime* mean? Which are Canada's Maritime Provinces?
3. What is special about the region of the St. Lawrence Lowlands?
4. What is the Canadian Shield? How did it get its name?
5. Who was Samuel de Champlain? What did he do?
6. What is a voyageur? How were they important to Canada's history?
7. What was the Quebec Act?
8. What are Canada's two territories? Why do few people live there?
9. What is the PQ? What does the PQ want?
10. What referendum was held in Quebec in 1980? What was the result?

SKILLS APPLICATION

MAP SKILLS

Look at the map and time line of Canada on page 453.

11. What is the smallest province?
12. Which province separates Alaska from the rest of the United States?
13. Name Canada's capital.
14. In what year did Manitoba become a province?
15. How many years after Alberta did Newfoundland join Canada?

TIME LINE SKILLS

Match the date or time with the event. Then make a time line. List each date with the proper event below it.

16. 1497
17. 1535
18. 1608
19. 1754–1759
20. 1867

A. Quebec is founded.
B. Canada becomes independent.
C. Cabot lands in Newfoundland.
D. French and Indian War is fought.
E. Cartier sails up the St. Lawrence River.

RESEARCH SKILLS

Use an encyclopedia or almanac. Copy this outline. Fill in the first two blanks with names. Tell how many members of Parliament are in each house and if they are elected or appointed.

Government of Canada

I. Queen or King of England: ______
  A. Prime Minister (executive): ______
  B. Judiciary (judicial)
  C. Parliament (legislative)
    1. House of Commons: ______ members, ______
    2. Senate: ____ members, ______

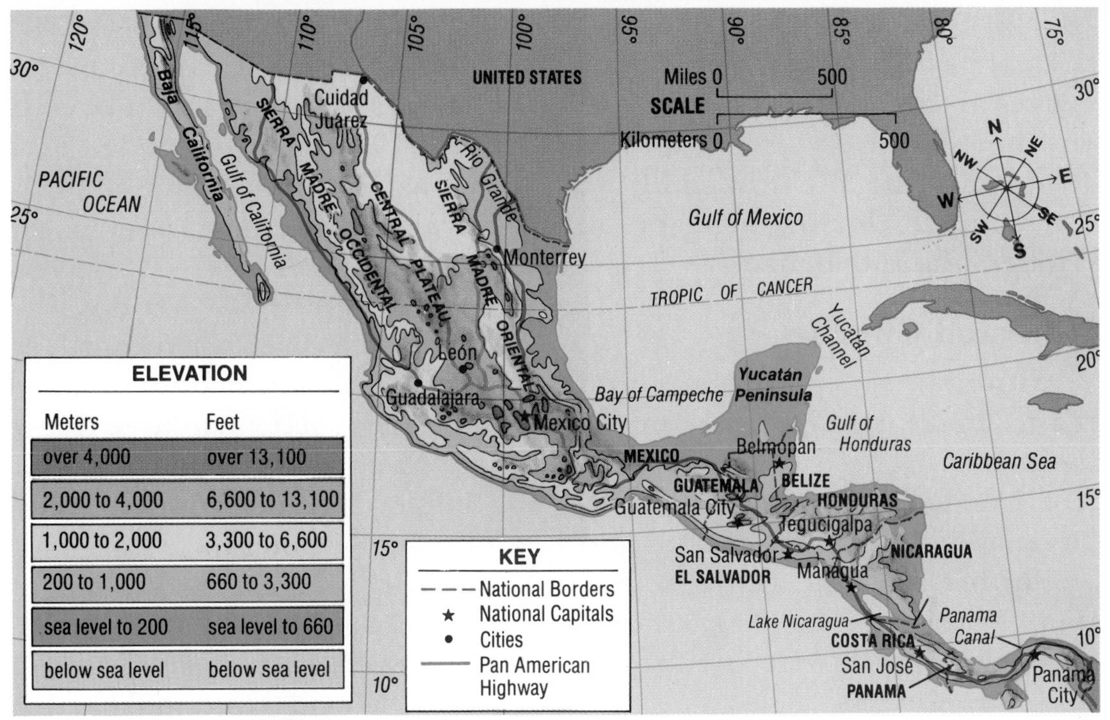

CHAPTER 2 MEXICO AND CENTRAL AMERICA

Lesson 1: The Geography of Mexico

FIND THE WORDS

active volcano **dormant volcano** **extinct volcano** **hacienda** **peon** ***ejido***

Mexico is south of the United States. The two nations share a border 2,898 kilometers (1,800 miles) long. Much of this border is formed by the Rio Grande.

Mexico is 1,972,547 square kilometers (761,604 square miles) in size. That is about one-fifth the size of the United States. However, Mexico has almost one-third as many people as the United States. That means that Mexico has a higher population density.

Like the United States and Canada, Mexico has many miles of coastline. On the west is the Pacific Ocean. In the northwest is a long, narrow peninsula, Baja (BAH hah) California. The main part of Mexico is shaped like a horn of plenty. Mexico's east coast curves around the gulf of Mexico. In the southeast, the Yucatán Peninsula juts into the gulf. In the south, Mexico borders on Guatemala and Belize.

Land and Climate

Mountains, plateaus, and plains make up Mexico's major landforms. These landforms affect Mexico's climates.The lowlands along the coasts are hot and wet or hot and dry. In the south, there are tropical grasslands and rain forests. In the north, there are deserts.

Inland, most of Mexico is mountainous or plateau. In the middle of the nation is the central plateau, or Mexican Plateau. Most of the Mexican people live on this plateau. Much of this land is more than a mile above sea level. The climate there is cool and dry.

The Mexican Plateau is enclosed by two ranges of mountains. On the west are the Sierra Madre Occidental. On the east are the Sierra Madre Oriental. The Sierra Madres come together south of the central plateau.

Violent changes in Earth's crust have shaped much of Mexico. Some of Mexico's mountains are active volcanoes. **Active volcanoes** may still erupt. **Dormant volcanoes** have not erupted for a long time. **Extinct volcanoes** no longer erupt at all. A belt of volcanoes runs across Mexico at about 19° north latitude. Volcanic ash has made the soil of the central plateau very rich.

Natural Resources

Mexico is rich in natural resources. The nation does not have much good, flat farmland. However, Mexico has such minerals as silver, gold, copper, lead, zinc, and petroleum.

Mexico's most valuable resource is petroleum. In the 1970s, rich new oil fields were found in eastern Mexico and offshore in the Gulf of Mexico. The government formed a company to produce the oil. Mexico has quickly become a leading oil producer.

Mexico's rivers are generally narrow and shallow. They are not good for transportation, but their water can be used for irrigation. Coastal waters provide many tuna, shrimp, and oysters.

Farming

Less than 15 percent of Mexico's land is suitable for farming. The biggest problem is lack of rainfall in the inland areas. Irrigation is very important.

In the past, farming in Mexico was done on huge estates called **haciendas** (HAH see EN duhz). The poorly paid farmers who did all the work were called **peons**

(PEE ahnz). This way of life lasted for hundreds of years.

Today, many farmers work on *ejidos*. An ***ejido*** (eh HEE doh) is a farm that is owned and worked by a group of farmers. The government gives the land to the group. Each farmer works a part.

Despite progress, small farmers in Mexico still live poorly. They have little land and poor tools. Their main crop is corn, but they also grow beans, sugar cane, citrus fruits, bananas, cotton, and coffee. In the north, some of the land is used to raise cattle.

POLITICAL MAP OF MEXICO

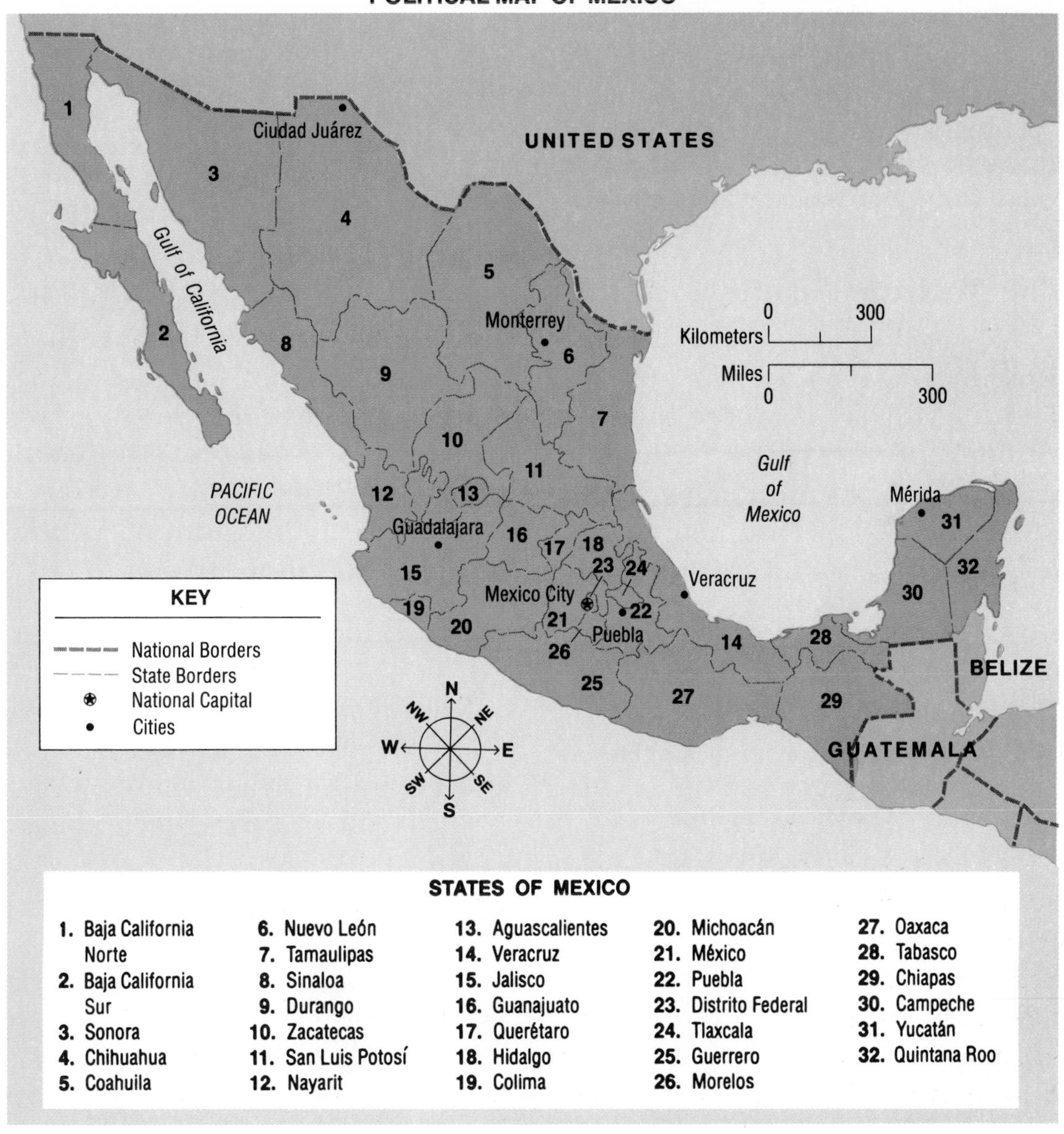

Mexico City, at 19° N latitude, 99° W longitude, may be the world's largest city.

The Mexican People

Mexico is one of the fastest-growing nations in the world. Today, Mexico has more than 75 million people. That number might reach 90 million by 1990. More than 16 million people live in Mexico City and its suburbs.

Of every 100 Mexicans, about 25 are American Indians. About another 8 of every 100 have Spanish or other European backgrounds. The remaining 67 out of 100 are mestizos.

Spanish is Mexico's official language. More than 90 American Indian languages are also spoken in Mexico. Most Mexicans are Roman Catholic.

Mexico City

Mexico's capital, Mexico City, is one of the world's oldest cities. Today, it is Mexico's center of government, business, industry, entertainment, and tourism. Because it is growing so fast, there are problems of overcrowding, traffic congestion, and smog. Mexico City also has a water problem. Since it has no rivers, water has to be pumped in and out over the mountains.

REVIEW

VOCABULARY MASTERY

1. ___ volcanoes are the least dangerous.
   Active Dormant Extinct
2. Today, many Mexican farmers work on ___.
   haciendas *ejidos* peons

READING FOR MAIN IDEAS

3. In what area of Mexico do most Mexicans live? Why? Why do so few live along the coasts?
4. What is Mexico's most valuable natural resource today?
5. What weather problem do many Mexican farmers face?

THINKING SKILLS

Mexico City is in a bowl-shaped valley ringed by mountains. The comfortable highlands climate and the hope for city jobs attract more and more people there. What do you think is likely to happen if this continues? Why?

Lesson 2: The History of Mexico

FIND THE WORDS

archaeology **anthropology** **vaquero** ***peninsulare*** **creole**

American Indians lived in Mexico for thousands of years before the Europeans came. Their cultures were different from those of the Indians who lived in the United States and Canada. The Indians in Mexico built large cities. They had governments that ruled over vast areas.

We know a lot about these people because of archaeology and anthropology. **Archaeology** (AHR kee OL uh jee) is the study of the ruins of past civilizations. Often, these ruins are buried in the ground. **Anthropology** (AN thruh POL uh jee) is the study of the ways different people live.

The first people to develop a civilization in Mexico were the Olmecs. They built cities. They also developed a calendar and carved huge stone heads.

The Maya lived on the Yucatán Peninsula. They were conquered by the Toltecs. Later, the Aztecs ruled in central Mexico. Find these civilizations on the map and time line on page 465. You studied them in Unit 2.

This modern painting shows people in the Aztec city of Tenochtitlán as imagined by Diego Rivera, one of Mexico's most famous artists.

The Spanish Arrive

The Aztecs had the last great American Indian civilization in Mexico. Then, in 1519, the Spanish under Hernán Cortés landed in Mexico. You read about how Cortés conquered the Aztecs.

The Spanish found that Mexico was rich in gold and silver. The Spanish wanted to take this gold and silver to Spain. They forced the Indians to work in the mines. Mexican gold and silver made Spain the richest nation in Europe in the 1500s.

The Indians were also needed to do farming and ranching. The Spanish taught some of the Indians to ride horses and round up cattle. These Indians were called **vaqueros** (vah KAIR ohz). They were the first cowboys.

The wealthy Spanish nobles in New Spain were called ***peninsulares*** (peh NEEN soo LAR es). They were born in Spain, which is on a peninsula. Only the *peninsulares* could serve as officials of the colony.

Just below the *peninsulares* in social position were the **creoles** (KREE OHLZ). They were Spanish people who were born in New Spain. Below the creoles in the social order were the mestizos, the people of mixed Spanish and Indian ancestry. Their rights and opportunities were very limited. At the bottom of the social order were the slave laborers, the largest group of all. American Indians and Blacks brought over from Africa were slaves.

The Fight for Independence

The Spanish kept a tight grip on Mexico for more than 250 years. By 1800, Mexico was like a volcano ready to erupt.

Miguel Hidalgo (mee GEHL ee DAHL goh) was the first to lead an armed uprising. He was a creole and was parish priest of the village of Dolores. On September 16, 1810, he made a famous speech called the "Cry of Dolores." Hidalgo called for freedom, equality, and the return of the land to the Indians. As a result of his speech, September 16 is celebrated as Mexico's Independence Day.

Hidalgo and his Indian followers fought bravely, but he was captured in 1811 and executed. The struggle for independence continued. Finally, in 1821, Spain gave up the fight. Mexico became independent.

Mexico's Early Struggle

The new nation faced many problems. It was poor, had few roads, and could not decide on the best form of government. Politicians fought each other for power. The landlords and the army kept their special privileges.

WHERE WE ARE IN TIME AND PLACE

EARLY INDIAN PEOPLES OF MEXICO

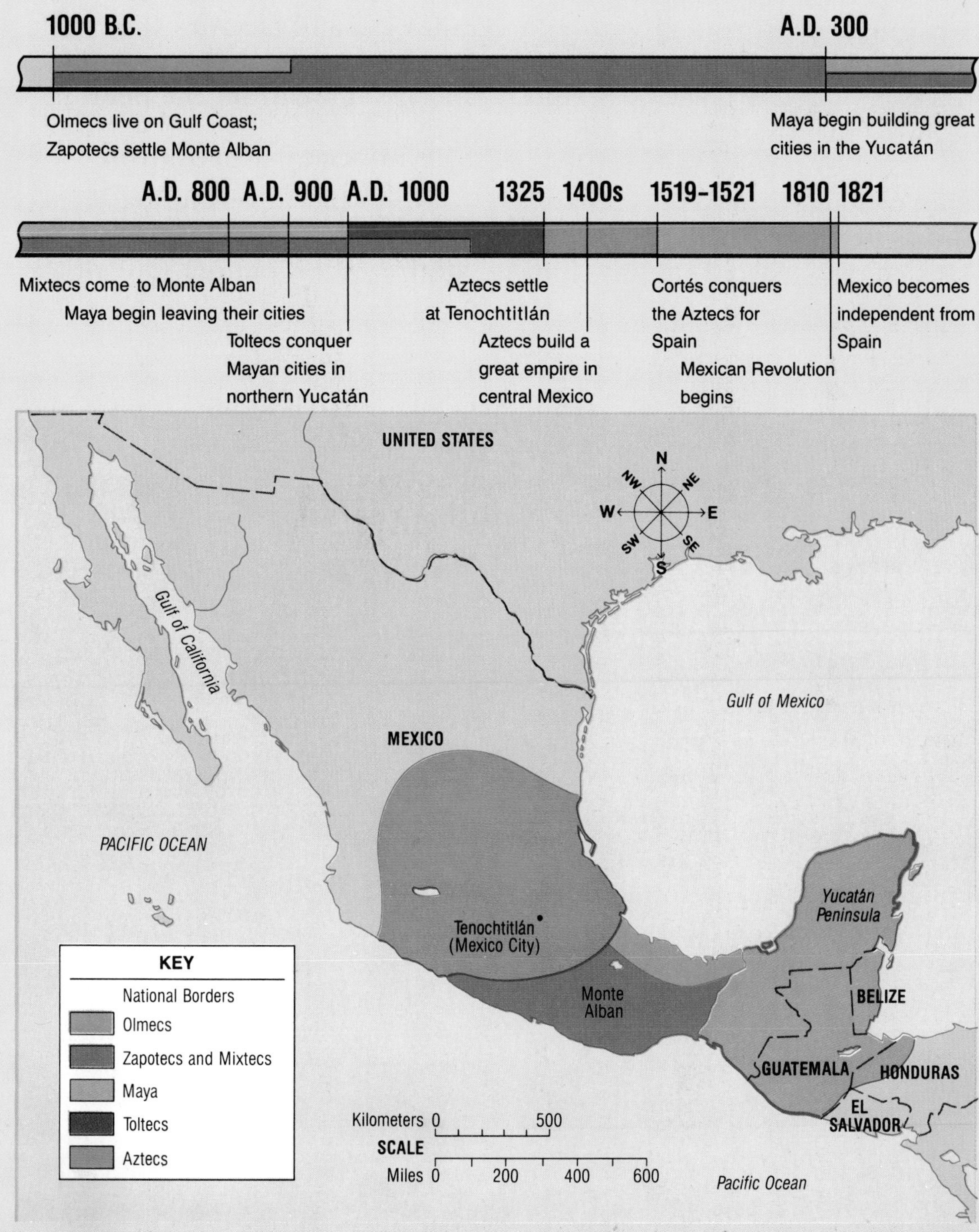

The new nation was much larger than Mexico is today. It included Texas, California, and all of the American Southwest. Soon there was trouble with the American settlers in Texas. In 1835, the Texans revolted and declared their independence from Mexico. From 1846 to 1848, Mexico fought the United States and suffered a disastrous defeat. Mexico was forced to give up most of its northern land.

The Mexican people were tired of wars and dictatorships. A period of reforms began. In 1858, Benito Juárez (bey NEE toh HWAH rehz) became Mexico's first Indian president. He wanted to make Mexico a true democracy. At this time, poor Indians and mestizos were still not much better off than they had been under Spanish rule. Juárez wanted to change this. However, his reforms were opposed by the rich.

Juárez also had a problem with some European nations. Mexico owed much money to Spain, Great Britain, and France. The Emperor of France made a European prince the Emperor of Mexico.

Once more the Mexicans took up arms. With American support, they won their country back. Juárez continued as president until his death in 1872.

After Juárez, a dictator took over Mexico once again. His name was Porfirio Díaz (por FIR ree oh DEE ahs). Díaz, a mestizo, turned Mexico into a modern nation. The economy improved. Roads, railroads, and factories were built. However, Díaz took away rights and freedoms from the poor.

The Mexican Revolution

In 1910, a revolution broke out. The poor fought the rich for control of the nation. One of the most popular revolutionary heroes was Pancho Villa (VEE yah). He led an army of peasants on horseback in northern Mexico and won many victories. Another hero was Emiliano Zapata (eh meel YAH noh sah PAH tah). His battle cry was "land and liberty!"

The constitution of 1917, which came out of the revolution, gave Mexico a strong democratic government. In the 1920s and 1930s, the large land holdings of the wealthy were broken up. Millions of landless people were given their own land to farm.

Mexico Today

Today, Mexico is a republic. Its official name is the United Mexican States. Mexico is divided into 31 states and a federal district in which the capital, Mexico City, is located. Like the United States, Mexico has a president and a congress. The president serves a 6-year term.

Large deposits of petroleum were discovered in Mexico in the 1970s. Today, refining petroleum and making petrochemicals are major industries in Mexico.

As neighbor nations, Mexico and the United States work together in many ways. The two nations trade with one another. The United States buys cattle and other farm products from Mexico. It also buys minerals such as natural gas and petroleum. Mexico buys machinery from the United States. Many Americans visit Mexico. Good relations are important to both nations.

REVIEW

VOCABULARY MASTERY

1. ___ is the study of the ruins of past civilizations.
   Anthropology   Archaeology   Architecture
2. ___ is the study of how different people live.
   Archaeology   History   Anthropology
3. ___ were the first cowboys.
   Creoles   Viceroys   *Vaqueros*

READING FOR MAIN IDEAS

4. Name four groups of people who developed civilizations in Mexico before the Spanish came.
5. What four groups made up the social order of New Spain? What rights did each group have?
6. Name two things Miguel Hidalgo did.
7. What was the Mexican revolution?

MAP AND TIME LINE SKILLS

List the civilizations on the time line in order, from oldest to most recent. Using directions and geographic terms, tell where each group lived.

RESEARCH AND WRITING SKILLS

Compare Benito Juárez with Porfirio Díaz. Which leader do you think was better for Mexico? Why? Use reference books.

Lesson 3: Central America

FIND THE WORDS

finca **subsistence farming** **barter**

Central America is a narrow bridge of land between Mexico and South America. On the map on page 472, you can see how Central America extends from northwest to southeast. Central America has two coastlines. There is little land between the Atlantic and Pacific oceans.

In a market square in Guatemala, local women display the pottery they have made.

It is more than 1,770 kilometers (1,100 miles) from one end of Central America to the other. At its widest point, this land is 483 kilometers (300 miles) across. At its narrowest point, it is only 64 kilometers (40 miles) across. Altogether, Central America is smaller than California.

There are seven small nations in Central America. They are Guatemala, Belize, Honduras, El Salvador, Nicaragua, Costa Rica, and Panama.

The Land and Climate

The land of Central America is much like southern Mexico. The climate is also similar.

The land along both coasts is lowland. It is usually wet and hot. The Pacific Coast has a tropical grasslands climate. The coast along the Caribbean Sea is tropical rain forest. Much of this land is swamp.

Inland, there are many high mountains. Many of them are active volcanoes. Some are over 3,220 meters (2 miles) high. The highlands are generally cooler and drier than the coasts. Most people in Central America live near the Pacific Coast or in highland valleys. Like Mexico, Central America has a central plateau.

Much of Central America sits on a large fault line, or crack in Earth's crust. There are many earthquakes in the region. Some have caused great damage.

Central America is mostly an agricultural area. The volcanic ash has made much of the soil good for growing certain crops. The Pacific Coast and highland areas are ideal for growing coffee. Bananas are grown in the rain forests of the Caribbean lowlands.

History

American Indians lived in much of Central America long before the Spanish discovered this region. The Mayan civilization extended into what is now Belize, Guatemala, and Honduras.

In 1513, a Spanish explorer named Vasco de Balboa landed in what is now Panama. From the Indians, he heard tales of a great sea. Balboa and his men set off through the jungle to find this sea. It took them more than 2 weeks to cross the Isthmus of Panama. Finally, from a mountaintop, Balboa saw the Pacific. When he reached the beach, he planted the Spanish flag.

At first, few Spanish settlers came to Central America. They went instead to Mexico or Peru because of the silver mines there. Eventually, the Spanish did have colonies in Central America.

In 1821, five nations in Central America became independent from Spain. These nations were Guatemala, Honduras, El Salvador, Nicaragua, and Costa Rica. At first, they became part of Mexico. Then, in 1823, they broke away from Mexico. Together, they formed a new nation, the United Provinces of Central America. In 1838, the United Provinces broke apart into five separate nations. Panama, the sixth Spanish-speaking nation in Central America, was part of the new Republic of Colombia. It became an independent nation in 1903.

The Panama Canal

For many years, people had dreamed of building a canal across Central America. This canal would connect the Atlantic and Pacific oceans.

In 1881, the French began digging a canal across the Isthmus of Panama. They found that the work was difficult, dangerous, and expensive. In 1887, they gave up.

President Theodore Roosevelt wanted the United States to build the canal. At that time, Panama was part of Colombia. The Colombian government would not allow Roosevelt to build the canal. So Roosevelt and the Americans encouraged the Panamanians to revolt against Colombia. Panama formed its own government in

The Panama Canal is an artificial waterway built across the narrowest part of Central America. The canal is near 9° N latitude, 80° W longitude.

1903. It gave the United States a strip of land 16 kilometers (10 miles) wide across the 40-mile Isthmus of Panama.

The canal was not finished until 1915. An army of workers had to hack through the jungle and move more than 200 million cubic meters (260 cubic yards) of earth. Doctors had to find ways to treat tropical diseases.

The United States paid Panama 10 million dollars for the strip of land known as the Canal Zone. The United States governed the Canal Zone. It also paid a yearly fee to operate the canal.

Many Panamanians felt that the United States had too much power in their nation. In 1978, the United States signed a historic treaty with Panama. It agreed to give the Canal Zone back to Panama in 1999.

Society

Central America is mainly a rural region. There are few large cities. There is little industry. Most of the people are farmers.

Coffee, bananas, cacao, and sugar cane are Central America's four main cash crops. They are grown for sale to other nations.

The major cash crops are grown on large plantations. Coffee plantations are known as *fincas*. A ***finca*** (FEEN kah) is a large estate that contains its own village. The estate may have a large house for the owner or manager. Workers usually live in small houses in the village. Often, the workers pick coffee beans by hand. Workers may be paid an hourly wage, or they may be paid according to how much coffee they pick.

Many farmers do not work on plantations. Instead, they have small patches of their own land. Usually, they grow just enough food to feed their own families. They may have a little food left over to sell at the local market. This kind of farming is called **subsistence farming.** *Subsist* means "to live on the least amount possible." Subsistence farmers often have poor land.

Subsistence farmers often have little money. They rely on barter. When people **barter,** they trade for things they need instead of paying cash.

In much of Central America, a few wealthy landowners have owned most of the land. This means that many poor farmers have little or no land. Poverty is a major problem in the region.

Politics

At times, most Central American nations have been ruled by dictators. Often, these dictators care little about the people. The people often have few rights.

In 1979, the Nicaraguans overthrew a harsh dictator. However, the new government has followed some Communist practices. Some Nicaraguans claim that they have little freedom. Political violence is continuing in Nicaragua.

In El Salvador, rebels have been fighting a civil war against the government. However, the elected leader of El Salvador has begun land reforms. If reform can be achieved, peace may come.

In several other nations in Central America, the army has the power to choose the president. Costa Rica, however, is different. It is a representative democracy.

One of Guatemala's major cash crops is coffee. Workers on the *fincas,* or coffee plantations, often pick the coffee beans by hand.

CENTRAL AMERICA AND THE CARIBBEAN

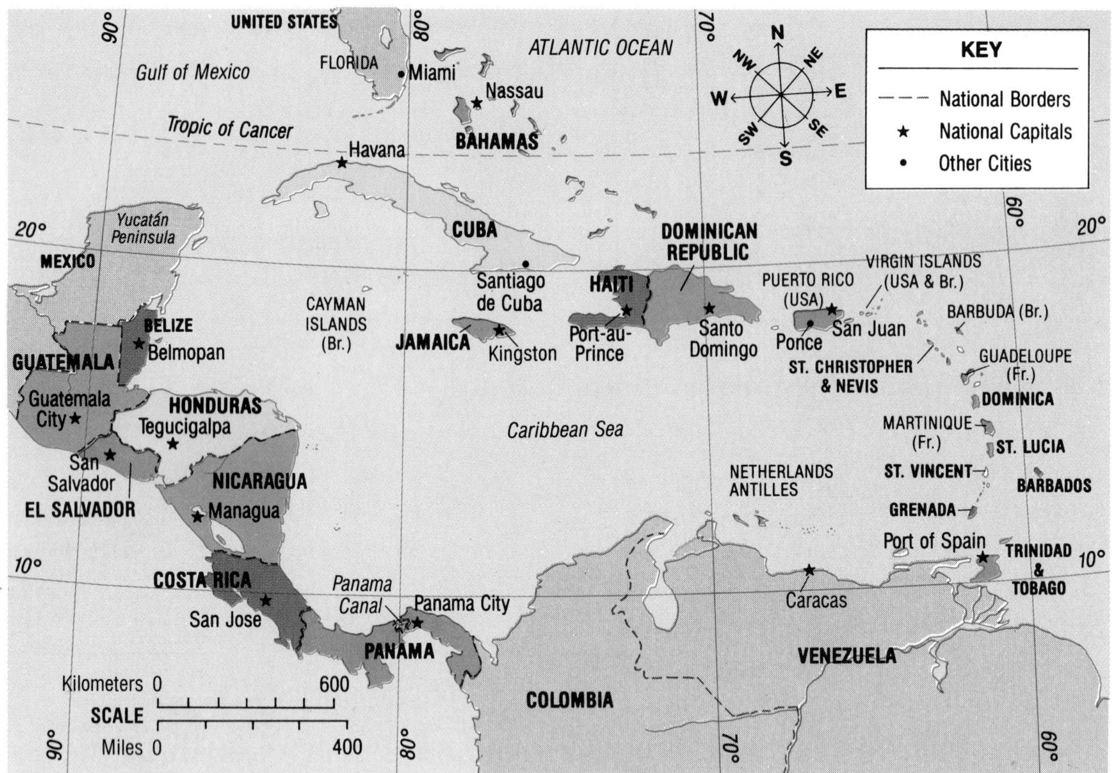

It has no army. The government of Costa Rica can therefore spend more money on education. Costa Ricans have the highest standard of living in Central America. They settle their problems peacefully.

REVIEW

VOCABULARY MASTERY

1. Small farmers in Central America often live by ___ farming.
   truck dairy subsistence
2. Coffee is grown on plantations called ___ .
   haciendas *fincas* *ejidos*

READING FOR MAIN IDEAS

3. Name the seven nations of Central America.
4. Describe the land and climate of Central America.
5. What land did Balboa cross to reach the Pacific Ocean?
6. What are Central America's main cash crops?
7. Why have most farmers in Central America usually had little land?

THINKING SKILLS

Why do you think President Roosevelt wanted the United States to build and control the Panama Canal? Do you think the canal is as important today as it was when it was opened? Why or why not?

CHAPTER REVIEW

VOCABULARY MASTERY

Use the words below to complete the chapter summary. Use each only once.

Active volcanoes	Extinct volcanoes
Dormant volcanoes	*fincas*
	haciendas
ejidos	peons

Some of the mountains of Mexico and Central America are volcanoes. __1__ may still erupt. __2__ have not erupted for a long time. __3__ no longer erupt at all. Volcanic ash has made the soil of some regions very rich.

In the past, farming in Mexico was done by poor __4__ on huge __5__. Today, many farmers own and work on __6__. In Central America, coffee is grown on large __7__.

READING FOR MAIN IDEAS

1. List Mexico's mineral resources.
2. What is the difference between haciendas and *ejidos*?
3. Who was Father Miguel Hidalgo? What did he do?
4. What parts of the United States were originally part of Mexico?
5. Who was Benito Juárez? What did he do for Mexico?
6. Who was Porfirio Díaz? How did he help Mexico? How did he hurt Mexico?
7. In what part of Central America do most people live?
8. Why are there many earthquakes in Central America?
9. How do volcanoes help Central American agriculture?
10. What did the treaty signed by the United States and Panama in 1978 say?

SKILLS APPLICATION

MAP AND TIME LINE SKILLS

Look at the map and time line on page 465.

11. Into what present-day nations did the Maya empire extend?
12. Which ancient people lived on the Gulf Coast? What color represents these people on the time line and map?
13. Was the Aztec empire north or south of the Zapotec empire? Did the Aztecs live before or after the Zapotecs?
14. What people conquered the Maya in the Yucatán?

RESEARCH AND WRITING SKILLS

Mexico has two major volcanoes: Particutín and Popocatepetl. Look in encyclopedias and almanacs to answer questions 15–20. Look under the following: "Mexico," "volcanoes," "Particutín," and "Popocatepetl."

15. When did Particutín start erupting?
16. Is it dormant now? If so, when did it stop erupting?
17. How did Particutín get its name?
18. When was Popocatepetl's last major eruption?
19. How tall is the volcano now?
20. What is the only mountain in North America taller than Popocatepetl?

SEQUENCING SKILLS

Rewrite the events below in proper sequence. Add the year for each.

a. The Mexican Revolution began.
b. Hidalgo led an uprising.
c. Mexico's constitution provided a strong national government.
d. Juárez became President.
e. Texas declared independence.

UNIT REVIEW

VOCABULARY MASTERY

Choose one of the lists of words below. Then write a paragraph or page using all the words from that list. You may use the words in the singular or plural. On a separate page, write the words and define them.

dominion	creole
habitant	hacienda
intendant	*peninsulare*
portage	peon
seigneur	*vaquero*
voyageur	viceroy

READING FOR MAIN IDEAS

1. What three oceans form natural boundaries for Canada?
2. Name the five geographic regions of Canada.
3. Why are Canada's forests an important resource?
4. What was the most important business in New France?
5. Why did the French and British fight a war in Canada? What was the result of that war?
6. What was the Quebec Act?
7. Where are Mexico's oil fields located? When were they found?
8. What are some of the problems that Mexico City faces?
9. In what year did Mexico become independent?
10. What were some of the problems that the new nation of Mexico faced?
11. Who were Pancho Villa and Emiliano Zapata?
12. What are Central America's four cash crops?
13. What are two causes of political problems in Central America?
14. What is the Panama Canal? Why is it so important?
15. What is subsistence farming?

THINKING SKILLS

16. By law, the king of France owned all the land in New France. Do you think this law was fair to the North American Indians? Do you think this law was fair to the habitants? Explain your answers.
17. What do you think are the benefits of a nation's being bilingual? What do you think are the problems?
18. Why do you think Mexico's farmers remain poor despite Mexico's national progress?
19. Explain why good relations between the United States and Mexico are so important.
20. In 1838, the United Provinces of Central America broke apart into five separate nations. Why do you think this happened?
21. Do you think the government of Panama was wise to let the United States dig the Panama Canal? Give reasons for your answer.

USE YOUR MAPS AND TIME LINES (pages 453 and 465)

22. What eastern provinces joined Canada after 1871?
23. Which Mexican Indians settled farthest south?
24. Which Indian settlement lasted the longest?
25. About how long did the Aztec empire last?
26. Where did the Olmecs live in relation to the Aztecs, Zapotecs, and Maya?

SKILL DEVELOPMENT

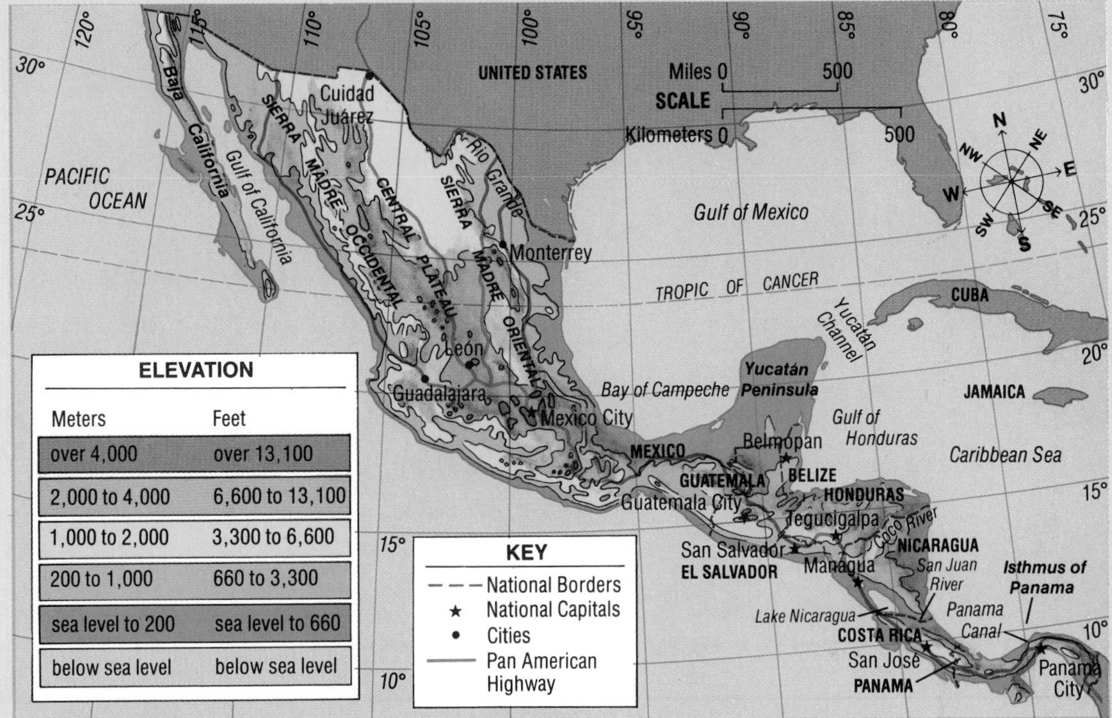

MAP SKILLS

Shown above is a physical map of Mexico and Central America. A *physical map* shows the height or shape of land. The elevation chart gives the color codes for the different heights.

1. How is a physical map different from a climate map?
2. What political information does this map include?
3. Most of the coastal areas shown are lowlands. About how many feet high are the lowlands?
4. What peninsula is all lowlands?
5. A mile is 5,280 feet. What is the color code for land that is a mile high and more?
6. List the cities along the Pan American Highway.
7. About how many miles is it from Ciudad Juárez to León along the highway?
8. Compare this map with the physical map of Earth on pages 476–477. Is the scale the same for both? Is Mexico the same size in both? Explain.
9. What is the color code for mountains? Where are most of them?
10. Near what city does the Rio Grande enter the United States?
11. What city is closest to 15° north latitude, 90° west longitude?
12. Give the latitude and longitude of Mexico City.

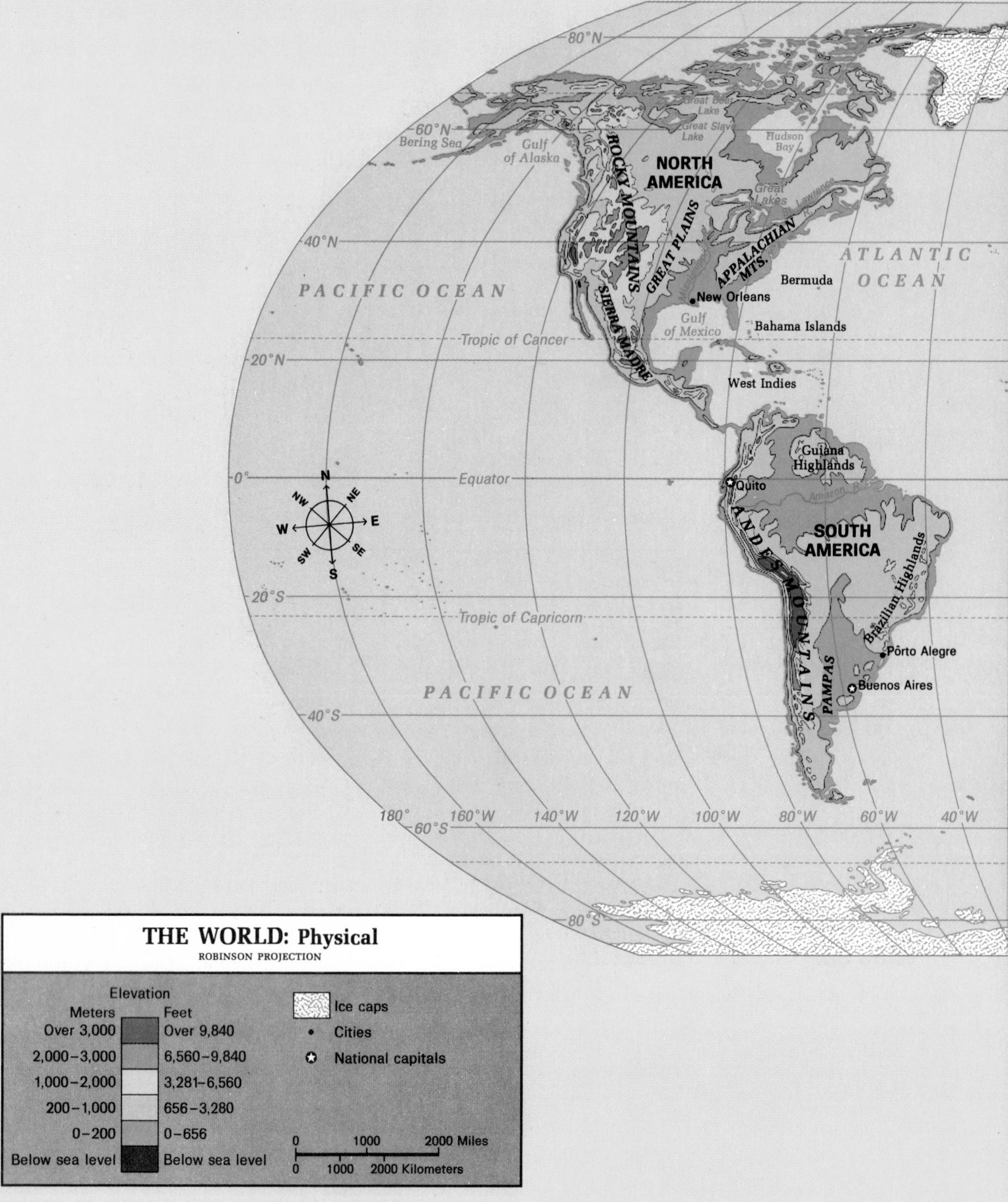
THE WORLD: Physical
ROBINSON PROJECTION
Elevation
Meters
Feet
Over 3,000
Over 9,840
2,000–3,000
6,560–9,840
1,000–2,000
3,281–6,560
200–1,000
656–3,280
0–200
0–656
Below sea level
Below sea level
Ice caps
Cities
National capitals
0 1000 2000 Miles
0 1000 2000 Kilometers
NORTH AMERICA
SOUTH AMERICA
PACIFIC OCEAN
ATLANTIC OCEAN
PACIFIC OCEAN
ROCKY MOUNTAINS
SIERRA MADRE
GREAT PLAINS
APPALACHIAN MTS.
ANDES MOUNTAINS
PAMPAS
Brazilian Highlands
Guiana Highlands
Great Bear Lake
Great Slave Lake
Hudson Bay
Great Lakes
Bering Sea
Gulf of Alaska
Gulf of Mexico
New Orleans
Bermuda
Bahama Islands
West Indies
Quito
Pôrto Alegre
Buenos Aires
Tropic of Cancer
Equator
Tropic of Capricorn
80°N
60°N
40°N
20°N
0°
20°S
40°S
60°S
80°S
180°
160°W
140°W
120°W
100°W
80°W
60°W
40°W
N
NE
E
SE
S
SW
W
NW

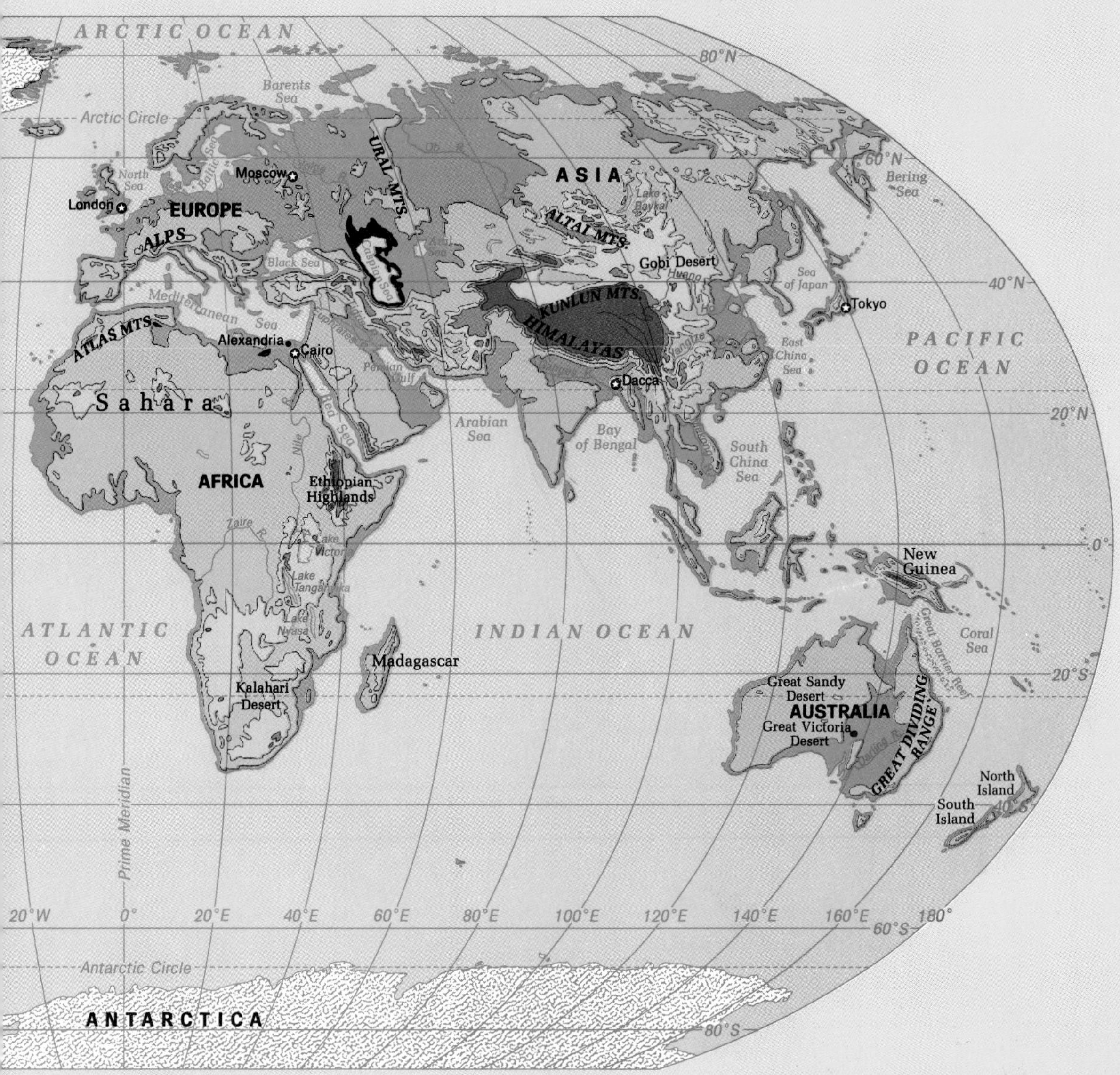
ARCTIC OCEAN
80°N
Barents Sea
Arctic Circle
URAL MTS.
60°N
Bering Sea
North Sea
Baltic Sea
Moscow
ASIA
London
EUROPE
Lake Baykal
ALTAI MTS.
ALPS
Caspian Sea
Aral Sea
Black Sea
Gobi Desert
Huang
Sea of Japan
40°N
Mediterranean Sea
KUNLUN MTS.
Tokyo
ATLAS MTS.
HIMALAYAS
Euphrates
Tigris
PACIFIC OCEAN
Alexandria
Cairo
Persian Gulf
Yangtze
East China Sea
Ganges
Dacca
Sahara
20°N
Red Sea
Arabian Sea
Bay of Bengal
South China Sea
Nile
AFRICA
Ethiopian Highlands
Zaire R.
Lake Victoria
0°
New Guinea
Lake Tanganyika
Lake Nyasa
ATLANTIC OCEAN
INDIAN OCEAN
Great Barrier Reef
Coral Sea
Madagascar
20°S
Great Sandy Desert
Kalahari Desert
AUSTRALIA
Great Victoria Desert
GREAT DIVIDING RANGE
Darling R.
North Island
South Island
Prime Meridian
20°W
0°
20°E
40°E
60°E
80°E
100°E
120°E
140°E
160°E
180°
60°S
Antarctic Circle
ANTARCTICA
80°S

THE WORLD: Political

ROBINSON PROJECTION

National boundaries

Disputed or undefined boundaries

0 1000 2000 3000 Miles

0 1000 2000 3000 Kilometers

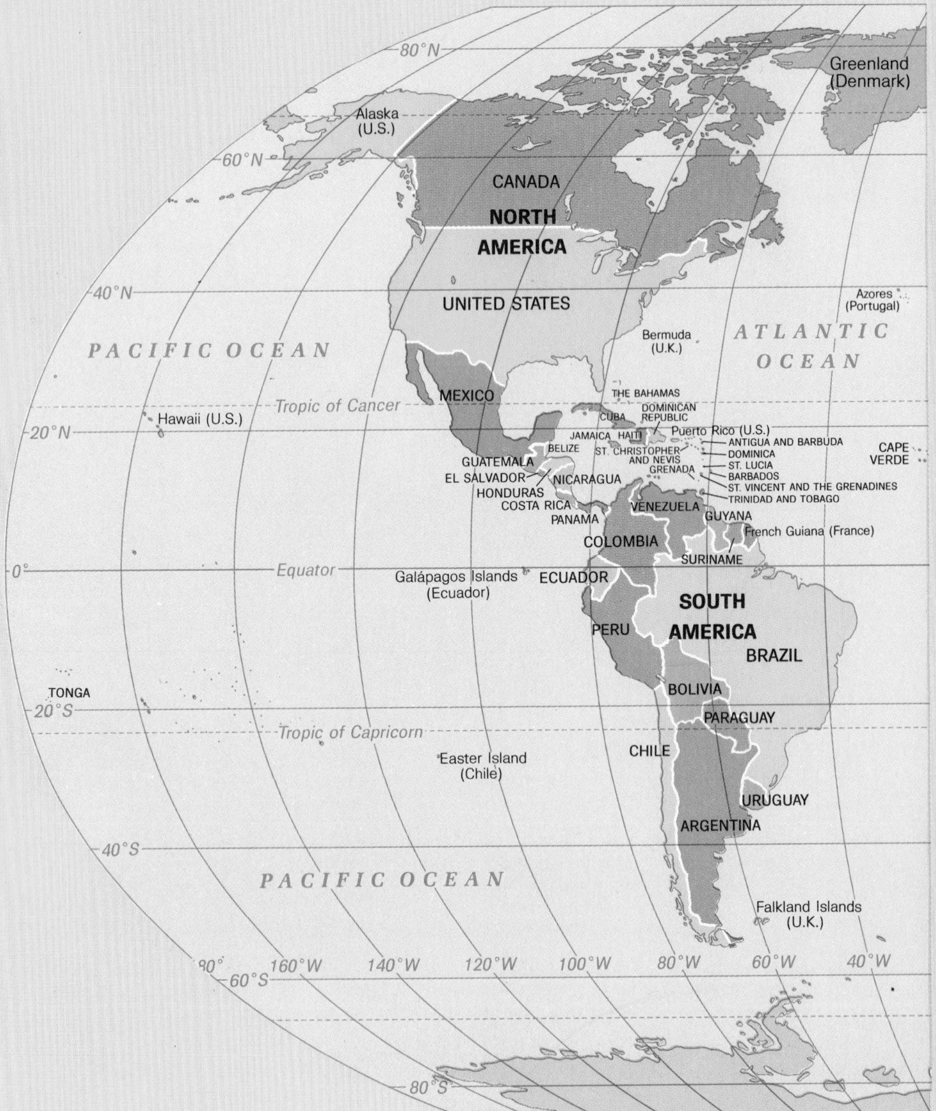

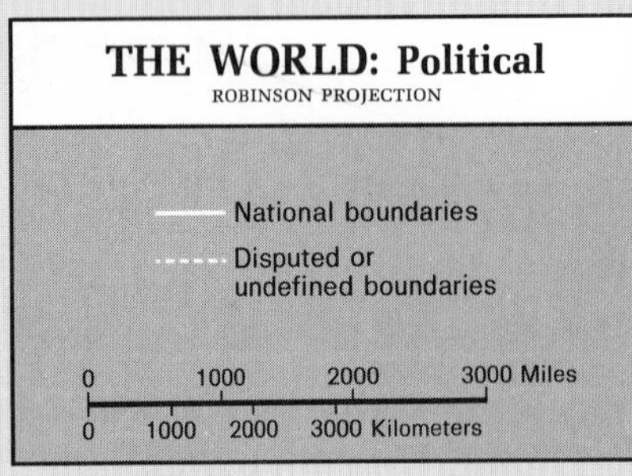

Alb. — Albania
And. — Andorra
Aust. — Austria
Bel. — Belgium
Czech. — Czechoslovakia
E. Ger. — E. Germany
Hung. — Hungary
Isr. — Israel
Leb. — Lebanon
Liech. — Liechtenstein
Lux. — Luxembourg
Mon. — Monaco
Neth. — Netherlands
P.D.R. of Yemen — People's Democratic Republic of Yemen
Switz. — Switzerland
W. Ger. — West Germany
Yugo. — Yugoslavia

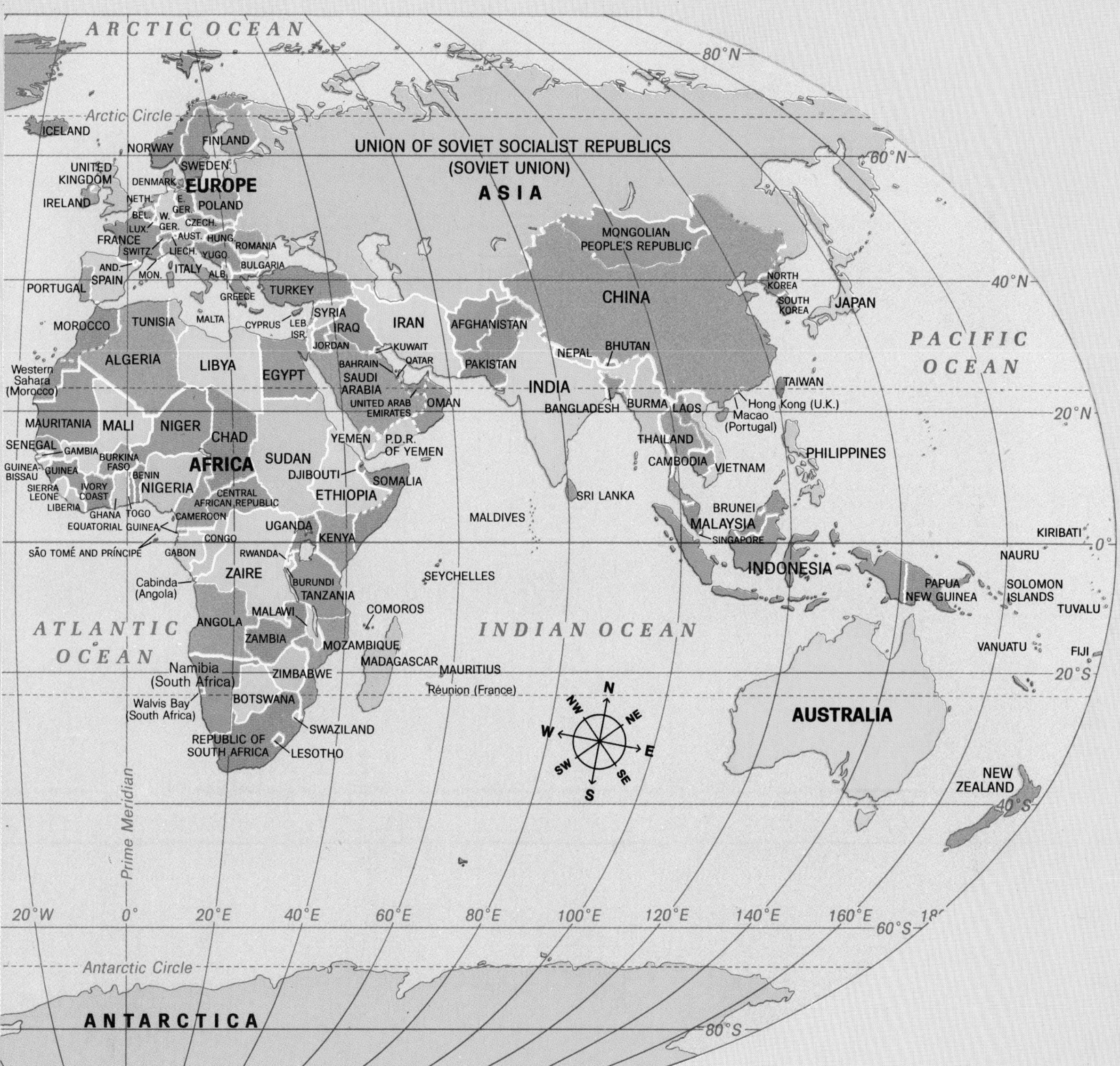
ARCTIC OCEAN
80°N
Arctic Circle
ICELAND
NORWAY
FINLAND
UNITED KINGDOM
SWEDEN
DENMARK
EUROPE
IRELAND
NETH.
E. GER.
POLAND
BEL.
W. GER.
CZECH.
LUX.
FRANCE
AUST.
HUNG.
ROMANIA
SWITZ.
LIECH.
YUGO.
AND.
MON.
ITALY
ALB.
BULGARIA
SPAIN
PORTUGAL
GREECE
TURKEY
MALTA
CYPRUS
LEB.
ISR.
SYRIA
IRAQ
IRAN
AFGHANISTAN
MOROCCO
TUNISIA
JORDAN
KUWAIT
BAHRAIN
QATAR
PAKISTAN
ALGERIA
LIBYA
EGYPT
SAUDI ARABIA
Western Sahara (Morocco)
UNITED ARAB EMIRATES
OMAN
MAURITANIA
MALI
NIGER
CHAD
YEMEN
P.D.R. OF YEMEN
SENEGAL
GAMBIA
BURKINA FASO
GUINEA-BISSAU
GUINEA
BENIN
AFRICA
SUDAN
DJIBOUTI
SOMALIA
SIERRA LEONE
IVORY COAST
NIGERIA
CENTRAL AFRICAN REPUBLIC
ETHIOPIA
LIBERIA
GHANA
TOGO
CAMEROON
EQUATORIAL GUINEA
UGANDA
KENYA
CONGO
SÃO TOMÉ AND PRÍNCIPE
GABON
RWANDA
ZAIRE
BURUNDI
TANZANIA
Cabinda (Angola)
MALAWI
COMOROS
ANGOLA
ZAMBIA
ATLANTIC OCEAN
MOZAMBIQUE
MADAGASCAR
MAURITIUS
Namibia (South Africa)
ZIMBABWE
Walvis Bay (South Africa)
BOTSWANA
Réunion (France)
SWAZILAND
REPUBLIC OF SOUTH AFRICA
LESOTHO
UNION OF SOVIET SOCIALIST REPUBLICS (SOVIET UNION)
ASIA
60°N
MONGOLIAN PEOPLE'S REPUBLIC
NORTH KOREA
SOUTH KOREA
JAPAN
CHINA
40°N
NEPAL
BHUTAN
PACIFIC OCEAN
INDIA
TAIWAN
BANGLADESH
BURMA
LAOS
Hong Kong (U.K.)
Macao (Portugal)
20°N
THAILAND
PHILIPPINES
CAMBODIA
VIETNAM
SRI LANKA
BRUNEI
MALDIVES
MALAYSIA
SINGAPORE
KIRIBATI
0°
NAURU
INDONESIA
SEYCHELLES
PAPUA NEW GUINEA
SOLOMON ISLANDS
TUVALU
INDIAN OCEAN
VANUATU
FIJI
20°S
N
NW
NE
W
E
SW
SE
S
AUSTRALIA
NEW ZEALAND
40°S
Prime Meridian
20°W
0°
20°E
40°E
60°E
80°E
100°E
120°E
140°E
160°E
60°S
Antarctic Circle
ANTARCTICA
80°S

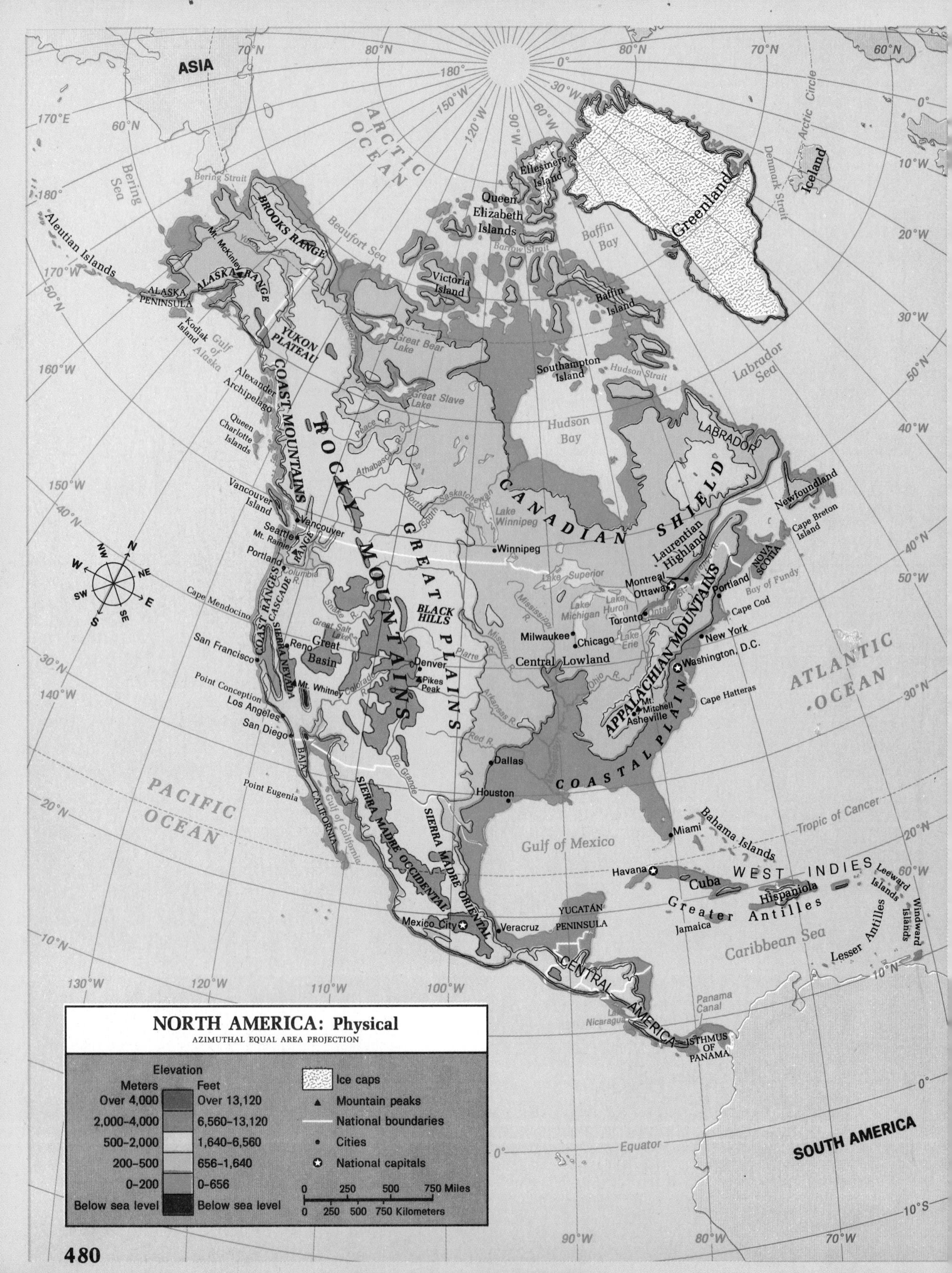

NORTH AMERICA: Physical
AZIMUTHAL EQUAL AREA PROJECTION
Elevation
Meters
Feet
Over 4,000
Over 13,120
2,000-4,000
6,560-13,120
500-2,000
1,640-6,560
200-500
656-1,640
0-200
0-656
Below sea level
Below sea level
Ice caps
Mountain peaks
National boundaries
Cities
National capitals
0 250 500 750 Miles
0 250 500 750 Kilometers
ASIA
ARCTIC OCEAN
Bering Sea
Bering Strait
Aleutian Islands
ALASKA PENINSULA
Kodiak Island
Gulf of Alaska
BROOKS RANGE
Mt. McKinley
ALASKA RANGE
Yukon
YUKON PLATEAU
Beaufort Sea
Mackenzie
Great Bear Lake
Great Slave Lake
Victoria Island
Queen Elizabeth Islands
Ellesmere Island
Barrow Strait
Baffin Bay
Baffin Island
Greenland
Iceland
Denmark Strait
Arctic Circle
Southampton Island
Hudson Strait
Hudson Bay
Labrador Sea
LABRADOR
Newfoundland
Cape Breton Island
NOVA SCOTIA
Bay of Fundy
CANADIAN SHIELD
Laurentian Highland
Lake Winnipeg
Winnipeg
Alexander Archipelago
Queen Charlotte Islands
COAST MOUNTAINS
ROCKY MOUNTAINS
Peace R.
Athabasca R.
North Saskatchewan
South Saskatchewan
Vancouver Island
Vancouver
Seattle
Mt. Rainier
CASCADE RANGE
Portland
Columbia R.
Snake R.
Cape Mendocino
COAST RANGES
SIERRA NEVADA
Reno
Great Salt Lake
Great Basin
San Francisco
Point Conception
Los Angeles
San Diego
Mt. Whitney
Colorado
Denver
Pikes Peak
GREAT PLAINS
BLACK HILLS
Missouri R.
Platte R.
Arkansas R.
Red R.
Rio Grande
Dallas
Houston
Lake Superior
Lake Michigan
Lake Huron
Lake Ontario
Lake Erie
Mississippi R.
Ohio R.
Milwaukee
Chicago
Toronto
Montreal
Ottawa
St. Lawrence R.
Portland
Cape Cod
New York
Washington, D.C.
Central Lowland
APPALACHIAN MOUNTAINS
Mt. Mitchell
Asheville
Cape Hatteras
COASTAL PLAIN
ATLANTIC OCEAN
PACIFIC OCEAN
Point Eugenia
BAJA CALIFORNIA
Gulf of California
SIERRA MADRE OCCIDENTAL
SIERRA MADRE ORIENTAL
Mexico City
Veracruz
YUCATÁN PENINSULA
Gulf of Mexico
Miami
Bahama Islands
Tropic of Cancer
Havana
Cuba
WEST INDIES
Hispaniola
Greater Antilles
Jamaica
Leeward Islands
Windward Islands
Lesser Antilles
Caribbean Sea
CENTRAL AMERICA
Lake Nicaragua
Panama Canal
ISTHMUS OF PANAMA
SOUTH AMERICA
Equator
N
NE
E
SE
S
SW
W
NW

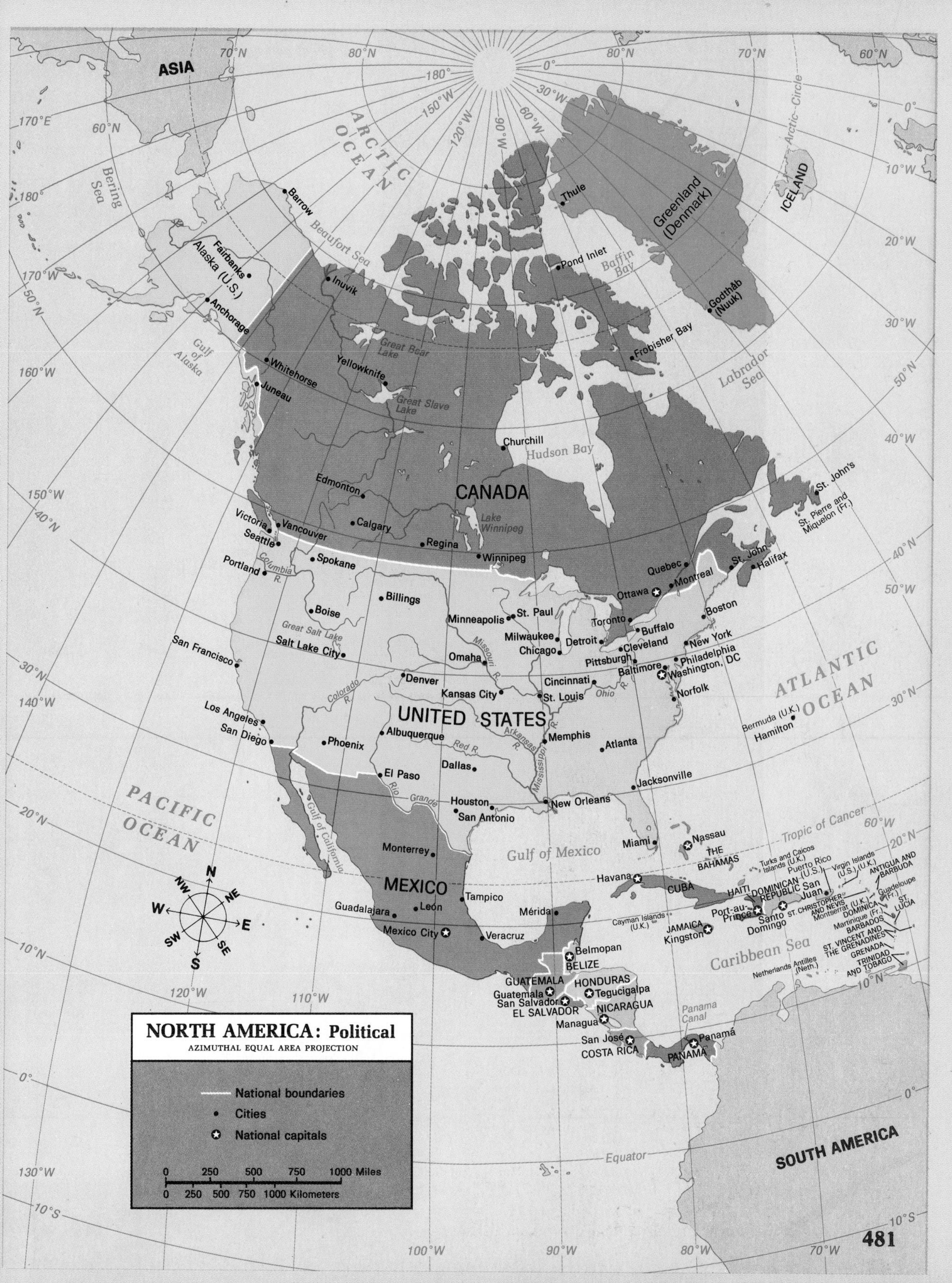

NORTH AMERICA: Political
AZIMUTHAL EQUAL AREA PROJECTION
National boundaries
Cities
National capitals
0 250 500 750 1000 Miles
0 250 500 750 1000 Kilometers
ASIA
ARCTIC OCEAN
Bering Sea
Beaufort Sea
Baffin Bay
Greenland (Denmark)
ICELAND
Arctic Circle
Labrador Sea
Hudson Bay
CANADA
UNITED STATES
MEXICO
Alaska (U.S.)
Gulf of Alaska
Great Bear Lake
Great Slave Lake
Lake Winnipeg
Great Salt Lake
Gulf of California
Gulf of Mexico
Tropic of Cancer
PACIFIC OCEAN
ATLANTIC OCEAN
Caribbean Sea
Equator
SOUTH AMERICA
Barrow
Fairbanks
Anchorage
Inuvik
Whitehorse
Juneau
Yellowknife
Thule
Pond Inlet
Godthåb (Nuuk)
Frobisher Bay
Churchill
Edmonton
Calgary
Regina
Winnipeg
Victoria
Vancouver
Seattle
Portland
Spokane
Columbia R.
St. John's
St. Pierre and Miquelon (Fr.)
Quebec
Montreal
Ottawa
St. John
Halifax
Toronto
Buffalo
Boston
New York
Philadelphia
Baltimore
Washington, DC
Pittsburgh
Cleveland
Detroit
Milwaukee
Chicago
Minneapolis
St. Paul
Billings
Boise
Salt Lake City
San Francisco
Omaha
Missouri R.
Denver
Kansas City
St. Louis
Cincinnati
Ohio R.
Norfolk
Colorado R.
Los Angeles
San Diego
Phoenix
Albuquerque
Red R.
Arkansas R.
Mississippi R.
Memphis
Atlanta
El Paso
Dallas
Rio Grande
Houston
San Antonio
New Orleans
Jacksonville
Miami
Bermuda (U.K.)
Hamilton
Nassau
THE BAHAMAS
Turks and Caicos Islands (U.K.)
Puerto Rico (U.S.)
Virgin Islands (U.S.) (U.K.)
ANTIGUA AND BARBUDA
Guadeloupe (Fr.)
ST. CHRISTOPHER AND NEVIS
Montserrat (U.K.)
DOMINICA
Martinique (Fr.)
ST. LUCIA
BARBADOS
ST. VINCENT AND THE GRENADINES
GRENADA
TRINIDAD AND TOBAGO
Netherlands Antilles (Neth.)
Havana
CUBA
HAITI
DOMINICAN REPUBLIC
San Juan
Port-au-Prince
Santo Domingo
Cayman Islands (U.K.)
JAMAICA
Kingston
Monterrey
Tampico
Guadalajara
León
Mérida
Mexico City
Veracruz
Belmopan
BELIZE
GUATEMALA
Guatemala
HONDURAS
Tegucigalpa
San Salvador
EL SALVADOR
NICARAGUA
Managua
San José
COSTA RICA
Panama Canal
Panamá
PANAMA
N
S
E
W
NE
NW
SE
SW

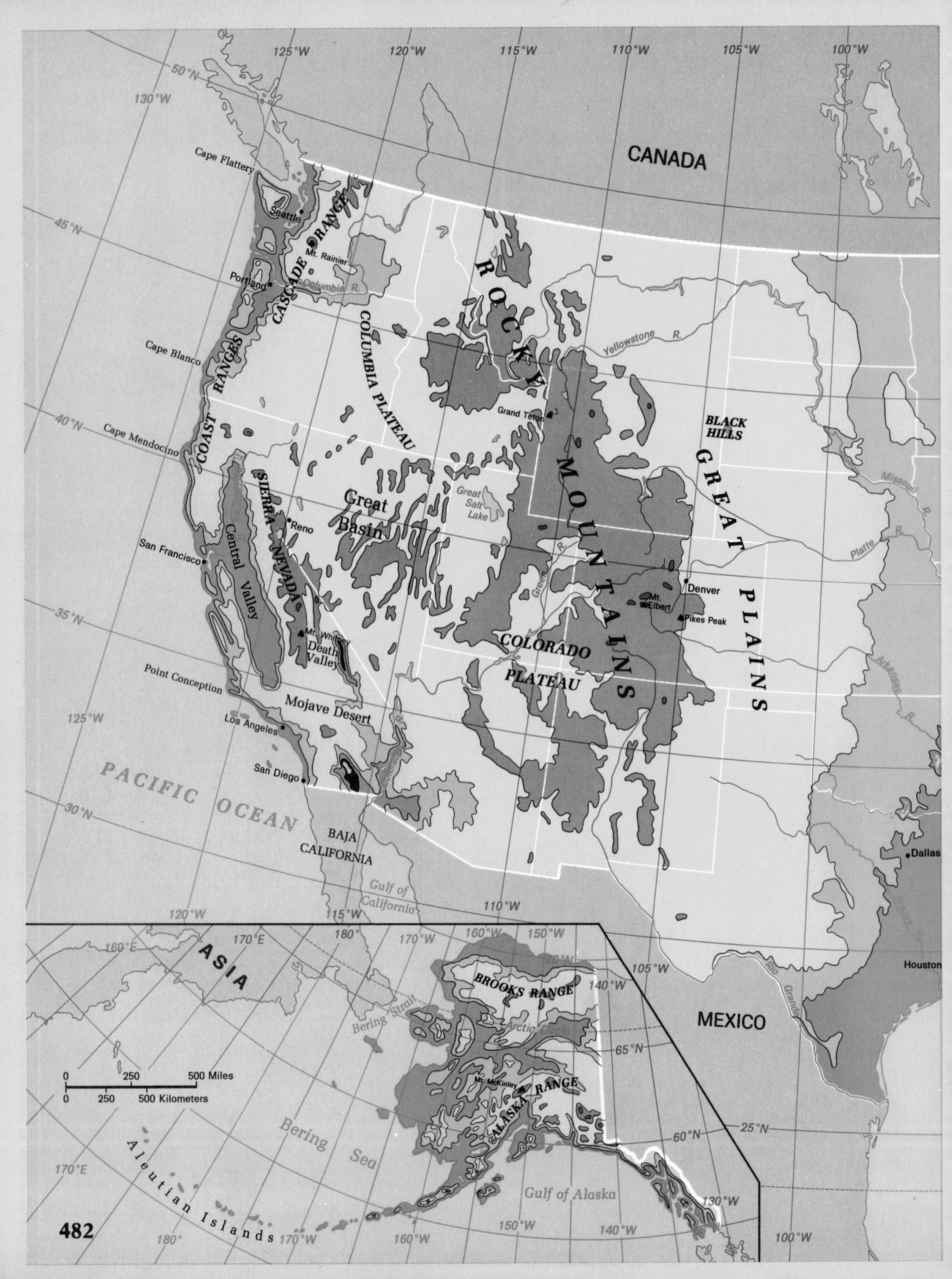
CANADA
ROCKY MOUNTAINS
CASCADE RANGE
COAST RANGES
COLUMBIA PLATEAU
SIERRA NEVADA
Great Basin
Central Valley
Death Valley
Mojave Desert
COLORADO PLATEAU
GREAT PLAINS
BLACK HILLS
PACIFIC OCEAN
BAJA CALIFORNIA
Gulf of California
MEXICO
Cape Flattery
Seattle
Mt. Rainier
Portland
Columbia R.
Cape Blanco
Cape Mendocino
San Francisco
Reno
Mt. Whitney
Point Conception
Los Angeles
San Diego
Great Salt Lake
Grand Teton
Yellowstone R.
Green R.
Denver
Mt. Elbert
Pikes Peak
Missouri R.
Platte R.
Arkansas R.
Rio Grande
Dallas
Houston
ASIA
Bering Strait
Arctic Circle
BROOKS RANGE
ALASKA RANGE
Mt. McKinley
Bering Sea
Gulf of Alaska
Aleutian Islands
0 250 500 Miles
0 250 500 Kilometers
50°N
45°N
40°N
35°N
30°N
25°N
60°N
65°N
70°N
130°W
125°W
120°W
115°W
110°W
105°W
100°W
160°E
170°E
180°
170°W
160°W
150°W
140°W

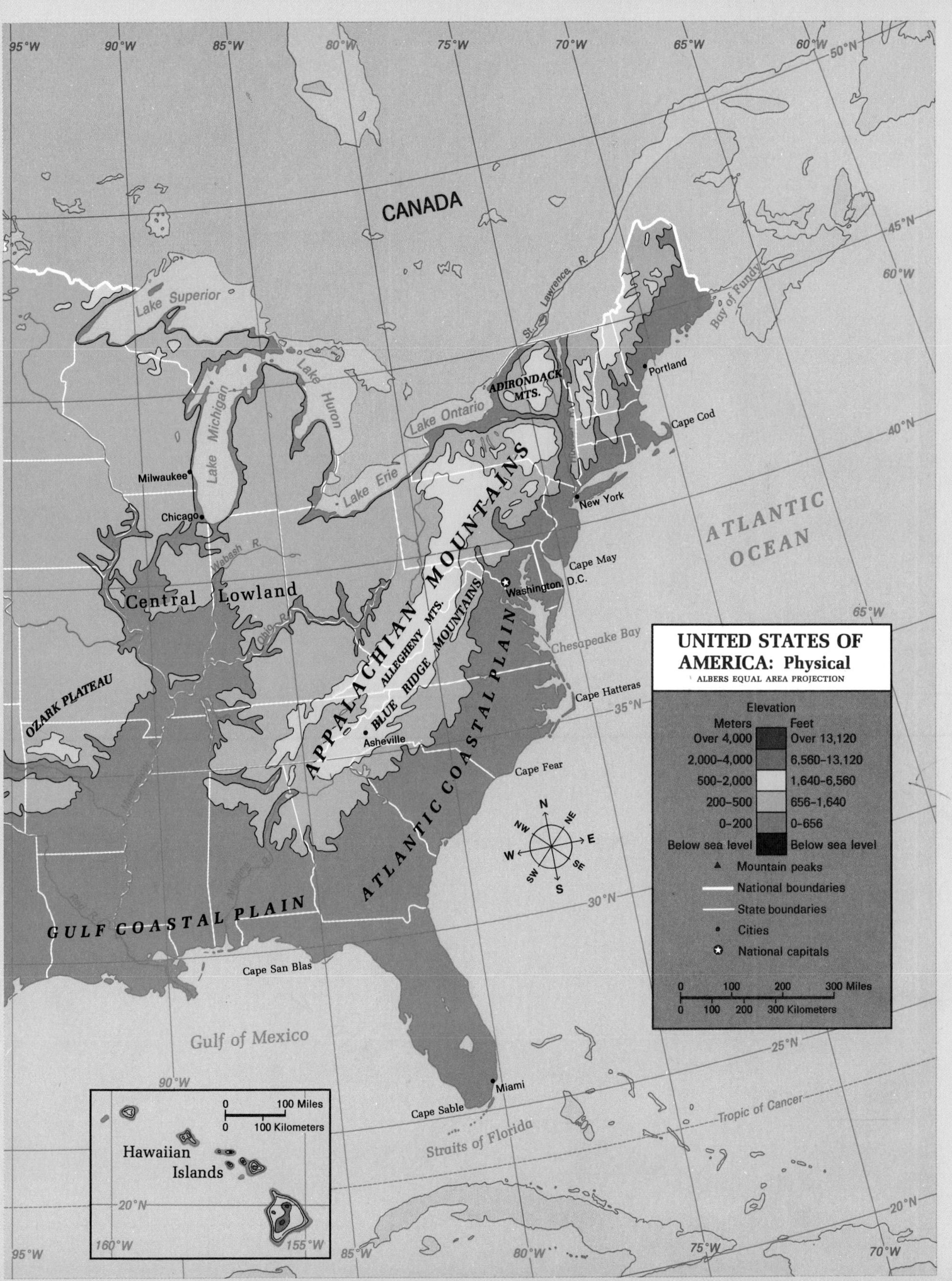

UNITED STATES OF AMERICA: Physical
ALBERS EQUAL AREA PROJECTION
Elevation
Meters
Feet
Over 4,000
Over 13,120
2,000–4,000
6,560–13,120
500–2,000
1,640–6,560
200–500
656–1,640
0–200
0–656
Below sea level
Below sea level
Mountain peaks
National boundaries
State boundaries
Cities
National capitals
0 100 200 300 Miles
0 100 200 300 Kilometers
CANADA
ATLANTIC OCEAN
Gulf of Mexico
Straits of Florida
APPALACHIAN MOUNTAINS
ALLEGHENY MTS.
BLUE RIDGE MOUNTAINS
ADIRONDACK MTS.
ATLANTIC COASTAL PLAIN
GULF COASTAL PLAIN
Central Lowland
OZARK PLATEAU
Lake Superior
Lake Michigan
Lake Huron
Lake Ontario
Lake Erie
St. Lawrence R.
Bay of Fundy
Wabash R.
Ohio R.
Chesapeake Bay
Portland
Cape Cod
New York
Cape May
Washington, D.C.
Cape Hatteras
Cape Fear
Milwaukee
Chicago
Asheville
Cape San Blas
Miami
Cape Sable
Tropic of Cancer
Hawaiian Islands
0 100 Miles
0 100 Kilometers
N
NE
E
SE
S
SW
W
NW
95°W
90°W
85°W
80°W
75°W
70°W
65°W
60°W
50°N
45°N
40°N
35°N
30°N
25°N
20°N
160°W
155°W

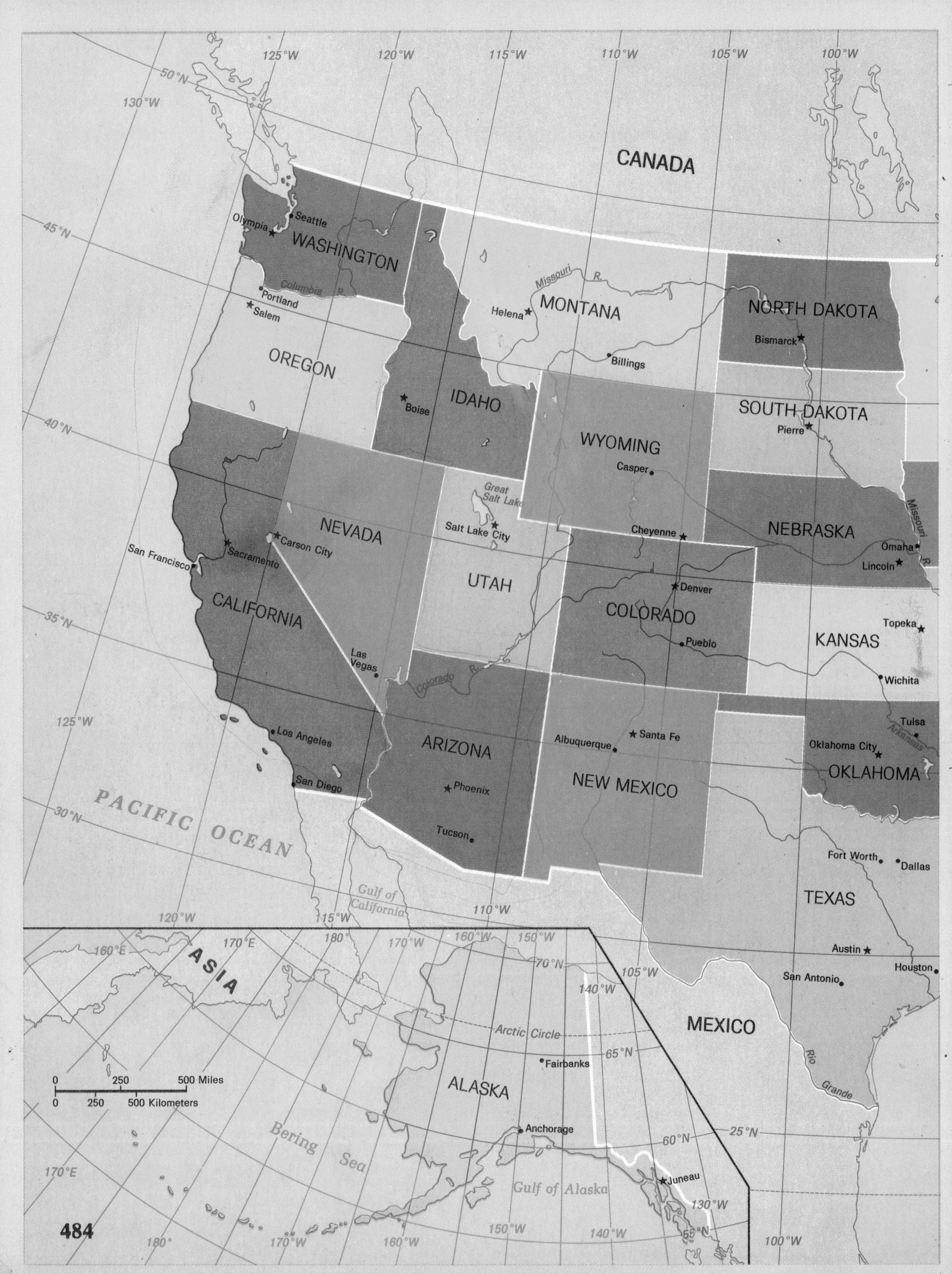
CANADA
WASHINGTON
Seattle
Olympia
Columbia R.
Portland
Salem
OREGON
IDAHO
Boise
MONTANA
Helena
Missouri R.
Billings
NORTH DAKOTA
Bismarck
SOUTH DAKOTA
Pierre
WYOMING
Casper
Cheyenne
NEBRASKA
Omaha
Lincoln
Missouri R.
Great Salt Lake
Salt Lake City
NEVADA
Carson City
Sacramento
San Francisco
UTAH
COLORADO
Denver
Pueblo
KANSAS
Topeka
Wichita
CALIFORNIA
Las Vegas
Colorado R.
Los Angeles
San Diego
ARIZONA
Phoenix
Tucson
NEW MEXICO
Santa Fe
Albuquerque
OKLAHOMA
Oklahoma City
Tulsa
Arkansas
TEXAS
Fort Worth
Dallas
Austin
Houston
San Antonio
Rio Grande
MEXICO
PACIFIC OCEAN
Gulf of California
ASIA
ALASKA
Fairbanks
Anchorage
Juneau
Arctic Circle
Bering Sea
Gulf of Alaska
0 250 500 Miles
0 250 500 Kilometers
50°N
45°N
40°N
35°N
30°N
25°N
125°W
120°W
115°W
110°W
105°W
100°W
130°W
170°E
160°E
180°
170°W
160°W
150°W
140°W
130°W
70°N
65°N
60°N
55°N

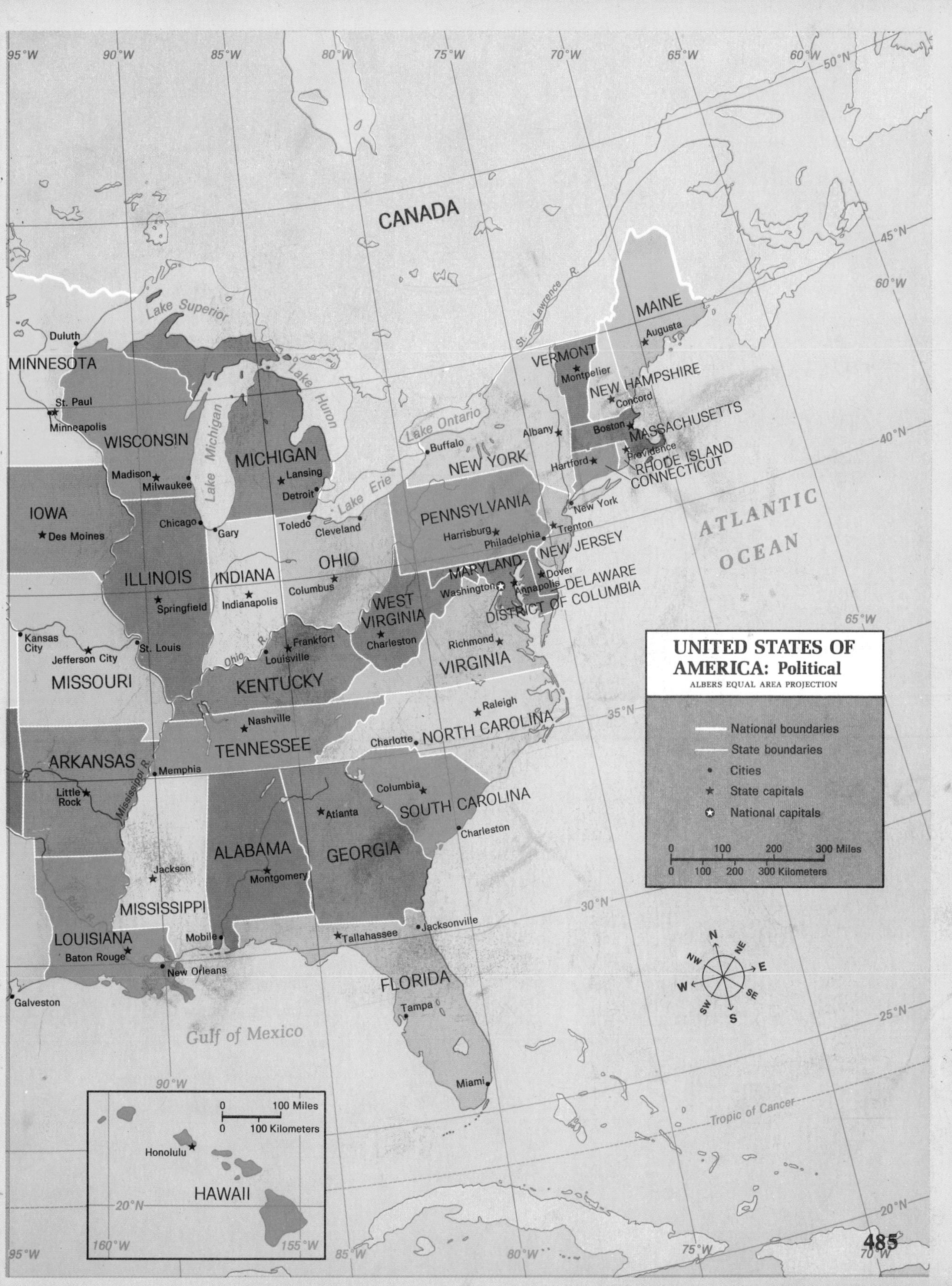
UNITED STATES OF AMERICA: Political
ALBERS EQUAL AREA PROJECTION
National boundaries
State boundaries
Cities
State capitals
National capitals
0 100 200 300 Miles
0 100 200 300 Kilometers
CANADA
ATLANTIC OCEAN
Gulf of Mexico
Lake Superior
Lake Michigan
Lake Huron
Lake Ontario
Lake Erie
St. Lawrence R.
Ohio R.
Mississippi R.
Red R.
Tropic of Cancer
MINNESOTA
WISCONSIN
MICHIGAN
IOWA
ILLINOIS
INDIANA
OHIO
PENNSYLVANIA
NEW YORK
VERMONT
NEW HAMPSHIRE
MAINE
MASSACHUSETTS
RHODE ISLAND
CONNECTICUT
NEW JERSEY
DELAWARE
MARYLAND
DISTRICT OF COLUMBIA
WEST VIRGINIA
VIRGINIA
KENTUCKY
MISSOURI
TENNESSEE
NORTH CAROLINA
SOUTH CAROLINA
ARKANSAS
MISSISSIPPI
ALABAMA
GEORGIA
LOUISIANA
FLORIDA
HAWAII
Duluth
St. Paul
Minneapolis
Madison
Milwaukee
Chicago
Gary
Lansing
Detroit
Toledo
Cleveland
Buffalo
Albany
Montpelier
Concord
Augusta
Boston
Providence
Hartford
New York
Trenton
Harrisburg
Philadelphia
Dover
Annapolis
Washington
Des Moines
Springfield
Indianapolis
Columbus
Charleston
Frankfort
Louisville
Richmond
Kansas City
Jefferson City
St. Louis
Nashville
Raleigh
Charlotte
Memphis
Little Rock
Columbia
Atlanta
Charleston
Jackson
Montgomery
Mobile
Tallahassee
Jacksonville
Baton Rouge
New Orleans
Galveston
Tampa
Miami
Honolulu
0 100 Miles
0 100 Kilometers
N NE E SE S SW W NW
95°W 90°W 85°W 80°W 75°W 70°W 65°W 60°W
50°N 45°N 40°N 35°N 30°N 25°N 20°N
160°W 155°W

NORTH AMERICAN AND CARIBBEAN NATIONS

Nation	Flag	Area sq mi	Area sq km	Population and Population Density	Capital City and Population
Belize		8,866	22,983	**155,000** 17 per sq mi (6.7 per sq km)	Belmopan 4,500
Canada		3,831,033	9,992,330	**25,100,000** 6.6 per sq mi (2.5 per sq km)	Ottawa 295,163
Costa Rica		19,730	51,100	**2,395,000** 121 per sq mi (47 per sq km)	San José 259,126
El Salvador		8,124	21,041	**5,140,000** 633 per sq mi (244 per sq km)	San Salvador 397,100
Guatemala		42,042	108,889	**7,815,000** 186 per sq mi (72 per sq km)	Guatemala 749,784
Honduras		43,277	112,088	**4,155,000** 96 per sq mi (37 per sq km)	Tegucigalpa 316,800
Mexico		761,604	1,972,547	**75,750,000** 99 per sq mi (38 per sq km)	Mexico City 8,988,200
Nicaragua		50,193	130,000	**3,060,000** 61 per sq mi (24 per sq km)	Managua 552,900
Panama		29,762	77,082	**2,200,000** 72 per sq mi (29 per sq km)	Panama 388,638
United States		3,679,201	9,529,081	**235,210,000** 64 per sq mi (25 per sq km)	Washington, D.C. 637,651

STATES OF THE UNITED STATES

State	Population/Admitted to the Union	Capital	Area Sq. mi.—Sq. km.	State Flag	State Bird	State Flower
Alabama (AL) Yellowhammer State	4,011,100 **1819**	Montgomery	51,609 133,667		Yellowhammer	Camellia
Alaska (AK) Last Frontier	462,700 **1959**	Juneau	586,400 1,518,776		Willow Ptarmigan	Forget-me-not
Arizona (AZ) Grand Canyon State	2,965,000 **1912**	Phoenix	113,909 295,024		Cactus Wren	Saguaro (Giant Cactus)
Arkansas (AR) Land of Opportunity	2,315,700 **1836**	Little Rock	53,104 137,539		Mockingbird	Apple Blossom
California (CA) Golden State	25,298,100 **1850**	Sacramento	158,693 411,014		California Valley Quail	Golden Poppy
Colorado (CO) Centennial State	3,128,100 **1876**	Denver	104,247 270,000		Lark Bunting	Rocky Mountain Columbine
Connecticut (CT) Constitution State	3,166,500 **1788**	Hartford	5,009 12,973		Robin	Mountain Laurel
Delaware (DE) First State	613,200 **1787**	Dover	2,057 5,328		Blue Hen Chicken	Peach Blossom

STATES OF THE UNITED STATES	Population/ Admitted to the Union	Capital	Area Sq. mi.—Sq. km.	State Flag	State Bird	State Flower
Florida (FL) Sunshine State	10,824,700 **1845**	Tallahassee	58,560 151,670		Mockingbird	Orange Blossom
Georgia (GA) Empire State of the South	5,790,800 **1788**	Atlanta	58,876 152,489		Brown Thrasher	Cherokee Rose
Hawaii (HI) Aloha State	1,021,100 **1959**	Honolulu	6,450 16,706		Nene or Hawaiian Goose	Hibiscus
Idaho (ID) Gem State	1,002,100 **1890**	Boise	83,557 216,413		Mountain Bluebird	Syringa (Mock Orange)
Illinois (IL) Land of Lincoln	11,527,900 **1818**	Springfield	56,400 146,076		Cardinal	Native Violet
Indiana (IN) Hoosier State	5,506,800 **1816**	Indianapolis	36,291 93,994		Cardinal	Peony
Iowa (IA) Hawkeye State	2,921,500 **1846**	Des Moines	56,290 145,791		Eastern Goldfinch	Wild Rose

STATES OF THE UNITED STATES	Population/ Admitted to the Union	Capital	Area Sq. mi.—Sq. km.	State Flag	State Bird	State Flower
Kansas (KS) Sunflower State	2,413,400 **1861**	Topeka	82,264 213,064	KANSAS	Western Meadowlark	Sunflower
Kentucky (KY) Bluegrass State	3,742,200 **1792**	Frankfort	40,395 104,623		Kentucky Cardinal	Goldenrod
Louisiana (LA) Pelican State	4,503,600 **1812**	Baton Rouge	48,523 125,675		Brown Pelican	Magnolia
Maine (ME) Pine Tree State	1,158,300 **1820**	Augusta	33,215 86,027		Chickadee	White Pine Cone and Tassel
Maryland (MD) Old Line State	4,324,400 **1788**	Annapolis	10,577 27,394		Baltimore Oriole	Black-eyed Susan
Massachusetts (MA) Bay State	5,786,400 **1788**	Boston	8,257 21,386		Chickadee	Arbutus
Michigan (MI) Wolverine State	9,197,400 **1837**	Lansing	58,216 150,779		Robin	Apple Blossom

STATES OF THE UNITED STATES	Population/ Admitted to the Union	Capital	Area Sq. mi.—Sq. km.	State Flag	State Bird	State Flower
Minnesota (MN) Gopher State	4,231,000 **1858**	St. Paul	84,068 217,736		Common Loon	Pink and White Lady's Slipper
Mississippi (MS) Magnolia State	2,629,800 **1817**	Jackson	47,716 123,584		Mockingbird	Magnolia
Missouri (MO) Show Me State	5,037,200 **1821**	Jefferson City	69,686 180,487		Bluebird	Hawthorn
Montana (MT) Treasure State	814,800 **1889**	Helena	147,138 381,087		Western Meadowlark	Bitterroot
Nebraska (NE) Cornhusker State	1,610,600 **1867**	Lincoln	77,227 200,018		Western Meadowlark	Goldenrod
Nevada (NV) Silver State	957,400 **1864**	Carson City	110,540 286,299		Mountain Bluebird	Sagebrush
New Hampshire (NH) Granite State	982,400 **1788**	Concord	9,304 24,097		Purple Finch	Purple Lilac

STATES OF THE UNITED STATES	Population/ Admitted to the Union	Capital	Area Sq. mi.—Sq. km.	State Flag	State Bird	State Flower
New Jersey (NJ) Garden State	7,552,700 **1787**	Trenton	7,836 20,295		Eastern Goldfinch	Purple Violet
New Mexico (NM) Land of Enchantment	1,413,700 **1912**	Santa Fe	121,666 315,115		Roadrunner	Yucca Flower
New York (NY) Empire State	17,555,500 **1788**	Albany	49,576 128,402		Bluebird	Rose
North Carolina (NC) Tar Heel State	6,168,200 **1789**	Raleigh	52,586 136,198		Cardinal	Flowering Dogwood
North Dakota (ND) Flickertail State	674,200 **1889**	Bismarck	70,665 183,022		Western Meadowlark	Wild Prairie Rose
Ohio (OH) Buckeye State	10,824,300 **1803**	Columbus	41,222 106,765		Cardinal	Scarlet Carnation
Oklahoma (OK) Sooner State	3,250,300 **1907**	Oklahoma City	69,919 181,090		Scissor-tailed Flycatcher	Mistletoe

STATES OF THE UNITED STATES	Population/ Admitted to the Union	Capital	Area Sq. mi.—Sq. km.	State Flag	State Bird	State Flower
 **Oregon (OR)** Beaver State	2,715,800 **1859**	Salem	96,981 251,181		 Western Meadowlark	 Oregon Grape
Pennsylvania (PA) Keystone State	11,887,200 **1787**	Harrisburg	45,333 117,412		 Ruffed Grouse	 Mountain Laurel
 **Rhode Island (RI)** Ocean State	959,300 **1790**	Providence	1,214 3,144		 Rhode Island Red	 Violet
 **South Carolina (SC)** Palmetto State	3,278,800 **1788**	Columbia	31,055 80,432		 Carolina Wren	 Carolina Jessamine
South Dakota (SD) Sunshine State	707,300 **1889**	Pierre	77,047 199,552		 Ring-necked Pheasant	 American Pasqueflower
Tennessee (TN) Volunteer State	4,762,400 **1796**	Nashville	42,244 109,412		 Mockingbird	 Iris
 **Texas (TX)** Lone Star State	15,566,000 **1845**	Austin	267,336 692,397		 Mockingbird	 Bluebonnet

STATES OF THE UNITED STATES	Population/ Admitted to the Union	Capital	Area Sq. mi.—Sq. km.	State Flag	State Bird	State Flower
Utah (UT) Beehive State	1,637,600 **1896**	Salt Lake City	84,916 219,932		Sea Gull	Sego Lily
Vermont (VT) Green Mountain State	529,100 **1791**	Montpelier	9,609 24,887		Hermit Thrush	Red Clover
Virginia (VA) Old Dominion	5,614,600 **1788**	Richmond	40,815 105,711		Cardinal	Dogwood
Washington (WA) Evergreen State	4,291,300 **1889**	Olympia	68,192 176,617		Willow Goldfinch	Coast Rhododendron
West Virginia (WV) Mountain State	1,983,000 **1863**	Charleston	24,282 62,890		Cardinal	Rhododendron
Wisconsin (WI) Badger State	4,833,800 **1848**	Madison	56,154 145,439	WISCONSIN 1848	Robin	Wood Violet
Wyoming (WY) Equality State	536,000 **1890**	Cheyenne	97,914 253,597		Meadowlark	Indian Paintbrush

PRESIDENTS AND VICE PRESIDENTS CHART

Name/Term	Political Party	Vice President	Facts about the President
1. **George Washington** (1789–1797)	Federalist	John Adams	The only President inaugurated in two cities, New York and Philadelphia.
2. **John Adams** (1797–1801)	Federalist	Thomas Jefferson	The only President whose son, John Quincy Adams, also became President.
3. **Thomas Jefferson** (1801–1809)	Democratic-Republican	Aaron Burr George Clinton	The only President to have served as Secretary of State before becoming President.
4. **James Madison** (1809–1817)	Democratic-Republican	George Clinton Elbridge Gerry	The British attacked Washington and burned the White House while Madison was President.
5. **James Monroe** (1817–1825)	Democratic-Republican	Daniel D. Tompkins	The first senator to become President.
6. **John Quincy Adams** (1825–1829)	Democratic-Republican	John C. Calhoun	Became a representative in Congress after he had been President. He was the son of President John Adams.
7. **Andrew Jackson** (1829–1837)	Democratic	John C. Calhoun Martin Van Buren	Was born in a log cabin and was the first President who did not come from an aristocratic family.
8. **Martin Van Buren** (1837–1841)	Democratic	Richard M. Johnson	The first President who was born a U.S. citizen and not a British subject.
9. **William Henry Harrison** (1841)	Whig	John Tyler	Harrison's grandson, Benjamin Harrison, was the 23rd President.
10. **John Tyler** (1841–1845)	Whig	No Vice President	The first vice president to succeed to the Presidency because of the President's death.
11. **James K. Polk** (1845–1849)	Democratic	George M. Dallas	Had served as the Speaker of the House of Representatives and the governor of Tennessee.
12. **Zachary Taylor** (1849–1850)	Whig	Millard Fillmore	Taylor's favorite horse, Whitey, was allowed to wander on the White House grounds.
13. **Millard Fillmore** (1850–1853)	Whig	No Vice President	Succeeded to the Presidency because of Taylor's death. His wife Abigail established the first White House library.
14. **Franklin Pierce** (1853–1857)	Democratic	William Rufus de Vane King	The only elected President who wanted his party to renominate him for a second term but was not renominated.
15. **James Buchanan** (1857–1861)	Democratic	John C. Breckinridge	Buchanan had served as the U.S. minister to Russia, senator from Pennsylvania, and Secretary of State under James Polk.
16. **Abraham Lincoln** (1861–1865)	Republican	Hannibal Hamlin Andrew Johnson	Operated a ferry boat across the Anderson River in Indiana when he was eleven. He was the first President to be assassinated.
17. **Andrew Johnson** (1865–1869)	National Union	No Vice President	Succeeded to the Presidency because of Lincoln's death. His wife taught him to write when he was about seventeen years old.
18. **Ulysses S. Grant** (1869–1877)	Republican	Schuyler Colfax Henry Wilson	Was general of the U.S. Army during the Civil War. Before that, he had worked in his father's hardware store in Illinois.
19. **Rutherford B. Hayes** (1877–1881)	Republican	William A. Wheeler	In 1879, President Hayes signed an act to allow women to practice law before the U.S. Supreme Court.
20. **James A. Garfield** (1881)	Republican	Chester A. Arthur	The second President to be assassinated. He was President for less than seven months.

Name/Term	Political Party	Vice President	Facts about the President
21. Chester A. Arthur (1881–1885)	Republican	No Vice President	Succeeded to the Presidency because of Garfield's death.
22. Grover Cleveland (1885–1889)	Democratic	Thomas A. Hendricks	The first President married in the White House.
23. Benjamin Harrison (1889–1893)	Republican	Levi P. Morton	The grandson of William Henry Harrison, the ninth President.
24. Grover Cleveland (1893–1897)	Democratic	Adlai E. Stevenson	Was the only President to serve two non-consecutive terms.
25. William McKinley (1897–1901)	Republican	Garret A. Hobart Theodore Roosevelt	The third President to be assassinated. During his Presidency, the U.S. acquired the Philippines and Puerto Rico.
26. Theodore Roosevelt (1901–1909)	Republican	Charles W. Fairbanks	Succeeded to the Presidency because of McKinley's death. He won the Nobel Prize for Peace for helping end the Russo-Japanese War.
27. William H. Taft (1909–1913)	Republican	James S. Sherman	Taft had served as governor-general of the Philippine Islands. He was the first President of 48 states.
28. Woodrow Wilson (1913–1921)	Democratic	Thomas R. Marshall	Won the Nobel Prize for Peace. He was the first President to appoint a woman, Annette Abbot Adams, to a sub-cabinet position.
29. Warren G. Harding (1921–1923)	Republican	Calvin Coolidge	Had been a newspaper publisher in Marion, Ohio. He died while serving as President.
30. Calvin Coolidge (1923–1929)	Republican	Charles G. Dawes	Succeeded to the Presidency because of Harding's death. During his administration, American Indians were given citizenship.
31. Herbert C. Hoover (1929–1933)	Republican	Charles Curtis	Had been a mining engineer in Asia, Africa, and Australia. While he was President, building of the Boulder Dam was started.
32. Franklin D. Roosevelt (1933–1945)	Democratic	John N. Garner Henry A. Wallace Harry S Truman	Before Roosevelt became President, he was stricken with polio. He was the only President to serve four terms. He died in office.
33. Harry S Truman (1945–1953)	Democratic	Alben W. Barkley	Succeeded to the Presidency because of Roosevelt's death. He had been a farmer, haberdasher, judge, and senator.
34. Dwight D. Eisenhower (1953–1961)	Republican	Richard M. Nixon	Had been a war hero as general and commander of U.S. forces in Europe during World War II.
35. John F. Kennedy (1961–1963)	Democratic	Lyndon B. Johnson	The fourth President to be assassinated. In 1957, he won the Pulitzer prize for his book *Profiles in Courage*.
36. Lyndon B. Johnson (1963–1969)	Democratic	Hubert H. Humphrey	Succeeded to the Presidency because of Kennedy's death. He had been a Democratic leader in the Senate and taught school in Texas.
37. Richard M. Nixon (1969–1974)	Republican	Spiro T. Agnew Gerald R. Ford	The first president to visit China, and the first to resign from office. His administration was destroyed by the Watergate scandal.
38. Gerald R. Ford (1974–1977)	Republican	Nelson A. Rockefeller	Became President when Nixon resigned. He was the first to serve as President and Vice President without being elected to either office.
39. James E. Carter (1977–1981)	Democratic	Walter F. Mondale	Emphasized human rights worldwide. He began the Camp David peace talks that led to an Israeli-Egyptian peace treaty in 1979.
40. Ronald W. Reagan (1981–)	Republican	George H. W. Bush	Had been an actor, and governor of California. During his term, the Columbia space shuttle did a 36-orbit journey around Earth.

GAZETTEER

Adirondack (AD uh RON DAK) **Mountains,** or **Adirondacks** part of the Appalachians (384)
Alabama Southeastern state of the United States, on the Gulf of Mexico (231)
Alaska Pacific state of the United States, in northwestern North America (25)
Albany capital of New York State; 43° N, 74° W (97, 123, 386)
Aleutian (uh LOO shun) **Islands** islands southwest of Alaska (24, 439)
Allegheny (AL uh GAY nee) **Mountains,** or **Alleghenies** part of the Appalachians (384)
Anchorage (ANG kur ij) city in the southern part of Alaska; 61° N, 150° W (434)
Annapolis (uh NAP uh lis) capital of Maryland; 39° N, 76° W (386)
Appalachian (AP uh LAY chun) **Mountains,** or **Appalachians** major mountain system of eastern North America, stretching from Canada to Alabama (28, 367)
Arizona (AR uh ZOH nuh) Mountain state in the southwestern United States (297, 423)
Arkansas (AHR kan SAW) South Central state of the United States (231, 404)
Atlanta capital of Georgia; 34° N, 84° W (400)
Atlantic Ocean ocean separating North and South America from Europe and Africa (80)
Augusta capital of Maine; 44° N, 70° W (378)
Austin capital of Texas, on the Colorado River; 30° N, 98° W (406)

Baja (BAH hah) **California** northwestern peninsula of Mexico (459)
Baltimore port city in north central Maryland; 39° N, 77° W (384, 390)
Baton Rouge (BAT in ROOZH) capital of Louisiana; 30° N, 91° W (406)
Beaufort (BOH furt) **Sea** part of the Arctic Ocean off northern Alaska (447)
Belize (buh LEEZ) nation in Central America, south of Mexico (460)
Bering Sea part of the Pacific Ocean between Alaska and Asia (29)
Biloxi (buh LOK see) port city in southern Mississippi; 30° N, 89° W (53)
Birmingham city in north central Alabama; 34° N, 87° W (400)
Bismarck capital of North Dakota, on the Missouri River; 47° N, 101° W (416)
Boise (BOI zee) capital of Idaho; 44° N, 117° W (426)
Boston capital of Massachusetts, a port on the Atlantic; 42° N, 71° W (116, 381)

California Pacific state of the southwestern United States (271)
California, Gulf of inlet of the Pacific Ocean east of Baja California (423)
Canada nation in northern North America (446)
Caribbean (KAR uh BEE un) **Sea** part of the Atlantic Ocean between Central America and South America (345)
Carson City capital of Nevada; 39° N, 120° W (426)
Central America narrow part of North America south of Mexico (468)
Charleston **1** capital of West Virginia; 38° N, 82° W **2** port city in South Carolina; 33° N, 80° W (238, 401)
Chesapeake Bay inlet of the Atlantic Ocean in Virginia and Maryland (105, 384)
Cheyenne (shy AN) capital of Wyoming; 41° N, 105° W (426, 430)
Chicago city in northeastern Illinois, on Lake Michigan; 42° N, 88° W (226, 253, 421)
Cincinnati city in southwestern Ohio, on the Ohio River; 39° N, 85° W (422)
Cleveland city in northeastern Ohio, a port on Lake Erie; 42° N, 82° W (422)
Colorado (KOL uh RAH doh) Mountain state of the western United States (404, 423)
Colorado River river in the western United States and in Mexico (423)
Columbia capital of South Carolina, in the central part of the state; 34° N, 81° W (396)
Columbia River river in southwestern Canada and the northwestern United States (440)
Columbus capital of Ohio; 40° N, 83° W (414)
Concord (KONG kurd) capital of New Hampshire; 43° N, 72° W (378)
Connecticut (kuh NET uh kut) New England state of the United States (376)
Connecticut River river of the northeastern United States (377)
Costa Rica nation in Central America (469)

Dallas (DAL us) city in northeastern Texas; 33° N, 97° W (411)
Delaware Middle Atlantic state of the United States, on the East Coast (123)
Denver capital of Colorado; 40° N, 105° W (430)
Des Moines (duh MOIN) capital of Iowa; 42° N, 94° W (414)
Detroit (dih TROIT) city and port in southeastern Michigan; 42° N, 83° W (420)
District of Columbia district in the eastern United States where the nation's capital is located; 39° N, 77° W (364)
Dover (DOH vur) capital of Delaware; 39° N, 76° W (386)
Duluth port city in northeastern Minnesota; 47° N, 92° W (417)

El Salvador nation in Central America (345)
Erie, Lake see GREAT LAKES (97, 374)

Florida Southeastern state of the United States, on the East and Gulf coasts (25)
Frankfort capital of Kentucky, a port on the Kentucky River; 38° N, 85° W (394)

Georgia Southeastern state of the United States, on the East Coast (51, 231, 392)
Grand Canyon gorge in northwestern Arizona; 36° N, 112°–114° W (86, 424)
Great Basin (BAY sun) desert region in the western United States (424)
Great Lakes five large lakes (Superior, Michigan, Huron, Erie, and Ontario) between the United States and Canada (30)
Great Plains plateau region of North America east of the Rockies (26, 283, 447)
Great Salt Lake large salty lake in northern Utah; 41° N, 113° W (30, 374)
Guatemala (GWAH tuh MAH luh) nation in Central America south of Mexico (66, 460)

Harrisburg capital of Pennsylvania, on the Susquehanna River; 40° N, 77° W (386)
Hartford capital of Connecticut, on the Connecticut River; 42° N, 73° W (382)
Hawaii (huh WAH ee) Pacific state of the United States, on Pacific islands (433)
Helena capital of Montana; 47° N, 112° W (426)
Honduras nation in Central America (468)
Honolulu (HON uh LOO loo) capital of Hawaii; 21° N, 158° W (277, 434)
Houston (HYOO stun) city and port in southeastern Texas; 30° N, 95° W (410)
Hudson Bay inlet of the Atlantic Ocean in northern Canada (29, 97)
Huron, Lake see GREAT LAKES (97, 374)

Idaho (EYE duh hoh) Mountain state of the northwestern United States (423)
Illinois (IL uh NOI) Midwestern state of the United States, on Lake Michigan (413)
Independence city in western Missouri; 39° N, 94° W (207)
Indiana Midwestern state of the United States, on Lake Michigan (374, 413)
Indianapolis (IN dee uh NAP uh lis) capital of Indiana; 40° N, 86° W (414, 422)
Iowa (EYE uh wuh) Midwestern state of the United States (413)

Jackson capital of Mississippi, in the central part of the state; 32° N, 90° W (394)
Jamestown first permanent English settlement in America; 37° N, 77° W (103)
Jefferson City capital of Missouri, a port on the Missouri River; 39° N, 92° W (416)
Juneau (JOO noh) capital of Alaska, in the southeastern part of the state; 58° N, 135° W (434)

Kansas (KAN zus) Midwestern state of the United States (72, 86, 284)
Kentucky Southeastern state of the United States (392)
Key West city on an island at the southwestern tip of Florida; 25° N, 82° W (53)

Lansing capital of Michigan; 43° N, 85° W (414)
Lincoln capital of Nebraska; 41° N, 97° W (416)
Little Rock capital of Arkansas, in the central part of the state; 35° N, 92° W (407)
Los Angeles port city in southwestern California; 34° N, 118° W (432, 439)
Louisiana South Central state of the United States, on the Gulf of Mexico (29, 98)

Madison capital of Wisconsin; 43° N, 89° W (416)
Maine New England state of the United States, on the East Coast (376)
Maryland Middle Atlantic state of the United States, on the East Coast (105)
Massachusetts (MAS uh CHOO sits) New England state of the United States (112)
McKinley, Mount highest mountain in North America, in Alaska; 63° N, 151° W (370)
Mexico nation in southern North America (459)
Mexico City capital of Mexico, on the central plateau; 19° N, 99° W (462)
Mexico, Gulf of part of the Atlantic Ocean east of Mexico (72, 98)
Miami (my AM ee) city in southeastern Florida; 26° N, 80° W (401)
Michigan (MISH ih gun) Midwestern state of the United States (98)
Michigan, Lake see GREAT LAKES (98, 374)
Minneapolis port city in southeastern Minnesota; 45° N, 93° W (420)
Minnesota (MIN uh SOH tuh) Midwestern state of the United States (98)
Mississippi (MIS ih SIP ee) Southeastern state of the United States (193)
Mississippi River longest river in the United States, flowing from northern Minnesota to the Gulf of Mexico (29)
Missouri (mih ZOOR ee *or* mih ZOOR uh) Midwestern state of the United States (240)
Missouri River second-longest river in the United States, flowing from Montana into the Mississippi River (369, 424)
Mitchell, Mount highest mountain in the Appalachians; 35° N, 82° W (393)

Mobile (MOH BEEL) port city in southwestern Alabama; 31° N, 88° W (53)
Montana Mountain state of the northwestern United States (423)
Montgomery capital of Alabama; 32° N, 86° W (339, 394)
Montpelier (mont PEEL yur) capital of Vermont; 44° N, 73° W (378)
Montreal (MON tree OL) city and port in Quebec, Canada; 46° N, 74° W (449)

Nashville capital of Tennessee, a port on the Cumberland River; 36° N, 87° W (396)
Nebraska (nuh BRAS kuh) Midwestern state of the United States (263, 291)
Nevada (nuh VAD uh *or* nuh VAH duh) Mountain state of the United States (423)
New England six northeastern states of the United States (90, 119)
New Hampshire New England state of the United States, on the East Coast (376)
New Jersey Middle Atlantic state of the United States, on the East Coast (384)
New Mexico Mountain state of the southwestern United States (64, 423)
New Orleans (OR lins; OR lee unz, *or* or LEENZ) port city in southeastern Louisiana; 30° N, 90° W (24, 411)
New York Middle Atlantic state of the United States, on the East Coast (72)
New York City port city in southeastern New York state; 41° N, 74° W (25, 388, 389)
Nicaragua (NIK uh RAH gwah) nation in Central America (468)
North America continent of the Western Hemisphere, bounded by the Atlantic, Pacific, and Arctic oceans (15)
North Carolina Southeastern state of the United States, on the East Coast (91, 106)
North Dakota (duh KOH tuh) Midwestern state of the northern United States (98)

Ohio (oh HY oh) Midwestern state of the United States, on Lake Erie (343)
Ohio River river in the eastern United States, flowing into the Mississippi (372)
Oklahoma (OH kluh HOH muh) South Central state of the United States (404)
Oklahoma City capital of Oklahoma, in the central part; 35° N, 98° W (406)
Olympia capital of Washington state, a port on Puget Sound; 47° N, 123° W (434)
Ontario province in eastern Canada (447)
Ontario, Lake see GREAT LAKES (97, 374)
Oregon (OR uh gun) Pacific state of the northwestern United States (282)
Ottawa capital of Canada; 45° N, 76° W (455)

Pacific Ocean ocean separating North and South America from Asia and Australia (28)
Panama southernmost nation in Central America, bordering Colombia in South America (468)
Pennsylvania (PEN sul VAYN yuh) Middle Atlantic state of the United States (374)
Philadelphia (FIL uh DEL fee uh) port city in Pennsylvania; 40° N, 75° W (126, 384, 389, 390)
Phoenix (FEE niks) capital of Arizona, on the Salt River; 34° N, 112° W (426, 430)
Pierre (PIR) capital of South Dakota, on the Missouri River; 44° N, 100° W (416)
Pittsburgh port city in southwestern Pennsylvania; 40° N, 80° W (388, 390)
Providence capital of Rhode Island, a port on Providence Bay; 42° N, 71° W (378)
Puerto Rico (PWEHR toh REE koh) commonwealth on islands south of Florida, part of the United States (80, 364)
Puget (PYOO jit) **Sound** arm of the Pacific bordering northwestern Washington state (433)

Quebec (kwih BEK) **1** city in southeastern Canada, on the St. Lawrence River; 47° N, 71° W (97) **2** province in eastern Canada (456)

Raleigh (RAH lee) capital of North Carolina, in the central part; 36° N, 79° W (394)
Rhode Island (ROHD EYE lund) New England state of the United States (376)
Richmond capital of Virginia; 38° N, 78° W (234)
Rio Grande (REE oh GRAND) river in the southwestern United States, dividing the United States from Mexico (372)
Rocky Mountains, or **Rockies** major mountain system of western North America, stretching from Alaska to New Mexico (423)

Sacramento (SAK ruh MEN toh) capital of California; 39° N, 122° W (271, 434)
Salem capital of Oregon; 45° N, 123° W (434)
Salt Lake City capital of Utah, near the Great Salt Lake; 41° N, 112° W (426, 430)
San Antonio city in southern Texas; 29° N, 99° W (340, 411)
San Francisco city in California, a port on the Pacific; 38° N, 122° W (90)
Santa Fe (SAN tuh FAY) capital of New Mexico; 35° N, 106° W (206, 426)
Seattle (see AT ul) port city in western Washington; 48° N, 122° W (440)
Sierra Madres (see EHR uh MAH drays) major mountain system of Mexico (460)
Sierra (see EHR uh) **Nevada** mountain range in eastern California (75)

South Carolina Southeastern state of the United States, on the East Coast (106)
South Dakota (duh KOH tuh) Midwestern state of the United States (98)
Springfield capital of Illinois; 40° N, 90° W (414)
St. Augustine city in northeastern Florida; oldest city in the United States; 30° N, 81° W (87)
St. Lawrence River river in eastern Canada, bordering New York state (94)
St. Louis (LOO is) city in eastern Missouri, on the Mississippi River; 39° N, 90° W (198)
St. Paul capital of Minnesota, a port on the Mississippi River; 45° N, 93° W (414, 422)
Superior, Lake largest of the Great Lakes (374)

Tallahassee (TAL uh HAS ee) capital of Florida, in the northwestern part of the state; 30° N, 84° W (54, 394)
Tennessee (TEN uh SEE) Southeastern state of the United States (231, 392)
Texas South Central state of the United States, on the Gulf of Mexico (64)
Topeka (tuh PEE kuh) capital of Kansas, in the northeastern part; 39° N, 96° W (414)
Toronto capital of Ontario, Canada, a port on Lake Ontario; 44° N, 79° W (449)
Trenton capital of New Jersey, on the Delaware River; 40° N, 75° W (386)

United States nation in North America, bounded by the Atlantic, Pacific, and Arctic oceans (15)
Utah (YOO taw *or* YOO tah) Mountain state of the western United States (423)

Vermont (vur MONT) New England state of the United States (376)
Virginia Southeastern state of the United States, on the East Coast (392)

Washington Pacific state of the northwestern United States (432)
Washington, DC capital of the United States; 39° N, 77° W (234, 390)
West Virginia Middle Atlantic state of the United States (366)
Whitney, Mount mountain in eastern California; 37° N, 118° W (433)
Wilmington port city in northern Delaware, on the Delaware River; 40° N, 76° W (126)
Wisconsin Midwestern state of the United States, on the Great Lakes (72)
Wyoming (wy OH ming) Mountain state of the northwestern United States (423)

Yucatán (YOO kuh TAN) **Peninsula** southeastern peninsula of Mexico; projecting into the Gulf of Mexico (66)

GLOSSARY

abolitionist (AB uh LISH un ist) a person in the United States before and during the Civil War who wanted to end slavery (225)
acid rain a kind of pollution that occurs when rain mixes with gases in the air (355)
active volcano a volcano that may still erupt (460)
adobe (uh DOH bee) sun-baked clay (71)
advertising the business of telling people about products or services (322)
aerial (A ree ul) **photograph** a picture taken from an airplane or a satellite (37)
aerospace (AIR oh SPAYS) **industry** the business that produces airplanes and spacecraft (438)
alien (AY lee un) a foreigner (278)
alliance (uh LY uns) an agreement between nations to support each other (313)
Allied Powers in World War I, Russia, France, Britain, Italy, Japan, and the United States (313)
Allies (AL EYEZ) in World War II, the United States, Britain, France, and the Soviet Union (330)
altitude height above sea level (423)
amendment a change in the Constitution (173)
ammunition (AM yoo NISH un) something that can be fired from a gun or exploded (155)
ancestor a member of a person's family who lived long ago (65)
anthracite (AN thruh SYT) hard coal (338)
anthropology (AN thruh POL uh jee) the study of the ways different people live (463)
antifederalist a person who was against the new U.S. Constitution in 1787 (169)
appoint to select for a certain job (172)
archaeology (AHR kee OL uh jee) the study of the ruins of past civilizations (463)
arid dry (370)
armistice (AHR muh STIS) an agreement to end a war (314)
Articles of Confederation the 1781 agreement that set up the first U.S. government (164)
assassinate (uh SAS uh NAYT) to kill a well-known person (313)
assembly (uh SEM blee) **1** a meeting **2** a group of representatives who meet to make laws (124)
assembly line a line of workers and machines in a factory, each doing a different thing to the product (248)
astronomer (uh STRAHN uh mur) a person who studies stars and planets (66)
atomic bomb a nuclear weapon (330)
Axis (AK sis) the military alliance of Germany, Italy, and Japan during World War II (328)

bail money pledged to get out of jail while awaiting trial (174)
barricade a defensive barrier (142)
barrier island a thin, sandy island that separates the ocean from the shoreline (393)
barter to trade for goods or services instead of using money (471)
bauxite (BAWK SYT) a mineral used to make aluminum (397)
bay a body of water mostly enclosed by land (29)
beef cattle cattle raised for meat (370)
benevolent (buh NEV uh lunt) kind (269)
bilingual using two languages (456)
bill a written plan for a new law (170)
Bill of Rights the first 10 amendments to the United States Constitution (173)
bison (BY sun) a large animal related to ordinary cattle; a buffalo (286)
bituminous (bi TOO muh nus) soft coal (388)
Black Codes laws limiting the rights of Blacks in the South after the Civil War (239)
blaze to mark a trail (190)
blizzard a heavy snowstorm with high winds (418)
blockade to keep a port or city blocked so that supplies cannot be brought in or sent out (234)
bog flooded ground; a swamp or marsh (380)
bonus an extra payment as a reward for special services (325)
border a line that divides two nations or parts of nations (43)
boycott to refuse to buy or use something as a form of protest (140)
breadbasket an area that produces large amounts of grain (126)
buffalo *see* BISON (286)
burgess (BUR jis) an elected representative in the colony of Virginia (105)

Cabinet the group of Presidential advisers who head the executive departments (177)
Canadian Shield the Laurentian Plateau of Canada, which is U-shaped like a shield (447)
candidate someone who runs for an office (176)
canyon (KAN yuhn) a deep, narrow valley with steep sides (424)
capital a city where the government of a state or nation meets (40)
capitalism an economy in which private individuals own property and businesses (337)
carcass the dead body of an animal (289)
cardinal directions north, south, east, west (42)
carpetbagger a Northerner who moved to the South after the Civil War to make money or gain political power (240)
cartographer (kahr TOG ruh fur) mapmaker (40)
cash crop a crop grown to be sold (107)
casualty (KAZ yoo ul tee) a person killed or injured in war (186)
census a count of the population, made by the government (366)
Central Powers in World War I, Germany, Austria-Hungary, the Ottoman Empire, and Bulgaria (313)
charter a government paper that grants a person or group special rights (114)
check to limit (170)
circumnavigate (SUR kum NAV ih GAYT) to sail completely around something (90)
citizen a person who is a member of a particular nation, state, or city (212, 280)
citrus fruit fruit such as oranges, grapefruits, lemons, and limes (398)
civilian (sih VIL yun) a person who is not in the armed forces (237)
civil rights rights that belong to people because they are citizens (339)
climate the average weather of a place (31)
coke a fuel made from bituminous coal (388)
cold war a tense condition in which nations are enemies but are not actually at war (337)
colony **1** an area of land ruled by a foreign or "parent" country **2** a group of people who settle in such a place (89)
commerce (KOM urs) the buying and selling of goods (377)
commercial (kuh MUR shul) referring to an activity done for profit (377)
Committees of Correspondence colonial groups that exchanged news about the British and shared plans for the American Revolution (158)
commonwealth a nation, state, or other area that governs itself (364)
communications (kuh MYOO nih KAY shuns) the area of business and art that includes radio, television, newspapers, and magazines (388)
communism (KOM yu NIZ um) an economy in which the government owns and runs all businesses and there is no private property (214)
commuting (kuh MYOOT ing) traveling back and forth from one community to another (381)
compass **1** a map drawing of arrows that point north, south, east, and west (42) **2** a tool with a magnetic needle that always points north (79)
compromise (KOM pruh MYZ) an agreement in which each side gives something up (168)
concentration camp a camp where prisoners of war are kept (329)
confederacy (kun FED ur uh see) a group of states or tribes that join together (73)
Confederacy the Southern states that fought against the Union in the Civil War (231)
congestion (kun JES chun) the crowding of people and vehicles on city streets (307)
Congress the legislative branch of government in the United States (170)
conservation (KON sur VAY shun) the careful use and protection of natural resources (354)

Constitution (KON stih TOO shun) the written plan of government and basic law of the United States (167)
construction (kun STRUK shun) building (253)
continent one of the seven large masses of land on Earth (15)
Continental Congress an assembly of representatives from the 13 American colonies (140)
Continental Divide a high ridge in the Rocky Mountains on each side of which rivers flow in opposite directions (423)
coordinates numbers and directions that give a latitude and longitude location (24)
cotton gin a machine that separates the seeds from cotton fibers (229)
credit the belief that someone who owes money will repay it (178)
creole (KREE OHL) a person born of Spanish parents in New Spain (Mexico) (464)
currency the money issued by a government (178)

dairy cattle cattle that produce milk (368)
dame school a school run by a woman in her home in colonial New England (119)
debtor (DET ur) a person who owes money (106)
declaration a formal statement (146)
deficit (DEF ih sit) a debt that occurs when a government spends more money than it has (355)
degree a unit of latitude or longitude (22)
delta an area of rich soil dropped by a river before it flows into the ocean (29)
dictator (DIK TAY tur) a ruler who has complete power over a government (328)
discrimination (dis KRIM uh NAY shun) treatment that is unequal or unfair (278)
distribution map a map that shows how things are spread out over an area (44)
division of labor the dividing up of work so that different workers do different jobs (247)
dominion a self-governing nation in the British Commonwealth of Nations (454)
dormant volcano a volcano that has not erupted for a long time (460)
downstream the direction in which a river flows (30)
draft a law that requires people to join the armed forces (235)
drain to carry away water (373)
drainage basin the land area drained by a group of rivers (373)
drought (DROWT) a long period with little or no rainfall (325)
dry farming a method of farming in areas with little rainfall to keep moisture in the soil (408)

earthquake a quick movement of Earth's surface that causes the ground to shake (433)
economy the way in which people produce and distribute goods and services (337)
ejido (eh HEE doh) in Mexico, a farm that is owned and worked by a group of farmers (461)
elect to choose by vote (170)
elevation (EL uh VAY shun) the height of land above sea level (40)
Emancipation Proclamation a document issued by President Lincoln on Jan. 1, 1863, that freed slaves in Confederate areas (236)
embargo (em BAHR goh) a ban on foreign trade of a particular product (344)
emigrant (EM ih grunt) a person who leaves one country or region to settle in another (204)
empresario (EM pruh SAHR ee oh) a land agent in Texas who brought in settlers (207)
energy power (353)
enterprise (EN tur PRYZ) new ideas and extra effort used to reach a goal (269)
entrepreneur (AHN truh pruh NUR) someone who sets up a new business (254)
environment a place's natural surroundings (354)
envoy (AHN voi) someone who represents one government in dealing with another (197)
equal-area projection a map that keeps land areas the right size but changes their shapes (36)
equator (ih KWAY tur) an imaginary line around the middle of Earth (17)
erosion (ih ROH zhun) the washing away or blowing away of the soil (326)
erupt to shoot out lava and gases (433)
escalate to greatly increase (343)
evidence visible proof (71)
executive (eg ZEK yuh tiv) **branch** the branch of government that carries out the laws (170)
expedition (EK spuh DISH un) a journey made by a group with a definite goal (97)
export *v.* (ek SPORT) to sell a product to another country *n.* (EKS port) a product sold by one country to another (121)
extinct volcano a volcano that no longer erupts (460)

fall line a place where the land level drops and the rivers form rapids and falls (384)
falls waterfalls (384)
famine a serious shortage of food that lasts for a long time (261)
fault a crack in Earth's surface (433)
federal of a nation made up of states (168)
federal district a special area set aside for a nation's capital (364)
federalist (FED ur uh list) a person who supported the new U.S. Constitution in 1787 (169)
fertile good for growing crops (368)
fertilizer a substance that adds minerals to the soil, making it more fertile (397)

fiber threads (229)
finance the management of money (388)
finca (FEEN kah) in Central America, a large estate with its own village (470)
fine money paid as punishment for a crime (174)
fishing ground a part of an ocean, river, or lake where many fish are found (120)
forty-niner someone who came to California in 1849 to look for gold (210)
Freedmen's Bureau an agency set up by the federal government to help former slaves (239)
free enterprise (EN tur pryz) an economy run by private individuals and businesses (337)
front the boundary between two air masses of different temperatures (417)
frontier (frun TIR) an unsettled area at or beyond the edge of a settled region (189)

geographer an expert in geography (16)
geographic region a large area where the landforms are similar (367)
geography (jee OG ruh fee) the study of physical facts about places on Earth (16)
geologist (jee OL uh jist) a scientist who studies Earth's physical structure (449)
geyser (GY zur) a hot spring that shoots water and steam into the air (431)
glacier (GLAY shur) a huge, slowly moving mass of ice that grinds down the land (374)
globe a round model of Earth (17)
gorge a deep valley formed by a river (404)
government the system by which laws are made and enforced (164)
Great Depression the period in the early 1930s when many businesses failed (324)
grenadier (GREN uh DIR) a type of British soldier (142)
grid a pattern of crossing lines (18)
growing season the time between the spring and autumn frosts when crops can best be grown (385)
gulf a part of a sea or an ocean that is partly enclosed by land (29)

habitant (ah bee TAHN) a settler in New France who worked for a seigneur (452)
hacienda (HAH see EN duh) in Mexico, a huge estate on which farming is done (460)
hardwood a tree that loses leaves in fall (398)
hemisphere (HEM uh SFIR) one of the four half circles that Earth can be divided into: Northern, Southern, Eastern, or Western Hemisphere (17)
hieroglyphics (HY ruh GLIF iks) a complicated form of picture writing (66)
hill land higher than the land around it (26)
Hispanic (hi SPAN ik) a person of Spanish background (213)
historian a person who writes or studies records of past events (15)
historical map a map that shows the world as it was, or as people thought it was, in the past (48)
history the story of what happened in the past (15)
House of Representatives one of two parts of the U.S. Congress (170)
hurricane a severe tropical storm with high winds and heavy rain (397)
hydroelectric power electricity produced by running water (377)

immigrant (IM i grunt) a person who comes to settle in a new country (259)
import *v.* (im PORT) to buy a product from another country *n.* (IM port) a product bought by one country from another (122)
inaugurate (in AW gyuh RAYT) to swear into office (183)
indentured (in DEN churd) **servant** a person whose way to the colonies was paid in return for a certain period of work without pay (102)
independence freedom from foreign rule (146)
indigo a blue dye taken from plants (107)
industrial (in DUS tree ul) manufacturing and selling many goods (252)
industry (IN duh stree) **1** steady effort to get work done **2** the manufacturing and sale of goods and services **3** all the businesses that supply a certain product or service (252)
inflation (in FLAY shun) a drop in the value of money, making goods cost more (355)
ingenuity native cleverness (251)
integration (IN tuh GRAY shun) the act of ending the separation of races (333)
intendant (ahn tahn DAHN) the governor of the colony of New France (452)
interchangeable parts machine parts of a standard size and shape (248)
intermediate directions northeast, northwest, southeast, and southwest (42)
interpreter (in TUR prih tur) a person who explains what is being said in another language (199)
interrupted projection a map with gaps, which changes the shape of ocean areas (36)
irrigation the system of supplying land with water that comes from somewhere else (370)
island a piece of land that is completely surrounded by water (28)
isolationism a national policy of not getting involved with other nations (329)
isthmus (ISS muss) a narrow strip of land connecting two large areas of land (83)
itinerary (eye TIN uh RER ee) a detailed plan for a trip (53)

judicial (joo DISH ul) **branch** the branch of government that decides whether laws have been obeyed or broken (170)
justice a Supreme Court judge (172)

key a list explaining the symbols and colors used on a map (40)

lake a body of water completely surrounded by land (30)
landforms the shapes of land on Earth, such as mountains, hills, plains, and plateaus (26)
land grant a gift of land by a government (207)
land speculator someone who buys land cheaply in order to sell it later for a profit (193)
latitude (LAT uh TOOD) distance north or south of the equator, marked on a map by lines that run east and west (18)
lava melted rock that pours out of a volcano (433)
legislative (LEJ is LAY tiv) **branch** the branch of government that makes the laws (170)
livestock farm animals (194)
lock an enclosed section of a canal in which the water level can be raised or lowered (417)
locomotive the part of a train that contains the engine (248)
locusts swarming insects that eat crops (283)
logging the cutting down of trees for wood (370)
longhorns cattle with long horns, formerly raised in the Southwest (283)
longitude (LON juh TOOD) distance east or west of the prime meridian, marked on a map by lines that run north and south (18)
Loyalist an American who remained loyal to the British during the Revolutionary War (151)
lumber timber sawed into boards or planks (120)

magnesium a light, strong metal (405)
malaria (muh LAIR ee uh) a disease spread by certain mosquitoes (299)
manufacture to make raw materials into finished goods by using machines (252)
manufactured goods products made in factories with machines (136)
map a flat drawing of all or part of Earth (34)
maritime on or near the ocean (447)
mass production the system of making a great many goods by using machines (246)
mathematician a person who studies numbers (66)
megalopolis (meg uh LOP uh lis) an area that has several large cities close together (389)
Mercator (mur KAY tur) **projection** a map on which the lines of latitude and longitude are both drawn straight and parallel. This makes land areas distorted near the poles. (36)
merchant (MUR chunt) a person who buys goods in order to sell them for a profit (121)
meridian (muh RID ee un) a line of longitude (18)
mesa (MAY suh) a steep hill with a flat top (26)
mestizo (mess TEE zoh) a person with Indian, Spanish, and sometimes Black ancestors (212)
migration (my GRAY shun) movement of people from one place to another (306)
mileage (MY lij) distance measured in miles (54)
mileage chart a chart that shows the number of road miles between cities (54)
mine a hole or tunnel dug under the ground for the purpose of taking out minerals (380)
mineral a substance found in the ground that is not a plant or an animal (388)
mining taking minerals out of the ground (370)
minute in geography, one-sixtieth of a degree (24)
mission a religious community founded to spread a particular faith (86)
missionary a person who travels to a new area to spread a religion (202)
mixed farming the raising of a combination of animals, grain, and hay (385)
Monroe Doctrine a declaration made by President Monroe in 1823 that European nations would not be allowed to set up any more colonies in the Americas (187)
mountain an area of very high, steep land that is much higher than the land around it (28)
mountain range a group of mountains (28)
mountain system a huge group of mountain ranges (28)
mouth the place where a river flows into another body of water (29)
muckrakers in the early 1900s, a group of people who brought wrongdoing to public attention (308)

national-origins system a system of immigration in which each nation's quota was based on its share of the United States population in 1920 (346)
natural boundary a feature of Earth, such as a river, that divides one place from another (44)
natural gas a mixture of gases found in the ground and used for fuel (388)
naturalize to give the rights of a citizen to someone from a foreign country (174, 280)
navigator 1 a person who directs the course of a ship **2** a person who explores by ship (89)
neutral (NYOO trul) not taking sides or not taking part in a war (313)
neutrality (nyoo TRAL uh tee) the refusal to take sides or take part in a war (179)
Nisei (NEE SAY) a person born in the United States of Japanese parents (334)
northwest passage a northern water route from the Atlantic Ocean to the Pacific Ocean (95)
nuclear (NOO klee ur) **energy** energy made in atomic reactors (354)

ocean one of the four very large bodies of salt water on Earth (29)
odometer (oh DOM uh tur) the instrument on a car that records the mileage (54)

parallel (PAR uh LEL) a line of latitude (18)
Parliament (PAHR luh munt) the lawmaking group, or legislature, in some nations, such as Great Britain and Canada (135)
pass a low place in the mountains (190)
patent an official paper from the government that gives an inventor all rights to the invention for a certain number of years (255)
patroonship (puh TROON SHIP) a large piece of land given to someone who brought 50 settlers to New Netherland (123)
peninsula (puh NIN suh luh) a piece of land mostly surrounded by water (28)
peninsulare (peh NEEN soo LAR ay) a Spanish noble in New Spain who was born in Spain (464)
peon (PEE ahn) a poorly paid farmer in Mexico who worked on a hacienda (460)
permafrost in a tundra region, the ground beneath the surface that stays frozen (436)
pestle a grinding stone (71)
petrochemical a chemical made from petroleum or natural gas (409)
petroleum a thick, dark liquid found in the ground and used for fuel; oil (370)
physical map a map that shows the height or shape of land (44)
piedmont (PEED mont) land that lies at the foot of a mountain, such as a plateau (384)
Pilgrims a group of English Protestants who believed that religious worship should be plain, simple, and strict (112)
pioneer (PY uh NIR) one of the first people to explore or settle in a new area (190)
plain land that is mostly flat (26)
plan a detailed map or diagram showing how a place is laid out (54)
plantation (plan TAY shun) a large farm where crops are raised (108)
planter a person who owns a farm on which cash crops are raised (108)
plateau (pla TOH) an area of high, flat land (26)
polar projection a map with the North Pole or South Pole at the center (37)
political boundary a line dividing two nations or parts of nations (43)
political map a map that shows the borders of cities, states, or nations (44)
political party an organized group of people who run candidates for public office (180)
pollution the putting of wastes into the air and water that could be harmful to living things (354)
population-density map a map that shows how people are spread out over an area (46)
porridge a souplike food (194)
port a place where ships can load and unload people and goods (123)
portage (POR tij) the carrying of boats and supplies over land between bodies of water (452)
possession an area that belongs to a nation but is not part of that nation (364)
poultry (POHL tree) chickens, turkeys, and ducks that are raised for food (380)
prairie (PRER ee) a large area of flat or rolling grassland with fertile soil and few trees (369)
preamble the introduction to a document (146)
precipitation (prih SIP uh TAY shun) the amount of water that falls from the air as rain, mist, snow, sleet, or hail (31)
premier (prih MIR) **1** the leader of a province in Canada (456) **2** a prime minister
President the leader of the United States (170)
prime meridian (muh RID ee un) the imaginary line at which longitude starts. It passes through Greenwich, England. (18)
prime minister the national leader in many nations (456)
process to prepare for sale or use (248)
product anything that people gather or make (46)
productivity (PROH duk TIV uh tee) the number of goods or services a worker can produce (355)
Progressives in the early 1900s, a group of people who started a movement to correct injustices (310)
Prohibition (PROH uh BISH un) the law, passed in 1919, forbidding the making or selling of alcoholic beverages (322)
projection the way sizes and shapes of places on Earth are changed on a map (34)
proprietor (pruh PRY uh tur) an owner (106)
prospector (PROS pek tur) a person who hunts for gold or other minerals (209)
province a part of Canada that is like a state in the United States (447)
Puritans a religious group that wanted to make the Church of England plain and simple (113)

Quakers the Society of Friends, a group of Protestants who believe that war is wrong (125)
quarry an open pit from which stone is taken (380)
quarter to house soldiers (140)
quinine (KWY nyn) a drug that is used to treat malaria (298)
quota (KWOH tuh) a certain share of the whole amount (346)

rapids rocky places in a river (384)
ratify (RAT uh FY) to approve (168)
ration (RASH un) to limit the amount of goods a person is allowed to buy (333)
raw material a product that has not been improved by manufacturing (136)
reaper a machine that cuts down a crop and drops it in piles (245)
rebellion a revolt against a rightful government (146)
reconstruction rebuilding (239)

Reconstruction the period (1865–1877) of control and occupation of the South by the federal government after the Civil War (238–239)
recycle to use again (354)
referendum (REF er EN duhm) a vote by the people to decide an important issue (457)
refine to purify (254)
reformer someone who tries to change things for the better (307)
refugee (REF yoo JEE) a person who leaves his or her country to escape danger or death (346)
relocation camp during World War II, camps where Japanese-Americans were imprisoned (334)
renewable resource a resource, such as a tree; that can be replaced after it is used (418)
repeal to cancel a law (175)
representative (REP rih ZEN tuh tiv) **1** a person chosen to speak or act for a group **2** a member of the House of Representatives (105)
republic a government without a monarch, in which the people elect their leaders (355)
reservation (REZ ur VAY shun) an area of land set aside for a group of American Indians (293)
resource anything on Earth that people can use to help them live (44)
revolution 1 a war in which the people of a country fight to change the government (135) **2** any great change in the way people work or live (244)
right a just claim to have or do something (169)
river a body of water that carries water away from the land (29)
river system a group of rivers that flow into another river (373)
road map a map that shows highways and other important roads (54)
route (ROOT) the path someone travels from one place to another (50)
rural area a country town, village, or farming region with fewer than 2,500 people (366)

salt pan an area of land covered with salt (424)
satellite (SAT uh lyt) an object sent into space to orbit Earth or another heavenly body (349)
scalawag (SCAL uh wag) a White Southerner who supported the Reconstruction government after the Civil War (240)
scale a diagram that shows what a map distance equals in real distance on Earth (40)
sea a body of water, smaller than an ocean, surrounded by land on two or more sides (29)
sea level the height of the ocean's surface (42)
season a period of the year with similar weather; spring, summer, fall, or winter (31)
secession (sih SESH un) in the Civil War period, the withdrawal of the Southern states from the Union (231)
secretary the head of any of the departments in the President's Cabinet (177)
segregation separation by race (240)
seigneur (san YUR) a French noble who controlled land in New France (452)
Senate one of two parts of Congress (170)
separatists (SEP ur uh tists) a group of people whose beliefs led them to separate from the Church of England (112)
service industry a business that provides a service instead of making products (400)
session (SESH un) a meeting or series of meetings of a legislature (326)
silt rich soil carried by a river (393)
skyscraper a very tall building (256)
slave a person owned by another person (108)
slogan an inspiring phrase (157)
smuggle to sneak something past the authorities illegally (137)
socialism an economy in which the government owns and runs the businesses but people keep some private property (337)
sod soil held together by the roots of grass (283)
softwood a tree with cones and needles (398)
sojourner (soh JURN ur) someone who plans to live in a place for a short time (269)
solar (SOH lur) **energy** energy from the sun (354)
sorghum (SOR gum) a grassy plant used as food for animals and to make syrup (408)
source the place where a river starts (29)
sponsor a person who agrees to be responsible for one or more refugees (348)
steppe (STEP) a grassy plain (404)
stereotype (STEH ree oh TYP) the false idea that everyone in a group is much the same (273)
stock shares owned in a company (324)
stockade a fence made of wooden posts, built for protection (73)
strait a narrow channel of water connecting two larger bodies of water (84)
strategy (STRAT uh jee) a plan of action (150)
strip mining mining done above the ground (418)
subregion a part of a region (364)
subsistence farming farming that produces only enough food for the farm family to live on (471)
suburb (SUB urb) a community near a city where people who work in the city live (322)
subway a railroad that runs underground (307)
suffrage (SUF rij) the right to vote (317)
suffragist (SUF ruh jist) someone who fights for the right to vote (317)
suit a legal action (174)
sulfur a yellow mineral (405)
sunbelt the warm, sunny area stretching across the southern part of the United States (399)
Supreme Court the highest court in the United States (171)
survey to measure land (185)
swamp a lowland usually covered by water (28)
symbol a sign that stands for something else (40)

taiga a forested area south of the tundra (449)
tariff (TAIR if) a tax placed on goods brought into a country from another country (227)
tax an amount of money paid by persons and businesses to support the government (135)
temperature the amount of heat in the air (31)
temple a place where people worship (67)
tenement an overcrowded apartment building in a poor area (264)
terms conditions of a treaty or an agreement (153)
territory an area that belongs to a nation but is not part of the nation (193, 364)
textile a piece of woven or knitted cloth (380)
thresher a machine that separates the grains of wheat from the rest of the plant (245)
tidewater water covering coastal land at high tide (393)
timber wood that can be used for building (120)
timberline on a mountain, the elevation at which trees stop growing (423)
time line a chart that shows the dates of important events in order (63)
time zone a geographical region within which all places have the same clock time (25)
tornado a small but very severe windstorm (405)
trade 1 a way of making a living by doing skilled work with the hands **2** the business of buying and selling goods (121)
trade route a line of travel over land or water used by traders carrying goods (79)
transcontinental (TRANS KON tuh NEN tul) going across a continent (271)
transportation (TRANS pur TAY shun) the movement of people or goods (370)
treaty an agreement between nations (153)
trench a deep ditch dug for defense (142)
trial by jury a court trial where a person is judged by others who are his or her equals (124)
tribe a group of people with a common ancestry (73)
tributary (TRIB yuh TER ee) a small river or stream that flows into a larger river (30)
truck farming the growing of different kinds of vegetables for sale (385)
tundra treeless land with permanently frozen soil beneath the surface (436)

U-boat a German submarine (314)
unconstitutional (UN kon stuh TOO shun ul) not in agreement with the ideas of the U.S. Constitution (172)
upstream the direction opposite to the flow of a river (30)
uranium (yoo RAY nee um) a heavy metal used to produce atomic energy (425)
urban area 1 a town or city with more than 2,500 people (364) **2** a city and its suburbs
urbanized (UR buh NYZD) having several communities very close together (380)

valley a lowland area between hills or mountains, often formed by a river (28)
vaquero (vah KAIR oh) in Mexico, an Indian who rode horses and rounded up cattle (464)
veto (VEE toh) to stop a bill from becoming law: a power of the President (171)
viceroy (VYSS roi) in New Spain, a governor who ruled an area for the Spanish king
volcano an opening in the Earth through which hot melted rock and gases can shoot up (433)
volunteer (VOL un TIR) someone who joins the armed forces of his or her own free will (235)
voyageur (vwah yah ZHUR) a person hired by the fur companies to transport furs and supplies in New France (451)

wagon train a group of people traveling together in wagons across the country (203)
War Hawks members of Congress who wanted war with Britain in 1812 (184)
wave a large group of immigrants arriving in a country around the same time (261)
weather the condition of the air in a place (31)
wood pulp wood ground up to make paper (380)

INDEX

abolitionists, 223–225, 235
Adams, Abigail, 159, 160
Adams, President John, 141, 153, 159, 160, 166, 181, 183
Adams, Samuel, 141, 158, 159
aerial photograph, 36, 37
Aguinaldo, Emilio, 279
Alabama, 193, 392–403
Alamo, 207–208
Alaska, 432–440
Aldrin, Edwin, 349
Alien Land Law, 278
Alliance for Progress, 338
Allied Powers, 313, 314, 315
amendments, 173, 236, 240, 319, 322
  Bill of Rights, 173–174
American Indians
  contributions of, 297–299
  of the Great Plains, 203, 286–295
  maps of, 296, 465
  on reservations, 292–295
  time line, 465
  see also specific tribe
American Revolution, 135, 139–145, 155–157
  leaders of, 148–153, 158–160
  map of, 149
Amundsen, Roald, 99
Anthony, Susan B., 319
Appalachian Mountains, 189, 368, 383–384, 393
Arab-Israeli conflict, 344–345
Arizona, 208, 423–431
Arkansas, 404–411
Armstrong, Neil, 349
Articles of Confederation, 164–166, 167

assembly line, 247–248, 321
Atchison, Davis Rice, 212
Atlantic Charter, 331
Atlantic Ocean, 377–378
Atlas, 476–485
atomic bomb, 330–331, 334, 337
Attucks, Crispus, 138
Austin, Stephen F., 206, 207
Austria-Hungary, 312–315
Axis, 328
Aztecs, 68–70, 84

Baffin, William, 96, 97
Baja California, 459
Balboa, Vasco de, 82–83, 85
banks, 178–179, 255
Banneker, Benjamin, 183
Battle of Bunker Hill, 142
Baumfree, Isabella, 224
Bay of Pigs, 338
Beckwourth, Jim, 202
Belize, 468–472
Bell, Alexander Graham, 255
Bill of Rights, 173–174
bills (and laws), 170, 171
Bing, Ah, 272
Black Codes, 239
Blacks
  in business and professions, 223, 224
  and civil rights, 339–341
  after Civil War, 238–242
  before Civil War, 108–111, 138, 144, 202, 220–232
  in Civil War, 235–237
  who fought slavery, 223, 224, 227
  in World War II, 333
Blackwell, Dr. Elizabeth, 317
Bluford, Guion, 350
"Bonus Army," 325
Boone, Daniel, 190
Boston Massacre, 137, 138
Boston Tea Party, 139, 158
boycott, 140, 340
Bradford, Cornelia, 126
"Brain Trust," 325
Bruce, Blanche, 240
Bureau of Indian Affairs (BIA), 292–293
Burgoyne, General, 148, 149
Burr, Aaron, 182

Cabinet, 177
Cabot, John, 82, 89, 93
Cabral, Pedro, 82, 85
California, 204–205, 208–211, 432–440
Cambodia, 343, 344
Canada, 97, 337, 446–457
  government of, 455–457
  history of, 451–454
  map of, 453
  time line, 453
capitalism, 337
Caribbean, map of, 472
Carnegie, Andrew, 254
Carson, Kit, 305
Carter, President Jimmy, 344–345
Cartier, Jacques, 92–96
Carver, George Washington, 242
Castro, Fidel, 338
Catt, Carrie Chapman, 318
Central America, 468–472
  map of, 459, 472, 475
Central Powers, 314, 315
Champlain, Samuel de, 96–97
charts
  American colonies, 115
  Canadian languages, 456
  climate zones, 32
  mileage, 54
  national government, 171
  North American nations, 486
  Presidents and Vice Presidents, 494–495
  states, 379, 387, 395–396, 407, 415–416, 427, 435, 487–493
  states where Hispanic-Americans live, 214
  U.S. rivers, 373
  U.S. territories, 365
Cherokees, 200
Chew, Thomas Foon, 275
Cheyenne, 286
Chiang Kai-shek, 335
China, 331, 338, 343
Chinese immigrants, 268–275
Chum Ming, 268–269
Churchill, Winston, 331
citizenship, 174, 212, 280
civil rights movement, 339–340
Civil War, 232, 233–237
Clark, George Rogers, 150, 151
Clark, William, 198–199
climate, 31–33
  chart of Earth, 32
  map of North America, 33
  zones, 31, 32
Cochise, 71
Cody, Buffalo Bill, 288
cold war, 336, 337
colonies, 101–127, 134–135
  chart of, 115
  maps of, 51, 109, 110
Colorado, 208, 423–431
Columbus, Christopher, 49, 79–82
  maps of voyages, 50, 77, 83
Comanches, 286
Committee of Correspondence, 158
Communism, 214, 330, 335, 337, 338, 343, 344
concentration camps, 329
Confederacy, 232, 233
Confederate Army, 234–237
Congress, 164–166, 170
Connecticut, 117, 376–382
Constitution, 109, 167–169
  amendments, 173–175
  Bill of Rights, 173–174
Constitutional Convention, 168
Continental Army, 141
Continental Congress, 140, 141, 159
Continental Divide, 423–424
Corbin, Margaret, 145
Cornish, Rev. Samuel E., 223
Cornwallis, General, 151, 152
Coronado, Francisco, 83, 85, 86
Cortés, Hernán, 82, 83, 84–85
Costa Rica, 468–472
cotton, 200, 229, 247
cotton gin, 229
Crockett, Davy, 207–208
Crow Indians, 202, 286
Cuba, 214, 338, 347–348
Cuban missile crisis, 338
Cuffe, Paul, 223

Daimler, Gottlieb, 254
Dakotas, 290
Dare, Virginia, 91
Daughters of Liberty, 158
Davis, Jefferson, 231
Dawes, William, 140
Declaration of Independence, 146–147, 160, 389
de la Costa, Juan, 49
de Lafayette, Marquis, 156
Delaware, 123–126, 383–390
de Leon *see* PONCE DE LEON
Democratic Party, 180
Democratic-Republican Party, 180
de Narvaez, Panfilo, 85, 86
depression, 274, 324–326
de Soto, Hernando, 83, 85, 88
de Vaca, Cabeza, 83, 85, 86
distribution maps, 44, 45
Douglass, Frederick, 223
Drake, E.L., 254
Drake, Sir Francis, 89–90, 93
Duluth, Daniel, 98

Earhart, Amelia, 317, 322, 323
Earth, maps of
physical, 476–477
political, 478–479
population, 46–47
economy, 337, 355–356
Eddy, Mary Baker, 317
Ederle, Gertrude, 317, 323
Edison, Thomas Alva, 256
Eisenhower, President Dwight D., 335
Electoral College, 178
Elizabeth I, Queen, 90, 91
El Salvador, 468–472
Emancipation Proclamation, 236
energy, 353–354
English explorations, 89–97
equal-area projection, 35–37
equator, 17, 20, 24
Era of Good Feelings, 187
Ericson, Leif, 78, 79
Eskimos (Innuit), 450, 451
Estebanico, 86
Europe
maps of, 52, 312, 327, 336
time line, 336
European exploration, 76–99
executive branch, 170–171
explorers, 78–80, 82–99
maps of, 49, 50, 77, 80, 83, 85, 93

factories, 222, 246–248, 308–309
Fascinating Facts, list of, 11
Fascist Party, 328
federal government, 168, 170
Federalist Party, 180, 181, 187
Ferdinand, King, 80
Ferraro, Geraldine, 342
Filipinos, 279–280
Florida, 53, 55, 200, 392–403
Ford, Henry, 321–322
Forten, James, 223
Fort Sumter, 232
forty-niners, 210–211
France, 312–315, 328–329
Franklin, Benjamin, 128, 141, 153, 159, 169
Freedmen's Bureau, 239
free enterprise, 337
French and Indian War, 135
French exploration, 89, 92–99
frontier life, 194–196
fur trappers, 202

Gadsden Purchase, 208
Garrison, William Lloyd, 225, 230
Gates, Horatio, 148, 151
Gates, Sir Thomas, 103–104
Gentleman's Agreement of 1907, 277, 279
George III, King, 153
Georgia, 106, 392–403
Germany, 312–315, 327–331
Gettysburg Address, 236
Glenn, John, 349
globes, 17–20
gold rush, 209–211
Gould, Jay, 254
government, 164
branches of, 170–172
and Constitution, 167–169
first, 164–166
new, 176–181
Grant, General Ulysses S., 236, 237
graphs
North and South in 1860, 228, 303
immigration, 259, 281
Great Britain, 312–315, 329–331
Great Depression, 324–326
Great Lakes, 97, 374, 384, 417
Great Plains, 282–285, 325, 369
Great Salt Lake, 205, 424
Greene, General Nathaniel, 152
Grimké, Angelina, 225
Guatemala, 468–472

Hamilton, Alexander, 177–181
Harding, President Warren, 322
Hawaii, 276–279, 432–440
Hays, Mary Ludwig, 144
Henry, Patrick, 138, 157
Hispanic-Americans, 212–214
historical maps, 38, 48–52, 64, 77, 80, 83, 85, 93, 96, 103, 104, 109, 110, 131, 149, 191, 203, 229, 265, 276, 312, 327, 336, 465
Hitler, Adolf, 327–328, 329
Homestead Act, 282
Honduras, 468–472
Hoover, President Herbert, 325
Hopewell people, 71–72
House of Burgesses, 105
House of Representatives, 170, 182
Houston, Sam, 208
Houston, Texas, 53
Howe, General, 148, 149
Howe, Julia Ward, 318
Hudson, Henry, 96–98, 123
Huntington, Collis P., 254
Hutchinson, Anne, 117
Idaho, 423–431
Illinois, 193, 413–422
immigrants to United States, 259–280
Chinese, 268–275
Europeans, 261–264
Filipinos, 279–280
graphs of, 259, 281
Irish, 261–262
Japanese, 276–279
maps of, 265, 276
time line, 265
immigration laws, 274, 277, 280, 346–348
indentured servants, 102, 108, 220
Indiana, 193, 413–422
Indians, *see* AMERICAN INDIANS or specific tribe
Industrial Revolution, 244–251
inflation, 355
Innuit (Eskimos), 450, 451
Inouye, Daniel, 342
integration, 333
inventors, 250, 255–256 *see also* specific inventor
Iowa, 413–422
Iran, 345
Iroquois, 452
Isabella, Queen, 79, 80
isolationism, 329
Israel, 344–345
Italy, 313–315, 328, 329

Jackson, General Thomas "Stonewall," 235
Jackson, Jesse, 340
Jackson, President Andrew, 186, 187, 200
Jamestown, colony of, 102–105, 108
Japan, 313, 329, 330–331, 334
Japanese immigrants, 276–279
Jay, John, 153, 180
Jay Treaty, 180
Jazz Age, 322, 323
Jefferson, Thomas, 141, 146, 156–157, 160, 166, 177–184, 197
Jews, 264, 328, 329
Johnson, Nancy, 250
Johnson, President Andrew, 239
Johnson, President Lyndon B., 343
Jolliet, Louis, 96, 98
Jones, Capt. John Paul, 150
Jones, John, 223
Joseph, Chief, 293
judicial branch, 170–172
justices, 172

Kansas, 413–422
Kelley, Florence, 311
Kennedy, President John F., 338, 343, 349, 351, 353
Kennedy, Robert, 353
Kentucky, 193, 392–403
Key, Francis Scott, 185
Key West, 53
King, Dr. Martin Luther, Jr., 340, 341, 353
Kiowas, 286
Korean War, 337–338
Kosciusko, Thaddeus, 156

landforms, 26–28
Laos, 343, 344
La Salle, Robert de, 96, 98, 99
latitude, 17–18, 20, 22–25
La Vérendrye, Pierre, 98
Lazarus, Emma, 267
League of Nations, 315
Lee, General Robert E., 235, 236, 237
Lee, Henry, 143
legislative branch, 170, 171
L'Enfant, Pierre-Charles, 183
Lewis and Clark, 198–199
Lincoln, President Abraham, 231–232, 234–237, 239
Lindbergh, Charles A., 323
longitude, 17–18, 20, 22–25
"Lost Colony," 91, 109
Louisiana Purchase, 197
Loyalists, 152, 155–156
Luey Gim Gong, 272
Lusitania, 314

Madison, President James, 168, 184
Magellan, Ferdinand, 84, 85, 185
Maine, 376–382
Mallory, George, 351
maps
  climate, 33
  distribution, 44, 45
  historical, 48–52; *see also* HISTORICAL MAPS
  physical, 44; *see also* PHYSICAL MAPS
  political, 44; *see also* POLITICAL MAPS
  population, 46–47, 362
  projection, 34, 35
  reading, 40–42
  road, 54, 55
  route, *see* ROUTE MAPS
  street, 56
  using, 53–56
Marion, General Francis, 152
Marquettes, Jacques, 96, 98
Marshall, James, 209
Maryland, 105–106, 123–126, 383–390
Mason, George, 111
Massachusetts, 113–115, 376–382
Maya, 66–68
Mayflower, 112–113
McClellan, George, 234
McCormick, Cyrus, 245
Meade, General, 236
Meat Inspection Act, 310
mercator projection, 35–38
merchants, 121–122
mestizos, 212, 462
Mexican-Americans, 212–214
Mexico, 459–467
  government of, 466–467
  history of, 463–467
  maps of, 459, 461, 465, 475
  people of, 462
  time line, 465
  and United States, 207–208
Michigan, 413–422
Middle Atlantic States, 383–390
  chart of, 387
  map of, 386
Middle East conflict, 344–345
Midwestern States, 413–422
  chart of, 415–416
  map of, 414
migration, 306
Minnesota, 413–422
Minuit, Peter, 126
Mississippi, 193, 392–403
Mississippi River, 29, 373–374, 396
Missouri, 413–422
Mitchell, Maria, 317
Monroe, President James, 187
Monroe Doctrine, 187
Montana, 423–431
Montezuma II, 85
Morgan, J.P., 255
Mormons, 205, 430
Morse, Samuel, 249
Mott, Lucretia, 319
Mountain States, 423–431
  chart of, 427
  map of, 426
muckrakers, 308–309
Mussolini, Benito, 328

Napoleon, 197
Natchez culture, 72–73
naturalization, 174, 280
Nazi Party, 328
Nebraska, 413–422
Nevada, 208, 423–431
New Amsterdam, 124
New Deal, 325–326
New England Colonies, 112–122
New England States, 376–382
  chart of, 379
  map of, 378
New Hampshire, 116, 376–382, 423–431
New Jersey, 123–126, 383–390
New Mexico, 64, 208
New Netherland, 124
New Orleans, 410, 411
New York, 123–126, 383–390
Nez Percé, 293
Niagara Falls, 389
Nicaragua, 468–472
Nisei, 334
Nixon, President Richard M., 343, 344
North America, maps of
  climate, 33
  historical, 64, 83, 104
  physical, 41, 480
  political, 23, 481
  resources, 45
North American nations, 486
North Atlantic Treaty Organization (NATO), 337
North Carolina, 106, 392–403
North Dakota, 413–422
North Pole, 17, 18
Northwest Passage, 95–99
  map of search for, 96
nuclear weapons
  atomic bomb, 330–331, 334, 337
  banning of, 338, 344

O'Connor, Sandra Day, 342
Oglethorpe, James, 106
Ohio, 193, 413–422
Oklahoma, 404–411
Olmecs, 463
Oregon, 202–203, 432–440
Otis, Elisha G., 256

Pacific States, 432–440
  chart of, 435
  map of, 434
Paine, Thomas, 157, 159
Panama Canal, 469–470
Parks, Rosa, 339–340
Paul, Alice, 318
Pawnee, 286
Pearl Harbor, 329
Penn, William, 125–126

Pennsylvania, 123–126, 383–390
People to Remember, 88, 117, 127, 143, 183, 199, 223, 224, 227, 293, 299, 319, 341
petroleum, 254, 353, 449
Philadelphia, 126, 167, 389, 390
Philippine Islands, 276, 279–280
physical maps, 41, 360–361, 459, 475, 476–477, 480, 482–483
Pilgrims, 112–113
Pitcher, Molly, 144
Pizarro, Francisco, 85, 86
plantations, 108–111, 222
Plymouth, 112
Pocahontas, 102
political maps, 12–13, 23, 43, 363, 365, 378, 386, 394, 406, 414, 426, 434, 453, 461, 472, 478–479, 481, 484–485
political parties, 180–181
Polk, President James K., 212
Ponce de León, 83–84, 85
Poor, Salem, 144
population
  maps, 46–47, 362
  of United States, 364, 366
Portuguese exploration, 79, 82, 85
Powhatan, 102
President(s), 170–171, 172, 176, 178, 212
  chart of, 494–495
prime meridian, 18, 21
printing press, 126
Progressives, 310–311
Prohibition, 322
Ptolemy, 21, 48, 49
pueblos, 71
Puerto-Rican Americans, 214
Puerto Rico, 364
Pure Food and Drug Act, 310
Puritans, 113–116, 119

Quakers, 125
Quetzalcoatl, 34–35

railroads, 248, 249, 254, 258, 271–272
Raleigh, Sir Walter, 91, 93, 259
Reagan, President Ronald, 345, 352–353
Reconstruction Period, 238–242
reformers, 307, 308–311
refugees, 346–348
relocation camps, 334
Republican Party, 180
resources, 44, 46, 353–354
  map of, 45
Revels, Hiram, 240
Revere, Paul, 137, 140
Rhode Island, 116, 376–382
Ride, Sally K., 350
Rillieux, Norbert, 223
road map, 55
Roaring Twenties, 322
Rockefeller, John D., 254–255, 308
Rolfe, John, 105
Roosevelt, President Franklin D., 325–326, 331
Roosevelt, President Theodore, 277, 310, 469
Ross, Betsy, 145
route maps, 50, 53, 64, 77, 80, 83, 85, 93, 96, 203
Russia, 312–315
  see also SOVIET UNION
Russwurm, John, 223
Ruth, Babe, 322, 323

Sacajawea, 199
Salt Lake City, 430
Samoset, 113
Sampson, Deborah, 144–145
segregation, 240, 242, 333, 339–340
Senate, 170
separatists, 112
Shays, Daniel, 166
Shays Rebellion, 165, 166
Shepard, Alan, 349
Shoong, Joe, 275
Shoshone, 199
Sioux, 286, 290
slavery, 108, 110, 122, 220, 236
Smith, Captain John, 102, 103, 112
Smith, James McCune, 223
socialism, 337
Social Security Act, 326
Society of Friends, 125
Sons of Liberty, 158
South Carolina, 106, 392–403
South Central States, 404–411
  chart of, 407
  map of, 406
South Dakota, 413–422
Southeastern States, 392–403
  chart of, 395–396
  map of, 394
South Pole, 17, 18
Soviet Union, 312–315, 330, 331, 337, 338, 344, 345, 349, 350
space program, 349–351
Spanish exploration, 79–88
Stamp Act, 135, 137
Standard Oil Co., 254, 308
Stanton, Elizabeth Cady, 319
Star-Spangled Banner, 185
Statue of Liberty, 267
steamboats, 248, 249
steam engine, 245, 253
steel industry, 253–254
Steffens, Lincoln, 308
Stowe, Harriet Beecher, 231
street map, 56
strip mining, 418
Stuyvesant, Peter, 124
suffrage, 317–319
Sumter, Thomas, 151
Supreme Court, 171–172

Taino people, 80
Taiwan, 335
Tarbell, Ida, 308
tariff, 227–228
Taylor, President Zachary, 212
telegraph, 249–250
telephone, 255
Temple, Lewis, 223
Temple Mound Culture, 72
Tennessee, 193, 392–403
Tennessee Valley Authority (TVA), 325, 397
Texas, 64, 207–208, 404–411
Thunderhawk, Zona, 286–288
time lines, 63, 82, 93, 105, 109, 135, 191, 197, 217, 231, 265, 336, 453, 465
time zones, 25, 443
Toltecs, 68
Trail of Tears, 200, 201
Treaty of Versailles, 315, 327, 328
trial by jury, 124
Truman, President Harry, 330, 333
Truth, Sojourner, 224
Tubman, Harriet, 227
Tuskegee Institute, 242
Twain, Mark, 377

U-boats, 314
Underground Railroad, 227
United Nations, 331
United States
  citizenship, 174, 212, 280
  physical maps of, 360–361, 482–483
  political maps of, 12–13, 43, 59, 363, 484–485
  population map of, 362
  schools in, 125
  territories, 365
  time zones, 443

Ushijima, George, 278–279
Utah, 208, 423–431

Vanderbilt, Cornelius, 254
Vermont, 376–382
Verrazano, Giovanni da, 92, 93
Vespucci, Amerigo, 82, 85
Vice Presidents, chart of, 494–495
Vietnam, 343–344, 348
Vikings, 77–79
Virginia, 91, 102–105, 392–403
voting, 239, 317–319

wagon trains, 203–204
Waldseemüller, Martin, 49–50
Walker, David, 223
Wampanoag, 113
War Hawks, 184
War of 1812, 184, 186
Warren, Mercy, 159
Washington (state), 432–440
Washington, Booker T., 242
Washington, DC, 123–126, 364, 383–390
Washington, George
  false teeth of, 177
  as general, 141, 143, 149–150, 156, 157
  as President, 143, 176–177, 179, 180, 181
Watt, James, 245
West Virginia, 123–126, 383–390
Westward movement, 189–193
Where We Are in Time and Place, 93, 109, 191, 265, 336, 453, 465
White, John, 91
Whitney, Eli, 229, 247–248
Williams, Roger, 115–116, 117
Wilson, President Woodrow, 314, 315
Winthrop, John, 114, 115–116
Wisconsin, 413–422
women
  in American Revolution, 144–145
  discrimination against, 340, 342
  rights of, 224, 317–319
  and suffrage, 317–319
  and World Wars, 317, 332
Woodlands culture, 73–74
World War I, 312–315, 327
World War II, 327–334, 336
Wyoming, 208, 423–431

Yom Kippur War, 344
Yucatán Peninsula, 66, 68, 460
Yung Wing, 274–275

CREDITS

Maps by R. R. Donnelley Cartographic Services: **12-13, 23, 41, 360-361, 476-485;** Maps by David Lindroth, Inc.: **18-20, 22,31, 33-35, 37, 45-47, 49-56, 59, 64, 77, 80, 83, 85, 93, 96, 109, 110, 130, 191, 203, 265, 276, 312, 327, 336, 362, 363, 365, 378, 386, 394, 406, 414, 426, 434, 443, 453, 459, 461, 465, 472, 475;** Time Lines and Charts by Boultinghouse & Boultinghouse, Inc.: **54, 63, 93, 109, 115, 135, 191, 197, 217, 231, 265, 336, 365, 373, 379, 387, 395-396, 407, 415-416, 427, 435, 453, 465, 486-495;** Art and Charts by Function Thru Form, Inc.: **27, 32, 42, 214, 259, 456;** Art by William Colrus. **69. 14:** NYPL Picture Collection. **15:** (T) Art Resource. **15:** (B) The Bettmann Archive. **17:** Robert Capece/McGraw-Hill. **26:** (M) Vautier-DeNanxe. **26:** (T) Daniel Brody/Stock, Boston. **26:** (T) Daniel Brody/Stock, Boston. **28:** (B) J.Claridge/The Image Bank. **28:** (BM) Dennis Stock/Magnum Photos. **28:** (T) C. Allan Morgan/Peter Arnold, Inc. **28:** (TM) Vautier-DeCool. **29:** (B) Shostal Associates. **29:** (M) Peter Frey/The Image Bank. **29:** (T) Michael Heron/Woodfin Camp. **36:** Mel Horst. **40:** Elihu Botnick/Woodfin Camp. **44:** Norris Taylor/Photo Researchers, Inc. **48:** Culver Pictures. **53:** Richard & Mary Magruder/The Image Bank. **53:** M. Serraillier/Photo Researchers. **53:** Van Bucher/Photo Researchers. **53:** Katrina Thomas/Photo Researchers, Inc. **55:** Baron Wolman/Woodfin Camp. **55:** Dennis Stock/Magnum Photos. **55:** Patrick Donehue/Photo Researchers, Inc. **55:** Van Bucher/Photo Researchers, Inc. **60–61:** John Gadsby Chapman/Collection of Mr. and Mrs. P. Mellon. **62:** The Granger Collection. **66:** R. Bunge/Bruce Coleman, Inc. **67:** Monkmeyer Press Photo. **68:** The Bettmann Archive. **69:** L.L.T. Rhodes/Taurus Photos. **70:** NYPL Picture Collection. **72:** Martin J. Dain/Magnum Photos. **73:** Shostal Associates. **74:** NYPL Pictures. **76:** The Bettmann Archive. **80:** The Bettmann Archive. **81:** Library of Congress. **87:** NYPL Picture Collection. **88:** Culver Pictures. **90:** David Muench. **91:** Lost Colony, Roanoke Island. **92:** NYPL Picture Collection. **94:** Richard & Mary Magruder/The Image Bank. **95:** Villard Atlas/Huntington Library. **98:** The Bettmann Archive. **99:** National Gallery of Art. **101:** NYPL Picture Collection. **103:** A.H. Robbins Company. **107:** Metropolitan Museum of Art, Garbisch Collection. **108:** The Bettmann Archive. **113:** The Bettmann Archive. **114:** New York Historical Society. **116:** Pilgrim Society. **117:** NYPL Picture Collection. **118:** Len Speier. **120:** (B) Boston Society. **120:** (TL) The Bettmann Archive. **120:** (TR) The Bettmann Archive. **121:** The Bettmann Archive. **124:** (B) Historical Society of Pennsylvania. **124:** (T) Museum of the City of New York, Davies Collection. **125:** Historical Society of Pennsylvania. **127:** NYPL Picture Collection. **132–133:** NYPL Picture Collection. **134:** Yale University Art Gallery. **136:** (L) Massachusetts Historical Society. **136:** (R) John Carter Brown Library, Brown University. **137:** Metropolitan Museum of Art. **138:** Culver Pictures. **139:** NYPL Picture Collection. **140:** Connecticut Historical Society. **141:** Delaware Art Museum. **142:** Delaware Art Museum. **143:** Metropolitan Museum of Art. **144:** (L) The Bettmann Archive. **144:** (R) The Bettmann Archive. **147:** Yale University Art Gallery. **148:** U.S. Naval Academy Museum. **150:** Valley Forge Historical Society. **151:** Indiana Historical Society. **152:** The Bettmann Archive. **153:** The Bettmann Archive. **155:** Maryland Commission of Artistic Property. **157:** (L) The Bettmann Archive. **157:** (R) The Bettmann Archive. **158:** Kennedy Galleries. **158:** (B) Museum of Fine Arts, Boston. **159:** (B) National Portrait Gallery, Smithsonian Institution. **159:** (T) Museum of Fine Arts, Boston. **160:** (B) Massachusetts Historical Society. **160:** (T) NYPL Picture Collection. **161:** (B) The Bettmann Archive. **161:** (T) NYPL Picture Collection. **163:** NYPL Picture Collection. **164:** The Bettmann Archive. **165:** The Bettmann Archive. **167:** Garbisch Collection, Virginia Museum. **169:** NYPL Picture Collection. **172:** William S. Weems/Woodfin Camp & Assoc. **174:** The Bettmann Archive. **176:** Library of Congress. **179:** (L) NYPL Picture Collection. **179:** (R) Yale

University Art Gallery. **180:** Archive of Bay Village, Smithsonian Institution. **182:** Library of Congress. **183:** New York Historical Society. **185:** Peale Museum. **186:** American Antiquarian Society. **189:** Washington University Gallery of Art. **190:** NYPL Picture Collection. **191:** The Brooklyn Museum. **192:** Chuck Place/The Image Bank. **194:** The Brooklyn Museum. Gift of The Brooklyn Institute of Arts and Sciences. **195:** The Bettmann Archive. **196:** The Bettmann Archive. **198:** Montana Historical Society. **199:** Museum of the American Indian. **200:** Museum of the American Indian. **201:** Woolaroc Museum. **202:** NYPL Picture Collection. **204:** The Butler Institute. **206:** (B) The Bettmann Archive. **206:** (T) Texas State Library. **207:** State Capitol, Austin, Texas. **209:** Southwest Museum. **210:** The New York Historical Society. **213:** Witte Museum. **213:** Witte Museum. **218–219.** Metropolitan Museum of Art. **220:** West Point Museum. **221:** (B) Kennedy Galleries. **221:** (T) New York Historical Society. **222:** Granger Collection. **223:** National Portrait Gallery, Smithsonian Institution. **224:** The Bettmann Archive. **226:** The Cincinnati Art Museum, Subscription Fund Purchase. **227:** NYPL Picture Collection. **229:** Jean Heiberg/Peter Arnold. **230:** (B) Culver Pictures. **230:** (T) The Bettmann Archive. **231:** National Portrait Gallery, Smithsonian Institution. **232:** (L) The Bettmann Archive. **232:** (R) Museum of the Confederacy. **233:** The Granger Collection. **234:** National Portrait Gallery, Smithsonian Institution. **235:** Library of Congress. **236:** Gettysburg National Military Park. **237:** Culver Pictures. **238:** Courtesy Abby Aldrich Rockefeller Folk Art Collection. **239:** Library of Congress. **241:** (B) Culver Pictures. **241:** (T) Library of Congress. **242:** The Bettmann Archive. **244:** NYPL Picture Collection. **245:** National Canning Association. **246:** Yale University Art Gallery, Garvan Collection. **247:** (B) NYPL Picture Collection. **247:** (T) Culver Pictures. **249:** (B) Culver Pictures. **249:** (T) NYPL Picture Collection. **250:** Culver Pictures. **252:** Culver Pictures. **253:** Museum of the City of New York. **255:** (L) Culver Pictures. **255:** (R) Culver Pictures. **256:** Library of Congress. **257:** Courtesy of AT&T. **260:** The Granger Collection. **262:** (B) Nebraska State Historical Society. **262:** (T&B) Culver Pictures. **263:** (T) Collection of San Antonio Museum. **266:** (L) George Eastman House Collection. **266:** (R) Library of Congress. **268–269:** Mark Sexton/Peabody Museum of Salem. **261:** The Granger Collection. **270:** The Bettmann Archive. **271:** Courtesy of Southern Pacific Lines. **272–273:** NYPL Picture Collection. **273:** NYPL Picture Collection. **274:** Olivier Rebbot/Stock, Boston. **277:** (B) NYPL Picture Collection. **277:** (T) Peabody Museum of Salem. **278:** (L) NYPL Picture Collection. **278:** (R) NYPL Picture Collection. **279:** (T) NYPL Picture Collection. **282:** NYPL Picture Collection. **283:** Nebraska Historical Society, Butcher Collection. **284:** (L) Courtesy of William Katz, Union Pacific Railroad. **284:** (R) NYPL Picture Collection. **287:** Walters Art Gallery. **288:** American Museum of Natural History. **289:** The Bettmann Archive. **290:** Gilcrease Museum. **291:** Granger Collection. **292:** Adam Woolfitt/Woodfin Camp. **293:** National Portrait Gallery, Smithsonian Institution. **294:** Dennis Stock/Magnum Photos. **295:** Peter Dublin/MGH. **297:** Arizona State Museum. **297:** Arizona State Museum. **298:** Chuck O'Rear /Woodfin Camp. **304–305:** Fred Ward/Black Star. **306:** The Bettmann Archive. **308:** The Bettmann Archive. **309:** The Granger Collection. **310:** The Bettmann Archive. **313:** The New York Historical Society. **315:** University of California, Berkeley. **316:** The Bettmann Archive. **318:** (BL) NYPL Picture Collection. **318:** (BM) The Bettmann Archive. **318:** (BR) Daniel Kramer. **319:** UPI Photo Library. **321:** E. Thelma Fink/Photo Researchers, Inc. **322:** (L) UPI Photo Library. **322:** (R) UPI Photo Library. **324:** (BL) Brown Brothers. **324:** (BR) The Granger Collection. **325:** FDR Library. **328:** (BL) The Bettmann Archive. **328:** (BR) The Bettmann Archive. **329:** U.S. Army. **330:** (TL) The Bettmann Archive. **330:** (TR) UPI Photo Library. **332:** The Bettmann Archive. **333:** (L) UPI Photo Library. **333:** (R) Culver Pictures. **334:** The Bettmann Archive. **335:** Wide World Photos. **337:** The Granger Collection. **339:** UPI Photo Library. **340:** (L) Cary Whitenton/Office of the Mayor/San Antonio, Texas. **340:** (R) Office of the Secretary of State, California. **341:** UPI Photo Library. **342:** (L) Lester Sloan/Woodfin Camp. **342:** (R) UPI Photo Library. **344:** Henri Bureau/Sygma. **345:** Bob Nicklesberg/ Woodfin Camp. **347:** (L) UPI Photo Library. **347:** (R) UPI Photo Library. **349:** NASA. **350:** (L) Randy Taylor/Sygma Photos. **350:** (R) Jacques Tiziou/Sygma Photos. **352:** Sygma Photos. **354:** Alec Duncan/Taurus Photos. **355:** National Park Service. **356:** (R) Will McIntyre/Photo Researchers, Inc. **367:** George Hall/Woodfin Camp. **368:** Edna Douthat/Photo Researchers, Inc. **369:** Chuck Lawliss/The Image Bank. **371:** Craig Aurness/Woodfin Camp. **372:** George Hall/Woodfin Camp. **376:** Clyde Smith/Peter Arnold. **381:** Dan Budnick/Woodfin Camp. **382:** Steve Dunwell/The Image Bank. **383:** Kenneth Garrett/Woodfin Camp. **385:** Tannenbaum/Sygma. **385:** Tannenbaum/ Sygma. **389:** Cletis Reaves/The Image Bank. **392:** M. Serraillier/Photo Researchers. **399:** Jacques Jangoux/Peter Arnold, Inc. **400:** Mike Yamashita/Woodfin Camp. **401:** R. Thompson/Taurus Photos. **402:** (B) Costa Manos/ Magnum. **402:** (T) Taurus Photos. **403:** William Strode/Woodfin Camp. **405:** Ron Church/Photo Researchers. **409:** Alex Webb/Magnum. **410:** Peter Beney/The Image Bank. **413:** David J. Maenza/The Image Bank. **419:** Craig Aurness/Woodfin Camp. **420:** Ellis Herwig/The Image Bank. **421:** Cliff Fairfield/Taurus Photos. **425:** Manuel Rodriguez. **428:** Annie Griffiths/Woodfin Camp. **429:** Eve Arnold/Magnum. **430:** David Hiser/The Image Bank. **431:** Leonard Lee Rue III/Monkmeyer Press Photos. **437:** Pro Pix/Monkmeyer Press Photo. **438:** Robert Frerck/ Woodfin Camp. **439:** Charles E. Schmidt/Taurus Photos. **440:** Gerhard Gscheidle/The Image Bank. **444:** (BL) Helen Marcus. **444:** (BM) Eric Wheater/The Image Bank. **444:** (BR) Lowell Georgia/Photo Researchers, Inc. **444:** (TL) Porterfield/Chickering/Photo Researchers. **444:** (TR) Michael Philip Manheim. **445:** (BL) Porterfield/ Chickering/Photo Researchers. **445:** (BM) Porterfield/Chickering/Photo Researchers. **445:** (BR) J. Williamson/ Photo Researchers. **445:** (TL) Lowell Georgia/Photo Researchers. **445:** (TR) Porterfield/Chickering/Photo Researchers. **446:** M. Funk/The Image Bank. **448:** John Tiszler/Peter Arnold, Inc. **449:** Burt Glinn/Magnum Photos. **450:** Russ Kinne/Photo Researchers. **451:** The Granger Collection. **452:** The Granger Collection. **455:** Craig Aurness/Woodfin Camp. **456:** Timothy Eagan/Woodfin Camp. **462:** Patti McConville/The Image Bank. **463:** Robert Frerck/Woodfin Camp. **467:** Marc Bernheim/Woodfin Camp. **469:** Bob Nicklesberg/Woodfin Camp. **470:** J.P. Laffont/Sygma. **471:** J.P. Laffont/Sygma.